Crimes of Loyalty

Crimes of Loyalty

A History of the UDA

Ian S. Wood

Edinburgh University Press

With love to Helen, Ben, David and Robbie

© Ian S. Wood, 2006

Transferred to digital print 2013

Edinburgh University Press Ltd
22 George Square, Edinburgh

Typeset in 10/12 Monotype Goudy Old Style by
Servis Filmsetting Ltd, Manchester, and
Printed and bound by CPI Group (UK) Ltd, Croydon, CR0 4YY

A CIP record for this book is available from the British Library

ISBN-10 0 7486 2426 0 (hardback)
ISBN-13 978 0 7486 2426 3 (hardback)
ISBN-10 0 7486 2427 9 (paperback)
ISBN-13 978 0 7486 2427 0 (paperback)

Contents

Acknowledgements

This book's title is derived from a dedication often to be seen on paramilitary Loyalist murals in Northern Ireland. It reads 'Their only crime was loyalty' and it usually accompanies names and faces of those killed in the conflict there. Many of them were killers too, though arguably not in a war of their own making.

Loyalty, or Loyalism, can never excuse the terrible killings and the torture which on so many occasions preceded them, and which members of the UDA/UFF carried out once they were convinced, as they often put it to me, of the need to 'fight fire with fire'. Such deeds necessarily occupy much of what follows, but my purpose has been not to excuse but to explain what, in an essentially decent community, drove countless mostly young working-class men to travel their chosen road.

Uppermost in my mind is the thought that no words spoken or written can bring back the dead of Northern Ireland's Troubles nor give comfort to the bereaved. That said, books – and there have been many of them – can help to give us a clearer view of what was, after all, the worst political and ethnic conflict in Europe's experience between 1945 and the break-up of the Soviet Union and former Yugoslavia.

Irish Republicans did most of the killing by far, and their victims numbered hundreds of Catholics. The UDA, although they took fewer lives than either the IRA or the UVF, were also a brutal combatant over nearly three decades and in these pages I have attempted to tell their story.

Enumerating all those who have helped me in the preparation of this work is a major task but one which must be undertaken here. I have acknowledged at the end of this book all who made themselves available to talk to me and my debt extends to those who did not wish to be identified.

The work of courageous journalists in Northern Ireland has provided me, as my endnotes show, with invaluable source material, as have the compilers of that deeply moving work *Lost Lives*. Hugh Jordan, David Lister, Colin Crawford, Jim Cusack and Henry McDonald, all created, with their writing, a breach in the wall through which I could follow at a somewhat slower pace. Hugh has always been generous with his time and his sources and he and Henry are friends whose company, either in Edinburgh or Belfast, I always enjoy. Jim McDowell has also provided good company, as well as help and encouragement and the odd pint when I needed one. The late Martin O'Hagan, too, was someone from whose knowledge

I could always learn. Unlike all of them, I had a return ticket when times were bad.

I also owe special thanks to Professor Graham Walker and to Dr Owen Dudley Edwards for their vital support and indispensable advice. Owen, in particular, took enormous trouble in reading my manuscript and identifying necessary changes. So too did Jane Tyler-Copper, who has used her keyboard skills tirelessly, along with her fine eye for detail, in making a lengthy text ready for publication. Jonathan Wadman did an essential and flawless job as copy editor. Roda Morrison at Edinburgh University Press has been a patient and supportive commissioning editor and I am indebted to Gloria Ferris for her hard work in promoting my book.

For unfailing help and hospitality over many years and endless good *craic* I want to thank Shaun McKeown and I want to add to his the names of Muriel Kinley and her late husband, my friend Maurice. Sammy Duddy and his wife Roberta have provided me with endless support and excellent company over many years.

Others whose names also belong in these acknowledgements are Dr Brian Barton, Dr Bob Purdie and my friend and former student Andrew Sanders. George Patten and Brendan Leckie have also, over time, provided me with invaluable help.

Gathering material for this book could sometimes be thirsty work. It would take too long to name all the licensed premises in Belfast and elsewhere whose friendly staff I could always rely on but a special mention is due here to John Lynn and John Bittles.

There are friends and colleagues too on this side of the sea whose company and encouragement have always kept me on course. They include, in no special order, John Brown, Ian Budge, Henry Cowper, George Hewitt, John Davidson, Mario Relich, Paul Addison, Ian Donachie and Gerry Douds, as well as Jim Seaton, who gave me the chance to write about Northern Ireland for the *Scotsman*.

Yvonne Murphy, Kris Brown, Alistair Gordon and Ciaran Crossey at the Political Collection in Belfast's Linen Hall Library have all given me indispensable help, as have staff in the newspaper annexe of Belfast Central Library and the National Library of Scotland. I must thank Carcanet Press for their permission to quote from Edwin Morgan's poem 'King Billy' and Blackstaff Press for allowing me to use extracts from John Hewitt's poems 'The Colony' and 'Once Alien Here'. Sammy Duddy was happy to let me quote from *Concrete Whirlpools of the Mind*. Mainstream Press gave permission for me to adapt some essential data from their unforgettable book *Lost Lives*. I must also thank Kelvin Boyes and the Loyalist Prisoners' Post-Conflict Resettlement Group for access to photographic material. Last but not least, I want to express my gratitude to Edinburgh University's Kerr-Fry bequest for once more providing generous funding for my work.

Ian S. Wood

Introduction

We marched in orderly lines
Thousands of us
Our stars of David sewn on
To our bright new rags
We clutched our possessions
As we marched along
They said our war was over

We sang quietly whilst on the move
Songs that our forefathers sung
And we were proud in the knowledge
That we were Jews
They said the meek would inherit the earth

As they herded us in we saw
The over-head pipes
They said it was to provide heat
But the odour of gas over-whelms us
When we were marching
We should have been fighting

This poem, entitled 'Our Way', was written by Sammy Duddy and appeared in a collection of his work published in Belfast in 1983.[1] The venture was supported by the Ulster Defence Association, in which the author had been active ever since its emergence more than ten years earlier. Andy Tyrie, the organisation's then commandant, wrote an introduction and the work was dedicated 'To all the long-suffering people of Ulster that they may see the light'.[2] The author has always said that he wrote 'Our Way' with the thought that Northern Ireland's Loyalist population could, like the Jews of Europe in the Second World War, end up acquiescing in their own fate, not genocide but the extinction of their identity and culture.

Duddy appears briefly in a recent book on Ulster Loyalists which dismisses him as 'Andy Tyrie's court jester'[3] without so much as a reference to his writing. All who have met him would agree that he is excellent company and an unfailing source of good *craic* but his poems capture something of the grief and trauma inflicted by the Troubles on both communities in Northern Ireland. He has escaped death more than once and threats forced him to leave his native

Shankill for a more secure Loyalist area of Belfast. This did not stop him performing a popular drag act in clubs and singing country and western, which he still did in a pub in North Belfast until another attempt on his life was made, early in November 2002, as part of a continuing feud within the UDA.

However, he has continued to work for the UDA, handling much of its publicity and also using his skills as an illustrator and cartoonist. Even when the organisation was drawn into the most brutal counter-terror in response to the IRA, it maintained a community role running advice centres for hard-pressed working-class people as well as for Loyalist prisoners' families. Duddy took his share of this even as the task became a thankless one while Loyalist communities and organisations such as the UDA succumbed to the temptations of crime and drug-dealing.

He has been a strong supporter of the UDA's political initiatives over the years, though realistic about their failure, and welcomes the Combined Loyalist Military Command's October 1994 ceasefire as well as the opportunity to campaign for a 'yes' vote in the 1998 referendum on the Belfast Agreement. If he now has serious doubts about the way that agreement is being implemented, they simply voice those of a community which sees old certainties crumbling amidst a peace process they feel is driven increasingly by an Irish nationalist agenda.

The community with which Duddy identifies does not belong to tennis clubs in Helen's Bay or have holiday access to villas in Tuscany. The people he grew up with and still lives among embody a distinction which has been analysed already, but which still needs to be made, between Ulster Unionists and Ulster Loyalists. These two traditions, it has been forcefully argued, have a clear class dimension: the former are mainly middle class and enjoy careers and lifestyles which have drawn them closer to contemporary 'mainland' British and European norms and values. The latter are a plebeian group whose self-image comprises a now uneasy loyalty to a Britain which they feel no longer understands them nor even wants their allegiance, and a loyalty as deep to their distinctive Ulster Protestant identity.[4]

The tension involved in these loyalties and the shifting relationship between them has been vividly reflected in the history of the UDA, still Northern Ireland's largest Loyalist paramilitary organisation. Thirty years ago it carried Union flags at its marches and rallies. It still does so but now they are outnumbered by Ulster standards and emblems, which also dominate entire localities where there is a UDA presence. Elements within its membership have now reverted to open support for Ulster independence, with which the organisation's leadership associated itself for a time in the 1970s, although in 1998 the UDA's political wing accepted devolved power sharing under the Belfast Agreement.

The Loyalism of the UDA, whether in Belfast housing estates or among the small farmers and traders of rural Antrim and Down is now, more than ever, the value system of those who have nowhere else to go and feel excluded from a world with little liking for them and even less desire to understand them. 'Late capitalism' has discarded most of them from the shipyards and engineering works where employment was once a badge of their sense of self-worth. They have had little part in the migration 'across the water' of young middle-class Unionists who, in growing numbers, are opting to study in English and Scottish universities and then to stay on after gaining their degrees.

Many Loyalists, left behind and fearful of their future, still identify with the UDA. Why they have done so, and still do, is the subject of this book, which will also explore the shifts and contradictions in UDA political thinking over the last thirty years as well as the organisation's claims to have played an effective military rather than a merely criminal and terrorist role in Northern Ireland's troubles.

NOTES

1. S. Duddy, *Concrete Whirlpools* of the Mind (Belfast: Ulidia, 1983), p. 40.
2. Ibid., p. 1.
3. P. Taylor, *Loyalists* (London: Bloomsbury, 1999), p. 84.
4. S. Bruce, The Edge of the Union: the Ulster Loyalist Political Vision (Oxford: Oxford University Press, 1994), pp. 70–1.

1

Joining Up: The Origins of the UDA

A pigeon fanciers' club in Leopold Street, off Belfast's Crumlin Road, may seem an odd place of origin for what became Northern Ireland's largest Loyalist paramilitary organisation. Yet David Fogel, a London-born former soldier who had served in Northern Ireland and then settled in Belfast, claimed that a meeting held there in July 1970 led to the formation of the Ulster Defence Association. The period was one of mounting tension. British troops had been on the streets since August of the previous year, when marches for civil rights and the Unionist government's response to them had precipitated serious sectarian violence.

As the Loyalist marching season got under way in the summer of 1970, trouble moved close to the Woodvale area in which Fogel lived with his Belfast-born wife and family. Almost a year earlier they had had to flee for their lives when gunmen had opened fire in the nationalist part of the nearby Ardoyne, but on Saturday, 27 June 1970 a Loyalist band parade along the Springfield Road prompted an attack from Catholic protesters. Bricks and paving stones were hurled at bandsmen and their supporters and soldiers answered with CS gas. Rioting spread quickly and once again live rounds were fired from Ardoyne, killing three Protestants on and near the Crumlin Road. 'In this instance the IRA were ready and waiting,' Gerry Adams later wrote in his memoirs.[1]

The shootings provoked a major Loyalist attack on the Short Strand, a small Catholic enclave on the edge of Loyalist East Belfast, and they made a deep impression on Fogel. 'A couple of days later', he recalled, 'I went along to join a group of men who were angry about it. All we were hearing about and reading was how the Catholics were getting a raw deal. Everything was being done to appease them. Yet there was all this violence. Law and order seemed to be taking a back seat.'[2] The meeting was in the 'pigeon house' as local people called it but Fogel was not impressed. 'I thought it was pathetic. Most of them were middle-aged men and all they were doing was moaning and exchanging rumours. It was all talk.'[3]

Fogel interrupted proceedings to say that mere talk was not enough. He impressed Charles Harding Smith, the man who had called the meeting and who lived only two streets away from the club. Harding Smith was an ex-shipyard worker who had become a tyre salesman working with his brother-in-law. He told Fogel what he wanted to hear, that Loyalists needed military training, and Fogel promised to recruit twenty local men, each of whom would bring a friend, for basic drill with dummy weapons as well as unarmed combat sessions and fieldcraft instruction in the country. 'It would be dishonest to pretend that real guns didn't exist,' Fogel said later. 'There were shotguns, legally held, too. We didn't have any illegal weapons then. We knew the shotguns would be used if the IRA came into our territory.'[4]

This was the beginning of the Woodvale Defence Association. Loyalists in other localities followed its example in response to increasing IRA attacks and their own growing doubts about British policy. Fogel, apart from his London accent, was typical of the many who 'joined up' at this time. After leaving the army he had worked as a machinists in Mackies' engineering plant but was made redundant in 1970 and lived off casual work when he could get it or unemployment benefit to pay rent on his house in Palmer Street, Woodvale. He talked later of a life not so different from that of the 'other side', a phrase Loyalists were using increasingly that year.

> Like most of the Catholics in the Falls – like half the working class in Britain – our house was small and old. It was the one thing we had in common with the Catholics. The parlour was a front room, leading straight off the street, with a scullery at the back, two bedrooms upstairs and an outside lavatory, no bathroom – for that we had to go round to the mother-in-law's.[5]

Andy Tyrie, who would rise to overall command of what became the Ulster Defence Association, grew up on the Shankill as one of a family of nine occupying a two-bedroom house. His father was an ex-soldier and his mother often took in sewing to supplement their income. He took whatever factory work he could get and found himself being drawn into the worsening conflict in 1970 and 1971.

His mother's finished needlework, he recalled, would often be sold at stalls on the Falls Road owned by Catholic traders. 'There was a close working relationship between the two communities. Even when the Troubles began the difference between the two communities was not overbearing in any way.'[6] Fear, as the situation worsened, forced Tyrie to define himself in terms represented by his father's military service and his own in the Territorial Army. In 1970 he was living in the new Moyard estate in West Belfast, but it provided no refuge from sectarian conflict and he joined a local group which sought to handle the problems of families fleeing into Moyard from other localities.

> What I found behind the scenes was that everything was being done to block Protestants from getting houses in the area. Protestants were being encouraged to leave the district and I became suspicious of people involved in house allocation. At one time I actually set up road blocks on my own and refused to let outsiders into the area. Things got really tough in my area and it soon became a focal point

for attacks on Protestant homes. We formed a defence group for all the Protestants of the area. I still believed that there was no reason why the two communities couldn't live together – but there were people who were not playing fair.[7]

Sammy Duddy also came from a large family. He grew up with eight brothers and sisters in the Hammer area of Belfast. He retells how, when on a childhood visit to the city's zoo, his parents asked for eleven admission tickets. The man in the zoo replied: 'Hold on a minute and we'll bring the animals out to see you.'[8] Duddy senior was a Londonderry man who had settled in Belfast and served in the RUC's B-Special reserve during the Second World War. He worked as a letterpress printer, a trade to which Sammy himself was apprenticed at the age of fifteen.

While still at school he had shown an aptitude for writing and would, on occasions, compose personalised Valentines for classmates in return for pens or Dinky cars. A sample of his work in this period, which he still quotes, reads as follows:

I held your hand in class today,
My mates think I'm a fool.
But you've a thirty six inch bust
And I've a six inch tool.[9]

Later he would both edit and contribute to UDA magazines as well as doing cartoons and illustrations for them, but, like many others, he initially joined a local defence association. 'It was vigilante stuff when things were hotting up, checkpoints and baseball bats.'[10]

Other very similar defence associations were formed during the remainder of 1970 and many more the following year as the IRA launched a series of attacks on the police and the army. These attacks took civilian lives as well and over a hundred deaths in 1971 were the work of Republican paramilitaries. Internment without trial was introduced as a desperate measure which did nothing to reduce the violence. The nationalists launched a civil disobedience campaign while Unionism drifted further into crisis with James Chichester-Clark resigning as Prime Minister in March. That month also saw the start of large protest marches, orchestrated by the Loyalist Association of Workers (LAW), whose leaders called for draconian security measures against the IRA.

Amid this escalating violence, paramilitary Loyalism on the Woodvale model remained localised and fragmented, each group assuming responsibility only for the defence of its own area. The worsening security situation impressed upon a growing number of activists the need for contact and co-operation among different vigilante groups. Meetings to bring this about began in the summer of 1971 and Ingram Beckitt, a dock worker from the Shankill, chaired one of the first meetings, in a Northland Street band hall, at which the name Ulster Defence Association was used. By January of 1972 a structure was beginning to emerge as well as a hierarchy of ranks within designated brigade and battalion areas.

When Duddy took his decision to join he had to present himself at a community centre near his home. A table was covered with a Union flag, on which lay a bible and a Sterling submachine gun. Not all present with him took the membership oath. The open display of a firearm deterred some from taking a major step beyond mere street defence work but Duddy was willing to be sworn in, believing that Loyalists now needed guns for their own protection.[11] Enough men in Duddy's locality and elsewhere joined with him for the new organisation to acquire a visible and formidable strength.

Alec Calderwood was far too young to join the UDA at this time, though he did so later and in 1982 received a life sentence for the brutal murder of a young Catholic. He was only seven years old in 1969 when British troops were deployed on Belfast's streets. He was born in Brown Square, off the Lower Shankill Road, 'a lovely wee community then, where you could leave your doors open, day and night, and you'd never get burgled'.[12] He earned his life-long nickname, Oso, because he was often seen waiting for an ice cream van with the name 'Mr Oso' painted on it. He was already in a junior Orange lodge when the Troubles started and Brown Square found itself in range of attack from the nationalist side of the army's rapidly built peace line.

What the Troubles really meant for him, however, was the presence of a company of the Royal Highland Fusiliers who were based in the Brown Square RUC station.

> I became their mascot. They let me into the station to make toast and tea for them. They bought me toys and they used to give me bread, butter and cheese to take home to my ma. Then there was the news that three of them had been shot dead, not any of the boys in Brown Square. I just went away and cried.[13]

These were the March 1971 killings of three young Scots off duty from their battalion who were lured by an Ardoyne IRA unit from a city centre pub to their execution on a lonely road in North Belfast. 'People started to say it was the IRA and I'd say: 'Who are they?' The answer would be: "They're Fenians." I started to want revenge for those boys.'[14] He had to wait for it, finally being accepted by the Lower Shankill UDA in 1978. He could neither read nor write, having been suspended from school at the age of eleven and a half for hitting a teacher with a chair. He stresses he was not the only one to emerge illiterate from Belfast's schools.

Calderwood still says he would rather have joined the Ulster Volunteer Force.

> They had something special, a mystique if you like. But I was from a big family, I had two sisters and four brothers. There were too many family already in the UDA for me not to join. That was it really. There was only the one way for me to

go after what had happened, the things I've told you about and what our community had gone through.[15]

Four or five miles away in the Braniel housing estate in east Belfast, a tough and streetwise teenager called Michael Stone also joined up. Brought up in the area by an uncle and aunt he has described as hard-working and affectionate to him, he had got into trouble at school and given up a shipyard apprenticeship after rising to a leadership role in one of the area's tartan gangs. Some of these had as many as 150 members and identified themselves by tartan scarves or patches on their denim jackets. This was possibly in tribute to the three very young Royal Highland Fusiliers whose deaths had such an impact on Calderwood, though they may also have been copying the Scottish rock band the Bay City Rollers.

The gang's forays into Catholic areas and Stone's relish for violence attracted the attention of the local UDA and its leader, Tommy Herron, but joining was not a problem. Stone had been deeply affected by the way a cousin who lived with and looked after sick and ailing parents had been evicted from his home in Ardoyne in the summer of 1971 by a vengeful Republican crowd. 'This sectarian attack on my family sowed the seeds of hatred and resentment that would stay with me for most of my adult life,' he wrote later.[16] As IRA attacks grew in indiscriminate ferocity, such as the bombing of a restaurant in Belfast's Cornmarket in March 1972, in which a young mother who was a family friend died of terrible injuries, Stone knew that he 'was on a path of no return, that would eventually take me to prison, or to my death'.[17]

Shortly afterwards Stone reported at a rendezvous on the edge of East Belfast with four other prospective UDA volunteers. Herron was there to meet them, and Stone, having been in the Army Cadet Force, was able to impress him by the ease with which he could dismantle, reassemble and load a 9mm Star revolver. The real test, however, which only Stone passed, was to use the weapon to kill a friendly Alsatian dog which Herron had brought with him. 'If you couldn't kill the dog, then you're not capable of killing a human being,'[18] Herron remarked as he took his leave, and Stone was sworn in to full membership the following week. His exploits would, in time, make him a figure of iconic status within the UDA.

Others, like Stone, joined the UDA in response to particular atrocities, sometimes ones which they had witnessed themselves. On 11 December 1971, at the height of a busy Saturday on the Shankill Road, the IRA, in revenge for a terrible Loyalist bombing of a Catholic bar, McGurk's, on North Queen Street a week earlier, planted a no-warning bomb in the Balmoral furniture store. The explosion brought most of the building down and hundreds of people dug at the rubble with their bare hands alongside police and troops in search of survivors. Of four victims killed, two were children aged two years and one year respectively. People still living in the area will talk even now of the young men they knew who joined Loyalist paramilitary organisations in the rage and fear which followed this attack. One who did, according to his son, was Tommy Lyttle, who later became a brigadier in the UDA.[19]

John White felt there was only one answer to acts like these: 'I'd seen the results of IRA operations, babies, children, pensioners beheaded, blown apart. I thought we should fight fire with fire.'[20] White, who, eighteen months later, committed two of the most frenzied and sadistic murders in Northern Ireland's Troubles, grew up with a large family on Belfast's Old Lodge Road. He had seven brothers and sisters, two of whom died young, and his father was an invalid from war wounds.

> My home wasn't a Loyalist one in a political sense but my father hated Catholics. He wouldn't have any in the house, even when one of my brothers had a Catholic girlfriend. Often he would talk of the Free State's treachery to Britain in the war in which of course he had served.[21]

The UDA for him initially was street defence. The family had left their home in the New Barnsley estate after the outbreak of the Troubles had turned the area into a dangerous 'interface'. After that, he describes his role as 'vigilante stuff, balaclavas, pick handles, all that',[22] though he held on to a job, having served an apprenticeship as a joiner. When, in June 1973, the Ulster Freedom Fighters emerged as the new cutting edge of UDA counter-terror, White was one of its founders and ready to kill for it.

Other Loyalists had already begun their journey down that road and some works on the Troubles attribute killings to members of the UDA well before it was formed. This of course is not to deny that murders were committed by Loyalists who later joined its ranks, and by the early months of 1972 it was 'outkilling' the UVF. This latter organisation, with a pedigree stretching back to the 1912 Home Rule crisis, proud of its ex-service ethos, secretive and disciplined, never aspired to a mass membership after its re-emergence in the mid-1960s. It soon brought the gun back to Belfast's streets, well ahead of the crisis arising from the Civil Rights Campaign. This fact has constantly been pressed into service by Republicans anxious to deny that Loyalist violence has simply been a reaction to their own and to argue that it has been more a response to the threat of political change.[23]

It is true that the first sectarian killings of the 1960s, if the final phase of the IRA's border campaign is left out, were indeed the work of Loyalists. These, however, were few in number and although Civil Rights and People's Democracy marches were physically attacked, a well-armed Loyalist community did not use guns against them.[24] The real escalation in Loyalist violence only came once it was clear that the IRA had embarked upon an all-out and indiscriminate offensive against the security forces and the majority community. Once this became a reality, UDA members, especially in 1972 and 1973, were responsible for many more killings than the UVF, which had suffered heavily from arrests of its members after the 1966 Malvern Street murder, for which Gusty Spence was convicted. It only reappeared with any capacity to kill in 1971 and most of its victims that year died in one single bombing, that of McGurk's bar.

Any analysis of Loyalist violence has to be linked carefully to the chronology of political events. When Britain suspended Stormont in late March 1972 and imposed direct government on Northern Ireland, it dealt a severe and lasting blow to the self-esteem of Ulster Loyalism and Unionism more generally. UDA killings in response to it and to continued IRA attacks intensified both in number and in the ferocity with which they were carried out. The journalist John Whale, a shrewd interpreter of the Troubles as they unfolded, was alert to the connection. 'Just as the Provisional IRA had been a response to pre-emptive violence used by the forces of order,' he wrote, 'so the UDA, though it had a long ancestry in Ulster history, was still at this stage a defensive reaction to violence from the Republican side. If that violence had ended then, when Stormont did, the UDA would certainly have remained watchful, but its growth would have been checked.'[25]

Even amidst mounting violence and with the ground shifting politically under Loyalists' feet, joining one organisation rather than another did require a choice, as David Ervine recalled more than thirty years later. He decided it had to be the UVF after Bloody Friday, 21 July 1972, when, with minimal warning to the emergency services, the IRA set off twenty bombs in Belfast in just over an hour. Television viewers the same evening saw RUC officers scraping human remains into plastic bags outside the Oxford Street bus depot, one of the targets. Nine people died and 130 were injured.

> The UDA was too loose and disparate for my liking. They took time to cohere from the original area defence associations. I was never too keen either on the street drills they went in for. The UVF had its own mystique. It was family history too as my grandfather had been in it. Mind you, lots of good lads I knew in East Belfast did join the UDA and that was never a problem for me. We all had to choose and we were all caught in a groundswell of feeling, of fear.[26]

Ervine was right about the UDA's preoccupation with open drilling on the streets. This was of course a way of both demonstrating its presence and providing footage for camera crews from the world's media but it was not all just show. In Woodvale, with David Fogel second in command to Charles Harding Smith, the local UDA unit entered 1972 with 150 members and trebled that number over the next twelve months. They exchanged fire with the IRA for the first time in December 1971 and Fogel looked after the instruction of new recruits: 'I taught them about unarmed combat – you know, how to break a nose, burst an ear drum, dislocate a spine.'[27] But he also set up lectures on police and army interrogation methods and urban guerrilla tactics.

Harding Smith's rise within the organisation was rapid. His power base in Woodvale was a strong one and by early 1972 he was speaking for it as chairman of its governing council, representing six brigade areas. As the security situation worsened he became convinced that the priority for the UDA was to expand and modernise its firepower. In April he and White went to London to make contact with arms dealers, claiming the funds were already there to cover major purchases. Recruitment continued in his absence and Fogel decided that, in response to the creation of a growing number of 'no-go' areas in the city controlled by the IRA, Loyalists must show their hand.

This appears to have been a decision he was able to make himself because Harding Smith and White were arrested in London at the end of April and charged with illegal purchase of arms. Jim Anderson, who ran a glazier's business on the Crumlin Road, took over as acting chairman and fully supported Fogel, who organised the sealing off of Woodvale with barricades and roadblocks at the end of May. Army and police units were as reluctant to act as they were in response to similar IRA initiatives and it was a triumph for Fogel.

> Before then we had been written off as a bunch of loonies: toy soldiers playing with wooden guns and crawling over fields in so-called training. Training for what, I used to be asked. That no-go area showed them. For the first time, ordinary Protestants were doing something for themselves.[28]

Press and camera crews gave the operation maximum coverage, as Fogel had hoped they would: 'After that there was no stopping us. In June three of us drove up to Stormont to see Willie Whitelaw, the British Cabinet Minister [who had been appointed Secretary of State for Northern Ireland when direct rule was announced on 24 March]. That same month we marched 23,000 strong and twelve abreast through the centre of Belfast.'[29] In fact, the new secretary of state was not initially over-impressed by Fogel and his fellow governing council members. 'I met the UDA leaders in mid-June,' he wrote in his memoirs. 'They arrived looking quite absurd in hoods and sunglasses.'[30]

Whitelaw made it clear that any further attempts to set up permanent barricades by the UDA would not be permitted and he left the meeting believing that such action would be postponed. The threat of more no-go areas was, however, renewed at the end of the month in Ainsworth Avenue, off the Shankill Road, at the height of which Fogel, Andy Tyrie and other UDA leaders negotiated directly with an army general. The full implications of this episode and its outcome will be examined in a later chapter which covers the UDA's paramilitary role and its relationship to the security forces.

Fogel's prestige on the Shankill soared as a result of the role he had played.

> I was big Dave. I even had two bodyguards who went everywhere with me. I was a bit of everything in those streets – policeman, magistrate, and welfare worker. I sometimes presided at unofficial courts. We bashed faces in if we thought someone guilty of, say, house breaking. There wasn't much trouble though.
>
> I've never been so busy. The parlour of our house was always full, neighbours, men from the UDA and Pressmen from all over the world. We even gave cups of tea to American Congressmen.[31]

The exercise by the UDA of a policing role in areas where the RUC's writ had for the time being ceased to run began to be of concern to Unionist politicians. Their concern grew as rumours spread about the extent of the organisation's fundraising and the way it was being carried out. White added fuel to the rumours when he told a broadcaster early in 1972 that raising £250,000 for arms purchases 'would be no great problem'.[32]

Wary as they may have been, Unionists could from early in the UDA's existence find themselves accepting its protection. James Molyneaux, a Unionist MP who later became party leader, found himself in this position early in July 1972 in Lisburn, when he attended the town's commemoration of the battle of the Somme and the sacrifice there of the Ulster Division. The parade organisers had been warned by the security forces of a possible IRA attack and of the only limited protection they could offer. A recently formed UDA unit from Dunmurry in South Belfast offered to line what it felt was the most vulnerable stretch of the parade route and marched into the town centre in order to do so.

Molyneaux and other Unionists and Orangemen leading the parade felt that they had at least to acknowledge the UDA's presence.

> You had the feeling that they knew you and vice versa, on Christian name terms. If they had taken off the masks most of the officers [he meant senior office bearers in lodges on the parade] and I would have recognised them. It was that type of contradictory position. They felt they had to band together to protect their community. However, even at the back of my mind, I was wondering, will somebody be able to keep control of all this?[33]

Apart from its increasingly visible presence on the streets and the intensifying attacks its members were launching on the nationalist community, the UDA in this period also issued a proliferating array of leaflets, bulletins and news-sheets to publicise and explain its role. Some of these ran for only a few issues. Others survive, undated. Often they were cyclostyled in the most basic way and proof-checking could be minimal. Yet these publications, brought out in haste and in response to rapid and violent changes, as well as ordinary people's contributions to them, remain a vivid and sometimes moving source on the anxieties and fears, even if crudely and brutally expressed, of a community which in a short space of time had seen all its old certainties turned upside down.

Symptomatic of this was the decision in July 1972 by the new Northern Ireland Office that there should be no 12 July parades. This was because of the communal violence caused by some major parades since August 1969 and because controlling processional routes would severely over-stretch the security forces. UDA publications called in vain for Orange lodges to resist this decision and forecast that new leaders would emerge within the Order to defy the authorities. Not all UDA members were Orangemen but they grasped the symbolism of the decision: 'The Twelfth without the marches is like a wedding without the bride,'[34] one contributor declared, predicting too that it would mean the end of Orangeism.

In fact the Orange Order survived though with diminishing power to influence events or the politics of a divided Unionism, and Loyalists clung to the notion of its marches being events which both communities could share in.

> On the 11th the crowds that were to be found around the bonfires all over the city were very mixed even in the supposedly bigoted areas of Sandy Row and Brown Square [off the lower end of the Shankill Road]. Of course there were always the old diehards. They existed on both sides. But they were few, very, very few.

This contributor to a cyclostyled UDA bulletin went on to invoke an image of pre-1969 Northern Ireland growing in prosperity and moving away from old hatreds but his tone altered when he argued that the trouble really lay with Captain Terence O'Neill's attempt to liberalise Ulster Unionism during his years as Prime Minister after 1963.

> He assumed that the Ulster Loyalist cared not about his birthright. This paternalistic moron made the assumption that the landed gentry who are educated in England continually think that they know what is best for the Ulster Loyalist. They keep forgetting that what distinguishes the Ulster Loyalist from the rest of the United Kingdom and the Nationalists is his stubborn independence, his criterion that he and he alone is the arbiter of his fate in human affairs.[36]

The writer accepted that there had indeed been justice in the demands of the civil rights movement but he argued that it had become an easy tool for Republicans and Marxists. Catholics in his view should bide their time without violence until they became a majority who could then vote themselves into a united Ireland. 'The Protestant, being what he is, will accept the situation then without any violence whatsoever.'[37]

Whether in the midst of a full-scale IRA campaign many Loyalists agreed with him on his final assertion must be debatable, but at least a UDA publication had let him say it. A recurrent theme in these bulletins and news-sheets is the superior skill with which nationalists and Republicans put their case.

> The claim that they and they alone were denied proper voting in local council elections was of course another blatant lie. They knew that the Protestant was subject to the exact same rules as the Roman Catholics but by skilful use of propaganda they implied to the world that they and they alone were the people deprived of voting rights under the existing system.[38]

Protestants were indeed denied local council votes in Northern Ireland before 1969 because the fault lines within the community there were the product of social class as well as sectarianism but the matter got crowded out of UDA publications in 1972 and 1973 amidst the brutal immediacy of events.

Alongside this degree of reflection on the politics of the Troubles, what often surfaced was a simple and very human regret at what people sensed was happening to them as individuals. The UDA early in 1971 printed a moving letter from a Second World War widow who had been appalled to witness pupils at her grandchildren's school in the Oldpark area requiring army protection from hostile nationalist crowds. 'I have become more and more dejected,' she wrote, 'at times I sit and cry my heart out. Normal conversation is a thing of the past, all that I hear are things said by people that I know to be untruths, spiteful things, hurtful things from people that I used to chat with, have cups of tea with. These same people now hurl abuse, bang binlids, allow themselves to be used as bomb throwers, their houses to be used as shelter for snipers and gunmen. Where, oh where is it going to end?'[39]

Her grandchildren's school, Finniston Primary on the Oldpark Road, had indeed become a sectarian flashpoint, requiring a permanent army presence at the start and finish of the pupils' day. Some parents resorted to a lengthy detour up the Cliftonville Road so that their children could use a safer rear entrance to the school. This was the vicious reality of the Troubles at street level and it affected deeply the unnamed Protestant woman who wrote in to the UDA bulletin. At the outset of the civil rights campaign, she admitted, she had felt some sympathy for the nationalist community.

> Like most moderates, I was fooled into supporting them at the start. But now I have to take my grandchildren to school because they are stoned if they go alone. The older children who go by bus were, I thought, safe. But this week their bus was stopped at 8.45 a.m. and even as the children were getting off the bus they were splattered with petrol by these animals – there, even now, I use words that weeks ago I condemned other people for using – and the last child had still to get off when the bus was set alight.
>
> I broke my heart as a daughter in 1918 when my father was killed in France and again as a wife in 1944. Must I break it again as a doting grandmother? Can I not have a little happiness before I die? Yet now I find myself condemning the army for standing by, for watching as our city dies in agony.[40]

Grief like hers, and of those either bereaved by IRA attacks or who had seen the results at close quarters, could quickly turn into fear and vengeful rage. This rage began to be directed at all things Irish and at the Irish state itself. Reports in 1972 of the Dublin government seeking powers to control illegal cross-border trading in pigs prompted an article in the *UDA Bulletin* declaring that the Republic was itself one large pigsty, second only to those occupied by the nationalist community in its own areas within Northern Ireland.[41] There had already been calls for Loyalists to refuse Irish currency, whether in banks, shops or social security offices, though little came of this campaign.[42]

An easier target for vilification was the nationalist enemy within, constantly expanding in numbers, it was claimed, and moving insidiously into former Loyalist areas with the connivance allegedly of growing numbers of

Catholic staff within the Housing Executive. This was the body which in 1971 had taken over the allocation and building of public-sector houses from local authorities. Its discrimination against Loyalists would be monitored, it was promised, and if it continued 'then the Ulster Defence Association will have to intervene in no uncertain manner'.[43]

Loyalists were urged to hold their ground and not leave Belfast, where long-term change in the religious composition of the city's population was already being anticipated. The siting of a new Catholic church was often identified as a signal of this process. In early 1972, work commenced on a church in Newtonabbey in North Belfast, a peripheral area of the city with a mainly Protestant population. 'This area is 74 per cent Protestant now,' the UDA told readers of its bulletin. 'If you let them get away with building a chapel you can say goodbye to Newtonabbey as a Loyalist area.'[44]

Newtonabbey in fact remained a predominantly Protestant area, partly because many Catholic families were intimidated out of it, but the call to 'protect' it and other Loyalist localities was a product of a daily worsening situation. It was also influenced by deep ethnic fear of the minority community. Sometimes this was expressed in the grossest caricatures of that community. Another issue of the *UDA Bulletin* referred to the Republican prisoners' compound at Long Kesh, or the Maze as it was later renamed, as a fumigation centre. Reports of an outbreak of scabies among prisoners there was attributed to 'the reaction of their bodies. The dirt that had been accumulated over the years had provided the bodies with bacteriological protection; however, the removal of this slime [necessary for fumigation purposes] removed the bodies' protection with the inevitable result of scabies.'[45]

From language like this it was a short trip to calls for the extermination of the enemy. In February 1972, the UDA's bulletin printed a letter which it claimed was from a woman reader, in which it was stated:

> I have reached the stage where I no longer have any compassion for any nationalist, man, woman, or child. After years of destruction, murder, intimidation, I have been driven against my better feelings to the decision – it's them or us. What I want to know is this, where the hell are the MEN in our community? Have they any pride? Have they any guts? Why are they not organized in, not defence, but commando groups? Why have they not started to hit back in the only way these nationalist bastards understand? That is, ruthless, indiscriminate killing. If I had a flame-thrower, I would roast the slimy excreta that pass for human beings. Also I'm sick and tired of you yellow-backed Prods who are not even prepared to fight for your own street, let alone your own loyalist people. When civil war breaks out, and God forgive me but I hope it's soon, I at least will shoot you along with the Fenian scum.[46]

Whether this letter was genuine or planted to deliberately raise the temperature and to mobilise support for Loyalist commando-style killer squads to take on and 'take out' the Republican enemy and its supporters is not really relevant. Killing by the UDA was already under way and was increasing, as was acceptance of it within the broader Unionist community. That was certainly the message from William Craig, formerly Home Affairs Minister in Terence O'Neill's Cabinet, when he told a huge Vanguard Unionist rally at Lisburn that same month: 'We are determined, ladies and gentlemen, to preserve our British traditions and way of life. And God help those who get in our way.'[47]

Victims of the UDA's murder gangs that began to operate out of hard-line Loyalist areas of Belfast in the summer of 1972 did not have to 'get in the way'. Simply being in the wrong place was enough to seal the fate of dozens of Catholics who were easy targets for its roving gunmen. The largest gang, in which John White was active, was based in the Shankill and may have numbered thirty members. One of them was Davy Payne, a sadist addicted to the use of knives to torture and mutilate those they abducted, including women, before killing them. Smaller units operated from East and North Belfast and from Sandy Row, close to the city centre.

Even as the UDA was drawn inexorably down a road which would lead it to take hundreds of lives, there were those within its membership who struggled to use its growing resources for other purposes. A new publication, the *Ulster Loyalist*, which began to appear in the latter part of 1972, regularly ran a 'Helping Hand' page to update readers on the UDA's contribution to 'community work'. This could include the type of action against anti-social elements in Loyalist areas which David Fogel had initiated in Woodvale. In February 1974 it advised people in the Sandy Row and Village areas that firm measures against teenage crime and vandalism were imminent. Local 'hoods' were warned that 'the necessary steps are being taken to seek you out and to deal with you in a manner which your behaviour deserves'.[48]

The paper's December 1973 issue had much space given over to the success of parties for pensioners and prisoners' children in East Belfast. In Upper Ardoyne, a local primary school, across the road from the Holy Cross girls' school which thirty years later would be made world famous by a Loyalist picket, 500 children attended a party organised by the UDA. A local army unit, the Argyll and Sutherland Highlanders, promised in advance to make their own rock group available for the event, security in the area permitting.[49] Earlier that year, over a hundred children from the Shore Road area, many of them with fathers in prison or interned, were given a holiday in England, organised and financed by the local UDA unit.[50]

This anxiety to set up activities and outings for children in Loyalist areas was rooted partly in fear of the cross-community initiatives of this period under which, and often with generous Northern Ireland Office support, Protestant and Catholic children would be taken on group holidays to locations outside the province. These projects may have achieved some success in bridging barriers though there could be no certainty of this. Alec Calderwood went on such a trip at the age of eleven and got into serious trouble in Holland for an assault on Catholic pupils.[51] One UDA publication left readers in no doubt about its view of such trips, condemning people who let their children go on them. In an article entitled 'Are you one of these parents?' it portrayed them as no more than a Catholic strategy to brainwash young Protestants: 'We know them to be liars: we know them to be hypocrites: we know now that they no more change their hatred of Protestants than a skunk changes its smell.'[52]

Some who joined the UDA in this period of extreme violence soon found that they had little relish for what was involved in its paramilitary role, especially as killers capable of psychotic violence against their own community as well as Catholics were let off the leash. It did, however, remain possible for such people to take a part in what they could convince themselves was the organisation's community role, especially providing advice and financial support for prisoners' families at a time when it was very hard for existing agencies to perform their most basic tasks in areas worst hit by the Troubles.

Sarah Nelson arrived in Belfast in 1971, just out of university, to take up a position as an unqualified social worker on the Shankill Road and later wrote an exceptionally vivid and moving account of her time there. She found herself among a population ignored by her academic peer group whose perception of the situation was heavily influenced by support for nationalism and Republicanism. The ordinary Protestant people she worked with close to the centre of the conflict seemed to her to feel as if they had little control over events and often drew only very limited reassurance from the UDA's appearance on their streets.

> Many families were overtaken by foreboding rather than relief or triumphalism. They did not know who some of these people were, even on their own streets. They were full of fear when their sons were mixed up in it or might become so, risking death, injury or jail and felt the young people were slipping further out of their control.[53]

Over time, many who had settled for contributing to the UDA's non-paramilitary role moved away from it and went into wider aspects of community work in Loyalist localities. Others remained in active membership while continuing, so far as they could, to support both its publicity and propaganda as well as its prisoners' support work and advisory services in hard-pressed Protestant areas. Sammy Duddy managed to do this for three decades.

The UDA's community role was certainly what drew Hester Dunn into it as a young mother who had moved into the Suffolk housing estate after growing up in East Belfast. A former go-go dancer without any political interests, she was drawn into local campaigns on road safety in which she felt Unionist councillors had been ineffectual. The Unionist Party in fact gave her work in its local office after she had led a street protest which resulted in a new pedestrian crossing being provided near her house after a child had been run over and killed. Suffolk was a mixed estate when the Troubles started, but rapidly became a dangerous interface area in which her Protestant neighbours by 1971 were under severe pressure to vacate their homes as nationalist crowds attacked them amidst mounting IRA violence.

As she became more active on behalf of beleaguered Protestant tenants in Suffolk, so she also became a target herself. She survived an attack by young Republicans but what most upset her was her small daughter's ostracism by Catholics in a nearby community centre where she had enrolled her for Irish dancing classes. On top of that came charges of public order offences. These were later dismissed by a court but involved eleven months on bail.

> The only people that I could see were doing anything were the Ulster Defence Association. I started to think if my court case had gone wrong and I'd been put in jail, who would have looked after me? The Ulster Defence Association. Then Andy Tyrie asked me did I want to work on a part-time basis.'[54]

Dunn remained with the UDA for many years and was encouraged by Tyrie to work on and write about women's issues, especially in *Ulster*, in which for a time she had a regular column. To sustain such a role was no mean feat in as heavily male an organisation as the UDA, but her presence at its Newtownards Road headquarters, chain smoking and often strikingly clad in tight black leather outfits, became familiar to many journalists and interviewers. One of these, the American Sally Belfrage, put it:

> Hester was obviously more than a mere receptionist – she appeared almost to choreograph the place, to know everybody's business and with an effective blend of chiding, wisecracking and mothering, to take on and tame the more threatening of the male species.[55]

Dunn was always fiercely loyal to Tyrie's leadership and left the organisation when he fell from power. Her own experiences as well as disillusionment with Ulster Unionism had brought her into the UDA and given her a significant role within it but she always accepted that, despite Tyrie's support for her work, there were limits to how far she could go.

Almost all those who rose to positions of leadership within the UDA in this initial period of its existence had come to have real doubts about what the established Unionist parties could offer the working-class Protestant people. 'Increasingly in Woodvale', David Fogel recalled, 'we also talked politics. We felt let down by the Unionists. We didn't want these middle class smarty pants ponceing down our streets once every five years asking for our votes and then never bothering to come back again until the next election.'[56] Fogel was impressed by the massive rallies mobilised by William Craig's Vanguard movement in February and March 1972. Many UDA men attended these and acted as bodyguards to leading figures but Fogel had his doubts about Craig because of his refusal to make a clean break with the Unionists.

He was unconvinced too by Craig's talk of a possible 'unilateral declaration of independence' by Loyalists and he talked to Dr Ian Paisley, whose new

Democratic Unionist Party was then pushing the case for the full integration of Northern Ireland with Britain. 'I personally thought there was a lot of sense in this but a majority of the Security Council disagreed,' Fogel later recalled.[57] It would take time for the UDA to come out for negotiated Ulster independence. In 1971 and 1972, many of its rank and file were content simply to support LAW, 'a front organisation for us' as Fogel called it,[58] though he recognised the importance of it in keeping Protestant trade unionists focused on the issue of tougher security measures against IRA attacks.

Others within the UDA did not share Fogel's doubts about Craig and this included his own Woodvale company. Their March 1972 bulletin pledged support for Vanguard on the grounds that 'this is NOT a political party, but an Organisation that is determined there will be no tampering with the constitution'.[59] Support for Unionists such as Craig and Paisley, Professor Steve Bruce has pointed out, could rise steeply when events let them present themselves as not mere politicians but prospective saviours of Loyalist Ulster.[60] The reality was that as many UDA members as wanted to could attend Vanguard's rallies, some of which drew enormous crowds, without the organisation itself having to be directly aligned to it.

Ernie Elliott, who became Fogel's second in command in the Woodvale UDA, though a tough character with whom few in the area would trifle, was convinced that the organisation could and should take on a real political role. This was not in fact the reason for him being murdered by other UDA members in December 1972, but Fogel remembered him as

> the man who always encouraged me to think in terms of politics. When I first met him I was a Conservative but he made me more left wing. He used to walk around Woodvale with Che Guevara's books stuffed in his pockets.[61]

How carefully he read the books, as opposed to displaying them, may never be known, but the period of his influence on Fogel saw successful threats of direct action and civil disobedience in Woodvale to pressurise the city council into restoring proper street lighting and repairing the pavements. It also saw attempts to make contact with the Catholic Ex-Servicemen's Association in nearby Ardoyne. Fogel felt they, in their street defence role, were a counterpart to the UDA and might co-operate with it in reducing and controlling interface violence. Charles Harding Smith, an inarticulate man, had few political ideas and discouraged political discussion at UDA Security Council meetings. Fogel thought this had a bad effect on them: 'We got so bored that Jim Anderson, the chairman, had to begin an attendance register, like we had at school.'[62]

Harding Smith's absence in London for much of 1972, after he and John White were charged with attempting the illegal purchase of firearms for the UDA, was an opportunity Fogel and Elliott had not anticipated. They did, it seems, use it to make some political contacts which their imprisoned leader would not have been happy with. These included talks in Dublin with Dessie O'Hagan, a leader of the Official Republican movement, which had called off its armed struggle against Britain's presence in Northern Ireland in May of that year on the grounds that it was only contributing to the worsening of sectarian divisions in the community.

They also met, in Fogel's home, two representatives of the British and Irish Communist Organisation, who were bitter opponents of the Provisional IRA and espoused the 'two nations' theory on the Irish question. This involved support for workers' struggles on either side of the border but saw Protestant Ulster as a nation in its own right whose best interests lay in the continuation of the Union with Britain. Fogel talked of them as

> the only Marxist group that recognises Ulster. It wants the Catholics to come out categorically for the recognition of the border. It's this which keeps the Catholic and Protestant working-class apart. Once the Prods lose their fear of Dublin then the way is open to a united working class.[63]

The talks were inconclusive but they do seem to have taken place. Fogel also recalled Tommy Herron, the UDA's East Belfast brigadier, attending and being 'quite interested'.[64]

Herron's presence at this meeting was used against him as tensions within the UDA rose during the period of Harding Smith's detention on remand in London. This gave Herron the chance to play a bigger role, which he clearly enjoyed. He missed no chance of talking to the media, claiming that his position as vice-chairman allowed him to do this during Harding Smith's absence. The fact that his mother was a Catholic fed rumours about him, especially when he made a statement on the need for the UDA to have no part in the killing of innocent Catholics. He went further and stated that Catholics in East Belfast who feared Loyalist attacks should approach him directly for protection.

This was too much for one UDA publication, the *Ulster Militant*, which devoted much of one issue to what Herron had said. In one article it declared:

> Any Protestant who threatens to take reprisal action against any other Protestant for his actions against the enemy is a traitor. Traitors deserve to be shot and should be shot and it is our hope that they will be shot.[65]

It also took up a claim by Herron that the UDA was there to protect all the people of Northern Ireland:

> Not the Loyalists, mind you, not the Protestants mind you, but all the people. This includes the Roman Catholics who have helped to rape our city, who have helped to bomb and murder Protestants. Only this week, they again, for the umpteenth time, shot at Finniston School on the Oldpark Road, a school for primary age children.[66]

Herron's alleged contacts with the Official Republican movement were also raised, partly in response to a recent article in the Dublin-based magazine *Hibernia*, which had claimed that there were active Marxists within the UDA receptive to the case for an Irish workers' republic.[67] 'Is this possible? Is it true?' the *Ulster Militant* asked.

> If it is, then it obviously explains the Vice-Chairman's preoccupation with Roman Catholics. If it is the policy of the UDA to protect and aid Roman Catholics while Protestants are still dying from Roman Catholic activities then we apologise to Tommy Herron for criticising him. But we feel it is necessary to add that it is time the rank and file were told about it. Don't you agree Tommy?[68]

Leading questions like these from within the UDA ought to have served as a warning to Herron, even though he still had a strong power base in the east side of the city. Herron is not remembered by those who knew him as living lavishly, though neither he nor his children appeared to be short of money. In fact no UDA leaders at this period were enjoying the affluent lifestyle later associated with it once the temptations of blatant criminality and drug-dealing took over. All that was still to come. Fogel recalled that he drew ten pound a week from the Woodvale unit's funds and was provided also with a second-hand Mini since he had to make trips to Stormont as well as visiting other brigade areas in the city.[69]

Fogel rejected press claims that Harding Smith and White had £350,000 or anything near it to spend on arms purchases at the time of their arrest. Fund-raising, he insisted, came from a membership levy of twenty-five pence a week, as well as collections at rallies and in pubs. Spending £4,000 to do up a club building in Woodvale had, he admitted, been possibly a public relations error, but as to the supply of liquor to it and other UDA clubs, he argued that 'it was obtained legally, at least by Belfast standards. So a man whose pub had disappeared would simply continue to order from the brewery and deliver to the clubs and he'd get his rake-off.'[70]

Bank robbery, Fogel also claimed, was something left to the UVF, and the West Belfast UDA tried mobile patrols of its own and cash rewards to bring under control the hijacking of vehicles carrying drink and cigarettes into the area. This could involve on occasions confronting non-political criminals.

> There were some hard men on the Shankill who we had to warn off. Usually a severe talking to was enough for them to see the error of their ways but those who remained stroppy received a thump. But in most cases, a warning like 'knock it off before you land up in Roselawn' was enough'[71]

Roselawn was one of Belfast's main cemeteries.

Rumours, however, continued to spread about UDA 'fund-raising' becoming a crude form of extortion. Harding Smith, on his return to Belfast, reacted with concern to this and to what he saw as a general increase in law-lessness. He pressed for the UDA to deal with these issues and to toughen up its own 'policing' role but the allegations persisted and the press began to take them up. 'I'm not a brave man but the money they are demanding would make business impossible,' a publican told a newspaper in June 1973. 'My life has been threatened. My pub receives six bomb scares a week. I don't know how long I can last out. I daren't go to the police. The UDA said they would get me wherever I was.'[72]

Herron, in the same newspaper, produced the manager of a pub close to the UDA's East Belfast HQ. The man, admitting he himself was in the UDA, declared: 'Since the UDA came in to protect us, we have had no trouble. Takings have doubled.'[73] Reporters, however, found other publicans, anxious to conceal their identities, who were rather less happy. They wanted to know where the money raised by 'protection' was going and who was paying for drinking parties in the UDA building. One man put it vividly:

> A UDA man comes round and says 'would you like to make a contribution to the UDA prisoners' welfare fund?' If I say no, it's common knowledge what will happen. You get a bullet through the door or you get your windows smashed. If you use my name or identify me, I'll be found out on some waste ground not moving.[74]

Few UDA members who were active in these years will now deny that such fund-raising methods were used and some, such as Jackie McDonald, who later became South Belfast brigadier, have talked openly about it.[75] A succession of court cases and convictions over the years offer further proof that this was how the organisation's firepower was financed and also how incomes, modest in many cases but lavish in some others, were put the way of unit and area commanders whose paramilitary connections cut them off from conventional employment.

Harding Smith's condemnation of such activity never needed to be taken too seriously. He wanted to retrieve and extend his power within the UDA, building from a power base in West Belfast which he felt had been compromised in his absence by the way Fogel and Ernie Elliott had run the organisation. Elliott, however, was brutally removed from the scene even before the Old Bailey court case against Harding Smith and White had collapsed. His body was found trussed up in a car just off Tates Avenue, which links Belfast's Lisburn Road to the fiercely Loyalist Village area. He had been killed by a shotgun blast in the face.

This was on 7 December 1972 and his funeral a few days later was a major event. Elliott's coffin was carried from his home on Leopold Street, covered in a UDA flag on which were laid his badges of rank in the organisation as well as his Orangeman's sash. A volley of shots was fired over the coffin by a UDA guard of honour and thousands of members in combat jackets and forage caps followed the cortège. Claims were made in the aftermath of his murder that Elliott was a victim of his socialist convictions and that Harding Smith wanted an example made of him because of these and his contacts with the Official IRA.[76]

There is little evidence to substantiate this. Elliott, it has been shown, was killed in a dispute between his own Woodvale unit of the UDA and members of one of its South Belfast companies who drank in a club in Sandy Row. Some Woodvale guns had been stored there for safekeeping and an argument developed over their return. An attempt by Elliott and another Woodvale man to take over the premises at gunpoint was foiled. Elliott received a vicious beating and was then killed with a shotgun, his body dumped only a short distance away.[77] The killing removed a close ally of Fogel, whose position was beginning to crumble even before Harding Smith returned to Belfast a week or so later. There is no basis for implicating Harding Smith in Elliott's murder, although it suited him well enough. In 1983, his name did not even figure in Belfast Crown Court when three Sandy Row men were brought to trial over Elliott's death, only for the case against them to collapse.[78]

Fogel's fall from power came quickly after Elliott's murder. It was hastened by the fact that Herron, aware of criticism within the UDA of his role, chose to support Harding Smith against the Woodvale commander. Fogel claimed that Herron did this because he was under threat and informed Jim Anderson, then co-chairman of the UDA with Harding Smith, that his running of the Woodvale company was being questioned.[79] On Saturday, 13 January 1973, Fogel was lured to Herron's East Belfast HQ on the pretext that two of his men were being held there over disciplinary matters. On his arrival, Fogel was placed under a form of arrest and held under guard for three hours in a room in the Newtownards Road building. It was put forcibly to him that he could only retain his position within the organisation if he accepted, without any qualification, Harding Smith's leadership.

As Fogel shortly afterwards told the press, he was not prepared to be anyone's puppet. He and his men in Woodvale, he argued, had been risking their lives during the months in which Harding Smith had been safely on remand. However, with Elliott dead and a wife and children to think about, Fogel decided to leave Northern Ireland and returned to the safety of London. In press interviews he set out his view of events:

> There is a power struggle going on and I don't want to be part of it. We are mixing with dangerous and evil men out for their own gains and not for the interests of the ordinary working-class people of Ulster.[80]

Harding Smith, he claimed, had been talking directly to the UVF, which was almost certainly true, because he seems to have decided since his return to Belfast that the UDA could learn from the UVF's discipline and perhaps take a share in the returns from bank robberies, which were its preferred form of fund-raising at this time.

Fogel was fearful of the UDA travelling down this road, even though, under his command in Woodvale, it was financing its activities by methods that would have landed it in court if the RUC had been able to act effectively against it. 'The UDA must stay within the law and not start robbing banks,' he declared. 'We must not be associated with anything illegal otherwise it will give the government a chance to clamp down on us.'[81] In fact it was to be twenty years before any government declared the UDA illegal, but as events would soon show, the fear that this might happen influenced Harding Smith too.

In February the *Ulster Militant* responded to the outcome of this power struggle in an issue published a year after the 'Bloody Sunday' killings in Londonderry, which it described as 'a good Sunday for Loyalist Ulster and its people'.[82] It went on to give strong support to Harding Smith, rerunning allegations and rumours it had already printed about Fogel. Harding Smith was commended for 'holding the UDA together and stopping a Communist takeover'. Herron was not mentioned by name but the 'elimination' was called for 'of all within the UDA whose actions weaken or divide it'.[83]

Herron was still suspect to many in the UDA, especially outside East Belfast. On 3 January 1973, the leadership circulated all members with a call for attacks on Catholics to stop. This was in fact obeyed for a three-week period only but Herron supported it in terms which prompted fresh questions about his role when he declared that killers who acted on their own authority should be eliminated. His action prompted the Official IRA, on ceasefire since May of the previous year, to use the executive of the Republican Clubs movement to propose to the UDA the idea of joint patrols to prevent sectarian killings restarting. The UDA quickly rejected this but Herron's involvement did not help him.[84]

His position was beginning to crumble and those close to him, such as Michael Stone, sensed it. Precisely because of this he had little option but to support, at least publicly, a new initiative from Harding Smith, who appeared perturbed by fears of a government ban on the UDA. He decided, in either May or June 1973, that the organisation's killers, already active against easy targets within the nationalist community, should operate under a new name. This was the Ulster Freedom Fighters, which rapidly became the 'flag of convenience' under which a hard core of UDA killers along with some UVF defectors began to operate.

Their first attacks came in response to an IRA bomb explosion in Coleraine on 12 June 1973, which killed six old age pensioners on a day outing. All of them were Protestants. IRA claims that they had inadvertently given the wrong location of the bomb in a warning call to the security forces had little bearing on the new UFF's decision to launch reprisal killings, which they began to claim responsibility for in communiqués to the media. Almost certainly the first of its victims was James Kelly, a 25-year-old Catholic from Larne who often hitchhiked back there from Belfast where his girlfriend lived. Five days after the Coleraine bombing his body was found close to the Larne–Belfast road at Corr's Corner. 'We gave him two in the head and one in the back,'[85] the UFF stated in a telephone call to a Belfast newspaper office. The call made no direct reference to the Coleraine deaths, referring only to the recent murder of Herron's brother-in-law, which is known to have been the work of other Loyalists.

John White, one of the UFF's founders, who was widely believed to issue menacing communiqués to the media under the alias 'Captain Black', has spoken about what lay behind its emergence:

> The feeling was that the UDA had got too big and that we needed to reorganise the real activists into small, streamlined units who could hit the IRA where it hurt most, by attacks on the communities which were not just making excuses for them but actively supporting them. It was simple and it was brutal, there's no point in denying that.[86]

Brutal it certainly was and indiscriminate too, but this escalation of Northern Ireland's war was also accompanied by the fullest attempt thus far in the conflict to justify the Loyalist position. This took the form of a statement handed by the UDA on 9 June to the *Sunday World* newspaper. It began with a review of the origins of the Troubles and an admission that there was justification for the demands of the civil rights movement. These, it argued, were so mishandled by the Unionists as to play into the hands of a Republican movement ready to regroup and resurrect what it described as the 'age-old conflict of the Scots-Irish versus the Irish-Irish'.[87] The equally old spectre was also invoked of betrayal by London governments who in reality thought of Loyalists as 'second-class Englishmen and half-caste Irishmen'.[88]

The British media were vilified for their incomprehension of the Loyalist position, as was Dublin:

> If the Southern Irish government wants us then it will have to win our hearts, rather than have us as bitterly hostile losers in a bombing war of attrition tacitly backed by them. Their own history should tell them that this will never work.[89]

Intensified armed action was offered as Loyalists' only option. If this precipitated a bloodbath the blame would be with British politicians and the British media. 'We the Scots-Irish are fighting for survival,' the statement concluded.[90]

The statement was not printed in full by either the *Sunday World* or the *Belfast Telegraph*, which also received a copy, but a month after the 9 June UDA communiqué, a reporter from the latter, along with one from the *Daily Telegraph*, were granted an exclusive interview by two men who described themselves as representing the UFF brigade staff. By this time the horrific murder of the SDLP Stormont Senator Paddy Wilson and a Protestant woman friend had taken place. The journalists were told by one of the men: 'Wilson and Andrews was a ritual killing. It was a godsend to get rid of vermin like that.'[91] 'Andrews' was Irene Andrews, who was, like Paddy Wilson, a victim of multiple stab wounds, but the UFF men insisted both of them had Official Republican contacts.

A statement handed to the two reporters reiterated many of the points made a month earlier but it went on to equate Protestant Ulster's fate with that of Israel:

Our backs are to the wall. We have more in common with the State of Israel, the Star of David on our flag. These brave people fought and won their battle for survival. We intend to win ours. And like the Jewish people, each time an act of aggression is committed against our people, we shall retaliate in a way that only the animals in the IRA can understand.[92]

This was the first time the UDA invoked the example of Israel, and it would be another three decades before it would buy in bulk Israeli flags for Loyalist areas to fly in response to the IRA's espousal of the Palestinian cause.

The document also incorporated an appeal to the Catholic and nationalist population to break with the IRA:

Throw these gangsters out of your midst. Until you do this you must bear the agony. Our fight is not with you but with the animals you shelter. We trust that when our fight is won – as win we will – Ulster will be filled with people working for a common purpose.[93]

The message was that there could and should be an equal place for Catholics in a future Ulster state, though the form of such a state was left vague, as was its relationship to the United Kingdom as a whole. Later policy documents from the UDA made a genuine attempt to clarify this.

The immediate issue for the UDA however, in the summer of 1973, was still Tommy Herron's future. The announcement of the UFF's formation was at least in part a compromise between Harding Smith's power base in the Shankill and Herron's in the east of the city. Earlier in the year, Jim Anderson had resigned from his position as joint chairman with Harding Smith. A meeting of UDA commanders responded by agreeing that one single chairman and commandant should be elected. A contest for this position between Herron and Harding Smith could well have been a damaging deadlock and Andy Tyrie, who had initially agreed to chair the meeting, came out as the victor, a compromise candidate acceptable to east and west as well as to the other brigade areas.

Herron's acceptance of this outcome, however, gave him no real protection. A warning came on 15 June when masked gunmen burst into his house on the Braniel estate and shot dead his eighteen-year-old brother-in-law, Michael Wilson. He was upstairs in bed, still recovering from the severe beating he had received from a crowd in the Catholic Short Strand area of the city. Herron's wife later told the inquest that the killers, on entering the house where she was with her five children, had first of all demanded to know where her husband was before they charged upstairs to kill his relative. Michael Stone had been on an errand for Herron and was close enough to the house to hear the screams of Herron's wife and children and to see the killers making their escape. He later asked Herron if he wanted retaliation against the IRA and received the reply: 'Wrong side kid.'[94]

There have been conflicting rumours ever since about Wilson's murder but his funeral was a major UDA event attended by thousands of mourners, many in full paramilitary uniform. Stone was convinced that Herron was living on borrowed time after this and in fact his turn came on 14 September, when he disappeared from East Belfast. He was last seen near the UDA headquarters and his body was later found in a ditch at Drumbo, County Down, with a single gunshot wound to the head.

To this day, the UDA has not come up with an explanation for Herron's killing, though in May 1976 one of its units shot dead a young Protestant in East Belfast, claiming he had been implicated. Other accounts have sought to explain it in terms of British undercover operations to neutralise or intimidate leftward-leaning elements within Loyalism.[95] Herron had had contacts with the Official IRA but these might not have been sufficient to get him killed. Others believed they saw the hand of Harding Smith, who fifteen months later would attempt to depose Tyrie and take overall control of the UDA. Yet another possibility is that Edward, or Ned, McCreery, an active UDA member, set up Herron's murder as a result of a dispute over money, using a woman to lure him to his death. McCreery was involved in many killings and when the UDA itself shot him dead in Aril 1992, rumours about his role in Herron's demise circulated once again.

Herron's funeral drew 25,000 people into the Braniel estate. Dr Ian Paisley conducted a service outside the family home before the coffin was brought outside for a UDA guard of honour to fire a volley over it. A trumpeter sounded the last post and the final act was at Roselawn cemetery, where a piper played 'Amazing Grace'. Whatever the reasons for his murder, Herron still had support within the UDA, especially in his own brigade area. Not all the organisation's publications had attacked him in the way the *Ulster Militant* had done. The *Ulster Loyalist*, which outlasted it, ran an article under the heading of 'A profile of courage and devotion', declaring that 'this brave man deserved well of his nation' and commending 'his indomitable resolution and splendid courage'.[96] The magazine later printed a ballad devoted to his memory and to be sung to the tune of 'Silent Night'.[97]

The UDA survived Herron's killing without serious damage and Tyrie's position as the successful compromise candidate for chairman and commandant remained secure. However, few would have predicted in 1973 that he would retain these positions for fifteen years, least of all Tyrie himself. He has offered his own explanations for this feat of survival:

> I came from West Belfast but I had connections in the east. People there accepted me because I wasn't Harding Smith and in the west they still saw me as local. I was careful too, once I was elected. I didn't spend too much time in bars and clubs. I was a family man. I didn't go hooring after women like some of them, so even people who might criticise me had no dirt to throw.[98]

Support for him was voiced in the UDA press, which as early as August 1973 began to refer to him as 'a Supreme Commander who will control all aspects concerning our organisation. He will direct a new look Inner Council with the emphasis on a closer liaison with all companies within the Province.'[99] Past mistakes, it was stressed, had to be rectified and the UDA strengthened 'until our beloved Ulster is once again free from all the rebel scum that has diseased our province for the past four years'.[100] Tyrie did indeed possess leadership skills which would soon be tested by new departures in British policy following the imposition of direct government on Northern Ireland.

NOTES

1. G. Adams, *Before the Dawn* (London: Heinemann, 1996), p. 139.
2. *Sunday Times*, 28 January 1973.
3. Ibid.
4. Ibid.
5. Ibid.
6. *Ulster*, October 1987.
7. Ibid.
8. *News Letter*, 22 February 2003.
9. S Duddy, interview with author, 15 October, 2002.
10. Ibid.
11. Ibid., also P. Taylor, *Loyalists* (London: Bloomsbury, 1999), p. 84.
12. A. Calderwood, interview with author, 7 July 2003.
13. Ibid.
14. Ibid.
15. Ibid.
16. M. Stone, *None Shall Divide Us* (London: John Blake, 2003), p. 24.
17. Ibid., p. 25.
18. Ibid., pp. 28–32.
19. D. McKittrick, S. Kelters, B. Feeney and C. Thornton, *Lost Lives: The Stories of the Men, Women and Children Who Died as a Result of Northern Ireland's Troubles* (Edinburgh: Mainstream, 1999), p. 129.
20. J. White, interview with author, 22 October 2001.
21. Ibid.
22. Ibid.
23. M. O'Doherty, *The Trouble With Guns. Republican Strategy and the Provisional IRA* (Belfast: Blackstaff Press, 1998), pp. 88–92.
24. This point was made to me on 31 July 2003 by Dr Bob Purdie, author of *Politics in the Streets: The Origins of the Civil Rights Movement in Northern Ireland* (Belfast: Blackstaff Press, 1990).
25. *Sunday Times*, 11 March 1973.
26. D. Ervine, interview with author, 6 May 2003.
27. *Sunday Times*, 28 January 1973.
28. Ibid.
29. Ibid.
30. W. Whitelaw, *The Whitelaw Memoirs* (London: Aurum Press, 1989), p. 123.
31. *Sunday Times*, 28 January 1973.
32. Taylor, *Loyalists*, pp. 102–3.

33. A. Purdy, *Molyneaux: The Long View* (Antrim: Greystone, 1989), p. 133.
34. *UDA Bulletin*, no. 14, 1972.
35. *UDA Bulletin*, no. 18, 1972.
36. Ibid.
37. Ibid.
38. *UDA Bulletin*, no. 17, 1972.
39. *UDA Bulletin*, no. 3, 1971.
40. Ibid.
41. *UDA Bulletin*, no. 18, 1972.
42. *UDA Bulletin*, nos 5 & 8, 1971.
43. *UDA Bulletin*, October 1971, not numbered.
44. *UDA Bulletin*, no. 12, 1972.
45. *UDA Bulletin*, no. 18, 1972.
46. *UDA Bulletin*, February 1972, not numbered. See also M. Dillon and D. Lehane, *Political Murder in Northern Ireland* (Harmondsworth: Penguin, 1973), pp. 56–7.
47. *News Letter*, 13 February 1972.
48. *Ulster Loyalist*, 28 February 1974.
49. *Ulster Loyalist*, 6 December 1973.
50. *Ulster Loyalist*, 1 September 1973.
51. McKittrick *et al.*, *Lost Lives*, p. 815.
52. *Ulster Militant*, no. 16, 1972.
53. S. Nelson, 'Belfast: walking the Shankill', in I. Wood (ed.), *Scotland and Ulster* (Edinburgh: Mercat Press, 1994), p. 24.
54. S Belfrage, *The Crack: A Belfast Year* (London: Andre Deutsch, 1987), pp. 152–3.
55. Ibid., pp. 141–2.
56. *Sunday Times*, 28 January 1973.
57. Ibid.
58. Ibid.
59. *Woodvale Defence Association News*, 8 March 1972.
60. S. Bruce, *The Red Hand: Protestant Paramilitaries in Northern Ireland* (Oxford: Oxford University Press, 1992), p. 86.
61. *Sunday Times*, 28 January 1973.
62. *Sunday Times*, 4 February 1973.
63. Ibid.
64. Ibid.
65. *Ulster Militant*, no. 16, 1972.
66. Ibid.
67. Ibid.
68. Ibid.
69. *Sunday Times*, 4 February 1973.
70. Ibid.
71. Ibid.
72. *Sunday Times*, 17 June 1973.
73. Ibid.
74. Ibid.
75. Taylor, *Loyalists*, pp. 169–72.

76. Dillon and Lehane, *Political Murder in Northern Ireland*, pp. 147–8.
77. Bruce, *Red Hand*, pp. 66–7.
78. McKittrick *et al.*, *Lost Lives*, pp. 300–1.
79. *Sunday Times*, 28 January 1973.
80. Ibid.
81. Ibid.
82. *Ulster Militant*, 3 February 1973.
83. Ibid.
84. Dillon and Lehane, *Political Murder in Northern Ireland*, pp. 161–2, also p. 167.
85. McKittrick *et al.*, *Lost Lives*, p. 369.
86. J. White, interview with author, 22 October, 2001. See also Taylor, *Loyalists*, pp. 115–16.
87. Dillon and Lehane, *Political Murder in Northern Ireland*, p. 281.
88. Ibid.
89. Ibid., p. 282.
90. Ibid., p. 283.
91. Ibid., p. 285.
92. Ibid., p. 286.
93. Ibid.
94. Stone, *None Shall Divide Us*, p. 44.
95. P. Foot, *Who Framed Colin Wallace?* (London: Macmillan, 1989), pp. 99, 103.
96. *Ulster Loyalist*, 22 September 1973.
97. *Ulster Loyalist*, 29 September 1973.
98. A. Tyrie, interview with author, 19 April 2000.
99. *Ulster Loyalist*, 20 August 1973.
100. Ibid.

2

Victory: The UDA and the 1974 Ulster Workers' Council Strike

౭

The year 1973 was another traumatic one for Ulster Loyalists. Although IRA no-go areas had been ended by military action the previous August, attacks on the security forces and on Protestant areas continued relentlessly. Protests orchestrated by the Loyalist Association of Workers (LAW) and the Vanguard Unionists made little apparent impact on British policy, while army measures in Protestant districts of Belfast thought to be supportive of the UDA and UVF became extremely tough, especially where the Parachute Regiment was deployed.[1] The year also saw the first internments of Loyalists, on 5 February. The two men concerned were active in an East Belfast UFF unit and were detained without trial after a grenade attack on a Catholic workers' bus. William Craig, the Vanguard Unionist leader, agreed to back a protest strike called by LAW and the UDA.

The strike was well supported while it lasted but it rapidly degenerated into destructive rioting in South and East Belfast, often led by tartan gangs. Snipers also opened fire on the security forces and one of them shot dead, by mistake it was at once claimed, a young fireman who happened to be a Protestant and was on duty in Bradbury Place, just north of the city centre. Unionist politicians reacted by trying to distance themselves from the protest's violent potential, which served only to deepen distrust for them within the membership of the UDA.

It was, however, William Whitelaw, appointed the previous year by Edward Heath as Secretary of State for Northern Ireland, who created the necessary pre-conditions for renewed co-operation between the UDA and Unionists, though without this being any part of his intention. While his priority in 1972 had to be firm action against IRA no-go areas, he also made time to work on a discussion paper, published on 31 October, which set out a range of constitutional options for Northern Ireland, as well as the promise of a referendum on whether or not partition and the border should continue.

This was held on 8 March 1973, in the face of a boycott of the polling stations by the nationalist population but those who turned out to vote 'yes' to the province's continued membership of the United Kingdom represented a decisive 58 per cent of the total population. Whitelaw felt this result cleared the way for a new experiment in devolved government, the main elements of which were initially to be the election by proportional representation of a new assembly, and a conference of elected representatives and the Irish and British governments to discuss possible new political directions for Northern Ireland. While power-sharing between the communities was not clearly set out ahead of the elections there was much speculation about it and the 28 June 1973 Assembly elections have been described as 'effectively a referendum on that possibility'.[2]

From the outset of the election campaign, Tommy Herron urged that the working-class Loyalists who had either joined or supported the UDA should have the chance to vote for candidates with whom they could identify. He himself, however, standing in West Belfast, found that it was a problem to convert the respect he had built up as a paramilitary 'hard man' into a significant vote. He won only 2,480 first-preference votes, while in North Belfast Tommy Lyttle fared worse. The UDA's only real victory was in Londonderry, where one of its local leaders, Glen Barr, was elected as much for his trade union and community work as for any paramilitary role he had played. Not for the last time a pattern of class deference in working-class Protestant voting worked against candidates with UDA or other paramilitary links and in favour of mainstream Unionist parties.

The overall result gave those in favour of power-sharing a majority. Brian Faulkner and his pro-Assembly Unionists won twenty-two seats, the SDLP nineteen and the Alliance gained eight. Against this bloc supportive of Whitelaw's intentions, Dr Ian Paisley's Democratic Unionist Party won eight seats, Vanguard seven and three independent Unionists opposed to power-sharing ware also elected. This put Faulkner in a strong position and he secured agreement from the SDLP and the Alliance to the formation of a devolved executive which he would lead as Prime Minister with Gerry Fitt of the SDLP as his deputy. The SDLP's reward for breaking with the northern nationalist community's traditional refusal to take part in six-county government was the formation of an inter-governmental Council of Ireland that would discuss cross-border issues, which many in the SDLP were swift to represent as a framework for Irish unification once the whole package was agreed by British ministers at the Sunningdale talks in December.

James Molyneaux, then Ulster Unionist MP for the Westminster constituency of South Antrim, later recalled how the night after the Sunningdale Agreement was reached his telephone rang constantly with messages of outrage at what had been agreed to. A few days later, he confronted Francis Pym, Whitelaw's successor as Secretary of State, in the House of Commons members' tea room:

Whether you know it or not, Francis, in your very short term in Northern Ireland you have achieved what no other politician, Unionist or nationalist, has ever been able to achieve – you have brought together in one force the self-styled working class and the professional class. They are as one now. They are utterly opposed to government policy.[3]

Molyneaux went on to tell Pym that his callers had 'cultured voices', that they 'were not hardliners from Lisburn or Rathcoole'[4] and that their views must be heeded. Within a month the Ulster Unionist Council rejected the Council of Ireland and Faulkner resigned as party leader.

Fortnight magazine, launched in 1970 for the expressed purpose of allowing both communities and all opinions to be represented in its pages, challenged the SDLP view of the Sunningdale Agreement:

> The first reality is that the Council of Ireland is not a vehicle for reunification, however much the Dublin government or the SDLP might wish to think of it as such. Nor should it be. It is legitimate to regard it as a means of bringing the two communities in Ireland into closer harmony, but that does not imply that unification is the ultimate goal.[5]

By the time the new Executive took office just over two weeks later on New Year's Day 1974, it was too late for Loyalists to be convinced that it was working to anything other than a nationalist agenda.

As early as October 1973, a contributor to the *Ulster Loyalist*, a UDA magazine distributed in Belfast, was comparing Faulkner's optimism about the Sunningdale Agreement with Neville Chamberlain's claims in 1938 that the Munich Agreement meant 'peace in our time'. Describing himself as an ordinary working-class Protestant family man, he drew sinister conclusions from the appointment of Paddy Devlin as Health and Social Services Minister in the Executive because of his IRA membership thirty years previously.[6] Devlin, in fact, had long since broken with militant Republicanism and earned much respect as a trade unionist and campaigner on social issues.

'What is any self-respecting Loyal Ulsterman to think,' he continued. 'Because of stupid, blind, blundering Unionist politicians like Mr Brian Faulkner we are left with two choices. Either emigrate and leave Ulster in the control of the Republicans, or take to the streets and overthrow the weak-minded representatives who are letting our heritage and everything our fore-fathers ever fought for slowly slip away. I myself would prefer to take the second choice, and I know that there are many thousands of Loyal Ulstermen who would make the same choice.'[7]

Language even more uncompromising than this can be found in the same magazine's editorial just eight weeks later, as the implementation of the Sunningdale package came closer. The framework for a united Ireland had already been created, an editorial declared, and it issued a call to action against it:

> The only negotiation tactics that are understood by Westminster are the tactics of force. We must take over the province with or without the support of the Roman Catholics. Every unionist that took part in the Council of Ireland committed

treason and must pay the price that all traitors pay. The Alliance Party and
Northern Ireland Labour Party members at the [Sunningdale] Conference must be
deprived of citizenship and deported, re-entry bringing an automatic death sentence. All their possessions must be forfeited.[8]

There was also a call for all Loyalist paramilitary action to be co-ordinated by
new leaders: 'The older generation are too gentlemanly, too hidebound with
tradition, too averse to the requirements needed to win this last battle for
Ulster.'[9] Vilification of Faulkner reached a new pitch, the question being put
to readers on a separate page why they might like to see him turned into a
lamp. The printed answer was: 'Because you could see him hang during the
day, burn at night and be extinguished in the morning.'[10]
    Ulster Loyalism has always been fuelled by the suspicion of treachery
within, 'Lundies' who would compromise with the enemy, but parallel to this
kind of language in UDA publications after the signing of the Sunningdale
Agreement was the posing of some real questions about Northern Ireland's
constitutional future. 'Are you prepared to go independent?'[11] readers of the
Ulster Loyalist were asked in its first editorial of 1974, which set out the possibility of a new constitution once power-sharing and the Council of Ireland
had been destroyed.
    More daringly, in a subsequent issue, readers were asked to consider, given
the continued ignoring of their rights by the Northern Ireland Office in
London, whether they should still stand up for 'God Save the Queen':

> We ask those who do not wish to stand to ascertain the general feeling in any
> Loyalist clubs they may go to and if they find that respect to the Queen is still
> expected then please leave before the anthem is played.[12]

This had the makings of a real debate about alternatives to the Sunningdale
Agreement, though how far the issues being raised really exercised the minds
of ordinary UDA members cannot be quantified. For many the appeal of vig-
ilantism and counter-terror against the IRA, which had already started to
degenerate into acts of nakedly sectarian murder, would always be greater.
Even so, in the midst of mounting crisis and continuing violence, UDA magazines such as the *Ulster Loyalist* still gave at least some space to discussion of
a better future for Northern Ireland and its people. Both Sunningdale and
debates about federalism were, it argued in a February 1974 issue, tainted by
the prospect of an all-Ireland outcome, yet the old shibboleth of 'a Protestant
Ulster for Protestant people' was no longer enough. This was not, an editorial stressed, because Northern Ireland had been a total failure, even though
thirty-five of its fifty years had been dominated by economic depression and
world war. The remaining fifteen years had seen real progress, 'though not
everybody shared in it, not all Protestants and certainly not all Catholics'.[13]
Power-sharing with Catholics in an independent Ulster thus needed to be
considered.

Even as these remarkable thoughts were aired in the pages of a UDA publication, distrust of established Unionism was reaching new depths. 'Loyalist Ulster's survival goes beyond what politicians can offer,'[14] the *Ulster Loyalist* had declared in an earlier issue, which queried the commitment of William Craig in his role as Vanguard leader and dismissed with derision the policy of full integration with Britain for which Dr Ian Paisley seemed to be pressing: 'Now the time has come for the paramilitary organisations to consider a military junta.'[15] This was not quite what would happen but political events across the Irish Sea relaunched joint action between the UDA and anti-Agreement Unionist politicians.

Barely two months into the life of the new Executive, Edward Heath, confronted by Britain's second national miners' strike within two years, gambled on a general election on the issue of trade union power and who should govern the country. His gamble failed and a minority Labour government was returned to office. In Northern Ireland, which then had twelve Westminster constituencies, the election was seen from the outset as a verdict for or against power-sharing and the Sunningdale Agreement. The pro-power-sharing parties failed to put together any sort of electoral pact and United Ulster Unionist Council candidates, representing Paisley's DUP, Craig's Vanguard Unionists and the anti-Sunningdale Unionists led by Harry West, took eleven of the available seats.

Faulkner's pro-Agreement Unionists won barely 13 per cent of the votes cast, while Unionists opposed to power-sharing took 51 per cent. 'It is clear from the Ulster Unionist Council's sweeping victory in the election', declared *Fortnight*, 'that there is no future in a policy of imposed or creeping unification.'[16] The result was clear proof of 'the determination of the Protestant community to maintain its separate identity from the "Irish nation" as it is defined in Dublin'.[17] Over-optimistically, however, *Fortnight* went on to argue that without any Council of Ireland a power-sharing executive could survive 'if the parties involved get on with an attractive social and economic programme'.

There would be scant time for that, as the UDA leadership could now embark upon a militant campaign against the Executive and all its works which could invoke the democratic will of the Unionist electorate. In early April 1974, the *Ulster Loyalist* alerted its readers to the existence of the Ulster Workers' Council, describing it as 'the coming together of men and women [though no women ever sat on it] of like minds, people who believe that the dream of Nationalists is near to hand, that is a United Ireland'.[18] The Northern Ireland that the Council would fight for, it was stressed, would be one free of privilege and discrimination and notice was served on politicians, 'whatever banner they operate under, that the workers are no longer tools to be used to forward their political ambitions but equal partners and that the future of Northern Ireland will no longer be decided behind closed doors between rival groups of politicians, each jockeying for the best advantage for himself and to hell with the workers.'[19]

Preparations for the Council's formation had in fact been going on for a period of nearly six months. Many of those active in this preparatory work had become known through their role in LAW but it had ceased to exist by early 1974, a victim of its own disagreements on Loyalist tactics such as rate and rent strikes as well as over the campaign against internment of Loyalists and how far it should be allowed to go. LAW's trade union and shop floor contacts still proved vital in mobilising support against the new Executive. Among the association's prominent activists was Hugh Petrie, an Amalgamated Union of Engineering Workers shop steward at Short Brothers and Harland. Three times wounded in action in the Second World War with British airborne forces, Petrie's speeches always commanded respect, as did those of Billy Kelly, a steward at the important Ballylumford electricity-generating plant at Larne.

Another key figure was Harry Murray, a shipyard shop steward who saw the need for LAW to give way to a more effective body. He attended what he always claimed was the first meeting of the future UWC in late October 1973, at Vanguard's headquarters on Hawthornden Road. From the start, his concern was to exclude paramilitary organisations from any protest campaign though he was wary too of Vanguard Unionist politicians manipulating trade unionists like himself. He was even more wary of Paisley, one of whose supporters and a member of his Free Presbyterian Church, Hugh Mallon, attended the meeting. This led to tension when Mallon was made secretary to the embryonic UWC and he was replaced by a UDA man, Jim Smyth, who had been editing *Ulster Militant*.

Because of Murray's suspicions, UDA members involved in these initial moves kept secret from him their involvement with it. A case in point was Bob Pagels, an activist in the Transport and General Workers' Union, who had become foreman at E. T. Green's, a big animal feed mill in Belfast's docks. Pagels had joined the UDA at its formation and became one of its company commanders in East Belfast but when Andy Tyrie came to sit in at one of the preliminary meetings which led to the setting up of the UWC, he recalls that they pretended not to know each other.[20] Other UDA men also had trade union backgrounds, such as Charles Harding Smith, who had been a steam hammer operator in Harland and Wolff's shipyard, and Tyrie himself.

Even leading Unionist politicians appear to have had only minimal knowledge of the Council's emergence and the extent to which strike action to bring down the Executive was part of its agenda. A probable exception, however, was David Trimble, in 1974 a lecturer in law at Queen's University, whose active support for the Vanguard movement had given him access to UDA members. 'Davy was always anxious to mix with the boys, the paramilitary men,' Glen Barr has been quoted as saying in 1973, though he stressed that Trimble only talked politics with 'the boys' and was never privy to UDA 'operations'.[21]

The other obvious exception was Craig, who, through Vanguard, had developed good contacts with Loyalist workers and supported the principle of strike action though not always agreeing with the decisions of what became the UWC. Craig was involved in the preliminary meetings which led to the Council's formation and then the decision on strike action. It was probably at one of these meetings, in February 1974, that the name 'Ulster Workers' Council' was agreed upon.

By then the Council was in being. Barr took the chair at its initial meetings and those in attendance included Murray, Kelly and Tom Beattie, another shop steward, from Ballylumford. Sometimes there were more than twenty, with Tyrie representing the UDA and Ken Gibson the UVF. Other smaller Loyalist paramilitary bodies were also present, such as the Orange Volunteers, founded in 1972 and closely linked to Vanguard, at whose mass rallies it had provided stewarding and security. Another was Down Orange Welfare, formed the same year from rural and small-town Orangemen. It was led by a retired army colonel, Peter Brush, who inevitably was nicknamed Basil, after the much-loved fox puppet Basil Brush, who featured in a children's television show at the time. Paisley, Craig and West were all co-opted to give anti-Agreement Unionists a secure presence on the council.

A smaller co-ordinating committee quickly grew out of this first meeting and it held its initial session at the UDA's headquarters in East Belfast on the Newtownards Road. The thirteen who attended were at once compared by Barr to the legendary thirteen apprentice boys who in 1688 had secured the gates of Londonderry against the army of King James VII of Scotland and II of England.[22] Numbers at this committee's meetings could vary and at least two members could get no publicity because of their links to the Red Hand Commando, the operational arm of the UVF, an illegal body widely thought to have been responsible for a series of sectarian killings.

The Northern Ireland Office appears to have had very limited intelligence on these developments and the Labour government's new Secretary of State had to learn quickly about events on the ground. This was Merlyn Rees, a Welshman who was at least able to impress his Stormont advisers with his interest in Irish and Ulster history. Few of his successors can have kept their police escort waiting anxiously outside while they browsed at length in the Queen's University bookshop. One review of his memoirs described him as 'a minister hooked on Northern Ireland'.[23] His father had served as a private soldier in Dublin during the Easter Rising of 1916 and his 'memoirs' are given over entirely to his attempts to grapple with the events which confronted him over his two-year period at Stormont Castle.

Some UDA members involved in pre-strike contacts with Rees liked him personally: 'He was easier to talk to than his deputy, Stan Orme, more conciliatory in his manner. We could have probably done business with him if it hadn't been for Harold Wilson,' recalled Pagels.[24] Tyrie thought so too. With Barr and other Council members, he met Orme for talks in London on the very eve of the strike. 'Stan Orme was perfectly hospitable to us but he was a hardliner. He told us we must call off any strike action, which he argued would simply play into the hands of the IRA.'[25]

Rees met representatives of the UWC on 8 April 1974. The occasion was not a success and he later described it as 'an angry, disjointed meeting'[26] held in an atmosphere of suspicion. UWC members later recalled that as they sat down to face the Secretary of State across a long table in his official suite, two plain-clothes men who they took to be from the RUC sat behind them, each with a hand permanently inside his jacket.[27] The Council's bargaining position was, however, quite carefully thought out and was based not on the case for an immediate end to power-sharing and the Council of Ireland, but on new elections to the devolved Assembly.

Other grievances and demands crowded the agenda, as Rees recalled in his memoirs.

> Their theme was clear: Sunningdale was undemocratic and had been shown to be so at the General Election. The executive was forcing the North into the South and was instrumental in the appointment of an 'IRA sympathiser', Frank Lagan, as Chief Constable in Londonderry.[28]

Rees was also put under pressure to admit that he was talking directly with terrorists when he met Dublin government ministers, 'who were not averse to relaxing the laws on contraception merely as a device to encourage eventual unification'.[29]

The treatment of Loyalist prisoners and angry exchanges over alleged shortcomings in security policy consumed additional time but Rees did not depart from his view that there was no case for new Assembly elections and that the Executive must, under the legislation which had created it, be given a full four years to prove itself. This was the substance of a press statement he subsequently released while UWC spokesmen told journalists that they felt they had got nowhere with him. Two days later Rees, back in London, sought to alert the Cabinet to growing Loyalist intransigence as well as the prospect that if the Council of Ireland were to be abandoned, the SDLP and the Dublin government would withdraw their support for the entire power-sharing experiment.

The UWC pressed ahead with its preparations for all-out strike action while Unionist politicians held back from supporting them, playing for time by holding a meeting at the end of April in a Portrush hotel from which Council spokesmen were excluded. All it came up with was the formation of a committee to 'consider' economic sanctions against the Irish Republic over what was seen as its role in the imposition of the Sunningdale package. Tyrie and Barr were by this time of the opinion that simply to go ahead with a strike was the best way to bring the anti-Agreement Unionists round to supporting them. On 13 May, Tyrie and Jim Smyth, who would handle much of the strike's publicity, travelled to Larne for a scheduled meeting of the UWC. Kelly and Hugh

Petrie joined them at the Laharna Hotel and they all took their seats before the Unionist politicians arrived. These included Paisley, Ernest Baird of Vanguard and John Taylor, though Craig was absent. Without preliminaries, Kelly announced that the strike was planned for the next day, just as soon as the Assembly had voted after yet another debate on the principle of Sunningdale and the power-sharing executive. After initial reluctance and some bluster from Paisley, who departed for Canada three days later on unclearly stated business, the politicians came round. 'In the course of one sunny day on the Antrim coast, political power passed almost effortlessly from the hands of the elected representatives of the Loyalists into those of the factory workers and paramilitary leaders who had appointed themselves.'[30]

This was one observer's assessment of events in an account he compiled for publication the following year. He might have added that the real shift of power was to the UDA, though in fact this power would not outlast the strike itself very long. Tyrie had become uneasy over the previous week or two about attempts to marginalise the UDA on the UWC and he seems to have blamed Harry Murray for these. The communiqué issued after the Larne meeting, however, had the impress of the UDA on it. It finished by declaring: 'If Westminster is not prepared to restore democracy, i.e. the will of the people made clear in an election, then the only other way it can be restored is by a coup d'état.'[31]

Questioned nearly thirty years later about the use of the phrase 'coup d'état', Barr's response was still an equivocal one:

> I think we used to bandy about dramatic words and use dramatic phrases in those days. I think we didn't fully understand what we were getting ourselves into. Here we were, a bunch of working class fellows and all of a sudden we were handed all this power and this responsibility in our communities.[32]

Even, so, he went on to say: 'The coup d'état was basically that we were going to take over the country ourselves rather than have it handed over to a united Ireland.'[33] That was precisely what the strike-coordinating body, and in particular the UDA, did, at least for the next two weeks.

The following evening, 14 May, after the predictable defeat of an Assembly resolution condemning the Sunningdale Agreement, Tyrie and Barr let Murray read out to the Stormont press room the announcement that the UWC was calling an indefinite strike in pursuit of the demand for new Assembly elections. He followed this with the news that there would be immediate reductions in electricity supply by over 200 megawatts throughout the province. Most of the media representatives present knew little about the UWC or who Murray was.

Some Loyalist accounts of the strike, which began on Wednesday, 15 May 1974, claim it as an almost bloodless victory over the British government. They ought not to do so, because it was accompanied by one of the worst single atrocities of the troubles: on Friday, 17 May, car bombs went off without warning in central Dublin at the height of the evening rush hour and also in Monaghan town, killing twenty-eight people and injuring hundreds more. The attacks were certainly meant as a warning to the Irish government over its role in the Sunningdale Agreement and power-sharing in the North, but are now generally believed to have been the work of the UVF rather than the UDA, though the collusion of British under-cover military units continued to be alleged.[34]

A major book on the UVF has in fact little to say on its role in the strike in Northern Ireland itself,[35] where almost from the start the UDA took a dominant role. UVF units played some part along with the UDA in effectively closing down the port of Larne on the first day of the strike but when a UWC delegation met Stan Orme, Tyrie detected an ambivalence in the UVF's attitude. This was when, in response to a direct question from Orme, Ken Gibson, their representative, declared: 'We are only here as observers.'[36] Tyrie drew the inference that their support was still only conditional.

Tyrie had other concerns that day. Earlier, he had turned up at the Vanguard Party head office in Hawthornden Road, which had been made available to the UWC's strike-co-ordinating committee, to find few people there and an atmosphere of uncertainty about what the response to the strike call was going to be. Many, in fact, turned up for work and there was confusion at some roadblocks and pickets, for example, over what bakery workers were supposed to do.

One North Belfast Loyalist was working as a baker in 1974 and set off for his shift on 15 May thinking that the strikers would not want to close down bakeries. He ran into a picket right away in the North Queen Street area of the city.

> They all had balaclavas on but I still knew who they were. I'd grown up with them after all. I told them they would still need bread but to start with they wouldn't let me through. Anyway, I managed to get to the bakery later and I got away a sack of potato flakes which did me and my wife fine because we had two wee ones to feed then. To start with, the pubs and clubs stayed open and that's where a lot of fellows headed. That soon changed. You could call it the women's voice. Wives didn't think their men should be striking just to sit in bars all day.[37]

Tyrie says now that he had no certainty on the first day what might happen. 'Other Loyalist strikes had gone nowhere and this one might be the same. We just didn't know at that point.'[38] Bob Pagels went to see Tyrie the night the strike was announced.

> I reached him at Roberta House, then the UDA's East Belfast headquarters. He asked us if we were sure we knew what we had started and of course none of us did. We'd no idea how long the thing might last. I had a wife and two small children to think about but I put out the word to my company to be ready in the morning. We all said we'd see each other the next day.[39]

Pagels arrived in Belfast docks early in the morning of Wednesday, 15 May, wearing his UDA camouflage jacket and cap, and was at once aware of cars parked in the Sirocco engineering works car park. 'It's not true I confronted managers and shop stewards with a gun in my hand,' he has said. 'I did address the men though. I appealed to them to think of the fate of Ulster and the threat of Rome Rule. That's what I believed then. I could have handled a united Ireland but never the dictatorship of any church, certainly not the Catholic Church. That's how I felt then.'[40] Nearly thirty years later, after surviving terrible head injuries in a work accident, Pagels, who has long since left the UDA, is a voluntary worker in a day centre for handicapped people and runs joint holiday schemes for them with nearby Catholic groups. He recalls the thoroughness with which the strike was organised:

> Harry Murray had been dead against any UDA role but I made it clear to him either that day or the next that I was with them. My real job was organising the distribution of animal feed. I was given an office and a phone to check what the farms needed. We made sure every farmer got at least the minimum they needed. It was all under control and we were ready for a long strike.[41]

There was only limited direct action on the first day, though at Ballylumford in Larne electrical power was switched down to 60 per cent of normal. The day ended with Rees and his advisers feeling that perhaps the UWC had overplayed its hand. The second day was different. Then the UDA began to emerge in force as the responsibility for making a reality of the strike shifted increasingly on to Tyrie's broad shoulders. Buses all over Belfast were hijacked to make roadblocks and picketing was intensified. 'The day that the workers called the strike, people went out to work,' Tyrie wrote much later, 'so I spoke to the UDA to devise a method to stop them. We used a subtle form of intimidation – no use lying about that – like taking pictures of people going to work with cameras without film.'[42]

By Thursday, factories, shops and pubs started to close down all over Northern Ireland and on Friday, 17 May, the UDA, acting through the UWC's co-ordinating committee, published its first list of essential services which it would allow to be, over varying periods, exempted from the strike. Rees reaffirmed his aversion to any compromises and the following day power cuts lasted for six hours as the electricity authorities announced they would proclaim a state of emergency the following day and an army unit in plain clothes secretly checked out Ballylumford only to report that they would not be able to operate it without the help of senior staff.

Late on Sunday, 19 May, the UWC decided to step up the number of barricades and roadblocks it was already operating in Belfast. Work had begun on more of these by eight o'clock on Monday morning, backed by a massive show of strength from the UDA. Some new barricades were set up within 500 yards of Belfast City Hall. The RUC and the army, under constant threat of attack from an IRA whose leaders saw no need to call a halt to their war because of the strike, did not act and the city came to a standstill. Driving into it was compared to 'entering the capital of a country in which a revolutionary army had just staged a coup d'état and in which the legitimate security authorities were uncertain to whom they owed their allegiance'.[43]

As important as overt coercion was a now rising groundswell of support for the strike's stated aim of new Assembly elections. Robert Fisk, covering events as a journalist, was quick to sense this: 'The Government's carefully nurtured belief that "loyalists" are staying away from work only because of intimidation seems to be further away from reality each day,' he wrote on 22 May.[44] He admitted the hijacking of cars for street barricades and the heavy UDA presence at roadblocks but also pointed out that chemist shops were staying open all day, food shops from 9 a.m. to 2 p.m. and post offices from 2 p.m. until 6 p.m. Welfare and advice centres were being run by the strike-co-ordinating committee and social security cheques as well as candles, tea and butter were getting delivered to old age pensioners by UDA men who alternated between this work and duty at the barricades.

'Survival', Fisk went on, 'is something the strike leaders have shrewdly learned to study. They have, however clumsily, begun to set up the framework of a crude system of social services to take the place of the state's. It is something the IRA perfected behind their barricades in Londonderry in 1972. And "Free Derry", with all its intimidation and its obvious gunmen, lasted for more than half a year.'[45]

Tyrie began to feel that the UDA could take a step back to let the trade unionists on the UWC take more of the responsibility for co-ordinating essential supplies and services:

> When the strike got up and running we said to Bob Pagels and the others – you deal with distribution of animal feed, you deal with petrol, and so on. It worked so well because most of them were either members, supporters or associates of the UDA. That made all the difference.[46]

On 22 May, one week into the strike, any movement of oil and petrol was stopped, so the use of private cars, already hazardous because of barricades and hijacking, became almost impossible. Queues at food shops lengthened as any movement of goods depended on authorisation by the UWC and its local activists. Charles Brett, a Belfast lawyer and former chairman of the Northern Ireland Labour Party, later wrote vividly of the atmosphere in the city at this time:

> In my office, as in many others, work continued after a fashion, though it was wise to keep well away from the front windows to avoid attracting the attention of roaming bands of tartan youths. But as the days went by, the amount of work actually done became less and less; and attendance at the office became something of a token. The lack of heating and artificial lighting was no great deprivation in the month of May: but as the ever longer and more frequent power cuts took effect,

so, without warning, electric typewriters, photocopiers and accounting machines suddenly became dead and useless.[47]

Central Belfast is low-lying and the basement of Brett's office lay below high-tide level, so his greatest fear became the closure by the strikers of sewage pumping stations and what might happen to masses of documents stored below ground level. The strike was called off before any of this happened, though the real danger of sewage floods was being discussed by the Executive in the final hours of its existence. Brett described the eerie emptiness of familiar streets as he cycled home by circuitous routes to avoid barricades to a Malone Road home without power or lighting:

> It was a curious experience to sit each evening in the gathering dusk – no street-lights anywhere, only the faintest of flickering lights in the windows of neighbouring homes – isolated in the midst of a community that had suffered almost total social break-down; wondering what would happen next. The feeling of helplessness was very great; no positive action whatever was possible. Was it a bit like this in the drawing rooms of St. Petersburg in October 1917?[48]

Brett's sense of isolation in his leafy residential Belfast suburb was the antithesis of how participants in the strike felt in the huge Rathcoole housing scheme on the northern edge of the city. John Gregg, who later served nine years in prison for the attempted murder of Gerry Adams and rose high within the UDA, had not long left school to work in Harland and Wolff's shipyard when the UWC announced the strike call. 'I'd been in the Ulster Young Militants [the UDA's youth wing] for a year already,' he recalls. 'It was either that or the Young Citizen Volunteers [the UVF's youth organisation] in Rathcoole. At first it was a bit like being in a gang and that's what a lot of young lads did. But there was more to it than that. We all knew there was a cause and big issues at stake.'[49]

Gregg was quickly caught up in the excitement of collective action.

> I was at all the big rallies and on the pickets too. I carried a gun to patrol the area, lots of us did. We'd been drilled and trained. My son, who's eighteen now, thinks it's wild when I tell him that! There was other work for us as well. Food had to be distributed properly. I was sent over to the Rushpark community centre, I remember, a few days into the strike, because hundreds of chickens had been brought in from the country. My job was to help lop the heads off them and have them ready to give out to our people who were there queuing for them. It was messy work. We gave out milk and bread too and delivered stuff to houses. It was well organised.[50]

Jackie McDonald also rose to a position of seniority within the UDA, in his case ultimately becoming its brigadier in South Belfast. He was in his mid-twenties in 1974 and had a good job as dispatches manager with the Balmoral furniture company when the strike began. However, he was also actively involved in the UDA in Dunmurry, where he lived. His recollections of events are vivid:

> It was a fantastic time. The weather was great and the sun shone. That helped us for a start. We knew what we had to do. Working from the local Orange hall we did our own mini-census of the area, round every house to find out if there were sick children or old people who couldn't get out. We bought bread and milk in bulk from the supermarket and sold them to people who came to the hall, as well as delivering to those who couldn't. We took over the local petrol station and drew up a list of people entitled to have their tanks filled, nurses, hospital workers. We issued our own passes and permits. It was real power while it lasted.[51]

McDonald admits it helped that social security payments continued.

> We were out of work but we got them all the same. That was thanks to Paddy Devlin on the Executive, who authorised payment through employers. I remember going in to one of my bosses wearing UDA combat kit and he stood up at his desk to salute me before he handed over my giro. We were using the firm's lorries for our barricades so not all the top men were sympathetic. One told me he had seen a police list of names with mine at the top. I told him we had one as well, with his at the top![52]

He has also been willing to talk about action taken against local businesses who would not close in support of the strike.

> They were mostly nationalist owned so they were warned then burned out. I remember though one wee man, a Catholic, who ran a shirt maker's shop. He told us he'd been burned out of other areas twice already by the Provos, so we left him alone.[53]

Sammy Duddy also has very clear memories of the strike fortnight.

> It was a great time. We were all in it together and with each other, like what you were told about London during the Blitz. We built Dutch ovens in our back gardens, easy to do, you just stacked up the bricks and lit a fire inside them with a bit of mesh or wire netting over the hole at the top. That way you could bake potatoes, no bother.

He did his share of barricades duty at the outset before being assigned to security at the Hawthornden Road headquarters, but he tells how, on the first full day of the strike, he helped hijack a bakery van. 'We paid over to the driver for the price of every loaf he was carrying. He took it too, then he probably just reported back to his bosses that he'd been robbed!'[54]

Right from the start, a principal fear in the minds of Andy Tyrie and other UDA leaders was confrontation with the army. This had happened before, notably during the Loyalist anti-internment strike of the previous year and in July 1972 General Sir Robert Ford, the Commander-in-Chief, Land Forces, had secured government authorisation for troops to open fire on the UDA when its members had tried to barricade Ainsworth Avenue, off the Shankill Road, an interface area close to the nationalist Springfield Road. A week into that strike however, control of major roads, especially in Belfast, became a real issue, partly because the Northern Ireland Office wanted them to be open to anyone wanting to join the TUC's 'back to work' march scheduled for Monday, 21 May.

The following day, after the failure of the march, many barricades remained in place but the army's 39 Brigade, operating in the Shaftesbury Square and Sandy Row area of Belfast, reported that community leaders had co-operated with its troops over the removal of most obstructions to traffic. The fact that the 'community leaders' were UDA men such as Tommy Lyttle and Sammy Murphy was not mentioned in the army's press release.[55] Nor was the very heavy deployment of troops and rooftop marksmen used to discourage resistance by the UDA. In return they were allowed to maintain their street patrols. The potentially bloody clashes which Tyrie feared had been averted but the outcome was far removed from recent talk by Stan Orme that the UDA was a fascist militia which had to be smashed.

Tyrie had served in the Territorial Army and has been known to express regret that his role in the UDA excluded him from being considered for service in the Ulster Defence Regiment. His concern was thus to minimise provocation to British troops during the strike. 'We played a cat-and-mouse game with them,' he remembers. 'If we knew the army was coming we would start taking down our barricades and rebuild them somewhere else. Their radio communications system was antique and we had Shankill Radio with a transmitter which could reach much of the city. We had a radio monitoring team with Pye receiving sets who could pick up most army orders.'[56] Tyrie admits to having considered the possibility that the army would open fire. 'It was a risk we had to take. I had no hatred for them as soldiers, nor had most Loyalists, but we were on opposite sides and we had to win.'[57] McDonald knew the risks too and took his share of them. 'We were patrolling one night in Dunmurry,' he recalls, 'close to what had really become an interface with Twinbrook, which by then was a nationalist estate. We felt it was our streets and homes we were protecting but one officer got heavy with us. I forget what regiment it was but he told us they would open fire if we didn't disperse. Maybe it was our combat kit that provoked him. Anyway I marched our boys, about forty of them, off to where most of us lived but I still remember the sound of rifles being cocked. Maybe they'd just have fired over our heads. Who knows? We took a chance.'[58]

A lot, McDonald still thinks, depended upon how different army units chose to operate.

Some of them would have you lying face down on the pavement for ID checks, standing on your legs, all that. We had a system of giving them different names each time to confuse them about our real numbers. That got trickier, though, once

they recognised you. Mind you, there were some of them we got on fine with.
Most nights during the strike there would be soldiers in for a drink with us in the
Orange hall.[59]

McDonald, in fact, was lucky to escape with his life during the strike when a
hijacked vehicle he was driving was fired on by the military police after a chase
down Lisburn Road and into Loyalist Sandy Row.

Leaving aside incidents like these, the disinclination of the army and
indeed the RUC to be drawn into major confrontations with the strike and
those who backed it was a decisive factor in the outcome. There was no IRA
ceasefire during the two weeks of the strike and its operational activity
remained at a low level, but military commanders were reluctant to commit
troops to major operations against Loyalists, especially the UDA. This
emerges clearly enough from most army accounts of its role in May 1974.

Whether the London government ever intended to use the army to break
the strike remains very doubtful. James Molyneaux, on the basis of his own
contacts with Harold Wilson and Merlyn Rees, never thought they would. He
saw them both as democrats averse to the use of military force against any
striking workers. Wilson's broadcast on the second Friday of the strike, in
which he talked of rebellion and called. Ulster Loyalists 'spongers' was, in
Molyneaux's view, a calculated method of bringing the crisis to a head and
clearing out of the way a failed constitutional package inherited from the previous administration.[60]

Molyneaux's belief that the army would not be used was shared by Brian
Faulkner, Prime Minister of the Executive. He thought that the weakness of
Rees's position lay in his knowledge that the army did not want to move
against the strike:

> We always found the army making excuses for doing nothing and very slow to
> respond to any suggestions put to them. The GOC [General Officer Commanding]
> in Northern Ireland, backed up by the General Staff and the Ministry of Defence
> in London, seems to have grossly exaggerated to the Government the likelihood of
> getting involved in a shooting war with the UDA if they took action against the
> barricades and the roaming gangs.[61]

Recollections of those close to the Wilson government stress the importance
of the army's belief that it could not handle the all-important task of maintaining electricity supplies.[62] General Sir Frank King, the General Officer
Commanding in Northern Ireland, is known to have communicated to the
Northern Ireland Office at the outset of the strike his reasons for wanting to
avoid the use of the army in any confrontational role.[63] Like the locally
recruited Ulster Defence Regiment, an integral part of the army, the RUC
showed itself ready to be guided by the army's reading of the situation.

For some military units, the strike seemed to ease the danger to them from
nationalist areas. Rathcoole was patrolled in the early days of the stoppage by

42 Royal Marine Commando and they sensed its potential to become a Loyalist no-go area. Yet, one of them later recalled,

> just down the road was Bawnmore, a real hard Catholic estate and when the UWC strike started, they were the first ones to turn up at the gate asking for extra patrols because they were frightened of what the outcome would be. Reports from the rest of the unit showed a similar attitude. In the New Lodge the Catholics were totally back to 1969: they were giving the lads sandwiches and cups of coffee because they were so pleased at the presence of the troops.[64]

Others were concerned by the security forces' inaction, like one former sergeant in the Queen's Own Highlanders:

> UDA men with their hoods and pick handles started to operate their checkpoints right outside our battalion's base. You began to ask yourself who was the law now. UDA pickets even stood talking to army patrols, sounding off about trouble at local discos and how they should be allowed to sort it out. In fact they were defying an elected government and we should have moved against these roadblocks. I still see it as a black day for the army that we didn't.[65]

This sergeant could not have known that an 'elected government' was not going to act; as the historian of the UDR put it, whatever individual soldiers or indeed police officers may have felt had little relationship to this reality:

> Early on the army made a judgement that there was little it could do in the face of so widespread a revolt. Their longstanding axiom that they could not fight on two fronts still stood. Both the RUC and the UDR, taking their cue from the army, kept their heads down in face of their own impotence.[66]

The army's role in bringing about the downfall of Northern Ireland's short-lived Executive fuelled rumours that it had 'taken sides' against the Labour government. There were those within the nationalist community who were ready to believe this and later in the year an article in the journal of the right-wing Conservative Monday Club was seized on by them. In this, an anonymous serving officer with operational experience in Northern Ireland claimed: 'The army has shown that it is not prepared to act under certain circumstances; it has shown a considerable distrust of Socialist politicians . . . It has emerged, in fact, as a force to be reckoned with in political circles.'[67]

David Trimble queried this view of events a year later when he reviewed Robert Fisk's book on the UWC strike. It was too soon for him to write publicly about how close to events he had actually been but he went to some pains to dispute that there had been any role played by the army comparable to that alleged in some accounts of the so-called Curragh mutiny of 1914. They had, Trimble argued, simply both realised the strength of support for the strike and made this known to politicians, as well as their disinclination to attempt to run key services, such as electricity supply, on their own. May 1974, he further argued, was not 'a conscious usurpation of the authority of the state', but a crisis in which 'the strikers stepped in to fill a vacuum deliberately left by the authorities'.[68]

The security forces did, however, respond to blatant and brutal indiscipline by Loyalists in Ballymena on 24 May, the second Friday of the strike. Several popular pubs in the town were owned by Catholics and had not closed in answer to the strike call so a drunken group of UDA men, with some UVF members as well, wrecked three of them. At a fourth, the Wayside Inn, they met resistance from the proprietors, brothers Brendan and Sean Byrne. Both men were shot dead but thirty Loyalists who had taken part were arrested by the RUC and one later received a life sentence for murder.

Andy Tyrie, who had travelled out of Belfast often with Glen Barr to as many localities as he could visit, was enraged by this episode, which was so much in conflict with his concern that the strike should minimise violence. The following day brought new anxiety for him as army units in Rathcoole launched an arrest operation against UDA members. 'I had to get up there quickly to talk to the boys. I'd spent the last ten days telling them not to be predictable. We were winning by then and there was nothing to gain from taking on the army.'[69] William Craig also went to Rathcoole and supported Tyrie's line at an angry meeting in Cloughfern Orange hall; their efforts headed off any over-reaction by UDA units in the area.[70] The UWC was indeed winning and that same day – Saturday, 25 May – army commanders made it clear to Rees that they could not run power stations unaided. His response was to task the army with the takeover the next day of petrol stations and storage depots, a decision he broadcast on radio, declaring it to be in fulfilment of the Prime Minister's undertaking that the government would maintain essential services. A total strike call was, within hours, the UWC's answer: gas, water, sewage disposal, food delivery – all, they promised in a menacing communiqué, would be stopped.

In fact, Harold Wilson's Saturday broadcast, in which he had represented the strike as simply the work of thugs and spongers seeking power for themselves, had virtually clinched victory for the UWC, such was the anger it provoked. It also, for a time, created the belief in the minds of Craig and others that the entire council was about to be arrested. Ernest Baird, Craig's deputy in Vanguard, rushed to Hawthornden Road to supervise the burning of numerous UWC files, membership lists and assorted documents relating to the strike. Trimble is now thought to have devised a plan for an alternative leadership to be formed from Assembly and Westminster Unionist members who would gather at the strike headquarters to be arrested while the core leaders would assume a clandestine role.[71]

Ten of the province's Westminster MPs did in fact gather at Hawthornden Road. A single candle flickered on the table round which the UWC had met but the security forces never turned up. The episode, anti-climactic though it may have been, is illustrative of the relationship that had developed between Unionist politicians and the strike, after their initial hesitation. Craig, of

course, had been in sympathy from the start, as had Trimble, though he held
no elected position at that time.

While fear within the UWC of its collective internment was still real, Barr
decided that direct contact with the Orange Order was worth trying. Martin
Smyth, Grand Master of the Orange Order in all of Ireland, was conveniently
out of the country so Tommy Passmore, Grand Master in Belfast, was
approached:

> The fear of internment was explained and we asked would the Order take over the
> strike. I was aghast at what he said, I've never forgotten it to this day. He said he
> couldn't instruct the Order to take over, it would have to go through all the levels
> twice. I asked him how long would this take. He said about three months. I told him
> we hadn't three hours, let alone three days, let alone three months and you're telling
> me you don't have the necessary machinery when your country is at stake. So we
> chased him.[72]

The momentum built up by the strike was a problem for Ian Paisley, because
prior to it he had associated himself with the policy of Northern Ireland's
full integration within the United Kingdom. He has espoused other conflicting policies in his time but integration was in real danger of being blown out
of the water as a constitutional option by a massively supported Loyalist
strike which was a real challenge to Westminster. Another reason for tension
between Paisley and the UDA was his jealousy of what he saw as their rapport
with his rival, Craig, but the doctor's arrogance did not help either.

On one occasion during the second week of the strike Paisley arrived late
for a full meeting of the UWC. Barr, from the chair, had made it known that
no latecomers would be admitted. Sammy Duddy was authorised to guard the
door and was armed. He has already described his altercation with Paisley
when the latter arrived and demanded admission.[73] This was refused and
Paisley was admitted only after his written request was slipped under the
door. His berating of Duddy made little impression on the meeting but there
was then further acrimony when he occupied Barr's chair during an adjourn-
ment of the meeting. On his refusal to vacate the chair, it was lifted with him
in it and moved down the table from the chairman's place. Duddy has added
that 'a gun up his nose helped to shift him', and also recalls that soon afterwards he had to dispose of his own revolver with some haste when RUC
officers were seen approaching the building.

> I noticed some pot plants downstairs so I shoved the gun into one of them and
> covered it over with earth. That did the job but I had to put in quite a bit of time
> cleaning it once it was safe to take it out.[74]

Relations deteriorated further when Barr began to suspect that when important decisions were taken, such as releasing animal feed to farmers, Paisley
was seeking to claim the credit with the media. Paisley and Harry West, Barr
has added, 'were trying to give the impression that they were running the

committee'.[75] He responded by using his authority to order the UWC switch-board to stop any outgoing phone calls by either of them. In the event, it was Paisley who, backed by Tyrie, moved that the strike be called off once the British government's cave-in was apparent and a return to work was starting.[76]

The Executive finally collapsed on 28 May. Cracks within it had begun to open up. Five days earlier West, the Environment Minister, had called for talks with the UWC and Brian Faulkner made it known he would abandon the Council of Ireland. Because of Loyalist roadblocks and the worsening fuel shortage, Faulkner had to be flown by army helicopter from his home at Seaforde in County Down to Stormont, pondering during the short journey the clear extent of the strike's success. 'From all over the Province came stories of how the rebels were in control and the community was taking the soft option of giving them at least passive support.'[77] His choice of the word 'rebels' was a revealing one for a Unionist politician talking about fellow Protestants.

He had made up his mind to tell his ministers that they must advise Rees to open talks with the UWC and that if he refused the Executive would resign. Apart from the SDLP ministers, the Executive agreed with him. Rees did refuse and Faulkner announced the Executive's resignation early in the afternoon. With the strike solid and a total electricity stoppage in prospect there was little option and the news soon reached Loyalist protesters whom Faulkner had seen from his helicopter gathering round Carson's statue outside the Stormont building.

Kenneth Bloomfield, secretary to the Executive and principal adviser to Faulkner, was with him as he read out the resignation statement and later wrote emotionally of the day's events: 'On our way back to Faulkner's office in Parliament Buildings, and quite without shame, I wept.' He had come to admire Faulkner and to have high hopes of the power-sharing experiment.

> I wept for the success of the hard men with the dark glasses, the balaclava helmets and pickaxe handles; I wept for the inevitability of a sweeping British judgement that we were all hopeless cases, doomed to endless conflict in an inferno of our own creation; I wept for the eclipse of local democracy.[78]

As he wept, he was within earshot of a Loyalist protest in the grounds of Stormont which was turning into a huge victory celebration, awash with flags and backed by bands starting to arrive from South and East Belfast.

Huge media coverage of the strike and its outcome followed and much of this focused necessarily upon the pivotal role played by the UDA. On 2 June, the *Observer* featured an article in which Neal Ascherson interviewed Tyrie about the strike and its implications. It was entitled 'The republic of Hawthornden Road' and Tyrie spoke of the success of the tactics used during the strike and how Loyalism had broken the mould of its own predictability. 'We've made a bloodless revolution,' he declared, and went on to assert:

'The types who want to kill everyone and burn everything are out.'[79] If he meant out of the UDA, his claim was a little premature but his immediate post-strike message was at least one that sounded conciliatory.

He pressed the case for the UDA to get round a table with Catholics to discuss real power-sharing, even if it involved talking to elected delegates of the IRA. Ulster's politics could be reshaped, Tyrie argued, in a way which could end once and for all the power of gentry-based and middle-class Unionism: 'They did politics for a hobby and now they come crawling to us from under their flat stones: they should be ashamed to show their faces.'[80]

Ascherson communicated to readers his fascination with what he heard from Tyrie and Barr and cast around in his article for analogies from his own experience.

> Where before did one hear hard men with gnarled trigger fingers proclaiming a new brotherhood of man, a rallying of different creeds under one patriotic flag (and a handful of foreign-paid agitators to be swept easily away?) It was France in May 1958.[81]

Then, the French right had claimed Moslem Algerians would rally to the rebirth of the nation. 'Some of the same delusions are stalking Belfast today,' Ascherson concluded,[82] but others clung to a class analysis of events.

Just five days later, the left-wing Labour weekly, *Tribune*, followed up with a much fuller exploration of how far the strike had had a real class content to it. Michael Walsh, its reporter, talked to many who had been actively involved and while he argued that the strike's success was further proof of Protestant domination of skilled work in key sectors of the Northern Ireland economy as well as in the civil service, 'moles' within which had kept the UWC well briefed about government intentions, he also accepted the key role of genuine trade unionists.

However, these, Walsh stressed, were not cast in the same mould as their counterparts in England or Scotland. He singled out Jim Smyth, who had acted as press spokesman, describing him as

> not the everyday idea of a working-class apostle. He is a former draughtsmen's shop steward, it is true. But last year Smyth was strenuously working to get himself nominated as a Vanguard candidate for the Assembly elections. Vanguard's politics have, admittedly, a sniff of socialism about them. But it is the party of Bill Craig and the socialism is that of Ernst Rohm.[83]

This became the connecting thread of the remainder of Walsh's article. His concern was to show that the trade unionists on the UWC were loyal primarily to Protestant Ulster rather than to any identifiably socialist concept of class struggle. The prominence they had achieved was mainly due to paramilitary links, he argued, and he mentioned Harry Murray in this context, but Murray was never in the UDA and was wary of its role. Others such as Barr and Bob Pagels certainly were, but Walsh admitted as 'a chilling fact for Socialists' that such men were 'for the moment – and it will probably be a lingering moment – the authentic voices of working class Protestantism'.[84]

In the final part of a lengthy article, Walsh made much of National Front support for the strike. This is clear from its magazine *Spearhead*, and in late 1973 it had set up a Belfast branch and launched the first edition of the *Ulster Worker*. Martin Webster, the Front's national organiser, refused to be drawn on its links with the UWC. Its role was never more than marginal, although, as in England, there was an element of support within the working class. The strike succeeded for many reasons unrelated to the Front's presence and John McMichael, once he became Second in Command of the UDA, gave it short shrift.

Walsh read too much into the Front's role although it arguably had more support from within a section of the UVF in the 1970s than from the UDA.[85] He was right, however, about the power exercised by the latter on the UWC and during the strike, correctly attributing this to the fact that, with the murder of Tommy Herron and the defeat of Charles Harding Smith, the UDA's feuding East and West Belfast brigades had been able to throw their joint weight fully behind the strike.

The conclusion to Walsh's article was a gloomy one:

> Now, boosted by their victory, the Loyalist Orders and their followers are bent on ensuring that Catholics won't even get the shadow of power-sharing. The terrifying thing is that, in pursuing that aim the Protestant working class may not even need their copy of *Spearhead* to point them on the way to national socialism.[86]

This simply did not represent the political route which the UDA under the leadership of Tyrie, Barr and McMichael would seek to travel.

Paddy Devlin lost little time going into print with his account of the fall of the Executive in which he had served. Privately published the next year, it was an angry tirade at what he perceived as London's infirmity of purpose during the UWC strike. He recognised the victory won by working-class Loyalism but, correctly as it turned out, doubted if its alliance with Unionist politicians would last long, describing it as 'merely skin deep'.[87] However, in his opinion, the class fault lines within Protestant Ulster had been opened up for all to see by the 'May days' of 1974. The UWC, he argued, 'were motivated in this action as much by a crude class hatred of the landed gentry and local business tycoons who for years had dominated Unionist party politics, as by their fears of a united Ireland via Sunningdale'.[88]

Other accounts of the strike also came out during 1975. T. E. Utley, an English Conservative journalist, saw it as an episode which 'revealed a whole new gallery of Ulstermen – hitherto obscure workers like Harry Murray, who had suddenly proved themselves capable of masterminding a revolution and administering a country'.[89] Their victory, in his view, was 'an example of what happens when a sophisticated political establishment loses contact with gut politics',[90] revealing 'a whole unsuspected world beneath the surface of Ulster politics'.[91]

Better known than Utley's quite brief work is Robert Fisk's still vivid and valuable account of events. He was never in doubt that the strike was a victory for working-class Loyalists: 'The strike had finally broken the English illusion that by persuasion or political coercion they could order the lives of the 1.5 million in this last corner of their Irish colony.'[92] For Fisk, however, the whole Irish question itself had to be redefined because the strike had begun 'the slow rending of the political chains which had bound Loyalist Ulster to Britain since before the First World War'.[93]

Fortnight magazine had been developing this analysis of militant Loyalists even before the strike started, and it saw the UWC victory as vindicating it.

> Ulstermen, which for this purpose means Protestant Ulstermen, are not Irish in the same sense as other (Catholic) Ulstermen. Attempts to make them so by political and economic pressures are more likely to have the effect of making them feel ever less Irish. For a long time the Ulster Protestants asserted their unIrishness by saying loudly to the world at large that they were British. Now that is clearly no longer the case, they are falling back on the assertion of a kind of Ulster nationalism.[94]

Merlyn Rees later wrote of how he too had begun to sense this during the strike. At the stylish Culloden Hotel at Cultra on the shore of Belfast Lough, he recalled, well-heeled late evening drinkers had jeered at him and called him a traitor when he arrived there at the height of the UWC strike:

> It was a spontaneous outburst of anger: we, the Brits, were the outsiders, always ready to sell good Loyalists down that mythical river into the Catholic South. What was uniting all these diverse social and economic groups of Loyalists in the province, from the paramilitaries to the CBI and the NILP [Northern Ireland Labour Party], from the industrial workers to farmers and middle-class professionals, was opposition to Sunningdale. When it was seen that I was not prepared to capitulate on the agreement the cement of Ulster nationalism hardened.[95]

Ulster nationalism and indeed the case for a form of Ulster self-government or even full independence featured increasingly in media coverage of the apparent vacuum left by the collapse of power-sharing and the role of Loyalist workers in bringing this about. On 22 June 1975, the *Sunday Times* carried the headline 'The retreat from Ulster is on – and it's working'. Below it, 'an epic change' was claimed to be opening up in Britain's relationship with Northern Ireland. Escape from an impasse which had confronted Gladstone and Lloyd George lay at hand: 'The ultimate release from the problem of conflicting loyalties will be the emergence of a genuine Northern Ireland identity.'[96]

In his book Fisk went much of the way with this, reading into the ceasefire which the IRA called at the start of that year proof of the London government's moving closer to disengagement: 'All the evidence points to a British assurance [i.e. to the IRA] that Ulster could not forever remain part of the UK.'[97] The strongest challenge to this thinking came from Brendan Clifford of the British and Irish Communist Organisation. They espoused the 'two nations' view of the Irish question, rejecting Marxist critiques of it as essentially an anti-imperialist issue, but Clifford asserted that the best form of self-determination for working-class Loyalists lay in remaining British within an integrated United Kingdom.[98]

Clifford has now abandoned the position he took in 1975 but his refusal to use the two-nations theory as a rationale for Ulster self-government was in turn attacked by the Scottish libertarian Marxist Tom Nairn, whose 1977 book, *The Break-Up of Britain*, devoted an extended chapter to the UWC strike and its implications. He berated the British left's traditional hostility to and incomprehension of Protestant Ulster, which in his view, led by its working class, was starting to move away from its old identification with an imperial Britain and to assert its right to real self-determination.

> Seven years of warfare have shown that they and they alone, can solve the problems of their own nation. These problems have been thrust more and more completely into their own hands. With the 1974 strike they drew a lasting limit to outside interference in their affairs.[99]

UDA leaders such as Tyrie and Barr were drawn into these debates with results that will be explored in a further chapter of this book. Amidst all the polemics prompted by the writings of Fisk, Clifford and others, something else thrust itself to the centre of argument and comment and that was the strategic role played in the events of 1974 by the UDA. *Fortnight* echoed this in one of its post-strike editorials: 'Behind all the various organisations and splinter groups lies a single body of men centred on the UDA.'[100]

Outside Belfast and in rural areas it conceded that local Orange lodges had given help and made halls available but 'in Belfast itself and the outlying estates however the centre of allegiance is more usually the local UDA'.[101] The UDA leaders of 1974 have never departed from this view of events. Barr, interviewed about the strike twenty years later, agreed that while other Loyalist organisations were involved,

> the UDA were the most important as they were the largest, with pockets around the country where the Orange Volunteers or UVF played the key role, but overall it was the UDA that played the greater role and influenced the strike most.[102]

Tyrie has put it more succinctly: 'We gave the strike movement the brains and the muscle that it needed to win.'[103]

With victory came an explosion of Loyalist joy, especially in working-class communities that had had little to celebrate over a five-year period in which much of their world had been turned upside down. Bonfires, street parties and marching flute bands all gave expression to their euphoria and for UDA leaders the temptation was to savour the moment. Their strike had succeeded more fully than any previously attempted by organised labour in the British Isles but victory brought with it the need to keep the UDA at centre stage in the political manoeuvres which followed the Executive's collapse. They would soon find out just how difficult this would prove to be.

Not all the key figures in the events of 1974 remained in the UDA. Bob Pagels did so for another seven years but his involvement was to cost him arrest and imprisonment. This marked the parting of the ways for him:

> I stayed friends with Andy Tyrie but after my release I told him I wouldn't be back. He accepted it. I'd done quite a lot after all and life moves on, it has to. I was happy to make the break and my wife was, too. She never had any time for the UDA or for any of that.[104]

He continues to work in the Island Centre for the Handicapped: 'I've been organising some buses for the people we look after here,' he told the author. 'There you are, back in 1974 one of my jobs was hijacking buses to build UDA barricades.'[105]

Barr had avoided involvement in the paramilitary side of the UDA. After the strike he took part, along with UDA leaders, in talks with Rees, but fell foul of the United Ulster Unionist Council, which had emerged to lead opposition to the Sunningdale Agreement. This was because in the October 1974 Westminster general election he opted to support a candidate of the Vanguard Unionist Progressive Party (VUPP), who stood unsuccessfully in West Belfast against the UUUC. In the Constitutional Convention, set up by the British government, he supported William Craig when the VUPP split over the issue of a voluntary coalition which might have included the SDLP had it come to fruition.

He remained deputy leader to Craig in the VUPP until February 1978, when it reverted to the status of the Vanguard movement and ceased to be a political party. Craig himself returned to mainstream Unionism, joining what had become the Official Unionist Party later that year, only to be isolated and destroyed politically by the DUP, which had come to see him as an enemy. Barr declined to follow him, preferring an independent stance and giving his support to the New Ulster Political Research Group, whose work in drawing up a policy document on an independent Northern Ireland will be looked at later in this book.

Barr finally withdrew from politics in 1981, the year the UDA formed the Ulster Loyalist Democratic Party. He later took over the running of a Londonderry training centre for unemployed young people from both communities and also worked on strategies to attract American investment to the city.[106] Like Pagels, he has re-emerged to talk to the media on anniversaries of the UWC strike and in 1998 he also served briefly on the Parades Commission set up by the Blair government.

Another key figure in the strike was Harry Murray. It was he who announced the UWC's strike decision to the media and he acted as a regular spokesman for it during the stoppage. He parted company with the UDA when the power-sharing executive fell. After stating, at an Oxford conference in July 1974, that he would talk to the IRA if they ended their war, he resigned from the UWC. The following year he stood unsuccessfully as an Alliance Party candidate in a North Down council by-election but gave continued support to the case for a new experiment in power-sharing. In 1982 he backed an effort to relaunch the UWC as a campaigning body which would support the case for job creation policies and working-class unity.[107]

Anniversaries of the strike were always opportunities for reflection on what might have happened had it been maintained for longer or if the British government had used military force to break it. Sinn Fein's newspaper in May 2004 devoted a full-page article to the events of thirty years earlier, pouring scorn on Britain's failure to act against the UWC and its alleged willingness to let the power-sharing executive collapse. Extraordinarily, the article made no reference to the Republican movement's contemptuous dismissal of the experiment at the time and the IRA's continuation of a campaign which would have exposed the security forces to a war on two fronts if they had been ordered to move against the strikers.[108]

At the end of 2004, new releases of relevant British Cabinet papers were a reminder of the sheer magnitude of the May 1974 crisis and of the demoralising effect it had on the Prime Minister, Harold Wilson. Soon after the end of the strike he drafted a confidential document for senior Cabinet Office staff, which showed vividly his fear of renewed action by Loyalists. 'All this', he went on, 'affects the drafting of any Doomsday scenario. In Doomsday terms – which means withdraw – I should like this scenario to be considered.'[109] It was one involving high risks, he conceded, where reactions from the nationalist community and the Irish government were concerned, but he set out the possibility of dominion status for Northern Ireland being negotiated and later put the idea to SDLP spokesmen in secret talks with them in June 1974.[110]

Thoughts like these from a Prime Minister conscious of his weakness after the UWC strike victory represent a climactic point in Loyalist and UDA power, one which they were not able to recapture. Whether UDA leaders were ready for the radical departure of full self-government on the back of their key role in the strike must remain debatable. In a television programme presented by Jim McDowell, the editor of the *Sunday World*, Pagels claimed that unilateral independence for Ulster was the UDA's aim.[111] The author has found no documents to confirm this, nor have other UDA participants in the strike, and most records of the UWC's debates and decisions were deliberately destroyed by it at the height of the crisis.

McDowell has also revealed that in comments not carried in the programme, Pagels has now contested the view that the strike was simply a reaction to the implementation of the Sunningdale Agreement, claiming that the planning of the stoppage had been started a full eighteen months before.[112] Again, this is a claim which needs to be substantiated but the documentation is no longer available. The record of what happened at the time still points to the ability of men such as Pagels, Barr, Andy Tyrie and others to improvise and rapidly adapt to a crisis which changed dramatically from day to day.

NOTES

1. A. Clarke, *Contact* (London: Secker and Warburg, 1983), pp. 44–56.
2. S. Bruce, *The Red Hand: Protestant Paramilitaries in Northern Ireland* (Oxford; Oxford University Press, 1992), p. 89.
3. A. Purdy, *Molyneaux: The Long View* (Antrim: Greystone, 1989), p. 134.
4. Ibid.
5. *Fortnight*, 14 December 1973.
6. *Ulster Loyalist*, 26 October 1973.
7. Ibid.
8. *Ulster Loyalist*, 20 December 1973.
9. Ibid.
10. Ibid.
11. *Ulster Loyalist*, 3 January 1974.
12. *Ulster Loyalist*, 31 January 1974.
13. *Ulster Loyalist*, 14 February 1974.
14. *Ulster Loyalist*, 31 January 1974.
15. Ibid.
16. *Fortnight*, 8 March 1974.
17. Ibid.
18. *Ulster Loyalist*, 6 March 1974.
19. Ibid.
20. B. Pagels, interview with author, 5 December 2002.
21. H. McDonald, *Trimble* (London: Bloomsbury, 2000), p. 41.
22. R. Fisk, *Point of No Return: the Strike Which Broke the British in Ulster* (London: Times/Andre Deutsch, 1975). See also an unpublished dissertation by F. Barlet for a valuable account of the UWC's origins.
23. *Labour Weekly*, 13 December 1985.
24. Pagels, interview with author.
25. A. Tyrie, interview with author, 3 December 2002.
26. M. Rees, *Northern Ireland: A Personal Perspective* (London: Methuen, 1985), pp. 58–9.
27. Fisk, *Point of No Return*, pp. 46–7.
28. Rees, *Northern Ireland*, pp. 58–9.
29. Ibid.
30. Fisk, *Point of No Return*, p. 48.
31. Ibid., p. 49.
32. P. Taylor, *Loyalists* (London: Bloomsbury, 1999), p. 129.
33. Ibid.
34. J. Cusack and H. McDonald, *UVF* (Dublin: Poolbeg, 2000), rev. ed., pp. 132–6.
35. Ibid.
36. Fisk, *Point of No Return*, p. 65.
37. North Belfast Loyalist, interview with author, 15 October 2002.

38. Tyrie, interview with author.
39. Pagels, interview with author.
40. Ibid.
41. Ibid.
42. *A Brief History of the UDA/UFF in Contemporary Conflict* (Belfast, 1999), p. 22. This title came out without a named author but was the work of John White. See also Glen Barr, 'Ten days in May: the UWC strike in 1974', *New Ulster Defender*, vol. 1, no. 10, 1994.
43. Fisk, *Point of No Return*, p. 92.
44. *The Times*, 22 May 1974.
45. Ibid.
46. *Brief History of the UDA/UFF*, pp. 22–3.
47. C. Brett, *Long Shadows Cast Before: Nine Lives in Ulster 1625–1977* (Edinburgh: John Bartholomew, 1978), p. 88.
48. Ibid.
49. J. Gregg, interview with author, 16 October 2002.
50. Ibid.
51. J. McDonald, interview with author, 2 December 2002.
52. Ibid.
53. Ibid.
54. Sammy Duddy, interview with author, 4 December 2002.
55. Fisk, *Point of No Return*, pp. 149–50.
56. Tyrie, interview with author. See also Fisk, *Point of No Return*, p. 157.
57. Tyrie, interview with author.
58. McDonald, interview with author.
59. Ibid.
60. Purdy, *Molyneaux*, pp. 112–15.
61. B. Faulkner, *Memoirs of a Statesman* (London; Weidenfeld and Nicolson, 1978), p. 263.
62. B. Donoughue, *Prime Minister: The Conduct of Policy under Wilson and Callaghan* (London: Jonathan Cape, 1987), p. 133.
63. D. Hamill, *Pig in the Middle: The Army in Northern Ireland 1969–1984* (London: Methuen, 1985), pp. 143–53.
64. M. Arthur, *Northern Ireland: Soldiers Talking* (London: Sidgwick and Jackson, 1987), pp. 99–100.
65. Interview with author; see I. Wood (ed.), *Scotland and Ulster* (Edinburgh: Mercat Press, 1994), p. 155.
66. C. Ryder, *The Ulster Defence Regiment: An Instrument of Peace?* (London: Methuen, 1991), pp. 77–8.
67. *Guardian*, 3 September 1974; see also *Monday World*, August 1974.
68. *Fortnight*, 21 November 1975.
69. Tyrie, interview with author.
70. Fisk, *Point of No Return*, pp. 213–14.
71. McDonald, *Trimble*, pp. 53–4.
72. *New Ulster Defender*, vol. 1, no. 10, 1994.
73. Taylor, *Loyalists*, p. 135.

74. Duddy, interview with author.

75. E. Moloney and A. Pollak, *Paisley* (Dublin: Poolbeg, 1986), p. 363.

76. Ibid.

77. Faulkner, *Memoirs of a Statesman*, p. 4.

78. K. Bloomfield, *Stormont in Crisis: A Memoir* (Belfast: Blackstaff Press, 1994), p. 220.

79. *Observer*, 2 June 1974.

80. Ibid.

81. Ibid.

82. Ibid.

83. *Tribune*, 7 June 1974.

84. Ibid.

85. S. Nelson, *Ulster's Uncertain Defenders* (Belfast: Appletree Press, 1984), pp. 172–3.

86. *Tribune*, 7 June 1974.

87. P. Devlin, *The Fall of the Northern Ireland Executive* (Belfast: Paddy Devlin, 1975), p. 83.

88. Ibid.

89. T. Utley, *Lessons of Ulster* (London: J. M. Dent, 1975), p. 120.

90. Ibid., p. 121.

91. Ibid.

92. Fisk, *Point of No Return*, p. 231.

93. Ibid., p. 235.

94. *Fortnight*, 7 June 1974.

95. Rees, *Northern Ireland*, p. 71.

96. Ibid.

97. Fisk, *Point of No Return*, p. 246.

98. B. Clifford, *Against Ulster Nationalism: A Review of the Development of the Catholic and Protestant Communities and Their Interaction with Each Other and with Britain: In Reply to Tom Nairn of* New Left Review *and Others* (Belfast: British and Irish Communist Organisation, 1975), pp. 60–6.

99. T. Nairn, *The Break-Up of Britain* (London: New Left, 1981), 2nd ed., p. 245.

100. *Fortnight*, 21 June 1974.

101. Ibid.

102. *New Ulster Defender*, vol. 1, no. 10, 1994.

103. Tyrie, interview with author.

104. Pagels, interview with author.

105. Ibid.

106. W. Flackes and S. Elliott, *Northern Ireland: A Political Directory 1968–1988* (Belfast: Blackstaff Press, 1989), pp. 74–5.

107. Ibid., pp. 196–7.

108. *An Phoblacht/Republican News*, 13 May 2004.

109. *Guardian*, 1 January 2005.

110. Ibid.

111. *Cabinet Confidential: Secrets of '74*, BBC Northern Ireland, 2 January 2005.

112. *Sunday World*, 2 January 2005.

3

After the Strike: Political Initiatives and Political Defeats

❧

'No solution could be imposed from across the water. From now on we had to throw the task clearly to the Northern Ireland people themselves.'[1] So wrote Harold Wilson quite soon after the collapse of the Executive.

His first move after this, however, was to extend direct rule in the province, which was agreed to in mid-July 1974 without a division being called in the House of Commons. Soon after that, the Assembly was scrapped and the formation in its place of a new Constitutional Convention was announced. The Wilson government still believed in power-sharing, though any Irish dimension to it was quietly laid to rest. Elections, however, offered the government little comfort. At the Westminster general election in October, the second of the year, only two 'Faulkner Unionists' were returned and the United Ulster Unionist Council, a coalition of the anti-power-sharing parties, won 58 per cent of the total vote.

They did even better when the elections to the new Convention were finally held in May 1975. When it convened it at once made clear its preference for a return to simple majority rule on the old Stormont model but with opposition (i.e. Catholic) members being guaranteed some committee chairs. The Vanguard Unionists' leader, William Craig, challenged this and in September came out for a voluntary coalition between Unionists and the SDLP. The split this caused ended Vanguard's political role and made Craig an easy target for Ian Paisley's Democratic Unionist Party, who ended his career by ousting him from his Westminster seat four years later. David Trimble supported Craig, taking the view that nationalists should be given the chance to 'come in from the cold' and was later able to argue that the UUUC had thrown away a chance for political and constitutional bridge-building.[2]

These developments and their politically sterile outcome did not entirely by-pass paramilitary Loyalism in general and the UDA in particular. The strike victory of May 1974 had seemed to offer a threshold of opportunity for mobilising the Loyalist working class against old-style Unionism. This was certainly a view held by some on the left who had chosen to support the strike, rejecting the more commonly held Marxist stereotype of the UWC as a neo-fascist Protestant backlash. The Workers Association, a small offshoot of the British and Irish Communist Organisation (BICO), had, during the strike, printed and distributed a bulletin strongly supportive of its aims. On 31 May 1974, the final issue of this bulletin declared:

> The attempt by [Merlyn] Rees and [Stan] Orme to treat Ulster as a colony has collapsed in disgrace: and so we bid farewell to these socialists who aspired to be colonial administrators. The general state of mind brought about in the Protestant community by the strike offers a greater opportunity for the working out of a democratic political settlement than has ever existed before.[3]

For a time indeed it seemed that the UDA leadership might well move in this direction, for in June 1974 it made known its readiness to hold talks with the SDLP and even the IRA. The Workers Association welcomed this while warning the UDA 'not to underestimate the determination of the UUUC leadership to retain their political control. Since the strike they have spared no effort to prevent the emergence of a Loyalist working class political voice.'[4]

In reality it was the Ulster Volunteer Force which entered the political arena sooner than the UDA. It had taken a minor part in the UWC strike at its central level but individual members had been active locally. After the end of it, some of them formed the Volunteer Party, whose programme has been described as being to the left of the Northern Ireland Labour Party.[5] They campaigned essentially for social justice within the Union. Glen Barr of the UDA appeared on the Shankill Road to declare his personal support for them and was, as a result, suspended from the UUUC. Their candidate in the October 1974 general election was Ken Gibson, who had sat on the UWC during the strike but he achieved only limited support in West Belfast, coming fourth with 2,690 votes.

Barr was not alone within the UDA in believing that it too had to find a political road to explore, even while it continued to wage war on the Republican enemy. The UWC, in his view, lacked the cohesion to find that road itself. He was right about that. It had been simply an umbrella body under which anti-Agreement Unionists and working-class Loyalists could gather for the agreed, albeit temporary, purpose of forcing the British Labour government into reverse. Whether the UDA could assume a political role on the back of its contribution to the victory of May 1974 was still problematic. Barr hoped so, and in his position as Vanguard's vice-chairman took Craig's side in the split within the 1975 Constitutional Convention on the case for a coalition with the SDLP. He resigned from Vanguard but his stance loosened his relationship with Andy Tyrie, whose enthusiasm for contact with the SDLP had cooled.

Tyrie had in fact supported a UDA ceasefire in July 1974, partly as a tactic to try and secure the release of members who had been interned as well as remission of sentences for those convicted. However, the continuing death toll that year and the next made it clear to everyone that some active and ruthless units were still being allowed to operate by a leadership uncertain of its ability to control them. Between the collapse of the power-sharing executive on 28 May and the end of 1974, UDA/UFF members were involved in at least nineteen killings, most of which fell into a grim pattern already set. The victims were late-night drinkers unwise enough to attempt walking home alone. Vulnerable staff in clubs and taxi offices, night shift workers awaiting transport: all were easy prey for UDA gunmen prowling in their cars along the ill-lit streets of Belfast's working-class areas. But there were others, including thirteen-year-old Catholic Joseph McGuinness from Upper Meadow Street in the New Lodge area of North Belfast. His mistake, on the night of 15 August, was to walk onto North Queen's Street to go with friends to a chip shop. As they approached the entrance to Duncairn Gardens, a dangerous interface throughout the Troubles, a Loyalist crowd yelled taunts at them, then a single shot was fired. He died soon afterwards. A man described in court as a UDA officer was later convicted of the killing.[6]

Another victim, whose fate shocked many Protestants and heaped condemnation upon the UDA, was Ann Ogilby, a 31-year-old single parent of a young daughter and also a Protestant. Nonetheless she was beaten to death in a UDA club in the city's Sandy Row area in late July 1974, her cries audible to her child outside the room where she had been taken. The exact motive for her murder was not established in court, though in February 1975, a man and no fewer than eleven women were convicted of involvement in her death. The judge in the case described the UDA as 'a vicious, brutalising organisation which took the law into its own hands'.[7]

The killing continued into the next year, in the course of which the UDA took twenty more lives although, as in 1974, the UVF claimed many more victims. Tyrie's position as commandant of the UDA was not strong enough for him to halt or bring under control such brutality as the murder of Ann Ogilby, any more than he could have halted other killings in this period, even if that had been one of his priorities. Continuing tensions within the organisation still threatened his position despite the key role he had demonstrably played in the UWC strike.

In November 1974, Tyrie accepted an invitation to go to Libya to meet its president, Colonel Gadafy, in order to explain to him the Ulster Loyalist position. Barr, Andy Robinson from Londonderry, Tommy Lyttle from West Belfast and Harry Chicken from Newtonabbey accompanied him on a bizarre trip which prompted wild speculation about contacts being made by the UDA with the Provisional IRA. They too were talking to Gadafy, but in reality no negotiations took place over any share-out of Libyan aid between the two organisations.[8]

Charles Harding Smith resented his exclusion from this Libyan venture, as indeed he begrudged Tyrie his rapid rise within the UDA. In early January, he announced that his West Belfast brigade was seceding from the organisation. The brigade area comprised mainly the Shankill and Harding Smith was trading on personal loyalty to him within this close-knit community, which was his power base. Lyttle's first reaction was to support him, though he later switched sides. Harding Smith had, however, damaged his own position by his treatment of David Fogel and rumours circulated about his role in Ernie Elliott's murder. He had also made a tactical error in quarrelling with and then ordering 'off the road' Davy Payne, a friend of Tyrie's, only for Payne to be promoted to the rank of brigadier in North Belfast, despite or even because of the ferocious reputation he had acquired.

Payne, however, remained a figure to reckon with, as Barr stated on the occasion of his death in March 2003:

> I owe my life to Davy Payne because there had been a plan within a section of the UDA to have me killed because I had been part of a delegation which had gone to Libya to have talks with Colonel Gadafy in 1974. Davy Payne went to those people and told them I was under his protection and I have no doubt that saved my life.[9]

Sammy Duddy realised that a new power struggle had started when the office from which he edited the *Ulster* magazine for the UDA was taken over by Harding Smith's men. 'I told them I had an article to finish but that made no difference since they put a gun to my head and told me to get out or be shot.'[10] Tyrie was placed under house arrest in his home in Glencairn and Harding Smith announced that a new Inner Council would meet shortly. At this point, Harding Smith's coup began to unravel. The East and North Belfast brigades boycotted the new Inner Council, as did the Londonderry brigade. Tyrie escaped from his house arrest and his supporters, including Duddy, organised a well-armed 'team' who drove into Glencairn to bring out their leader's family.

'Harding Smith was no loss,' Duddy later recalled; 'he thought he could throw his weight around, intimidate people. He was just a bully in my view. I saw a lot of things about him that I didn't like. I caught him once knocking a wee girl about in a room in the Shankill office. He'd wanted to get photos of her, you can guess what kind, too. He was bad news. He thought he was bigger than the UDA.'[11] Harding Smith soon found out that he was not. On 14 January he was shot in the Shankill Road office in a well-prepared attack by a marksman who had taken up his position in a shop opposite. The Inner Council went through the motions of expressing regret over the injuries which put Harding Smith into hospital. He was shot again almost as soon as he was discharged. Once more he survived, but departed for England, where he worked as a commercial delivery driver for a biscuit firm in Yorkshire and later died of natural causes.

This violent sequence of events was interpreted by some commentators as merely a squalid struggle for control of UDA funds, but Harding Smith's motive is more likely to have been to win back overall power for himself. *Fortnight* magazine argued that 'what it all adds up to is an absence of any credible and coherent policy on either side and a return to the tactics of simple gangsterism in the resulting impasse'.[12] This, however, was a mistaken analysis because Tyrie used his survival in power to encourage debate among those in the UDA who were prepared at least to consider alternatives to the gun.

One such alternative for UDA members with trade union experience and connections was to join campaigns such as Save the Shankill. This began in 1974 to combat plans for a Belfast ring road which threatened to cut the area apart. It was also a response to planned redevelopment of the district, involving the demolition of many old streets to build high-rise flats and chain stores which would force out local businesses.[13] Tyrie and the UDA's Inner Council encouraged members to take an active role in protests, which indeed stopped some of the worst threats to the area's distinctive character.[14] Whole streets were saved for rebuilding by the Housing Executive instead of demolition and high-rise building was held at bay. No disaster comparable to the awful Divis tower block on the nearby Falls Road was ever inflicted on the Shankill.

Tyrie's support for initiatives like these was instrumental in creating the Ulster Community Action Group (UCAG), a loose grouping of community organisations from Protestant areas in East and North Belfast. A prominent member of BICO, who had helped bring out its supportive strike bulletin in May 1974, advised UCAG and acted for a time as its chairman. BICO still had high hopes of class-based politics developing within Protestant Ulster, particularly Belfast. 'The strike has shown once and for all', it declared in a 1975 pamphlet, 'that the community is sufficiently well-organised, determined and united to resist any attempts to push it around; and that it can do that without indulging in a bloodbath or mindlessly submitting to a Hitler-type leader.'[15]

Community activists committed to tackling the real problems of the Shankill and other areas could only welcome the contribution some UDA members could make.[16] For some of these, the priority they gave to what they were doing could mean leaving the UDA altogether and for others, inevitably, a real choice had to be faced between this sort of work and carrying on the war against the IRA and communities which were thought to sustain it.[17] Real paramilitary hard-liners were probably not attracted for very long to these alternative roles.

For Tyrie, the bigger picture was still Northern Ireland's political future and the nature of its constitutional relationship with Britain. After the success of the UWC strike, invitations began to reach participants in it to attend academic seminars and events such as the annual conference of the British and Irish Association in Oxford in July 1974. Contacts made at these gatherings and the exposure to much talk of cross-community peace initiatives led heroes of the strike such as Harry Murray to break with the UWC and Bob Pagels ultimately to leave the UDA.

In late March 1975, under the auspices of the Dutch Council of Churches, fourteen senior UDA members spent three days in Amsterdam hearing about how the political system of the Netherlands worked through mechanisms devised to achieve compromises between culturally and religiously different populations.[18] They also had the chance to listen to, and take part in, a debate on constitutional alternatives to the Union with Britain, in which the case for Ulster independence was pushed quite hard but also challenged by a representative of BICO, who argued that integration within the United Kingdom remained Loyalists' best option and that independence was being pressed by a British government beginning to think in terms of disengagement from Northern Ireland.[19] One major event in which the UDA took part was a conference held at Amherst, Massachusetts, in the late summer of 1975. It was organised by local academics and businesspeople with an interest in Irish affairs. Historians and academics from both sides of the Atlantic were invited, as well as Ulster Unionists and Republicans with Provisional IRA links. Unionists and the SDLP declined to take part, though the Reverend Martin Smyth, a senior figure in the Orange Order, who was to enter the Westminster Parliament as a Unionist in 1982, did attend. So too did Seamus Costello, who had led a breakaway from the Official Republican Movement and formed what claimed to be the more militantly Marxist Irish Republican Socialist Party. Its and his links to the INLA brought about his assassination in Dublin two years later.

Since those with Provisional IRA connections were refused entry visas by the American authorities, Costello found himself the only representative of a distinctively Republican viewpoint in the series of debates which took place. The UVF did not take part but Tyrie, Barr and Sammy Smyth were there to put a Loyalist view. Accounts of the conference underline Tyrie's authority within the UDA. Costello made a case, in one session, for talks amongst paramilitary organisations to halt sectarian killings. Interest in this built up but then

> the whole thing was brought to an end by Barr on a nod from Tyrie who stuck to the UDA line that there would be no talks until the rank and file had given their consent. Tyrie said little during the conference but when he did his troops obeyed to the letter.[20]

Smyth made a forceful contribution on civil rights in Northern Ireland, stressing for American listeners that this was an issue for Protestants as well as Catholics. Also present was the Irish historian Liam de Paor, who in 1970 had written *Divided Ulster*, a Penguin Special, sympathetic in tone and content to the civil rights campaign. He gave what the UDA deputation later admitted was their first real chance to hear Irish history presented in a nationalist but also scholarly context. What seemed to some observers a darker side to the proceedings was that, despite the current IRA ceasefire, 'the UDA ran a continual and rather nasty joke about kneecapping with electric drills' (i.e. instead of using guns).[21]

This macabre humour was kept up during an afternoon off when conference members were taken to a local country fair near Amherst. The United States Army had a stand for recruitment and publicity and this included a jeep with an automatic weapon mounted on it. Two UDA members grabbed hold of Costello while Tyrie jumped on the jeep and pointed the weapon at him, simulating the sound of it being fired with a shout of 'you're dead'.[22] Costello is said to have made light of the incident and was later overheard in conversation at the bar with Tyrie, addressing him as 'just one commander-in-chief to another'.[23]

The most significant event at Amherst, however, was when Barr was given the floor to set out what he stressed were at this point his personal views on the case for full Ulster independence and a new identity for Ulster people. 'Ulstermen', he stressed, must no longer be 'second class Englishmen or second class Irishmen as they had been until now'. Events since 1969, he argued, supported his analysis.

> The Nationalists had shown that they could destroy the old Stormont system. But so too the Loyalists had shown that they could bring down a power-sharing executive, though that in itself was no great loss, since it institutionalised our communal differences. What it amounted to was that each side had the power to destroy whatever was brought forward.[24]

Only in an independent Ulster could non-sectarian politics develop, Barr continued, but he stated that the European Community would have to be involved if this new status for Northern Ireland was to be economically viable. He acknowledged the difficulties that would be involved in any transitional process and the destabilising factor of continuing Loyalist violence. This violence, he predicted optimistically, would base any rationale it had under a new constitution acceptable to both communities but he avoided the issue of whether this constitution would be a republican one or built upon allegiance to the British crown. The latter was clearly an issue on which he needed to declare himself but he stressed in his address that he wanted to test opinion on this preliminary statement of his ideas.

There had been talk of Ulster independence as some kind of Doomsday option for Loyalists in UDA publications prior to the formation of the UWC in 1974. Some media analyses of the strike and its victorious outcome had interpreted events as proof of the emergence of a recognisable Ulster nationalism, as indeed had the Secretary of State for Northern Ireland at the time, Merlyn Rees. The Amherst gathering served to raise the profile of debate on independence, though there were also sceptics who took the view that the idea had tacit encouragement from elements within the British government who now favoured disengagement from Northern Ireland. Attendees at Amherst later recalled the presence of a mysterious Sean Hopkins claiming to represent the long-defunct Campaign for Democracy in Ulster and joking at the bar about being 'your friendly neighbourhood spy' as well as talking of his army contacts.[25] Media interest in this debate continued. The *Irish Times* gave extensive coverage to the Amherst conference and the UDA's part in it, claiming that 'it was able to achieve the dignity of a forward-thinking political group',[26] and in October it applauded the news that at a UDA meeting convened for November 1975 in Belfast, independence would be on the agenda: 'The UDA will now be discussing seriously a concept that has gained powerful support in the highest echelons of paramilitary Loyalism.'[27]

The UDA's magazines began to show an interest in independence, influenced clearly by the organisation's Scottish contacts. Roddy MacDonald, the UDA's leader in Scotland in 1975 and 1976, who was later imprisoned on charges of illegal handling of guns and explosives, put the case for Ulster independence under the Crown, in a contribution to *Ulster* magazine on its Tartan Warrior page.[28] The next issue, however, carried a fuller and much more thoughtful treatment of the question.

This article was unsigned but its author was clearly well versed in Scottish history and the current political situation there. England, he or she argued, should welcome movements for independence within the British Isles 'as a means of regaining their own lost sense of identity and direction'.[29] The piece quoted a passage by the Scottish Catholic and nationalist writer Sir Compton Mackenzie, but carefully substituted at every necessary point, the word 'Ulster' for 'Scotland' or 'Scottish'. 'Your immediate duty', it told readers, 'is to recreate yourselves, for only in recreating yourselves will you recreate that nation of Ulster.'[30] The article concluded, however, by accepting that a likely majority of Protestant people in Northern Ireland were not yet persuaded of the case for independence, though, as in Scotland, support for it could be built.

This intermittent, though continuing, debate within the politically minded element of the UDA has to be seen within a context of political impasse in Northern Ireland. The Constitutional Convention set up by Rees folded amidst acrimonious scenes in March 1976 and the immediate future appeared to be one of continued direct rule by London-appointed ministers. It was accompanied by a shift in security policy, with primacy being accorded to a reorganised and much expanded RUC and Ulster Defence Regiment. This was 'Ulsterisation', which meant locally recruited police and soldiers, nearly all Protestants, bearing the brunt of IRA attacks. Forty-two of them were killed that year while British army casualties dropped correspondingly.

A new Secretary of State succeeded Rees in August 1976. Roy Mason identified himself strongly with the new policy while showing little inclination for new constitutional initiatives or experiments. Unionism remained divided, with Dr Ian Paisley coming out for a return to Stormont-style rule. The Official Unionist Party gave at least token support to that, though others were influenced by Enoch Powell, MP for South Down since 1974, who was making the case for full integration with Britain as the ultimate protection for the Union.

Out of these anxieties there grew yet another Unionist pressure group, the Loyalist Action Council, later renamed the United Unionist Action Council, originally a sub-committee of the UUUC. Its remit was to press both for devolution of power back to Northern Ireland and a tougher security policy to reduce the loss-rate of the RUC and the UDR. The Action Council quickly formed a paramilitary wing, the Ulster Service Corps, which in counties Tyrone and Armagh began its own patrols, some of which carried legally held firearms. Paisley told the House of Commons that he had taken part in some of these and, along with Ernest Baird, an East Belfast chemist who had been active in Vanguard, appealed for all Loyalists to support the new Action Council.

His own party, the DUP, already did so, and they were joined by the Independent Orange Order and the Apprentice Boys of Derry, as well as a number of trade unionists who had been active three years earlier in the UWC. Its leadership, however, had changed. Some of the militants of 1974 had left it but Jim Smyth and Billy Kelly, key figures in bringing out the Ballylumford power station workers, were still there and Paisley and the Action Council had high hopes of them. A serious initial blow was the refusal of Harry West, the OUP leader, and the Reverend Martin Smyth, Grand Master of the Orange Order, to join it. Both had serious doubts about the Council's ability to force British policy into a reversal comparable to that of 1974. Their doubts proved to be well founded, especially when Paisley began to press the case for renewed strike action by Loyalist workers in pursuit of the Action Council's demands.

It was at this point that Paisley and his party colleagues approached the UDA, with whom relations had been severely strained since 1974. Like the UVF, its leaders felt that Paisley had not honoured promises to try to secure representation for them on the UUUC, for which they had provided the muscle needed to defeat the Sunningdale power-sharing initiative. The UDA had also been extremely critical of Paisley's treatment of William Craig within the Council over his declared support for a new experiment in coalition between Unionists and the SDLP. In August 1976, Paisley was enraged when Andy Tyrie put these points to him, denouncing his 'brazen effrontery'.[31]

The DUP leader went on to describe Tyrie as 'a man who leads an organisation whose members in the past months have been tried in the courts and have pleaded guilty to or been found guilty of the most diabolical of crimes'.[32] Knowledge of Paisley's own recent talks with themselves as with other paramilitary groups was a ready weapon in the UDA's hands and their reaction was to threaten to go to the press with what they knew. They backed off from doing this but Paisley had to repair relations with Tyrie as any strike was clearly going to need UDA support.

The UDA began to have its doubts as 1976 slipped into 1977. Paisley kept up an acerbic attack on the OUP, especially West, and also alienated the Orange Order by leaking to the press details of secret talks between Smyth and the SDLP. The talks had not committed Smyth or the Order to anything, but the vitriol of Paisley's language guaranteed that any strike action would go ahead without the declared support of the biggest Unionist party or of the Orange Order. Paisley himself began to exhibit doubts and, when the Loyalist Action Council met on 23 April, appeared to many of those present to be against strike action. He also shifted his ground on what the Council should demand, arguing that it should limit itself to the need for a radical over-haul of security policy since the British government was unlikely to respond to any call for implementation of the Constitutional Convention's case for a restoration of Stormont-style majority rule.

The UDA itself went divided into the strike action which soon followed. Jim Smyth, a key figure in planning the tactics and public relations of the UWC strike three years earlier, became alarmed at seemingly belated attempts to organise support in Loyalist workplaces, especially the all-important Ballylumford power station at Larne. He was over-ruled, however, by the Inner Council, which claimed it had intelligence reports of support building up within the workforce. On 19 April, Tyrie joined a huge rally in support of strike action in Portadown. It brought the town to a standstill and hastened confrontation with the new Secretary of State, who, one week later, received an ultimatum from the Loyalist Action Council giving him a seven-day period within which to give commitments both on security policy and on the recommendations of the Constitutional Convention.

Mason proved to be a very different opponent from Rees. He also had much better intelligence about the strengths and weaknesses of the planned strike. On 29 April, he later claimed, he received documentary proof of UDA plans to take control of key services in Loyalist areas once the strike was called. Folders circulating 'suggested the work of someone with good administrative – or perhaps army – experience'.[33] Their contents revealed plans for a local controller to take responsibility for areas of 400 households, looking after food and fuel distribution and organising first-aid and medical teams as well as dispatch riders:

> All the elements were in place for a long siege, and of course the UDA and others in the strike were simultaneously encouraging their followers to make a point of picking up their Social Security benefits. The intention from the start was that the campaign against the government would be largely funded by public money.[34]

Mason's contacts with the Action Council, however, gave him a rather different perspective. He at once sensed the mutual distrust between Paisley and the UDA. His briefing on the balance of power within the Council was good and he quickly decided that Baird was hardly a figure to reckon with and was in fear of his life.[35] Jim Smyth himself confided to the Secretary of State his doubts about how well the strike had been prepared and how Tyrie 'had been given a hard time by the wives of his followers'.[35] On the night of 2 May, he also recalled later, Glen Barr telephoned him from abroad, warning of planned UDA attacks on the security forces that same night. These did not materialise and Barr was not involved in planning the strike.[36] Even so, Mason went into it with advantages not available to his predecessor.

Once the strike began it quickly became clear that the RUC and the army were ready to act against roadblocks and barricades and to maintain essential services. Police Land Rovers were used to force UDA men off Belfast's Newtownards Road and Tyrie was drawn into an angry confrontation with the officers in command. As he later admitted, this was exactly what Loyalists needed to avoid if the strike was going to succeed.[37] It was only the first full day of the attempted stoppage and while many factories and offices closed down, as well as Belfast's major shipyards and the port of Larne's ferries, the Ballylumford power workers, despite intense pressure, remained at work.

Open intimidation by roving groups of UDA men was a much more obvious factor than it had been three years previously but this of course was itself a sign of weakness. The point was clear to one careful observer of events, writer Sarah Nelson:

> During the strike – and despite media portrayal of ruthless, determined intimidators – the reality in many Loyalist areas starkly revealed paramilitary discomfort. UVF and UDA men hanging around the Shankill looked forlorn and sheepish; few gave the impression of believing in what they were doing or seeing much point to it. They looked like people who had been divided over the strike, knew the reality of public support and were acting under orders. Tyrie's hardline political policy has cost them serious loss of face and threatened to remove the remains of their public support.[38]

With the RUC and army dismantling roadblocks almost as fast as they went up and both West and William Craig coming out openly against the strike, support began to crumble. By Friday, 6 May, the fifth day of action, it was obvious to many that the strike was losing support. That same day, the Ballylumford power workers voted by a clear majority against strike action. They had by-passed both Paisley and the Loyalist Action Council, or the United Unionist Action Council as it had somewhat over-optimistically renamed itself, by accepting an invitation to meet in person with the Secretary of State. This was his moment to reveal a new security initiative to them. It was based on an expansion of the RUC to 6,500 full-time officers, who would have the latest weapons issued to them. Its Divisional Mobile Support Units would be expanded too, anti-terrorist legislation was to be reviewed and intensified undercover operations by the SAS and other army units were also promised.

The strike was called off on 12 May, an outcome predicted by commentators with knowledge of the tensions existing between Paisley and the UDA. Writing close to the strike's collapse, *Fortnight* magazine analysed carefully the differences between the situation in 1977 and the huge support there had been for strike action three years earlier, when the UWC's mandate was vastly different from that of Paisley and Baird's Action Council. 'The basis of its campaign', *Fortnight*'s editorial declared, 'is a general dislike of Mr Mason's security policies, despite the evidence that they are in fact working in wearing down the IRA and a renewed call for action on the Convention's report. Neither of these seems likely to command the active or tacit support from the majority community as did the emotional dislike of the Sunningdale package.'[39]

Some UDA hard-liners naïvely thought that, even without the power workers' support or that of Paisley, the strike could continue. Tyrie, though he had come to share their opinion of Paisley, did not agree with them. 'As the power men did not come out,' he told a newspaper shortly after the end of the strike, 'we would have had to resort to violence to keep people from work and there was no way we were going to do that. Look, the Protestant community will not be forced into anything they don't want to do.'[40] He said much the same in an interview with this author several years later, adding: 'We should have known enough not to let ourselves be used the way we were by Paisley. At least that was a lesson we learned from what was a total failure for us.'[41]

As the strike wound down the UDA asked for Barr's advice, which was that they extricate themselves as best they could from a confrontation which offered only the certainty of defeat. Interviewed many years later about his view of events, Barr blamed the outcome on self-serving Unionist politicians, especially Paisley:

> They created a fallacy that we'd defeated the Brits in 1974. We hadn't. We'd brought down [Brian] Faulkner, forcing the British to remove Sunningdale. In 1977, out of selfishness and ego on Paisley's part, 1974 was murdered, giving the British and the Irish the confidence to implement 1985 [meaning the Anglo-Irish Agreement]. During the 1977 strike I was approached to give Tyrie advice. I told him to get out and let Paisley carry the can or he'd carry it for Paisley, as did happen in the end.[42]

For Paisley, the outcome of the 1977 strike was a humiliation which, to many, called in question his political judgement. Nonetheless, and perhaps typically, his career survived, though he would never again be able to take for granted the support of the UDA. Their antagonism to him was confirmed by the strike and his role in it. His religious fundamentalism was never compatible with the very secular Loyalism of the UDA, and his regular denunciations of drink in his sermons could easily have been meant for the organisation's social clubs with their late-night or sometimes non-existent licences. 'He knew how to talk up the tension and call on Loyalists to get out on the streets but he was even better at getting out of the way himself,'[43] Sammy Duddy later reflected, and he has said that one of his poems, 'The Evil Orator', was a thinly disguised description of Paisley.[44]

After 1977 and certainly for as long as Mason remained at the Northern Ireland Office, new political initiatives stayed on hold while UDA gunmen, using the name Ulster Freedom Fighters as a flag of convenience, continued to kill but at a diminished rate compared to the early and mid-1970s. Tyrie knew that it must revert to the task of finding a political voice and in January 1978, he gave his support to the formation of the New Ulster Political Research Group (NUPRG). He persuaded Barr to be its chairman. This was Barr's opportunity to work on some of the ideas which he had tested at the Amherst conference at Massachusetts two and a half years earlier. Harry Chicken and Tommy Lyttle supported him and John McMichael, from Lisburn, who was active in the UDA's paramilitary operations, took the position of NUPRG secretary.

A few months later, McMichael gave readers of the UDA's magazine, *Ulster*, some indication of the group's thinking. In a carefully argued article, he devoted much of what he said to attacking the continuation of direct rule as essentially unstable and a convenient way for any London government to reverse overnight its policy on Northern Ireland. Total integration of the province within the UK, which Enoch Powell supported and was trying to convert his Unionist colleagues to, was simply a way of giving a veto on any constitutional change to a majority of Westminster MPs, few of whom, he pointed out, were ever even in the chamber when Northern Ireland's problems were on the order paper. Other options he considered and dismissed were any return to the old Stormont model, federalism, power-sharing as set out under the 1973 Sunningdale Agreement, or joint rule in any form by London and Dublin. The way ahead, he concluded, had to be 'in a special type of negotiated independence'.[45]

Duddy followed this up in the same issue with a reiteration of the UDA's growing distrust of the politicians working-class Loyalists had once voted for instinctively:

> Not one Unionist MP is worth his salt. Not one Unionist MP can be entrusted with the future and the lives of the people of this province. The whole charade is crumbling. Gaping holes are appearing in the once-great wall of Unionism and time will tell of the intrigue and treachery perpetrated by Unionists in our name.[46]

Tyrie followed him in the next issue with an equally contemptuous dismissal of Unionist politics and alluded to what he called 'two years of political investigation conducted by the UDA'.[47] This was probably a reference to the NUPRG, though it had not in fact existed for as long as that, but Tyrie declared that over this time he had begun to think increasingly about what Northern Ireland's two communities had in common.

A six-county Ulster state could, he argued, 'take its rightful place in the world and not be seen as a country with a death-wish'.[48] Its creation could, over time, drain away support for the IRA; he also claimed, however, that its opposition to any form of six-county independence was already on record. There was a simplistic element to this thinking but at least some of the UDA leaders had now embarked on a journey which had taken them a long way from the mental certainties with which they had joined it in 1972. In Tyrie and Barr's case, this had involved travel abroad to meet academics and, at Amherst, Catholics and Republicans. Barr had gone back to the United States on a month-long study trip in 1978 financed by the State Department. There were also almost certainly contacts with the Northern Ireland Office at this time. Some civil servants there, while not necessarily converts to Ulster separatism, were still happy to draw the UDA into political dialogue as an alternative to violence.[49]

Breaking the NUPRG's self-imposed refusal to talk to the press about its deliberations, Barr gave an interview late in 1978 to the Dublin magazine

Magill. The UDA, he assured its readers, was 'no longer a Protestant army at the beck and call of Loyalist politicians'[50] and he dated this change to the 1977 strike.

> It was clear to us that as with the UWC strike in 1974, we were being used by politicians for their own narrow, sectarian ends. The UDA determined that this would never happen again and realised as well that if there was going to be a political solution it would have to be based on something different to an appeal to old flag-waving loyalties.[51]

A UDA and NUPRG discussion paper probably from this period took careful notice of the case against Ulster independence, especially the economic arguments, and tried hard to address the question of what form of independence might be attainable, how close it might be to existing Commonwealth and dominion models and what kind of relationships with the Irish state and the European Economic Community could be negotiated. Power-sharing rather than simple majority rule was regarded as essential and the end of any Stormont-type relationship to Britain would, it was argued, make it impossible for the majority to disregard the minority community's rights.[52] Belief in a distinctive and ancient Ulster identity underpinned the growing confidence of these UDA deliberations. This was because a new history was emerging for Loyalists in this period and many of them, especially UDA members, were eager to clutch at it. The Gaels, according to it, were not the first inhabitants of Ireland but had simply driven out the Cruthin, who had once ruled the ancient kingdom of Ulaid. This was claimed to have extended well beyond what later became the border of Northern Ireland. Defeat in 563AD at the battle of Moira led to a Cruthin diaspora which took most of them to the Pictish kingdom of Dalriada. Their descendants' eventual return to settle in Ulster in the Plantation period was claimed as proof that Ulster's Protestant community were historically not colonists at all but linked by ethnicity and bloodlines to an original population.

While few Irish historians or ethnographers believed this, it did provide a secular identity for Loyalism removed from the religious fundamentalism of Dr Ian Paisley and the often very literal and unexamined allegiance to the British crown that was characteristic of traditional Unionism. It also gave Loyalists a weapon to use against Republicans anxious to categorise them as 'Brits' whose best option was to 'go home'. Dr Ian Adamson, an active member of the OUP, was a prolific contributor to the literature of this Cruthin-based history of Ulster.[53] Copies of his books became available at the UDA's East Belfast headquarters and this author has a copy of one of them, *The Identity of Ulster*, which was given to him by John McMichael.

The UDA's own magazines also began to give significant space to articles about the Cruthin and early Ulster history both before and after Barr and his colleagues finally went public with their thoughts on a new political direction for Northern Ireland. In the August 1978 edition of *Ulster*, Sam Sloan, a

UDA member from the Shankill, took readers through the arguments that Adamson sought to popularise in his books and finished by quoting from him: 'We affirm that Ulster is a Pictish and not a Gaelic nation. Both Gaelic and English are languages of conquest, although both have words and features which are older than the conquerors, including the name of Ireland itself.'[54]

Adamson contributed to a subsequent issue, writing under the auspices of the NUPRG. He invoked an ancient Ulster identity rooted in the affinity of Cruthin and Pict and finished his résumé of the historical case for it with his own affirmation of allegiance: 'This land of the Cruthin is our homeland and we are its children, the sons and daughters of the Picts. We have a right to belong here, we have a right to be heard here, we have a right to be free.'[55]

Early in 1979, Barr returned to the United States with Tommy Lyttle for a two-week tour, during which they met politicians, civic groups and trade unions, as well as taking part in radio phone-in programmes. Writing about it on his return for the UDA magazine, he claimed that nearly every audience had been sympathetic to the ideas for which the organisation's leaders would soon be declaring their public support: 'The American people', he assured readers, 'are hungry for the true facts about Ulster and are fed-up with the biased reporting they receive. They are anxious to help and encourage the Ulster people find a solution to the problem.'[56]

Fifteen months after its formation, the NUPRG delivered its report at the end of March 1979. It was entitled *Beyond the Religious Divide* and was based on the case for the negotiated independence of an Ulster state which would have the United States' political system as its model. This can be taken as proof of the American contacts made by Tyrie and Barr and perhaps too as a tribute to the Ulster Presbyterian democrats who had played a major part in the American Revolution. The Ulster state envisaged would have a written constitution, a bill of rights and a separation of executive and legislative powers. All elections would be by the single transferable vote system and proportional representation would determine the election of all committees and their chairmen in the proposed legislative assembly. A Supreme Court, presided over by a judge from outside Ireland, would interpret and apply the constitution. Britain and Ireland would have to withdraw all claims of sovereignty over the province though the report looked to British financial support over a 25-year transitional period.

The report ran to forty closely argued pages and rested on the belief that its implementation would allow both sides to claim victory and thus retain their self-respect: Republicans would be able to say that Britain had withdrawn from the six counties while Protestants could equally claim that unification with the Irish state had been laid to rest. 'It is the only proposal which does not have a victor and a loser,' the report's introduction declared. 'It will encourage the development of a common identity between the two communities regardless of religion. It offers first-class Ulster citizenship to all of our people because, like it or not, the Protestant of Northern Ireland is looked upon as a second-class British citizen in Britain and the Roman Catholic of Northern Ireland as a second class Irish citizen in Southern Ireland.'[57]

Press comment on *Beyond the Religious Divide* was extensive. Under the headline 'UDA unveils proposals for an independent North', the *Irish Times* gave the document extensive coverage and compared the UDA's analysis favourably with that of Fianna Fáil, the then ruling party in Dublin.[58] The *Guardian* ran a headline, 'Separate province only solution to the Troubles', but gave a full summary of the report.[59] It later interviewed Tyrie and though he was put under pressure from the paper over UDA/UFF killings, he still defended the 1979 document.[60]

Other coverage from papers both in the Irish state and in Northern Ireland was given in summary form in the UDA's *Ulster* magazine[61] but they gave pride of place to the response of Professor Bernard Crick of Birkbeck College in London. His *New Statesman* article on *Beyond the Religious Divide* was reprinted in full, partly because he had given unpaid constitutional advice both to Vanguard and the UDA since the period of the Constitutional Convention in 1975. Some UDA leaders, Crick recalled, were initially extremely vague about what 'going political' might mean:

> It was a matter of taking them through some of the basics, getting out leaflets, canvassing, all that. They were a tough lot and they had come through a lot but they were not stupid. Barr in fact was highly intelligent. He was self-taught but quick on the uptake. I got on well with him.[62]

Some of his talks dating back to the Convention period, Crick feels, did feed into the work of the NUPRG, though 'negotiated independence for Ulster' went well beyond his own position.

> We need to remember how much they had come to distrust British politicians. The independence argument developed out of that though Glen [Barr] was into the idea of the Cruthin and an ancient Ulster identity to which Loyalists could lay claim. He used the word 'Brit' as if it was an expletive and he was not alone in that.[63]

For much of 1979 and into the following year interest in *Beyond the Religious Divide* continued. Over one four-week period from 2 October, Barr, Lyttle and others involved in the report's publication took part in eight discussion events on its recommendations in Ulster and one in the Netherlands, and Barr gave two interviews for BBC Northern Ireland and Canadian television.[64]

For some who had been active Republicans since the start of the Troubles the UDA's apparent search for a political role had to be welcomed. Seamus Lynch stayed with what became the Official Republican movement after the 1970 split caused by the Provisionals and strongly supported both its May 1972 ceasefire and its espousal of socialist politics. In 1977, the movement renamed itself Sinn Fein: the Workers Party and that same year Lynch was elected to Belfast City Council and went on to become Northern chairman and national vice-president when it became simply the Workers Party five years later. He drew some real hope from the fact that *Beyond the Religious Divide* came out at a time when the UDA seemed to have reduced random attacks on Catholics though it was still committed to killing known Republicans.

> I had grown up as a socialist Republican, I believed what Wolfe Tone said, that the English connection must be broken and here was the UDA and its research group talking about exactly that. We couldn't ignore it. I'd had contact with one or two of them, like McMichael. He had started to see that Unionist politicians had used Protestant working people, rather than ever doing much for them. If the UDA could contribute to raising political awareness among ordinary Loyalist people, I was ready to listen.[65]

On the back of *Beyond the Religious Divide* were printed the lines:

> He who cannot compromise is a fool.
> He who will not compromise is a bigot.
> He who dares not compromise is a slave.

Yet whether this document offered any real basis for the kind of historic compromise its authors had in mind must remain problematic. For Loyalists it offered nothing on the position of the Crown, nor on an Ulster state's position, if it was to have one, within the Commonwealth. McMichael later gave ground on these issues, admitting that they mattered greatly to the majority population.[66] A bigger issue was and remained the document's provenance. Even though its paramilitary strategy had changed, the UDA's ferocity in the early 1970s was still a vivid memory for Catholics who were being asked to trust an element within it which had opted to 'go political'.

Republicans were certainly not going to settle for anything less than a 32-county Irish state. Their press gave little attention to *Beyond the Religious Divide*, while constitutional nationalists in the SDLP were already listening to predictions of demographic change which, over time, could bring a peaceful end to partition, or so they hoped. The UDA–NUPRG document hardly confronted this possibility even though being 'outbred' by the minority was an almost ancestral Loyalist fear. For McMichael, the immediate need was to 'talk up' the virtues of *Beyond the Religious Divide* in the hope of winning over Catholic opinion. 'We'll just continue what we've been doing during the past year,' he declared in 1981. 'It will become more and more obvious that the UDA is taking a very steady line, that we're not willing to fall into line behind sectarian politicians. It will take time. What people forget is that we also have to sell the idea to Protestants.'[67]

Time was precisely what McMichael did not have, as the worsening crisis in the new H-blocks of the Maze prison, formerly Long Kesh, and the demands of IRA prisoners drew Northern Ireland into the deeply divisive crisis of the 1981 hunger strikes. Even so, it was midway through that year that McMichael and Tyrie gave their support to the formation of the Ulster

Loyalist Democratic Party, to campaign for the policies set out in the UDA–NUPRG document. Barr had voiced doubts that this could be achieved by contesting elections and, pleading ill health, took no part in setting up the new party, so McMichael was elected as chairman. Barr's view was that established Unionism would do its best to crush any new Loyalist party and his own treatment by the OUP was still vivid in his mind from August 1974, when the South Down Unionist constituency party had unanimously struck off his name for adoption as their candidate despite his key role in the UWC strike.[68] A UDA candidate, Sammy Miller, had already won a council seat for North Belfast at a by-election in January 1981. He stood as an independent Loyalist, but held the seat in the full council elections a few months later, surviving an IRA attempt on his life in the course of his election campaign. Another council by-election in August of the same year gave the new Loyalist party its chance. Billy Elliott, a former bodyguard of Tommy Herron who later became a UDA brigadier, failed to be elected, but won more than a thousand votes, 38 per cent of the total cast, against strong OUP and DUP candidates.[69]

What seemed to McMichael to be the ULDP's real chance, though, came with the murder by IRA gunmen of the Reverend Robert Bradford, OUP member of the Westminster Parliament for South Belfast. Bradford, an evangelical Christian who lost no opportunity to vilify Republicanism and the H-block hunger strikers, had become an obvious IRA target. The UDA, however, it has been claimed, were implicated in his death in the sense that his severe criticisms of its clubs and fund-raising had led it to withdraw bodyguards it had previously agreed to provide for him.[70] The single RUC officer with him when he was shot dead in a community centre in his constituency was unable to save him.

This murder sent shockwaves through Unionism. James Prior, the new Secretary of State, was jeered and abused at Bradford's funeral, which was accompanied by widespread protest stoppages of work by Protestants. Dr Ian Paisley, who had been close to Bradford, called for tax and rent strikes by Loyalists and announced the formation of a new paramilitary body for which he claimed he was helping to recruit. Because it was to supplement the RUC and UDR, he called it the 'Third Force'. He told a Newtownards audience that he was mobilising men 'willing to do the job of exterminating the IRA'[71] but stressed that he wanted them recruited by the Crown. Little was heard of it after its first parade and the UDA took no part in it. Some Loyalists were quick to label it the 'Third Farce' and McMichael attached more importance to the by-election in South Belfast occasioned by Bradford's death.

Even so, a UDA response distinct from Paisley's was thought to be necessary and a few days after the murder, the Inner Council called for a boycott of the Westminster Parliament by Unionist members on the grounds that it had 'failed in its prime function of the protection of life and property in Ulster. Therefore, the Ulster people have no moral obligation to owe their allegiance to a failed administration.'[72] No more, in fact, came of this than of the call for a new Ulster Security Council, with a place on it for the UDA, to co-ordinate the war on terrorism; McMichael's immediate concern was clearly the impending by-election.

The South Belfast constituency lay within the UDA brigade area which McMichael commanded and when he was adopted as the ULDP's candidate he had high hopes of potential support within fiercely Loyalist working-class localities such as Sandy Row, the Village and Donegall Pass, as well as housing estates such as Taughmonagh to the south of them. Since Bradford's murder, there had been no killings claimed by the UDA/UFF, though several by the UVF, and McMichael hoped that this would help to secure a hearing for the ideas in *Beyond the Religious Divide*. He threw himself into the campaign with optimistic energy, as Tyrie has recalled:

> John never did things by halves. He thought he had to look right as a candidate so he got a smart dark overcoat for knocking on people's doors. The weather was mild though, and it was far too heavy but he wouldn't take it off. I can remember the sweat on him while he was canvassing the Loyalist areas.[73]

Although the constituency was mainly middle class, McMichael sought to mobilise the several thousand working-class Loyalist votes that were also there but the result was a humiliation for him. Out of more than 43,000 votes cast, he received only 575, less than 2 per cent of the total. The Official Unionists had put up the Reverend Martin Smyth, who won the seat comfortably. His connections with the constituency and his position as Grand Master of the Orange Order made him a strong candidate but the Reverend William McCrea, standing for the DUP, got out a strong vote, as did the Alliance Party. Those of the small Catholic electorate who voted did so either for the Alliance or the SDLP. The very name of McMichael's party would have alienated most of them as did his known role within the UDA, which involved him in sanctioning and setting up many of its killings, even though these had stopped during his election campaign.

One writer on Northern Ireland who knew McMichael at this time described him as

> a clever and ruthless enemy of Republicanism. On one level he was a man who sought to give working-class Loyalism a political ethos which was not simply rooted in the Unionist tradition but capable of being moulded to take Northern Ireland along an independent route or towards a degree of shared-responsibility government with Catholics. Behind the political rhetoric, however, he was also a leader of the UDA's military wing, the Ulster Freedom Fighters.[74]

The South Belfast electorate's verdict was a severe blow to him, even if it merely confirmed 'respectable' Unionism's continuing hold on the Protestant working class. 'He was devastated' was the recollection of Seamus Lynch, who had met him and stayed in contact with him.[75] It was the beginning and the end of whatever parliamentary ambitions McMichael may have had but not the end of the political road for the UDA.

NOTES

1. C. O'Leary, S. Elliott and R. Wilford, *The Northern Ireland Assembly 1982–1986: A Constitutional Experiment* (London: C. Hurst, 1988), p. 38.
2. H. McDonald, *Trimble* (London: Bloomsbury, 2000), p. 61.
3. *Workers Association Strike Bulletin*, no. 10, 29 May 1974.
4. *Workers Weekly*, 1 May 1975.
5. S. Nelson, *Ulster's Uncertain Defenders: Protestant Political, Paramilitary and Community Groups and the Northern Ireland Conflict* (Belfast: Appletree Press), p. 181.
6. D. McKittrick, S. Kelters, B. Feeney and C. Thornton, *Lost Lives: The Stories of the Men, Women and Children Who Died as a Result of the Northern Ireland Troubles* (Edinburgh: Mainstream, 1999), p. 472.
7. Ibid., pp. 467–8.
8. S. Bruce, *The Red Hand: Protestant Paramilitaries in Northern Ireland* (Oxford: Oxford University Press, 1992), pp. 103–5.
9. *Irish News*, 19 March 2003.
10. S. Duddy, interview with author, 7 July 1999.
11. Ibid.
12. *Fortnight*, 24 January 1975.
13. *Fortnight*, 25 November 1977.
14. Nelson, *Ulster's Uncertain Defenders*, pp. 194–6.
15. *What Happened on the Twelfth*, Workers Association pamphlet (Belfast, 1975).
16. T. Lovett and R. Percival, 'Conflict and community action in Northern Ireland', in P. Curno (ed.), *Political Issues and Community Work* (London: Routledge and Kegan Paul, 1978).
17. *Irish Times*, 13 July 1976.
18. *Fortnight*, 11 April 1975.
19. B. Clifford, *Against Ulster Nationalism: A Review of the Development of the Catholic and Protestant Communities and Their Interaction with Each Other and with Britain: In Reply to Tom Nairn of* New Left Review *and Others* (Belfast: British and Irish Communist Organisation, 1975), p. 83.
20. *Fortnight*, 12 September 1975.
21. Ibid.
22. Ibid.
23. Ibid.
24. Ibid.
25. Ibid.
26. *Irish Times*, 6 September 1975.
27. *Irish Times*, 30 October 1975.
28. *Ulster*, May 1976.
29. *Ulster*, June 1976.
30. Ibid.

31. E. Moloney and A. Pollak, *Paisley* (Dublin: Poolbeg, 1986), p. 369.
32. Ibid.
33. R. Mason, *Paying the Price* (London: Robert Hale, 1999), p. 177.
34. Ibid.
35. Ibid., p. 180.
36. Ibid.
37. A. Tyrie, interview with author, 3 December 2002.
38. *Fortnight*, 13 May 1977.
39. Ibid.
40. *News Letter*, 19 May 1977.
41. A. Tyrie, interview with author, 19 April 2000.
42. *New Ulster Defender*, vol. 1, no. 10, 1994.
43. Duddy, interview with author.
44. S. Duddy, *Concrete Whirlpools of the Mind* (Belfast: Ulidia, 1983).
45. *Ulster*, August 1978.
46. Ibid.
47. *Ulster*, September 1978.
48. Ibid.
49. A. Aughey, *Under Siege: Ulster Unionism and the Anglo-Irish Agreement* (Belfast: Blackstaff Press, 1989), pp. 123–9.
50. *Ulster*, January 1979, reprint of *Magill* article.
51. Ibid.
52. UDA–NUPRG draft discussion document, undated, probably 1978, courtesy of Professor B. Crick.
53. I. Adamson, *The Identity of Ulster: The Land, the Language and the People* (Belfast: Ian Adamson, 1982), also his *The Cruthin: The Ancient Kindred* (Newtownards: Nosmada, 1986).
54. *Ulster*, August 1978.
55. *Ulster*, May 1979.
56. *Ulster*, February 1979.
57. *Beyond the Religious Divide* (Belfast: NUPRG, 1979), p. 2.
58. *Irish Times*, 30 March 1979.
59. *Guardian*, 30 March 1979.
60. *Guardian*, 16 September 1980.
61. *Ulster*, April 1979.
62. B. Crick, interview with author, 31 March 2003.
63. Ibid.
64. See *Ulster*, vol. 2, no. 6, 1979.
65. S. Lynch, interview with author, 22 October 2001. See also P. O'Malley, *The Uncivil Wars: Ireland Today* (Belfast: Blackstaff Press, 1983), pp. 353–4.
66. O'Malley, *Uncivil Wars*, pp. 332–3.
67. Ibid., p. 340.
68. S. Heffer, *Like the Roman: The Life of Enoch Powell* (London: Weidenfeld and Nicolson, 1998), pp. 727, 730.
69. Bruce, *Red Hand*, p. 240.
70. UDA source, 12 April 1985.

71. P. Taylor, *Loyalists* (London: Bloomsbury, 1999), p. 177.
72. *Ulster*, December 1981.
73. Tyrie, interview with author.
74. M. Dillon, *The Dirty War* (London: Hutchinson, 1990), p. 292.
75. Lynch, interview with author.

4

The Campaign against the Anglo-Irish Agreement and 'Common Sense'

ᐯ

James Prior, as Secretary of State, embarked upon a 'rolling devolution' programme for Northern Ireland, part of which was to be an elected assembly
with powers only to 'scrutinise' Westminster legislation. Elections to it were
held in late October and the ULDP put up just two candidates in North
Belfast, who between them polled 5 per cent of first preference Unionist
votes. It took no part in the Westminster general election the following year
or in the contest for Northern Ireland's three seats in the European Parliament
in 1984.

This apparent retreat from testing electoral support for UDA policies did
not mean an end to politics within its publications or to political thinking
among leaders such as Andy Tyrie and John McMichael. Both were only too
happy to engage in political debates with journalists and interviewers who
called in at the organisation's new headquarters in Gawn Street, off the
Newtownards Road. The red-brick houses beside it were overshadowed by
the massive yellow cranes of Harland and Wolff's shipyard, then still a big
employer of Protestants, and tight security controlled access to the building.

Tyrie usually sat at the far end of an imposing mahogany table with crossed
Ulster standards on the wall behind him as well as the UDA crest with its
motto 'Quis Separabit' (Who Shall Divide Us). Books had begun to appear
on the shelves, copies of Ian Adamson's work, particularly *The Identity of
Ulster*, sets of which were sometimes given out to visitors. There was also
Robert Taber's classic text on guerrilla insurgency, *The War of the Flea*, widely
studied in the 1970s and 1980s at Sandhurst and the army's Staff College at
Camberley. Incongruously, some might have thought, there was also at one
point a life of Gandhi. 'This place is turning into a fucking library'[1] was on
one occasion the reaction of Billy Elliott, who had become a UDA brigadier.

Discussions with both McMichael and Tyrie could range from early Ulster
history and the virtues of the Cruthin to political strategies for Loyalism and
on from there to the merits of selective assassination of known Republicans
as a tactic as well as the UDA's frustration at not being able to work more
closely with the security forces.[2] Sometimes security men as well as UDA
brigadiers would be brought in to listen. The author can recall one meeting
with a group of Scottish students after which Tyrie said to him: 'It's good for

our men to hear clever people like you talking.'[3] The Gawn Street office, it should be added, had other functions. Weapons were found there during an RUC raid in 1982 and charges were brought but later dropped.

Maintaining the degree of political credibility which the New Ulster Political Research Group and *Beyond the Religious Divide* had achieved for the UDA remained a priority even when it was openly making the case for the murder of Republicans. 'What I've always said', Tyrie told the *Guardian* in September 1980, 'is if you want to shoot someone, for hell's sake, shoot the right person.'[4] In the same interview, however, he was careful to bring his questioner round to the UDA's recent identification of itself with the case for an independent Ulster.

The following year, both Tyrie and McMichael talked to a newspaper interviewer in the aftermath of a speech by the former Labour leader and Prime Minister James Callaghan in which he had appeared to support the independence option. McMichael compared the situation to the Western Front in the First World War, with two sides mired in the rival positions of a united Ireland and a Northern Ireland forever a part of the United Kingdom. 'What we have done is get out of the trenches and have a look around,'[5] he declared. Any solution would need both sides to give ground: 'The minority will not identify with the British community but they are going to have to accept that the other community are not going to be drawn into Ireland in any circumstances.'[6]

Loyalists would end up giving more ground, McMichael predicted, under the formula set out in *Beyond the Religious Divide*. 'We will have to sacrifice our membership of the UK at some time in the future but not to accept a united Ireland. We are going to take the greatest risk.'[7] Tyrie backed McMichael with his own gloss on the 1979 document but, as in the *Guardian* interview the previous year, the conversation returned to the case for the selective assassination of known Republicans. Their 1980 interviewer acquired a poster with which his paper overlaid his article. It showed a revolver in shadow with its trigger cocked along with the words 'The future belongs to the few of us still willing to get our hands dirty – Political Terror – it's the only thing they understand. Ulster Freedom Fighters'.[8]

Ulster magazine kept up the argument too, running an unsigned article, 'Independence, no other solution', which recycled the essential points of *Beyond the Religious Divide*, pointing out that despite its innate sectarian tensions the six-county state had achieved the status of 'an entity which was recognisably different from either Britain or the Irish Free State'.[9] Independence for it was set out as an effective way to outmanoeuvre Republicanism: 'The ideology of the Provisional IRA could not cope with a new Ulster state, since they could not claim with any degree of conviction that an indigenous government of Ulster politicians would be colonial or imperialist.'[10]

Despite McMichael's rejection by South Belfast Loyalist voters, the flow of articles continued. Sammy Duddy made his own contribution with an article in which he argued that the pattern of job-creating British investment was shifting significantly from Northern Ireland to the Republic. This, in his view, was part of a larger strategy of quiet withdrawal: 'It is hardly surprising, therefore, that more and more Ulster Protestants are beginning to feel less and less British when they witness the decline of a once proud state.'[11] Of the others who still clung to their British allegiance, he declared, in words that were close to his fine poem 'Our Way': 'Their over-riding blind faith is akin to that of 6,000,000 Jewish citizens who marched proudly to the gas chambers during World War II instead of resisting.'[12]

Ulster returned to this theme in its May 1984 issue. A contributor identified only by the initials A.F.B. compared the internal divisions and weakness of Protestant Ulster to that of the Jews in German-occupied Europe[13] and also invoked the memory of the UWC's victorious strike ten years earlier. It was the subject of a full-length anniversary article in the same issue. 'In any other country,' the writer declared, 'such a rebellion would have meant the overthrow of the government'[14] and he urged the same solidarity on Loyalists in response to the recently set up New Ireland Forum, which was studying possible new structures and processes which might promote a resolution of the 'Northern question'.

Heroic early history was not ignored, however. An adaptation of the poem *The Death Call of Cuchulainn, Champion of Ulster*, retelling the death of Ulster's ancient hero and claiming that he fell in battle against the invading armies of Queen Maeve of Connaught, had appeared in the journal's April issue[15] and in February 1985 readers were alerted to the importance of the pre-Christian site of Eamhon Macha, or Navan in its anglicised form, the fort near Armagh where other Irish kings and clans had once rendered tribute to the Uluti.[16] A much longer article in the July–August issue that year celebrated Eamhon Macha or Navan as proof of how the Cruthin people had defended ancient Ulster against the depredations of the Gael and it urged Loyalists to take pride in their identity and culture.[17]

McMichael's interventions in the UDA's magazine, and in the press more generally, became regular occurrences both before and after his bid for election to Parliament. In April 1984, he gave a wide-ranging interview to the *Guardian*. In the course of it he predicted an intensification of attacks on Republican targets, something he was well placed to do since he was directing them himself from his Lisburn power base within the UDA's South Belfast brigade. Asked about the inter-governmental New Ireland Forum then meeting in Dublin, his reaction was that it would have little to offer Ulster Protestants. Neither joint Anglo-Irish sovereignty over the North nor Irish federalism would be acceptable to them, he stressed.

Because of this, he went on, he had to treat his role within the UDA as one of 'preparing the Ulster Protestant community for a head-on collision to decide whether in fact it will survive as a people on this island'.[18] The alternative, in his view, might well be 'because the two combatants within that possible conflict are pitched so close in strength, Ulster Protestants and Catholics may sit down round a table and negotiate what the future of the Ulster people will be.'[19] In his declared opinion, Protestant Ulster's bargaining position in such a situation would have to be self-determination. The words 'Ulster independence' were not mentioned.

Self-determination rather than independence was also the theme of a special article McMichael contributed to the July–August 1984 'special bumper edition' of the UDA magazine. The time had arrived, he stated, to break free from a negative siege mentality and to argue for the rights of an Ulster nation. The Northern Ireland Assembly should be reconvened as a constitutional forum to formulate a written constitution amendable only by a referendum vote. This was backed by a passionate affirmation of an Ulster identity. 'We have been so set on being seen to be nothing but British that we have denied our birthright, allowing Irish nationalists to take the best of it and bastardise it into Gaelic mythology.'[20]

By this time, the New Ireland Forum, set up in May 1983 to bring the three main parties in the Irish state into dialogue with the SDLP on cross-border constitutional issues, had reported after many months of deliberation involving politicians, clergy and academics from both sides of the border. It was severely critical of British policy since the onset of the Troubles but it set out three options: a unitary state, achieved by consent; a federal Ireland; or a joint-authority formula. Under the last, the London and Dublin governments, with strong encouragement from President Ronald Reagan, who saw some political mileage for himself in any moves towards a settlement of the Irish conflict, would have equal responsibility for all aspects of the running of the province. These findings were anathema to Ulster Unionists and unacceptable to Margaret Thatcher, but the Forum changed the political atmosphere by the contacts and dialogue it had made possible. Even the IRA's almost successful attempt on the Prime Minister's life at Brighton in October 1984 did not divert her from developing formal talks between the London and Dublin governments.

The April issue of *Ulster* reacted with predictable foreboding, identifying 'the sinister and ongoing conspiracy between Westminster and Dublin to continue an Anglo-Irish solution despite the wishes of Ulster'.[21] This, it argued, could be defeated by a radical overhaul of paramilitary Loyalism's military capabilities. 'The battle for Ulster is now,'[22] it told readers, and this theme was taken up in other issues, though they shifted the emphasis to the Thatcher government's close relationship with the Reagan administration in Washington. Borrowing from claims made in speeches by Enoch Powell, it was also argued that American intelligence services, notably the CIA, were pushing for an all-Ireland solution to the conflict in which an end to partition would be negotiable in return for an end to the Irish state's neutrality.[23]

Powell put his claims of American involvement in a planned betrayal of Northern Ireland in sometimes extravagant language and had been doing so at least since 1980. In that year, during a speech in his South Down constituency, he had told the audience that the IRA was a lesser danger to the Union than the CIA and what he described as 'that nest of vipers, that nursery of traitors which is known as the British Foreign Office'.[24] The UDA did not demonise Anglo-American intentions in quite these terms but the premonition of the Thatcher government's talks with Dublin leading to an imposed deal grew as the summer of 1985 slipped by.

It was a summer which saw Sinn Fein making significant gains in council elections, winning a total of fifty-nine seats despite Unionist exhortations to the electorate to smash Republicanism. Writing in *Ulster*, McMichael argued:

> Sinn Fein cannot be smashed because Sinn Fein is the IRA. Ulster is not a political game, it is a war game and unless we are prepared to play the game to the full we should not play at all.[25]

The UDA was already in the process of reorganisation for this ultimate 'war game' even as McMichael wrote these words. He was a key figure in this process, driven in part by an increasingly shared Loyalist fear that the RUC was no longer to be depended upon as 'their' police force to be relied on unreservedly in the defence of 'their' Ulster.

Developments in policing policy during the 1985 marching season influenced this fear powerfully, particularly in relation to traditional Orange Order parades in Portadown, where the religious composition of areas close to these parade routes had changed. Amidst rumours of Dublin pressure in the inter-governmental talks for more even-handed policing, the RUC announced that while the traditional pre-Twelfth Sunday church parade in Portadown to and from Drumcree would be allowed to use the established route, other parades on and after the Twelfth would be denied passage through Obins Street and the Tunnel, where disorder was feared. This latter decision and its enforcement led to serious Loyalist rioting which spread into the town centre.

Tension was not reduced by interventions from politicians. The SDLP MP Seamus Mallon visited the scene during the violence and when asked about Dublin involvement in the decision to reroute parades, told the press: 'I would be very disappointed if they had not made representations.' Meanwhile Sammy Wilson, the DUP press officer, was quoted by the *Irish News* as saying that Loyalists should not feel ashamed of confronting 'policemen who bowed to the demands of Dublin.'[26] Individual UDA men were inevitably involved and the organisation's magazine treated events in Portadown as further proof of an Ulster heritage under threat.

In the immediate aftermath of this crisis, McMichael gave another interview to the *Guardian*. In it, he looked beyond events in Portadown to the wider issue of the Thatcher government's intentions and the possible outcome of its talks with the Irish leaders. 'The British should realise now that we will not accept Dublin interference in our affairs. The potential for Protestant violence is as great now as it always was.'[27] He could have added that this was in some measure because of his own paramilitary role within the UDA, though for the interview's purpose he concentrated on his political role and reiterated UDA demands for a written constitution for Northern Ireland which would guarantee the border, with change possible only through a two-thirds referendum majority.

Again, Ulster independence was omitted, and had been in other UDA statements over the last year or two. The priority was beginning to be seen as a defensive fight for Loyalists seeking to hold what they had rather than moving into the uncharted territory mapped out in *Beyond the Religious Divide*. One immediate decision McMichael and Andy Tyrie took was to give UDA backing to the Portadown Action Committee, which had been formed in July to oppose the rerouting of parades. It remained in being after the violence of that month had subsided and announced the impending formation of the United Ulster Loyalist Front (UULF). McMichael agreed to sit on its co-ordinating committee, which was formed at a packed meeting in Portadown.

He was one of thirteen, representing the Orange Order as well as the two main Unionist parties, but he was clear in his own mind that the Front would have to fight on broader ground than the parades issue. 'This is a new strategy to block off a power-sharing deal imposed on us simply to please Dublin. They'll back off if they see real resistance here, even if Charlie Haughey doesn't find his own reasons to pull the plug on it,' McMichael declared later in August. 'We need the Unionists on board, just as we did in 1974 but politicians who treat this as just another bandwagon will live to regret it.'[28]

The Front emerged briefly on Belfast's streets for a rally within a few days of the Anglo-Irish Agreement being signed. In scenes reminiscent of the early 1970s, combat kit, bush hats and dark glasses were worn in an affirmation of UDA and UVF co-operation. Open shows of strength on the streets were not really part of the UVF's ethos and much more time would be needed before there was real operational co-ordination between the two organisations.

The new Front had in fact only a limited life but out of it grew the Ulster Club movement. Its credo was revealed at a rally on 1 November in Belfast's Ulster Hall when a young Orangeman who had been active in the July protests in Portadown declared that the formation of a network of Ulster Clubs was a way to uphold Ulster people's right to full citizenship of the United Kingdom and to fight the erosion of their Protestant heritage. Full and equal UK citizenship was of course not necessarily compatible with Protestant supremacy in its old form but the clubs grew rapidly. McMichael felt that, with Protestant Ulster fearful for its future, the clubs should be supported because they could be a way of mobilising people who would be deterred from joining any paramilitary organisation. He was reported as also backing the movement because Ulster Clubs had also been formed in 1912.[29]

The clubs, it has been argued, were in reality too diverse an umbrella grouping to be politically effective[30] or to make any real impact on British policy. Events moved quickly in the final months of 1985 and nobody within the new but short-lived UULF, the Ulster Clubs, the Unionist parties or the paramilitaries was prepared for the Agreement, drawn up without any reference to them and signed on 15 November by Margaret Thatcher and the Irish Taoiseach, Garret FitzGerald, at Hillsborough Castle.

FitzGerald would later admit that he and his Dublin colleagues had 'over-estimated the extent of briefing'[31] given by the British side to Unionist leaders and under-estimated the shock it would be for a cautious constitutionalist like James Molyneaux, the Official Unionist Party leader, who by 1985 had moved close to Enoch Powell's position on the case for the province's integration within the United Kingdom. One minister, not long arrived in the Northern Ireland Office, who had immediate premonitions was Richard Needham. 'No marketing plan had been devised to explain to the Northern Ireland public why the Anglo-Irish Agreement was the only way forward,' he was to write in his memoirs: 'there was no broadcast from the Prime Minister to the Ulster people, no explanatory leaflets, no detailed plans for briefing key decision-making groups.'[32]

*

The Agreement provided for regular British and Irish consultation at ministerial level to promote cross-border co-operation and to deal with security, legal and political matters. The last named was defined as covering discrimination, the status of the Irish language and the display of flags and emblems. A permanent secretariat of civil servants from both sides of the border was set up ahead of the actual signing and based at Holywood in East Belfast. Article 4 said that both governments supported the devolution of power to Northern Ireland on the basis of consent throughout the community. Any change in the province's constitutional status, it was also stressed, would not take place without majority consent. Even so, as Unionist constitutional authorities were quick to point out, a major change was involved through Britain's admission that it could no longer determine adequately and alone the welfare of a proportion of its own people.[33]

It could also be argued that under the Agreement the aspiration to Irish unity was given full recognition but with no demand from Britain that in return for its concessions, Articles 2 and 3 of the Irish constitution, which defined Northern Ireland as part of the 'national territory', should be amended. The fact that Fianna Fáil denounced the treaty from the Dáil's opposition benches because it represented, in their view, renewed Dublin acquiescence in a British presence in the North and that Sinn Fein called it a 'disaster' which simply underwrote partition had no effect on the reaction of Ulster Unionists. To all shades of Unionist opinion, the Agreement was a shocking betrayal, especially as it came from a Prime Minister whose preferences for a time had seemed increasingly integrationist and influenced by colleagues such as Ian Gow and Powell. Unlike in1912, however, Unionism had to fall back on its own resources rather than look to Westminster for any significant support.

The campaign against the Agreement built up a rapid initial momentum and drew massive support to a protest rally on 23 November, which brought central Belfast to a standstill. Uncompromising rhetoric, especially from Dr Ian Paisley, whipped the huge crowd to a frenzy yet in reality it served to mask the real difficulties of forcing British policy into reverse.

Much of the next issue of *Ulster* was devoted to the Agreement, although space was made for a two-page Ulster Culture spread, celebrating those who had joined Edward Carson in the fight to block the 1912 Home Rule Bill, while another article extolled Ulster's historic ties to Scotland and North America. The editorial talked of 'Ulster's darkest hour'[34] and other contributions vilified a Prime Minister 'who betrayed the people of Rhodesia/ Zimbabwe by delivering them into the hands of a terrorist, Robert Mugabe, and then had the audacity to dance with him at a social function'.[35] Once again, American influence on British policy was claimed as a significant factor behind the Agreement: 'the Union is dead,' readers were told, 'killed neither by us nor by the Provos, but by successive English governments. Let the spirit of Ulster nationalism awake and assert itself. To survive we must govern ourselves.'[36]

The trouble with such calls to action was that the UDA had already drawn well back from the demand for an independent Ulster even though Tyrie still described himself as an Ulster nationalist whose birthright had been sold out. This was in 1986 when he was talking to Sally Belfrage,[37] but such talk, whether in interviews or articles in *Ulster*, was in reality backed by little more than exhortations to Loyalists to join the Ulster Clubs to combat the Anglo-Irish process. Exactly what doing this would achieve was not set out and the call to join was accompanied by the somewhat ambivalent injunction to 'hope for the best, prepare for the worst'.[38]

For some, the degree of Unionist hostility to the Agreement created the potential for the UDA to move to centre stage in a way that it had not been able to since 1974. However, Tyrie and McMichael did not see it that way. Their assessment of the situation was that the UDA should support and infiltrate resistance to the Agreement without asking to take it over, especially when the UUP and Paisley's DUP formed a coalition to fight government policy. Unionist protests took varied forms. Party representatives refused to attend meetings with British ministers, officials and Unionist-controlled councils suspended business and Unionist MPs resigned their seats to force a set of by-elections intended to be a referendum on the Agreement.

These were held in fifteen constituencies across Northern Ireland on 23 January 1986 and pro-Agreement parties such as the SDLP, the Alliance and the Workers Party could poll only 21 per cent of the total vote. Although the anti-Agreement Unionists did not reach their target vote of 500,000, leaders at once claimed the result as a massive endorsement of their position.

McMichael accepted this but argued that the result must be followed by with-drawal from Westminster:

> The message to the MPs is clear – come home (this battle must be fought on Ulster soil): organise and lead a campaign of non-co-operation and civil disobedience. Make Thatcher understand that Ulster cannot be governed without the consent of the majority and will not be governed by any coalition which involves a foreign and hostile power.[39]

This was also the view of the Ulster Clubs' spokesman, Alan Wright, although he was correctly sceptical about whether it would happen. He claimed the clubs could help to make Northern Ireland ungovernable and welcomed the pres-ence within them of UDA members while stressing that they had joined as individuals. Asked if paramilitary elements might take over the clubs, Wright's answer was evasive: 'That's a long way off. If the withdrawal of consent and civil disobedience fail to bring down the Agreement, then you will see force being met with force.'[40]

Attacks on the Prime Minister intensified in UDA publications. From being vilified as the dancing partner of Robert Mugabe, she was accused of having 'tried to don the mantle of a British de Gaulle, with proclamations of patriotism going hand-in-hand with betrayal of those who believed she would keep the British people strong and free'.[41] Equating the cause of Unionist Ulster with French settler rule in Algeria was a dubious tactic, as was linking it in the same article to Afrikaner rule in South Africa and the sovereign rights of the Falkland Islanders for which a British force had gone to war four years previously. In truth these sustained attacks on Margaret Thatcher were a sub-stitute for a distinctive UDA strategy to force on her some kind of retreat from the Agreement.

When a day of province-wide strikes and protest action for 3 March 1986 was called for by the Ulster Clubs and Unionist leaders, the UDA's Inner Council responded by saying that it would not take part as an organisation but that its members would be free to join in individually. This was a clear indication of the UDA leadership's continuing distrust of Unionist politi-cians, who had drawn them into the ill-planned and abortive strike action of 1977. Even as the Day of Action was launched, *Ulster* was still attacking the Unionist leaders for 'merely stalling in order to try to think of some "nice" tactics to employ in order to avoid using nasty unconstitutional methods which will confront our enemies on our ground in the way they fear while we understand'.[42]

*

Paisley and James Molyneaux had flown to London prior to the calling of the Day of Action to see the Prime Minister. All they achieved was agreement that a conference on devolution of power back to Belfast be held in the near future.

Molyneaux rashly treated this as a reason for telling the press that deadlock had been averted. Paisley was more circumspect and was quickly on the telephone to his party colleagues in Belfast to contradict Molyneaux by insisting that no concessions had in fact resulted from the Downing Street meeting. Even so he had to face a stormy executive meeting of the DUP on his return home. For a time the initiative seemed to be slipping to his deputy, Peter Robinson, who had gone on record with the view that the planned Day of Action could be a preparation for a mobilisation equivalent to that achieved in 1974 by the UWC.[43]

The 3 March Day of Action made a major impact despite a sustained campaign by the Northern Ireland Office to talk down its significance and blame in advance any success it might have on simple intimidation. This was not absent on the day, but, as *Fortnight* magazine wrote, 'even if the pickets had stayed at home there would have been a virtual shutdown in the province'. Comparing the protest with the slow and uncertain start to the 1974 strike, it reported 'a standstill by noon – well before the violence began'.[44] Towns such as Larne and Carrickfergus were deserted from early in the day; the only traffic in motion being police and army patrols or vehicles driven by organisers and supporters of the strike.

In most large factories the strike was strongly supported, causing power cuts and serious curtailment of public transport. Police in Land Rovers arrived at one factory in Lurgan to evacuate 200 women who had not joined the strike. They were besieged by angry Loyalists who set the building on fire, and several towns, including Omagh, Kilkeel, Rathfriland, Comber and Larne, were sealed off for much of the day by barricades of cars, tractors and felled trees. Violence, however, increased as the day wore on. The RUC received a flow of allegations of intimidation and came under attack when they responded to disorder in Belfast city centre after a large protest rally. Forty-seven officers were injured during the day's disturbances and the force fired a total of sixty-five plastic baton rounds.

Paisley and Molyneaux had little option but to denounce the violence although Paisley predicted more of it would happen unless the government was prepared to compromise over the Anglo-Irish Agreement. McMichael was swift to claim the Day of Action as a success but denied that it had been seen as a prelude to all-out strike action. Its organisation, he stressed, had been localised and the violence, which he dismissed as minimal in relation to the numbers involved, was, he argued, a result of Unionist MPs and Assembly members not playing their full part. As a show of strength he believed 3 March had been a real success:

> The workers are finding their feet and rapidly organising but are geared only to the industrial sector. The three groups which did show their ability to organise, produce and control large bodies of people were the paramilitaries, the Ulster Clubs, and the farmers.[45]

By 'the paramilitaries' he clearly meant the UDA and he went on to quote unnamed Unionist politicians who, he claimed, had told him that the violence of 3 March, while not something they welcomed, was also a reality they must get used to if the campaign was to succeed. 'We are burning bridges behind us,' he continued. 'For possibly the first time Loyalists have come face to face with the possibility of defeat. We can smell a united Ireland and are battling for our existence and our homeland.'[46] Only a suspension of the Agreement could avert a collision course with the government. Given his active and ruthless military role within the UDA, McMichael's language was ominous but he still did not exclude the negotiation of an alternative to the Agreement. 'It's time to get talking'[47] were the concluding words of his article, which carried with them a signal that the UDA still did not think the political road was closed to it.

The violence of the Day of Action continued, shifting its focus to localities affected by the RUC's announcement of the rerouting of traditional Orange Order parades. This was seen as proof of the hand of Dublin at work through the joint consultation mechanisms of the Anglo-Irish Agreement, and the Easter start of the Loyalist marching season was accompanied by serious rioting, especially in the Orange citadel of Portadown. Plastic baton rounds fired there by the RUC led to the death of a young Protestant and to intensified attacks on police homes, which had already become a target since the Agreement.

By the end of 1986, well over 500 such attacks had been recorded by RUC headquarters and 111 police families were attacked or threatened more than once. Bricks and petrol bombs were used and on occasions shots were fired too, though the force sustained no fatal casualties.[48] The UDA was widely believed to have been behind many of these attacks, something later readily admitted by one of its brigadiers, Jackie McDonald. 'That was a sign of the times,' he recalled, 'because this was a unique situation that no-one had experienced before. We didn't want the Agreement but Maggie Thatcher was saying "This is what you're getting".'[49]

Speaking close to the events themselves, Andy Tyrie moved away from the initial caution with which he had approached the 3 March protests. Asked by the press in late April 1986 what he felt about Sinn Fein spokesmen's claims that the nationalist community was at serious risk from the escalating violence, he replied:

> They are right to feel that way. I am not going to calm down Protestants any more. The only language Mrs Thatcher understands is that of violence. I am revelling in the fact that the Protestant people are fighting back. We are fighting for our survival. There is no control now. Everybody is pitching in. The Protestants have seen that violence by the IRA has paid off. Do you think there would have been an Anglo-Irish Agreement without it?'[50]

Tyrie's interviewer took his remarks as a warning signal of a deteriorating situation and proof of elected politicians being swept aside by paramilitary hard men. Violence did indeed worsen over the summer months, especially in Portadown over the intractable issue of rerouted Orange Order parades in July, and the UVF embarked upon a savage killing spree, many of its gunmen being once more available after the collapse of most of the cases brought against it through the RUC's use of supergrasses over the previous two years. The UDA was left behind, killing only four people in the remainder of the year, though it carried out a number of unsuccessful attacks.

Those four killings were acts of sickening brutality. The first victim, thirty-year-old Margaret Caulfield, was in fact a Protestant whose crime had been to marry a Catholic. She was shot dead on her bed, beside her husband, who was badly wounded. Usually reliable sources attributed the murder to the UFF and one of the killers may have been Ned McCreery, who carried out many murders during the Troubles. Mrs Caulfield was killed on 7 May 1986; UDA killers struck again in late August. Paddy McAllister, a 47-year-old Catholic taxi driver and father of four, lived in Rodney Drive, off Belfast's Donegall Road, an address for a Catholic dangerously close to the fiercely Loyalist Village area. Two gunmen burst into his home on the evening of 26 August and shot him eight times in the head and chest. One of his children ran in from the street to find his father already dead.

*

Seven weeks later, the UDA struck again. Their next victim was Kathleen Mullan, aged seventy-six, who was shot dead in her farmhouse near Ballynahinch, County Down, along with her son, Terry. She may have been killed by a bullet fired at him which passed through his arm and entered her upper body. The UDA claimed to have acted on intelligence based on the Mullan family's Republican and IRA links, but this has always been denied by relatives and Terry Mullan's name has never been put on any IRA memorial or roll of honour. The UDA's final victim of 1986 was another Catholic, Peter Bradley from Antrim, who died from terrible head and brain injuries from a beating he received on 9 December in a Lisburn bar frequented by UDA men. Murder charges were made but later dropped when potential witnesses all declined to help the RUC with their investigation.[51]

None of these killings, outnumbered as they were by those of the UVF in what remained of 1986, contributed to any definable military campaign against the IRA or the INLA. The victims were not hard to locate or to kill and the same could be said of UVF murders over the same period. Loyalist gunmen could claim no 'prestige' killing comparable to that of John Bingham, UVF commander in North Belfast, shot dead by the IRA in September. The falling off in UDA/UFF operations was in part a result of an ongoing restructuring within the organisation. This was intended to raise its operational capacity for the Doomsday situation which might lie ahead. Tyrie and McMichael were both closely involved in it yet neither of them had abandoned belief in the importance of a new political initiative by the UDA.

The need for it grew in their minds, as the protest campaign against the Anglo-Irish Agreement had clearly begun to falter while the government remained resolute. Academic and legal contacts dating back to the days of Vanguard and the UWC had been maintained, notably with David Trimble. New approaches were made to him once the decision was reached that *Beyond the Religious Divide* needed to be replaced by a new formulation of Northern Ireland's constitutional future. Tyrie claimed that four years of consultation went into this process,[52] which led to the publication of *Common Sense* at the end of January 1987.

He has also acknowledged the advice which was freely given from outside the UDA, especially from Trimble: 'We consulted him on the *Common Sense* document because he was a constitutional expert. We could never have put the document together without asking people what they thought and that included Trimble.'[53] A Belfast businessman with legal expertise was also consulted, but still wishes his identity to be protected, according to Tyrie.[54]

Someone else who was brought in to discuss the document was Seamus Lynch, who had sat on Belfast City Council in 1985 and then became Six Counties chairman of the Workers Party. With the agreement of party colleagues he accepted an invitation from McMichael, whom he had already met at a social event in the European Community's Belfast office, to look over the draft document. 'When we met,' Lynch recalled, 'I put all my cards on the table. He knew of my background in the Official IRA and then the Workers Party and I laid it on the line that my problem was the UDA's blatantly sectarian murdering of Catholics. If that stopped, I told him we could talk, maybe even work politically on some issues.'[55]

Given McMichael's reputation at this time, Lynch showed courage in talking to him at all and setting out his own position so unequivocally.

> John McMichael replied that he wanted to bring killing to an end but was isolated over this within the UDA, where any real political thinking was distrusted by the gunmen. He repeated he wanted to get beyond the sectarianism of which I had told him the UDA should be ashamed. This first meeting set the ground rules for further contact and for us to achieve some rapport. I had to assure myself he was genuine and I sensed the risks that political action could mean for him.[56]

The outcome of these initial contacts was indeed that Lynch received a draft copy of *Common Sense* to look over and comment upon.

> I suggested some changes so that its language really could reach my community. I think I could claim an input into the general shape of the document though of course I still saw the UDA's militarism as the real problem. I could also see that people like Glen Barr and Harry Chicken were wary of him. After their work on *Beyond the Religious Divide* they felt he was moving towards some kind of takeover where he would be the main political spokesman.[57]

Further contact followed and McMichael invited Lynch and his wife to his home in Lisburn for a meal:

> My wife had serious doubts about that, I can tell you, but I put it to her that I shared her view of the UDA's murderous reputation. In my view they were as sectarian in their killing as the Provos but our visit might help to change that.[58]

Driving by night in as violent a year as 1986 to a Loyalist stronghold such as Lisburn was not a matter for someone of Lynch's background to embark upon lightly but in fact he remembers the evening going well:

> We had a nice time. I sat there looking at him and listening to him, a youngish working-class fellow just like me, drawn into a conflict and trying to find a way through it. There he was, helping his wife Shirley with the meal and with a young child in the house. We did a lot of talking. I tried to stress to him that our move-ment had had to re-examine itself and its allegiances in order to go political and that this had meant stopping killing. If he could do that, I would help him in any way I could. That was my last meeting with him. I still think there was good in him.[59]

Also consulted, indeed brought back into play, was Professor Bernard Crick, known to Loyalists since the days of the Vanguard movement in the 1970s. He had remained a regular visitor to Northern Ireland and a frequent com-mentator in its affairs, which, earlier in 1986, he wrote, 'are as fascinating to me as rare diseases are to a doctor'.[60] He had continued to believe in the potential of the power-sharing experiments attempted in 1974 and then debated in the abortive Constitutional Convention but had little faith in Unionist politicians who would not compromise at least with constitutional nationalism. This was a good reason for the UDA to make contact with him, and Joe English (writing under the alias John Montgomery which he often used), the South-East Antrim brigadier, sent him a draft of *Common Sense* for his comments later that year.[61]

Common Sense was presented to the media under the auspices of the New Ulster Political Research Group but its true provenance was clear since, apart from Tyrie, the signatories were UDA brigadiers. One of these, Davy Payne, chose the pseudonym Cecil Graham, almost certainly because he was linked in many people's minds to some particularly sadistic killings in the early 1970s. Only Tyrie and McMichael, drawing intelligently on the outside help already referred to, had taken a systematic interest in the document's prepa-ration. It was they, and particularly McMichael, who handled media ques-tions on its proposals.

Common Sense began with a predictable and categorical rejection of the Anglo-Irish Agreement, arguing that it could bring no peace with it 'because it is a contract between two governments and not an agreement between those in the cockpit of the conflict – Ulster Protestants and Ulster Catholics.'[62] Rejection, it was stressed, could in itself solve nothing and the document went on to a thoughtful and well-balanced look at the origins of the current conflict and the two communities' perceptions of each other. Like *Beyond the Religious Divide*, it set out the case for a written constitution which could only be changed by a two-thirds referendum majority, a bill of rights and a supreme court to protect individual liberties.

'There is no section of this divided Ulster community which is totally innocent or indeed totally guilty, totally right or totally wrong,' McMichael wrote in the introduction to *Common Sense*. He declared: 'We all share the responsibility for creating the situation, either by deed or by acquiescence. Therefore we must share the responsibility for finding a settlement and then share the responsibility of maintaining good government.'[63] From there, it was a short step to making the case for power-sharing under a new name provided that the minority community gave a commitment to supporting Northern Ireland's continued existence.

There was to be no return to simple majority rule, which, *Common Sense* argued, 'in deeply divided societies is likely to be profoundly undemocratic. The only democratic system is one that allows participation in government by a coalition of all groups, majority and minority, on a more or less permanent basis.'[64] This would be secured by proportionality at every level, with ministerial places allocated on the basis of proportions of votes gained. In many ways all this foreshadowed the Good Friday Agreement of 1998 with its commitment to fully equal citizenship and its concern to free Protestants from their siege psychology as well as Catholics from their equally deep fear of domination by the majority built into the state since partition.

Common Sense called for an immediate constitutional conference, chaired by a nominee of the Secretary of State but one acceptable to it. The conference's remit would be to draft a new constitution but of course an obvious impediment to this was always going to be the continued existence of the Anglo-Irish Agreement. A way round this was not offered by *Common Sense* but even so the general response to it was very favourable. To many commentators it was proof that paramilitary Loyalism could look beyond the stockade and offer an even-handed analysis of conflict and its causes, as well as proposing a way forward from it.

The *Irish Times* printed *Common Sense* in full in its centre pages and quoted many of the points which McMichael had made at its Belfast launch. It described the document as 'a blueprint for consensus coalition government'.[65] The Belfast-based *News Letter* called it 'a patently honest and open appeal to political leaders in Northern Ireland to join together in building a future for all in a spirit of tolerance and co-operation'.[66]

The Unionist parties' response was at best lukewarm, a product of their uneasy relations with paramilitary Loyalism but also of a period in which both Dr Ian Paisley and James Molyneaux had moved close to an integrationist view of what the province's relationship with Britain should be. An exception was the OUP secretary, Frank Millar, who made clear his view that the UDA document should be seriously considered because 'it concentrated

Unionist and Loyalist minds on the problem of the minority community in Northern Ireland',[67] even if it might be shown to be defective on some points of constitutional detail.

From within the nationalist community, both John Hume, the SDLP leader, and Cardinal O'Fiaich, Archbishop of Armagh and Primate of all Ireland, welcomed *Common Sense* at the very least for its recognition of the failure of majority rule over so many years as much as for the new constitutional formula it offered. Sinn Fein gave a half-page analysis of the document in its weekly paper, identifying what it claimed was 'a political about-turn which seems to have taken place within the organisation'.[68] By this it meant the UDA's move away from Ulster independence. In fact there had been little reference to it in UDA statements over almost a four-year period but Sinn Fein represented *Common Sense* as a retreat from this policy to a power-sharing deal similar to the one tried and abandoned in 1974.

The UDA, in Sinn Fein's view, had

> finally realised that a significant fraction of the Northern Ireland Catholic middle-class is eager to settle for some stake in the Six-County state. This document is an appeal to these Catholics. It is also an attempt at influencing the other Unionist groupings to adopt the only 'realistic' method of shoring up and stabilising the Northern state.[69]

This was Sinn Fein speaking as the political arm of an IRA in the process of intensifying its own armed campaign but it found no problem in dismissing the UDA's political credibility because of the killings its members were carrying out.

Danny Morrison, Sinn Fein's director of publicity, accorded some significance to what was in the document. He accepted that its contents represented 'a more forthright and ambitious approach than those of the two main Unionist parties' but he still saw it as 'a means of entrapment for the nationalist community and aimed at stabilising the union with Britain, which republicans will never accept'.[70]

Tyrie responded swiftly by denying any fundamental conflict between independence as a long-term aim and the creation by agreement of an executive and legislature with cross-community support. The success of such an experiment, he argued, would isolate the IRA politically and prepare the ground for viable devolved government. *Common Sense* made only one reference to Sinn Fein but Tyrie stressed that he would welcome its participation in the proposed constitutional conference if it called a ceasefire.[71]

For several weeks after the launch of *Common Sense*, Tyrie remained optimistic about the response to it. Indeed he and Hester Dunn, who was running the UDA's women's department, insisted that support for its proposals was coming in not just from traditionally Loyalist areas but from within the nationalist community too. Their commitment to *Common Sense* was welcomed by Professor Bernard Crick and he wrote of it as a contribution to a larger debate about the decentralising of power within the United Kingdom as a whole.[72]

Disenchantment for Tyrie and McMichael, particularly the latter, came with the realisation that both Paisley and Molyneaux had no intention of talking to them about *Common Sense* and indeed were hostile to it. Paisley even dismissed it as a surrender to a nationalist demand for power-sharing, which Loyalist mobilisation had defeated in 1974. McMichael did his best to explain that he saw the document as a way for the Unionist parties to retrieve the political initiative by offering an imaginative devolutionary package which would put the SDLP under pressure to decide whether it was worth trading off the Anglo-Irish Agreement for an internal cross-community settlement.

Expressing his frustration to a Dublin newspaper after *Common Sense* had come out, McMichael inevitably had to face questions about fire bombs planted a few days earlier in central Dublin by the UFF. 'It's not a matter of *Common Sense* in one hand and a fire-bomb in the other,' he told his interviewer. 'We are interested in selling our proposals and further action by the UFF would only make that more difficult.'[73] Given his own military role, this was a disingenuous answer but in other articles and interviews he continued to press the case for *Common Sense* as the only alternative to a worsening spiral of violence. This certainly seemed to be happening as another marching season drew near and as Charles Haughey, whose Fianna Fáil party had returned to power in Dublin, announced that his office would take over responsibility for implementing the Anglo-Irish Agreement from the Department of External Affairs.

*

McMichael lost no chance in this period to talk to the Dublin media in order to leave them absolutely sure about Loyalist resolution against the Agreement as well as the alternatives set out in *Common Sense*. His loss of patience with British policy, however, began to show. Speaking of Margaret Thatcher in April 1987, he declared:

> She is determined to break Ulster Loyalism, which she disparages and distrusts, as well as buying time and some peace by temporarily pacifying Nationalist aspirations. But it hasn't even done that. What has this pact achieved? Community polarisation has worsened. Alienation, so called, is now truly here. The security forces are attacked by both sides now. The Provos have been encouraged. It looks like these two Governments have paid a high price in blood for their constitutional tinkering, their test-tube baby.[74]

There were limits beyond which the case could not be taken and the UDA leadership's ability to put it was challenged from a source they had not foreseen. This was the Campaign for Equal Citizenship (CEC), formed in 1985 by the Shankill-born barrister Robert McCartney. His concern was to make the case for the full integration of Northern Ireland within the United Kingdom. This, McCartney argued, was more important than the *Common Sense* proposals, which put the constitutional cart before the horse. He was supported by the British and Irish Communist Organisation (BICO), which since 1974 had retained a nose for anything it thought smacked of Ulster nationalism.

In its paper, BICO vilified McMichael for having 'joined the ranks of swamp things which infest this stinking provincial marsh. Swamp things love wordy, paper, constitutions, cocktails in the Culloden Hotel, legislative devolution.'[75] The paper's editor was a member of the CEC and his intervention served simply to confuse debate over *Common Sense* and what the Unionist response to it should be. By this time many in the UDA who supported it were becoming sceptical of any impact it might have and it played little part in the Westminster general election held in June.

The Ulster Loyalist Democratic Party made no attempt to put up candidates and Tyrie, when questioned about the UDA's role, claimed that it was giving active support to some Unionists whose anti-Agreement credentials it could trust. He declined to name them in case UDA support might work against some of them.[76] No new anti-Agreement party emerged, unlike in Scotland, where the Orange Order supported a short-lived new Unionist Party, which in the event contested no seats but identified eleven where it felt tactical voting could defeat Conservatives who had supported government policy over the Agreement. Seven of these seats were lost to the opposition parties but this was more likely to have been the result of the then deeply unpopular poll tax imposed upon Scotland ahead of England by the Thatcher government.

Tyrie made it clear that neither the UDA nor its political wing had made any contact with the Scottish party, though *Ulster* magazine did give it supportive coverage in the post-election issue.[77] He even expressed the hope that McCartney might come round to supporting *Common Sense* in his bid for election in North Down.[78] In fact there was little chance of this. Standing as an independent Unionist, McCartney fought a lively campaign in support of what he called 'real Unionism' based on equal citizenship in an integrated relationship with the United Kingdom.[79] Steve Bruce's verdict probably remains correct: 'However much some people were impressed by the fact of a paramilitary organisation producing a reasoned and imaginative policy document, the major parties ignored it and there was no pressure from the public for them to do otherwise.'[80]

Even so, significant space continued to be accorded to *Common Sense* in editions of *Ulster*. An interview with Tyrie appeared in its October issue, in which he insisted that its analysis and proposals were still there as a basis for dialogue on a non-violent future for Northern Ireland. Asked how this dialogue could be maintained given the negative response of the Unionist parties, he said that either the UDA could support a new political party wholly independent of it or its members could seek to work within the existing parties. *Common*

Sense, he insisted, 'was accepted by a substantial number of people as the only way forward that has been seen to come from the grassroots Unionist community'.[81]

Within only a few weeks of Tyrie giving that interview, McMichael was killed by an IRA bomb fitted under his car at his home in Lisburn. His death did not, as has sometimes been claimed, destroy the prospects of the UDA seizing the political initiative with *Common Sense*. That would always have been extremely difficult given the power of the existing Unionist parties and the degree of working-class Loyalist support for them. Nonetheless, UDA members able and willing to talk and think politically continued to invoke what became known as the McMichael principles and *Ulster* magazine continued to find room for articles about them even as the IRA stepped up its killing campaign.

The Ulster Democratic Party, formed in 1989 from the original ULDP, campaigned for policies based on *Common Sense* and McMichael's son Gary became active in it. The party's electoral success was very limited but it did play quite an important role in the negotiations which brought to birth the Belfast Agreement in 1998. Many of the power-sharing mechanisms incorporated within it were close to those outlined in *Common Sense* ten years earlier. Hundreds more lives were claimed by the Troubles during that intervening decade but at least the UDA's second attempt at a major political initiative achieved something.

Fourteen years after John McMichael's death, a contributor to the *Irish News*, Roy Garland, wrote generously of him: 'It was his intention to move into the world of politics, put an end to racketeering, abolish sectarianism and enable the Unionist working-class to make their unique contribution to the future of Northern Ireland.'[82] It was an assessment which, however, avoided the reality that McMichael had earned his influence in the UDA through the single-minded and ruthless paramilitary role he had played within it. Had he lived, McMichael would have had to choose between the power base he had secured and using it to take the UDA on to a political road. The dangers of attempting this might well have proved greater than the rewards.

NOTES

1. A. Tyrie, interview with author, 3 December 2002.
2. Tyrie, interview with author, *Scotsman*, 23 January 1984.
3. Tyrie, interview with author, 15 April 1985.
4. *Guardian*, 16 September 1980.
5. *Scotsman*, 7 July 1981.
6. Ibid.
7. Ibid.
8. Ibid.
9. *Ulster*, October 1981.
10. Ibid.

11. *Ulster*, December 1982.

12. Ibid.

13. *Ulster*, May 1984.

14. Ibid.

15. *Ulster*, April 1984.

16. *Ulster*, February 1985.

17. *Ulster*, July–August 1985.

18. *Guardian*, 2 April 1984.

19. Ibid.

20. *Ulster*, July–August 1984.

21. *Ulster*, April 1985.

22. Ibid.

23. *Ulster*, June 1985.

24. S. Heffer, *Like the Roman* (London: Weidenfeld and Nicolson, 1998), p. 830.

25. *Ulster*, July–August 1985.

26. R. Jones, J. Kane, R. Wallace, D. Sloan and B. Courtney, *The Orange Citadel: a History of Orangeism in Portadown District* (Portadown: Portadown Orange Lodge District No. 1, 1996), pp. 48–9.

27. *Guardian*, 29 July 1985.

28. J. McMichael, interview with author, 23 August 1985.

29. *Fortnight*, 2 December 1985.

30. A. Aughey, *Under Siege: Ulster Unionism and the Anglo-Irish Agreement* (Belfast: Blackstaff Press, 1989), p. 75.

31. G. FitzGerald, 'The origins and rationale of the 1985 agreement', in D. Keogh and M. Haltzel, *Northern Ireland and the Politics of Reconciliation* (Cambridge: Cambridge University Press, 1993), p. 200.

32. R. Needham, *Battling for Peace: Northern Ireland's Longest-Serving British Minister* (Belfast: Blackstaff Press, 1998), pp. 81–2.

33. Aughey, *Under Siege*, pp. 53–7.

34. *Ulster*, December 1985–January 1986.

35. Ibid.

36. Ibid.

37. S. Belfrage, *The Crack: A Belfast Year* (London: Andre Deutsch), p. 156.

38. *Fortnight*, 10 February 1986.

39. *Ulster*, February 1986.

40. *Fortnight*, 10 February 1986.

41. *Ulster*, February 1986.

42. *Ulster*, March 1986.

43. E. Moloney and A. Pollak, *Paisley* (Dublin: Poolbeg, 1986), pp. 395–6.

44. *Fortnight*, 24 March–20 April 1986.

45. Ibid.

46. Ibid.

47. Ibid.

48. C Ryder, *The RUC: A Force under Fire* (London: Methuen, 1989), pp. 329–30.

49. P. Taylor, *Loyalists* (London: Bloomsbury, 1999), p. 182.

50. *Observer*, 20 April 1986.

51. See D. McKittrick, S. Kelters, B. Feeney and C. Thornton, *Lost Lives: The Stories of the Men, Women and Children Who Died as a Result of Northern Ireland's Troubles* (Edinburgh: Mainstream, 1999), pp. 1036, 1047, 1052, 1055 for the details of these four murders.
52. Tyrie, interview with author, 13 February 1987.
53. H. McDonald, *Trimble* (London: Bloomsbury, 2000), pp. 98–9.
54. Tyrie, interview with author, 19 April 2000.
55. S. Lynch, interview with author, 19 April 2000.
56. Ibid.
57. Ibid.
58. Ibid.
59. Ibid.
60. *Scotsman*, 3 May 1986.
61. The author is indebted to Professor Crick for the loan of this undated letter.
62. *Common Sense: Northern Ireland – an Agreed Process* (Belfast: Ulster Political Research Group, 1987).
63. Ibid.
64. Ibid.
65. *Irish Times*, 30 January 1987.
66. *News Letter*, 31 January 1987.
67. *Irish News*, 30 January 1987.
68. *An Phoblacht/Republican News*, 5 February 1987.
69. Ibid.
70. *Irish News*, 30 January 1987.
71. Tyrie, interview with author, 13 February 1987.
72. *Scotsman*, 22 February 1987.
73. *Sunday Tribune*, 14 February 1987.
74. *Irish Times*, 6 April 1987.
75. *Workers Weekly*, 19 April 1987.
76. Tyrie, interview with author, 3 June 1987.
77. *Ulster*, July–August 1987.
78. Tyrie, interview with author, 3 June 1987.
79. Aughey, *Under Siege*, pp. 163–5.
80. Bruce, *The Red Hand: Protestant Paramilitaries in Northern Ireland* (Oxford: Oxford University Press, 1992), p. 239.
81. *Ulster*, October 1987.
82. *Irish News*, 15 October 2001.

5

The UDA at War

Alex, or 'Oso', Calderwood, whose reasons for joining the UDA have been mentioned in Chapter 1, had been drinking in a pub on the Lower Shankill Road before setting off to walk home on the night of 3 January 1980. As he drew near to Berlin Street he saw a crowd which had gathered:

> They had two fellows up against the wall and someone I knew shouted to me that they were Fenians and had I got a gun on me. He knew I was in the UDA. One of the two they had caught made a run for it but they hung on to the other one. I took him along the street a little way to a derelict garage and there was a loose slab of concrete there. I was a big strong fellow and I picked it up and smashed his skull in with it. I beat him to death and I felt good about it. It wasn't drink, I'd have used a gun if I had had one. I was judge, prosecutor, you name it – and executioner. I took that young fellow's life.[1]

The victim was Alexander Reid, aged twenty, a Catholic from Ardoyne who worked as a labourer. He was married and had a small child. He and the friend who escaped had made the mistake of taking a taxi up the Shankill Road with the intention of getting out of it to cut across to their homes in Ardoyne. An RUC patrol vehicle was stopped in Berlin Street and officers in it were told of moans coming from the garage. They found Reid, already dead and lying face down in a pool of blood with his skull shattered. Over the next few days, many death notices offering prayers for the repose of his soul appeared, as they did throughout the Troubles for murder victims, in the pages of the nationalist *Irish News*. One notice was from the committee and members of the Shamrock Social Club in Ardoyne, of which Reid's father was a founder member. It read: 'If his murderers had known this young man as we knew him, they would hang their heads in shame.'[2]

The only murderer was Calderwood, although three friends of his who had been identified in the crowd in Berlin Street were wrongly convicted of killing Reid before he was. For Calderwood, Reid's murder proved to be a turning point, though not right away. Soon after it, he was sent to a young offenders' institution on conviction of burglary. There he was befriended by a Catholic whom he later saved from likely execution by the UDA after he, like Reid, had strayed into the Shankill late at night. In mid-June 1981, Calderwood flagged down a police vehicle near the Shankill Road and made a full confession to the murder of Alexander Reid. Since he was still not yet eighteen when charged, he received a sentence of indefinite length. During it he learned to read and write. He also underwent a Christian conversion and broke with the UDA. Since his release he has worked in cross-community church groups and in the probation service and has met a cousin of his victim in the course of his work.[3]

Calderwood has never sought to justify the brutal killing of an innocent victim as an act of war or a military operation but at the time he did it he was an active member of C Company in the West Belfast battalion of the Ulster Freedom Fighters. In no sense a separate body from the UDA, the many killings claimed by the UFF from the summer of 1973 onwards confused the security forces, initially at least, and protected the UDA itself from being proscribed. As happened again at the end of the 1980s, C Company was a particularly ruthless unit when Calderwood joined it: 'We did the business. We were an effective killing machine,' he recalls. 'Yes, that meant killing ordinary Catholics, spreading terror, giving it back. We did it. We were volunteers but under orders and for me, Catholics were the enemy. I'd no hesitation in my mind that they should be hit, taken out, killed. I'm being truthful. I'm a very different person now but that's how it was, how I was.'[4]

C Company during Calderwood's time regularly robbed business premises. One raid, he recalls, 'went wrong'. The target was a shoe shop.

> The Peelers caught us just as we were ready to move out 2,000 pairs of shoes. We'd have got rid of the lot, sold them on in clubs and pubs. Sure, a few quid came our way. You took a cut and you were glad of it. It was hard to hold down a job if you were as active as I was. Any cash topped up your social security if you were eligible for that. If shops and pubs were not paying up what the UDA thought was due to them, we would sort them out. We accepted, we assumed that our leadership used cash from these sources for the cause. You accepted the deal as it was. We followed orders, like foot soldiers in an army.[5]

In what real sense, however, was the UDA an army? Lurid and often menacing murals in Loyalist areas in Belfast and elsewhere proclaim that it was, and indeed still is, and regular commemorations of UDA members killed in the Troubles and more recently drive home the message. Whether the UDA/UFF really impeded the ability of the IRA and other Republican paramilitary groups to wage war on Northern Ireland and the British presence there, or indeed influenced the Sinn Fein and IRA leadership's decision ultimately to settle for a political road rather than continued armed struggle, will be a principal concern of this book, as will the twists and turns in its relationship with the security forces.

In so far as the UDA was effective in its initial street defence and vigilante role in Loyalist areas fearful of IRA attacks, it owed a good deal to former soldiers. David Fogel was only one of them, though he achieved a particularly important role for himself during the crisis year of 1972. One astute British reporter observed and later recalled the importance of men with military experience in the early UDA:

> The leaders often tended to be ex-Territorials or regular soldiers, hard, ruthless and shrewd but often very likeable; they were adept at wheeling and dealing and had a remarkable flair for understanding what 'makes people tick'. With the merciless form of selection of the UDA those who ended up at the top were often of high calibre. But their hard men required action and for the leaders to remain at the top they had to provide it. So in many ways the UDA needed contact with the Army much more than the other way round. It was always anxious to be considered as a 'Third Force' i.e. after the army itself and the RUC.[6]

The army initially took a guarded and cautious view of the UDA's emergence. It had to in 1972, a year of carnage and horror which killed seventy-nine of its soldiers, all victims of IRA gun and bomb attacks, and stretched its resources to the limit. UDA members were responsible for dozens of Catholics' deaths without claiming responsibility for them as an organisation and it was as hard for the army to stop these as it was for it to halt or neutralise the IRA's much greater onslaught. A more immediate threat to the army was the UDA's clear desire to show its strength on the streets. In full view of television and press cameras, army units held back from any response to the UDA's first no-go area, which it set up in Woodvale at the end of May. UDA spokesmen let it be known that the operation would be repeated elsewhere.

This was indeed what happened, though barricades around other Loyalist areas were often erected only at weekends in order not to inflict hardship on people who needed to get from them to their work. In some places, UDA commanders actually gave out assurances that vehicles taken to build barricades would be returned to their owners after the weekend. The army's fear was that these no-go areas were not just to protect Loyalist communities under threat from the IRA but had the potential to be used as bargaining counters against them.[7] When the army did move to take down barricades, as in East Belfast on the night of 21 May, serious violence erupted and lasted for several hours.

On 29 May the Official IRA announced a ceasefire based on its leaders' analysis that continued war would drag the community into sectarian catastrophe. Rumours spread that the Provisional IRA might be planning to do the same and on 26 June it announced what turned out to be only a very temporary ceasefire. William Whitelaw's promise that the British government would reciprocate intensified Loyalist fears that the Northern Ireland Office and London were prepared to talk to the IRA. In an atmosphere of growing suspicion the West Belfast UDA took an initiative which was a clear challenge to the army.

This took the form of extending its original Woodvale no-go area. Masked men with picks and pneumatic drills took over a corner of Woodvale at its southern end where a number of small streets joined the Springfield Road. One of these was Ainsworth Avenue, previously a mixed locality but one from which most Catholics had fled in 1969. The army was advised that if the UDA's barricades were extended, some fifty remaining Catholic families would be confined within the enlarged no-go area. Officers of the King's Regiment told the UDA that the new barricades would have to come down. This was in the early evening of 3 July but the UDA's response was to move large numbers of its men into Ainsworth Avenue.

An army brigadier then arrived as the UDA assembled several thousand men very close to the troops in position at the interface. He talked with UDA leaders to play for time, as the soldiers of the King's Regiment were heavily outnumbered. The talks moved into a small and increasingly over-crowded house on Ainsworth Avenue. UDA leaders and activists who arrived on the scene included Fogel, Tommy Herron, Jim Anderson, Sammy Doyle and Andy Tyrie. They were joined by General Sir Robert Ford, overall commander of British land forces in Northern Ireland. He assessed the situation then decided that the danger to troops under his command justified a phone call to Whitelaw, seeking authority to order them to open fire unless the UDA stayed where they were.

Thirty years later, giving evidence to the Saville inquiry into an infinitely worse confrontation between British troops and the population of Londonderry, the general recalled how 'he, i.e. Whitelaw, gave that authority. I contacted the leaders of the UDA. We knew who they were and after considerable discussion persuaded them that what I told them was the truth.'[8] Whitelaw later wrote that 'General Ford played his hand brilliantly'.[9] In one obvious sense this was true, as the UDA leaders agreed to take down their barricade if any army checkpoint was set up on the interface and if they could maintain patrols behind the site of the original barricade.

Whitelaw's view was 'that UDA men being permitted to move unarmed in a road behind an army checkpoint was a far cry from an armed force manning a permanent concrete barricade which had been the UDA objective'.[10] It was better, he went on, 'to allow the UDA to claim a meaningless victory, for their leaders knew the truth and so did the Catholic families involved'.[11] This was a justifiable view for him to take, though Andy Tyrie for one has continued to contest it[12] and some accounts have represented it as a 'major victory for the UDA'.[13]

Perhaps it was in the sense that senior British officers, including a general, had been seen to negotiate directly with the UDA in order to defuse a crisis which could have put the army in an almost impossible position if it had opened fire on Loyalists. The UDA had guns in Ainsworth Avenue too and its battalions from North and West Belfast marched off in celebratory mood. Fogel spoke a few months later about how he had sat with Ford,

> haggling over a strip of land like two Chinamen. Maybe it was the UDA's finest hour. At last the poor people of West Belfast who for years had been living in the shadow of the middle-class Unionists were doing something for themselves.[14]

Another confrontation with the army followed quickly, this time in South-West Belfast in an area where IRA attacks had driven Protestant families out of entire streets. One of these was Lenadoon Avenue, where vacant houses were made available by the authorities to Catholics intimidated out of other areas, notably Rathcoole on the northern edge of the city. The UDA's South Belfast brigade took the view that this was giving ground to the enemy and massed its men close to the avenue to stop the Catholics moving in. The army arrived in strength on 9 July and at once came under pressure from the local IRA unit to hold back the UDA. Officers tried to mediate but an angry Catholic crowd started to stone soldiers, who replied with CS gas and plastic bullets. IRA marksmen opened fire, a clear indication of the two-week truce being over, an outcome generally satisfactory to the UDA.

Confrontations like these with the army were a risky business for the UDA. It had grown far too fast to be able to arm any more than a few of its units. Fogel admitted in May 1972 that it had not the firepower to take on either the army or the IRA.[15] Awareness of this created a heightened interest in guerrilla strategy and tactics. The following month there were reports of an Inner Council document being circulated among units and members urging them to learn both from the IRA's methods and from its mistakes. It also made the case for 'producing an equal or greater amount of terror among their followers than they can among us,'[16] an ominous justification of the serial killing of Catholics already taking place. The Stern gang, Irgun, Guevara, Lenin, Castro and an 'old IRA' hero, Michael Collins, were all quoted as names UDA activists could learn from.[17]

Army units, notably the Parachute Regiment, could also provide brutal reminders of their readiness to 'go in hard' against Loyalists. In August 1972, this regiment's First Battalion provided Woodvale with what Fogel described later as a 'rude awakening'. He added: 'We realised that some of the allegations against the army by the Taigs might have been true.'[18] These events prompted an ill-judged 'declaration of war' on the army by Tommy Herron, acting on his own authority and without the means to back it up. It simply led to even rougher tactics from army units operating in Loyalist areas.[19]

Proof of this came on the night of 7 September 1972, when the First Battalion of the Parachute Regiment made a series of house searches in the Shankill Road area and also seized bomb-making equipment and a radio from the UDA's Wilton Street headquarters. Soldiers claimed they had been stoned and then had come under fire before opening fire themselves. Two men were shot dead. One of them was later described by witnesses at the inquest as a harmless drunk and the other inadvertently drove his car into the line of fire from the army. Lieutenant-Colonel Derek Wilford, who had commanded the battalion on Bloody Sunday in Londonderry in January, defended its behaviour but the next day an angry Protestant crowd demonstrated outside Tennent Street RUC station, which paratroopers had been using as a base. A UDA statement declared: 'Never has Ulster witnessed such licensed sadists and such blatant liars as the 1st Paras. These gun-happy louts must be removed from the streets.'[20]

The two men killed on 7 September had no UDA connections, unlike eighteen-year-old Robert Warnock, who was shot dead a week later by an off-duty RUC officer. He and an accomplice had attempted to hold up a bar at Castlereagh in East Belfast and then opened fire on the officer, who returned lethal fire with his own revolver. Fogel had wanted UDA men to keep out of armed robbery, whether of bars, banks or shops, but Warnock could not be disowned. The East Belfast UDA provided a guard of honour and a colour party for his funeral and his name later appeared on UDA memorials.[21] Warnock's brother, even younger than he was and a junior UDA member, was crushed to death by an army vehicle only a few weeks later during further Loyalist rioting in East Belfast.

Men in one unit of the Ulster Defence Regiment, formed in 1970 to replace the old RUC B-Special reserve force, actually refused to carry out their duties until the Parachute Regiment was withdrawn from the Shankill area. Tension between the UDA and the army smouldered on into October and erupted again in the middle of the month with rioting and gun battles in which army units claimed 500 shots had been fired at them. Two Protestants were killed and once again Herron denounced both army and government, saying: 'To hell with the British army. To hell with the Whitelaw administration. The British government and British army are now our enemies.'[22] A two-day truce restored calm but resentment remained over the army's role.

Meanwhile, the UDA went on killing Catholics as and when it could target them. One source attributes 71 murders to it during 1972,[23] though many of these killings were not in fact claimed by any Loyalist organisations at the time. Some victims died from appalling beatings or multiple stabbing. Davy Payne, who rose high within the UDA's command structure, was known for his fascination with knives and his readiness to use them.[24] He was almost certainly involved in the mutilation and murder of Senator Paddy Wilson and Irene Andrews in late June 1973.[25] Other victims, however, died mercifully quicker deaths at the hands of UDA gunmen.

Where the UDA was acquiring its firearms, as well as the ability to use them, became a matter of obvious concern within the nationalist community. Many of its members had handled weapons while in the army but rumours were rife about former members of the RUC's B-Special reserve having been allowed to retain their guns after it was disbanded in late 1969. The newspaper of the Official Republican movement made free with this allegation as well as claiming that former 'B-men' were active in a rash of private gun clubs where weapons and the necessary skills in using them could be passed on to para-military recruits. It referred to over thirty such clubs including one at the Rolls-Royce engineering plant, where Andy Tyrie had once been employed.[26]

Such rumours are difficult to substantiate thirty years later, but the issue resurfaces in the recollections of those who were drawn into an active paramilitary role. Michael Stone has claimed that apart from 'shipyard specials', handguns illicitly made by Loyalists employed by Harland and Wolff, where he had worked for a time, he gained access to guns and adequate practice in using them at a well-equipped gun club in North Down. Its facilities, he also says, were used by lawyers, some judges and RUC officers.[27]

From belief in such rumours it was but a short step to accepting even more serious claims of security force collusion with the UDA. One volunteer who joined early on, 'Geoff Mitchell' (not his real name), told an interviewer:

> As time went on, our information got better: we began to get co-operation, you see. I'll not be too specific, you won't expect that, but there were those in the police who felt their hands were tied and knew ours weren't and they'd give us some help now and again. Information, or something more than that once in a while: there were instances where weapons went missing, let's not say more.[28]

On the night of 3 October 1972, a murder particularly horrible even by the standards to which Belfast descended took place in the eastern part of the city. James McCartan, a 21-year-old Catholic originally from the Markets area, attended a party in the Park Avenue Hotel in East Belfast. For a Catholic to do such a thing in a fiercely Loyalist area was a grievous error. He was seized by a group of men as he left the party and driven to a UDA 'safe house' where he was repeatedly kicked, beaten with a pickaxe handle and stabbed at least 200 times. Close to death, he was hooded, bundled into a car and driven to where police later found his body, near Mersey Street bridge, with three bullet wounds in his head.

In October 1973, Albert Baker was sentenced to life imprisonment when he made a plea of guilty to this and three other murders. It emerged from the trial that Baker was a former soldier who had deserted from the Royal Irish Rangers to join the UDA in East Belfast, where he quickly acquired a brutal reputation. His confession implicated other UDA men, including Ned McCreery, a UDA commander in the area, but they were acquitted in 1974 because of inconsistencies in Baker's evidence. What gave a dramatic dimension to Baker's own trial and the subsequent one arising from it was the allegations he made about the UDA's relationship with the army and its undercover and intelligence services. UDA leaders were, he claimed, 'untouchable', so long as they followed British orders and Herron's fate later in 1973 was, he suggested, sealed by his refusal to do this.

In repeated letters from prisons in England to, among others, Father Denis Faul, a priest who took up several civil rights cases arising from the Troubles, and Ken Livingstone MP, Baker both stuck to and elaborated on his story. He accused the RUC as well as the army of active complicity in killings committed by UDA members. Some writers on the conflict have been willing, probably too willing, to believe him. Livingstone was one of them, declaring: 'If only one quarter of what Baker told me is true, it would be enough to demolish both the government's policy and its record in Ireland.'[29] He had in mind the Thatcher government, but Baker's claims, of course, related largely to events during the lifetime of the 1970–74 Heath government. In fact, both in open court and in his later letters from prison, Baker was unable to provide the names of security force members he claimed had acted in collusion with UDA killers. He also omitted any reference to the large number of Loyalist murder suspects, especially UDA men, whom the army and police arrested and detained in 1972 and 1973 only to have to release many of them because of insufficient evidence for a conviction.

Army units serving their tours of highly dangerous duty in Northern Ireland in 1972 had to live with and sometimes accept the UDA's presence in Loyalist areas. This could mean responding toughly to it when it tried to confront them but also negotiating with it, or attempting to, as at Ainsworth Avenue or Lenadoon. For the UDR, first deployed in 1970, relations with the UDA were always going to be problematic because sustained IRA attacks on it had rapidly turned the regiment into a predominantly Protestant force quickly demonised by Republicans for what was claimed to be, at the very least, its empathy with armed Loyalists.

Initially, there was no impediment to UDA members joining the regiment. After the mid-October violence on the Shankill Road, the UDA gave a full paramilitary funeral to 23-year-old John Todd, who was killed on the 17th, a night of clashes between local people and the army. He was also a private in the UDR, which never incorporated his name in its roll of honour.[30] Soon after this, the regiment's commanding officer, Brigadier Denis Ormerod, said on television that he accepted that some of his men might belong to the UDA and that they would only be disciplined or dismissed if their UDA membership led to military misconduct.

He appeared to many to be contradicting his own early assertions about the importance of the UDR having a non-sectarian role and the *Belfast Telegraph* voiced moderate Unionist opinion by condemning what he had said, declaring that 'membership of a British regiment should be totally incompatible with membership of a sectarian organisation'.[31] British Cabinet papers from this period seem to indicate that the view of advisers to the government in London were not too far removed from those espoused by Ormerod. Indeed, they could be seen as betraying a rather different view of Loyalist violence from that taken of Republican paramilitarism.

A memorandum in late November 1972 from the Ministry of Defence to the Cabinet Office, marked 'Prime Minister (for information)', emphasised the continued legality of the UDA. It went on to assert that 'an important function of the UDA is to channel into a constructive and disciplined direction Protestant energies which might otherwise become disruptive'.[32] It is revealing that this was still being said after some serious attacks on the army by the UDA and after dozens of murders of Catholics, which were widely believed by the security forces to be the work of its members. As to the UDR, the document went on to say that 'it was not considered desirable or practical to make membership of the UDA a bar in itself to membership of the UDR'.[33]

UDR soldiers who had also joined the UDA were to be warned not to let membership of it affect their performance of military duties, and dismissal was set out as a clear possibility if this happened. A new 'Regimental Routine Order' was cited under which officers of suspect loyalty could be asked to resign and other ranks dismissed. 'We do not expect that this change will result in any more than about fifty dismissals,'[34] the memorandum concluded.

Anxiety about the UDR's supposed or actual Loyalist and UDA sympathies continued within the nationalist community. Events during the May 1974 UWC strike reinforced this. However, as argued earlier, the regiment's disinclination to take on Loyalist strikers was also a product of its integral membership of a British army which had little relish for a trial of strength with Loyalist paramilitaries as well as its costly efforts to contain IRA attacks. This could lead to attitudes to the UDA which were, at the very best, ambivalent in tone.

One officer, whose disguised published reflections on events have already been drawn upon in Chapter 2, wrote:

1972 was the year of the UDA. Like Napoleon and Hitler, the Army had long worried about a war on two fronts, and this it got with the rise of the UDA – a paramilitary manifestation of the growing fear of the Protestant working class that it was being sold down the river by Whitehall. In order to combat this threat, the Army chose quite deliberately to give the UDA tacit support. The UDA virtually ran East and North Belfast. It was the threat of UDA intervention that led to Motorman, the Army's operation in August 1972 to end IRA 'no-go' areas, and it was the threat of UDA action on the Catholic ghettos in Belfast that led to even higher troop levels. Almost too late, in the winter of 1972, the Army realised that it had assisted in the birth of a monster. It sought to act but was only able to cage the beast: the secret of its destruction had been lost with its birth.[35]

Trying to keep the beast caged might well serve as a description of the security forces' response to the UDA in this period, and nationalist anxiety about sympathy for it among some soldiers and RUC officers was not easily allayed. The 31 July 1975 massacre of the Catholic Miami Showband pointed clearly to paramilitary links between some UDR members and the UVF and there was little to stop UDR men leaving the regiment to join either the UVF or the UDA. In 1985 the UDA appointed, only for a brief period as it turned out, a press officer who had held a commission in the UDR[36] and Andy Tyrie talked of UDR men who 'had come over to us'.[37] A 1984 issue of *Ulster* listed with pride the number of UDA life sentence prisoners in the Maze who had records of service with the security forces.[38]

Of the forty-one 'lifers' in this article, nine, it was claimed, had served in the regular army, five in the UDR, six in the Territorial Army and four in the RUC. 'These men had everything to lose and nothing to gain, by defending their country.' The author of the article went on to declare: 'To call them "criminals" is in itself criminal.'[39]

Frustration at the constraints within which the security forces found them-selves operating against the IRA could lead young Protestants into the UDA. One of them, from County Antrim, who does not want his identity to be known, talked to this author of his own experiences:

> My war started in the UDR. I joined full time when I was eighteen, to be a soldier. There was a police and army tradition in my family. They believed in law and order, they were Unionist voters and breaking the law would have been alien to them. Pay in the UDR wasn't brilliant and our lives were on the line, especially when a lot of us volunteered for a transfer to active duties in Armagh city. The IRA were really calling the shots there. I saw the bodies. On New Year's Eve 1985 we were alter-nating there with the RUC, an hour at a time on street patrols.
>
> The Provos had set a bomb to go off in a litter bin and it blew two RUC men apart. I was there when the ambulance came. It was a mess. The wife of one of them arrived in a hysterical state and we had to hold her back in case the body was booby trapped. I'll never get it out of my mind. I did three years in Armagh and I lost count of the funerals I attended. I got to the point where I'd had enough so I resigned from the regiment. I joined the UDA for revenge and to take a real war to the IRA. We thought we could do it better than the security forces and we did. I was on a lot of successful operations until I was caught. I went down on a four-teen-year sentence for illegal possession of explosives, a reduced charge from that of conspiracy to murder. I'm not ashamed of what I did but I paid a price and so did others. I had married and I put my family through six years of hell as a pris-oner. I missed years of my children's lives.[40]

Joining the UDA did not necessarily mean handling or using firearms, espe-cially in the days of its early mass membership. Some never did but those with weapons training and a willingness to use them would more often than not be recruited into the UFF. No special oath for this appears to have been required and the ex-UDR soldier whose recollections have just been quoted moved into the UFF almost as a matter of course. The UFF's emergence in June of 1973 initially confused the media in Northern Ireland as it issued its first com-muniqués claiming responsibility for a series of killings. 'Investigations by the security forces in the city's Protestant areas so far indicate that the UFF is an organisation formed by dissident UDA men,' the *Irish News* reported. It was in fact formed to hold the UDA together and avert the possibility of it being proscribed.

The *Irish News* was closer to the mark when it went on to claim that the UFF 'have been joined by a few breakaway members of other Protestant extremist organisations, including the outlawed UVF'.[41] The following day it drew closer to the truth when one of its reporters wrote that the security forces believed the UFF 'were working on instructions from the UDA command, though under a different name to protect the UDA's thin veneer

of respectability'.[42] He then retreated to his newspaper's mistaken belief in
the UFF being some kind of dissident group when in fact they were simply
UDA members who thought that a war against the IRA had to mean killing
Catholics and as many of them as possible.[43]

Killing relentlessly, without pity and often sadistically, was what the UFF
did, for the remainder of 1973 and for the three years that followed it. In each
of these years they were easily surpassed in capacity to kill by Republicans
and in 1974, 1975 and 1976 by the UVF. Then, until the end of the decade
and beyond it, there was a marked falling off in UFF and Loyalist killing as a
whole, as these figures for 'claimed' killings show:[44]

'Claimed' killings, 1973–80

	Provisional IRA	Official IRA	Other Republicans	INLA	UDA/UFF	UVF
1973	125	2	10	0	44	34
1974	129	7	13	0	41	79
1975	94	9	15	12	20	100
1976	139	1	18	5	50	71
1977	68	4	2	0	12	14
1978	60	0	2	0	2	8
1979	91	1	4	8	10	7
1980	45	0	5	8	9	4

Figures like these can never begin to describe the horror of these years, particularly in working-class areas of Belfast where murder gangs like Lennie
Murphy's Shankill Butchers, fuelled by alcohol and sectarian hatred and
under no real organisational control, dragged the conflict to some of its lowest
depths.[45] The UVF, to which Murphy and most of his gang had given a loose
allegiance, was prepared to go very public in its conception of terror as a
weapon against the IRA: 'There is only one way to control an area or ghetto
that harbours terrorists or insurgents', a magazine it controlled declared in
September 1976, 'and that is to reduce its population to fear by inflicting upon
them all the horror of terrorist warfare. Where these means cannot, for whatever reasons be used, the war is lost.'[46] The UDA would not have dissented
from this analysis.

Research into the chronology of carnage in Northern Ireland in the 1970s
and later can only be a harrowing and upsetting task. Looking for patterns to
it takes nothing from the humanity of the victims or the enduring grief of
those close to them. The contribution to it of the UDA/UFF lends itself
easily to the accusation that their targets were ordinary, mostly innocent
Catholics, swiftly identified from where they lived or worked or simply the
direction in which they were walking late at night if they risked doing that, as

all too many, especially the young, inevitably did. The belief that this was the priority of the UDA, and Loyalists more generally, is deeply ingrained within the Republican psyche and some commentators have reinforced it.

Chris Thornton, a fine journalist writing retrospectively of the Troubles, argued that of 181 victims of Loyalist and mainly UDA killing in 1972 and 1973, only one had been in the IRA. The UDA simply took over, he claimed, where the UVF had left off in 1966 after the arrest and conviction of Gusty Spence and others for the Malvern Street murder.[47] To accept his case without reservation is, of course, to come as close as makes no difference to an essentially Republican view of what drove paramilitary Loyalist violence in these awful years, but at the very least Republican sources which claim to enumerate their movement's victims need careful checking.

Along with the numerous IRA memorials which have been built and dedicated all over Northern Ireland in recent years, there is now a major published source, *Tirghra: Ireland's Patriot Dead*. The Gaelic word *tirghra* means 'love of country'. This book was launched with much ceremony at a Dublin hotel in April 2002. Specially bound and embossed copies were presented to the families of 364 IRA volunteers and Sinn Fein party activists whose names formed the roll of honour of which the book consists.[48] Over the period from the UDA's emergence to the end of 1979, the book names just two Republicans killed by the UDA/UFF, both in 1976. One of them was Colm Mulgrew, a Sinn Fein organiser in North Belfast, shot dead at his home by UDA gunmen on 5 June. The other was Maire Drumm, a charismatic speaker at IRA events and assiduous political worker for the movement. Loyalist assassins dressed as doctors shot her dead in her bed in Belfast's Mater Hospital, where she was awaiting eye surgery, on October 28.

'That was an important hit for us and good for Loyalist morale,' a UDA member has told the author. 'It was a joint UDA/UVF job, not just our boys on their own. It was carefully planned but local too. Don't forget some teams didn't even need cars, they lived so close. Drumm was taken out from the Lower Shankill. It was so close to the Mater. Jim Craig [a UDA leader shot dead in an internal power struggle in 1988, the IRA claiming the credit] tried to claim the credit for setting it up. I had to listen to him bumming and blowing about it but it wasn't true. That's just what he was like.'[49]

Mulgrew was a less significant figure than Drumm and at the inquest into his murder the coroner described him as a perfectly innocent victim of a random sectarian killing. His name did, however, later appear on Republican rolls of honour alongside those of active IRA volunteers, as well as in *Tirghra*. When his killers arrived at his home off North Belfast's Limestone Road, it was barely an hour after two Protestants had died in an IRA bomb attack on the nearby Times Bar at the junction of York Road and Mountcollyer Road.[50]

In the following month's issue of its magazine *Ulster*, the UDA was prompt in claiming that Mulgrew's Republican connections made him a legitimate Loyalist target. Under the heading 'Innocent Catholics?'[51] it names seven other Catholics killed until that point in 1976. One of them, Anthony McNeill, was found by police late on 20 June in a lane close to Alliance Avenue and near a UDA drinking club. His throat was slit, he had multiple deep knife wounds and terrible head injuries. Police evidence suggested that after drinking in the by then predominantly Catholic Ardoyne area, he had simply strayed fatally into Loyalist territory, in search of a taxi.[52] His name never appeared on any Republican memorial and Mulgrew's was the only one of those listed that did.

Even so, the *Ulster* article went on to assert: 'We can say without fear of contradiction that 98 per cent of "innocent Catholic" victims have in fact contributed, by their actual presence or giving information, to assisting the murder of Loyalists.'[53] Other reportage in a similar vein would appear in UDA statements and magazine articles over the years and to this day UDA members claim that far more of those killed by it and the UFF were part of a terrorist network than the Republican movement will ever admit, even ten years into the 'peace process'.

For the historian of events as recent as these, the problem is one of which sources can be relied on and whose personal testimony to be guided by. For the period from the UDA's emergence in 1972 to the end of the decade, *Tirghra* lists over eighty IRA volunteers, mostly inexperienced in handling explosives, who were killed by their own devices exploding prematurely. Another six are of those killed in accidental shootings and there are eleven victims of car crashes. Just three Republican deaths are attributed to the UDA/UFF, two fewer than those admitted to having been caused by the old Official IRA, from which the Provisionals split in early 1970.

From sources such as *Tirghra*, the Officials, or 'Stickies' as they became known because of their preference for stick-on Easter 1916 commemorative lilies, emerge as more effective killers of Provisionals in the 1970s. *Tirghra* attributes to them five killings of volunteers and active IRA members in the 1972–79 period, including three senior members. One of them was Seamus McCusker, the Provisionals' Northern Command intelligence officer, shot dead on 31 October 1975, and another was James Bryson. His death from wounds in late September 1973 is claimed in some accounts to have resulted from a gun battle with the army in Ballymurphy, though Officials in the area certainly regarded him as a target.[54]

To this day those active in the UDA during this period are deeply sceptical of the claims and explanations that Republicans offer about the IRA's death roll in the Troubles. 'Republicans have always been good at rubbishing Loyalists' ability to take on the IRA. It's been easy for them and they've had a fair bit of help from elements within the media.'[55] This was and is still Andy Tyrie's view. 'Ulster Protestants have always made good soldiers but bad terrorists. Conspiracy, guerrilla war, that was always a Republican tradition but we never had it. When we decided we had no choice but to take on the Provos we had to find them, target them, and that wasn't easy.'[56]

Tyrie has never denied that ordinary and often innocent Catholics were victims. 'Who started the pub attacks and the car bombs?' he asks. 'We'd created a big organisation, with increasing access to guns, full of Loyalists who were deeply afraid, whose blood was up. Yes, there was sectarian murder and I did my best to keep it under control. Don't forget, we thought the UDA's role was going to be a temporary one but of course it wasn't. We had no leadership or management training, but we killed far more IRA men than they'll ever admit. That's why it's a problem to put a figure to it.'[57]

Nevertheless, Tyrie has insisted, the UDA/UFF had their successes from early on. 'If we were so stupid, how were our boys able to enter and take over a UDR camp and clear it out of weapons?'[58] He was referring here to a series of raids on and thefts from UDR bases over a period of time between 1972 and 1987.

He takes pride too in the UDA's 'Operation Greencastle' on 8 March 1975, when the Donegal village of the same name was the target of a raid by two UDA/UFF units which crossed from their side of Lough Foyle to take their war back into the territory of the Irish Republic. Their objective was Irish trawlers in the harbour believed by Loyalist intelligence sources to be importing weapons and explosives for the IRA. Major hazards were the British army base at Magilligan, only two miles away, and also Royal Navy patrol boats operating on the lough, but the raid went ahead, led by Andy Robinson, a former Royal Marine Commando who became a UDA brigadier.[59] He now runs a bed and breakfast business in the south of Scotland, but Tyrie remembers him as 'one of our best, as good as John McMichael'.[60]

The raiding party claimed to have captured a significant cache of automatic weapons and ammunition as well as a rocket launcher and night-sights for a rifle, before using incendiary devices to set the trawlers alight. Two were destroyed and three severely damaged. An Irish police diving unit made a lengthy inspection of the hulls of other vessels in the harbour and the raid was widely reported in the Irish press along with unconfirmed claims that agents from a Soviet bloc state had been landed by submarine in Donegal to assist the IRA.[61]

In propaganda and arguably military terms Greencastle was a victory for the UDA/UFF and no lives were lost as a result of it. Yet during that year of 1975, they killed twenty people, a sharp drop from the previous two years, and in 1976 they went back on the offensive, killing another fifty victims. Against the accusation that these were mostly the defenceless and innocent, Jackie McDonald's response is:

From where we were sitting the nationalist community were the IRA's eyes and ears. Often knowingly but sometimes unwittingly they carried intelligence back into their areas that the IRA could use against us, to set up attacks. We had to hit people like that, for our own security and to warn off others. There was no choice. We would go after them if we had the information but if they strayed into our areas we saw them as suspects. It was like a spider's web. They came within our reach and they would get hit.[62]

McDonald accepts that security force operations, as well as accidental explosions, killed far more active Republicans and IRA volunteers than the UDA/UFF were able to reach. 'We needed time,' he stresses. 'We got better at finding and hitting IRA targets but they were mostly well guarded. It was never easy to get to them in their own areas.'[63] Sammy Duddy makes the same point but cites the role of the security forces too:

> The Peelers and the army on the ground could make it harder for our boys to hit targets. We knew of cases of active IRA men living in houses close to, even opposite, army and RUC bases and they never got touched. We didn't want to be shooting RUC men and British soldiers but there they were, on the ground in places where we needed to operate. It was even as if some IRA men were being protected. Yes, we sometimes thought that.[64]

Republican infiltration of government agencies and public bodies in order to gather potentially 'military' data is something else Duddy mentions as a factor in the UDA/UFF's often seemingly random killing.

> We didn't know who to trust. How could we? When you went for your dole cheque the fellow at the counter could be a 'sleeper' for the IRA, sending out details from a Loyalist area. They had a finely tuned intelligence operation. They were into computers long before us, some of their operators were geniuses. We could be sure of nothing, they infiltrated the civil service, councils, you name it. I did a piece for *Ulster* in 1987, naming an IRA 'mole' in the Holywood Road DSS office but I was pulled in for it by the RUC. They told me I could be charged with incitement to murder and that if your man was hit the rap could be complicity in murder. He was transferred to a different office quite soon. Maybe the police thought we wouldn't advertise an imminent hit. I don't know but I was pulled in by them three times in two years over stuff like that.[65]

Pressed on the ambivalence of his views on the security forces' role Duddy agrees:

> Yes, we wanted to see them really go after the Provos and we wanted to help them but they kept making it harder for us. They got no thanks for it from the Provos either, who castigated them even when they were getting protection from them. We had our successes, though, we got to more of them than they have ever admitted.[66]

This refrain in UDA recollections is thoughtfully examined in a recent book on the organisation. Its author accepts that it was to the IRA's advantage to minimise the capacity of Loyalists to eliminate active members but he also argues that the IRA would often respect the wishes of families who did not want it to be known that children, brothers or sisters had been in it. There are indeed well-documented cases of IRA volunteers keeping their activity a secret from their families and insurance companies and claims for compensation from the state could also be jeopardised if a dead volunteer's role was admitted.[67]

Even though UDA members active in these years agree that its operations killed more IRA members than the Republican movement will concede, they also accept that by the late 1970s there was a clear decline in its capacity to kill. John White has recalled that in 1978, the year he was sentenced for the murders of Senator Paddy Wilson and Irene Andrews, while the IRA claimed sixty-two lives, the UDA/UFF killed just two. 'We had completely lost the plot. A lot of that was down to the police and special branch. They had amassed a frightening amount of intelligence on us, closing down nearly all of our operations.'[68]

Duddy agrees with his viewpoint but offers a broader explanation of the falling off in operations:

> UDA commanders were mostly unemployed men. They had to be because it was a full-time job. People in work couldn't do it. We grew so fast in those days. There was never a formal system of payment but it was accepted that commanders could draw a percentage of the funds we raised. Some, never Andy Tyrie, mind, took a lot more than they were entitled to and it began to show: new cars, holidays in Spain. The RUC weren't stupid. They knew that if they leant hard enough on a brigade or unit area, lifted commanders and took them to Castlereagh a few times the level of activity would drop. And they had their informers too. We were well infiltrated.[69]

Another factor was Tyrie's belief that the UDA had done enough sectarian killing of Catholics. 'Most of that was because of the amount of autonomy brigade and unit areas had in the early days. It was an eye for an eye, a Catholic for every Protestant, but it was taking us nowhere,'[70] he has told the author. 'I was sickened every time I heard about the death of a Catholic taxi driver or shopkeeper. We wanted to go for the IRA and republicans but we couldn't locate them, we didn't know who they were. The bottom line was that if the IRA killed us, some of us were going to kill them.'[71] 'Them' in this context clearly means ordinary Catholics but Tyrie was clear that at the risk of radically reducing the organisation's rate of killing, 'we needed to go for real high-profile hits. We'd got too defence minded, we needed to go on the attack.'[72]

Tyrie agrees with Duddy's analysis of the UDA's operational problems and identifies Tommy Lyttle in particular as an impediment to attacking and eliminating 'real' Republican targets. Lyttle, who died in 1995, is widely known to have been a police informer, though he served on the UDA's Inner Council with Tyrie and became West Belfast brigadier until his arrest in 1990 under the Stevens inquiry into alleged collusion between the security forces and paramilitary Loyalists.

> He helped blunt the cutting edge I wanted to achieve through a real overhaul of our organisation. He just didn't want the risks involved if we got some high-profile hits against the Provos and people who provided back-up for them.[73]

Tyrie also wanted the UDA to be associated with some serious political thinking and 1978 had seen the publication of *Beyond the Religious Divide*, followed
three years later by the formation of a UDA-backed political party (see
Chapter 3). By the start of 1979, however, there was a much greater likelihood
of Republicans seizing the political initiative due to a worsening crisis in
Northern Ireland's prison system. This had arisen from the government
policy to phase out 'special category' status for paramilitary prisoners. John
McMichael, promoted by Tyrie to the rank of South Belfast brigadier, was
quick to see the potential political momentum which Republicanism could
build from the prison issue and took the view that the UDA/UFF should
target prominent activists in the prisoners' support campaign.

Like other Ulster Loyalists, McMichael was also enraged by the apparent
ease with which, on 30 March 1979, the Irish National Liberation Army had
assassinated Airey Neave, Margaret Thatcher's shadow Secretary of State for
Northern Ireland. A hardliner on security policy in the province, Neave had
retained links with MI6, which he had joined during the Second World War.
His death appears to have been a one-off operation by INLA supporters who,
once they had wired up his car with a powerful bomb, were allowed to fade
into obscurity by the organisation.[74] Many in the Irish Republican Socialist
Party, i.e. the INLA's political arm, and others associated with it were known
supporters of the demands of Republican prisoners on the H-blocks of the
Maze. McMichael's view was that they should be targeted for this as well as
for Neave's murder.

The first victim was John Turnly, a member of the National H-Blocks
Committee. His family were landowners in County Antrim and he had been
a British army officer before becoming drawn to Irish nationalism. He joined
the SDLP and was later a founder member of the small Irish Independence
Party. On 4 June 1980, he was shot nine times, in the presence of his Japanese
wife and two small children, by UDA gunmen who had driven into the coastal
village of Carnlough, where he was to address a meeting. Four UDA men
from the Larne area were charged later with Turnly's murder, three of whom
received life sentences. A fourth was given a lesser twelve-year sentence for
manslaughter. One of the convicted, Robert McConnell, told the court after
the verdict that he had worked for the SAS and he named a sergeant and corporal who he claimed had provided him with the weapon he had used in the
killing. Whether he hoped for a reduced sentence or made his claims as part
of a UDA strategy to claim state support, and thus a degree of legitimacy for
Turnly's killing, remains problematic.[75]

The fact that RUC officers and detectives admitted at the trial that they had
followed orders to destroy, because of their 'sensitivity', notes of interviews
with McConnell's brother Eric, also convicted, fuelled suspicions of some
form of state involvement. In fact, Turnly, who made no secret of his politics
and was well known locally, was not a particularly difficult target. This was
not true of the Queen's University lecturer in Social and Economic History,

Dr Miriam Daly, who was killed just six days later in the Republican stronghold of Andersonstown in West Belfast, where she lived with her family. She was on the National H-Blocks Committee and had also briefly been a member of the IRSP but had left it over the issue of its relationship to its military wing, the INLA. On a speaking tour of the United States in 1976 she declared that, in her view, the IRA were fighting British imperialism in the only way they could. From the UDA's point of view, she had made herself a target. Some UDA members still believe she had been involved in Neave's death but the *Irish Times* claimed that her husband Jim was the real target.[76]

Daly's killing was professionally carried out. Her killers entered and took over her house after a period of heavy military activity in the area. They cut the telephone line and tied her up while they waited for her husband to return home. When he failed to arrive, they used a pillow to muffle the sound of the shots they drilled into her. They left her where she was, still tied up and in a pool of blood, for her children to find when they came back from school. She was given a paramilitary funeral, with INLA gunmen in masks firing shots over her coffin, and her name is still on the organisation's memorial in Milltown cemetery. No specific claim to this killing was made at the time by the UDA/UFF though they had issued generalised threats to the H-block support campaign as a whole.

One account declares that the Daly killing 'had an SAS look' to it and belief in special forces involvement has also persisted over two further killings of Republicans in October 1980. At around one o'clock on the morning of 15 October, two masked men sledgehammered their way into a house deep within the Andersonstown area and not, like Daly's, situated on a main road. The gunmen knew exactly who they were looking for and in which upstairs rooms to find them. Their victims were both heavily involved in the IRSP. The widow of one of them, Queen's University graduate and former teacher Ronnie Bunting, recalled the precision and professionalism of the killers' movements as they shot her husband and then his friend, Noel Lyttle, who was sleeping in the same room as their infant son. As they retreated down the stairs she struggled with one of them but the other man, despite this, was able to shoot her accurately in the arm and upper body. She was shot again in the face by the first man once he had shaken her off and she remained on the critical list in hospital for forty-eight hours before she began a slow recovery.[77]

Neighbours alarmed by the noise and the hysterical crying of the Buntings' two older children called the RUC, who found a gruesome scene. One former detective sergeant, Johnston Brown, has admitted that he was for some time convinced that a special army unit or even the SAS had been at work. He later abandoned that belief in the light of information which came to him about John McMichael's influence within the UDA:

> Sure, those fellows were good. It was precision stuff. They knew exactly what they were there for. It was military drill, just as Bunting's widow said. I've never forgotten

going into the other room to take a close-up look at Lyttle. He'd obviously tried to haul on his trousers. Strange, he might have had a slim chance if he'd gone through the window without them. Anyway, they had given him what scene of crime police called a 'third eye'. One bullet was neatly drilled into his head, just above the nose.[78]

This sequence of killings was certainly seen by the UDA as decapitating the INLA/IRSP by going for its political and intellectual nerve centre. The organisation indeed never recovered its cohesion and some writers on British counter-insurgency in Northern Ireland clung to the view that British special forces were operating in collusion with the UDA or were simply dealing out reprisals on their own for Neave's assassination.[79] Others see the UDA's role in this period simply as an application of the 'counter-gang' strategy previously tested in British colonies against local dissidents and guerrillas. In this interpretation, the UDA would operate within parameters set out for it by state intelligence agencies.

> Since McMichael was never charged with murder but, on the contrary, was continually paraded on the British media, the logical conclusion is that he himself was a British agent brought up through the ranks and available to bring a lull or cull to the murder of Catholics if the general political situation so required. Such agents are always expendable.[80]

This is the view set out in one study of SAS operations in the province by an author who claims that McMichael 'had earned his pips on the ground by personally killing three Catholics'.[81] Since the writer's sympathies are clearly nationalist, it may of course also be purely a restatement of the opinion that in order to succeed, Loyalist paramilitary operations had to have the support of the 'secret state'.

UDA members will now readily admit that their organisation carried out these killings and that McMichael co-ordinated them, nor do they dissent from Martin Dillon's belief that the killers were exceptionally well briefed.

> McMichael privately confessed to associates that the squads were professionally trained and had access to good intelligence, and that he had contacts within the RUC and UDR who kept him informed of the whereabouts of targets and when necessary would provide information about security forces' movements in areas prior to and following an assassination.[82]

McMichael was to take many secrets with him to an early grave. Always affable and helpful to interviewers, he was also clearly a ruthless man, whose rise within the UDA would certainly not have been assisted by a disinclination to kill. Those who were close to him in the UDA still have little except praise for his role. 'I decided John should be overall military commander. I assigned that title to him,' Andy Tyrie recalls. 'He was tasked to set up and co-ordinate all our major operations and that's exactly what he did, while carrying on his political role, which he was extremely good at. We needed a real cutting edge as a Loyalist strike force and John gave us that. He was a political soldier, the best I could have had working for us. We trusted each other totally. There was a problem, though, because the power his position gave him was resented in some of our brigade areas.'[83]

Jackie McDonald was active in the UDA's South Belfast brigade and was close to McMichael, acting for a time as one of his bodyguards.

> John's role was crucial, he was the best but he didn't run a one-man show. A collective decision back then was needed for us to get our act together, to get away from tit-for-tat stuff and to go for the real enemy. We needed better intelligence and the Inner Council and Brigade staffs were sometimes meeting three times a week to set things up. Things got close to a rota system once our intelligence improved; all our brigades and units wanted a share of the action.[84]

Sammy Duddy remembers the period in very similar terms:

> John was the man, he was ideal for a role that was military and political. His contacts were second to none. Thanks to him we got some top hits. It all got almost competitive to the point where the Inner Council would assign operations or 'sanctions' as they were sometimes called. The location of a target could determine which unit would do a hit. There could be months of surveillance first but there had to be co-operation with and from the units based closest to the target. John used a nucleus of no more than nine operators. Ray Smallwoods was one of the best of them.[85]

Smallwoods later became a very competent political spokesman for the UDA and the Ulster Democratic Party. He was shot dead by the IRA on 11 July 1994.

Operations could still go wrong. One of them, which earned Smallwoods a lengthy prison sentence, was the attempt to kill Bernadette McAliskey, the former MP for Mid-Ulster and civil rights activist who had given very public support to the demands of the Republican H-block prisoners. The attack which was carried out on her home near Coalisland in County Tyrone caused severe injuries to McAliskey and her husband. They survived, due to the prompt arrival of a Parachute Regiment patrol who gave them first aid as well as apprehending the three-man UFF unit which had been assigned to the operation. A cartoon celebrating a near miss against the 'witch's lair' appeared in *Ulster* magazine[86] and McDonald, who was held and questioned about it by the RUC for seven days, has subsequently said: 'The attack would be seen as a failure but it was one hell of an effort.'[87] John McMichael thought so too and made a point of being in court when Smallwoods and his associates were convicted.

Inevitable questions were asked in the nationalist community about why an army unit close enough to the scene to block off the attackers' escape route and give medical help to the victims could not also have prevented the attack. This is Duddy's recollection from information he received at the time:

> Everything was set up, the getaway vehicle was there, the house's telephone was cut but John knew something had gone wrong, but there were informers on our own

Inner Council: Tommy Lyttle and Jim Craig and another one, too. Major hits were discussed in their presence. The army knew about that one, no question.[88]

Duddy recalled McMichael's unease in the aftermath of the failed attack on Bernadette McAliskey: 'John was uneasy but it wasn't the right time for him to make a move. The tension was there. You could sense it. It was a power struggle in the making, a deadly business as it turned out.'[89]

An even more dramatic near miss came three years later, when a 'sanction' was set up against the Sinn Fein president and MP for West Belfast, Gerry Adams. 'The boys were practically queuing up for the chance to do that one,' McDonald recalls. 'There was a risk involved in it too, no question, because we knew the IRA would hit back, not just at us but against the Protestant community. What was important was that we had to get the signal to them that we could reach their top man, that he wasn't fireproof. South-East Antrim Brigade got the job in the end.'[90]

Adams's own account of how he survived the attempt on his life is a graphic one. After attending court in the centre of Belfast in a minor public order case, he was in a taxi with bodyguards and colleagues heading for the Falls Road when the gunmen drew level with them in another vehicle. 'The car window came in around me. I felt the thumps and thuds as the bullets struck home. The crack of the gunfire came after. Everything was in slow motion,' Adams has recalled. His antennae, he has said, had been 'screaming danger, danger. Jesus, Joseph and Mary, I give you my heart and my soul . . . I mouthed the prayers we had been taught in childhood while the car windows and upholstery exploded around me.'[91] Adams was hit and seriously injured by five of the shots fired into the taxi and needed emergency surgery at the Royal Victoria Hospital.

John Gregg, one of the three-man team assigned to the attempt to kill Adams, always believed that the security forces had been alerted to it:

It's still a big regret of mine that we didn't do the job and finish him off. It was all set up and we were a good team but we were set up too. There were just too many coincidences.[92]

Duddy shares Gregg's view.

They were set up, no mistake about it. The UDR had an intelligence officer up in Rathcoole, working from high up in a big block of flats with a view of the whole area. We reckoned he had cameras, binoculars, the lot. He probably clocked big Grugg [Gregg's nickname] and the team who were to do the hit. They had help too from one of our own, a UDA commander in the area. We never got to him. He's still around, living outside Belfast in the country.[93]

Even so, Gregg and his accomplices came close to what would have been a hugely prestigious kill for a UDA whose success rate had been minimal over the previous two years. He later told Michael Stone in prison that he had deliberately avoided using a semi-automatic machine gun or a high-velocity rifle because rounds fired from them could easily have passed clean through Adams's body and killed or wounded anyone else in the line of fire. One of his revolver rounds in fact hit Adams in the neck and Gregg recalled his victim rising out of his seat, pushing his head and neck as far into the car roof as he could, leaving just his upper body exposed: 'Gregg's choice of weapons saved Gerry Adams' life that day, purely because he wanted to reduce civilian casualties.'[94]

The UDA's *Ulster* magazine had no reservations about acclaiming Gregg and the two other members of the South-East Antrim unit. Adams, it declared, had been shot 'as a soldier in the conflict' and it went on to assert 'pride that young men are still prepared to sacrifice everything to do what every Ulster Protestant felt like doing' and questioned 'whether the IRA can really believe that Ulster Protestants are forever going to allow themselves to be shot like fish in a barrel without responding.'[95] On the conviction, the following year, of Gregg, Colin Gray and Gerry Welsh, the magazine lauded them as 'national heroes who deserved Victoria Crosses'.[96]

The failed attempts to kill Adams and McAliskey along with the 1980 murders of prominent H-block campaigners and INLA supporters stand out in a period within which the UDA/UFF appeared to many to have lost its cutting edge. Airey Neave's biographer attributes its limited successes in 1980 primarily to the role of British undercover forces co-ordinating Loyalist operations against 'soft' Republican targets in order to satisfy the new Prime Minister, Margaret Thatcher.[97] This is also the view taken in a major book on SAS operations on Northern Ireland in this period[98] but both are influenced by a belief that Loyalists by definition needed the state machine behind them to operate at all.

This mindset is of course the product of a simplistic and one-dimensional view of Loyalism amongst people who see Northern Ireland's conflict as nothing more than an anti-imperialist struggle. It ignores the variegated nature of and class tensions within Loyalism and where an organisation like the UDA is concerned, it needs to deny it any capacity for autonomous action either politically or in a paramilitary context.[99]

Another study of British undercover operations in the late 1970s and into the following decade takes a sceptical view of what the UDA accomplished, as it does of claims of a structure of collusion between its gunmen and the security forces. 'Despite the Adams incident it must be noted that if ever anybody in the intelligence world did commission Loyalist terrorists to kill senior IRA figures, they failed to do so,'[100] and its author argues that from 1977 until 1987 the IRA executed more of its own members for informing than were ever eliminated by the UDA or Loyalists in general.

In the early 1980s, in spite of some of the claims made within the UDA for John McMichael's role, it simply had not resumed killing at a rate likely to force any change in government thinking about the organisation's legal status.

On 5 January 1987, a year in which the UDA did in fact significantly step up its killings, Mr B. A. Blackwell, a civil servant in the Northern Ireland Office's Law and Order Division, made the point that the position under the law of all paramilitary bodies was kept under constant review. He added:

> While individual members of the UDA have been convicted of acts of terrorism, it is not itself a terrorist organisation. Sinn Fein is similarly not proscribed, despite its close relationship with and open support for the IRA. The fact that membership of an organisation is not illegal does not, however, confer any immunity from prosecution on its members if they commit criminal acts.[101]

The two years prior to this memorandum had seen very limited operational activity by the UDA/UFF, though the maverick gunman Michael Stone had become active again in circumstances about which, as will be discussed later, he has given contradictory accounts in press interviews and in his memoirs. He now claims to have accepted in court the responsibility for killings he did not carry out in order to protect other Loyalists but he was certainly the killer, on 16 November 1984, of Paddy Brady, a West Belfast milkman and Sinn Fein activist claimed by the UDA to also be an IRA intelligence officer.[102]

Another decision by the UDA's leadership at this time was to promote the former Black Watch soldier Brian Nelson to the rank of intelligence officer. It took time for the Inner Council to suspect his double role as an informer working for the army's highly secretive Force Research Unit. With Tommy Lyttle and at least two other Inner Council members already feeding information to the RUC Special Branch and possibly army intelligence as well, it is unsurprising that there was no immediate move against Nelson. Andy Tyrie has recently described how he started to have his doubts about Nelson but points out that Lyttle's role was a bigger concern:

> I assigned him the job of doing surveillance on Pat Finucane [the nationalist lawyer later killed by the UFF in 1989]. One of his offices was down near Cromac Square and I wanted Tommy to check all movements into and out of it. We had our suspicions of Finucane but Tommy didn't want to be involved. He told me he was afraid he'd be hit in retaliation, because he was a brigadier, if our boys took out Finucane.[103]

'Taking out' any targets by the mid-1980s had become a problem for the UDA because of the role of informers within it such as Lyttle, as well as infiltration of its membership by RUC and army agents.

> Guns were doctored so that they failed to fire during operations, safe houses were kept under surveillance, operations were patently set up by the security forces so that UDA/UFF men could be apprehended en route to or returning from them. Elements within the security forces were clearly determined to put the UDA out of business.[104]

Tyrie and McMichael were well aware of this, as well as of the lavish lifestyles enjoyed by some commanders and Inner Council members who were disinclined to compromise their positions by sanctioning high-risk operations. In 1985, however, they took one major initiative, which was to form the Ulster Defence Force (UDF). Its remit was to give selected UDA members intensive and specialised training in fieldcraft, military tactics and intelligence-gathering, as well as the use of weapons and explosives. Golden wings inscribed with the words 'Sans Peur' were issued to those who completed their training over a fixed number of weekends. Regular articles and photographs appeared in *Ulster* on the UDF's progress and its recruiting posters were widely distributed in Loyalist areas.

Tyrie still takes pride in the work done by the UDF and the quality of its instructors.

> We needed and we got ex-soldiers, plenty of them, especially former senior NCOs, to organise the training. We made mistakes too. We took on one former UDR captain who had been to Trinity College, Dublin as well as Sandhurst, but we soon realised he was on the take, embezzling funds and using our name to try to buy a new BMW car on HP. We even let him do press work for a short time until we found out about him. He lasted about six weeks with us.[105]

Ulster magazine stressed that there would be no mass recruitment to the UDF until the time was right and claimed it was the nucleus of a 'new Loyalist army at the ready'. It wrote too of financial support for the UDF from 'a sophisticated network of legal businesses'[106] which was making possible ambitious training programmes. Tyrie still declines to speak in any detail about these sources but he does insist that a new breed of young militants gained from their UDF training and emerged after 1989 as the gunmen who restored to the UFF's West Belfast C Company its ferocious reputation.

Tyrie has always insisted that the UDF was a success but that success brought its own problems because 'once we got some of the young hotheads off the streets, and in some cases out of real trouble, and gave them their training, they came out of it straining at the leash. It wasn't easy to keep control of some of them.'[107] Many of them did indeed go through UDF training and wanted to follow it up right away with the real business of killing. One of these was William 'Mo' Courtney, who is at the time of writing in Maghaberry prison, charged with the murder in late May 2003 of another UDA activist, Allan McCullough. In conversation with the broadcaster Peter Taylor, he recalled the frustration of young and militant recruits who went through their UDF training only to be restrained from attacks on the nationalist community: 'The hierarchy people upstairs seemed to be holding us back. They were holding the reins. They didn't want the shootings and the bombings.'[108] Courtney's judgement was correct in its essentials and he also voiced his resentment at the comfortable lifestyles of most of the 1980s leaders. It is unlikely that he had Tyrie and McMichael in mind, but they certainly saw the

UDF's role in relation to a longer-term Loyalist strategy rather than using it for immediate attacks on Catholics.

The UDF was formed in April 1985 in anticipation of the Anglo-Irish Agreement and its existence could be used as a way to convince Loyalists, especially young ones, that the UDA was serious about an ultimate trial of strength with the British government. A huge effort was in fact committed by the UDA to the campaign against the Agreement once it was signed in November. This campaign, as has been shown earlier, included often violent street protests as well as strike action and co-ordinated attacks on RUC officers' homes through 1986 and into 1987.

The early months of that year were dominated by a brutal feud within the INLA which claimed many lives, but on 8 May the IRA suffered its worst single reverse in the conflict when an entire eight-man unit was wiped out by the SAS in a carefully prepared ambush at Loughall, County Armagh. Apart from the shooting dead of Larry Marley by the UVF at his Ardoyne home on 3 April, Loyalists had achieved no successes against the IRA at the time of the Loughall operation, though in February a UDA/UFF unit had set off some fire bombs in central Dublin.

The SAS liquidated the entire core of the East Tyrone IRA at Loughall, but the UDA's reaction was to attribute the operation to the British state's desire to avenge the IRA's murder of Lord Justice Maurice Gibson, one of Northern Ireland's senior judges. He was killed in his car with his wife by a huge IRA landmine planted close to the Irish border at Killeen, County Down, on 25 April. 'There is no significance in Loughall in terms of a new security policy,' *Ulster* magazine declared. 'There is no new security policy. There has been no tightening of the border, neither has there been an increased security presence inside Ulster as numerous shootings since Loughall have testified. It is not in the interests of our English masters to defeat the IRA. The "acceptable" level of violence is just as acceptable now as it was in 1971. What the authorities have showed by their Loughall action is that the IRA can murder as many "ordinary" people as they wish, but if they as much as touch the colonial establishment, or make England look foolish, they will be swiftly rebuked.'[109]

The phrasing of this response to Loughall was revealing. Talk of 'our English masters' and the 'colonial establishment' traditionally came from Republicans but the UDA's recourse to it was a reminder of its growing distrust of British intentions since the Anglo-Irish Agreement and of its relaunching of Ulster self-government as a policy in the *Common Sense* document which it had brought out at the start of the year. That is the article's real significance, rather than its explanation of the Loughall ambush, which took much longer to set up than the two weeks which had followed Gibson's death.[110]

The year had started badly for the UDA. Early in March, 23-year-old Lorraine McCausland, a separated mother of two, was found by police half naked and face down in a stream near a Loyalist club in the Tyndale area of North Belfast. She had been battered to death with a slab of concrete and was not the first Protestant woman to have been the victim of UDA justice for some real or imagined transgression against the organisation.[111] A few week later another Protestant from the same area died a very similar death. He was Hugh McFarlane, who had got caught up in a fight in the Ballysillan Arms, a pub on the Upper Crumlin Road frequented by UDA men.[112]

Episodes like these, with their evidence of heavy drinking and gratuitous brutality, were not calculated to do anything for the UDA's image at a time when Tyrie was wanting to review the organisation's whole structure as well as to associate it with the positive political thinking of the *Common Sense* document. The leadership also wanted it to resume an offensive role against the Republican enemy and in fact its gunmen went back to work between late May and the end of the year, killing a total of six victims. Michael Stone still claims that one of these, Dermot Hackett, a bread delivery driver in County Tyrone shot dead by the UFF on 23 May, was an IRA intelligence officer and that, at his trial in 1989, he made a plea of guilty for Hackett's killing to protect a teenage Loyalist linked wrongly to it by the RUC.[113]

Hackett's family continue to deny that he was in the IRA. One of the UDA's victims who had been actively involved in it and interned in 1971 was Francisco Notarantonio, aged sixty-six, shot dead at his Ballymurphy home on 9 October 1987. His killing is now thought to have been set up by Brian Nelson to divert the UDA from a much more important target, Frederico Scappatici, a highly placed security forces informer within the IRA whom it was state policy to protect. The gunman, assigned his first killing by the UDA/UFF, was Sam 'Skelly' McCrory, who went to live in the west of Scotland after his release from a prison sentence under the terms of the 1998 Belfast Agreement.[114]

Other UDA/UFF attacks in these months came close to killing known Republicans. Alex Maskey, elected four years earlier to be Belfast's first Sinn Fein councillor, was lucky to survive a shotgun attack at his home in Gartree Gardens, West Belfast, in June, and Brendan Quinn, a Sinn Fein activist, had also narrowly missed death in a gun attack in North Belfast the previous month.

These attacks and murders were overshadowed by the carnage caused at Enniskillen on 8 November, when the IRA detonated a powerful bomb at the town's war memorial as people assembled for the annual Remembrance Sunday ceremony. This savage blow at the very heart of Unionist Ulster created immediate fear of a ferocious Loyalist backlash but this did not materialise, partly because of the impact of an emotional appeal by Gordon Wilson, the father of one of the victims, that there be no reprisals. There was, however, one revenge killing, the day after the Enniskillen bomb, in which UDA/UFF gunmen mistook the identity of a target and shot dead nineteen-year-old Adam Lambert, a Protestant student on a work placement at a West Belfast building site.[115]

Even before Enniskillen, there was unease within the UDA over what seemed to many its faltering response to IRA terror. Very few high-profile

Republican targets had been successfully attacked during the year and there
was sceptical reaction to claims made for operations such as the one in Belfast's
New Lodge area in August 1987, when a three-man UDA unit abseiled on to
the roof of the Artillery Flats to capture an Irish tricolour and take it back to
the Loyalist stronghold of Ballysillan.[116] There were uncorroborated press
reports around the same time of a UDA plot to assassinate the Irish Taoiseach,
Charles Haughey. Tyrie was dismissive of them and denied that Haughey was
even a priority target for the organisation.[117]

The following month Tyrie gave a robust defence of the UDA's role in an
Ulster interview, though he clung to the fiction of the UFF's 'separate identity'
from the UDA and pledged 'moral support in their strategic and non-sectarian
campaign against Republican terrorists'.[118] Not everyone was convinced, least
of all the contributor of an article to the magazine's November issue, a UDA
activist in the Lisburn area who had worked closely with John McMichael.
Writing under the alias of 'Rosetta', he was highly critical of the way the UDA's
operations had become confined to Belfast and to the north and west of the
city when Loyalists in Londonderry, South Down, Armagh and right along the
border were under constant threat. Far too many operations were, he argued,
being aborted through poor security and, he implied, forewarning of the police
and army. A close look at all members had become essential, 'especially those
who are guilty of loose talk and too much alcohol'.[119]

Rosetta's strictures were aimed at the UVF as well but his prime target was
the UDA, which, he urged, must carry out a major reshuffling of battalion
staff if it was to resume an offensive role. Was it, he sarcastically asked, about
to go into hibernation for another winter? As the second anniversary of the
Anglo-Irish Agreement drew near, Loyalists were at a crossroads. They could
either entrust the war against the IRA to the army and the police or seize the
initiative themselves: 'Sadly the security forces are unable and the politicians
unwilling, to really smash the Republican movement. It is high time Loyalist
security forces took a hand.'[120] As events would show, there was support for
Rosetta's wake-up call to the UDA but he had issued it at a sensitive time for
the organisation. In August, a programme in the television series *The Cook
Report* had made dramatic allegations about racketeering and extortion
carried out by the UDA. Roger Cook, impersonating a building contractor,
was filmed paying money under threat to Eddie Sayers, a mid-Ulster Inner
Council member of the UDA. This was later used as evidence to convict
Sayers but the programme also named Jim Craig as a major co-ordinator and
beneficiary of multiple protection operations in West Belfast. This was not
news to the UDA and at the time of Craig's death the following year, a highly
knowledgeable Belfast reporter wrote that by 1984 he was collecting payments
from seventy-two Belfast firms.[121]

Craig grew up in the Shankill area and had acquired a criminal record when
the Troubles started. His involvement in them earned him a period in prison
during which he formed close contacts with the UDA, for a time taking charge

of its prisoners in Crumlin Road gaol and later in the Maze. It has been recalled that he maintained his authority with a heavy hammer which he would use to smash the fingers of troublemakers.[122] On his release in 1976, his rise within the UDA continued, taking him into its Inner Council, but he also became a prime suspect of C13, the RUC's anti-racketeering squad. Their task was a hard one. A major case against Craig collapsed in 1985 after he had identified from the dock even heavily disguised witnesses for the prosecution. The author can remember seeing him shortly after this, celebrating with his minders in a pub in the centre of Belfast.

This acquittal encouraged him to show off his wealth even more flamboyantly. He is reputed to have invited senior RUC officers to a lavish wedding reception for his daughter and could turn on charm as readily as he could convey menace. The author Sally Belfrage wrote of him as

> the most personally powerful man I had ever met, with an air of animal force that inspired awe at the idea of its ever being let loose. He was also as drunk as I had seen anyone in my life who could still more or less negotiate a sentence and a sequence of steps.[123]

She met him at an 11 July party at the UDA's East Belfast HQ and was in due course propositioned by him. He does not appear to have taken her refusal amiss and later lurched to a microphone as midnight drew near to lead the company in 'The Sash'.

Despite this ritualistic profession of Loyalist allegiance, Craig had a network of contacts with Republicans, some of which dated back to his time as a prisoner. He was not averse to using and expanding these contacts in order to divide up territory for protection purposes but suspicions grew that, in return for financial favours, he was feeding information to both the IRA and the INLA. He was linked in the minds of many in the UDA to a sequence of IRA killings of leading Loyalists in the 1980s in North and West Belfast. These involved Lennie Murphy, leader of the notorious Shankill Butchers gang loosely affiliated to the UVF, who was killed in 1982; Billy McCullough, a UDA commander killed in 1981; and John Bingham and William 'Frenchy' Marchant, both senior UVF figures, shot dead in 1986 and 1987 respectively.

These suspicions could not be immediately substantiated but Craig was ordered off the Shankill Road by the Inner Council, with some of whose members his relations had become antagonistic. McMichael appears to have backed this decision though he had also accepted a substantial sum of money from Craig to restore the struggling financial position of the Admiral Benbow pub in Lisburn, which he owned. There was no acrimony, it would appear, between himself and Craig comparable to that felt for him by Tommy Lyttle, who blamed him for making his daughter pregnant. But being put 'off the road' did not stop Craig operating elsewhere and McMichael's South Belfast brigade allowed him to continue 'fund-raising' in their area.

Jackie McDonald was later convicted, along with three other UDA members, for extorting money under threat. South Belfast was his area and a court heard him on tape saying: 'The only way that anybody in our sort of business can survive is if witnesses don't go into the jury box. They just don't get there.'[124] Craig was dead by then, but McDonald has readily admitted to working with him while expressing regret for not seeing sooner that his personal greed was far greater than his loyalty to the cause of Ulster.[125]

In autumn 1987, the Inner Council agreed to set up an inquiry into Craig's activities. Some think that, whatever the nature of McMichael's own relationship to Craig, he had been shaken by the damage resulting from *The Cook Report*. He gave orders for Craig's movements and contacts to be monitored but Andy Tyrie thinks he was becoming careless about his own personal security:

> He was a prime target for the Provos, he had a brain, that was enough for them, and he gave us a public face that the media liked. Their view also was that he must have sanctioned the 1984 attack that nearly killed Gerry Adams, so they had him in their sights. John was in demand, he liked it and he liked the limelight and he played up to it. He told me how he used to practise his replies to likely interview questions in front of a mirror. I kept telling him to be careful but he liked a social life, he liked being seen.[126]

On the night of 22 December 1987, McMichael's eighteen-year-old son Gary was with friends at a packed rock concert in Belfast's Ulster Hall. The band performing was Stiff Little Fingers. Some way into the event a note was passed to the lead singer, who announced Gary's name and said he was to phone home. Gary McMichael later said that he knew at once what had happened.

> That night my father had been going out with some turkeys to take to Loyalist prisoners' families for Christmas. Even though he'd been warned that an IRA unit had come up the week before to get him he didn't take security precautions. That night he was going to take along my half-brother Saul, who was three, but he changed his mind.[127]

In fact, he had been away from home for two weeks, as his wife told the inquest, but he returned on the evening of the 23rd to take out his car. The IRA unit, led by Sean Savage, who was shot dead barely three months later by the SAS on Gibraltar, had fitted a powerful bomb underneath the vehicle, timed to explode as soon as the ignition was switched on. It inflicted terrible injuries on McMichael, who died in the ambulance which came for him.

His funeral in Lisburn was a big event attended by both Unionist politicians and members of the SDLP. Three thousand mourners, many in UDA combat kit, marched through the town behind the coffin and at the burial service the Rev. Canon R. H. Lowry described McMichael as having been 'a man of great intelligence and ability, a man of great kindness and one who had been working towards peace'.[128] An even more generous tribute was paid by Cardinal Tomas O'Fiaich, Archbishop of Armagh and Primate of Ireland, who called him 'untiring, fresh and constructive and ready to cross the religious divide to find a solution for Northern Ireland'.[129]

These were fair acknowledgements of his attempts to find a political road for Loyalism and his active support for the *Common Sense* document published earlier in the year. John McMichael, however, as his son Gary has said, was no saint.[130] He had literally 'called the shots' as a UDA brigadier and Inner Council member and in his time been active in measures of intimidation to force Catholics out of his home town. He had willingly ridden two horses, the political and the paramilitary. In the situation as it then existed in Northern Ireland this was perhaps, to quote the Clydeside socialist Jimmy Maxton, the only way for him to stay in the circus at all.

An Phoblacht, in whose pages the IRA had been quick to claim responsibility for the 'execution' of McMichael, describing him as the UFF's military commander, poured scorn on the tributes to him. Reading them, it declared, any outsider 'would have been led to believe that his life's work was the *Common Sense* document and that he never had any involvement in the murkier side of Loyalism: the Ghandi [*sic*] of Six County politics had been murdered'.[131] *An Phoblacht* went on to admit that the *Observer* and the Dublin-based *Sunday Tribune* had, in fact, raised major questions about McMichael's paramilitary role. Whether the IRA had really acted alone or without help from inside the UDA added to the divisions within the UDA at the end of a year in which its political campaign against the Anglo-Irish Agreement had reached a cul-de-sac, its 'operational' role against the IRA had faltered, and, in the most public way, it had been accused of blatant racketeering.

NOTES

1. A. Calderwood, interview with author, 7 July 2003.
2. *Irish News*, 7 January 1980.
3. Calderwood, interview with author.
4. Ibid.
5. Ibid.
6. D. Hamill, *Pig in the Middle: the Army in Northern Ireland 1969–1984* (London: Methuen, 1985), p. 126.
7. S. Bruce, *The Red Hand: Protestant Paramilitaries in Northern Ireland* (Oxford: Oxford University Press, 1992), pp. 60–1.
8. *An Phoblacht/Republican News*, 31 October, 2002.
9. W. Whitelaw, *The Whitelaw Memoirs* (London: Aurum Press, 1989), pp. 123–6.
10. Ibid.
11. Ibid.
12. A Tyrie, interview with author, 3 December 2002.
13. Bruce, *Red Hand*, pp. 61–2. See also Hamill, *Pig in the Middle*, pp. 108–10.
14. *Sunday Times*, 28 January 1973.
15. *Sunday Times*, 21 May 1972.
16. Ibid.

17. Ibid.
18. *Sunday Times*, 28 January 1973.
19. A. Clarke, *Contact* (London: Secker and Warburg, 1983).
20. D. McKittrick, S. Kelters, B. Feeney and C. Thornton, *Lost Lives: The Stories of the Men, Women and Children Who Died as a Result of Northern Ireland's Troubles* (Edinburgh: Mainstream, 1999), pp. 261–2.
21. Ibid., p. 263.
22. C Ryder, *The Ulster Defence Regiment: An Instrument of Peace?* (London: Methuen, 1991), pp. 57–8.
23. McKittrick *et al.*, *Lost Lives*, p. 1475.
24. J. Holland, *Hope against History: The Ulster Conflict* (London: Coronet, 1999).
25. S. Phoenix and J. Holland, *Phoenix: Policing the Shadows – the Secret War against Terrorism in Northern Ireland* (London, Hodder and Stoughton, 1996), p. 235. See also Chapter 1 of this book.
26. *United Irishman*, August 1972.
27. M. Stone, *None Shall Divide Us* (London: John Blake, 2003), pp. 34–5.
28. T. Parker, *May the Lord in His Mercy Be Kind to Belfast* (London: Jonathan Cape, 1993) p. 319.
29. K. Livingstone, *Livingstone's Labour: A Programme for the Nineties* (London: Unwin Hyman, 1988), pp. 128–30.
30. Ryder, *Ulster Defence Regiment*, pp. 58–9.
31. *Belfast Telegraph*, 9 November 1972.
32. Cabinet Papers, 29 November 1972, PREM 15/10/13, letter from MoD to PM.
33. Ibid.
34. Ibid.
35. *Monday World*, August 1974. The officer wrote under the pseudonym Andrew Sefton.
36. *Scotsman*, 26 February 1986.
37. Tyrie, interview with author, 10 February 1985.
38. *Ulster*, September 1984.
39. Ibid.
40. Former UDR soldier, interview with author, 5 December 2002.
41. *Irish News*, 18 June 1973.
42. *Irish News*, 19 June 1973.
43. Ibid.
44. McKittrick *et al.*, *Lost Lives*, p. 1475.
45. M. Dillon, *The Shankill Butchers: A Case Study of Mass Murder* (London: Hutchinson, 1989).
46. *Combat*, September 1976.
47. *Irish News*, 15 June 1997.
48. *Tirghra: Ireland's Patriot Dead* (Dublin: Republican Publications, 2002).
49. West Belfast UDA member, interview with author, 9 October 2003.
50. McKittrick *et al.*, *Lost Lives*, pp. 651–2.
51. *Ulster*, July 1976.
52. McKittrick *et al.*, *Lost Lives*, pp. 656–7.
53. *Ulster*, July 1976.

54. McKittrick *et al.*, *Lost Lives*, p. 393. See also M. Dewar, *The British Army in Northern Ireland* (London: Arms and Armour, 1985), pp. 86–7.
55. Tyrie, interview with author, 17 November, 2003.
56. Ibid.
57. Ibid.
58. Ibid.
59. Ryder, *Ulster Defence Regiment*, pp. 179–80.
60. Tyrie, interview with author, 17 November 2003.
61. *Fortnight*, April 1975; *Irish Times*, 10 March 1975; 'Down memory lane: Operation Greencastle', *Ulster*, January 1983.
62. J. McDonald, interview with author, 7 October 2003.
63. Ibid.
64. Duddy, interview with author, 9 October 2003.
65. Ibid.
66. Ibid.
67. C. Crawford, *Inside the UDA: Volunteers and Violence* (London: Pluto Press, 2003), pp. 43–4.
68. Ibid., p. 94.
69. Duddy, interview with author, 9 October 2003.
70. Tyrie, interview with author, 17 November 2003.
71. Crawford, *Inside the UDA*, pp. 46–7.
72. Tyrie, interview with author, 17 November 2003.
73. Ibid.
74. P. Routledge, *Public Servant, Secret Agent: The Elusive Life and Violent Death of Airey Neave* (London: Fourth Estate, 2002), pp. 353–4.
75. Bruce, *Red Hand*, pp. 205–6.
76. *Irish Times*, 27 June 2003.
77. J. Holland and H. McDonald, *INLA: Deadly Divisions* (Dublin: Torc, 1994), pp. 158–61.
78. J. Brown, interview with author, 6 May 2003.
79. R. Faligot, *Britain's Military Strategy in Ireland: the Kitson Experiment* (London: Zed, 1983), pp. 113–15.
80. R. Murray, *The SAS in Ireland* (Cork: Mercier Press, 1990), p. 261.
81. Ibid., p. 260.
82. M. Dillon, *The Dirty War* (London: Hutchinson, 1990), p. 292.
83. Tyrie, interview with author, 19 April 2000.
84. McDonald, interview with author, 7 October 2003.
85. Duddy interview with author, 9 October, 2003.
86. *Ulster*, March 1981.
87. *Sunday Times*, 28 February 1999.
88. Duddy, interview with author, 9 October 2003.
89. Ibid.
90. McDonald, interview with author, 7 October 2003.
91. *Irish News*, 27 September 2003.
92. J. Gregg, interview with author, 2002.
93. Duddy, interview with author, 9 October 2003.

94. Stone, *None Shall Divide Us*, pp. 221–2.
95. *Ulster*, April 1984.
96. *Ulster*, April 1985.
97. Routledge, *Public Servant, Secret Agent*, pp. 340–4.
98. Murray, *SAS in Ireland*, pp. 259–60.
99. J. McCauley, 'Cuchullain and an RPG: the ideology and politics of the Ulster Defence Association', in E. Hughes (ed.), *Culture and Politics in Northern Ireland 1960–1990* (Milton Keynes/Philadelphia: Open University Press, 1990).
100. M Urban, *Big Boys' Rules: The Secret Struggle against the IRA* (London: Faber and Faber, 1992), p. 59.
101. Murray, *SAS in Ireland*, p. 261.
102. McKittrick *et al.*, *Lost Lives*, p. 1000.
103. Tyrie, interview with author, 17 November 2003.
104. Crawford, *Inside the UDA*, p. 40.
105. Tyrie, interview with author, 19 April 2000. See also note 37.
106. *Ulster*, April 1985.
107. Tyrie, interview with author, 17 November 2003.
108. P. Taylor, *Loyalists* (London: Bloomsbury, 1999), pp. 204–5.
109. *Ulster*, July–August 1987.
110. Urban, *Big Boys' Rules*, pp. 224–37.
111. *Lost Lives*, pp. 1063–4.
112. Ibid., pp. 1072–3.
113. Ibid., p. 1081. See also M Stone, *None Shall Divide Us*, pp. 80–2.
114. D. Lister and H. Jordan, *Mad Dog: The Rise and Fall of Johnny Adair and 'C' Company* (Edinburgh: Mainstream, 2003), p. 49.
115. *Lost Lives*, pp. 1098–9.
116. *Ulster*, September 1987.
117. *Guardian*, 21 September 1987.
118. *Ulster*, October 1987.
119. *Ulster*, November 1987.
120. Ibid.
121. *Independent*, 17 October 1988.
122. Ibid.
123. S. Belfrage, *The Crack: A Belfast Year* (London: Andre Deutsch, 1987), p. 350.
124. *Belfast Telegraph*, 31 January 1990.
125. Taylor, *Loyalists*, pp. 171–2.
126. Tyrie, interview with author, 19 April, 2000.
127. *Observer*, 13 March, 1994.
128. *Observer*, 27 December 1987.
129. *Guardian*, 24 December 1987.
130. G. McMichael, interview with author, 9 February 2000.
131. *An Phoblacht*, 31 December 1987.

6

Fighting On

Andy Tyrie could not have had a worse beginning to 1988, under pressure as he was from critics of his leadership and from those who wanted John McMichael's death fully investigated as well as avenged. On the night of 8 January on the road from Tandragee to Portadown, the RUC stopped two Ford Granada cars and found the boots of both vehicles stuffed with weapons. There were sixty-one AK47 assault rifles, thirty Browning pistols, 150 grenades and 11,500 rounds of ammunition. Most of the consignment was from South Africa and paid for by bank robberies in the area. What the police had stumbled on was only part of a larger load brought into Belfast docks a few weeks earlier. It was intended for distribution to the UDA, the UVF and Ulster Resistance. This latter body had been formed in autumn of 1986 from a fusion of the Ulster Clubs and Dr Ian Paisley's much-ridiculed 'Third Force'. Typically, Paisley had noisily committed himself to the new grouping and attended some big rallies in its support but was careful to distance himself from gun-running and law-breaking by it.

The RUC had in fact intercepted the UDA's share of the weapons and ammunition and the leading vehicle which they stopped was driven by Davy Payne, who, after a chequered career in the organisation, had recently been reinstated by Tyrie as its North Belfast brigadier. He had held the command there before but his unpredictable violence had made him difficult to work with and he was 'stood down' by the Inner Council. Many thought he had acted recklessly over the UDA's load of weapons, as the UVF and Ulster Resistance were later able to collect their share without detection. At his trial, along with three other UDA men, Payne claimed he had been 'set up' from within the Inner Council and the day after his arrest the *Irish News* had quoted a police reference to information from a 'well-placed paramilitary source'[1] which they had acted upon.

Later in 1988 and after Tyrie's resignation from his positions at the head of the UDA, the organisation sanctioned the publication of a sustained attack on Payne. This described him as a torturer and also a fantasist who had made false claims over his own role in the UDA and over the preparation of the 1987 *Common Sense* document. It also accused him of complicity in John McMichael's murder because his own corruption was under investigation after an extended period in which the leadership had avoided a proper inquiry into his activities.[2]

Payne was sentenced to nineteen years' imprisonment and gave nothing away at his trial. The circumstances surrounding his arrest raised new questions about Tyrie's running of the UDA and his appointments within it. Questions were being asked too about his replacement of the murdered McMichael at South Belfast by Jackie McDonald, whose initial readiness to work with Jim Craig would soon land him in prison. Overshadowing these matters was the urgent need for a thorough investigation of the McMichael killing and of how an IRA unit had been able so easily to enter and leave the solidly Loyalist Hilden estate in Lisburn. Tyrie had already authorised a full inquiry but the Gawn Street building where he worked was firebombed on the evening of 5 January and this was followed by a phone call to a local radio station warning Tyrie and another unnamed brigadier to leave Northern Ireland within seven days. The caller claimed to represent a previously unheard-of body, the Loyalist People's Reaction Force.

The murder inquiry was slow in getting under way but to many within the UDA and also outside its ranks, Craig was the obvious suspect. He had already gone on the offensive against both the Central and Ulster television companies, announcing in January that he would take legal action over their screening the previous year of the *Cook Report*'s allegations against him. Jack Kielty, a well-known County Down building contractor who had co-operated with the programme's researchers, made it known that he would go into court as a witness for the companies, but on 25 January he was shot dead in his office in Dundrum by a three-man UFF unit whose members were all later convicted of his murder.[3]

Craig clearly had reasons for wanting Kielty dead, though his complicity in the murder was never proved. There was, as it turned out, little time for the police to do that, but all his movements were monitored with increasing care by the UDA, especially his apparent freedom of access to hard-line Republican areas of Belfast. Craig's days were numbered and on 15 October 1988 he died, along with an old age pensioner, in a hail of bullets when two UFF gunmen burst into the Castle Inn in East Belfast, where he was playing pool. The UFF later claimed Craig was 'executed for treason'[4] and alleged he had been involved in McMichael's murder. Paramilitary ritual at his funeral was conspicuous by its absence, as were leading members of the UDA.

Tyrie accepts that Craig's transgressions were more than sufficient to cause his death at the UDA's hands but he has remained unconvinced that Craig 'set up' McMichael for the IRA to kill him.

> John was always someone the Provos wanted to hit. They'd have taken their chance whenever it came, but why, when he was under real pressure anyway over the *Cook Report* programme and a lot else, would Jim Craig have taken the risk of setting up as senior a figure as John, a brigadier? They got on well, they were friends. Jim put

in £20,000 to keep John's pub afloat. It was just as well, because John was no businessman! We all know Jim had Republican contacts. It was no secret, no more than
the fact that his wife was a Catholic. He was an easy scapegoat once John had been
killed, that's all. I'm not denying he had faults, bad ones.[5]

Gary McMichael has claimed in writing that he knows the names of his
father's killers[6] and he has repeated the claim in an interview with the author.

It was the IRA who planted the bomb, no question. I could give you the names. It
was Semtex, which Loyalists were not using in 1987. My father was a big target so
it would have been an Army Council matter. If they could do it with help from
within the UDA, so much the better for them. There was a corrupt element who
feared my father more than they did Andy Tyrie. He saw the need to clean them
out but he hadn't the balls for it. He had his problems, trying to stay on top by
managing rival factions and preferred my father to take on the task.[7]

He recognises that his father used money which came to him through Craig
to solve business problems, and worked with him in other ways.

The difference between him and Craig was that, while he knew funds had to be
raised often ruthlessly and from criminal sources, it was to 'fight fire with fire' and
to hit the IRA where it hurt; he never got into collusion or co-operation with them,
which was what Craig had been doing. I suppose my father's mistake was not getting
his retaliation in first.[8]

Gary McMichael's interpretation of events is one which puts Craig clearly in
the frame as the prime suspect for guiding the IRA to his father.

The journalist Martin Dillon claims to have had access to a UDA report
on Craig which he says was only completed after Tyrie resigned from the positions he held in the organisation in March 1988. This document, according
to Dillon, provides much detail on how Craig had maintained his Republican
contacts[9] but does not answer the questions posed by Tyrie. 'Too many
people', he argues, 'were influenced by the intervention of Jack Hermon (the
Chief Constable of the RUC) after John's death.' Hermon, stressing that he
was choosing his words with care, told the media that they should look
'within Loyalism' for an explanation of the McMichael murder. Tyrie still
thinks that it was set up not within the UDA but from the Maze prison and
by one of its officers inside it, John Hanna, rather than by Craig outside. It
was to Hanna, in his view, that the Chief Constable was referring.

Hanna, Tyrie claims, used his position within the prison to collect information on John McMichael during his visits to Loyalist inmates, because
though a Protestant, he had become infatuated with Rosena Brown. She was
a well-known actress who had performed both on stage and on television but
also acted as an intelligence officer for the IRA. Her importance to their campaign is documented in the memoirs of Martin McGartland, who penetrated
the organisation as a British agent.[10] 'It adds up,' Tyrie has said. 'I heard John

talking about conversations he had with Hanna during visits to the Maze. He was able to have John's movements checked, even in Lisburn itself, and the Provos had his exact address, his car registration number, all that.'[11] In 1990, Hanna was given a life sentence for aiding and abetting the killing, two years earlier, of Brian Armour, a prison officer at the Maze and vice-chair of the Prison Officers' Association.

Brown was named in court during Hanna's trial but not charged over the Armour murder, though she was later convicted and sentenced for illegal possession of explosives. She was released in 1999 under the terms of the Belfast Agreement.[12] Since then, she has worked with a West Belfast theatre group and does not respond to questions about her role in the IRA. Hanna died in prison from cancer, taking many secrets to the grave. So too did McMichael and Craig. In the case of the latter, however, it has recently been claimed that video evidence of his IRA contacts was passed to the UDA's Inner Council by Brian Nelson, who saw Craig's incrimination and murder as a way to enhance his own credibility within the UDA. Nelson's army intelligence handlers, it is suggested, saw Craig as expendable in order to secure the position of a key agent.[13]

McMichael's death was not just a deeply felt personal blow to Tyrie. It removed a close ally on the Inner Council while cancer removed another, Alan Snoddy, the South-East Antrim brigadier. Always a loyal supporter of Tyrie, he had become too ill to remain active and died in September 1988. Tyrie's position was crumbling as he felt he could trust neither Tommy Lyttle nor Billy Elliott, while Davy Payne, controversially reinstated by him, was in prison awaiting trial. There was also Nelson to worry about and Tyrie claims that he was warning the Inner Council about him well before his own departure. 'The trouble was that people like Tommy Lyttle still trusted Nelson, or seemed to,' he recalls. 'Yes, he kept the intelligence coming but I knew he was suspect. I had surveillance done on him, Sammy Duddy did some of it, but he was laughing at us.

'I met him after I had finished with the UDA. It would be later on in 1988 and he was off to do road haulage work in Germany, or so he said. I reckon his army minders wanted him out of the way for a bit. I remember he told me I was well out of the UDA, whom he described as a "bunch of dickheads" for not catching on to what he was doing.'[14] It is questionable whether Tyrie would have had the support he needed for a move against Nelson and on 7 March he received a clear warning when he spotted an explosive device fitted under the driver's seat of his car, which for security reasons he usually parked some distance from his home in Ballybeen in East Belfast.

Sammy Duddy claims that he foresaw a move being made against Tyrie.

> Okay, Andy always checked his car and maybe it was meant as a warning to him to stand down. Even so it could still have killed him if he had been careless like John McMichael. It was Craig and Tommy Lyttle who set it up. I know it was because

I overheard them talking about it in the Gawn Street office. I went straight out to a public callbox to tell Andy and then of course the Peelers pulled me in for questioning about it. Craig and Lyttle hated each other, that was no secret, but they both had their reasons for wanting Andy out.[15]

Four days later there were reports of the commanders of five UDA brigades meeting in North Belfast to vote on Tyrie's position. Jackie McDonald, who had taken over in the south of the city, and Joe English, acting for the South East Antrim brigade in place of the seriously ill Snoddy, voted for Tyrie but the other three carried the vote against them. This precipitated a very big meeting of both members and UDA officers from all the city's brigade areas but not outside it. In Tyrie's recollection there were over 600 present.

It was a tense business. You could feel it, but I sensed they didn't want to make the decision themselves. There were calls for it to be left to an Inner Council vote after people had made their criticism. I might just have won that but I decided to go. I wanted out and I had done for three years. It had become a shitty job and I was sick of it. We were riddled with informers at the top and I'd had enough.[16]

He was given little time in which to clear his office. Duddy recalls with distaste how he was ordered by Lyttle and Elliott to accompany the former leader in order to check what items he put into the bin liner bag they had provided for him.[17] Tyrie had survived for as long as he had by never being too closely identified with any one brigade area. This had made him a good compromise candidate for the leadership at a fraught and violent time in 1973. His growing preference, however, for trying to centralise the command structure and for personally appointing brigadiers alienated an element within the organisation who had joined it when such positions were still filled by a rough and ready election process. His concern to reduce sectarian killing by the UDA and to involve it in political initiatives also lost the support of those who came to feel it had ceased to be a killing machine which the IRA really feared. Not corrupt himself, Tyrie was also under pressure for being slow to act against those who were.

The changes which followed Tyrie's departure were soon apparent in the Gawn Street headquarters building. The imposing long table, at one end of which he had always sat, disappeared along with the crossed Union and Ulster flags. So too did a Rangers calendar and a copy of Rudyard Kipling's poem 'If'. An unprepossessing round table appeared, at which journalists would be invited to sit, usually with Lyttle and English, though easy media access could no longer be taken for granted. Lyttle would joke with interviewers about the missing flags, even promising to restore them if the demand was there, and made much of the different symbolism of the round table. All this was rapidly overshadowed by events in West Belfast on 16 March 1988.

Several thousand Republican mourners, including Gerry Adams and Martin McGuinness, had assembled that day in Milltown cemetery for the

interment of three IRA members shot dead in Gibraltar ten days earlier by
the SAS. Just as the burial service was getting under way, Michael Stone
launched a single-handed attack which gave the world's media some of their
most brutal footage from Northern Ireland's conflict. Claiming later that his
targets were Adams and McGuinness, Stone used fragmentation grenades, a
Browning pistol and a Ruger Magnum revolver to kill three people in the
cemetery and cause injuries to sixty others. His Russian-made grenades were
fitted with a time delay fuse to make them explode a few seconds after being
thrown. However, he threw his first grenades too soon. They would have
caused a huge death toll if they had exploded in mid-air, showering shrapnel
over a wide area of the packed burial ground.

Even so, Stone's ability to penetrate West Belfast and to get so close to
killing the IRA leadership sent shockwaves of fear through the Republican
movement and its supporters. These fears were savagely exemplified three
days later by the terrible beatings given to two off-duty British corporals from
the Royal Signals who inadvertently drove their car into the funeral cortège
of one of the Milltown victims. The two soldiers were thought to be either
Loyalist gunmen or members of the special forces and were eventually shot
dead by IRA men who were called to the scene. 'It was blind panic, just that.
I was there and I panicked with everyone else. The soldiers were never SAS
or undercover guys. They were just in the wrong place at the wrong time,'[18]
was the recollection of eye witness Joe Austen, a Sinn Fein councillor.

Sinn Fein was quick to describe the cemetery killings as an organised
Loyalist attack, though in fact Stone had little time to prepare in comparison
with some of the other targets he had previously stalked. The UDA was
equally swift to disclaim responsibility for Stone or any knowledge of him.
This was primarily the work of Lyttle, who telephoned UDA commanders to
tell them to keep to this line. Jackie McDonald, who had succeeded
McMichael as South Belfast brigadier, has recalled his unease over this:
'Tucker [Tommy Lyttle] just wanted a quiet life then along came someone
with the balls to walk into Milltown and take on the Provos. Stone got close,
he could easily have taken out Adams and McGuinness.'[19] Duddy does not
limit the blame to Lyttle:

> After Milltown, two UDA brigadiers from two Belfast battalions telephoned the
> IRA to say they didn't know Michael Stone. They said he was just a rogue Loyalist
> acting without authorisation. But Michael was UDA, he was a travelling gunman
> who went after the IRA and Republicans and he needed no authority for that
> because that was his job. Those two brigadiers were scared in case the IRA would
> retaliate against them or their areas which would mean trouble, so they disclaimed
> Michael, one of our best operators.[20]

Claims and counter-claims have been made from then on about the nature of
Stone's relationship to the UDA, not least by Stone himself, who has published his memoirs and given press interviews since his release from prison in

1999. By the time of his trial a decade earlier in late February 1989, he was already a Loyalist folk hero and his acceptance by UDA prisoners on H-Block 7 of the Maze prison was assured. At the trial, which finished on 3 March, Stone made pleas of not guilty but refused to speak or co-operate in his own defence. He was convicted of the Milltown killings and of three others, along with a series of charges of conspiracy to murder and of unlawful wounding. The presiding judge passed concurrent sentences with the recommendation that Stone serve at least thirty years. Among Loyalists in the public gallery who rose to cheer him and also to taunt the families of those killed at Milltown was Johnny Adair, already active in C Company of the UDA's West Belfast battalion.[21]

Once sentence was passed and Stone arrived at the Maze, the UDA devoted much of an issue of *Ulster* to him. The cover of the magazine's March edition featured Stone at bay in Milltown, still firing as his pursuers closed in on him, and an article on an inside page praised him as a hero with a mission to eliminate men who were 'the engine-room of the IRA's murder campaign in Ulster'.[22] Although Stone's getaway driver had failed to appear on the hard shoulder of the motorway at the cemetery's edge when he made his escape attempt, *Ulster* acclaimed his deeds as those of a lone hero: 'Not for him the skulking dead of night attack such as is a feature of IRA activity. Not for him the sniper's rifle or the 200 yard long trip-wire. Michael Stone stood bravely in the middle of rebel scum and let them have it.'[23] Stone, correctly as it turned out, interpreted this tribute as a sure sign of change. 'The UDA's old guard was disintegrating. The UDA that denied me in 1988 and told the press I was too extreme to be a member was starting to fall apart.'[24] It was, but time was still needed for a real shift of power within it.

Two years into his sentence, Stone agreed to be interviewed by the journalist Martin Dillon. In 1992 Dillon brought out a book which he claimed was based on Stone's life story as well as the interviews he had agreed to do. Stone was the child of a mixed marriage. The author drew large conclusions from this as well as from the fact that his Catholic mother abandoned him in infancy after the family had moved to England. He also claimed that in 1980 McMichael had brought Stone back into the UDA without reference to the rest of its leadership and with a roving commission for him to carry out intelligence operations both in Belfast and in rural areas as well as liaising when necessary with UVF units. He writes too of McMichael sanctioning operations, which in the end were abandoned, to kill two Republican leaders, Owen Carron and McGuinness.[25]

The book also asserted that, once the date of the funeral of the three IRA members killed in Gibraltar was set, Stone, with McMichael dead, approached other UDA leaders about a possible attack in the cemetery, but it was made clear to him that they were afraid of the likely IRA reprisals which might follow. One or two, in Dillon's account, were prepared to consider planting bombs in the cemetery ahead of the funeral, only for Stone to veto the idea on the grounds that bombs might miss the prime targets, IRA leaders, in what he saw as 'pay-back time' for Enniskillen and other atrocities against Loyalists.[26]

Dillon's book was dismissed by some in the UDA who read it and one of the organisation's magazines called its price 'the biggest rip-off since Robert Maxwell's pension fund'.[27] The author, it went on, 'happily paints Michael Stone as a half-English, half-Catholic, womanising lunatic, ignoring or barely touching on Stone's obvious political motivations'.[28] With McMichael's son Gary embarking on a political career in the Ulster Democratic Party and anxious to promote the principles of the *Common Sense* policy document once more, there was also pressure on Stone from within an element in the UDA to deny that he had been recruited by and had worked closely with the murdered leader.[29]

This Stone duly did, in a letter to Gary McMichael which was also made available to the Belfast *Sunday Life* newspaper and to UDA publications. In it, Stone wrote contemptuously of Dillon's claims, describing him as having

> shown his true colours in casting a shadow over your late father's good name. I find this personally objectionable, as this closet Republican has used my name in an attempt to discredit a man I respected as a Loyalist and a politician who sought a peaceful end to this conflict.
>
> It is my loss that I never met your late father, he was a good man and I profoundly regret the understandable anger and distress Dillon's publication has caused your dear family.[30]

Since his release from prison, Stone has repudiated this denial, claiming that he only agreed to it because the McMichael family was upset by media coverage of Dillon's book linking him to John McMichael. 'In front of McMichael's grieving family I denied the relationship with the man I called my friend.'[31] He now says he feels ashamed of what he did and excuses himself in part because of pressure brought to bear on him by the UDA's South Belfast brigade to issue his statement.

'I did know John McMichael. I worked with John McMichael on a regular basis. Operationally, our work brought us into close contact and he was a trusted friend and ally,'[32] Stone has now declared. McMichael was indeed an astute co-ordinator of operations who would have recognised Stone's value while letting him have as much autonomy as he wanted as a killer. Andy Tyrie, who appears in Stone's memoirs simply as someone who let the 'right people' know about his availability to the UDA,[33] has recently described meeting Stone a few days before Milltown:

> He told me all about what he was planning and that he could do it. I replied 'We'll see' but I suppose my message for him was to go ahead. He had the nerve, the balls for it, I could see that. It didn't need an Inner Council decision. He got so close. It was a pity they got him the wrong grenades.[34]

While Stone certainly acted alone in Milltown once he was able to enter the cemetery, his published account of events claims much for the back-up he had, and not just from within the UDA. He makes no mention of Tyrie, referring only to a 'senior member of the UDA'[35] who gave him the organisation's 'official' clearance for what he was planning. In an elaborate description of his preparations, he describes being given his pick of weapons from an Ulster Resistance cache at a secret location outside Belfast, and also how he was driven back into the city by a member of the RUC.[36]

Stone always took pride in the thoroughness of any operation he undertook and Milltown, despite the very limited time had had to plan his attack, seems to have been no exception. He claims he had detailed information about police and army movements as well as assurances that soldiers and RUC officers were not going to be deployed in the cemetery because of serious clashes with mourners at recent IRA funerals, notably that of Larry Marley in Ardoyne the previous year. These data, he insists, came to him indirectly.

> I was never handed a file by a member of the security forces, although I do concede that the files were very professional both in presentation and content, especially the aerial photography. I am not aware of any Loyalist paramilitary group that had its own air corps.[37]

Stone's statements of course need to be tested against evidence which may emerge from inquiries ongoing at the time of writing into alleged collusion between the security forces and Loyalist paramilitaries. One killing in particular which still has a central relationship to these inquiries is that of Patrick Finucane, a skilful and tenacious lawyer with Republican connections and sympathies who was shot dead at his North Belfast home by Loyalists on 12 February 1989. This was while Stone was in gaol awaiting trial and he claims he spotted Finucane, while on a prison visit, listening in a cubicle to one of his interrogations by Special Branch officers.[38] Finucane's murder was a signal of change within the UDA, undertaken as it was by an increasingly restless younger element within C Company of the organisation's West Belfast battalion who wanted what they saw as real action and prestige kills.[39]

Although *Ulster* ran an article justifying and applauding Finucane's killing, its pages in 1989 and indeed over much of the previous year reflected other UDA preoccupations arising from both McMichael's death and Tyrie's fall from power. Rosetta continued to call for the organisation to put its house in order:

> It simply cannot afford to gloss over the reports of collusion with republican paramilitaries or overlook the blatant extortion practiced by some members. The UDA, after seventeen years should be adult enough to face up to – and then face down – these problems. There are rotten apples in the barrel, the organisation has admitted so in the past, who are ruining the UDA's image with the Loyalist community.[40]

Removing the 'rotten apples', he stressed, was essential if the offensive was to be resumed on both the political and military fronts. Tyrie's departure, he argued, would serve no purpose if the same men were left in charge of the UDA's active units.

The power struggle anticipated by some in the media did not materialise but there was fairly open talk of a new leadership structure. Along with the continuing inquiry into McMichael's murder, there would be, members were assured by the Inner Council itself, an overhaul of the organisation to maximise its operational role.

> The days of two men delivering the UDA to politicians are over. Things were like that in the UDA for six years or more but that leadership era is over. People have great affection for John McMichael but John and Andy didn't consult the men. We do and we listen and we are not going to be the muscle for politicians.[41]

Other issues of *Ulster* referred to the work of a 'Special Assignment' section of the UDA whose remit was clear. A 9 November 1988 deadline was offered for all who had in any way worked against the organisation to come forward with full confessions. The alternative for not doing so was made fairly explicit:

> This section will in future, investigate any allegations of behaviour detrimental to the Loyalist cause. This will include allegations of racketeering, gangsterism and misuse of the organisation's name for self-gain. We are determined to stamp out all those who would betray the Loyalist people and ourselves.
>
> If you are involved with PIRA etc., come forward NOW – there will be no further warnings on this matter.
> ALL INFORMERS BEWARE.[42]

The Special Assignments section is likely to have sanctioned Jim Craig's murder in October 1988. The UFF, in a statement soon after it, declared that he had been 'executed for treason'[43] and he had been under surveillance since before McMichael's death. So too had James McVeigh, a 31-year-old Protestant living on the Suffolk estate in West Belfast. He had been passing information to the IRA and even set up for assassination a UDA man in a shopping centre in the city, though Loyalists uncovered the plan and the intended target survived. When McVeigh was picked up for questioning, he thought the IRA had come for him.

> I thought that because they knew so much. They knew the names of my three Provo contacts and a contact telephone number. They knew of my meeting places and they knew I had set up a UDA man and that the murder was to take place in the Park shopping centre. I said I could set him up again and that they would get him this time. Then they told me who they were.[44]

McVeigh saved himself by telling his interrogators all they wanted to know ahead of the amnesty deadline set by the UDA and announced in *Ulster*. He was given thirty-six hours to leave Northern Ireland and wasted little time in making the necessary arrangements to do so, taking his family with him. The UDA told him he was a lucky man, staying alive only because of the amnesty, which in fact ended on 28 November.

During 1988 the UDA/UFF maintained their killing rate of the previous year. Their twelve victims added up to only one more than those claimed by the UVF and were hugely outnumbered by the sixty-nine murders carried out by the IRA and the INLA. The twelve included those shot dead by Stone at Milltown, as well as Craig and the innocent old age pensioner caught in the burst of fire which killed them both in the Castle Inn in October. Two killings in the latter part of the year were the work of the increasingly active West Belfast C Company and have been a focus for continued inquiry and controversy ever since. They also figured prominently in the June 1992 trial of Brian Nelson.

The first of these two victims was the 29-year-old Terence McDaid, a bricklayer by trade, who lived in Newington Street, off the Antrim Road in North Belfast. On the evening of 10 May 1988, he and his wife had just put their children to bed when two masked gunmen burst into the house and shot McDaid seven times in the head and chest. He died on his own sitting room floor with his children screaming hysterically at the top of the stairs. The killers were from the UFF's C Company and at Nelson's trial it was revealed that he had given them the name and photograph of McDaid's brother, Declan, when they approached him for information on Republican targets. He was an active Republican and had a strong facial resemblance to his brother. The killing of Terence McDaid arose from a case of mistaken identity and Nelson's handlers in the army's undercover Force Research Unit reacted with anger to it, only to be told by him that his remit was intelligence, not actual operations.[45]

On 23 September 1988, Gerard Slane, aged twenty-seven, was killed at his home in West Belfast in very similar circumstances. A five-man C Company unit arrived at the house on the Falls Road and four of them forced their way in and shot Slane dead as he came down the stairs to investigate the noise they had made in breaking in. His wife and children found him dead on the landing, with much of his face blown off by the concentrated gunfire at close range. Once again, the UDA had been given a photograph of their victim by Nelson and an *Ulster* article claimed that Slane had active links with the Irish People's Liberation Organisation, which had broken away from the INLA.[46] At the inquest, the RUC questioned the likelihood of this, though Slane had been in court two years earlier over a rifle found by security forces in the outside lavatory of his house. Sentence was suspended, however, because the judge in the case accepted his claim that the weapon had been hidden there not long before the search without his knowledge.[47]

Slane might have had some Republican involvement and it has been claimed that his widow Teresa was offered, but declined, a Republican funeral for him.[48] As with McDaid, what might have sealed his fate was that he had a brother who was active in the IPLO. In the close-knit community of Republican West Belfast, guilt by association in the minds of Loyalist gunmen was easily acquired and information from Nelson was enough to activate killers from the UFF's C Company who lived no great distance away on the other side of the army's fortified 'Peace Line', which was intended to separate nationalist and Loyalist West Belfast. It ran right up alongside Clonard Monastery, one of whose priests officiated at Slane's funeral. This was yet another terrible occasion, at which a grief-stricken Teresa Slane had to be almost held up by her family to walk behind her husband's coffin.

Although the 'young guns' of the Shankill were straining at the leash, their opportunities to kill in 1989 did not expand at the rate that they had hoped for. After the murder of Patrick Finucane, claimed by the UDA as 'the most senior member of the Provisional Irish Republican Army that has so far been executed',[49] the UDA/UFF carried out only five killings over the remainder of the year. This was despite new revelations about intelligence data reaching both the UDA and the UVF through the security forces in a court case involving a part-time UDR soldier, Joanne Garvin. She was convicted in May of passing confidential files and photographs to Loyalists, using her contacts at the army's Girdwood barracks in North Belfast. One of her contacts was a corporal in the Royal Scots, Cameron Hastie.[50]

A Belfast-based reporter described the case as 'a stark illustration of the inevitability of locally recruited members of the security forces coming into contact with extreme Loyalist elements'.[51] Garvin, under questioning by RUC detectives, told them of occasions on which she had heard soldiers 'talking about leaving material for Loyalist paramilitary groups when their regiments left'.[52]

How far such intelligence was effectively used was another matter and part of the problem was that the UDA's old guard was still represented within its command structure, especially by Tommy Lyttle in West Belfast. By this point, however, Lyttle was living on borrowed time where his credibility was concerned. He had for several years been feeding information to the RUC's Special Branch as well as keeping operations in his brigade area on a tight rein. Lyttle's work for Special Branch was not lavishly paid but it gave him a significant degree of protection from the IRA and allowed him to indulge his enthusiasm for greyhound breeding and racing. He became a familiar figure at a dog track in North Belfast frequented by Republicans and over time the inevitable questions were asked about why he was never an IRA target. He remained a genial enough figure when talking to the media though he became increasingly evasive on specific questions and clearly preferred to talk on general issues. He also liked to reminisce about his days as an amateur boxer and a childhood and early life which he insisted was just as much defined by poverty and limited expectations as that of Gerry Adams or any other Republican.[53]

He also had other preoccupations. His son John, now a journalist in London, is homosexual and 'came out' in the 1970s to join a Belfast gay scene where religious and sectarian labels were not important issues. He has been quoted as saying that because of who his father was he must have been the only gay man on the Shankill not to have been beaten up.[54] He has also said that being gay and taking Catholic partners was a way of asserting himself against a background dominated by Lyttle senior's role in the UDA and has recalled how his father had one of those Catholic partners followed. UDA manpower was used for this but Tommy Lyttle explained to him that possibly dangerous Republican connections must be checked out. When John was arrested with other gay men in Belfast in 1976, he was able to cope well with police interrogation methods, having been thoroughly drilled in them and how to respond by a father who might not initially have anticipated his arrest on charges of gay sex, which remained illegal in Northern Ireland until 1982.[55]

Lyttle had been alarmed at the implications of the Finucane murder but nemesis for him was the killing in Rathfriland, County Down, of Loughlin Maginn, a 28-year-old Catholic, on 25 August 1989. Maginn had been stopped and questioned on many occasions by army and RUC patrols but the UFF claimed the responsibility for shooting him dead in his home. Then and since, the UDA has insisted Maginn was a legitimate target[56] but the truth of his alleged IRA links was queried by the media. In response, the UDA/UFF claimed to have acted on police intelligence and gave out to journalists RUC files and photomontages in which Maginn and many others figured.

The RUC reacted furiously to these claims. Its new Chief Constable, Hugh Annesley, asked John Stevens, Deputy Chief Constable of Cambridgeshire Police, to conduct an inquiry into allegations of collusion between the security forces and Loyalist terror groups. A series of arrests began of UDA members and one of them was Lyttle. He appeared at a preliminary hearing before a Belfast court on 16 January 1990, to be charged with the withholding of information that could have prevented acts of terrorism. 'What am I doing here? I'm working for you anyway'[57] is, reportedly, what Lyttle said to detectives who arrived to question him after his arrival in prison.

By the time Stevens was ready to report his findings in the spring of that year, nearly sixty arrests had been made. These included Tommy Lyttle Junior; William 'Winkie' Dodds, a UFF gunman; Matthew Kincaid; and also Sammy Duddy, against whom charges were later dropped. The most significant arrest, as events would soon show, was that of Brian Nelson. For journalists in Belfast, an immediate problem became just who to make contact with in the UDA: its Gawn Street headquarters in East Belfast stayed virtually empty for several weeks, apart from a security man who took phone calls and looked after a closed-circuit camera alarm system. Not all the UDA's leading figures were arrested, as its spokesmen boasted to the press, claiming advance information of police raids authorised by the Stevens team.[58]

Ulster magazine remained in production despite the Stevens arrests and sought to put forward a brave face on events. It attributed the arrests made under the inquiry to a state strategy of punishing the UDA/UFF for being too effective. 'The UFF challenged the security apparatus because they sought out and executed the terrorists who the British failed to engage.'[59] This, it claimed, along with the increasing politicisation of the UDA, had added to the pressure to criminalise it as an organisation. It admitted that abuses within had played into the state's hands but in fact the proscription of the UDA was still a full two years away.

Rumours were already circulating that when the Stevens report came out, it was much more likely to blame the UDR for collusion than the RUC. This was reason enough for the same issue of *Ulster* to heap praise on the regiment for its localised unit structure and for the grass roots Loyalist support it had, especially in country areas.

> It has all the factors necessary to form the framework of a People's Army. On its own, the UDR poses a major risk to those who are intent on forcing Northern Ireland into an all-Ireland state. But it is the inevitable link-up with the UDA which poses the ultimate threat. This completion of rural and urban fighting forces would provide the united front needed to fight for democracy.[60]

Many Loyalists may have believed this but the UDR, in its existing form, was soon a casualty of the fall-out from the Stevens report.

The report was published in May 1990 but only in a 29-page summary form. This was despite the fact that it had access to more than 2,500 documents obtained from Loyalist sources containing sensitive security force information on Republican and IRA suspects and had interviewed 1,900 witnesses. The report accepted that leakages of information to Loyalist paramilitary groups had taken place but declared that these were not 'institutionalised' but the work of individuals, fifty-nine of whom had already been charged. The RUC as a force was largely cleared of blame but tighter vetting procedures for UDR applicants were called for since many of those arrested and questioned were members of the regiment. To the UDA this was proof of a dual-state strategy under the Anglo-Irish Agreement to break up the UDR and neutralise the UDA,[61] leading members of which were awaiting trial as a result of the Stevens investigation.

Tommy Lyttle's arrest, however, was hardly a blow to the UDA. It was almost certainly he who *Ulster* magazine had in mind when, in its July–August 1990 issue, it claimed that three brigadiers and eighteen active members of the organisation had been approached by the RUC Special Branch regarding the passing of information to it. This could only be, an article suggested, because 'a good informer has been lost'[62] by it. Lyttle had been given bail after the initial charges against him but was then rearrested on suspicion of trying to intimidate likely witnesses at his trial. In July of 1991 he was found guilty of the major charges against him and sentenced to seven years' imprisonment.

Even while awaiting trial, Lyttle had become an isolated figure, deeply suspect in the eyes of many fellow prisoners. Duddy, who was a remand prisoner at the time, recalled this:

> Out in the exercise area Tucker would be the last to be asked to make up the numbers for a game of football if he got asked at all. Mind you, he had rank, so he had an easier time than some. For those who had broken UDA rules, inside the prison or out, there were punishment kickings and beatings sanctioned by senior men serving their time. I saw it happen. They would form a circle with the offender in the middle. Tucker Lyttle was never in line for that but prison must have been a lonely time for him.[63]

Michael Stone was particularly resentful of Lyttle for the way he had been disowned after Milltown. Soon after he began his sentence, the latter arrived at the Maze to see him and they had an angry encounter. Lyttle demanded information about the Milltown attack and what sort of back-up had been available to him. Stone refused to tell him anything and claims that he drew his own conclusions from the fact that prison officers cleared the entire visiting area for Lyttle's visit.[64] After serving his sentence, most of it well away from UDA men and with conforming non-political prisoners at Maghaberry, Lyttle lost no time in leaving Belfast and later settled at Donaghadee in County Down, where he died of a heart attack in October 1995 at the age of fifty-six. 'If you play, you pay' is a maxim sometimes heard from observers of Northern Ireland's paramilitary world. For many years 'Tucker' Lyttle played for both the UDA and the state. Luckily for him the UDA did not execute either serving brigadiers or those like himself who had been 'stood down'. Johnny Adair would later pay the price for sanctioning a breach of this rule.

Lyttle's arrest and subsequent imprisonment, along with that of Jackie McDonald and Andy Aiken – a figure close to the Inner Council – who had both been convicted in January of the previous year, prompted much speculation about which direction the UDA would take. This had begun in response to John McMichael's murder and Andy Tyrie's departure but it reached new heights in 1991 as UDA/UFF attacks and killings once more started to intensify.

The first of these was on 27 January at a house in Rosapenna Court in the Oldpark area of North Belfast, where a Catholic scaffolder, Sean Rafferty, was shot dead in front of his five children as he prepared their Sunday dinner. It is now known to have been ordered by Adair during a drinking session in a Shankill bar and to have been carried out by gunmen from C Company of the UFF's West Belfast battalion.[65] A week later, six incendiary devices were found in several central Dublin hotels, and in a phone call to the BBC they claimed to have planted twenty in total. None of the six exploded but the Gardai said they believed there was a UFF unit in the capital planning to set off more devices.[66]

A source close to the UDA/UFF leadership said that the bid to firebomb stores in Dublin showed that new UFF leaders were 'trying to put themselves in the same league as the Provos' and were 'a more vicious group than the older crowd'.[67] The Dublin operation, like nearly all others attempted by Loyalists since the May 1974 bomb massacre there, was ineffectual but in Belfast the UDA/UFF killed again twice during April. Both victims were taxi drivers, traditionally easy targets for Loyalist gunmen. One was Samuel Bell, a father of five who was shot on the night of 3 April. The second, a fortnight later, was John O'Hara, aged forty-two, a father of five daughters whose widow Marie had lost her first husband to Loyalist gunmen in 1975. His funeral was yet another appalling scene for the media to cover as the victim's coffin was carried the short distance from the family home on Mountpottinger Road in East Belfast to St Matthew's Church in the Short Strand. At the Requiem Mass, the Bishop of Down and Connor, Dr Patrick Walsh, reminded mourners that less than two months earlier he had confirmed one of the O'Hara daughters. 'Love binds, hatred breaks,' he told the congregation, 'and ultimately hatred breaks the heart of the one who hates. Only love can overcome hatred.'[68] It would need time for that to happen to O'Hara's killers, who made taunting phone calls to the taxi office where he had only just begun working.

This killing preceded a Loyalist announcement of a 'universal suspension of aggressive operational hostilities' from midnight on 30 April, in order to create a more favourable atmosphere for talks on the province's constitutional future announced by the Secretary of State, Peter Brooke. He had mentioned this initiative on 26 March, promising a 'three-stranded' process which would cover problems within Northern Ireland, North–South relationships and Britain's role. The Loyalists' move took many commentators by surprise, as did the wording of the ceasefire communiqué. Suspension of armed action, it declared, was being ordered 'with a sincere and genuine desire to see a peaceful and acceptable solution to our political differences'.[69] There was, however, one important proviso. The statement cautioned the IRA against any deliberate disruption of the talks by raising the level of violence. 'Let them therefore be warned that the combined command will order defensive, and where fitting, retaliatory action if so required.'[70]

The ceasefire was a politically sophisticated move, intended to wrongfoot the IRA and to modify paramilitary Loyalism's uncompromising image. As important was the emergence, early in 1991, of the Combined Loyalist Military Command, which issued the ceasefire announcement. It represented the UDA, UVF and the Red Hand Commando, a body with whom the UVF had reached a working agreement in 1972 to co-operate closely while retaining separate organisational identities. The new Command was to co-ordinate both paramilitary action and political initiatives and the UVF has always claimed much of the credit for bringing it into being, with the UDA simply being invited to join.[71] David Ervine, a former UVF prisoner who became a political activist and was elected in 1998 to the Northern Ireland Assembly, has gone some way in accepting this claim but has added:

> It was a case of escalating the war in order to end it. Plan A under the CLMC's remit was to step up the war but with the thought always that there could still be a political way out. That was certainly Gusty Spence's view.[72]

Predictably, Gary McMichael has claimed a bigger role for the UDA and for its political wing, the Ulster Democratic Party, in the CLMC and its ceasefire initiative. He stresses the key role of Raymond Smallwoods, convicted in 1981 for his part in the attempted murder of Bernadette McAliskey. After serving his sentence Smallwoods emerged as an intelligent spokesman of working-class Loyalism. In 1991, according to McMichael, he was already a key figure:

> I was just on our party executive, starting to gain some experience, so I preferred to let Ray take the lead but our problem was that the media's focus was so much on the IRA that any Loyalist initiative was never going to get that much recognition. The Brooke talks failed but we learned a lesson, never to let ourselves be excluded as we were then from any constitutional or peace initiative.[73]

By mid-June the Brooke talks were beginning to collapse and the IRA continued to kill, regarding them simply as a means for Britain to force the pace towards a purely internal and partitionist political settlement. In May they killed two RUC officers and another former member of the force in a spate of attacks in Belfast and County Fermanagh. They also shot a Belfast fruit and vegetable trader for supplying army bases and planted some huge bombs in Protestant towns and villages. Loyalists, growing increasingly uneasy about both the talks and their own ceasefire, felt the need for retaliation and this took place on 25 May, although without the CLMC's April announcement being repudiated. This was because the operation was carried out in the Irish Republic.

The victim was a Sinn Fein councillor, Eddie Fullerton, a builder by trade, married with six children and a well-known figure in the small town of Buncrana in County Donegal. On the night of the 25th, UFF gunmen sledgehammered their way into his home and shot him dead as he came down the stairs from his bedroom to investigate the noise. The killers were from a Lisburn unit of the UDA's South Belfast brigade who drove across the border to reach their target. Some reports at the time claimed they then hijacked a car but Henry McDonald, the distinguished *Observer* journalist and expert on Ulster terrorism, now thinks local Loyalist sympathisers took them in a farm vehicle. He has also found that Ned Greer, a key figure in setting up that operation and others as well was, like Brian Nelson, a double agent working for army intelligence.[74] Greer had begun to be suspected within the organisation and his abrupt disappearance, almost certainly into protective army custody, was later reported in *Ulster* magazine.[75]

Fullerton's killing appears to have been set up by the UDA/UFF and executed without reference to the CLMC. This would be true of many more carried out after the ceasefire ended, especially by Johnny Adair's C Company gunmen. David Lister and Hugh Jordan, in their compelling and meticulously detailed study of Adair and the killing machine he ran, make only two references to the Command in the entire book.[76] The Fullerton attack was, however, the only killing by Loyalists over the ten weeks of the ceasefire but even so the UVF element within the CLMC had from the start been wary about UDA discipline and about its ability to control C Company.

With the removal of the constraints imposed by the ceasefire, both the UDA and the UVF launched a wave of attacks on targets in the nationalist community. By the end of 1991 their combined total of killings was close to that of the IRA, the UVF claiming twenty-four to the UDA/UFF's figure of seventeen. The latter represented a menacing growth in UDA activity and it would be maintained and relentlessly increased until the IRA's own ceasefire at the end of August 1994. Probably the only joint operation carried out under CLMC auspices and certainly the only one claimed in its name was an unsuccessful rocket-propelled grenade attack on 13 December 1991 on the canteen block of Crumlin Road prison in Belfast, where IRA and INLA prisoners were known to be having their evening meal.

The attack failed, the rocket bouncing off a grille on one of the canteen windows without exploding. It was a response to the fact that Loyalist prisoners from both the UDA and UVF were held in Crumlin Road and that they had been victims of a bomb left by IRA men who had used the canteen separately from the Loyalists for their evening meal on 24 November. The explosion and flying metal debris in a confined area caused dreadful injuries and killed two Loyalists, Rab Skey from the UDA and the UVF's Colin Caldwell.

The author was given a vivid account of this episode by a UDA member:

I was a remand prisoner then and it was a horrific time. It was an old prison and segregation never really worked. Facilities like the canteen had to be shared on an alternating basis. That was how the Provos got their bomb in, just for us. I was there when it went off. The radiator was a really old one and it just turned into flying shards of jagged, red-hot iron. I was right beside Colin Caldwell and he had an iron spike through the back of his head and into his throat. I just stayed with him and talked to him, told him he'd be OK but he was in a terrible state. I'll never get it out of my mind. Once the medical people arrived we were all sent to our cells but the Provos soon got word that one of our boys was dead and more badly injured. They went berserk on their floor. I can hear them still, cheering, whooping, banging their doors, their food trays, anything they could get.

A week later, by which time Colin of course had died, the screws let us have a brief memorial ceremony in the exercise yard for him and Rab, but the Provos were ready. They were up at their cell windows with tins and basins of piss and shite to throw down on us through the grilles. They must have been saving it up. You couldn't believe the hate in there, the fights I saw. I once saw one on a landing. It was impossible to avoid each other totally in the limited space there was. Anyway, on this occasion one of our lads actually managed to sink his teeth into a Provo prisoner's throat. That was the level we got to, all of us. We were barely human at times. My God, I never want to go back to that.[77]

NOTES

1. *Irish News*, 9 January 1988.
2. *Ulster*, November 1989.
3. *Sunday Times*, 31 January 1988.
4. D. McKittrick, S. Kelters, B. Feeney and C. Thornton, *Lost Lives: The Stories of the Men, Women and Children Who Died as a Result of Northern Ireland's Troubles* (Edinburgh: Mainstream, 1999), p. 1148.
5. A. Tyrie, interview with author, 19 April 2000.
6. G. McMichael, *Ulster Voice: in Search of Common Ground in Northern Ireland* (Boulder, CO/Dublin: Roberts Rinehart, 1999), p. 29.
7. G. McMichael, interview with author, 9 February 2000.
8. Ibid.
9. M. Dillon, *The Dirty War* (London: Hutchinson, 1990), pp. 454–6.
10. M. McGartland, *Fifty Dead Men Walking: The Heroic True Story of a British Secret Agent inside the IRA* (London: John Blake, 1997), pp. 191–8.
11. Tyrie, interview with author.
12. McKittrick *et al.*, *Lost Lives*, p. 1148.
13. *Observer*, 11 June 2000.
14. Tyrie, interview with author.
15. S. Duddy, interview with author, 9 November 2003.
16. Tyrie, interview with author.
17. Duddy, interview with author.
18. J. Austen, interview with author, 10 April 1988.
19. J. McDonald, interview with author, 7 October 2003.
20. *Belfast Telegraph*, 18 October 2003; see also C. Crawford, *Inside the UDA: Volunteers and Violence* (London: Pluto Press), p. 63.
21. M. Stone, *None Shall Divide Us* (London: John Blake, 2003), p. 213.
22. *Ulster*, March 1989.
23. Ibid.
24. Stone, *None Shall Divide Us*, p. 228.
25. M. Dillon, *Stone Cold: The True Story of Michael Stone and the Milltown Massacre* (London: Hutchinson, 1992), pp. 59–61, 69–71, 145–6.
26. Ibid., pp. 142–3.
27. *Loyalist*, vol. 1, no. 5, 1992.
28. Ibid.
29. McDonald, interview with author.
30. *Warrior*, vol. 1, no. 5, 1993. It is produced by the North Antrim and Londonderry UDA.

31. Stone, *None Shall Divide Us*, p. 104.
32. Ibid., p. 105.
33. Ibid., p. 5.
34. Tyrie, interview with author, 17 November 2003.
35. Stone, *None Shall Divide Us*, p. 119.
36. Ibid.
37. Ibid., p. 201.
38. Ibid., pp. 197–8.
39. D. Lister and H. Jordan, *Mad Dog: The Rise and Fall of Johnny Adair and 'C' Company* (Edinburgh: Mainstream, 2003), pp. 53–66.
40. *Ulster*, April 1988.
41. *Ulster*, May 1988.
42. *Ulster*, November 1988.
43. McKittrick *et al.*, *Lost Lives*, p. 1148; see also the *Scotsman*, 17 October 1988.
44. *Scotsman*, 29 November 1988.
45. N. Davies, *Ten-Thirty-Three: The Inside Story of Britain's Secret Killing Machine in Northern Ireland* (Edinburgh: Mainstream, 1999), pp. 130–4.
46. *Ulster*, November 1988.
47. Lister and Jordan, *Mad Dog*, p. 50.
48. Davies, *Ten-Thirty-Three*, p. 126.
49. *Ulster*, March 1989.
50. *Independent*, 7 November 1989.
51. Ibid.
52. Ibid.
53. T. Lyttle, interview with author, 12 April 1989.
54. Obituary of Tommy Lyttle, *Guardian*, 21 October 1995.
55. *Sunday Best: Sleeping with the Enemy*, BBC Radio 4, 14 September 2003.
56. J. McDonald, in P. Taylor, *Loyalists* (London: Bloomsbury, 1999), p. 206.
57. RUC source quoted by Tyrie, interview with author,17 November 2003.
58. *Independent*, 9 January 1990.
59. *Ulster*, March 1990.
60. Ibid.
61. *Ulster*, May 1990.
62. Ulster, July–August 1990.
63. Duddy, interview with author.
64. Stone, *None Shall Divide Us*, pp. 107–9.
65. Lister and Jordan, *Mad Dog*, pp. 78–9.
66. *Irish News*, 7 February 1991.
67. Ibid.
68. *Irish News*, 20 April 1991.
69. *Guardian*, 18 April 1991.
70. Ibid.
71. J. Cusack and H. McDonald, *UVF* (Dublin: Poolbeg, 1997), p. 274.
72. D. Ervine, interview with author, 6 May 2003.
73. G. McMichael, interview with author.
74. *Observer*, 20 April 2003.

75. *Ulster*, April 1993.
76. Lister and Jordan, *Mad Dog*, pp. 180–1.
77. Former UDA prisoner who does not wish to be named, interview with author, 5 December 2002.

7

Simply the Best: the Rise of Johnny Adair and C Company

◌

Outside the forbidding walls of Crumlin Road prison the killing continued and increased. The UVF played their part in it but over the period from the ending of the Brooke talks and the Loyalist ceasefire to the end of the year, UDA/UFF gunmen went to work with a ferocity not seen in many years. They claimed a total of ten victims, seven in Belfast, though one was later admitted to have been a case of mistaken identity. Media speculation over the emergence of a 'new breed'[1] of Loyalist killers became intense and it was fuelled too by statements in the UDA's renamed journal, the *New Ulster Defender*.

'Due to results obtained by the UFF and also by the Stevens inquiry team', it told readers in the new year of 1992, 'the organisation has been able to reorganise and restructure itself. The end result is that the Ulster Defence Association is a very much different organisation from that of the eighties.'[2] John Stevens, a later issue argued, should be applauded for 'removing senior UDA personnel, now expelled, who had been in the employ of the security forces for some time'.[3] Their role, it claimed, had fitted well with the strategy of Sir Maurice Oldfield, who had been brought out of retirement from MI6 by Margaret Thatcher, to overhaul and co-ordinate intelligence operations in Northern Ireland after she took office.

The Stevens inquiry, the *New Ulster Defender* argued, had led to good Loyalists also being taken off the streets and having to serve sentences. Eric McKee, William 'Winkie' Dodds and Matt Kincaid were among those it would have had in mind, but its view of the UDA's immediate future was an optimistic one: 'It is unlikely that the security forces will either recover the ground they have lost since the Stevens inquiry, or become a more potent threat against our republican enemies than that posed by Loyalists themselves.'[4] Privately, there were certainly those within the RUC who accepted this analysis:

> We've got a problem now, no question of it. There's a new bunch of boys in there who are capable of anything. They scare me, even the thought of them, but they have discipline too. They've been ready to learn lessons from the Provos. We're into a different ball game with them.[5]

Johnny Adair was one of this 'new bunch'. A Scottish journalist met the UDA's Inner Council in October 1991 but younger activists were also present, flanking Joe English, who took most of the questions. He reminded his interviewer 'that they were just children during the 1970s'[6] but he then made a point of introducing 'a young man in his early twenties with blond, spiky hair, blue eyes and a blue suede jerkin. "Things are brilliant now," this member declared. "We're free to do more than in the past. There was virtually nothing done by the UFF last year but this year it's way up." '[7] This was Adair, older in fact than the reporter thought, though talking was something he did little of when first asked to sit in at Inner Council meetings. The author can recall an occasion in April 1992 when he took a group of students to meet UDA spokesmen in the Shankill Road office above Frizzel's fish shop, which was destroyed by an IRA bomb eighteen months later. English again took the chair and the students asked a series of questions about the political situation and the UDA's role. Adair, in expensive-looking casual wear, was present but silent and although his eyes moved constantly round the group, his interest appeared to be only intermittent in what was being said.

Adair's rise was part of a remilitarisation of the UDA which the previous year's arrests under the Stevens inquiry had helped to speed up. He has been quoted as saying later that Stevens 'had got rid of all the shite'.[8] This remilitarisation was an uneven process but Adair was always central to it. Once in prison, Tommy Lyttle was replaced as West Belfast brigadier by Tommy Irvine, who was happy to let C Company go its own way in the Lower Shankill, which Adair was turning into his personal power base. After Irvine's arrest under the Stevens investigation, command of the brigade was given to Jim Spence from Woodvale. When he too was arrested and held for questioning, the command passed to Ken Barrett, later to be charged with the murder of Pat Finucane. Barrett proved ineffectual and, from prison, Lyttle tried to use what was left of his power to impose his own brother-in-law, Billy Kennedy, as brigadier. This provoked a crisis meeting at Langley Street social club in December 1990, which after some angry exchanges forced out the old guard and cleared the way for Adair to take full command of C Company. The intensified killing by them through 1991 and beyond flowed directly from these events.[9]

Johnny Adair was born in October 1963 and brought up in the Lower Oldpark, a very tough locality close to nationalist areas and the scene of constant street violence as the Troubles worsened after 1969. He attended school on an irregular basis and appears to have been under very little parental control. He did some casual work in a sawmill where his father was employed but this mattered little to him compared with the lure of the streets, along with alcohol and glue-sniffing. With friends such as Sammy McCrory, Donald Hodgen, 'Fat Jackie' Thompson and the brothers James and Herbie Millar, he formed a skinhead gang who got involved initially in petty then increasingly violent crime. Adair and some of the gang also formed a rock band called Offensive Weapon, whose raucous performances were outlets for raw sectarianism and support for the National Front, who were, in the early 1980s, trying to establish a presence in Belfast. There was little support for this venture from the UDA leadership and none at all from John McMichael, who told the author he wanted them 'run out of town'.[10]

Adair's criminality earned him a series of minor convictions but it also gave him his first contact with the UDA, who threatened him with a knee-capping for an assault on an old age pensioner. McCrory, his accomplice and close friend, did in fact receive this punishment but Adair was given the option of joining the Ulster Young Militants, the UDA's youth wing, which he agreed to do. This was and remained the organisation's way of redirecting the high-octane energy of teenagers like Adair and his friends. The author has had access to a report which RUC detectives began to compile on Adair. By 1993, it was already in the process of becoming a thick dossier. The conclusion to its introduction merits quotation:

> One could sum up Adair's childhood and adolescence as a period when he formed his intolerance for and hatred of the Catholic community. Due to a combination of lack of control by his parents and existing social conditions, it is clear he revelled in being a member of an unruly, violent group. The number of arrests for disorderly behaviour, assaults on police, riotous behaviour etc indicate a youth developing a dislike of authority and a disregard for the consequences of his actions.
>
> He was also the victim of a serious assault by youths from the local R.C. community during his late teens and this undoubtedly added 'fuel to the fire'. In short, he was a wild and reckless character, with a strong sense of tribal loyalty.[11]

Between 1985 and 1987 Adair, like many others, undertook quite extensive training in the Ulster Defence Force, set up by Andy Tyrie and McMichael to toughen up the quality of UDA recruits. He emerged from this anxious to prove himself but at a time when UDA/UFF activity had fallen to quite a low level. Johnston Brown, a former RUC detective sergeant who knew the Shankill area extremely well, recalled:

> C Company and indeed most of the West Belfast brigade were nothing much then. We knew who the key players were but we didn't rate them much: ageing men, drinking in clubs. They would have two or three Catholics a year hit, just for appearances' sake, you might say. Johnny certainly didn't rate them. I knew him from away back and I knew what a bad wee bastard he was, but it was the UVF boys he admired. He was fascinated by them, especially the team that operated out of the Liverpool Supporters club at the top end of the Shankill. He even used to call them the Mujahideen. I suppose he picked that up from TV news stuff on the war in Afghanistan.[12]

The relatively few UDA/UFF operations carried out in this period could be entrusted to already experienced gunmen, though young enthusiasts might be 'blooded' too. McCrory got his chance with the killing of Francisco Notarantonio in October 1987 and C Company was involved in a sequence of further murders, including those of the previously mentioned Gerard Slane in September 1988 and Pat Finucane in February 1989. More followed that year and in 1990, when a succession of victims were mown down in high-speed, precision operations by masked squads in protective clothing who left no forensic tracings behind them and whose getaway routes and transport were thoroughly planned in advance.

The security forces had their suspicions of Adair's role and early in August 1990 he was arrested after the killing of John Judge, a 34-year-old Catholic who lived just off Belfast's Springfield Road. On the evening of 31 July, C Company gunmen, using a hijacked taxi and exploiting the fact that the security gates were open on Lanark Way, which linked the Shankill to the Springfield Road, shot their victim five times as he stood outside his home with friends during a birthday party for one of his three children. However, neither Adair, nor McCrory nor Thompson, who were arrested with him, were accused of Judge's killing. Instead, they were charged with three attempted murders over the June–July period, with illegal possession of arms and of threats to a girlfriend with whom Adair had recently quarrelled.

The case was not skilfully handled by the RUC and, in the face of inadequate evidence, all the charges were dropped and the men released in early December. Adair had in fact been directly involved in a series of killings in the period prior to this but only in the sense that he had gathered the necessary intelligence, 'picked the team' and organised transport. He was already proving extremely good at all this and increasing his authority and status in the process. The 1993 RUC report already referred to him as

> an extrovert and forceful personality. Although he had no significant schooling, he is an extremely bright and intelligent character. Adair is a streetwise and cunning individual who has, for a number of years, eluded police efforts to bring him to justice. All of the above combine to create in the eyes of his followers a heroic, charismatic leader. Adair thrives on the reputation he has built up and wastes no opportunity to enhance it.[13]

This last character trait would be his eventual undoing but the RUC were right in their assessment of a formidable enemy.

Brown did not take long either to recognise Adair's quality.

> I don't know what his IQ was but he was able to run rings round us. He would pick targets, often at random to start with though he began to target the Provos very effectively as he got more confident. He set things up really fast, sometimes over drinks in a club, then he would call a hit team together and keep them incommunicado in his house in Hazelfield Street until it was time to move. Often the final decision was made in the kitchen with Gina, Adair's common-law wife, doing the tea. He'd shout out 'kitchen' when he wanted the team together. I saw it happen.

I did close-up surveillance, don't forget, I talked my way into his confidence. 'We're soldiers, taking the war to the enemy,' he would tell me, but he never missed a trick over his alibi. He'd be down in a club or a bar with plenty of people to see him by the time the target was taken out.[14]

Brown's surveillance and eventual entrapment of Adair is one of the most extraordinary and courageous episodes in the entire history of the RUC. Over a period of many months, this self-effacing but indefatigable officer, who more often than not didn't even carry a firearm, used every opportunity to talk to Adair, in the street and in his home, to study his character traits. He also spun him stories of IRA and INLA observation of his movements, which he could abort by having colleagues arrest the non-existent 'spotters'. On one occasion, he managed to make Adair believe that the RUC had got Gina off on a drink-driving charge, when in reality the alcohol in her blood sample had tested below the legal limit. 'I remember him saying, "Thanks, big man," but it was all part of a long game to let him think I was on his side, that we were still "their" police force.'[15]

Older members of the UDA began to worry about Adair's rising profile and the frequency of the attacks on the nationalist community which he seemed to be able to organise. The anxiety reached up to Inner Council members such as Joe English but also to Adair's brigadier, Jim Spence, who feared that C Company was getting out of control. He even voiced these fears to Brown, who recalled Spence complaining to him that C Company was financing itself from the takings of the Langley Street social club bar and had no accountability for its actions. 'I want to take down that bastard Adair but I can't wind in the wee fucker at all,' Spence once told him.[16] It was the tenacity and courage of Brown and his police colleagues that would do the job of 'winding in' Adair but it would also take time. Meanwhile, C Company's reputation grew and gaudy murals started to appear in Loyalist areas, celebrating its exploits and using the words of Tina Turner's hit 'Simply the Best'.

Increasingly Adair began to feel that C Company's status entitled it to 'intervene' in other brigade areas he deemed to be 'under-performing'. None of these was far from his own base, since Belfast is not a huge city. A case in point was North Belfast, which had recruited strongly in the early period of the Troubles but had also undergone numerous command changes. As with the organisation as a whole, its killing capacity had dwindled in the 1980s and its leadership quality had deteriorated, as one of its very active members, Eddie McLean, recalled in conversation with the author:

Things needed to change. There were too many hard men who were just hoods, not real Loyalists. Tigers Bay especially was a mess until Johnny brought a team in to sort it out. They were good. If they wanted to operate in our area they would make contact. I was kept in the picture. I knew about every target. They would be watched for weeks, sometimes months, then we'd send back all the intelligence needed by the team Johnny picked for the hit . . . I set up the safe houses, the escape routes. I was directly involved in six C Company hits, all good ones, all successful.[17]

One particularly brutal operation outside the Shankill which Adair was involved in was in South Belfast, a brigade area, like the East, for which he had little respect. This was prompted by an IRA ambush at Teebane crossroads in County Tyrone between the towns of Omagh and Cookstown on 17 January 1992. The eight victims were all Protestant building workers who were returning from repair work on the army base at Lisanelly, killed by a roadside bomb packed into a plastic bin. A car and a school bus with twelve pupils in it passed the spot just moments before the huge explosion which left a crater more than six metres wide and a metre deep. The six survivors had to be treated for very severe injuries.[18]

Although an emotionally disturbed RUC officer took three lives before shooting himself in a one-man attack on Sinn Fein's Falls Road office on 4 February, a Loyalist response to Teebane was a certainty and it came the following day. Adair had contacts with South Belfast, particularly with Joe Bratty and Raymond Elder, two of the more active UDA members there, and helped pick a target, Sean Graham's betting shop on the mainly Catholic Lower Ormeau Road. He also provided a C Company gunman to take part in the attack. On 5 February at 2.00 p.m. the small shop was full when two gunmen in masks and boiler suits emerged from a car parked across the road from it on University Avenue. It was the work of moments for them to enter Graham's, firing indiscriminately with an automatic rifle and a revolver. The impact, in a confined area, confronted ambulance crews and a local priest with an appalling sight when they arrived on the scene.

Only three of the people in the shop escaped serious injury and five were killed, including fifteen-year-old James Kennedy. Two years later his mother died, from what her husband claimed was a broken heart. 'She talked about James a lot, he was her life. She never really got over it.'[19] Interviewed by the *Irish Times* soon after this, he was quoted as saying: 'The bullets that killed James didn't just travel in distance, they travelled in time. Some of those bullets never stop travelling.'[20] As the gunmen backed out of the shop they were heard yelling: 'Remember Teebane.' It too was a terrible atrocity, as sectarian, the *New Ulster Defender* insisted, as the attack on Graham's. In an article, 'Teebane: the truth', it censured the media for avoiding saying this and it also invoked a maxim of Clausewitz on 'the rapier sword of revenge' as a legitimate weapon of war.[21]

The Sinn Fein-controlled Lower Ormeau Residents' Action Group vehemently attacked Alasdair McDonnell, a local doctor and SDLP councillor and now a Westminster MP, for daring publicly to link the betting shop slaughter to the Teebane bomb. He was accused of trying to shift the blame onto the IRA in order to draw support away from Sinn Fein to his own party in the Westminster election due later in the year. The truth was, as journalist

Suzanne Breen pointed out, that after Teebane, Catholics across Northern Ireland simply held their breath in readiness for certain Loyalist retaliation while stepping up their security precautions as far as they could. She also stressed that she had heard little demand among Lower Ormeau residents for the IRA to respond with attacks on pubs or betting shops in nearby Protestant areas such as Donegall Pass or the Annadale Flats further up the Ormeau Road. The hardest line taken was that if the IRA knew the identity of the killers at Graham's it should 'take them out when the time was right'.[22] In due course this would happen, though not before other Catholics from the locality would die at Loyalist hands.

Only the day before the massacre at Graham's, sentence was passed in Belfast Crown Court on Brian Nelson after a trial which, for those close to victims of C Company's hit squads, reopened many wounds. Several of the victims had been targeted with intelligence data Nelson had fed to the UDA/UFF while at the same time working in close co-operation with the army's highly secretive Force Research Unit. The trial in fact raised more questions than it answered because an original total of fifteen charges, including the murders of Terence McDaid and Gerard Slane, were dropped. The killing of Pat Finucane did not figure among the original charges. In all, Nelson admitted to five charges of conspiracy to murder, one of possessing a sub-machine gun and fourteen of possessing information likely to be of use to terrorists. After a glowing tribute to his work from an anonymous British intelligence officer, now known to have been Colonel Gordon Kerr, who later became military attaché to the British embassy in Beijing, Nelson was given concurrent sentences of ten years.

His punishment was widely agreed to be lenient and he was quickly spirited out of Belfast to serve only five years. The case had huge implications for the handling of covert operations by the security forces and Kerr, who claimed in court that Nelson had used his double role to save lives, could give few examples of this. Others have argued that Nelson had no qualms about letting innocent Catholics be murdered, even when this angered his army handlers,[23] and also that, having been a failure as a soldier, he took a sick relish in the power he could exercise as a double agent. 'Pitting your wits against those you seek to compromise acts like a drug,' Nelson confided to a journal he kept in prison. 'The more you experience it, the more you want it, regardless of the moments of intense fear.'[24]

Almost everything about the way the trial was conducted served to prevent the full extent of Nelson's role being revealed. There was no reference to the sectarian brutality of which he was known to be capable, neither was there any hint of claims he had made in his journal that the RUC Special Branch and army intelligence had known of the UDF's training programme in the 1980s but had been careful not to interfere with it. A video recording of one of the UDF's exercises, according to Nelson, was actually made available to the security forces. Another eleven years were to pass before any of this was made public, either in the press[25] or in the Canadian judge Peter Cory's report into a series of unsolved murders including that of Finucane.

Had not the original charges against Nelson been dropped, his trial would have put the UDA itself under a great deal of scrutiny. In the period after John McMichael's death and Andy Tyrie's resignation questions continued to be asked about how much they had known about Nelson's double role. 'If the Crown Forces wanted people dead and wanted us to do it, we were the people to do it. We had the same enemy,'[26] an unnamed Loyalist paramilitary has told the journalist Martin Dillon. For British military intelligence to use the UDA to keep up the pressure on the IRA and to expose its inability to protect ordinary Catholics from Loyalist attack could help to edge the IRA leadership onto a political road which some of them, notably Gerry Adams, had already settled for. Using loyal 'counter-gangs' against an identified enemy both to put military pressure on it and to influence its political thinking was a well-tried British strategy which had pre-dated the conflict in Northern Ireland and been tested in Kenya, Aden, Cyprus and Southern Rhodesia (Zimbabwe).[27]

When the Stevens inquiry was set up Nelson was reported to have given all his files to the army for safekeeping. The Stevens team took four months to learn of their existence. Copies of most of this material were kept by the UDA and the author has been reliably informed by one of its active members that a good deal more, when Nelson was arrested, 'went straight to us and onto our computers. His trial in one way wasn't good news for us though it blocked off a flow of information about us to the security forces. But it didn't halt the process of us getting our act together, quite the opposite.'[28] Some of this material almost certainly helped Adair and his C Company team to ratchet up the rate of killing they carried out in 1992 and indeed right up to the IRA's 1994 ceasefire.

More recently, it has been reported by a Belfast journalist with exceptionally good sources that Adair in fact had direct contacts with army intelligence and with one officer senior in rank to Kerr. 'Adair's finger prints', he has claimed, 'have been found on at least a dozen military intelligence dossiers uncovered by the Stevens inquiry team into collusion between Loyalists and the security forces.'[29]

*

Adair liked to brag to Johnston Brown and other RUC officers of his sources within the security forces but he had his own distinctive methods, such as cruising nationalist areas in a car with a cardboard cut-out figure of a Celtic player dangling inside the rear windscreen. He was even known to go jogging into such areas wearing a Celtic strip and if stopped by the security forces would be happy to identify for them the houses or bars used by those he claimed were in the IRA. Whatever the source, the end result was more killing both in Belfast and beyond it. Three victims were shot dead in early 1992 in

Moira, Lisburn and Kilrea, and on 29 March fire bombs damaged a store in Dublin city centre.

Time was also taken out to settle accounts with members of the organisation thought to have betrayed it. On 14 January 1992, two gunmen shot dead David Boyd, a 41-year-old builder who lived in the Dundonald area of Belfast. A UFF statement claimed he had been a police informer. On 15 April, a much more prominent member met the same fate. This was Edward 'Ned' McCreery, the brother of the former Northern Ireland and Manchester United winger David McCreery. He ran the Avenue One bar on East Belfast's Templemore Avenue and had a violent record in the UDA going back to the early 1970s. In a statement after he had been shot dead at his home, the UFF said its 'Special Assignment Section', first referred to by it after Jim Craig's murder in 1988, had executed McCreery as part of an 'ongoing investigation into various degrees of corruption and collusion' by certain past Loyalist leaders. The statement concluded: 'No further warnings, either public or private, will be given.'[30]

It is unlikely that this 'disciplinary' killing involved Adair and there were press reports of unease over it. 'Protestants don't like Protestant killing Protestant,' one Belfast Sunday paper was told and the UDA Inner Council also sought to distance itself from rumours that Tyrie was under threat from it over matters arising from his extended period as Commandant and chairman of the UDA.[31]

After this it was back to business with C Company. Two weeks later a masked gunman walked into the Springfield Road pharmacy in West Belfast, while an accomplice waited outside for him on a Suzuki motor bike. His target was Philomena Hanna, a mother of two aged twenty-six, whom he shot six times at close range in the head and upper body. The UFF, in its usual statement a little later, claimed the victim was an IRA intelligence officer, but RUC detectives said there was no evidence to support this. What she had been by all accounts was someone willing to serve both communities, who regularly delivered prescriptions and bottled oxygen to elderly Protestants living on 'their' side of the nearby peace line.[32]

Murdering a young pharmacist at her place of work was an easier undertaking than targeting leading IRA members. Adair found this out in July 1992 when he picked a four-man team from C Company and also the South Belfast brigade to kill Brian Gillen, an IRA Belfast commander who later became a member of its Army Council. Also targeted were Martin Lynch, another IRA leader, and two women volunteers, and Adair acquired information about an address they were using in Andersonstown in West Belfast. The operation was set up only twenty-four hours before it was mounted early on Saturday, 18 July but it turned into a disaster when the unit, comprising 'Fat Jackie' Thompson, Sammy McCrory and two less experienced members, Tommy Potts and Matthew McCormick, drove into a well-prepared police and army ambush on Finaghy Road North. The four, who were lucky to survive some intense fire from the security forces, were all arrested and later given prison sentences.[33]

This outcome was a bad blow to Adair because Gillen had become a target he was obsessed with and also because Thompson and particularly McCrory were very close friends. It did not however deter him from going ahead with plans for more attacks but by the summer of 1992 the Northern Ireland Office and John Major's government in London were under growing pressure to take away from the UDA the legal status which it still enjoyed. Successive governments had pondered but avoided the issue since the emergence of the UFF in 1973. That organisation had been proscribed almost at once but the UDA, for all its closeness to it, was allowed to maintain a legal presence through its clubs, advice centres and intermittent interventions in politics. For some within the security forces this was a situation they could live with, as in their view a legal UDA could be more readily infiltrated than a proscribed one. Events unleashed by the Stevens inquiry made this view much less tenable.

By the beginning of 1992 Sinn Fein had added its voice to the growing demand for a ban on the UDA even though Martin McGuinness had previously been dismissive of Loyalism's operational capacity. Indeed, the previous Easter had seen him address a very large rally at Milltown cemetery to mark the seventy-fifth anniversary of the 1916 rising and he had used the occasion to pour scorn on the Loyalist paramilitaries, comparing them to the 'motivated military force' that was the IRA. He also asked his audience the somewhat rhetorical and redundant question 'How many of the security forces have Loyalists killed?' and drew a huge cheer from his listeners when he declared: 'Loyalists are cowards and their military rating is zero.'[34] By the end of 1991, neither he nor his audience were likely to have been thinking in these terms.

The SDLP had long before this been making the case for a ban on the UDA and one of their spokesman, North Belfast councillor Brian Feeney, did so forcefully on the television programme *This Week* on 30 April 1992. Michael Mates, a minister at the Northern Ireland Office, also took part in the programme and tried to avoid the issue, though accepting that the UDA was 'getting more sophisticated'. He went on to say that the organisation

> is from a part of the community that believes they are under threat. It has a right
> to protest and to associate within the law but none of this is to say that there are
> not rowdy, hooligan and possibly criminal elements within it.[35]

The government, he stressed, would keep its legal position under review. Asked recently by the author whether he should have been more forthright on the whole issue, Mates replied:

> I was speaking carefully at the time because, when I appeared on that programme,
> we were in the process of making assessments. I therefore had to be very careful
> what I said.

I remain of the view that the UDA/UFF came into existence and became militant and organised originally because they thought their communities were under threat. The fact that they then embraced criminal and terrorist elements is another matter and it was because of those elements that it was eventually banned. Whether it should have been banned earlier is not for me to say: there are many considerations which led us to decide that the time was right for banning. I still think that if the IRA were to disband the Protestant paramilitaries would wither on the vine.[36]

As speculation about an imminent ban grew, UDA spokesmen clung to the claim that it still had a role distinctive from that of the UFF. 'It's a separate body,' an Inner Council member told a journalist on 18 June 1992. 'It's there to offer community advice and information. If the IRA stopped its campaign it would still have a role as a community support group, perhaps a political pressure group, but as long as they are here, carrying on their programme of genocide against the Protestant people, we'll be here.'[37] By then, however, the reality was that the UDA was existing on borrowed time as a legal body.

When the new Secretary of State for Northern Ireland, Sir Patrick Mayhew, did announce, on 10 August 1992, that the UDA was to be made illegal, he told Parliament that a detailed review had satisfied him that it was 'actively and primarily engaged in criminal and terrorist acts'[38] but would not be drawn on specific reasons for the policy change involved. Most commentators reacted to the ban as proof of government concern at the new muscle of an organisation which was starting to match the killing capacity of the IRA, but they doubted what real effect it would have.

Feeney, who sat on the city council for one of Belfast's worst killing grounds, agreed but took some satisfaction from the ban being 'an important message for the nationalist community, that those who are organising the killing of Catholics are not going to be tolerated as a legal organisation'.[39] Dr Ian Paisley also voiced doubts about what the ban would achieve and wanted to know why it had been so long delayed. He allowed himself to sound equivocal over how far he accepted UDA responsibility for recent murders and claimed that the hand of Dublin was behind the ban as well as the government's concern to restart inter-party talks. He also offered his own view that government policy was 'to keep Sinn Fein a non-proscribed organisation so that it can talk to them'.[40]

Paisley's belief that British ministers would talk to Sinn Fein proved to be correct, though of course this was initially done through intermediaries. His scepticism, shared by others, over whether the UDA ban would either halt or reduce Loyalist killings was supported by a poster proclaiming 'business as usual' which appeared on a window of the UDA's Shankill Road HQ on the Monday after the ban was announced. The building itself remained empty after the ban and one newspaper reporter went so far as to say that it had become 'one of the safest places to be in Ireland'.[41] His words now have an unintended irony given the carnage caused by the IRA's attack on it less than eighteen months later but his point was that there was so little reaction to the Secretary of State's decision because the UDA was well prepared for it and had been tipped off in advance.

In the same newspaper one UDA spokesman told an interviewer that the security forces had come round to the case for a ban because they had lost their grip on the organisation. 'We were banned because they couldn't direct us any more,'[42] he claimed, and he also linked the ban to the fact that MI5 had recently taken over responsibility for counter-terrorist intelligence and surveillance. This had indeed been announced in Parliament in May 1992, after an at times messy turf war between MI5 and Special Branch.[43]

The *New Ulster Defender*'s view was that the ban would have little effect on the security situation:

> Not only has the UDA declared that it has no intention of going away, but history shows clearly that proscribing organisations does nothing to reduce their support or their ability to operate. Indeed many experts suggest that the opposite is the case. So it can be said that the ban will suit the UDA in many ways.[44]

In the same editorial, however, the magazine reminded readers that the UDA still had a political analysis of the conflict and of ways out of it: 'The UDA have publicly declared their support for the creation of fair and just institutions of government for Northern Ireland as agreed and endorsed by the people in free elections.'[45] Compromise and accommodation were still attainable, it stressed, though there could be no compromise on Northern Ireland's continued right to exist. Given the ongoing level of Loyalist and IRA killing in 1992, this was relatively conciliatory talk for the UDA to offer.

It was, however, offset by another article in the same issue, which was bitterly dismissive of the SDLP's claims that it could lead the way to what its leader, John Hume, had started to call 'an agreed Ireland'. This, it was argued, was simply a phrase with which he could mask the strategy of drawing British ministers into a joint sovereignty agreement with Dublin. Out of this, a simple arithmetical majority could then be invoked to justify the coercion of the Unionist majority in the North. The SDLP was castigated as a party which simply rode on the back of the IRA while protesting its own non-violence. It was a short step from these accusations to calling the SDLP part of a 'Pan-Nationalist Front'.[46]

Johnny Adair's interest in political analysis, from the UDA or any other source, was minimal. His reaction to the ban, once it was stated that it would come into effect on midnight of 10 August, was a typical piece of mischievous bravado. He presented himself at Tennent Street RUC station and asked to see Johnston Brown in order to announce his formal resignation from the UDA. Accompanying him were Jim Spence and Curtis Moorehead, who were both subsequently charged with terrorist offences and, in Moorehead's case, convicted. Their conversation was duly recorded by Brown and, in the growing dossier being built up on Adair, it could be linked to countless police sightings of him with leading UDA members and also entering and leaving its Shankill Road building.[47]

To Adair's brutal and visceral logic, the ban on the UDA pointed only in one direction, that of carrying on and stepping up the killing. The first victim to be targeted by him after the August ban was an eighteen-year-old Catholic schoolboy, Gerard O'Hara, who lived with his mother and sister in North Queen Street, a traditionally dangerous area where Catholic homes on the edge of the nationalist Carrick Hill and New Lodge estates lay within walking distance of the fiercely Loyalist Tigers Bay area. Just before 5.00 p.m. on 27 September, two masked C Company gunmen burst into the O'Hara home and killed their victim with a total of seventeen shots, though his mother Bridie begged them to shoot her instead. One of them, she later recalled, looked her in the eye as he went on firing. The Secretary of State, in a response to the murder, paid his own tribute to Bridie O'Hara's 'enormous act of love'[48] in offering her life for that of her son.

His sentiments could not have been further removed from those of the men who organised and carried out the attack. Eddie McLean, responding to media coverage of the boy's death and interviews with his mother ten years later, had this to say to the author: 'I was in on that. It was a fair target. The family was involved. His brother, an active Provo, had been sunning himself in their front garden half an hour before C Company moved.'[49] Asked about the victim's probable innocence and his mother's attempt to save him, his response was:

> Listen, I'd have shot her myself. She was a Provo, she was back-up for them. She washed their clothes in that house after they had been out killing my people. As for the boy, he'd have been a Provo too if he had lived long enough. It was an act of war. I had no remorse over it, none. We got a target, we got a result and I organised what the C Company boys needed to do the hit.[50]

In October and early November of 1992, the IRA intensified its own campaign with a wave of attacks on the security forces. One of these, on the RUC's forensic science laboratory building, wrecked over a thousand homes in the Belvoir area of Belfast. Central London was targeted once again with a fire bomb attack on the Hyde Park Hilton Hotel while massive damage was caused by bombs in the predominantly Protestant towns of Bangor, Coleraine and Glengormley. On 6 November, a UFF statement promised that further bombs would be answered with 'attacks against the republican community as a whole'. They had killed since Gerard O'Hara's murder but just a week after their newest threat they singled out an easy target in North Belfast.

This was James Murray's betting shop on the Oldpark Road, mostly used by Catholics who lived in an area traditionally called the Bone, on the edge of Ardoyne. On the afternoon of Saturday, 14 November, UFF gunmen staged a grim repetition of events on the Lower Ormeau Road at the start of the year. In the brutal slang of paramilitary Belfast they carried out a 'spray job' on the shop and its customers. One man fired an automatic weapon from the doorway and another smashed open the windows to hurl a grenade through it. As he did so he shouted: 'Youse deserve it, youse Fenian bastards.' Two men were killed instantly and another, who had survived captivity at Japanese hands in the Second World War, died later in hospital. Thirteen others were treated for injuries, in some cases very severe ones.[51]

In all these murders, Adair's role was as the co-ordinator, picking the targets and the killers he decided to assign to them. Though physically aggressive and with a proven history of violence, it is probable that he did not carry out any killings at this point himself. He had almost certainly been involved in operations where he had missed targets but he was clearly fascinated by killing and would boast about 'hits' he had not carried out himself.[52] The Oldpark Road betting shop killing was followed by a raucous celebration in a Loyalist club in South Belfast with Adair occupying centre stage. 'Johnny could set up operations, he could motivate a unit, no question, but he was a fantasist,' Jackie McDonald has said. 'He lived in his own world and he always had to be at the centre of it.'[53]

The coming of 1993 saw no remission from killing for Northern Ireland's people. The UVF carried out the year's first murders on 3 January, but the UDA/UFF came hard on their heels and in fact claimed twice as many victims over the year as a whole. Increasingly they showed themselves able to target active Republicans, killing several of them, while among those who survived were Gerard McGuigan, Annie Armstrong and Bobby Lavery, all elected Sinn Fein members of Belfast City Council. Only a few weeks before the attempt on his life, Lavery had seen his own son fatally shot by UDA/UFF gunmen who broke into the family home on 8 August. Ominously too for Sinn Fein, the home of Gerry Adams was also targeted in an unsuccessful grenade attack.

Seamus Mallon, SDLP member of Parliament for Newry and Armagh, made a desperate plea at the start of the year to Loyalist gunmen to meet him face to face so that he could hear what conditions they might want to set out as a basis for ending their killings. He met with no response from the Combined Loyalist Military Command, which in reality exercised little real control over the way the UDA/UFF had operated since it was set up. Unlike the UVF, the UDA/UFF did issue a communiqué in response to Mallon, refusing categorically to meet him.[54] Four weeks later it set off incendiary bombs at the Belfast homes of two of his party colleagues, Dr Alasdair McDonnell and Dorita Field, both city councillors. They, like Mallon, were described as members of the Pan-Nationalist Front, a phrase first coined by Adams, as readers of the UDA magazine were reminded.

Raymond Smallwoods certainly took this view and was not inhibited in expressing it in his role as a spokesman for the Ulster Democratic Party. Reminiscing to the author in April 1993 about his conviction twelve years earlier for his part in the attempted murder of Bernadette McAliskey, he declared:

Back then I'd have happily killed John Hume. He and his party rode on the back of
the Provos and they still do. He has called Ulster Unionism 'a boil to be lanced'.
What else can he mean than by the surgery of Irish unification? Sinn Fein at least
are open about their goals and their methods while the SDLP claim to condemn
violence but profit from it politically. Without it Hume would never be where he
is and he wouldn't have got his Anglo-Irish Agreement either. It's all the logical
extension of a strategy based on an obscene and monumental lie which seeks to
deny Ulster's Protestantism and Britishness.[55]

Smallwoods was beginning to be thought of as a 'coming man' who could
think and talk politically and who had the ear of the Inner Council. He was
also clear in his own mind that Loyalists must fight on and accepted that this
could mean those with no Republican involvement being killed along with
known IRA men. Exactly this happened at Castlerock in County Londonderry
on 25 March 1993, when UDA/UFF gunmen opened fire on a building
worker's van. They shot dead James Gerard Kelly from Maghera, who was later
admitted by the IRA to be an active volunteer, as well as three workmates
unlucky enough to have shared a lift to work with him. The following day a
UDA/UFF spokesman was quoted in a newspaper as saying: 'It is a terrible
thing that anyone should lose their life but, if you are talking in terms of
success rates, yes, this week has been a success and it's still only Thursday.'[56]

Penetrating UDA/UFF operations in Belfast was proving harder than it had
ever been for the security forces. Their spokesmen readily admitted to the
press that Loyalist paramilitaries and the UDA/UFF in particular posed as
great a threat as they had at any point in the last fifteen years because of a
hugely improved ability to avoid forensic or any other form of detection of
their operations.[57] This reality owed everything to the organisational skills of
Adair and his rampant C Company gunmen recruited from the streets of the
Oldpark and Lower Shankill.

Women who shared Adair's bed, other than Gina, his common-law wife
and mother of his children, have said that when he came to them after a killing
had been set up and carried out, simply describing what had happened gave
him a sexually charged excitement. The fact that nearly all C Company's
killings were done by others selected by Adair does not appear to have got in
the way of this.[58] He also took a proprietary pride in individuals such as
Stephen McKeag, one of its most ruthless killers. Johnston Brown has
recalled Adair introducing McKeog to him as his 'top gun'[59] and this accol-
ade was later formalised in an award ceremony in a Shankill club. Like Adair,
McKeag grew up in the area and knew him well but his background was a religious one and he was a much less extrovert character. He brought a cool discipline to the business of killing, which Adair admired and perhaps envied.
His first victim was the pharmacist Philomena Hanna and others followed,
including Gerard O'Hara and the men who died in the Oldpark Road bookmaker's shop.

Through the summer and autumn of 1993 C Company continued to kill and Adair basked increasingly in the notoriety this brought him as its commander and then as West Belfast brigadier. He appears to have claimed this rank for himself when Jim Spence was arrested once again, and the RUC report on Adair accepted that he had become responsible for most UDA/UFF attacks in Belfast and beyond. It called him the 'single most powerful member of the UDA/UFF by a substantial margin'.[60] Later that year detectives taped Adair describing his position:

> In the whole of Northern Ireland the ball's at my feet. If I say go, it goes. If I say stop, it stops. I say make the bombs and we'll scare the Peelers for forty-eight hours. I've got some fucking power, I'll tell you. How did I get to the top? Scratching my balls, do you think? Do you think I bluffed my way there?[61]

He was, of course, progressively incriminating himself, without ever seeming to realise it, by his incurable boasting, since everything he said was being noted by Brown and other detectives. Brown recalls a naïve quality which co-existed with Adair's streetwise operational cunning. On one occasion over tea with the detective in his house, Adair started to tell him how he ran C Company. Brown intervened to say: 'Well, I'll just have to put you in prison then, won't I?' to which Adair roguishly replied: 'You'll have to catch me first, big man.'[62] On another occasion, Brown even joked with Adair when he and some of his C Company team were all talking at once. To great hilarity, he urged them to talk only one at a time so that the bug in the room light could pick up their voices. Later that day a colleague told Brown that the house was indeed bugged for sound, albeit not in the light.[63]

Adair had sniffed glue as a teenager and dabbled in the beginnings of the Belfast drug scene but Brown and his colleagues noted carefully the evidence of his increasing addiction as C Company worked towards a crescendo of killing while moving into drug-dealing themselves.

> The extent of his drug abuse has been further accelerated by the fact that his team members are selling large quantities of drugs as a means of making substantial sums of money. The readily available supply of free drugs has caused him to develop an increasing habit.[64]

This was apparent to everyone who observed Adair at this time and of course C Company's dealing brought him spending money well beyond any legal income he could claim. Police checks on the contents of his home and the value of the cars he drove made this mismatch abundantly clear.

As 1993 drew towards its close, media interest in Adair grew, though without his actual name being used in journalists' copy. The *Guardian*'s Maggie O'Kane featured him in a rather melodramatic article entitled 'For Queen and Country'. She met him with the UDA's Inner Council for a question-and-answer session in which he took little part, but he later offered to drive her round the Shankill and then up to the Cloughfern Arms pub in Rathcoole.

When she asked him if he had ever previously had a Catholic in his car he replied: 'Only a dead one.' Her description of his stocky build, short hair with blond highlights, tattooed arms and gold earring in his right ear would have left the *Guardian*'s probably few readers in the area in no doubt as to who she was writing about and she used the nickname 'Mad Dog', which some RUC officers had begun to apply to him.[65]

A very similar article appeared three days later in the *Irish Independent*. Under the title 'Face to face with the UFF's top assassin' it described Adair clearly enough, without mentioning his name, as

> a bundle of nervous energy, talks fifteen to the dozen, racing along, flinging the names of IRA men in Belfast across the room. The addresses he personally knows because he has targeted their homes, cruising around the estates of West Belfast as well as the tightly knit Nationalist areas in North Belfast.[66]

As with the *Guardian* piece, much was made of Adair's perverse pride in the IRA's numerous attempts to kill him.

These had indeed become part of his legend but on the very next day after the *Irish Independent* interview, the IRA tried again. Early in the afternoon of Saturday, 23 October, a two-man unit from Ardoyne left a powerful Semtex bomb in Frizzel's fish shop on the Shankill Road, immediately below premises which had been used by the UDA's Inner Council as well as its West Belfast commanders. This ended after the August 1992 ban, after which only a prisoners' aid group made occasional use of the building. Thomas Begley, one of the men who planted the bomb, was killed as were nine shoppers and passers-by in a huge explosion which brought the building above down upon the shop.

Fifty-seven others were injured, some badly. Three women and two school-girls were among the dead and rescue services faced an appalling task clearing away the rubble to uncover the many bodies buried under it. The IRA later claimed that the bomb was intended to have a short fuse on it, allowing just enough time to evacuate the shop but not enough for anyone upstairs to escape. There was, of course, nobody upstairs. IRA intelligence had failed and Begley, an inexperienced and possibly expendable volunteer in the organisation's eyes, had made an error in priming the device.[67] Psychologically, the attack was a traumatic blow to Protestants, their arch-enemies being seen to have launched an indiscriminate strike in a historic heartland of Loyalism on a busy Saturday.

The UDA/UFF responded chillingly to the Shankill bomb, issuing a statement that same afternoon promising that all units would be fully mobilised by six o'clock in the evening. 'John Hume, Gerry Adams and the nationalist electorate', it warned, 'will pay a heavy, heavy price for today's atrocity. To the perpetrators we say "There will be no hiding place. Time is on our side." '[68] Reprisal killings followed swiftly from both the UVF and the UDA/UFF in the days after the bombing, while the Shankill buried its dead amidst scenes of grief which left even hardened camera crews emotionally drained.

Adair was convinced the bomb was intended for him. He declared that an IRA 'spotter' must have observed him either entering or leaving the building above Frizzel's shop to collect a prison visiting pass in order to see his old friend Sammy 'Skelly' McCrory in the Maze. This, he claimed, would have been seen by the IRA as justification for the killing. At the Maze that weekend, Michael Stone later recalled listening to a wild tirade on the bombing from Adair:

> I got the distinct impression there was no regret on his part at the loss of civilians, the deaths of mothers and their children, or the fact that the very heart of his community had been bombed to kingdom come. I knew the deaths of the nine were a badge of honour rather than an unspeakable human tragedy when he said to me: 'I'm very important, Mikey. Those people lost their lives because the Provies wanted me.'[69]

In Stone's version of this meeting, Adair went on to promise reprisals for the Shankill bomb. These, he claims, were to include simultaneous attacks on Catholic churches at Sunday Mass in the Belfast area. According to him, Adair's words were that he would order picked hit squads to target churches then 'spray the fucking places with AKs, kill them all and let God sort them out'.[70]

The massacre of Catholic congregations at Mass could well have pushed the conflict in Northern Ireland over the edge and into the abyss of civil war. Only intensive activity by the security forces prevented it and for the first time in the history of the Troubles, many churches found themselves under police and army guard while priests urged worshippers to disperse as quickly as possible after Mass. One UDA member active at this time has told the author how Adair did indeed order an attack on the Holy Family church just off the Limestone Road in North Belfast:

> He wanted a congregation to be hit when they were in there for Mass. I organised the gear and the car for them and Johnny picked the team. I worried though because it would have been ordinary Catholics we got, not necessarily IRA men.[71]

Asked about this in a prison interview with the author more than ten years later, Adair disclaimed all knowledge of any such operation being planned. When confronted with Stone's recollection of his reaction to the Shankill bombing and the claims that he had sanctioned church attacks as a reprisal, Adair's response was predictable:

> Michael was a good Loyalist, unlike a lot of fuckers in the UDA who were all mouth, but he made up things. Don't forget he says things in that book about me being gay. That's a joke. I've probably shagged more women than all the UDA's brigadiers put together.[72]

Pressed further on the issue, Adair simply shook his head and looked away. As others who have had contact with him have observed, Adair can be highly selective about what he wants to remember.

Mercifully, a major atrocity was averted at the Holy Family church.

> Our boys drove over from the Shankill and out of Tigers Bay to do the hit. They were a good team, fully tooled up, but when they got there big high iron gates were locked, blocking off access past the priest's house and the parish offices. Getting over the gates and back out would have taken time and the Peelers and the army were all over the area so they called it off.[73]

Father Sean Emerson, the Holy Family priest then and now, has confirmed that the gates were indeed secured before services during such tense periods and that at any weekday or Saturday evening Mass at least a hundred people would have been in the church and more on a Sunday.[74]

The Rising Sun bar at Greysteel, close to the shores of Lough Foyle and just a few miles from Londonderry, was without a doubt selected as a target because it was well away from Belfast, where security force activity was intense after the Shankill bomb. It was impossible, however, for the security forces to be everywhere. 'How many pubs are there in Northern Ireland?' one RUC officer asked the press in response to questions being put to him about the attack.[75] Another was quoted as saying: 'The Loyalist groups used to be a joke. We could find out almost anything we wanted. But now we have no significant intelligence.'[76]

The UDA man quoted here was willing to admit that a massacre of the Holy Family congregation would, in political and moral terms, have been a disastrous own goal for Loyalism. He was, however, ready to justify the organisation's attack on the night of Saturday, 30 October on the Rising Sun. Seventy people were in the bar waiting for a country and western band to perform when two men in camouflage kit and balaclavas burst in. One of them shouted 'Trick or treat' before they opened rapid fire with an AK47 assault rifle and a Browning automatic pistol. Nineteen people were hit in the fusillade of fire and eight of them were killed, seven Catholics and one Protestant who had served in the Ulster Defence Regiment. Their work was done in minutes and they withdrew to a getaway vehicle, leaving a scene of blood-splattered chaos behind them. Two women were among the dead, one aged just nineteen; another casualty was the 81-year-old father of the bar's owner.

Justifying Greysteel was not a problem for Loyalists. 'You must appreciate', one of them told the press, 'that to the UDA and UFF this is their Alamo. They feel they have nothing left to lose. They are in a war situation, and as the Provos have told us for twenty years, sometimes innocent people get hurt. When politicians say Loyalist violence hardly strengthens the Union with Britain they are missing the point. "Loyal" these days means something new. The Tories can't be trusted, so it's Loyalty to Ulster and its people. No-one else counts.'[77] Stephen Irwin, the Greysteel killer who had called 'Trick or treat' before opening fire, had no regrets when interviewed some time after he was sentenced in 1995 along with Torrens Knight, Jeffrey Deeney and two others involved in the back-up operation. 'I don't know what I'll feel in ten years' time,' he told an interviewer, 'but I've never felt remorse about what I did. We were using IRA tactics against the IRA and the republican community. It was Old Testament justice, an eye for an eye, a tooth for a tooth.'[78]

Five years later, Eddie McLean suffered a family bereavement shortly after serving most of a three-year sentence in the Maze. He received a card from UDA prisoners, including Adair, offering him their sympathy. Irwin signed the card simply as 'Stevie Greysteel'.[79] Irwin, Knight and Deeney were all members of the UDA's North Antrim and Londonderry brigade, a unit which had been only intermittently active in recent years although it had carried out the Castlerock killings seven months before Greysteel. Irwin's account of the Rising Sun attack describes the order for it coming from Belfast[80] and other UDA members are clear in their own minds that it was sanctioned by C Company on the Lower Shankill. Adair himself was under arrest at the time of the attack, having been taken, along with others, into Castlereagh RUC station for questioning on 28 October.

A West Belfast UDA member has talked to the author about the decision to target Greysteel:

> C Company had information that senior IRA men drank in the Rising Sun and the area was strongly nationalist. Unfortunately they were not there on Hallowe'en but our boys acted on the briefing they had been given from C Company here in Belfast. Torrens Knight was an important contact for them. He had been spending quite a bit of time with us on the Shankill. Of course I regretted the fact that innocent Catholics were killed, as well as a Protestant, but Knight, Deeney and Irwin believed their intelligence briefing had been right and they simply acted on it.[81]

The Hallowe'en massacre ended a terrible week in which twenty-three lives had been taken. The sight on television of John Hume weeping unashamedly at the funeral of some of the Greysteel victims captured the despair that many were starting to feel. Fear had become tangible and streets in Belfast and other places in Northern Ireland emptied at night in an atmosphere reminiscent of the worst killing times of the 1970s.

Yet even amidst these forebodings, political movement was taking place. Just a week after Greysteel the Irish journalist Eamon Mallie reported in the *Observer* that the IRA had been in secret contact with British intelligence. Sir Patrick Mayhew responded with a series of denials but three weeks later admitted that there had indeed been contacts though not, he insisted, negotiations. Republicanism, though still ready to wage war against both Loyalism and the British state, was developing a political strategy too. In February of the previous year, in its policy document *Towards a Lasting Peace*, Sinn Fein for the first time had avoided any reference to a precise period for British withdrawal and it also included an acknowledgement of Unionist rights, though not, it stressed, any right to a veto 'on the national rights of the Irish people as a whole'. The IRA's Army Council had in fact called off operations against British military targets in continental Europe though this was not made public and in January 1993, Gerry Adams made his first visit to the United States to talk to Americans for a New Irish Agenda, a group of Democrats and businessmen close to the new president, Bill Clinton, whose commitment to work for peace in Northern Ireland was on record.

Outwardly, Sinn Fein still took a hard line on the future of Northern Ireland as a political entity. In an article entitled 'No civil rights without national rights', its weekly paper declared in August 1993 that 'no reform short of its abolition can remedy the fundamental injustice of the six county state'.[82] It also cited a recent statement by Martin McGuinness that no further IRA ceasefires would be called without firm assurances of British withdrawal, though he avoided setting out any set period of time for this. Sinn Fein also showed signs of being willing to consider as an interim compromise joint British and Irish sovereignty over Northern Ireland, which had been recently set out as a basis for ending IRA violence in a British Labour Party document drafted by Kevin McNamara MP.

The UDA's response was to look for what it called 'hairline cracks' in the Pan-Nationalist Front. Sinn Fein and the SDLP, it argued, were beginning to falter in their reaction to the current level of Loyalist attacks, which could put at risk all the gains that nationalism had made. Sustained IRA violence could only raise the level of these attacks and 'move the British to a much harder anti-Irish stance in order to placate the Loyalist men of violence'. Hawks within the Pan-Nationalist Front would favour fighting on but others, not just within the non-violent SDLP, would oppose them.[83] It was an analysis rooted in a belief in a rationale for Loyalist attacks which went beyond the UDA itself.

Earlier in the year a phone-in poll conducted by the News Letter had shown 42 per cent of callers supporting Loyalist violence. Almost half of 4,000 callers said it was acceptable in some circumstances and what the Irish News described as a 'resounding' 82 per cent believed Loyalists would stop killing in response to a real IRA ceasefire.[84] The UDA's publications alluded to this evidence, claiming that 'Loyalists from all classes and walks of life openly commend this organisation as being the only force preventing a United Ireland active in Ulster today'.[85] Yet alongside uncompromising talk of this kind and amidst the carnage of October and November 1993, there were voices within or close to the UDA leadership which still signalled possible areas of compromise.

The December issue of the organisation's major Belfast publication predictably described the Shankill bomb as an act of Republican genocide and it also ran a lengthy article, originally published in Dublin four years earlier, on the erosion of a Protestant community in what it portrayed as a relentlessly sectarian and clerical Irish state. Even so, the same issue accepted Hume's commitment to non-violence but challenged what it saw as his political strategy of talking the British government into the role of a persuader of Unionists that their longer-term interests could only be in a united Ireland.

'A new Ireland' could be acceptable, it declared, if it was 'an island at peace with itself, where both jurisdictions can co-operate in areas of mutual benefit and where the legitimacy of both states is recognised by each'.[86]

These were the voices of the renamed Ulster Democratic Party, in close touch with the UDA but not directly of it, whose spokesmen, such as Gary McMichael and David Adams, would take it gradually into the peace process that began to unfold the following year. In an article entitled 'Scenarios for peace' they stated:

> The challenge for all of us is to learn to accept and to cherish diversity and protect all aspirations. Therefore what Unionists are looking for from Reynolds, the Irish Republic's Taoiseach or Prime Minister, and Hume, and Adams for that matter, is an indication that they accept this diversity and that they see Unionists as more than dysfunctional Irishmen.[87]

NOTES

1. *Guardian*, 17 August 1991, also *Fortnight*, no. 301, December 1991.
2. *New Ulster Defender*, vol. 1, no. 1, 1992.
3. *New Ulster Defender*, vol. 1, no. 2, 1992.
4. Ibid.
5. RUC Chief Inspector, interview with author, 8 December 1991.
6. *Scotland on Sunday*, 27 October 1991.
7. Ibid.
8. D. Lister and H. Jordan, *Mad Dog: The Rise and Fall of Johnny Adair and 'C' Company* (Edinburgh: Mainstream, 2003), p. 66.
9. Ibid., pp. 75–7 for a full account of this meeting.
10. J. McMichael, interview with author, 10 June 1987.
11. RUC profile of Johnny Adair, 1993, Appendix 1, p. 1.
12. J. Brown, interview with author, 6 May, 2003.
13. RUC profile of Adair, Appendix 3, paragraph 1.4.
14. Brown, interview with author.
15. Ibid.
16. Ibid.
17. E. McLean, interview with author, 19 November 2003.
18. D. McKittrick, S. Kelters, B. Feeney and C. Thornton, *Lost Lives: The Stories of the Men, Women and Children Who Died as a Result of Northern Ireland's Troubles* (Edinburgh: Mainstream, 1999), pp. 1268–9.
19. Ibid., p. 1279.
20. *Irish Times*, 5 February 1994.
21. *New Ulster Defender*, vol. 1, no. 1, 1992.
22. *Fortnight*, no. 304, March 1992.
23. N. Davies, *Ten-Thirty-Three: The Inside Story of Britain's Secret Killing Machine in Northern Ireland* (Edinburgh: Mainstream, 1999), pp. 94–8,129–35,188–91.
24. *Independent*, 9 June 1992.
25. *Sunday Business Post*, 4 April 2004.

26. M. Dillon, *The Trigger Men* (Edinburgh: Mainstream, 2003), p. 255.

27. F. Kitson, *Low Intensity Operations: Subversion, Insurgency, Peace-Keeping* (London: Faber and Faber, 1971); see also R. Faligot, *Britain's Military Strategy in Ireland: the Kitson Experiment* (London: Zed, 1983).

28. North Belfast UDA member who does not wish to be named, interview with author, 7 October 2003.

29. *Observer*, 27 April 2003.

30. *Irish News*, 16 April 1992.

31. *Sunday World*, 26 April 1992.

32. McKittrick *et al.*, *Lost Lives*, p. 1288.

33. Lister and Jordan, *Mad Dog*, pp. 97–101.

34. M. McGuinness, Milltown Cemetery address, 31 March 1991, author's notes.

35. *This Week*, Granada Television, 30 April 1992.

36. Rt Hon. Michael Mates MP, letter to the author, 26 February 2004.

37. *Irish News*, 18 June 1992.

38. *Guardian*, 11 August 1992.

39. Ibid.

40. Ibid.

41. *Sunday Press*, 16 August 1992.

42. Ibid.

43. P. Taylor, *Brits: The War against the IRA* (London: Bloomsbury, 2001), pp. 321–2.

44. *New Ulster Defender*, vol. 1, no. 3, 1992.

45. Ibid.

46. Ibid.

47. RUC profile of Adair, Appendices 4.4, 4.5.

48. McKittrick *et al.*, Lost Lives, p. 1298.

48. McKittrick *et al.*, Lost Lives, p. 1298.

49. E. McLean, interview with author, 19 November 2003.

50. Ibid.

51. *Guardian*, 16 November 1992. See also McKittrick *et al.*, *Lost Lives*, pp. 1301–2.

52. Lister and Jordan, *Mad Dog*, pp. 50–1.

53. J. McDonald, interview with author, 7 October 2003.

54. *New Ulster Defender*, vol. 1, no. 5, 1993.

55. R. Smallwoods, interview with author, 8 April 1993.

56. *Irish News*, 26 March 1993.

57. *Scotsman*, 5 January 1993, also *Sunday Life*, 11 April 1993.

58. Lister and Jordan, *Mad Dog*.

59. Brown, interview with author.

60. RUC profile of Adair, p. 3.

61. Ibid., 19 November 1993.

62. Brown, interview with author.

63. Lister and Jordan, *Mad Dog*, p. 138.

64. RUC profile of Adair, p. 5.

65. *Guardian*, 19 October 1993.

66. *Irish Independent*, 22 October 1993.

67. *Scotland on Sunday*, 31 October 1993.

68. *Irish News*, 25 October 1993.
69. M. Stone, *None Shall Divide Us* (London: John Blake, 2003), pp. 254–5.
70. Ibid., p. 255.
71. McLean, interview with author.
72. J. Adair, interview with author, 9 June 2004.
73. Ibid.
74. Fr S. Emerson, interview with author, 22 November 2003.
75. *Scotland on Sunday*, 7 November 1993.
76. Ibid.
77. Ibid.
78. C. Crawford, *Inside the UDA: Volunteers and Violence* (London: Pluto Press, 2003), p. 196.
79. North Belfast UDA member, interview with author, 19 November 2003.
80. Crawford, *Inside the UDA*, p. 197.
81. West Belfast UDA member, interview with author, 16 November 2003.
82. *An Phoblacht/Republican News*, 26August 1993.
83. *New Ulster Defender*, vol. 1, no. 7, 1993.
84. *Irish News*, 1 April 1993. See also S. Bruce, *The Edge of the Union: The Ulster Loyalist Political Vision* (Oxford: Oxford University Press), pp 38–9.
85. *New Ulster Defender*, vol. 1, no. 7, 1993.
86. *New Ulster Defender*, vol. 1, no. 8, 1993.
87. Ibid.

8

Ceasefire and an Uncertain Peace

ॐ

Neither the UDA nor its political spokesmen were prepared for the major initiative which the London and Dublin governments announced on 15 December 1993. This was the Downing Street Declaration, in which the two countries' leaders pledged their support for a new political framework within which relationships could develop in Northern Ireland and between Britain and Ireland. The principle of national self-determination on the basis of consent on both sides of the Irish border was accepted and Paragraph 4 of the Declaration enlarged upon this. It asserted that

> the Prime Minister, on behalf of the British government, reaffirms that they will uphold the democratic wish of the greater number of the people of Northern Ireland on the issue of whether they prefer to support the Union or a sovereign united Ireland.

Whatever comfort these words may have offered, it seemed to many Unionists and Loyalists to be undermined in the very next sentence. This stated that the British government had

> no selfish strategic or economic interest in Northern Ireland. Their primary interest is to see peace, stability and reconciliation established by agreement among all the people who inhabit the island and they will work together with the Irish government to achieve such an agreement, which will embrace the totality of relationships.

This last phrase, 'the totality of relationships', was one which John Hume had often used in his critique of the view that there could be no internal political settlement in Northern Ireland which denied a role to Dublin.

All this was a long way from Margaret Thatcher's assertion that Northern Ireland was 'as British as Finchley', while the promise that if the IRA ended its war there could be a role for it, after a brief period to test its sincerity, in talks about the political and constitutional future sat uneasily with John Major's earlier admission that even talking to Sinn Fein 'would make my stomach turn'. Attached to all copies of the Declaration, issued by the Northern Ireland Information Service, was a list of undertakings and reassurances to Unionists about the Union not being at risk and how a majority view would always be accepted.

Major was neither the first nor the last British Prime Minister to see a solution to the 'Irish question' as his passport into history but he was uncertain of how the Declaration would play among a majority community ever more distrustful of British intentions. Early opinion polls showed majority support for the 15 December statement, but once reduced to the sum of their parts, these in fact showed that there was a huge predominance of support amongst nationalist opinion while under half of Unionists took an affirmative view.[1]

Nonetheless, the Ulster Unionist Party's leadership gave the Declaration guarded and cautious support. Predictably, the Democratic Unionist Party rejected it out of hand. Its deputy leader, Peter Robinson, called it 'humbug and hogwash'[2] and on the same day Dr Ian Paisley made a sustained and bitter attack on Major in the House of Commons. The Combined Loyalist Military Command had no inclination to be associated with this and made it clear that it would prefer to reserve its position on the Declaration.

The Command had been informed by Dublin of the preparatory talks between the two governments which led to the Declaration. As with military operations, its power to co-ordinate a political response proved limited. The UDA was offered, but rejected, a secret channel for communication with Dublin but the UVF showed itself willing to stay in touch with the process. Fergus Finlay, an adviser to the Irish Foreign Minister, Dick Spring, developed a good working relationship with Gusty Spence and David Ervine, who met him in Belfast in their capacity as spokesmen of the Progressive Unionist Party, though both had the ear of the UVF leadership. In fact, they at once recognised their own input in the draft declaration, especially in Paragraph 5, with its emphasis on full freedom of expression and equal social and economic opportunity as a necessary part of any political settlement.[3]

Finlay was careful to see that all Loyalist paramilitary groups, including the UDA, were given access to copies of the Declaration ahead of its actual publication, but Gary McMichael later argued that the Downing Street document was tainted by its links to the parallel Hume–Adams dialogue. 'The link between the two initiatives ensured that the Declaration was doomed from the beginning,' he wrote six years later. 'A large section of Unionists refused to view it as anything other than a translation of the secretive process which had the IRA at its centre regardless of the actual contents of the document.'[4]

These suspicions, however, did not add up to a case for outright rejection of the Declaration either in his mind or in that of the CLMC. 'They needed time and they had learned how to play for it,' Sammy Duddy recalled. 'They had set out their stall back on 10 December with a very clear statement of our position and they could judge the Declaration against it.'[5] He was referring to the Combined Command's *Six Principles*, which it had made public on 10 December. This, incorporating the thinking both of the UDA's 1987 *Common Sense* document and the UVF statement titled 'Sharing Responsibility', set out in unequivocal terms the case for Northern Ireland's place in the United Kingdom but with fully democratic and accountable devolved government, a bill of rights and agreed cross-border structures to further co-operative relationships with the Irish state.[6]

Sensibly, the CLMC in fact did play for more time, reiterating its 10 December principles and also making clear that it would not be rushed into a premature response to the Downing Street document. It also considered but rejected the case for a Christmas ceasefire to reduce tension in the community, at least temporarily. McMichael pressed the case for this only for the IRA to get wind of it and destroy any potential such a move might have had. It issued a statement saying its answer would be to halt attacks on Loyalist organisations but not on the security forces. The CLMC settled instead for a pre-Christmas press release which called for a forum to be instituted in which all constitutional parties could set out their views on the Declaration.[7]

The CLMC statement was quite a skilfully drafted piece of work. The UVF leaders were in active consultation with Ervine and Spence, who both wanted Loyalism to find a non-violent and political role for itself, while the UDA's Inner Council was listening to the analysis of McMichael and, at this point a more influential figure, Raymond Smallwoods. The latter, after his release from prison, had emerged as a forceful and articulate speaker whom journalists were beginning to seek out for his impressive presentation of the Ulster Democratic Party's views. Smallwoods and McMichael could rely on a fair hearing for their opinions from Joe English, still a senior figure on the Inner Council, who is remembered by leading figures in the Workers Party for his willingness to talk to them and even to think of himself as politically on the left.[8]

English, however, had to allow for the reality of an Inner Council majority who were deeply distrustful of the Downing Street Declaration and wanted an outright rejection of it. The UVF view was a more circumspect one because it had been in closer touch with the process leading to the Declaration than the UDA. It has been claimed that some in the UVF were ready to support a Loyalist ceasefire to test IRA intentions and put maximum political pressure on Sinn Fein,[9] but memories in the CLMC of how their summer 1991 ceasefire had been ignored were still fresh. The December statement took care to make clear that Loyalists were still at war: 'In the interim period and in the absence of any response from the Provisional murder gangs, the CLMC will pursue its stated policy in relation to IRA violence.'[10]

Events in the New Year of 1994 soon provided proof that these words were meant to be taken literally, yet at the same time the CLMC was prepared to let talking continue. Senior churchmen like the Reverend Roy Magee of the Presbyterian church and Archbishop Robin Eames of the Church of Ireland acted as facilitators and intermediaries for continued dialogue, helping to set up an important meeting in late January at the Park Avenue Hotel in East Belfast. UDA and UVF representatives attended to listen and respond to the analysis of local academics. The Unionist parties stayed away, though John Taylor, Westminster MP for Strangford, telephoned a message of support. Ervine left the gathering feeling that it had helped the political process forward.[11]

Optimism was more of a necessity than ever as no remission from the killing seemed in prospect, least of all from the IRA and INLA. From the start of the year until the Provisional IRA's ceasefire announcement on 31 August, they killed twenty-six people and launched numerous other attacks with guns and car bombs. Only six of their victims were members of the security forces and in Belfast itself intensive surveillance and patrolling by the army and RUC had blunted the edge of IRA attacks to the point where just two RUC officers were killed in the city prior to 31 August.

Loyalist killing also continued unremittingly and in contrast to 1993, the UVF did more of it than the UDA. One reason for this was that the RUC's lengthy entrapment of Johnny Adair at last took him off the streets. On 16 May he was arrested and later charged with directing terrorism but not brought to trial until the following year. He was not, however, charged with a murder that he is widely thought to have carried out towards the end of the previous year. The victim was Noel Cardwell, a Protestant in his mid-twenties from the Lower Shankill area, who suffered from poor health and was on constant medication. He also had a mental age of twelve. On only the most tenuous evidence, he was accused of giving police the names of UDA members and Adair ordered that he be held for interrogation.

This took place in a flat used for the purpose near Adair's home on the night of 13 December. The interrogation involved a brutal beating of Cardwell, who was later shot in the head at close range and left to die, which he did in hospital some hours later after a neighbour had found him and called an ambulance. Gary McMaster, a UDA man who admitted being present during both the questioning and shooting, was later brought to trial on unrelated charges. In the course of the trial he named Adair as the executioner and it is possible that this was in fact the first killing he had carried out in person.[12]

Questioned about this killing while he was in Maghaberry prison after his release under licence had been revoked a second time, Adair told the author he had no knowledge of it:

> Listen, I didn't know all that was going on. I wasn't there. Them boys were doing their own thing. If he was a tout, he'd get one behind the ear, no question, but I was never involved. That cunt McMaster named me in court to try and make things easier for him. They all thought they could blame me'.[13]

Earlier in the same interview Adair had been emphatic about the control he had over C Company and its operations in this period.

The fact that Adair had two sisters who were educationally sub-normal added to the revulsion felt by many in the area over Cardwell's killing, but the power of Adair and C Company made it dangerous for anyone to voice such

feelings. For others it was simply proof of his growing confidence and ruth-
lessness, which were reflected in C Company operations as the new year got
under way. These began with a series of unsuccessful attacks on the homes of
Sinn Fein councillors. Adair was always ready to point out that near misses
should never be discounted because they served notice on the Republican
enemy that Loyalists could bring the war almost literally to their doorsteps.
'I set up a real Loyalist war machine,' he told the author ten years after
these events. 'The boys knew what needed to be done and we took the war
right to them fuckers and they knew it. We took our chances. I can show you
my bullet wounds. It was a war for Ulster, whatever anyone calls me now. You
ask the Provos which UDA commander they really feared and they'll say
Johnny Adair.'[14]

On the evening of 10 January, however, there was a new and ominous
development. The Rock Bar, a popular venue on the Upper Falls Road, the
very heart of nationalist West Belfast, was attacked early in the evening by
two masked men who used a shoulder-held rocket-propelled grenade
launcher to fire at the building. The missile hit an upstairs safety grille over a
window and detonated in the street, causing a huge explosion. As their
getaway vehicle raced from the scene, the two men opened fire on the bar but
there were no fatalities. The rocket would, of course, have wrought carnage
had it gone off in the crowded upstairs lounge at which it was aimed. Adair
was arrested and held at Castlereagh RUC station for forty-eight hours and
boasted to officers there about the new weapon. 'It was almost like listening
to a wee lad going on about a new toy,'[15] recalled Johnston Brown, the officer
who questioned Adair about the incident.

Police had in fact located and seized a rocket launcher in the Shankill area
before Christmas. They treated the Rock Bar attack as proof that the UDA/
UFF had others, part of their share of the 1988 consignment of weapons
brought into Northern Ireland from South Africa. The IRA had had rocket
launchers for some time, and indeed Beechmount Avenue, off the Falls Road,
traditionally a starting point for Easter 1916 commemoration parades, had
been renamed RPG Avenue after a successful attack with the new weapon on
a British army patrol. Parity of Loyalist firepower with that of the IRA was
however, a matter of 'major concern',[16] as the RUC told the press a few days
after the Rock Bar's narrow escape.

Further such attacks followed, including one on Connolly House in
Andersonstown, which housed Sinn Fein's offices, and at the beginning of
April the party's press office, where Sebastopol Street joins the Falls Road,
suffered extensive damage when an RPG warhead crashed into the front of
the building, which was unoccupied at the time. C Company were back at the
scene just three days later, when workers repairing the office's exterior structure were attacked from a car which slowed outside the office for gunmen to
open fire. Fresh murals celebrating the 'rocket team on tour' began to appear
in the Shankill area, though in fact more lives were taken by simply targeting

victims at work or in their homes. Such a case was Theresa Clinton, wife of a Sinn Fein activist, who died in her home off Belfast's Ormeau Road from multiple bullet wounds after gunmen opened fire through the glass of her sitting room window on 14 April.

Bigger Republican targets such as Brian Gillen, an IRA Belfast brigade officer who later joined the organisation's Army Council, eluded C Company's gunmen but Adair is adamant to this day about the degree of success he claims these attacks achieved: 'I deal only with facts,' he has declared to the author from prison, in response to the question of whether he had been responsible for innocent victims' deaths. 'Ninety per cent of all UFF operations in the early nineties were carried out by C Company. Among their targets were members of PIRA, Sinn Fein and the INLA, and indeed their homes and party offices in republican strongholds throughout Belfast. Among those attacked were many elected councillors who were legitimate targets.'[17]

Adair's justification for what the UDA/UFF was doing was at the time shared within its ranks, and this offset whatever hope was to be drawn from the fact that it, like the UVF, had not openly rejected the Downing Street Declaration. Indeed, intermittent dialogue was still being channelled through the CLMC's contacts with intermediaries of the Dublin and London governments. What optimism this generated was dealt a blow in early January 1994, however, when a chilling document drafted by the UDA was made available to a Belfast newspaper.

It was printed in very limited numbers and with tight restrictions applying to its distribution. No individual at any time was authorised by the UDA to have more than two copies and he or she was always to be accompanied by another member while in possession of them. The document's remit was to analyse the likely situation after a British withdrawal or acceptance by a London government 'of Pan Nationalist Front conditions for a United Ireland'. In such a situation, it was argued, the UDA's objective would have to be to 'establish an ethnic Protestant Homeland' through the 'repartition of the existing state of Northern Ireland'.[18] This, the document stressed in its foreword, had indeed been considered as an option by the Thatcher government in the period prior to the signing of the Anglo-Irish Agreement. The truth of this claim was later confirmed by two former advisers to the Prime Minister, her private secretary, Charles Powell, and Sir William Armstrong, later Lord Armstrong, the Cabinet Secretary, in a BBC television documentary, *Endgame in Ireland*.[19]

'That the British Cabinet dismissed this as a viable solution', the UDA document declared, 'does not undermine the viability of partition as a military objective. The government dismissed Repartition for fear that the Unionists would perceive such a move as a betrayal and a further act of appeasement of the Pan Nationalist Front. The fact remains however that repartition was considered as an option and as such had to have a military perspective to the political considerations that repartition would bring.'[20]

Claiming contact with the security forces, the UDA went on to assert that 'British military intelligence suggests that at least two and probably three counties in Ulster are already lost. Surrendering two or three counties to the Irish Republic would alleviate much of the security problem.'[21]

In the remaining three or three and a half counties the predominantly Protestant population, it was argued, 'would have an automatic cultural identity with the security forces. Security would be enhanced and any isolated pockets of dissident Irish nationalists more easily contained and policed.'[22] The repartitioned state would be secured by locally recruited defence units under a central command structure and it was accepted that there would be a Catholic population stranded behind the redrawn contours of the province who would have to be 'expelled, nullified or interned'. Expulsion would reduce the demand on food and, it was accepted, give extra manpower to the Republican enemy. 'Nullification', a macabre euphemism for ethnic killing, was described as 'difficult' but also as an option which, like expulsion, would reduce pressure on food and other resources. Internment of Catholics would be a commitment for Loyalist defence forces in the new state but would provide 'useful bargaining chips'[23] in possible negotiations.

Accompanying the proposals was a detailed breakdown from census figures of 'men in militarily useful trades', showing how these were distributed between the two communities. This was designated as part of a 'Loyalist battlefield analysis' and a set of maps was also incorporated in the package, coloured in and marked to show the possible contours of a 'British Ulster', 'Irish Ulster' and ethnically cleansed areas. The demands on Loyalist firepower involved in securing and sealing off target areas were admitted and the ultimate alternative was set out as 'a withdrawal of Ulster Protestants to the mainland and the destruction of everything left behind, leaving nothing but a huge repair bill to the Irish Republic'.[24]

The UDA had based this Doomsday plan on the work of Dr Liam Kennedy, a lecturer in social and economic history at Queen's University in Belfast. In 1986 he had brought out a book entitled *Two Ulsters: A Case for Repartition* and three years later he contributed his views in summary form to a book of essays on possible ways out of conflict for Northern Ireland. His premise was that for the state in its existing form there was in fact no solution to sectarian conflict. 'The border of 1920', he argued, 'was a rough recognition of contemporary realities'[25] but was not designed to 'reflect as far as possible the spatial distribution of nationalists and unionists'. Any rationale for partition, in his view, should have been to bring into being 'a smaller but politically more homogenous Northern Ireland statelet'.[26]

Kennedy's work was accompanied by maps illustrating possible boundaries for 'British' and 'Irish' areas of Ulster and these were identical to the ones used by the UDA in their document. He was quick to accuse them of plagiarising his work in what he described as 'a sloppy piece of so-called research'[27] but there were those who welcomed the UDA's initiative. Sammy

Wilson, speaking for the DUP, called it a 'very valuable return to reality', and added that 'while some will no doubt denounce and ridicule their plan, nevertheless it shows that some loyalist paramilitaries are looking ahead and contemplating what needs to be done to maintain our separate Ulster identity'.[28]

Others took the view that, whether or not there had been any plagiarism, the document, with its talk of the 'nullification' of Catholic localities and ethnic cleansing, needed to be taken seriously. 'The detail of this document and timing of its disclosure will be a cause for deep concern in the political world,' one press commentator wrote. 'The fact that UDA leaders saw fit to have this document commissioned demonstrates their pessimism about the future of the province. And the fact that it has been leaked now shows that they hold out little hope for the current peace process.'[29]

Raymond Smallwoods denied suggestions that he had been involved in drafting the document but he certainly took it seriously when questioned about it by the author the following month

> I was not consulted but the scenario set out is a perfectly plausible one. We may well be heading for a Bosnian situation and perhaps a three-and-a-half-county Northern Ireland. I agree with what Sammy Wilson has said about a return to reality. We've seen twenty years of genocide directed against us and Loyalists need to start thinking in these terms. Our rights now count for so little that it's time we stopped pretending about our future.[30]

Adair, despite his seniority within the UDA, has disclaimed any knowledge of the document. This may well serve as proof that he never had much interest in, or grasp of, political initiatives, even one so extreme and dangerous. Given photocopies of press coverage of the 1994 proposals on repartition while in prison ten years later, he voiced no opinion on them, repeating that his role at that time was a 'military one only.'[31]

In the immediate aftermath of the January document Adair had other preoccupations. The following month Courtney Kennedy, niece of the assassinated American president, arrived in Belfast for a court case involving her husband, Paul Hill, one of the freed 'Birmingham Six' bombers. He had brought an appeal to Belfast Crown Court against a conviction for murder dating back to 1974. Courtney, her mother Ethel and her brother, Congressman Joe Kennedy, spent thirteen days in the city, travelling to the court daily to observe proceedings. Adair took the view that, given the family's Irish nationalist sympathies, their presence was an affront to Loyalists and they were therefore a legitimate target for attack. He set to work on plans to destroy their car with a rocket-propelled grenade on one of its daily journeys. The plan was ultimately aborted because the Kennedy party's security was intensified after police spotted Adair close to the court building where the appeal was being heard.[32] One senior RUC officer on duty at the time has recalled how Adair, in his tracksuit, had jogged up to greet him with the words: 'Hi, big man, I don't suppose you know where yer man Kennedy's going for his lunch but we do.'[33]

The hardening of attitudes revealed in talk of a repartitioned state was observable in other UDA statements in early 1994. In April, two brigadiers, Joe English from South-East Antrim and John Reid from North Belfast, talked to a newspaper reporter who wanted to assess their reaction to the IRA's brief Easter ceasefire, which had just ended in renewed attacks on the security forces. They were unimpressed and took it as proof of the IRA still having its eye on the prize of British willingness to negotiate with it. They did not allude to the repartition document but talked of a new and wider-ranging policy statement on Ulster independence within the European Union. This, they stressed, had to remain the fall-back position for Loyalists if they were finally convinced that Britain wanted to disengage from Northern Ireland.[34]

'We've a great deal of faith in our own ability. We are a very independent people. There are people within Northern Ireland who are more than capable of running this country,'[35] the two brigadiers told their interviewer, insisting that an Ulster mini-state would accept European Union law and be ready to be part of a larger political entity once the relationship with Britain was felt to have run its course. This was a reversion to some of the political thinking developed by John McMichael and others in the late 1970s; as with him, such thinking was inseparable from taking the war to the Republican enemy. English and Reid assured the *Guardian* that the UDA was ready for a long haul and that recruitment was better than ever. 'We are very pleased', they added, 'with the amount of assistance that we're getting from people who share our views but would perhaps not be prepared to join us and can give us support in other ways.'[36]

These themes were taken up by another senior UDA man only a week later in an interview with the *Observer*, which was careful to conceal his identity. He too promised intensified armed action against the IRA and the 'Pan-Nationalist Front' because the 'British Government hasn't had the will to deal with the IRA. There has been a policy of containment instead of an offensive policy.'[37] An offensive policy was maintained by the UDA in the weeks that followed but on 16 May, the RUC made a long-prepared move, arresting Adair and nearly twenty others active in C Company. Adair's initial reaction was that this was simply another police initiative to keep him temporarily off the streets.

In this he was seriously mistaken. After four days at Castlereagh interrogation centre he was transferred to the remand wing of Crumlin Road prison prior to being informed that he was to be charged with the direction of terrorism, a blanket accusation that would make conviction much easier than attempts to prove him guilty of any specific killings. His first night in Crumlin Road was accompanied by sustained rioting in Loyalist areas in his support, with RUC patrols coming under gun and petrol bomb attacks. As already described, Adair's arrest was the culmination of a protracted operation to ensnare and incriminate him which had gone on for almost three years.

To this day, Adair denies that he contributed significantly to his later conviction by his own reckless bravado and careless talk, as well as by his readiness to believe in the goodwill towards him of detectives such as Johnston Brown, who were in fact carefully spinning an elaborate web within which to trap him. 'Johnny just never got it,' Brown has said. 'All we needed to do was to keep him talking and let him think we saw him as being on our side against the Provos. A bit of flattery went a long way, too. If I said to him, as I did a few times, "Your team's the best, Johnny," he'd be all smiles, in almost a child-like way.'[38]

Adair's version of events which he has given to the author is a predictably self-justifying one in which he stresses the length of time the police needed to bring him to trial:

> The authorities had been trying for many years to have me charged with serious offences. In 1989, for the first time in the history of the conflict, they used a woman supergrass to have me and some of my friends charged and taken off the streets. [This is a reference to Kathy Spruce, a former girlfriend, whose accusations against him first brought Adair into the public eye, though the police case on this occasion collapsed.] Thankfully, the charges were dropped after four months behind bars.[39]

He has gone on to claim that the police response to his growing notoriety varied:

> A number of attempts were made to recruit me as an informer. In one attempt they used a suitcase filled with £50,000. When this failed they passed my details to the PIRA in an attempt to have me taken out by them. I never hid my opinion on Republicans whenever I was stopped at RUC checkpoints. This was used against me to form part of the evidence, along with over 200 police, army, prison officers and civilian witnesses all willing to testify against me but it still took years before they could secure a conviction against me.[40]

Attempts to 'turn' Adair with offers of cash are more likely to have been the work of the RUC's Special Branch, which had serious disagreements with the strategy pursued by Brown. His methods succeeded and Adair has never given up a promise to have revenge on Brown and his family. Their home later came under attack and this forced them to move house. Hugely expensive security installations protect their new property against the likelihood of Adair's revenge.

Adair's arrest and that of other key figures in C Company such as Winky Dodds and Donald Hodgen brought a lull in UDA/UFF killings. The next seven Loyalist murders were all the work of the UVF, who then, on 18 June, proceeded to emulate the brutality of the Greysteel attack by shooting dead six Catholics, one of them eighty-seven years of age, in a bar in Loughinisland near Downpatrick, where they were watching World Cup football on television. The UDA had not ceased to operate but events proved that it was vulnerable to attack even as its killings declined in frequency.

At nine o'clock on the morning of 11 July, Raymond Smallwoods was shot dead outside his home in Lisburn by an IRA unit of four men and a woman who had taken over the house opposite in order to lie in wait for him. Security force sources believe the assassin, who fired several shotgun blasts, may well have been Brian Gillen, whose killing Adair had tried and failed to set up. To many, this murder was proof of the priority they felt the IRA had always had of striking at the political brain of Loyalism. As chairman of the UDP and a council election candidate in Lisburn, Smallwoods was an approachable and skilful exponent of a working-class Loyalist analysis of Northern Ireland's conflict and possible ways out of it.

Not long before his murder he had spoken to the author confidently about the UDP's electoral prospects, though admitting to frustration at the still limited proportion of UDA funds which were going towards political campaigning: 'They have resources,' he declared. 'That's an understatement and it's no secret. If more of them found their way to us we could have put up 200 candidates at the last council elections.'[41] Smallwoods's growing interest in political action had given him contacts with Protestant and Catholic clergy who were working to promote dialogue between the two communities. Prominent among these were the Reverend Kenneth Newell, minister at the Fitzroy Presbyterian Church in South Belfast, and Father Gerry Reynolds, a Redemptorist priest of magnetic personality from Clonard Monastery in West Belfast, where Gerry Adams sometimes attended Mass and also sat in on political discussions.

Both men were invited to the wake for Smallwoods, which was held in a Lisburn housing estate. Extraordinarily perhaps, for a society living through such a spasm of killing as Northern Ireland was in the summer of 1994, Reynolds was asked to lead the gathering in prayer with senior UDA figures joining in.[42] He and other priests are known to have protested to the IRA about the killing though Smallwoods was probably not in reality any sort of dove within the UDA. Deeply distrustful of any likely IRA ceasefire, in conversation only weeks before his death he remained uncompromising in his hostility to Republicanism and unrepentant about his own past.

An *Observer* journalist noted, as did the author, that when Smallwoods gave interviews he would begin by referring to the UDA as 'them' but once relaxed over a drink or a cup of coffee, would quickly and without realising it, start talking instead of 'us'.[43] He was fatalistic about the possibility of his own death though always meticulous in the way he would check his car for explosive devices that might be fitted underneath it. A UDA activist close to him was quoted as saying that his murder was 'a final fling, a final show of strength, a final bloodbath before Sinn Fein go to the talks table'.[44]

In fact it was not the 'final fling'. The IRA had other targets in mind in the run-up period to its ceasefire, amongst both the UVF and the UDA. On 31 July, outside the Kimberly bar off Belfast's Ormeau Road, one of its units ambushed and shot dead Raymond Elder and Joe Bratty, senior UDA men in the area who were widely believed by the nationalist community to have carried out the massacre at Sean Graham's betting shop in February 1992. Adair, in prison awaiting trial, was incandescent with rage, both at the ease with which the IRA reached its targets and at the lack of rapid and adequate retaliation. 'The IRA', he subsequently told the authors of an invaluable book about him, 'knew the fucking brains and balls was in jail. If I had been out it would have been different.'[45]

It might well have been, but even Adair out of prison would have had to respond to the IRA's 31 August announcement of an indefinite cessation of hostilities. Their tortuous road to this decision has now been very fully explored. One view sees the road originating off the French coast in October 1987 when the *Eksund*, a ship carrying a huge supply of Libyan arms, was seized by the French navy as a result of a tip-off to British intelligence from a senior figure in the IRA. If this disaster indeed aborted a massive all-out offensive against the security forces in Northern Ireland and ensured only the prospect of protracted military stalemate, then it can be seen as a milestone in the peace process even though the IRA never lost its capacity to kill.[46]

Within the organisation, debate, driven increasingly by the dominant influence of Gerry Adams, came to focus on the political dimension to armed struggle or indeed on alternatives to it. British intelligence was kept informed of these developments and John Major, working in close contact where Irish events were concerned with both Dublin and Washington, became, in the summer of 1994, guardedly optimistic. 'As we moved through June and July,' he wrote in his memoirs, 'evidence that the Provisionals were moving slowly towards a ceasefire began to mount.'[47]

Gary McMichael has recalled the expectancy of this time: 'The IRA cessation was imminent and we were aware of that and even had a reasonable understanding that it would be some time in August.'[48] Intensified IRA attacks and the killings of Smallwoods, Bratty and Elder convinced him that a major Republican initiative was coming. 'The escalation of IRA activity over the preceding months supported the anticipation that there would be a storm before the lull.'[49] The IRA, he was certain in his own mind, wanted to provoke Loyalists to a degree that would stop them taking the lead in what he called the 'ceasefire stakes'.

This was also the view of David Adams, who, like McMichael, was close to the thinking of the Loyalist leadership. He has claimed that

> the conditions were in place for the announcement of a Loyalist ceasefire in June or July of 1994 but the murders of Smallwoods, Bratty and Elder put that ceasefire back more than three months. There was no doubt that the killings were a concession to the hardliners within the IRA before they called their own ceasefire. There was a belief that if Loyalists had called their ceasefire first, we would have stolen the limelight from Republicans. It was clear to us that the IRA was trying to push Loyalists away from calling the ceasefires but instead it made us more determined.[50]

If this IRA tactic had failed they would then, in McMichael's opinion, have wanted Loyalist attacks to continue after their own ceasefire 'to give them maximum standing as peace-makers while Loyalists would be seen as peace-breakers'.[51]

These were considerations that weighed heavily with Loyalists when the IRA ceasefire was finally announced. A few days earlier the IRA's Army Council had met at a secret location in Donegal to make its decision. This took the form of a five-to-one vote, with one abstention, in support of a four-month cessation of operations, but to the disquiet of hardliners the announcement on 31 August was made without reference to any time limit.

Even as the rumour mill went into overdrive about a likely IRA ceasefire Loyalists continued to kill. On 8 August, Kathleen O'Hagan, a mother of five and seven months pregnant, was shot dead by UVF gunmen at her home near Cookstown in County Tyrone. Her husband returned home to find his children, the eldest only eight years old, huddled around their mother's bullet-riddled body. The UDA/UFF killed three more victims before the IRA announcement. Their details constitute yet another sad catalogue of working-class Catholics easily targeted at their workplaces or, in the case of one of them, Sean Monaghan, abducted from near his home off the Falls Road and dumped in the Loyalist Woodvale area with four bullets in his head.

They killed again on the day following the ceasefire. John O'Hanlon, prematurely described in one newspaper caption as 'the last victim of the Troubles', was a 31-year-old Catholic from North Belfast who was helping a friend change the wheel on his car when gunmen opened fire on him from a passing vehicle. Another friend was quoted as saying:

> He was just in the wrong place at the wrong time. What is the price of peace? How many people have to be killed before both sides sit down and give peace a chance? I think he will just be forgotten like the rest of them. He will be a statistic like all the others.[52]

Many in the UDA, or close to it such as McMichael, had grave doubts about the IRA's intentions. The weeks prior to their ceasefire had been a stressful time for him, involving as they did the murder of his close friend Smallwoods and direct death threats to himself. When the ceasefire announcement finally came on 31 August hundreds of Republicans took to the Falls Road in cars and black cabs waving Irish tricolours.

> The triumphalist nature of the occasion did not encourage euphoria on the nearby Shankill Road or in any other Protestant area. Republicans were portraying the ceasefire as the last stage of their struggle, cementing fears that a deal had been cut with the British government and that we were not seeing all of the picture.[53]

The UVF element within the combined Loyalist leadership used its Dublin contacts to try to talk down these fears. Gusty Spence and David Ervine were given assurances from sources close to the Reynolds government that there was no 'hidden agenda' and, more urgently, that an imminent visit to Dublin by Gerry Adams to meet the Taoiseach and John Hume would not mark the launch of any new pan-nationalist coalition. Reports in the *Irish Times* backed up this message[54] but just eight days after the IRA announcement, the CLMC made it known that they would not call a ceasefire until they had answers to a series of questions raised by the IRA's initiative.

These questions covered the need for proof of the genuine nature of the IRA ceasefire, of there being no secret deals between the IRA and the British government and of there being no threat to Northern Ireland's constitutional position. Also set out as a matter needing clarification was the intentions of the INLA, while London was warned not to do anything to 'facilitate the illusion of an IRA victory'.[55] Hard work was done, mainly at this point by the UVF and its political spokesmen, to spread reassurance within Loyalist areas. Marches were organised and new graffiti painted up accepting the IRA's surrender but the UVF and the UDA let it be known that their capacity to launch attacks was intact.

As proof of this the UVF, on 12 September, set off a bomb on a train arriving in Dublin's Connolly station from Belfast. The explosion caused minor injuries to two women passengers and further hoax calls brought traffic chaos for over two hours to the centre of the Irish capital. Both the UVF and the UDA were quick to endorse the attack. The UVF issued a statement calling it 'a warning to the Dublin government that Northern Ireland is still British and we will not be coerced, forced, or persuaded into a united Ireland'.[56] McMichael described it as 'a very clear message to Albert Reynolds regarding the haste with which he has embraced Gerry Adams'.[57]

Although a Loyalist response to the IRA ceasefire came sooner than many commentators anticipated, the process leading up to it was never likely to be easy. The UVF's magazine came close, in its September issue, to making the case for a Loyalist ceasefire, a former life sentence prisoner arguing that the IRA really had given ground under pressure from London, Dublin and Washington. The ceasefire, he stressed, had been called without Republicanism's historic goals having any guarantee of being achieved.[58] Making this case to the UVF membership was easier than to the UDA's. The UVF's tradition of secrecy, strong centralised leadership and limited membership eased the process. Its prisoners constituted simply an integral unit whose views would be given a hearing but who were under the organisation's overall discipline.

The UDA, with its looser command structure and much larger membership, needed longer to arrive at an agreed viewpoint. Its prisoners too had a different status from those of the UVF and were consulted individually by the Inner Council and other senior members of the organisation over almost a two-week period before a meeting was held on 10 October to inform the UDA's political wing that support had indeed coalesced behind a ceasefire. McMichael was present and though without any record of paramilitary activism himself, he put the view that a ceasefire might be premature and that more time was needed to prepare the organisation for the political initiatives it would have to take. He was, however, as he knew himself, in no position to divert the Inner Council from a course of action that now had the military men's support and above all that of the prisoners, even of Johnny Adair and Michael Stone. As he later recalled, on the eve of the Loyalist ceasefire one UDA Inner Council member simply told him: 'Son, you will just have to work with the tools you are given.'[59]

Fernhill House, in its attractive grounds looking down on the Shankill Road, now houses a fine museum of Ulster history. It was the symbolic setting for the CLMC's ceasefire announcement on Thursday, 13 October. Belfast battalions of the original UVF had drilled and paraded there between 1912 and 1914. Bodies of the victims of roaming Loyalist killer gangs had also been dumped there during the darkest years of the Troubles. The CLMC statement in fact took many by surprise. Prepared and read out by Spence, it laid down no specific conditions other than that the IRA's ceasefire be maintained. Unlike the IRA's announcement, the Loyalist ceasefire's wording, while paying tribute to UVF and UDA volunteers who had 'kept the Union safe', incorporated regret for the human price of the struggle. 'In all sincerity we offer to the loved ones of all innocent victims over the past twenty-five years abject and true remorse. No words of ours will compensate for the intolerable suffering they have undergone.'

The thirteenth of October at Fernhill House was a day for Loyalism's political spokesmen. Brigadiers and operational commanders stayed away or kept in the background. Andy Tyrie was present but it was six and a half years since he had led the UDA. So too was John White, who was sitting next to Spence as the ceasefire statement was read out by him. His prominence had a chilling effect on many in the audience because the awful sadism of the murders of which he was convicted had not been forgotten. That said, he had played a significant role in assessing feelings about a ceasefire among UDA prisoners prior to the Inner Council making its decision and clearly relished the increasingly public role this gave him.

His name was not mentioned by Stone in an interview he gave to the Christmas 1994 issue of the *New Ulster Defender*, in which he set out his reasons for backing the ceasefire. Asked what had influenced his personal decision to support the UDA/UVF leadership, Stone replied:

> A number of factors contributed to it. The constitutional guarantee by John Major, his personal promise of a referendum on any political developments which are expected in the near future, also the sincerity of leading Ulster Unionists, backed by respected church leaders, in conjunction with our long-suffering Loyalist community, convinced us that to be seen standing in the way of peace would be perceived as unjustifiable in the present political climate.[60]

Asked about the role of Loyalist prisoners in giving the ceasefire their support, Stone's answer was that it had been 'in a word, paramount. No-one will ever realise the heated debates and soul searching which took place. All the pros and cons were taken into consideration before we gave our overwhelming support for a universal ceasefire under the terms of the CLMC.'[61]

He went on to voice his personal repugnance at the thought of Loyalist leaders talking to Sinn Fein but added: 'The reality is that Sinn Fein do have a political mandate and they have acknowledged the futility of their armed struggle in that they called a complete cessation of violence.'[62] Whether the IRA leaders saw their ceasefire in such terms was another matter, but Stone's public endorsement of the Loyalist response to it was hugely important.

His sentiments were echoed throughout the issue of the magazine in which he was interviewed. Its columns were largely given over to McMichael and David Adams, who had visited the United States in October to put Loyalism's political case to interested Congressmen and Senators and to refocus attention on the UDA's 1987 *Common Sense* document. The editorial also took a positive view of the political potential offered by both ceasefires while offering a warning to Irish nationalism of the fragility of peace. 'Do not throw it away by seeking more from the loyalist community than they can possibly give.'[63]

The moment of opportunity for working-class Loyalist politics opened up by the ceasefires was a real one, although, as after the Ulster Workers Council strike in 1974, it would yield very limited political dividends. James Molyneaux, whose leadership of the UUP would end the following year, made only a low-key response to the ceasefires while Dr Ian Paisley was widely believed to have advised the Loyalist leaders against theirs. Only six weeks earlier he had been predicting civil war in Northern Ireland. He was now a tired but still bellicose figure who simply could not relate to the remarkably pluralist language of the CLMC's ceasefire statement, with its acceptance of the need for Northern Ireland's two communities to respect each other's different traditions and allegiances.

For Paisley the best, perhaps the only, card to play was the prospect of an Anglo-Irish strategy of betrayal which would sacrifice the Union as part of a continuing peace process. On 1 February 1995 he and doubters among Molyneaux's colleagues were offered what they needed when the *Sunday Times* ran extracts of the framework document which the British and Irish governments were working on. Prematurely the paper claimed that 'the British and Irish governments have drawn up a document that brings the prospect of a United Ireland closer than it has been at any time since partition in 1920'.[64]

The full document came out three weeks later and called for a North–South co-operation agency which would function outwith the control of any Belfast-based assembly. It would have wide powers covering agriculture, fisheries, industrial development, transport, health and much more. In reality, harmonisation of practice in such areas, given different fiscal and legal systems, would have been an extremely long-term exercise and Sinn Fein's central demand for a British withdrawal was not even mentioned. Nonetheless, alarm bells began to ring within Unionism and ominously hostile graffiti prompted by the document started to appear on walls in Loyalist areas of Belfast.

Adams and McMichael responded critically but constructively to the framework document. Predictably, they criticised what they saw as its emphasis on an all-Ireland element to any political settlement. They argued that it was too early for that and also stressed its exclusion of any bill of rights to cover both communities. In addition, they regretted the absence of any British Isles element to the document, linking this to the Major government's uncompromising hostility to any devolution of legislative power to Wales and Scotland. If and when this came, they argued, any devolved Northern Ireland executive and assembly could have an equal place, alongside the Irish state, in a consultative Council of the Isles.[65] Provision for this was indeed later incorporated into the 1998 Belfast Agreement. Their concern was to be critical on points of detail but not, like Paisley, simply to use the document as a crude weapon against an already ongoing peace process.

Mainstream Unionist suspicion of the framework document stalled political progress for the remainder of 1995. So too did the British government's reiterated disinclination to talk directly to parties linked to paramilitary organisations which had made no moves towards disarming. The UDA and UVF took the view that they should wait for Sinn Fein to show some willingness to co-operate with an international commission on weapons. In mid-September that year, the Secretary of State, Sir Patrick Mayhew, did at least meet UDA and UVF leaders to hear their thoughts about ways in which their weapons might at some point be 'decommissioned'. McMichael took part and reported that the contact had been useful but that Sinn Fein's intransigence was still the rock on the road to any agreement on the weapons issue.[66]

As political stalemate continued tension began to mount over the issue of Loyalist prisoners. Phased release, either for them or for IRA prisoners, was never going to come ahead of a comprehensive political settlement. Even so, Loyalist areas sprouted graffiti and murals calling for prisoners to be freed and the *New Ulster Defender* took up the matter in its first 1995 issue, with John White reminding the Major government that prisoners' support for the Loyalist ceasefire had been a key factor in making it possible. Serious violence in fact erupted in the Loyalist blocks of the Maze prison in March even though the prisoners, for all practical purposes, ran the blocks. Eighteen prison officers sustained injuries and fifty more suffered smoke inhalation from fires started during rioting which destroyed much of one block.

The UDA was not directly involved in orchestrating this prison protest, which was led by the UVF, and it also kept itself at a distance from the potentially serious disorder which broke out in July 1995 over the Portadown District of the Orange Order claiming its right on the Sunday prior to the twelfth to march from its church service back into the town centre down the predominantly nationalist Garvaghy Road. Drumcree church and the Garvaghy Road became the scenes of tense confrontation between Orangemen and security forces, who initially implemented government orders to halt the parade close to the church. The RUC's Chief Constable reversed his decision to ban it and in the face of non-violent nationalist protests the parade went ahead, with the local MP, David Trimble, and Paisley taking part and rashly claiming it as a great Loyalist victory for which commemorative medals were issued by the Orange Order. Trimble's role was a factor in securing him the Ulster Unionist leadership when the party's council voted in September on the succession to Molyneaux.

All this was but the forerunner of infinitely more violent conflict over the parade issue in subsequent years. The UDA's disinclination to become involved as an organisation was a relief to the authorities but at the same time they knew that it remained fully and formidably armed and in control of what it saw as 'its' areas. Even as political spokesmen such as Adams and McMichael talked the language of reconciliation and bridge-building, this control could take the form of blatant extortion. At Belfast Crown Court two UDA members made pleas of guilty to extorting money from businesses in the Shankill area for the organisation[67] and in June members of both the UDA and the UVF were convicted of similar offences as well as of blackmail.[68] The fact that these offences dated back to before the Loyalist ceasefire did little to persuade observers of the Loyalist paramilitary scene that such activity belonged to the past.

On 25 August 1995 the CLMC issued a statement outlining its current position. It reiterated its commitment under its ceasefire to political action and stressed that, while still armed, the organisations it represented would resort to no first strikes against the IRA or the nationalist community. There was also the inference to be drawn from the wording that Loyalists would disarm if real movement came from the IRA on ridding itself of its weapons. Sammy Duddy, who had returned to political work for the UDP, drew encouragement from this statement: 'If the ceasefire fails,' he told the author, 'it won't be our doing. The ball's in the Provos' court now and we need to keep it there. We'll keep our powder dry, as Carson told us we should in 1912, but there's not many of our boys who want to get the guns out at the moment. They are there, so are the Provos', but we'll not use them unless we have to.'[69]

In case anyone might doubt the support they still had, the UDA and UVF mounted a massive show of strength in a parade into central Belfast on the first anniversary of the Loyalist ceasefire. The CLMC had called for this and McMichael later claimed that of the estimated 40,000 people who took part and lined the route, at least half were UDA members.[70] Although styles had changed and bush hats and parkas were no longer in evidence, some found it eerily reminiscent of the early 1970s. Questions were once again asked about Loyalist paramilitarism and Trimble, ahead of President Clinton's hugely popular visit to Belfast, moved to defuse them by approaching the UDA and UVF through an intermediary on the notion of them starting a process of weapons-decommissioning ahead of the IRA.

Trimble admitted to the press that he had made this approach, saying: 'If only the Loyalist paramilitaries would move, even without waiting for the IRA, then I think it would deprive the IRA of any possible scintilla of justification for holding on to their weapons.'[71] He claimed to have appealed to the Loyalists on previous occasions to begin the process but within both the UDA and UVF there were what turned out to be well-justified doubts over how long the IRA was going to maintain its ceasefire. The UDA's Inner Council was quick to reject Trimble's call but they left it to McMichael to pass on their reaction to the media. 'It was seen as an attempt to try and manipulate the paramilitary organisations,' he told them. 'They have had enough bitter experience of that in the past and they were not prepared to fall into another trap.'[72]

NOTES

1. *Irish News*, 22 December 1993.
2. *Irish News*, 16 December 1993.
3. H. Sinnerton, *David Ervine: Uncharted Waters* (Dingle: Brandon, 2002), pp. 146–51.
4. G. McMichael, *An Ulster Voice: In Search of Common Ground in Northern Ireland* (Boulder, CO/Dublin: Roberts Rinehart, 1999), p. 49.
5. S. Duddy, interview with author, 24 February 1995.
6. McMichael, *An Ulster Voice*, p. 48.
7. Ibid., pp. 52–4.
8. J. Lowry and D. O'Hagan, Workers Party spokesmen, interview with author, 25 March, 2004.
9. S. Bruce, *The Edge of the Union: The Ulster Loyalist Political Vision* (Oxford: Oxford University Press, 1994), pp. 94–5.
10. Ibid.
11. Sinnerton, *David Ervine*, p. 155.
12. H. Jordan, *Milestones in Murder: Defining Moments in Ulster's Terror War* (Edinburgh: Mainstream, 2002) p. 202.
13. J. Adair, interview with author, 9 June 2004.
14. Ibid.
15. J. Brown, interview with author, 6 May 2003.
16. *Sunday Life*, 16 January 1994.
17. Adair, letter to author, 20 April 2004.
18. *Sunday Life*, 16 January 1994.
19. *Guardian*, 16 June 2001.
20. *Sunday Life*, 16 January 1994.
21. Ibid.
22. Ibid.
23. Ibid.
24. Ibid.
25. L. Kennedy, 'Repartition', in J. McGarry and B. O'Leary (eds), *The Future of Northern Ireland* (Oxford: Clarendon Press, 1990), p. 141.
26. Ibid., p. 143.
27. *Belfast Telegraph*, 17 January 1994.
28. Ibid.
29. Ibid.
30. R. Smallwoods, interview with author, 12 February 1994.
31. Adair, telephone conversation with author, 2 June 2004.

32. *Sunday Life*, 5 October 2003.
33. Former RUC superintendent, interview with author, 22 September 1994.
34. *Guardian*, 9 April 1994.
35. Ibid.
36. Ibid.
37. *Observer*, 17 April 1994.
38. Brown, interview with author.
39. Adair, letter to author.
40. Ibid.
41. Smallwoods, interview with author.
42. E. Mallie and D. McKittrick, *The Fight for Peace: The Secret Story behind the Irish Peace Process* (London: Heinemann, 1996), p. 309.
43. *Observer*, 17 July 1994.
44. Mallie and McKittrick, *Fight for Peace*, p. 310.
45. D. Lister and H. Jordan, *Mad Dog: The Rise and Fall of Johnny Adair and 'C' Company* (Edinburgh: Mainstream, 2003), p. 176.
46. E. Moloney, *A Secret History of the IRA* (London: Allen Lane, 2002), p. 33.
47. J. Major, *The Autobiography* (London: HarperCollins, 1999), p. 457.
48. McMichael, *An Ulster Voice*, p. 58.
49. Ibid.
50. *Irish News*, 26 July 2004.
51. McMichael, *An Ulster Voice*, p. 59.
52. D. McKittrick, S. Kelters, B. Feeney and C. Thornton, *Lost Lives: The Stories of the Men, Women and Children Who Died as a Result of Northern Ireland's Troubles* (Edinburgh: Mainstream, 1999), p. 1378.
53. McMichael, *An Ulster Voice*, p. 61.
54. *Irish Times*, 6 September 1994.
55. *Herald*, 3 September, 1994.
56. *Guardian*, 13 September 1994.
57. Ibid.
58. *Combat*, September 1994.
59. McMichael, *An Ulster Voice*, p. 65.
60. *New Ulster Defender*, vol 1, no. 12, 1994.
61. Ibid.
62. Ibid.
63. Ibid.
64. *Sunday Times*, 1 February 1995.
65. *New Ulster Defender*, vol. 1, no. 13, 1995.
66. *Guardian*, 13 September 1995.
67. *Irish News*, 18 January 1995.
68. *Irish News*, 23 June 1995.
69. Duddy, interview with author, 5 September 1995.
70. G. McMichael, interview with author, 9 February 2000.
71. *Guardian*, 4 December, 1995.
72. Ibid.

9

Signing Up to Peace? The UDA's Road to the Good Friday Agreement

The year 1996 and the first half of 1997 was a period dominated by the IRA's resumption of hostilities and also by dramatically heightened tension over the Loyalist marching season, especially the Portadown Orangemen's demand to parade their traditional Pre-Twelfth Sunday route from Drumcree church back into the town centre. Renewed IRA attacks and successive Drumcree crises posed urgent questions for the UDA and its political spokesmen but the organisation's political wing did at least achieve some modest success in elections, at the end of May 1996, to the new Forum, set up by John Major's government for constitutional talks. However, its candidates did not campaign jointly with those backed by the UVF and ominous tensions between the two bodies became apparent and were a factor in the break-up of the CLMC.

The IRA's bombing of the Canary Wharf complex in London on 9 February 1996 took two lives and injured dozens of people as well as causing colossal destruction. Other attacks followed and central Manchester miraculously escaped with no loss of life when another huge bomb was set off there on Saturday, 15 June. At the time, and later in his memoirs, Gerry Adams claimed implausibly not to have known in advance of the IRA's return to war.[1] These attacks had been in preparation for some months and were a simple if brutal way to avoid a split within the ranks at a time when London, despite the IRA's 1994 ceasefire, was still refusing to talk to Sinn Fein ahead of arms-decommissioning or to move on the issue of prisoner releases.

The CLMC met in response to the Canary Wharf attack a few days later and UDA members on it agreed to the drafting of a joint statement with the UVF. It declared:

> From a position of confidence, strength and sophistication, we have withstood the recent provocation of IRA bombs on the mainland which have killed our innocent British fellow citizens.
>
> These atrocities cannot be permitted to continue without a telling response from this source. We are poised and ready to strike to effect. We will give blow for blow. As in the past, whatever the cost, we will gladly pay it.[2]

The CLMC met once a week in the period immediately after Canary Wharf. Its message to Loyalists was to keep calm and it kept up its contact with

Loyalist prisoners. Gary McMichael was particularly active in liaison work between the Command and UDA/UFF prisoners, visiting them three times a week in the aftermath of the IRA ending its ceasefire. John White at this time told the author that it would be easier for the CLMC to hold the line if the IRA did not resume major attacks in Northern Ireland itself. He added, however, that there would be 'a limit to Loyalist patience if more of our fellow British citizens are killed by IRA bombs in English cities'.[3]

Vigorous police action in London and elsewhere involving the arrests of IRA members and in one instance the shooting dead of one of them allayed Loyalist fears. The IRA's campaign in Northern Ireland, as some in the security services had predicted, remained low key, though an exception to this was its bomb attack on the army's headquarters at Thiepval Barracks in Lisburn. This took the form of a car bomb planted within the complex on 10 October 1996. A warrant officer caught in the blast died later from multiple burns and terrible injuries. Lisburn, however, is a predominantly Protestant town and virtually all the civilian work force employed at Thiepval were Protestants too.

The sight, on army video footage shown on television news programmes, of civilian workers fleeing from the first bomb only to be caught in a second explosion near the camp's medical block was a savage reminder of what the IRA was still capable of. Protestant anger was deepened by the way Adams dismissed the attack as merely 'an incident', and Sammy Duddy told the author:

> If the Provos want to push ordinary Protestant people into a war situation, this is how to do it. Adams and [Martin] McGuinness may have come off the Provos' Army Council but this was planned weeks ago so Loyalists find it hard to believe they knew nothing about it.[4]

The Lisburn attack came at a difficult time for the UDA. Some of its prisoners had begun to express doubts about the political direction of the peace process and early in June nine of them, including the Greysteel gunmen Torrens Knight and Stephen Irwin, were expelled from the UDA wing in the Maze for voicing their opposition to a new mural displaying a white dove of peace painted in a corridor by other prisoners. Subsequently they agreed to be rehoused in a wing run by dissident UVF men who later emerged as the nucleus of Billy Wright's Loyalist Volunteer Force. Rumours were rife about splits within the UVF, and the CLMC, whose days as a cohesive body were numbered, held several hours of tense deliberation the day after the Lisburn attack.

The UDA/UFF response would have been a different one if Johnny Adair had still been at liberty, though he let it be known from prison that he supported the principle of a Loyalist ceasefire. This owed much to the growing influence upon him of White, who cultivated the role of a spokesman for the peace process. Adair had, in fact, in May 1995, made a plea of guilty to the charge of directing terrorism and had been sentenced to sixteen years. His only hope of early release lay with political dialogue amongst the parties bearing fruit and the ending of armed action by both Loyalists and Republicans. The future was still uncertain in 1996 and he faced an extended period in prison. He began to use his time pumping iron in the Maze gymnasium as well as transforming his appearance by shaving his head and injecting himself heavily with powerful steroids.

John Gregg, on his release from prison for his part in the attempted murder of Gerry Adams in 1984, had returned to his home ground in the sprawling Rathcoole estate in North Belfast, where he quickly made himself a figure to reckon with. He was given the South-East Antrim brigade command in place of Joe English, who was 'stood down' for what Workers Party spokesmen claim was his willingness to enter into political dialogue with them.[5] English was important enough to be part of the joint Loyalist delegation to Washington in 1995 but he had dared to make allegations about senior UDA figures in Rathcoole being involved in the expanding drug trade there.

Community workers, clergy and others had become concerned at blatant drug-dealing in the area but Gregg chose not to use his ferocious reputation to halt it. Though probably not a dealer himself, he was widely believed to have settled for a policy of turning a blind eye to it provided the UDA was accorded a fixed share of all transactions. English, relieved of his command, continued to object to the organisation's involvement and was expelled from it, becoming an ostracised 'non-person'. Gregg, it must be said, eschewed the ostentatious lifestyle of his fellow brigadier in East Belfast, describing himself to the author as a 'home bird'.[6] His main indulgence was travelling with his son to Rangers games in Glasgow and pounding the bass drum in a local flute band, the Cloughfern Young Conquerors.

In Gregg's area as in others, the UDA's main concern, even in a period of renewed IRA operations, was to consolidate control on the ground and to build up a new membership. Gregg openly told the author how the post-ceasefire period had seemed to him a chance to maximise recruitment from Newtonabbey and Rathcoole up to Larne and Carrickfergus while not actually coming out against the Loyalist ceasefire. This, he stressed, he had supported only as a way to help his friends get out of prison.[7]

Factors like these and Adair's absence from the scene had the end result that virtually no significant operations were launched against Republican targets over the seventeen-month period of the IRA's renewed 'military' campaign. This was a vacuum which dissident Loyalist killers would begin to fill as tension reached boiling point over the marching season in the summers of 1996 and 1997. The only victim of the UDA/UFF directly was John Slane, who was shot dead in his home in the Broadway area of West Belfast on 14 March 1997, though his death was widely agreed to have been a case of mistaken identity.[8]

On 11 June 1997 a UDA gunman, acting without the organisation's authority, killed another victim. This was Bobby 'Basher' Bates, once a member of the dreaded Shankill Butchers gang whose sadistic killings had terrorised nationalist Belfast in the 1970s. Bates had been released from prison a few months before, claiming to have found God while serving his lengthy sentence. His killer, who shot him dead outside an evangelical advice centre on the Woodvale Road where he had been helping out, acted to avenge the killing of Robert Curtis Moorehead twenty years earlier. He had been a UDA victim of the Butchers, though nearly all their victims were Catholics, and was battered to death by some of them, including Bates, in the toilet of the Windsor bar on the Shankill Road, as a result of a quarrel with them. Bates's killer was related to Moorehead but cannot be named for legal reasons. He was protected by the UDA, then spirited out of the Shankill to a different area of Belfast.[9]

Over this same period the UDA lost three of its members but none of them was the victim of IRA attack. Thomas 'Tucker' Annett had a record of involvement with the UDA in South Belfast and also had ordinary criminal convictions. He had been on good terms with Adair but on the night of 12 July 1996, traditionally a time of parties in Loyalist areas to follow on from those of the 'eleventh' night, he was beaten to death in a drunken fight with visiting Scottish bandsmen who were said to have taken it in turns to kick him unconscious and batter his head with bottles from the nearby Kimberley bar. Police told the press that the victim was 'well known to them'[10] but nobody was charged with his murder.

Almost exactly a year later Brian Morton, described as 'a dedicated member' of the organisation at his funeral, was killed by a pipe bomb which exploded prematurely while he was handling it near a towpath by the river Lagan in the Dunmurry area of South Belfast. Some reports suggested he was in fact the second in command of the UFF in South Belfast. Gary McMichael and David Adams represented the Ulster Democratic Party at his burial, which was also attended by Jeffrey Donaldson, the Ulster Unionist MP for the Lagan Valley seat.[11]

Three and a half months later, Glen Greer was driving off from his house on the Loyalist Kilcooley estate in Bangor, County Down, when his car was wrecked by a powerful bomb fitted to it. Neighbours saw him with a severed leg trying to crawl away from the burning vehicle. He died later in hospital, leaving a wife with three children and expecting a fourth. It was widely believed that he had been under threat for some time from the UDA for acting as a police informer. The device which killed him was based on Powergel, though Loyalists made limited use of car bombs. A neighbour's jaundiced comment to the press was: 'Loyalists have finally worked out how to make a car bomb that doesn't fall off or fail to ignite and their first victim? One of their own.'[12]

The UDA made no claim to having carried out this killing and there was speculation that it was the product of deteriorating relations between the UDA and the UVF, who had taken it upon themselves to eliminate a Loyalist informer. Frankie Curry, a self-confessed serial killer with a long record in the UVF, later told the press, close to the time of his own murder in a Loyalist feud, that he had killed Greer.[13]

The one significant Republican target singled out for attack in this period by the UDA/UFF was an Ardoyne man, Eddie Copeland. Three years earlier his seniority in the IRA had been referred to in the House of Commons by David Trimble and he was regarded with particular loathing by Adair and C Company, who had made more than one attempt to kill him. He had been a close friend of Thomas Begley, the Shankill Road fish shop bomber, and many Loyalists believed that Copeland had in fact set up that attack. However, the reason for the attempt on his life on 28 December 1996 was an IRA attack just a few days earlier on Nigel Dodds, a former Lord Mayor of Belfast and Democratic Unionist Party candidate in the approaching Westminster elections.

What shocked Unionist and Loyalist opinion was that that gunmen had opened fire on Dodds at the Royal Victoria Hospital, where he was visiting his seriously ill seven-year-old son, a victim of cerebral palsy. Copeland was targeted for a reprisal attack and sustained serious injuries when a bomb fitted under his car exploded as he tried to drive it away from his mother's house in Ardoyne. No organisation claimed responsibility for the attack but the CLMC certainly did not rush to condemn it and a senior UDA member in West Belfast gave the author to understand soon afterwards that the attempt on Copeland's life had been sanctioned by the organisation as a way of showing that Loyalists could reach targets even in strongly Republican areas.[14]

What had, in this period, as much potential as the IRA's renewed campaign to reactivate Loyalist killing was the unresolved Drumcree crisis. For the Orange Order and for many Loyalists outside its ranks this remained unfinished business despite the victory of July 1995 when the security forces had permitted a parade along the disputed Garvaghy Road. This was a victory which nationalist residents were determined to stop being repeated the next year. Led by a former IRA activist and ex-prisoner, Brendan McKenna, they kept their case in front of the media and built a network of contacts with other residents' groups, on Belfast's Lower Ormeau Road, Dunloy in County Antrim and Bellaghy in South Londonderry amongst other places.

Orangemen and Unionists still believe that the Republican movement worked closely with these groups to 'talk up' the parades issue as part of a post-ceasefire strategy to broaden the base of its support in Catholic and nationalist areas. In 1998 they were able to quote none other than Gerry Adams on the matter. Secretly tape-recorded remarks he had made at a Sinn Fein meeting in County Meath were leaked to the media. In the course of these he had said:

> Ask any activist in the North, did Drumcree happen by accident, and he will tell you 'no'. Three years of work on the Ormeau Road, in Portadown and parts of Fermanagh and Newry, Armagh and in Bellaghy, and up in Londonderry. Three years of work went into creating that situation and fair play to those who put the work in. They are the type of scene changes we need to focus on and develop and exploit.[15]

Fear that this was the reality behind the growth of nationalist residents' groups led hardliners within the Orange Order, in September 1995, to form their own campaigning group called the Spirit of Drumcree. They were motivated not just by what they believed was an Orangeman's right to walk traditional parade routes but by the belief that the Grand Lodge of Ireland would be over-cautious on the issue. The order's Portadown District did not support the group and was alienated by its often aggressive rhetoric and by the leading questions some of its spokesmen began to pose about the whole ethos and structure of the Orange Order.

Traditionally the Loyalist marching season in Northern Ireland begins on Easter Monday with a major parade organised by the Apprentice Boys of Derry. In 1996 this was scheduled for Portadown, but affiliated clubs across the province normally paraded locally with their bands to transport which would take them to the appointed venue. For South Belfast's Ballynafeigh club, this meant crossing the Ormeau bridge and marching down the Lower Ormeau Road with its mainly nationalist population. Their preferred route would also have passed Sean Graham's betting shop, scene of the February 1992 massacre and the target on occasion since then of some vicious taunts from marching Orangemen and their supporters on the pavement.

Well ahead of Easter Monday, Sir Hugh Annesley, the RUC's Chief Constable, made it known that any parade beyond the bridge would be forbidden. Early on the morning of 8 April police armoured vehicles and the RUC's mobile support unit, with army units in reserve, sealed off the bridge before the Ballynafeigh club's arrival. They and their band turned back after a formal protest and amidst vocal anger from a growing crowd of flag-waving Loyalists. 'All this for one fucking bookie's shop,' one woman told the author. 'They're just here to protect IRA murderers who live down that road.'[16] For some hours, a sullen stalemate continued with protesters increasing in numbers.

At this point the UDA's preference was not to be drawn into confrontations over the parades issue. Like the UVF, its relationship with the Orange Order had always been an ambivalent one. Individual members could join lodges and indeed hold office in them. If convicted of criminal acts, the decision whether or not to discipline or even expel them was usually one devolved to individual lodges, or clubs in the Apprentice Boys' case. Both organisations officially disowned paramilitarism, though over the years lodge premises had on occasions been made available to the UDA for meetings and sometimes for more than that. 'We could never take their support for granted, not when it mattered,' Sammy Duddy later told the author. 'Sometimes they would let us store our gear in their halls but then one of them was always liable to go to the Peelers and shop us.'[17]

He had made cheerful fun in his published poems of what some Loyalists like to call 'parade Protestantism' and was conspicuous by his absence on the Ormeau Bridge on Easter Monday 1996. In so far as the UDA had any presence there, it was through its political wing, the UDP. Gary McMichael appeared during the course of the morning to appeal for calm and also present was Pauline Gilmore. She had had a close relationship with Edgar Graham, the Queen's University law lecturer and active Unionist whom the IRA had murdered in 1983. She later joined the UDP and admitted to having contacts with active UDA members in South Belfast.[18] She became the key figure in Order, a campaign for Protestant rights in the Ormeau area. She later fell out with the UDP but on Easter Monday was ready to put the case against any rerouting of the Apprentice Boys' parade to the media present at the bridge.

The stand-off on the Ormeau Bridge lasted until late afternoon, when many of the Apprentice Boys with their bands and supporters, well fuelled with drink, arrived on the scene from Portadown to launch sustained and well-orchestrated attacks on the RUC with bricks, bottles, scaffolding poles and petrol bombs. The author recalls a police sergeant saying to him, in the midst of all this: 'Do you remember the film *Zulu*? The difference between here and Rorke's Drift seems to be that the Zulus have got the Union Jacks.' The police lines held, though plastic baton rounds had to be fired, and over a period of some hours the rioters were pushed back up the Ormeau Road but it was the most serious street violence Belfast had seen since the 1994 ceasefires.

Tension rose throughout the community, not least because of uncompromising rhetoric at some of the Republican movement's Easter 1916 commemorations on the same day and on the previous Sunday. At the New Lodge ceremony on the morning prior to the Ormeau Bridge riot, Barry McElduff, a Mid-Ulster Sinn Fein spokesman, told a cheering crowd that there was 'no room for the Union Jack in North Belfast or anywhere else in the North of Ireland. No English politicians will ever get their hands on IRA weapons. There's only one legitimate army in Ireland and that's the IRA.'[19]

The countdown from these events to what both the media and the security forces began to call Drumcree Two was rapid. As widely expected, Annesley announced on 6 July that, once again, it was the RUC's intention to block the Portadown Orangemen from marching down the Garvaghy Road. This was a Saturday and David Trimble, addressing Scottish Orangemen at Stirling, made dramatic and possibly inflammatory use of the news in his speech to them. He told his audience about massive RUC and army deployment in Portadown and declared that the security forces were on a collision course with the Unionist people, adding: 'Enough is enough. We've had it up to here.'[20]

As thousands of Loyalists poured into Portadown to support the district lodge there, the murderous potential of the situation became brutally apparent. Thirty-one-year-old Michael McGoldrick, a Catholic from nearby Lurgan who was married with one child and with his wife expecting another, had taken summer work as a taxi driver after graduating in English and Politics from Queen's University. Near midnight on Sunday, 7 July, he set off to collect a fare from a bar on the Portadown Road only to be found a few miles away the following morning, dead in his vehicle with two bullet wounds in the back of his head. This was not the work of the UDA/UFF but of dissident gunmen in the Portadown area who were in the process of breaking away from the authority of the UVF. It is almost certain that McGoldrick's murder was ordered by Billy Wright, a much-feared figure in his own area and beyond it. Clifford McKeown, later convicted of the killing, in fact described it as a 'birthday present' for Wright.

Local newspapers had attributed a series of killings to him and Martin O'Hagan, a reporter with the *Sunday World*, had nicknamed him 'King Rat'. Wright resented this deeply and vowed vengeance on O'Hagan. This was eventually taken but not until three years after Wright's own death in prison at the hands of INLA killers. Wright had come out openly against the Loyalist ceasefire and the peace process and had become an increasingly public figure as the Drumcree crisis worsened, speaking about the situation directly at one point with Trimble. This was on Thursday, 11 July,[21] by which time much of Northern Ireland had been brought to a standstill by Loyalist blockades and roadblocks in support of the Portadown Orangemen.

Attacks on the security forces at the Garvaghy Road barricade close to Drumcree church worsened from one day to the next with a Tannoy system blasting out a combination of Loyalist tunes and blatant threats to RUC officers whose names and home addresses were often announced. Like the UVF, the UDA held back from involvement in a crisis which appeared to be spiralling out of control. The UVF command was aware of the degree of its local members' support for Wright but the UDA had its own dissidents too. Some of them, to show their support for the protest, stole a heavy mechanical digger from a quarry on the edge of Portadown and drove it to an area just behind Drumcree church. There they welded onto it armour plating acquired from Mahon army barracks in the town and also fitted it with a bullet-proof windscreen.

It was then driven on to Drumcree Hill, just beside the church, where, on the morning of Tuesday, 9 July, the security forces got their first glimpse of it. Alongside it was a tractor towing a slurry spreader and word soon got about that the armour-plated digger was to ram police and army lines, allowing the tractor driver to spray either toxic slurry or even lighted petrol over police and soldiers. UDA men involved in all this told the journalist Hugh Jordan years later that the digger's appearance was crucial in undermining the RUC Chief Constable's will to enforce the parade ban.[22] It may have been a factor but it was only one among a series of others analysed in a definitive account of the episode.[23]

Claims were made at the time that the digger was driven by Alex Kerr, who had until lately been UDA brigadier in South Belfast. He had always been regarded as a hardliner whose doubts about the peace process had drawn him into the orbit of Wright. For this and also for allegations he spread about other brigadiers he was stood down by the Inner Council and arrested later in the year by the RUC on charges of illegal possession of firearms. As the July

1996 Drumcree crisis intensified, Kerr was seen there in Wright's company but it now appears that he was not the digger's driver any more than Wright had organised its acquisition.[24]

As the Twelfth drew closer, so did the prospects of thousands more Orangemen arriving at Drumcree to support the protest. Despite the biggest army presence anywhere in Northern Ireland since the 1994 ceasefires, the RUC was exhausted and over-stretched by the crisis. With a heavy commitment of British troops to Bosnia in 1996, there was a limit to the back-up the army could provide, though its commanding officers were prepared for a much more active role if the Chief Constable asked for it. Annesley opted, however, to let the Portadown District Lodge march down the Garvaghy Road after all on Thursday the eleventh. This provoked a violent nationalist reaction and rioting spread rapidly to other areas, only subsiding on the sixteenth. By then, 24,000 petrol bombs had been thrown and 6,000 plastic bullet rounds had been fired by the police. Some 149 RUC officers and 192 civilians were injured and one man was crushed to death by an army vehicle in Londonderry.[25]

More than 250 people driven from their homes by communal violence and threats had to be resettled. Policing the crisis had cost £10 million and rehousing the homeless and replacing burnt-out buses and public buildings added another £7 million to the bill. The cost to the RUC's relationship with the nationalist community was greater still. Yet all this was the prelude to an even worse crisis over Drumcree the following year, 1997, which was both preceded and followed by sectarian killings. Some were of a particularly brutal nature, such as those of eighteen-year-old Catholic Bernadette Martin, shot dead on 15 July in the house of her Protestant boyfriend at Aughalee, and of James Morgan, a teenage Catholic schoolboy, whose battered and mutilated body was found on 27 July, dumped in a water-filled animal carcass pit near Castlewellan in County Down. These murders were not, however, the work of the UDA but of young Loyalist dissidents acting under Wright's influence.

IRA gunmen continued to kill until their leadership called a second ceasefire on 19 July 1997. This, along with the Orange Order's crucial decision to reroute some particularly contentious 12 July parades in Belfast and elsewhere, gave some respite to both the security forces and a recently elected Labour government which had not felt confident enough to enforce a ban on the Drumcree parade. Once again, Northern Ireland had come close to the edge of the sectarian precipice, with the INLA threatening that its gunmen would fire into Orange Order parades on the Twelfth if they went ahead as planned.

As in 1996, the UDA sought to claim some credit for keeping its membership out of the worst of the Drumcree-related violence. Sammy Duddy, in conversation with the author, held to his view that there was no reason for the UDA to fight the Orange Order's battle for it. He admitted, however, that there could have been a breaking point and that we might have had to let our boys off the leash. We didn't want pointless rioting and destruction in our own areas but the other side did their best to provoke us. If they had killed that wee fellow McCann, that might just have done it.[26]

The 'wee fellow' was Craig McCann, fifteen years old and a promising footballer who had been offered a trial with Chelsea. On the night on 7 July 1997 he was engaged in a traditional task for boys in Loyalist areas, guarding the local bonfire in readiness for the Twelfth. This was in Ainsworth Avenue, one of Belfast's grimmest interfaces, opening off the Shankill Road right on to a reinforced section of the army's peace line dividing the area from nationalist West Belfast. The night was a violent one, with rioting in many areas over the ongoing 'Drumcree Three' crisis, and McCann was hit by a burst of automatic fire from a masked gunman who climbed on to the 'peace wall' from its nationalist side to pick his target.

The attack on a group of unarmed teenagers was calculated and deliberate. McCann was not caught in any crossfire between gunmen and security forces, as some newspapers reported. 'The Peelers and the army, from where they were, would have had to be firing round a corner to hit him,' one Ainsworth Avenue resident told the author soon afterwards.[27] McCann survived, though there was a fear for a time that he might lose an arm. Had he not lived, his death would have been a sectarian murder by Republicans and Duddy was under no illusions as to what it might have led to. 'We can just about control the Shankill,' he told the author in the aftermath of the McCann shooting and went on to confirm reports that masked and armed UDA men were seen in Woodvale and elsewhere 'just to reassure the local people, a wee reminder that our boys were still there'.[28]

In the backwash of the successive Drumcree crises and amidst continued political uncertainty, sporadic violence by the UDA continued, often in the form of intimidatory fire and pipe bomb attacks on Catholic homes. This had been a feature of the violence of the summer of 1996 and in March the following year a Rathcoole man received a six-month sentence in a Belfast court after admitting that he had, under what he claimed was duress, used his car to drive UDA members to houses which they had attacked and damaged in the previous July.[29] Continued attacks of the same type in Rathcoole, Glengormley, Larne and Carrickfergus were also the UDA's work and it was widely known that they were sanctioned by John Gregg, or 'Grugg', as he was also known. Also in March 1997, security forces had to defuse ninety pounds of explosives fitted to a device left outside a Sinn Fein advice centre in Belfast's New Lodge area. UDA responsibility for what might have been carnage in a built-up area was talked about but not claimed by it.

The slow-drip effect of incidents like these fed rumours about the viability of the Loyalist ceasefire. In July 1996, at the height of that year's Drumcree crisis, a Unionist newspaper had described the ceasefire as 'hanging by a thread'[30] and the very public behaviour of UDA and UVF dissidents such as

Kerr and Wright intensified the speculation. In that same year, copies of a video began to be distributed in Loyalist areas denouncing the October 1994 ceasefire as an act of treachery and vilifying the political spokesmen of the UVF and UDA as 'bought men' acting as the stooges of British intelligence services.

Although poor in image quality, the video was well edited and clearly the work of someone with excellent access to both BBC Northern Ireland and Ulster Television footage. Its message was the uncompromising one that Loyalist Ulster's fate was in its own hands. Raymond Smallwoods among others, it claimed, had been murdered with British connivance because he was an impediment to any agreement with Dublin over Northern Ireland's future. The same fate, it went on to argue, had been intended for Johnny Adair when Frizzel's fish shop on the Shankill Road was bombed on 23 October 1993. The Reverend Roy Magee, a Presbyterian minister who had been a key figure in expediting the Loyalist ceasefire, was used on the video too in an interview in which he declared that 'terrible things had had to be allowed to happen'[31] in order to make the peace process possible.

James G. MacLean, a leading Scottish Orangeman who has good Ulster Loyalist contacts, has recalled scores of copies of the video being in circulation. The fact that a Scottish voice was used for the commentary is, in his view, a ruse to conceal its real origins. He has no doubt in his own mind that it originated in Northern Ireland but disclaims any knowledge of its creators. Never convinced himself of the IRA's good intentions or of the durability of the peace process, he recalls his own reactions at the time: 'I was amazed at the content, that early, when both the UDA and UVF were still officially optimistic about events, but it made an impact, I'm certain of that. It fed scepticism among Loyalists.'[32]

It is in fact more than likely that the video was the work of a fundamentalist Protestant pastor who has had an intermittent but sinister role in the history of the Troubles. He cannot be named here for legal reasons but has had a proven ability to avoid arrest or being charged with any offences despite close links with extreme elements in paramilitary Loyalism. This has led some to suspect that he may also have worked as an agent for British intelligence. One bizarre cause he has espoused is that of the British Israelites, a fundamentalist Loyalist group who claim that the Ulster Protestants, not the Jews, are the true lost tribe of Israel, and he also has links with the far-right American organisation Aryan Nation, one of whose founders, Richard Butler, also a self-styled pastor, died in September 2004.[33]

The pastor has edited *Rome Watch International*, a four page 'newsletter' which denounces Catholicism in the most rabid language, with a heavy emphasis on child sexual abuse by clergy and religious orders. He is also the author of a series called Prophecy Study Booklets, heavily laced with quotations from the book of Revelation and seeking to prove the Catholic Church to be the embodiment of paganism and the anti-Christ. He has a degree from

London University and has also published a number of booklets on Ulster Protestant history.

He has held teaching positions in schools in Northern Ireland but is known to be homosexual and also to have been close to the late William McGrath, an active Loyalist and Orangeman finally brought to trial and convicted in 1981 of the sexual abuse over an extended period of boys placed under his care when he ran the Kincora home in East Belfast. McGrath was also a member of a shadowy and secretive Loyalist society called Tara, now known to have had links with British intelligence. To this day, former RUC officers will speak off the record of the numerous obstructions placed in the path of their investigation of this squalid case.

The pastor circulated a series of pamphlets anonymously denouncing the alleged treachery of the UDA and UVF leadership. He also wrote most of the shortlived *Ulster News*, which in one of its issues called the October 1994 ceasefire statement 'a grovelling defeatist diatribe' and those who drafted it 'paid collaborators'.[34] Some of this material called on 'true Loyalists' such as Wright and his Portadown lieutenant Mark 'Swinger' Fulton to link up with UDA dissidents in order to form a new 'Ulster army' which could smash both the IRA and the Belfast Agreement. The UDA's Inner Council came close to identifying the challenge to it and the autumn 1996 *New Ulster Defender* ran an editorial alerting members to the danger. It described it as

> centred in the Mid-Ulster area, but with active assistance of unsavoury elements from other areas of Northern Ireland, an unholy alliance of drug dealers, media junkies, criminal elements, and believe it or not, fundamentalist clerics active in trying to bring about a collapse of the Loyalist ceasefire.[35]

In reality, the CLMC, which was the target of many of these attacks, no longer had a significant role in events. Speculation over its future had pre-dated the 1996 Drumcree crisis with Joe English telling the press that it was no longer functioning. He was well placed to know, though his own position was crumbling rapidly, but he put much of the blame on the Mid-Ulster UVF, who had in March of that year brought Dublin airport to a standstill with a hoax car bomb but without informing the CLMC. 'That was a big breach of trust,' English declared. 'Under no circumstances will the Combined Loyalist Military Command meet until all parties can be assured there will be no similar breach of trust.'[36] His premonitions were well founded though the Command held some further meetings in the latter part of the year.

A much greater blow to the Command's credibility was of course its failure to discipline Wright after his open defiance of it during and after that year's Drumcree crisis. He was given until September to leave Northern Ireland or be killed, a threat also made to Kerr. The UDA could at least say that it had already expelled him from its ranks and sent a hit squad to his home town of Cookstown, County Tyrone, though their intention to kill him had been foiled by the heavy presence of security forces in the area. Shortly before the ultimatum for Wright, the UDA also moved against areas where it suspected there might be support for him. On the night of 28 August more than a hundred UDA men took over the streets of Dromore, in County Down, wrecking the houses of two men known to be close to Kerr. Fire bombs were thrown and furniture flung into the street. Afterwards, armed UDA units toured the town's bars, reading out a prepared statement calling for loyalty to the CLMC.[37]

A show of strength like this was not, however, enough to make a reality of the Command's authority in face of the support for Wright and his breakaway LVF, which grew rapidly in and around Portadown after the CLMC's 1 September statement. Some of this support was very clearly orchestrated by the DUP, who had no relish for the UVF's political wing, the Progressive Unionist Party, becoming a significant force within Unionism. Wright's relationship to the DUP was indeed identified by an anonymous contributor to the UVF's magazine in September 1996[38] and the UDA leadership broadly accepted this view of his role, while also fearing the appeal that his breakaway LVF might have for some of its own membership, who were attracted to this group's readiness to target and kill Catholics.

LVF members were indeed implicated in the murder of Sean Brown, president of the Bellaghy Gaelic Football Club in South Londonderry, and also those of Bernadette Martin and James Morgan. These were carried out subsequent to Wright's own removal from the scene by his arrest and conviction in March 1997 for the intimidation of a witness in a local court case. The UVF's failure to discipline him or act against him heightened tensions within the CLMC. At the October rally which it called outside Belfast City Hall to mark the third anniversary of its ceasefire, only UDA members turned up. They heard Gary McMichael, David Adams and other speakers press the case for the UDA's political wing to be part of the negotiating process already set in motion by the new Secretary of State, Mo Mowlam.

The UVF's absence from the rally, for the second year running, fed press speculation about the future of the CLMC. The UVF had also absented itself from what were intended to be joint demonstrations in support of the release of Loyalist prisoners but Billy Hutchinson, a former UVF prisoner speaking for the PUP, denied that there were grounds for the CLMC breaking up. Even if this happened, he argued, both the UVF and the UDA could and should continue to play a part in the current negotiations at Stormont.[39]

The rally concluded with the sound system blasting out Tina Turner's 'Simply the Best', which had become the anthem of the UFF as well as a vocal section of Rangers' home support at Ibrox Park in Glasgow.[40] Paramilitary bands and colour parties then marched off to Loyalist areas of the city in what Belfast's SDLP Lord Mayor called a 'repugnant' display which he promised he would ask the RUC to investigate.[41] However, nothing appeared to come of this.

The paramilitary symbolism of the October rally had not been intended to undermine Loyalist support for continuing to talk to the new Secretary of State but by the end of the year UDP spokesmen such as Adams and McMichael were beginning to feel frustration over where the new government's agenda might be leading. Key to the talks was guarantees for the phased release of Loyalist prisoners as opposed to concessions like extended Christmas parole time. Unilateral action by the Dublin government in releasing nine IRA prisoners without prior consultation with Mowlam or Loyalist leaders was a blow to the whole process. 'Nothing is going our way,' Adams told the press on 23 December,[42] as he left the Maze after talks with UDA prisoners.

Their views remained vital but there were reports that they had come close to withdrawing their support for the Loyalist negotiators at the Stormont talks. McMichael issued a statement which read: 'Within the Loyalist community there is a very severe feeling of alienation and people are starting to question the value of this process.'[43] He also announced that the UDP would review its own participation in the talks before their scheduled resumption on 12 January. At this stage he was still confident that the party had a role to play. It had won two seats in the 1996 Forum elections and had succeeded in getting four candidates elected at the May 1997 council elections. Its annual conference in October was a well-attended and upbeat occasion and most of the November issue of the *New Ulster Defender* was given over to speeches made and policy resolutions carried. However, danger still stalked Loyalists who aspired to follow a political road.

For some commentators, some of this danger came from the final breakup of the CLMC. This had been predicted throughout the year but its demise had no major impact on events. All it had ever been was an umbrella body under whose aegis disparate organisations could issue agreed statements such as the 1991 and 1994 ceasefires, but it had little in the way of any operational role, and, as the 1996 and 1997 Drumcree crises had shown, Loyalist violence had a brutal momentum which was virtually independent of it.

More danger came from inside the UDA, from those who had become open in their scepticism about where the peace process was going yet preferred to remain with the organisation. This was true of the North Antrim and South Londonderry brigade area, which retained a good membership but, in operational terms, had been only intermittently active over the years, though its gunmen had carried out the Castlerock and Greysteel attacks in 1993. Billy McFarland was the area brigadier, a rank he had risen to after an active period in the 1970s in which he was ultimately convicted of a series of bomb attacks on nationalist-owned businesses and properties.

McFarland, known as 'the Mexican' because of his dark moustache and swarthy looks, expanded his interests in the building business after his release and used his position to discourage blatant racketeering and drug dealing, themes echoed in the brigade's magazine, *Warrior*. Increasingly its pages came to develop a political position markedly different from that of the Belfast leadership. Some saw this as proof of rural Loyalist Ulster's capacity to arrive at a semi-detached relationship with a heavily urban leadership. Billy Wright's Mid-Ulster UVF unit had done this too and burnt its bridges with its Belfast command but this was not a road McFarland wanted his brigade to follow.

Instead, he encouraged contributors to *Warrior* to set out their individual views of what kind of future Ulster Loyalists could create for themselves and he was happy to promote new talent within the organisation. A case in point was an articulate young Glaswegian, Jim Wright, a Transport and General Workers' Union shop steward in a bus-building plant outside Ballymena, who also had a strong background in Scottish Loyalism and had joined the UDA before he settled in Antrim and married a local woman.

As the IRA resumed its attacks in 1996 and as British intentions became even less clear to Loyalists, *Warrior* began to espouse an Ulster nationalist position reminiscent of John McMichael's in the early 1980s after the launch of *Beyond the Religious Divide*. This was also a reaction to what was represented as a Belfast-based Loyalist leadership's readiness to be wined, dined, patronised and deceived in both London and Washington by politicians whose real agenda was to impose a future on Northern Ireland which would be decided by negotiations with Dublin.

Rejecting any form of Irish federalism or Anglo-Irish joint authority, *Warrior* argued that what it called 'the British family of nations' was perfectly compatible with full Ulster self-government, just as it would be with that of Scotland, Wales and England itself. Blood ties were invoked to support the case[44] and readers were told:

> As a nation our sovereignty is only complicated by a minority 'Irish' community within our borders, whose allegiance lies with the Irish republic, not Ulster. This is the only problem we have with our identity, contrary to what our enemies like to believe.[45]

The growing size of Ulster's 'Irish minority' was excluded from this analysis which led logically back to the repartitionist position of the UDA's plagiarised January 1994 document. If and when an Ulster state was brought into being, *Warrior* argued, those Irish people who could not accept it had a choice, to move back to their own country.[46] What kind of choice this was for people who saw themselves as Irish but whose homes and ancestry in Ulster stretched over generations was not explained.

All of this was a reminder that Ulster Loyalism did not have to be Unionist any longer in the old and literal sense of the word. Contributors to *Warrior* were influenced by a small Ulster independence movement which had maintained a presence in rural Antrim and other areas outside Belfast, producing papers and small magazines such as the *Ulster Nation* and the *New Ulster Patriot*. These made space for the views of right-wing ethnic nationalist movements which had emerged in post-Cold War Europe and also ran articles celebrating the virtues of the old rebel Confederacy of the southern states in America and the Ulster exiles who had supported it.[47] These publications can still be bought through Loyalist outlets in Belfast but made little impact on a UDA leadership there which still in 1997 and 1998 wanted to remain on the inside track of the peace process.

Their ability to do that was gravely compromised by the murder on 27 December 1997 of Billy Wright in the Maze prison. At the time of writing, an inquiry is continuing into how this was allowed to happen and one prolific writer on the conflict in Northern Ireland has claimed that Wright had in fact been an informer for British intelligence services who had become surplus to their requirements in the post-ceasefire period.[48] Key questions remain about the ease with which Wright's INLA killers were able to reach him across the roof from their own block and Richard Sullivan, a Belfast journalist, set out these questions in detail in one of his articles.[49]

At the time of Wright's murder the UDA's political spokesmen were still taking part in the Stormont talks, unlike Dr Ian Paisley's DUP and the United Kingdom Unionist Party, headed by the barrister Robert McCartney, which had both withdrawn when Sinn Fein was admitted in July once the IRA had reinstated its ceasefire. By the year's end Unionists were still refusing to speak directly to Sinn Fein but progress was being made and talks had moved on to the so-called three strands on political relationships within Northern Ireland, between it and Dublin, and between Britain and Ireland as a whole. Weapons decommissioning was the obvious stumbling block in the process but it had been handed over to a special committee. All this was the groundwork necessary for ultimate success but the brutal backlash prompted by Wright's murder became a dire threat to it and to the UDA's ability to remain part of it.

In death, Billy Wright was guaranteed iconic status within Loyalism. Portadown's town centre closed down for his funeral and murals depicting him went up within days of his burial. Young Loyalists across Northern Ireland began to adopt cropped hair and closely trimmed beards in tribute to him. The first killing to avenge Wright came quickly, just hours after his death, when LVF gunmen from Mid Ulster attacked a hotel outside Dungannon, killing a doorman who was a former IRA prisoner, though any of his colleagues would have been seen as legitimate targets.

Some of those close to Wright, especially Mark 'Swinger' Fulton, also from Portadown, had believed for some time that they could draw an element of the UDA back to war. For them, their hero's murder was the moment they had been waiting for. There was the thought too that the accession to their ranks of hardened ex-UDA gunmen would make it more difficult for the UVF to initiate effective disciplinary moves against them. Fulton, who quickly followed Wright to overall command of the LVF, had known Johnny Adair for some years and had maintained contact with him after he was sentenced in 1995.

The next killing in revenge for Wright was the work of the UDA/UFF although it was the LVF which claimed it in a statement, adding: 'This is not the end.' The victim was Edmund Treanor, a 31-year-old Catholic employee of the Housing Executive, who was having a drink on the last night of 1997 with his girlfriend in a bar on Belfast's Cliftonville Road. He died in hospital three hours after being shot at close range by two gunmen using an Israeli-made Uzi sub-machine gun, and five other people in the bar had to be treated for injuries. At the time police suspected UDA/UFF involvement and the attack was indeed the work of Adair's C Company. It was Stephen McKeag, winner of the unit's 'top gun award', who killed Treanor but the UDA's Inner Council felt they could not ignore an open breach of the Loyalist ceasefire, especially after reports that McKeag had been spotted in the getaway vehicle immediately after the murder with a woman 'whooping and squealing with delight and laughter', according to a witness.[50]

It summoned McKeag to explain himself but he brazened it out, claiming that the 1994 ceasefire and subsequent statements from the CLMC, while it still existed, simply precluded 'first strike' attacks by Loyalists. Wright's murder, he said, altered the situation and made retribution an obligation for other Loyalists. In what soon came to seem a crucial loss of nerve, the Inner Council backed off from disciplining McKeag, fearing the disunity within the UDA which might result. Their inaction enhanced the confidence of those who favoured a link-up with the LVF and gave out a signal that the organisation's leadership might not impose its authority on individual units.[51]

Gary McMichael knew that a crisis had been reached and on Wednesday, 7 January 1998 he went to London to speak directly with Mo Mowlam, rather than wait for her next visit to Belfast, which would in any case have been soon. McMichael was accompanied by David Adams and Jackie McDonald, among others, and they asked to see the Secretary of State alone, without civil servants present. She has recalled the tension of this meeting in her memoirs:

> I listened to their hushed voices, looked at their serious faces. Gary McMichael's confidence was clearly shaken by what was happening around him. His face was straight, but the eyes were giving it away. His people thought the process was all going one way, towards the republicans.[52]

Four days into what was clearly going to be a bloody New Year, UDA/UFF prisoners in the Maze, 130 in number and the biggest Loyalist grouping there, met to deliberate on the situation. Even before Wright's murder, their attitude to the peace process had been hardening over issues such as the repatriation of IRA men from British to Irish prisons and what some of them felt was a premature visit to 10 Downing Street by Gerry Adams and Martin McGuinness. The questions already being asked about Wright's death were also ringing alarm bells about their own safety in prison or when out on parole. When a vote was taken on whether they still supported the peace process, 60 per cent of the UDA/UFF men in the Maze answered 'no'.

McMichael, always an open and approachable person, was indeed under severe pressure. The lack of a real paramilitary track record was always a weakness in his position, so Jackie McDonald's presence was important in

Figure 1 *This cartoon illustrates the problems of the UDA's political wing trying to hold back the militants (December 1981).*

Figure 2 *This was the UDA's response to their failure to kill Bernadette McAliskey, the former MP, in 1981 (February 1982).*

Figure 3 *Artwork from assorted UDA magazine covers.*

Figure 4 *Andy Tyrie emerged after a brutal power struggle as a compromise candidate for the leadership of of the UDA in 1973. He remained as its Inner Council chairman and 'supreme commander' until 1988.*

Figure 5 *Andy Tyrie's most trusted lieutenant and ultimately his second in command. John McMichael was a skilful and ruthless co-ordinator of UDA/UFF attacks but was also interested in finding a political road for Loyalism. He was killed by an IRA bomb in late 1987.*

Figure 6 *Memorial to the victims of the UDA/UFF massacre of Catholics in Sean Graham's betting shop on Belfast's Lower Ormeau Road in February 1992.*

Figure 7 *UDA/UFF colour party, Remembrance Sunday, 2002, in the White City Estate, North Belfast.*

Figure 8 *Johnny Adair in the Maze prison after being sentenced in 1995 for 'directing terrorism'. He later shaved his head and took up body-building with the aid of powerful steroids.*

Figure 9 *The title of Tina Turner's hit 'Simply the Best' was adopted by the UDA in the Lower Shankill area of Belfast after Johnny Adair took control of it and converted it to a ruthless killing machine.*

Figure 10 *Colour party of UDA/UFF prisoners in the Maze prison preparing for Remembrance Day, c. 1996. Note hand-made replica weapons.*

Figure 11 *May 1998 Ulster Hall rally: UDA/UFF leaders back Ulster Democratic Party call for a 'yes' vote. Note cartoon figure of Dr Ian Paisley.*

Figure 12 *UDA supporters on the march in the referendum campaign (May 1998).*

Figure 13 *Sammy Duddy, cartoonist, illustrator, poet, country and western singer and former drag artist, who was a very early recruit to the UDA and still does political work for it.*

Figure 14 *The UDA marks out territory in Belfast.*

Figure 15 *A North Belfast mural in memory of Glen Branagh, a sixteen-year-old member of the UDA's youth wing killed by his own pipe bomb during a riot on North Queen Street in November 2001. The mural was soon defaced by attackers from the nationalist New Lodge area close to it.*

adding urgency to the visit. The minister's version of events is that it was McMichael who urged her to go to the Maze to talk directly to the UDA prisoners[53] but another possibility is that the idea was hers and that the UDA deputation gave it their immediate support. In any event, Mowlam cleared her decision with civil servants and Cabinet colleagues, helped by the fact that David Trimble had already been to the Maze to speak to both UDA and UVF prisoners. Her visit to the Maze, surrounded by huge publicity, took place only two days after her meeting with McMichael.

Whilst there, she talked with UVF and IRA prisoners but, given the LVF's hopes of drawing the UDA into reprisal killings for Wright's murder, her meeting with UDA/UFF men was the crucial one. As Labour's shadow Secretary for Northern Ireland, Mowlam had been to H-Block 7 in 1996, when she had met Michael Stone and Adair. Both were there to greet her on 9 January. With them in the Governor's office on the block were Bobby Philpott and Glen Cunningham, each serving long sentences, and Sammy 'Skelly' McCrory, Adair's oldest friend and UDA officer in command inside the prison. He had laid down a dress code of white shirts and dark trousers in place of the shorts and singlets normally worn by prisoners because of the heat within the blocks.

John White, who not so long before had held McCrory's position, was also present, and joined the prisoners in a semi-circle of chairs formed around the Secretary of State for a 45-minute question-and-answer session. All took part, with the conspicuous exception of Adair, who was out of his depth in any political dialogue and was already in contact with the LVF outside the prison as their murderous campaign to avenge their fallen leader got under way. Mowlam later recalled her audience being 'straightforward and intense, rather than aggressive'[54] as she tried to impress upon them that, while both Loyalists and Republicans must be ready to make concessions, there was no sell-out being planned on Northern Ireland's place within the Union.

She spoke mainly to a prepared fourteen-point brief, though in the relaxed style which had already come to be expected of her. Most of the points were a reiteration of existing positions necessary for a settlement, but the penultimate one was vital. It dealt with the need for an agreed process of prisoner releases 'in the context of a peaceful and lasting settlement' although she made it clear that organisations which resumed killing could not expect to benefit from this. Less than two hours after she had left the prison, McMichael provided vindication for her visit with an announcement to the press that the UDA/UFF prisoners were now prepared to give political talks another chance.

Mowlam's visit to the Maze did not stop the UDA killings. The claim that it did has been described in one account of events as 'one of the most enduring myths of the Northern Ireland peace process'[55] but she was certainly correct in identifying the special position of the UDA's prisoners. When news of the visit was announced, the UVF prisoners were initially reluctant to meet her, though out of courtesy they agreed to do so. Their reluctance lay in the fact that they saw themselves as no more important than any other group within the organisation where opinions on the peace process were concerned.

This was a position, it has been pointed out,[56] that was close to that of the Republican movement, which accorded respect to prisoners and their opinions but believed that prison was not the right place for talks with ministers. UDP spokesmen such as McMichael and White, on the other hand, were able to communicate to Mowlam their view of UDA prisoners as having a veto over whether the organisation should, through its political wing, remain in the Stormont negotiations at all. The public perception, shaped by television footage from H-Block 7 with its ferocious murals, that convicted murderers could exercise such power over the UDP may well have worked against it in the Assembly elections later in 1998 which were to follow the Belfast Agreement.

Murderers within the UDA's ranks were back into action all too soon after Mowlam's visit to the Maze and the resumption of the all-party talks at Stormont. The first of the year's victims was Terry Enright, shot dead by gunmen who pulled up in a car outside the nightclub close to Belfast's Donegall Street where he was working as a doorman. Born in 1969, the year the Troubles started, Enright was married to a niece of Gerry Adams but had no Republican involvement. He had taken the evening job to raise extra cash for a new kitchen in his home and had earned much respect for his daytime work with problem children in West Belfast. His funeral was one of the biggest seen there since the hunger strikes of 1981. Adams, delivering a tribute to Enright in the presence of his widow and two small children, came close to losing his usually tight self-control.

The LVF were swift to claim the killing. In a coded statement to a Belfast newspaper, they declared it was in retaliation for Billy Wright's murder and also a warning to the Dublin government to 'drop its illegal claim over Northern Ireland and to stop interfering in the north'.[57] The UVF believed that the killer was one of their own dissidents who had become a supporter of Wright, but the vehicle used in the attack was later found in an area of East Belfast where the UDA had strong support. The police also pursued the possibility that the murder weapon had been made available from a UDA source.

This was only the start of a sequence of callous killings, reminiscent of the worst periods of the Troubles. The LVF continued to claim them but several were in reality the work of the UDA's West Belfast brigade. The leadership in fact had little option but to let its killers off the leash. 'We all knew that,' Sammy Duddy later told the author. 'What could the Inner Council do? If they held our boys back, the LVF could have recruited them. We'd have been the losers. They have the gear but they're a bunch of headless chickens who can't think beyond killing. They've no real politics in their heads though some of them mouth off a load of stuff they've learned off Paisley.'[58]

The fear of the LVF's ability to poach UDA members was real. It had been reinforced by reports that the gunman who had killed the former 'Shankill Butcher' Bobby Bates the previous June had already defected. Reports in the press, drawing upon both Loyalist and security force sources, suggested that he joined the LVF to gain better protection for himself since he was under sentence of death from the UVF, who wanted Bates avenged. 'It doesn't surprise me at all that this boy has linked up with the LVF,' a Loyalist source was quoted as saying. 'He knows the UVF will kill him when they get their chance. The frightening thing is he now has to prove himself to the LVF to be protected. He is capable of anything.'[59]

The LVF killed again only days after Enright's murder. Their victim was another easy target, a young Catholic named Fergal McCusker who was walking home in Maghera after a night out with friends. On the same day, 19 January, the INLA intervened in a way that guaranteed a UDA response. Jim Guiney, a close friend of McMichael who had held local rank in the South Belfast brigade of the UDA as well as being the Master of his local Orange lodge, ran a small business selling carpets at Kingsway, Dunmurry. At 11 a.m. that day he was at work in his shop, which was advertising a special sale, when the INLA men, one disguised in a wig, entered and shot him dead at close range. They made their escape to a getaway vehicle which police found burnt out later in the day in the Twinbrook area of West Belfast.

The UDA's response was as swift as it was brutal. Barely eight hours later, its gunmen struck on the Ormeau Road, leaving a Catholic taxi driver, Larry Brennan from Friendly Street in the Markets area of the city, bleeding to death in his vehicle from four gunshot wounds in the chest. News of these killings reached Adams and Martin McGuinness, who were in London the same day for what proved to be a tense meeting with Mowlam and Tony Blair, in which they set out Sinn Fein's objections to the British and Irish governments' latest negotiating initiative. This was a document which they felt smacked too much of a purely internal settlement because it gave the proposed new assembly veto powers over the decisions of any North–South ministerial council which might be set up.

They returned to a Belfast where once more fear was tangible, with pubs and restaurants closing early and the streets emptying by early evening. Renewed killing overshadowed the detail of negotiations in London and Stormont. Starting on 21 January, UDA gunmen killed three Catholics in the space of four days, though without claiming the responsibility. Benedict Hughes was shot dead by a single gunman as he started his car outside his place of work, a vehicle supply firm on the Donegall Road. The following day, Ronnie Flanagan, the RUC's Chief Constable, linked the UDA/UFF to the murder of Hughes, as well as of Brennan and Edmund Treanor. His call for an end to the violence went unanswered, with gunmen from C Company striking again in North Belfast on 23 January. Their victim was Liam Conway, a Tyrone man who was working a mechanical digger on a gas pipe-laying operation close to Ardoyne. Conway was described as a quiet and inoffensive man who lived with and looked after two brothers with impaired sight.[60]

Only hours after this latest killing, the UDA/UFF gave a statement to its political spokesmen at Stormont to release to the press. In it they claimed that since August 1995, a 'no first strike' policy had been maintained despite severe provocation. It went on to declare: 'The current phase of republican aggression by the INLA made a measured military response unavoidable. That response has now concluded.'[61] This admission by the UDA of its role in the continuing spasm of killing was an acute embarrassment for McMichael and his UDP colleagues, who had accepted denials from the Inner Council that UDA men were behind any of these murders.

McMichael had indeed reiterated this denial in public after the New Year's Eve murder of Treanor, despite the evidence pointing to UDA/UFF involvement. Two days later he told the press:

> I think that we are going in the wrong direction if we are going to continue to fingerpoint at different people. The LVF have claimed this and the logic behind the fingerpointing at the UFF does not stand up to scrutiny. The LVF exist in opposition to the Loyalist ceasefire, in opposition to the policies of both the UFF and UVF, so I don't see any sense in collusion in any respect.[62]

Embarrassment at the UDA/UFF admission of their part in the 'measured military response' to Billy Wright's murder turned into something much worse for the UDP. The very next day, C Company picked out a traditionally easy target, a Catholic taxi driver. The victim was John McColgan, a young father of three children. His body was found dumped on a grass verge at the roadside on Hannahstown Hill on the edge of West Belfast. The killers were passengers who had called him late in the evening and the back of his head was shattered by five revolver shots fired at close range. His widow made a moving plea for there to be no retaliation. She was later seen to be overcome and almost helpless with grief on her way to the Requiem Mass which preceded the burial at the City Cemetery.[63]

Speaking to an interviewer soon afterwards, Jackie McDonald justified the UDA/UFF response to Guiney's murder, calling it

> the nature of the beast. Some people would call it a knee-jerk reaction but it's just a product of the times. If someone attacks us, we have to attack back. We developed because of IRA violence. We came into being because of what the IRA was doing to this country. We agreed to hold a ceasefire, but once people attack us, although we are on ceasefire, we still have to respond against the people who attacked us.[64]

To many, the McColgan killing raised the obvious question of how much control the UDA still had over self-appointed executioners who could flout a statement like the one issued at Stormont the previous day. It posed equally obvious questions about the credibility of McMichael's position and that of his UDP colleagues. 'They couldn't tell Gary right away what was really happening,' Sammy Duddy later reflected. 'How could they? There was a score to settle over Billy Wright, even though he was never one of us. He had his own agenda but he was a hero to a lot of Loyalists and there was no way the UDA could let the LVF take all the credit for avenging him. Even so the leadership wanted us to stay in the Stormont talks so Gary just had to have the wool pulled over his eyes.'[65]

McMichael himself, in conversation with the author two years later, accepted this as a description of how the UDA had acted.

> Billy Wright was murdered at a time of crisis. Morale in our party and the PUP was low. When the killings started, I went to the Inner Council and urged them to stay out of reprisals and to my face they denied any UDA responsibility. The phrase used at the time was 'no claim, no blame' but there was a real problem and it was grass roots anger. I think they probably felt they were protecting my political position by denying responsibility. It all got a lot harder for me of course when they came out with their 23 January admission of involvement.[66]

Pressure mounted by the hour for the UDP's suspension from the Stormont talks. The case against them was that they were in effect operating an 'on–off' ceasefire, in clear breach of US Senator George Mitchell's formula of non-violence as a principle that all participants in the talks must observe. McMichael saw it coming but blamed the Alliance Party for leading the demand for it. 'I am sick to the teeth of their sanctimonious attitude,' he wrote on 25 January 1998. 'They quickly come out in condemnation of violence, regardless of its origin, but then they retreat back to their comfortable homes, their conscience clear and certain that they have fulfilled their moral responsibility.

'Meanwhile, members of my party have often put themselves in harm's way, in an effort to change people's minds and diminish the potential for political violence.'[67]

The following day, McMichael and his colleagues pre-empted the Secretary of State's decision by announcing their withdrawal from the talks, which had transferred to Lancaster House in London. After hours of tense exchanges, the UDP left the Long Gallery to inform the press of their imminent suspension. Later in the day, Mo Mowlam told a press conference that

> the British and Irish governments have decided that the UDP is no longer eligible to participate. The UFF have themselves admitted responsibility for a series of appalling murders which have created fear on the streets of Northern Ireland. The evidence before us was beyond doubt that the Mitchell principles of non-violence had clearly been breached.'[68]

The UDP had in fact been offered, but had refused, the option of disowning any connection to the UDA/UFF but even so the Irish Foreign Affairs Minister, David Andrews, made it clear that the party's return to the talks would be considered if a full UDA/UFF ceasefire was restored.

Writing in the press the day after his party's suspension, McMichael denied that, as a party, they should be singled out for violating the Mitchell principles while Sinn Fein remained in the talks. 'The UFF', he argued, 'are not the architects of the current spiral of inter-community violence but were nonetheless unfortunately sucked into it. The UDP faced its responsibility, investigated the issue and once UFF involvement was clear, used our influence to urge the UFF to reinstate its ceasefire and come clean.'[69] The IRA had indeed been involved in the violence of the previous weeks and Sinn Fein would soon join the UDP in being suspended from the talks.

At this point, as McMichael had predicted in his 28 January article, there was an end to UDA/UFF participation in the bloody and indiscriminate cycle of retaliation for Wright's murder. It needed firm action from the UDA's Inner Council and for brigadiers such as Jackie McDonald to rein in the gunmen of Johnny Adair's C Company, who had tasted blood again and wanted more of it. This exercise of what remained of the Inner Council's authority was more important than any appeals from Mowlam, in the Maze prison or outside it, though defectors who had gravitated to the LVF would continue to kill in the weeks that followed.

Proof that the reinstated UDA/UFF ceasefire would hold came twelve days later, when the IRA once more turned their guns on Loyalists. Ever since their 1994 ceasefire, using the cover name Direct Action against Drugs, they had targeted and killed inconvenient drug dealers who insisted on operating without clearance from them. One of them was Brendan 'Bap' Campbell, whom they shot dead outside a restaurant on Belfast's Lisburn Road on the night of 9 February 1998.[70] However, on the following day, they singled out a UDA member.

Their victim was Robert Dougan, aged thirty-eight. He was killed in Dunmurry, close to where Guiney had died two weeks earlier, outside the Balmoral Textiles building where he was waiting in his car to pick up a friend. A lone gunman approached him and opened fire at close range, killing him instantly. Dougan's role in the UDA had made him a target long before this and he had survived two previous attempts on his life. Four men were arrested soon afterwards in the Twinbrook area after a stolen vehicle, believed by police to have been used for the attack, was found there, but charges against them were later dropped.

Suspicion fell immediately on the INLA, given that they had claimed the responsibility for Guiney's death. The Irish Republican Socialist Party, speaking for them, was quick to deny that it had been involved and police suspicion shifted to the IRA. They issued no denials. Killing Dougan was their way of showing that they could still respond to Loyalist terror even if their war against the British state was effectively at an end

Dougan's funeral was a major UDA event. The cortège left his home on the Suffolk estate in West Belfast, accompanied by a guard of honour formed by members of the Upper Falls Protestant Boys flute band, in which he had played. Paramilitary standards were placed on his coffin and his widow, Lesley, told the media that he had been 'a dedicated member of the UDA and a true Loyalist. He fought against Republicans for many years and he knew some day he might die for his beliefs.' She added: 'I think our country is going to need more people like Bobby in the near future. We all want peace but it just isn't going to come.'[71]

Her fears were widely shared as Sinn Fein was predictably suspended from the all-party talks by the Secretary of State, although, as it turned out, for a shorter period than the UDP. Crucially this time, the UDA did not seek to avenge Dougan and although brutal killings by dissident Loyalists and by the INLA continued during March and April, the parties at Stormont were given the breathing space they needed to resume their talks. McMichael later claimed this as a vindication of his role and that of UDP colleagues such as David Adams. 'The Inner Council listened to us. We got through to them. We got a result that made the road to the Belfast Agreement easier than it might have been.'[72]

He still anticipated further IRA attacks after the Dougan murder but these did not materialise. That killing proved to be a one-off act which was not intended to set up a pretext for the Sinn Fein leadership's withdrawal from the talks process. They no more wanted to do that than did the majority on the UDA's Inner Council. McDonald in particular believed it was essential for his organisation to give the peace process a chance provided it offered real guarantees that the Union was safe.

> We had to be certain of that before we agreed to anything else. That was always the bottom line for us. In January and February we hit back when we had to but it was never our intention to put the talks in jeopardy. We'd been through too much to want that.[73]

On 19 March, with the UDP's suspension from the all-party talks over, McMichael and Adams gave an important signal when they decided to confront Dr Ian Paisley and his followers at a large and intimidating anti-peace process rally in Lisburn. The event had been publicised as a Unionist meeting so they felt they had the right to attend and voice their views, especially since McMichael was the elected councillor for the area in which the meeting was being held. When they arrived in the Orange Hall hired for the occasion, they received an ugly reception from both the platform party and the audience. They were shouted down and threatened and one of their supporters was assaulted as he left the hall.[74]

The experience was enough to convince them of the hazards that lay ahead for Loyalists who were prepared to support the Stormont negotiations. It had been made clear to them, however, from no less a source than Senator Mitchell, that they were wanted back in the talks, along with Sinn Fein. He had told them that back in January at the very moment of their suspension, saying, as he later recalled it: 'Whatever you do, I hope you'll be able to say that you support the process and that you want to come back in as soon as possible. You guys have made a good contribution to this process.'[75]

When the Senator returned to Northern Ireland in late March, he convened a fresh and, he stressed, final round of talks. Their period of suspension at an end, the UDP were back at the negotiating table, as were Sinn Fein. Intense drama and expectation built up as Mitchell announced from the chair that he was setting a specific deadline for agreement, failing which the whole process would be abandoned. His deadline was 19 April, Good Friday, chosen with its symbolism very much in his mind.

The UDP's presence, representing paramilitary Loyalism along with the PUP, was not decisive nor even central to the outcome, but McMichael and Adams, as well as David Ervine and Billy Hutchinson, did contribute to the development of a positive and purposeful atmosphere, one into which trust and even a degree of warmth began to filter through. What determined ultimate success, of course, was the readiness of the Sinn Fein leadership to sign up to a partitionist settlement, but one which gave them the certainty of exercising some real power both in the northern state and in cross-border bodies created under the Agreement. David Trimble, for his part, had to talk his colleagues into accepting a deal that secured the Union at the price of sharing power with what they had every reason to believe was still the IRA's political wing.

Acrimonious scenes followed the endorsement of the Agreement by the negotiating parties apart from the DUP, as Paisley's followers clashed with members of the UDP and PUP in the precincts of Stormont. Their leader had been noisily barracked in the media tent the night before the announcement of the Agreement, when once more he had set out his intransigent case against it. By the time it had been made public, Paisley had already left the scene, apparently isolated and humiliated. Before long, however, he would be back at the centre of Northern Ireland's political stage.

Writing some months later about the extraordinary process in which he had been such a key figure, Mitchell felt able to look ahead with guarded optimism:

> There will be many setbacks along the way, but the direction for Northern Ireland is firmly set. No society in human history has been able to enjoy the complete absence of violence. Our own American society, of which we are justly proud, is regularly scarred by horrific acts of violence. So it is unfair and unrealistic to hold the people of Northern Ireland to a standard that has never been met elsewhere. There will be among them the deranged, the regressive, the criminal. Individuals will die in early and untimely ways. But the organised political violence of the past thirty years, which killed and injured thousands, is over for now.[76]

Of those thousands referred to by the Senator, 408 had been killed by the UDA/UFF, callously and often sadistically. In West Belfast's Milltown cemetery, the Republican plot contains no gravestones with inscriptions which refer to UDA/UFF killers. This is equally true of other burial grounds in Northern Ireland maintained by the Republican movement. Its spokesmen will readily cite this as proof that the UDA's war, and that of Loyalism more generally, was waged against those who were the easiest targets and by extension, those who were innocent.

Conversely, for many years to come the UDA is likely to claim, as it has done to the author, that its gunmen had more successes than Sinn Fein and the IRA will ever admit to. Even if it was to turn out that they killed half the number of IRA volunteers who died from their own bombs exploding prematurely in the 1970s, an appalling death roll would still be left of those who were simply caught in the wrong place, shot down by assailants who often lived close enough, especially in West and North Belfast's confined maze of streets, to monitor their movements to and from home, work, shops, pubs and clubs.

The less fortunate were abducted, beaten and tortured to death or had their throats slit, sometimes in the back rooms of clubs and bars. Their broken bodies would be dumped in alleys, on roadsides, in car parks or in country lanes outside Belfast, left for the security forces to identify and inform their families. Few wars have that much real glory to them and the UDA's had less than most, for all the grandiose symbolism of its murals and memorial events. On 13 October 1994, when the Combined Loyalist Military Command's ceasefire statement was read out, there was indeed much to apologise for, as Gusty Spence and the others who drafted it had the grace to admit.

NOTES

1. G. Adams, *Before the Dawn: An Autobiography* (London: Heinemann, 1996), pp. 324–5.
2. J. Cusack and H. McDonald, *UVF* (Dublin: Poolbeg, 1997), p. 339.
3. J. White, interview with author, 19 February 1996.
4. S. Duddy, interview with author, 12 October 1996.
5. D. O'Hagan, Workers Party spokesman, interview with author, 26 March 2004.
6. J. Gregg, interview with author, 16 October 2002.
7. Ibid.
8. D. McKittrick, S. Kelters, B. Feeney and C. Thornton, *Lost Lives: The Stories of the Men, Women and Children Who Died as a Result of Northern Ireland's Troubles* (Edinburgh: Mainstream, 1999), p. 1405.
9. Private information supplied to the author from West Belfast UDA, 27 January 2004.
10. *Belfast Telegraph*, 17 July 1996.
11. *Irish News*, 12 July 1997.
12. *Guardian*, 27 October 1997.
13. McKittrick *et al.*, *Lost Lives*, pp. 1468–70.
14. *Scotland on Sunday*, 29 December 1996; also West Belfast UDA member, interview with author, 4 January 1997.

15. C. Ryder and V. Kearney, *Drumcree: the Orange Order's Last Stand* (London: Methuen, 2002), p. 133.
16. Author's notes; see also *Scotsman*, 10 April 1996.
17. Duddy, interview with author, 12 April 1996.
18. *Belfast Telegraph*, 15 November 1996.
19. Author's notes.
20. Author's notes.
21. *Belfast Telegraph*, 16 July 1996.
22. *Sunday World*, 4 January 2004.
23. Ryder and Kearney, *Drumcree*, Chapter 7.
24. *Sunday World*, 4 January 2004.
25. Ryder and Kearney, *Drumcree*, pp. 171–5.
26. Duddy, interview with author, 8 July 1997.
27. Ainsworth Avenue resident to author, 8 July, 1997.
28. Duddy, interview with author, 8 July, 1997.
29. *Irish News*, 7 March 1997.
30. *News Letter*, 15 July 1996.
31. *Sell-Out and Surrender: The Hidden Story of the Irish Peace Process*, anonymous video, 1996.
32. J. MacLean, interview with author, 29 July 2004.
33. *Guardian*, 10 September 2004.
34. *Ulster News*, vol. 1, no. 5, 1996.
35. *New Ulster Defender*, September 1996 (unnumbered).
36. *Sunday Life*, 19 May 1996.
37. *Sunday Life*, 1 September 1996.
38. *Combat*, September 1996.
39. *Irish News*, 14 October 1997.
40. *Irish News*, 13 October 1997.
41. *Irish News*, 15 October 1997.
42. *Guardian*, 24 December 1997.
43. Ibid.
44. *Warrior*, no. 6, 1996.
45. Ibid.
46. Ibid.
47. See J. Docherty, 'Imagining Ulster: Northern Ireland Protestants and Ulster identity', unpublished Queen's University Ph.D., 2001.
48. M. Dillon, *The Trigger Men* (Edinburgh: Mainstream, 2003), pp. 29–32, 45–6.
49. *Sunday World*, 27 September 2003.
50. *Irish News*, 2 January 1998.
51. Private information to the author from a West Belfast UDA source, 25 January 1998. See also D. Lister and H. Jordan, *Mad Dog: The Rise and Fall of Johnny Adair and 'C' Company* (Edinburgh: Mainstream, 2003), p. 204.
52. M. Mowlam, *Momentum: The Struggle for Peace, Politics and the People* (London: Hodder and Stoughton, 2002), p. 183.
53. Ibid.
54. Ibid., p. 188.

55. Cusack and McDonald, *UVF*, p. 370.
56. *Fortnight*, December 1998–January 1999.
57. McKittrick *et al.*, *Lost Lives*, p. 1423.
58. Duddy, interview with author, 28 January 1998.
59. *Observer*, 4 January 1998.
60. *Irish News*, 24 January 1998.
61. Ibid.
62. *Irish News*, 3 January 1998.
63. McKittrick *et al.*, *Lost Lives*, p. 1427.
64. P. Taylor, *Loyalists* (London: Bloomsbury, 1999), pp. 246–7.
65. Duddy, interview with author, 28 January 1998.
66. G. McMichael, interview with author, 9 February 2000.
67. *Ireland on Sunday*, 25 January 1998.
68. *Irish News*, 27 January 1998.
69. *Guardian*, 28 January 1998.
70. J. McDowell, *Godfathers: Inside Northern Ireland's Drug Racket* (Dublin: Gill and Macmillan, 2001), pp. 54–62.
71. *Irish News*, 14 February 1998.
72. McMichael, interview with author.
73. J. McDonald, interview with author, 7 October 2003.
74. G. McMichael, *An Ulster Voice: In Search of Common Ground in Northern Ireland* (Boulder, CO/Dublin: Roberts Rinehart, 1999), p. 199.
75. G. Mitchell, *Making Peace: The Inside Story of the Making of the Good Friday Agreement* (London: Heinemann, 1999), p. 136.
76. Ibid., p. 187.

10

War within Loyalism

〜

Senator George Mitchell's premonition that Northern Ireland's sorely tried people would have to go on living with residual paramilitary violence was well founded. Gunmen, both Loyalist and Republican, had continued to kill until the very eve of the Belfast Agreement and other killings would follow it. More horror lay ahead in another turbulent summer of contested parades and the worst single atrocity of the Troubles at Omagh in August, where a bomb planted by dissident Republicans took the lives of twenty-nine people as well as unborn twins.

There was also the issue of paramilitary prisoners, whose phased release had been written into the Agreement. Whether they would support its letter and spirit once they were back within their own communities was a risk the Ulster Unionists and the British and Irish governments had agreed should be taken. It would be a very big risk where Johnny Adair was concerned since, despite his protestations of support for the peace process, he was known to be in increasing contact with the rogue gunmen of the Loyalist Volunteer Force and also to be envisaging a dramatic enlargement of his role within the UDA once he was released under licence.

The Agreement, however, set in motion a period of intense political activity, as its terms required referendum votes on both sides of the border as well as elections to the new power-sharing assembly. Like their counterparts in the Progressive Unionist Party, Gary McMichael and his colleagues had to gamble heavily on the Agreement's acceptability to a sceptical Protestant electorate. From the start of the referendum campaign there was pressure for a 'yes' vote from the Northern Ireland Office, which gave a lucrative contract to McCann-Erickson, an advertising agency with a Belfast office, to produce publicity in favour of the Agreement and to carry out research into shifts in voters' opinions.[1]

Huge coverage was given to Tony Blair's interventions in the campaign. His eleventh-hour note to David Trimble at the Stormont talks, stressing his commitment to rapid movement on IRA weapons-decommissioning and exclusion of any party from the new power-sharing executive found to be in violation of democratic and non-violent norms, was much quoted. He reiterated these in a written pledge to the people of Northern Ireland on 20 May, as the ballot drew closer and Belfast's three newspapers supported his call for a 'yes' vote, even though the *Belfast Telegraph* came under some pressure from the Northern Ireland Office for giving too much space to the 'no' case.[2]

Sinn Fein took a tactically low profile, preferring to leave it to the SDLP and the Ulster Unionists to energise the 'yes' campaign. Working under the aegis of the United Unionist Committee, the Democratic Unionist Party and the United Kingdom Unionist Party, led by North Down Westminster MP Robert McCartney, had what some commentators felt was the easier task of occupying a simple negative stance. Their publicity was much given over to lurid leaflets claiming to show a future of 'gunmen in government' and the RUC taken over and transformed by paramilitaries. In fact, the 'yes' campaign faltered to a degree that alarmed both Downing Street and the Northern Ireland Office, at least until the televised U2 concert at Belfast's Waterfront Hall, at which Trimble and John Hume drew a huge ovation from the audience when they went on stage to affirm their support for the Agreement.

That was on 19 May, just three days ahead of the actual vote. Well before this, the UDP had thrown its resources into a robust campaign in support of the Agreement. Old warriors such as Andy Tyrie returned to the political fray and at the Loyalist Prisoners Resettlement Office on the Shankill Road, from where much of the party's canvassing was organised, the steel security grilles on the windows were raised to make space for a rash of 'yes' posters.

The climax of the UDP's effort was its 14 May rally at the symbolic venue of the Ulster Hall. A few days earlier, the DUP had failed to fill it, but on the fourteenth easily enough UDP supporters marched on the hall from Loyalist areas of the city. They formed up in a noisy parade behind UDA standards and flute bands but they also carried placards in support of a 'yes' vote. Sammy Duddy, one of the event's organisers, contributed mocking life-sized effigies of Dr Ian Paisley, to be displayed inside the hall for the amusement of the audience.

Even before the rally got under way, the atmosphere was transformed by the arrival in the hall of Michael Stone to a hero's welcome, not unlike that accorded in Dublin a few days earlier at the Sinn Fein Ard Fheis to the recently freed members of the IRA's notorious Balcombe Street gang, who had terrorised central London in the late 1970s. Like theirs, Stone's reception was fully covered by television cameras but not everyone in the UDP was happy about it.

In fact, Stone was out of prison on a routine parole and had already gone on record with his support for the peace process but the rally organisers had not been told that he was going to attend. 'It caught us on the back foot,' Duddy later recalled. 'It was his people from East Belfast who wanted him there. He was the local hero but it was all a bit triumphalist for my liking when he came into the hall. We had to think about the sort of signals we were giving voters and people watching television. To be fair, Michael didn't try to speak, or upstage anyone else, but we were left with the explaining to do.'[3]

McMichael was even more concerned, as he later remembered:

> It was a total screw-up which did us no good. Of course the context in people's minds was IRA gunmen appearing to a huge welcome at the Sinn Fein Ard Fheis in Dublin. That caused a Unionist outcry even if they declared their support for the Good Friday Agreement. Stone's presence in the Ulster Hall was an own goal. Inevitably, the media concentrated on it, rather than on our support, and his, for a 'yes' vote. We hadn't even known about his parole but once out, he had every right to go. I've since heard that he thought twice about it but on his home ground in the east, people would have been offended if they had thought he would be unwelcome or snubbed in some way by us. Tactically it was a disaster, there's no question of it.'[4]

In the event it was not enough of an own goal to eat into the Loyalist vote which McMichael and Duddy knew the UDP had to mobilise. As to Republican West Belfast and other areas where Stone's very name still caused fear and loathing, voting, when it fell due on 22 May, showed an electorate well drilled in support of Sinn Fein policy to work with the Belfast Agreement. The outcome, predicted with remarkable accuracy by the *Guardian* four weeks earlier, was a 71 per cent 'yes' vote. It was a huge relief to the London and Dublin governments and was greeted emotionally by many local politicians in Belfast's King's Hall as the votes were counted.

A critical obstacle had been surmounted but the vote, which was not broken down in any detail for the media, either by existing Westminster constituencies or area by area, masked a deep split within Unionism. A community once monolithic in its support for the 'big house' leadership of Lord Craigavon and Lord Brookeborough had divided almost in half over the issue of what should be Northern Ireland's constitutional future and its relationship to the Irish Republic.

The UDP glossed over this in what proved to be one of the final issues of the *New Ulster Defender*. Under the heading 'Why Yes?' it declared:

> We voted for a new start for our children and our children's children. We voted 'yes' because we feel that not all Catholics are republicans. We voted 'yes' so that our elected representatives could stand up in councils and other meeting-places to let our voice be heard. We voted 'yes' because we are certainly not running and hiding from the enemy. By voting 'yes' we can bargain from a position of strength rather than from a position of weakness.[5]

The article went on to stress that the war was not over but that the Belfast Agreement and the referendum result had altered the nature of the battlefield. It also delivered a blistering attack on Paisley, for his propensity to lead from the back and for his 'vanishing acts' when things got dangerous. It was a rerun of what all too many working-class Loyalists who had suffered at the sharp end of the Troubles thought of the 'big man' and his constant calls to arms over the years. Derision was also poured on Robert McCartney, who shared several platforms with Paisley in the 'no' campaign. 'He imagines himself head and shoulders above ordinary mortals down there on the Gold Coast of County Down. The only bombs he ever heard being detonated were those in Belfast – across Belfast Lough from his castle.'[6]

This was the abrasive and confident voice of a plebeian Loyalist politics which had been heard before, in 1974 during the Ulster Workers Council Strike and again when documents such as *Beyond the Religious Divide* and *Common Sense* had been launched. Whether the UDP, with its admitted relationship to the UDA, could find the right voice to activate a working-class Loyalist electorate was soon put to the test in the elections to the new assembly, scheduled for the following month.

In this contest, Sinn Fein's chances of mobilising a large vote were immeasurably greater than those of either of the Loyalist paramilitary parties. It was over twenty years since Danny Morrison had told the movement's Ard Fheis in Dublin that the road to power for Republicanism was 'with an Armalite in one hand and a ballot paper in the other.' Since then Sinn Fein had worked tenaciously to build a strong electoral base though never at the expense of an ongoing armed campaign which took infinitely more lives, including Catholic lives, than those of both the UDA and the UVF. The winding down of IRA action since 1994 had paid political dividends. In the May 1997 Westminster general election, held prior to the second IRA ceasefire, Sinn Fein polled just under 127,000 votes, electing Martin McGuinness as well as Gerry Adams, a performance far beyond the reach of the Loyalist parties.

In many ways, the Assembly elections proved to be almost a rerun of the referendum. As McMichael later put it, 'the proximity between the April Agreement, May referendum and June election became a seamless period, and therefore the issues remained unchanged. People were not interested in the practical and social issues that candidates presented to them.'[7] Essentially, the campaign was dominated by an overspill of the pro- and anti-Agreement split within Unionism. There was no such split inside the nationalist community, where the contest was, as it has continued to be, one for supremacy between the SDLP and Sinn Fein.

The electoral system for the Assembly agreed at the Stormont talks was one which made it vital for a small party like the UDP to maximise its vote in working-class areas. Given the proliferation of Unionist parties competing with each other, this proved difficult to do. In the Shankill, six rival Unionist candidates fought for the last of the West Belfast constituency's seats. John White, the UDP candidate, polled poorly. 'Anyone could have predicted it,' was Duddy's verdict. 'People here have got memories. Our people have never agreed with everything that Loyalists did and he went down after all for two of the worst killings of the Troubles and they were just the ones he was found guilty of.'[8]

McMichael, while not seeking to minimise the horrific murders White had committed, made the point that both Sinn Fein and the PUP had fielded former life sentence prisoners as candidates.

After all, John White had been rated good enough by us to be one of our party's Stormont negotiators and he had shaken hands with John Major in 10 Downing Street. Dropping him would have been a false piece of image management. Who would have been fooled?[9]

Despite his defeat, White continued for some time to act as a UDP spokesman but nearly all who had dealings with him, including the author, recall an inescapable chill factor to his personality even when he was attempting bonhomie.

In the Lagan Valley constituency, McMichael got a significantly better vote than White did in Belfast but it was still not enough. 'It was the Ulster Unionists who aborted my chances,' he later reflected. 'They stopped Jeffrey Donaldson from standing because he had jumped ship, he walked out of Stormont before the Good Friday Agreement. That upset a lot of Unionists and created a protest vote that went to Paddy Roche of the UK Unionist Party. So there was a tactical middle-class Unionist vote which by-passed me as a pro-Agreement candidate.'[10] The single transferable vote system operating in the elections would have only worked for him if enough transfers had gone to him but the 'Donaldson factor' prevented this.

In fact, the elections dealt the UDP what proved to be a fatal blow with none of its candidates succeeding, while the PUP was able to secure the return of David Ervine and Billy Hutchinson to the new assembly. An electoral agreement between the two parties might have averted this outcome but it was never a possibility. Tensions between the two paramilitary organisations with which the parties were linked precluded it. These went a long way back but had once again become public and had been a major factor in the break-up of the Combined Loyalist Military Command.

Another real problem for the UDP was the perception by many voters of its close relationship to the UDA/UFF. Mo Mowlam's January negotiations with prisoners convicted of murder had reinforced this view of a party who could take no serious initiatives without the support of convicted killers. Both Sinn Fein and the PUP proved much more skilful at creating a distance between themselves and both their paramilitary wings and the latter's prisoners. Hutchinson, indeed, made it abundantly clear that even if UVF prisoners had come out against the peace process it would have made no difference to his party's stance in the Stormont negotiations, though he admitted such a loss of support would have been a problem to be addressed.[11]

In the post mortem which followed the UDP's election failure, McMichael did his best to look honestly at the party's nature and the problems it created.

Sinn Fein can now talk about having a double mandate, votes, Assembly seats, as well as the Provos' 'armed struggle' yet they deny that they speak for the IRA. We've been a lot more open and maybe paid for it, I mean about our relationship to the UDA/UFF. We've tried to build a mandate on it without having control over what they do. The January killings and our suspension from the talks prove that.

Our links to the UDA/UFF are like Sinn Fein's publicly claimed relationship to the IRA, in which it now suits them to deny they speak for it or can control it. Publicly we will say we represent UDA thinking but the reality is that we really are not the UDA/UFF.[12]

There would have been few votes in trying to clarify these nuances in the party's position and its electoral failure boded ill for the future. The biggest Loyalist paramilitary body had been left with no political reward for the extent to which it had supported the peace process and the eventual Belfast Agreement. The UDP still had four councillors, including McMichael himself in Lisburn, but it had no voice in Stormont as the new Assembly tried to find its way. David Adams, who had stood in South Belfast, took his and the party's rejection particularly badly, as he later admitted in an interview:

It is very hard to have been at the heart of the political landscape and now totally outside everything that is happening. We were working sixteen hours a day for years. Much of what we have said for ten years is enshrined in the agreement.[13]

Whether UDA political spokesmen such as Adams and McMichael could have used seats in the Assembly to give an effective voice to a new kind of working-class Unionism is debatable. Hutchinson and Ervine attempted this and in the process gravitated to groups like the Women's Coalition and to left-leaning community activists, but ran the risk of alienating their own support base. The UDP's failure in the June elections had serious implications, however, for it left the UDA without any apparent reward for its part in the peace process as yet another Drumcree crisis built up with all its potential to inflame and further alienate Loyalist opinion.

By the time the 1998 marching season was under way, a Parades Commission with statutory powers to stop or reroute parades had been created by the new Labour government. Glen Barr, once a UDA hero for his role in the May 1974 strike, though he had never had a paramilitary role within the organisation, sat briefly on the Commission but resigned once it became clear to him that the Portadown Orangemen's Garvaghy Road parade was going to be banned. The Commission's ruling drew predicable fury from the Orange Order and speculation grew once more over what the Loyalist paramilitary response would be.

The UVF had to admit that its mid-Ulster units with Orangemen in their ranks would be ready to give active support to the Portadown district. The LVF, although now officially 'on ceasefire' was still in contact with Johnny Adair and this fed rumours that under his influence from the Maze prison, UDA members would be 'on the hill' behind Drumcree church to give support to the hardliners who had already split with the UVF. Late in June UDA dissidents in South Belfast are known to have met with the LVF to discuss joint action at Drumcree. The UDA as an organisation held back from any involvement in the days of violence directed against the security forces at Drumcree once the parade ban was clearly going to be enforced and it was able to disclaim responsibility for individual members who took part.

Petrol and blast bombs were hurled at police and army lines and at one point masked men opened fire on them with live rounds. However, their lines held, aided by layers of barbed wire and a massive concrete barrier at the crossing point onto the Garvaghy Road. One UDA member, whose photograph is proudly displayed on the wall of the Imperial bar in Ballymena, managed to crawl under the wire, a considerable feat, only to be promptly arrested on his emergence at the police and army side. Inevitably, violence once more spread across the province and only began to subside with the awful deaths, in the early hours of 12 July, of the three small Quinn brothers in a Loyalist fire bomb attack on the house in Ballymoney in North Antrim where they lived with their Catholic mother.

Even this horror was eclipsed by the carnage of the Real IRA's bomb attack on Omagh the following month. Loyalist resentment continued to fester in Portadown and on the night of 5 September, during attacks on the RUC near Drumcree Hill by a large crowd, Constable Francis O'Reilly was hit by a blast bomb. He was a popular local officer and in fact a Catholic convert to Presbyterianism. His injuries left him on a life support machine but he died from the effects of red-hot metal fragments which had pierced one of his eyes and entered his brain.

Responsibility for the fatal attack on O'Reilly was claimed by a new Loyalist grouping which called itself the Red Hand Defenders and which began to act as a magnet for young disaffected and ruthless members of both the UDA and UVF. Some of them had come under the influence of the evangelical pastor described in the previous chapter and he continued to nurture and encourage their visceral hatred of the Belfast Agreement and of the nationalist community as a whole.

On 30 October 1998 the RHD struck again, carrying out a gun attack on a bar on the Colinglen Road in West Belfast. Nobody was killed or wounded but on the following night they found an easy victim, 35-year-old Brian Service, a Catholic building worker who was walking back to his parents' home in the Mountainview area up the Crumlin Road from Ardoyne. He died in the Mater Hospital after being shot several times in the head as he walked along Alliance Avenue, close to the fiercely Loyalist enclave Glenbryn. Some accounts claim that the murder weapon had earlier been blessed by the said pastor in a house in Woodvale before it was passed over to the killer, a gunman with previous links to the UVF.[14]

One press report attributed this killing to the LVF[15] but they in fact were close to at least a token act of arms-decommissioning, which they allowed General John de Chastelain's decommissioning body to make public on 18 December 1998. As mentioned above, Service was actually murdered by the Red Hand Defenders, whose name began to serve as a convenient cover for mostly young Loyalists who simply wanted to go on killing Catholics without

implicating the UDA or UVF or because they had already split w.
Service's death came the day before a key deadline under the Belfast Agre
by which areas of cross-border co-operation between Northern Ireland and
Irish Republic were to be agreed. The main impediment to this end and to Sin.
Fein's joining the new Executive was IRA weapons-decommissioning, a process
unlikely to be hastened by renewed Loyalist killing.

Alarm bells in the minds of those who had invested all their hopes in the
Agreement were rung only four weeks after Service's murder when another
Loyalist organisation, the Orange Volunteers, seemed to emerge from the
shadows. On 15 November, a heavily armed and masked group of men staged
a show of strength for Ulster Television at a secret location. They told a
reporter that they were pledged to fight and destroy the enemies of Ulster and
that any IRA prisoners freed under the Belfast Agreement would be legitimate
targets. They went on to declare: 'Ordinary Catholics have nothing to fear
from us. But the true enemy will be targeted and that's a lot wider than just
Sinn Fein and the IRA.'[16] Ten days previously they claimed to have been
behind the bombing of a bar near the village of Crumlin but this was their first
contact with the media.

In fact the group, borrowing a name used early in the Troubles by Orange
lodge members willing to take on vigilante work, had links with the same
pastor who had been in close contact with the RHD. Like them, it remained
small but there were rumours that through the pastor's contacts it might have
access to arms brought into Northern Ireland by the Ulster Resistance organisation in 1988 and hidden since then in the North Armagh area. In the event,
the Orange Volunteers limited themselves to fire and pipe bomb attacks on
Catholic homes. Like the Red Hand Defenders, they were a flag of convenience
for an element within the UDA which wanted to step up such attacks, especially in John Gregg's South-East Antrim brigade area, but to carry them out
on the same 'no claim, no blame' basis as the UDA killings at the start of the
year in revenge for Billy Wright's murder.

These attacks, which had been maintained during the marching season at a
high level of intensity, increased during the final weeks of 1998 and into the
early months of the following year and were often coupled with overt intimidation of Catholic families by other methods. Over 1999 as a whole, more
than 230 pipe bomb attacks were launched by Loyalists, mainly by the UDA's
youth wing, the Ulster Young Militants. Nobody was killed by these but suspicions were widely voiced of UDA involvement in two killings which took
place within forty-eight hours of each other in March 1999.

The first of these was in Lurgan on Monday, 15 March, when Rosemary
Nelson, a well-known solicitor, was killed close to her home when a bomb
fitted to her car exploded under the driver's seat. It severed her legs from her
body and inflicted dreadful abdominal injuries from which she died less than
two hours later in Craigavon Hospital. Her eight-year-old daughter Sarah was
within earshot of the explosion at Tannaghmore Primary School, just a

hundred yards away. Nelson had acted successfully for nationalist and Republican clients both in her own town and in nearby Portadown. It emerged too that an element within the RUC resented her work and had sometimes let this be apparent in their dealings with her.

Her killing was claimed by the RHD but there was immediate press speculation that the UDA had been involved.[17] One active member of the organisation dismissed such suggestions. 'Rosemary Nelson was never a Provo. If we have to start killing again we would find more important targets,'[18] he declared. However, he accepted that there was a former UDA man living in Portadown known to possess bomb-making skills. He was a Scot from West Lothian who had settled in the area and set up a small business there. Fanatical in his opinions, he had, with some help over necessary parts from the West Belfast UDA, constructed the bomb which killed Nelson.

Inevitably the solicitor's work had drawn her into some contact with leading local Republicans as well as the Garvaghy Road Residents' Association in Portadown, whose leader, Brendan MacCionnaith, or McKenna, was a former IRA prisoner. Her murder was seen by RUC spokesmen as a calculated attempt by Loyalists to drive up tension in an always volatile area and get a reaction from the Provisional IRA which would destabilise or even wreck the whole peace process.[19] Questions have continued to be asked as to how the bomb which killed Nelson was driven into and then wired up in a nationalist part of Lurgan which until not long beforehand had experienced intense activity by the security forces. The RUC certainly had reason to fear her forensic skills but with its entire future as a force under examination by the Patten commission, it is unlikely to have wished to be implicated in her murder.

Two days after the killing, Frankie Curry, a well-known Shankill Loyalist with a long paramilitary track record in the UVF, was shot dead on waste ground close to Malvern Street. This was the scene of the killing of a young Catholic barman in 1966 which had led to the conviction of Curry's uncle, Gusty Spence. Curry was expelled from the UVF in 1996 over his support for Billy Wright, but he had later gravitated towards the RHD. He had mastered bomb-making skills which he was ready to make available to them and may even have given the new grouping its name.

At the time of his murder, Curry had made his home in Portadown but had returned to the Shankill to see his mother and also to seek help from John White about some job applications he had made. Once back 'on the road' even his brutal reputation gave him no protection from enemies with scores to settle and he appears to have ignored police warnings about the danger to him.[20] Not all his victims as a Loyalist assassin had been Catholics and police had already questioned him about his role in the murder in July 1998 of William Paul, a Bangor-based Loyalist, in a quarrel over drug money. The UDA was angered by Curry's killing, fearing it might be blamed, but was philosophical about his death:

Nephew or not, Curry had become a thorn in Gusty Spence's flesh and that of the UVF. Their leaders are on the defensive now over the peace process and there were scores to settle because your man had become a loose cannon even when he was in the UVF.[21]

There was in fact no immediate follow-up to Curry's killing but pipe and fire bomb attacks on Catholic homes intensified. So too did the picketing, by often violent Loyalist crowds, of the Catholic church at Harryville in the predominantly Loyalist town of Ballymena. This long-running protest was prompted by the Parade Commission's ban on a parade at Dunloy, a village just a few miles to the north. As another marching season arrived, attacks on homes became more ferocious and on 5 June, in Portadown, a pipe bomb killed a Catholic grandmother, Elizabeth O'Neill, in her own home.

One of the few people who appeared to believe that UDA members were not using the names of the Orange Volunteers and the RHD to take part in these mounting attacks was Gary McMichael. Responding to the narrow escape from a gun attack of Frank Pettigrew, a West Belfast Catholic community worker, he told the press in late May:

As far as I am aware the leadership of the UFF is still committed to the peace process, so I don't see how that can be reconciled with the allegations that it is linked to this random violence. We will not have any relationship with people who are engaged in violence to oppose the peace process.[22]

In his role as spokesman for a party with an increasingly uncertain future, though it was still in contact with the UDA leadership, condemnation of continued attacks on Catholics was all McMichael could offer. In July of 1999 however, the UDA's Inner Council acted as tension rose predictably over Orange Order parades. In Belfast the County Grand Lodge demanded the right of all the city's lodges to parade to Ormeau Park, which lay close to the still contested Ormeau Bridge. The Parades Commission required the parade to march down Ravenhill Road and to hold its rally in an area of the park well away from any nationalist protests on the lower side of the bridge.

The Inner Council called for a peaceful demonstration and the South Belfast brigade urged upon members the importance of any protests against the rerouting being non-violent. 'Any display of violence or aggression will dishonour the objective of the demonstration and play into the hands of republican propagandists,'[23] the brigade's statement read, and Jackie McDonald's influence on it was clear as he tightened his grip on the organisation in the south side of the city, where membership was very large and in fact extended as far as Lisburn and the surrounding area.

The Twelfth and the continued impasse at Drumcree was inevitably accompanied by some violence but not on the scale of the previous year. This owed much more to effective action by the security forces than to the UDA, which was increasingly preoccupied with its own deteriorating relationship with the UVF. Symptomatic of this was the final demise, in 1997, of the Combined Loyalist Military Command. Some of the reasons for this have been described in Chapter 9, but in fact the two organisations had always co-existed uneasily.

David Ervine remarked in a conversation with the author that he would 'rather have been a private in the UVF than a general in the UDA',[24] though he also went on to pay tribute to the genuine Loyalist motivation of many of his peer group who had joined the UDA. At the outset of the Troubles, the UVF, with their disciplined, centralist structure, relatively small and often ex-service membership, and their avoidance of the media, reacted to the UDA as ill-equipped interlopers, not to be taken any more seriously than the Wombles, the animal characters who lived under Wimbledon Common in a popular children's television series. To this day, the UDA are still quite often referred to as the Wombles.

They in turn quickly nicknamed the UVF the 'Blacknecks' because on the occasions when they appeared in uniform they wore black polo sweaters under their combat jackets. Activists in and well-wishers to the two organisations tended also to drink in their own separate bars and clubs, as they still do, but rivalry and banter in 'neutral' premises could quickly turn into vicious drink-fuelled fights. Their politics were also different. The UVF has always been more literal in its Unionism and happier to display Union flags rather than Ulster standards on their own. Politically, while Spence as a prisoner came to think of himself as a socialist [25] and encouraged debates on working-class politics, the UVF never travelled along the road which took the UDA to its espousal of the cause of Ulster independence or, at the very least, real self-government.

The UVF supported the Ulster Workers Council strike in May, 1974 and one of its members, Ken Gibson, sat on the Council, but the organisation was never keen on mass shows of strength on the streets, though in East Antrim its members did play some part in the shutting down of the electricity supply. The awful massacre of people in Dublin and Monaghan by bomb attacks calculated to intimidate the Irish government was the UVF's work but in fact the strike generated a vicious feud with the UDA. This originated over the UVF's failure to close all its drinking clubs during the strike. A UDA order to close a club in Tigers Bay in Belfast led to a fatal shooting, then a brutal sequence of reprisal kidnappings and killings which cost eleven lives. This feud poisoned relationships between the two organisations and in January 1977, one of the victims of the Shankill Butchers, who were loosely linked to the UVF, was a UDA member, James Curtis Moorehead.[26]

Intermittent attempts were made to rebuild relations and sometimes joint parades were held and reported, at least in UDA publications. One such event was a joint parade and wreath-laying ceremony by colour parties of both organisations to mark Remembrance Sunday in 1986,[27] but the UVF's journal, Combat, tended to ignore the UDA, giving only half a page to Michael Stone's one-man attack on Republican mourners at Milltown in 1988 and referring to him only as 'a freelance paramilitary'.[28] John McMichael, it has been claimed, sought to co-ordinate some joint UDA/UFF operations outside Belfast and the formation in 1991 of the CLMC was wrongly thought of by some commentators as heralding more of such co-ordination.

The Command's role, as shown in an earlier chapter, was mainly to prepare the ground for and announce the short-lived 1991 Loyalist ceasefire. Only one operation was set up and carried out under its auspices, an unsuccessful rocket attack on the Republican wing of Crumlin Road prison in December of that year. There were indeed occasions when UDA/UFF communication was so poor that prepared attacks had to be abandoned because the 'other side' had gone ahead with its own operations without any consultation.

A case in point occurred on 14 March 1984, when UDA/UFF gunmen tried and failed to kill Gerry Adams in the centre of Belfast. A UVF team, fully armed, were lying in wait in a vehicle close to the Westlink roundabout, no great distance away, in the expectation that Adams and his entourage would drive up to where they were waiting in order to reach the safety of the Falls by way of Grosvenor Road. They heard from their radio that the Sinn Fein president had been attacked in his taxi near the law courts and had to abandon their own carefully planned operation to kill Adams and those travelling with him.[29] Similarly a UVF plan to kill a leading South Belfast Republican eight years later, in February 1992, also had to be called off at short notice when troops and police flooded the Lower Ormeau Road area after the massacre at Sean Graham's betting shop, carried out by UDA/UFF killers.[30]

Such unity of purpose as the two bodies achieved within the CLMC and with the October 1994 Loyalist ceasefire announcement unravelled rapidly. What caused this, apart from long-simmering suspicions, was mounting anxiety among many UDA members and supporters regarding the high media profile of the PUP, the UVF's political wing, and the readiness of spokesmen for it such as Ervine and Billy Hutchinson to enter into post-ceasefire dialogue with the nationalist community. At street level, territorial antagonisms which had never really gone away resurfaced in the form of increasingly vicious fights in and near bars and clubs where UDA and UVF men clashed.

On 19 May 1996, under the headline 'Loyalist gang wars reach boiling point',[31] a Belfast Sunday newspaper reported the fall-out from a brutal mêlée outside the Alexandra bar on the city's Loyalist York Road. Serious injuries resulted among those involved and trouble spread quickly to the Shankill, where the RUC reinforced its patrols to head off further violence. The UDA claimed their men had been attacked first but at Belfast Crown Court a year later a Shankill Road man admitted he had driven to the Alexandra bar with four car loads of UDA men armed with batons and baseball bats to retaliate against the UVF.[32]

Ominously, this violence was exacerbated by the relentless inflow of drugs into Northern Ireland. Rumours were rife in the spring of 1997 of the UDA blaming the UVF for putting into street circulation contaminated ecstasy tablets, which they believed had killed one of their members, Stephen Kingsberry. He appears to have taken some of these while celebrating his release from the RUC's Castlereagh holding centre, where he had been questioned for forty-eight hours about an attempted armed robbery.[33]

Violent incidents continued and one of the worst was in Londonderry on the last Saturday of August 1997, when thousands of members of the Apprentice Boys converged on the city for their annual parade to celebrate the ending of the siege, three centuries earlier, by the armies of the Stuart King James VII of Scotland and II of England and his patron, Louis XIV of France. To lower tension, the RUC banned the parade from part of its traditional route along the city's walls. Some disorder resulted but was overshadowed by bloody encounters between Loyalist flute bands. Many of these had for long had rival paramilitary links and two of them, the UVF-linked Shankill Protestant Boys and the UDA-linked Cloughfern Young Conquerors, met in head-on combat at the city's railway station after the parade.

Both were large bands and much drink had been consumed during the day. With no regard for the terror they caused to uninvolved bystanders and children, the 'musicians' and their supporters fought each other with fists, boots, broken bottles and glasses and any other weapons which came to hand. John Gregg, who combined his command of the UDA's South-East Antrim Brigade from his Rathcoole base with playing the bass drum in the Cloughfern band, reminisced cheerfully to the author about this bloodbath, though in fact he lost the sight of one eye, which was gouged out by one of his assailants.[34]

With no CLMC in being to even attempt to control this spiralling violence, the atmosphere in some working-class Protestant neighbourhoods began to resemble that in nationalist areas in the 1980s, when a bloody struggle for power within the INLA led to a brutal sequence of killings before priests at Clonard Monastery acted to bring the situation under control. One always perceptive Belfast reporter, Brendan Anderson, realised that the internecine Loyalist violence was in fact symptomatic of a deep and growing malaise in localities where the UDA and UVF had traditionally drawn support: 'The tension between the two paramilitary groups is fed by the sense of bewilderment amongst the Unionist people who believe they have been left rudderless while their whole way of life is being changed by forces beyond their control.'[35]

Mutual suspicion between the UDA and UVF was increased rather than diminished by the April 1998 Belfast Agreement, although their political wings both actively supported it. The UDP's failure to secure any seats in the new legislative assembly, even with candidates of the calibre of Gary McMichael and David Adams, was a blow worsened by the high profile achieved by Ervine and Hutchinson from their success in the elections. The contacts and the media attention this gave them fuelled UDA suspicions of their real agenda.

These suspicions were voiced in unequivocal terms by the UDA's North Antrim and South Londonderry brigade. 'While the UDP has politically followed the traditional Loyalist ideology with its emphasis on a fundamentalist Protestant working class conservative ethos,' they argued, 'the PUP have already alarmingly deviated towards an ethos of left-wing Marxist Socialism.'[36] They blamed this on the contacts that UVF prisoners such as Gusty Spence and Ervine had made with members of the official Republican movement while serving their sentences but they also stressed that this was a pattern limited to some areas of Belfast and had no real roots in rural Loyalism, where the 'personality cults' of Spence, Ervine and Hutchinson held little sway.

It became common for UDA spokesmen to refer to the PUP, and by inference the UVF, as the 'peace people', and Sammy Duddy was particularly cynical about their denial of any complicity in Frankie Curry's murder in March 1999:

> The UVF need to come clean on this but then David Ervine and Billy Hutchinson would have to be suspended from their assembly seats if they do that. They've bent over backwards to compromise with Sinn Fein. They are practically in bed with them. We've been monitoring their movements and we don't like what we have found. Some of them have been socialising with leading Republicans and in some cases visiting their houses, yet we know the IRA are doing regular surveillance on our own people. We've even spotted IRA vehicles here on the Shankill Road.[37]

The lingering antagonism between two organisations supposedly brought into being by a common enemy was clearly voiced in a short and lavishly illustrated history of the UDA published late in 1999 and widely believed to have been compiled by John White. In the section entitled 'Casualties' he declared:

> It is sad and quite ironic that the UDA had more men murdered by the UVF than by the IRA. In fact the UVF has been responsible for murdering twenty seven members of the UDA. In many cases these crimes were carried out for no other reason than rivalry and disrespect for an organisation which the UVF saw as a threat to its power base and influence in the Loyalist community.[38]

He went on to refer to 'the deep resentment among many UDA members towards the UVF that still comes to the surface from time to time'.[39]

The book came out at just such a time and with tension growing as the date of Johnny Adair's release from prison under the terms of the Belfast Agreement drew near. This finally took place on 14 September 1999 as part of an ongoing process returning convicted paramilitaries to their communities. Adair emerged through a turnstile into the Maze prison car park just before 11 a.m. He gave a clenched-fist salute to White and about twenty-five supporters, one of whom had draped two UDA flags over the turnstile as a welcome.

Physically 'bulked up' by his many hours in the prison gymnasium as well as from a hefty intake of steroids, Adair was dressed in blue jeans, black T-shirt and a reversed baseball cap. He listened in silence as White told reporters that the newly freed prisoner would be taking part in 'cross-community work' in Belfast and also working with the Shankill Prisoners Aid and Resettlement Group. Explaining his own presence outside the prison, White said he had 'come here this morning to thank Mr Adair personally for his role in the peace process from its inception. Mr Adair has given unwavering support for the peace process.'[40] As incredulous reporters recorded all this, Adair was hurried to a waiting car and wasted no time in donning a bullet-proof vest before being driven away.

The *Irish News*, in its editorial, reacted with predictable cynicism to the whole event, calling it 'a nauseating display of triumphalism' and added that 'suggestions that Adair might have a contribution to make to the peace process will be regarded with contempt by relatives of his many victims'.[41] Personal security was Adair's main priority on his release. During a prison parole four months earlier he had survived an attempt to shoot him by a drugs dealer during a concert by the band UB40 in the Botanic Gardens, which he had recklessly decided to attend with Gina Crossan, whom he had finally married in the Maze prison in early 1997. Amidst much speculation about his plans, Adair moved into a house in Boundary Way on the Lower Shankill, an estate fiercely loyal to the UDA though there were some UVF families in the area. He would be well protected there and the building's security was almost as expensive as its interior fittings, TVs and stereos.

In the initial period after Adair's release, White seldom stayed far from his side. Adair looked up to him as some kind of mentor despite the grotesque double murder for which White had been sentenced and the rumours of his involvement in other killings and in the torture of UFF victims. Two decades on from his conviction, White, with an Open University degree acquired in prison, wanted to enhance his profile as a supporter of the peace process while enjoying a lifestyle he claimed was funded from successful property speculation achieved with the help of a brother in the building trade The security forces and, in particular, the RUC's drug squad were not convinced. White's nickname 'Coco' began to be seen amidst wall graffiti in Loyalist areas and was a direct reference to what was believed to be his role in handling lucrative quantities of cocaine and Ecstasy tablets on the relentlessly expanding Belfast drug market.

Ervine recalls listening to White describing himself as 'a patriotic drug dealer'[42] and Jackie McDonald, who was taking a tough line against UDA drug involvement in his South Belfast brigade area, remembers a meeting in an East Belfast hotel when he saw both White and Adair emerging from the toilet with white rings round their nostrils. 'They'd been in for a snort and I told them their make-up was showing. They weren't too pleased.'[43]

White had been putting the case to the UDA's Inner Council for a major initiative by it on weapons-decommissioning well ahead of Adair's release. In May of 1999, however, he sounded a warning about the adverse effect on such a move of the continuing Stevens inquiry into Loyalist collusion with the security forces, especially over the 1989 murder of Pat Finucane. He told the press of real Loyalist anger over this: 'If UFF personnel are going to be arrested it will have a serious effect on whether the UFF would continue to support the peace process.'[44]

Even with these premonitions, White still pressed the case for some significant decommissioning by the UDA and in early December it was announced by the leadership that it would meet with the International Commission on Decommissioning, chaired by General John de Chastelain. White took part in the talks which resulted. So too did UDA brigadiers John Gregg, Jackie McDonald and 'Winkie' Dodds and also a smartly suited Adair, who accepted White's arguments. 'I did support the view that Loyalists should bring about an act of decommissioning,' he told the author recently. 'This was in order to put the republicans under pressure and help to speed up the dragging peace process.'[45]

The talks with de Chastelain achieved little of a concrete nature, as White admitted to the press late in January 2000. In the absence of any movement on arms from the IRA, no decommissioning from the UDA leadership would be likely, he stated. He went on, however, to underline his own view that a bold move on arms by Loyalists had real political merit. He argued that 'it would help put pressure on the IRA and lessen the number of excuses they have for not decommissioning'[46] and claimed to have 'an awful lot of support by people who have been key players in the UFF in terms of military activity'.[47] He also accepted that 'some occupying key positions within the movement remain unconvinced'.[48]

Even with Adair's support, White would still have had trouble talking round a majority of the Inner Council but what aborted any UDA move on arms was the action of the Stevens inquiry. Early in 2000 it confirmed that it had identified six UDA members it suspected of involvement in the Finucane murder and that their names, along with relevant forensic evidence, had been passed to the Director of Public Prosecutions. White and Adair were adamant that the arrest of any of these men would mean the end of any talk of UDA arms-decommissioning.[49] This was a response born of resentment at the way the Finucane family and the Republican movement had conferred iconic status on the murdered lawyer. They presented his case as in some way special because of who he had been at the very moment when Northern Ireland was being urged to try to break free from the burden of its recent history.

Other lawyers had been callously murdered by the IRA because they were opponents of paramilitary Republicanism. One of them was Dr Edgar Graham, a law lecturer shot dead within the precincts of Queen's University, where he taught. Sylvia, Lady Hermon, now a Unionist MP for North Down, was studying law at Queen's in 1983 when this killing took place. She has recalled her horror in the university union building on hearing the cheers and stamping of Republican students when, as part of a security alert, news of the murder came through on the public address system.[50]

Finucane had known Republican sympathies and contacts. A police officer recalls him going into court in Belfast wearing a black armband after the death on hunger strike of Bobby Sands[51] and in February 2004 his son Michael gave the Bobby Sands memorial lecture to a West Belfast audience, an event fully reported in Sinn Fein's weekly newspaper and attended by past and present IRA members.[52] To Unionists and Loyalists, the clamour over the Finucane case and calls for a full public inquiry into it seemed proof that the Republican movement, far from accepting the Belfast Agreement's agenda of reconciliation embodied in prisoner releases and the appointment of a once senior IRA man as Education Minister, was in fact pushing for publicly funded investigations into crimes from the recent past chosen on a selective basis and involving mostly victims from their own community.

Over and above the implications of John Stevens's ongoing investigation and at the very moment when White and Adair had espoused a significant UDA move on decommissioning, Loyalist suspicions of Republican intentions were reignited by events across the Atlantic. Several IRA men were arrested in Florida and charged with being part of an operation to buy and ship to Northern Ireland 'clean' weapons, i.e. guns without any incriminating forensic history. Such a weapon was used in October 2000 in West Belfast to kill a Real IRA leader, Joseph O'Connor. These arrests of clearly still active Provisionals sealed the fate of any UDA arms initiative, regardless of White's support for it and his ability to talk Adair round to it. Had it succeeded it could only have strengthened David Trimble's increasingly beleaguered position as Ulster Unionist Party leader.

Whether Adair fully grasped this is another matter. In any event he maintained and indeed increased his contacts with Portadown-based Loyalist dissidents whose allegiance was to the LVF and who saw themselves as sworn opponents of Trimble as well as keepers of the flame lit by Billy Wright. In doing this, Adair could only deeply antagonise the UVF, whose authority Wright, by his defiance, had openly mocked in 1996. Over a longer period, he also enraged the UDA's Inner Council and created in their minds the belief that he planned to take over the whole organisation. At every stage, Adair was encouraged by White, who came to resemble his *eminence grise*, always at his side and ready to explain and justify what he was doing, something that his protégé was not always good at doing in his dealings with the media.

The sequence of events which was to destroy Adair's power base within the UDA has been documented in vivid detail in two recent books by journalists with intimate knowledge of paramilitary Loyalism as well as resourcefulness and courage,[53] so this chapter will cover what happened in summary form. The 'community work' which White claimed Adair would be undertaking after his release soon took the very public form of covering every available kerbstone on the Lower Shankill in red, white and blue paint and also ordering in bulk from Taiwan sky-blue banners emblazoned with the insignia of the UDA and often of C Company too. These began to be displayed in particular profusion in the area stretching from where the Adair family lived in Boundary Way to Carlisle Circus, a junction which led into North Belfast. In response, the crimson flags of the UVF started to appear in areas where they had a presence further up the Shankill and beyond Agnes Street, which became something of a frontier as relations between the two organisations worsened.

This phoney war of the flags took on an uglier edge as a direct result of events in Portadown early in 2000. On 10 January, Richard Jamieson, a senior UVF commander in the town, was shot dead outside his home. He had become an outspoken opponent of what he claimed was LVF drug-dealing and urged public support for the RUC in any measures it took against those involved. Two weeks earlier he had also been present at the local football team's social club, where a savage fight broke out between UVF men armed with baseball bats, hammers, axes and knives and drunken LVF members who had gathered to honour the memory of Billy Wright. The ferocity of the UVF onslaught left over a dozen of them needing hospital treatment.

Jamieson's funeral was unmistakeably a UVF event and was preceded and followed by the methodical vandalising of the rival organisation's murals. Brutal revenge for Jamieson's death came just four weeks later when two Portadown teenagers, Andrew Robb and David McIlwaine, were abducted in the early hours of 19 February then hacked and beaten to death. Their appallingly mutilated bodies were found 200 yards apart on a road close to the village of Tandragee. An RUC scene-of-crime officer was shaken by what he found: 'Some of the wounds were so big you could put a fist through them,' he told a newspaper. 'Their throats had been slashed. The attack was extremely vicious.'[54]

Robb had once been photographed in Wright's company but his connection to the LVF had been only a tenuous one. On his last night alive, and unknown to him and McIlwaine, local UVF members had been in the same nightclub and had singled them out as being in some way implicated in the Jamieson murder. In fact, the mid-Ulster UVF was under pressure from Belfast to avenge Jamieson and the two teenagers were easy prey. Within hours of their deaths, Portadown's graffiti writers were at work and the message 'UVF – child killers' began to appear on walls and hoardings.

At Robb's funeral on 21 February, an ominous development was the arrival of Adair and White, with some well-known members of the UDA's West Belfast C Company, to join the cortège.[55] Three days later there was an appeal by the UDA's Inner Council for an end to internecine Loyalist killing but few believed this was likely to happen. Back in Belfast the war of the flags mutated into one of murals, with Adair ostentatiously supervising the painting up of new and provocative works celebrating Wright's memory . When one of these was defaced in late April he led a thousand people in a protest march down the Shankill Road.[56]

Wright was depicted in one of the new murals not by name but simply as 'King Rat – Loyalist martyr'. Another chilling one appeared in late June in

Dover Street, just off the Lower Shankill Road. It listed recent Loyalist mas-
sacres of Catholics, including those at Greysteel and Sean Graham's betting
shop on the Ormeau Road. Inscribed below them were the words from Van
Morrison's lyric 'Coney Island', which went: 'Wouldn't it be great if it was
like this all the time?' They had also been used in a Northern Ireland Office
broadcast urging continued support for the peace process. In face of angry
protests which went beyond the nationalist community, White disclaimed
UDA responsibility although the mural celebrated only killings it had carried
out. Late in July 2000 the mural was finally painted over, in front of invited
members of the media, by Frank McCoubrey, Deputy Lord Mayor of Belfast
and a UDP councillor. Amidst jeers from some bystanders, he told journalists
he had acted 'after discussions with local people' whom he did not name.[57]

Murals which came under attack were cleaned up and restored under
Adair's guidance, and deranged humour, as often in Belfast, crept in with
unused wall spaces being labelled as 'reserved' for the UVF or the UDA as
the case might be. As the 2000 marching season got under way, Adair converted the Lower Shankill into a garish Loyalist theme park with murals
appearing on every available gable celebrating Loyalist paramilitary history,
but also portraying the Queen and Diana, Princess of Wales. As tension grew,
White denied allegations that there was a strategy to provoke the UVF but he
did admit to the press that 'the situation here on the Shankill is fragile and it
is serious'.[58] He denied any formal UDA–LVF links but did say that both he
and Adair had 'friends' in the latter organisation. 'You can't cut off friendships made over years,' he insisted. 'We're supporting them and respecting
the memory of Billy Wright, not because they're LVF but because they're
Protestants and Loyalists.'[59]

White had even claimed earlier that an opinion survey had been conducted
in the Lower Shankill as part of a 'community project'[60] to assess opinion on
the new murals. It would have needed a brave householder to refuse the use
of his or her gable wall to Adair and his roving mural artists. On the related
issue of the UDA's relationship to the LVF, Adair stayed close to the line
taken by White, admitting to his own 'strong friendships' with LVF members
but insisting: 'If you are asking me formally if there is dual membership of
the LVF and the UDA, or a formal partnership, I am telling you there is no
formal linkage.'[61] Soon after giving this interview, Adair departed for a
holiday in Jamaica with his family, declining to explain how he could finance
it, having had no regular employment since his release from the Maze.

The ongoing war of flags and murals was accompanied by bomb and gun
attacks and on 26 May Martin Naylor, a shipyard worker who lived well
beyond the Shankill in the Silverstream area of North Belfast, was shot dead
next door to his home as he helped a neighbour build a garden wall. Billy
Hutchinson of the PUP, who had known the victim, was quick to blame the
LVF, though Naylor may not in fact have been the intended target. The week
was a tense one, with another man who had UVF connections surviving an

attempt on his life in the city just two days earlier, and journalists and police on the ground had the strong sense of a simmering feud waiting to explode.[62]

Adair, however, simply grew more confident as the marching season gathered momentum. On Friday, 16 June, he appeared at Cliftonpark Avenue, a section of a parade route traditionally followed by Loyalist flute bands in what was known as 'the tour of the North'. This parade had often led to violent clashes with the nationalist population where its route went close to their areas. Adair made a show of concern for maintaining order and even provided UDA stewards for part of the route. A local newspaper described the bands marching 'under the control of stewards and under Mr Adair's watchful eye.'[63] White dutifully told journalists: 'We thought it was proper to come here and have some marshals on the ground to ensure that the likes of hangers-on who create trouble don't do that.'[64]

The 'stewards' and 'parade marshals' were UDA men and White and Adair were using an opportunity to present the media with C Company's 'acceptable face'. Yet on the very same day, large UDA banners were hung across the Loyalist end of North Queen Street within sight of nationalist households further along a thoroughfare which had for long been a notoriously violent interface. This would not have happened without Adair's sanction. North Queen Street lay just inside the UDA's North Belfast brigade area but in 2000 it was under the erratic leadership of 'Jimbo' Simpson, known to graffiti artists in the area as 'the Bacardi brigadier'. Adair had set up operations in North Belfast before his arrest in 1994 and could still influence events there.

The banners in North Queen Street compromised the 'peace-keeping' initiative a mile or so away in Cliftonpark Avenue and only days later a UFF communiqué warned that the organisation's ceasefire was at risk because of continuing attacks on Protestant homes at interface areas. The statement, read out in a social club by masked C Company members, was at once criticised by Gary McMichael[65] and extraordinarily, given his closeness to Adair, also by White. Some in the security forces had their doubts as to the origins of these attacks, which they thought might well have been staged by C Company to justify 'reprisal' assaults on Catholic homes. The communiqué was in fact issued without other UDA brigades being informed and three days later it was graciously withdrawn. It had been a muscle-flexing exercise by C Company, a show of strength to alarm the minority community with a follow-up to it in conciliatory mode.

How little such gestures in conciliation were worth became clear as the crucial month of July drew close. Graffiti around the Lower Shankill displaying the message 'Roll on Drumcree 2000' had been appearing for many weeks and they became more menacing as Portadown Orangemen and the security forces prepared for yet another confrontation. Once again the Parades Commission announced a ban on any march down Garvaghy Road while the Orange Order's biggest parade in Belfast would once again have to follow a route to Ormeau Park which took it well away from any nationalist areas. The Order's response was initially an inflammatory one with calls for all Orangemen in Northern Ireland to rally at Drumcree, and another huge operation was mounted by the security forces to secure the Garvaghy Road and to seal off Portadown.

In this atmosphere of palpably mounting tension, with promises by Orange Order spokesmen to bring Belfast to a standstill, Adair made his move, travelling to Portadown with almost the entire membership of C Company to join the Orangemen's protest. On 3 July they formed up outside Drumcree church wearing tight T-shirts all showing the slogan 'UFF – Simply the Best'. One of Adair's two huge, though in fact docile and friendly, German shepherd dogs, Rebel, was also present, wearing the regulation T-shirt. Later the same day, Adair was given a hero's welcome and was caught cheering by television cameras while masked LVF gunmen fired shots into the air beside a bonfire on the Corcrain housing estate. The provocation to the UVF could hardly have been more obvious.

Even yet, Adair seems unable, or perhaps unwilling, to see this. Asked by the author about both his presence at Drumcree in July 2000 and the Lower Shankill 'mural war', Adair's reply was:

> I would have stood shoulder to shoulder with any Loyalists, no matter what badge they wore. I had nothing against the LVF or the UVF in 2000 and I would have shared my support for the Orange men [sic] on the hill with any Loyalist. Billy Wright RIP was one of the best UVF leaders ever produced by them and I had a lot of respect for him because of the hardline stance he took against the enemies of Ulster.[66]

As rumours of hostility to his 'grandstanding' at Drumcree grew in other UDA brigade areas, Adair came under more pressure to explain his behaviour. Interviewed by two Belfast journalists, Hugh Jordan and Jim McDowell, he insisted implausibly that he was still working for peace: 'I was at Portadown as Johnny Adair, Loyalist, not as a paramilitary,' he told them. 'I have the right to support whatever protest, whatever it may be, and to do it peacefully.'[67] He denied he had any responsibility for the mounting tension and violence on Belfast's streets and elsewhere but stumbled over his answers when asked why, if it was so important for him to be at Drumcree, he had never joined the Orange Order or any of the other loyal orders. He simply replied: 'I don't know.'[68]

Only two days after Adair gave this interview and after a day of Loyalist protests and street blockades in support of the Portadown Orangemen had brought much of Belfast to a standstill, John White told the author that in his view the Drumcree issue was 'a busted flush'.[69] He argued that the Orange Order could achieve nothing, other than a compromise with the Parades Commission, without the paramilitaries. 'Without them,' he declared, 'the whole thing is futile. Why should the Orangemen expect others to fight their battles for them?'[70] He was echoing a view expressed by others in the UDA yet, as disquiet was growing over Adair's increasingly volatile behaviour, the question could be asked as to why White had not used his influence to keep him away from Drumcree.

On the eve of the Twelfth, Adair, hungrier than ever for the attention of the media, agreed to talk on national television to Martin Bashir, who had achieved global fame for his *Panorama* interview with Diana, Princess of Wales. Adair's performance was often a faltering one as he was pressed hard on matters such as his role in rising sectarian tension, as well as the sources both of his income and his suntan. The programme, entitled 'Mad Dog the Ulsterman', ended with Adair denying that any 'mad dog' had ever existed. Talking to the author soon afterwards in an office used by White, Adair described Bashir as 'a real gentleman'.[71] The office was destroyed ten days later by a UVF bomb.

On the following day, the Twelfth parades passed off relatively peacefully. Adair reappeared at Drumcree with a smaller member of C Company members carrying a UFF banner, and in his own fiefdom on the Lower Shankill, masked gunmen were once again filmed firing volleys beside a massive bonfire the night before the Belfast parade. Tension, however, remained high, not least because Andrew Cairns, a young UVF member, was shot dead after a fight at a Loyalist bonfire in Larne and a man with UDA links was charged with the killing.[72] Nor did Michael Stone's emollient words on his release from prison on 24 July have much effect. In a brief statement to the press, he described himself as 'a volunteer in the UDA involved in a thirty-year war. It was not of my doing.'[73] However, he expressed regret for all the deaths that had resulted as well as his support for the Agreement, under whose terms he had been released.

Adair spent much of August in almost perpetual motion, overseeing the completion of new murals and decorations and giving interviews as well as orders to underlings in C Company. Meanwhile blatant drug-dealing could be observed barely two minutes' walk from his home in Boundary Way, a short street awash with flags. A derelict flat in North Boundary Street was the nerve centre of operations with even ten-year-old children being supplied. Local people made contact with a Belfast newspaper to report what they saw but were afraid to give their names. 'Drug dealers run the show,' one householder said. 'All we can do is sit and watch as they deal out this poison to children, we are powerless to do anything about it. Anybody who stands up to them is taking their life in their hands.'[74]

It simply is not possible that Adair and his C Company lieutenants cannot have known about what was going on. Nothing happened on the Lower Shankill at this time without their authorisation. The area was patrolled by young supporters in baseball caps and sports gear, often accompanied by not-so-young minders who had no hesitation in threatening journalists and ordering them off the estate. According to them, they were protecting the area from attacks by Republicans in the nearby New Lodge and Carrick Hill estates, an issue White was happy to talk up in yet another newspaper interview he gave on 12 August: 'The UFF feels it has no choice but to protect its territory in the only way it knows how,' he declared.[75]

He went on to admit that such incidents gave Loyalists the excuse which many of them in any case wanted to attack Catholic homes. Just who was setting up some of the attacks in Loyalist areas was indeed a matter for speculation both by the security forces and by the media. This speculation intensified after Adair claimed to have had a narrow escape at midnight on 15 July from a pipe bomb attack on the Oldpark Road. The explosion was close to Ardoyne and Adair was in one of two cars driven by UDA men at the time. He at once claimed that the attack was the work of Republicans but declined to make the vehicle in which he had been travelling, and which was damaged by the explosion, available for police examination.[76] Pipe bombs, the RUC pointed out, were used almost exclusively by Loyalists and UDA sources told a Sunday newspaper that the pipe bomb was intended for an attack on Ardoyne but had gone off prematurely.[77]

Shortly afterwards, Sammy Duddy confirmed to the author that this was indeed the case:

> That was no murder attempt on Johnny. The *Sunday World* got it right. Those boys were on a bombing run up the Oldpark and into Ardoyne when things went wrong and their pipe bomb blew on them. The Provos have never used pipe bombs. Everybody knows that.'[78]

This simple but potentially lethal weapon was used again in the days that followed in attacks in North Belfast, Larne and Carrickfergus, and White stretched credibility further by claiming that the UDA/UFF ceasefire was still intact: 'I think until guns are used and someone is shot they are not in breach,'[79] he was quoted as saying amidst growing rumours that Adair's rearrest was imminent.

There were other unfounded reports that Adair had taken a flight to Spain out of Belfast airport. In fact he was putting much of his energy into the preparation of a 'festival of Loyalist culture' to be held in the Lower Shankill area on Saturday, 19 August. This event, in fact, had the support of all the UDA's brigades. Some of them, like South Belfast, agreed to take part rather than let the occasion be monopolised by Adair and C Company. The 'cultural' content of the day was to be confined to a parade of masked colour parties, UDA units and dozens of flute bands sympathetic to the organisation from all over Belfast and beyond it. Its climax was to be the formal dedication of new murals on the Lower Shankill estate. It was also, ironically, in the light of what it unleashed, publicised in leaflets as a 'fun day' for children, with bouncy castles and other activities organised by Duddy.

The day began peacefully, with around 8,000 marchers making their way up the Shankill Road for a memorial service at Woodvale Park. They then formed up to parade back down the road and to Adair's home ground for the main event of the afternoon, passing without incident the Rex bar, traditionally a meeting for the UVF, many of whose members and supporters were within it and on the street outside. The last band in the parade, however, in a calculated act of provocation, unfurled and waved a large standard emblazoned with the initials and insignia of the LVF. This at once unleashed a bloody fracas, with Rex bar drinkers hurling themselves at the offending colour party as well as the band and those marching with it. As word of this reached the head of the column nearly a hundred vengeful UDA men raced back up the road and attempted to storm the bar, whose customers had barricaded themselves inside it.

Prominent Adair associates, some openly carrying and using firearms, were captured on film as the fighting went on until RUC officers and troops were able to separate the two sides. Adair later blandly told the author that he had not been involved as he was helping to organise events near Boundary Way, where a speakers' platform had been set up.[80] The platform party included some bemused and uneasy UDA brigadiers, especially Jackie McDonald, whose premonitions about Adair had been growing almost by the week, and the Deputy Lord Mayor of Belfast, Frank McCoubrey, who was wearing his red robe and chain of office. Afterwards, he had to face demands for his resignation, even though he had been unaware of what was to happen.

After a brief speech by White, a firing party in combat kit and balaclavas – and a mini-skirt in the case of Gina Adair – took the stage to blast off volleys into the air with AK47 assault rifles. This show of force set the scene for what happened next, though attacks on the homes of local UVF families had already started. A third and final onslaught on the Rex bar was launched later in the evening while Adair hosted a bonfire party and firework display on the site where the afternoon 'festival' events had been held. Much drink was consumed and the 'drug house' as it was commonly called, in nearby North Boundary Street, did brisk business.

Though deaths resulting from these events were not long in coming, none took place on the Saturday or Sunday. However, what became quickly apparent was the havoc wreaked by C Company and its supporters on the homes of those thought to be less than loyal to Adair or, worse than that, UVF sympathisers, which some isolated individuals and families on the Lower Shankill still were. Best known of these was Gusty Spence, whose house on Denmark Street was broken into and wrecked by C Company members. He was fortunate to be staying away that weekend in his caravan on the coast at Groomsport.

The house of Spence's son-in-law, 'Winkie' Rea, got the same treatment, even his Orange lodge collarette being ripped up and a portrait of Sir Edward, later Lord Carson, a true Ulster Loyalist hero, smashed up. Less lucky were householders in Hopewell Avenue, who had to abandon their homes with only the clothes they were wearing. The fire-blackened frontages of their houses, with vandalised belongings dumped in small front gardens, were gaunt images for the media to highlight in the next few days. Untouched of course were homes which flew the UDA and C Company standards. Amidst this frenzy, guilt by association was easily and arbitrarily decided and then acted upon.

Chris McGimpsey, a much respected UUP councillor for the area, found his small office on the Shankill Road overrun with mothers and children made homeless by events and seeking help while husbands and partners hid in safe houses further up the road. 'I feel like emigrating just at present,' he told the author on 28 August, though in fact he continued, with his secretary, to work round the clock to rehouse dozens of families. 'Decent people will be quietly asking the Housing Executive for transfers out and the Lower Shankill will become a ghetto controlled by thugs.'[81]

Some thought this had already started to happen. It was certainly the view of David McKittrick, a veteran writer and journalist who had spent his early childhood in the Shankill until his parents moved away. Amidst the grim fall-out from events on Saturday, 19 August, he pondered the impact on the area of lost employment in traditional industry and continuing low levels of educational aspiration:

> Over the years most of the more ambitious families have done as we did and gone to live in less troubled communities. The loss of potential leaders and useful role models has left a district in which paramilitary groups hold sway.
>
> For an under-educated youth in a district where learning is scorned and jobs are few, joining a paramilitary organisation confers instant status, together with a sense of belonging and the possibility of material gain from activities such as selling drugs. The scourges of drugs, unemployment and above all paramilitarism, mean the Shankill's deterioration is likely to continue.[82]

At least McGimpsey was at his office every day at a time when more senior members of his party were not to be seen on the Shankill at all. So too, wholly in character, was Duddy, who never failed to open the Loyalist Prisoners Post-Conflict and Resettlement office and dispense cups of coffee and tea there even as the violence continued and the predictable killing got under way. Listening to the stories of homeless women, like one ordered out of her house at gunpoint simply because a teenage son played with the Shankill Protestant Boys Flute Band, which had traditionally UVF links, or viewing the devastation at the lower end of the road, it was easy to think of James Joyce's description of Ireland as 'a sow that eats its own farrow'. He used these words in the anger of exile but in August 2000 it was possible to apply them to the once vibrant Loyalist heartland of the Shankill.

For several days buses from the city centre stopped going up the Shankill Road and the fleet of black taxis operating out of North Street, which had served the area for many years, though widely known to be owned by the UVF, altered their route for the safety of drivers and passengers. In a bizarre irony created by the feud, this involved travelling up the Falls Road then rejoining the Shankill on safer territory beyond Agnes Street, where Adair's writ did not run in the way that it did further down the road. Schools were also disrupted by the violence. Parents with UDA or UVF links clashed outside them as they waited to collect their children. At one school on Malvern Street, many pupils were kept away by parents while other schools took to operating separate exits for pupils according to family allegiances.

Ultimately, over 300 families had to be rehoused. Most of them were from the Lower Shankill, victims of their real or imagined links to the UVF. Further up the Shankill Road, on its middle and upper sections, people with UDA loyalties but vulnerable because of them in an area where the UVF's presence was stronger also had to leave their homes in haste. Probably around forty families fell into this latter category. Politically prominent figures were obvious targets and Billy Hutchinson, who had used the media to excoriate Johnny Adair and C Company, had his home in Ambleside Street shot at and bombed. He left the area temporarily, amidst mocking graffiti from C Company activists.

Not all the graffiti took Adair's side. Indeed, he had misjudged the extent to which the UDA as a whole wanted to be drawn into open war with the UVF. All its brigades outside West Belfast, encouraged by Jackie McDonald's example, wanted no part of it and even in West Belfast, A and B Companies based in the Woodvale and Highfield estates were disinclined to be drawn in. Worse still for Adair was the fact that his former prized killer, 'Top Gun' Stephen McKeag, gave him no support. By this time McKeog was living off a lethal mix of hard drugs and alcohol, as well as painkillers he needed for injuries he had sustained two years earlier in a motorbike crash. He had distanced himself from C Company though they gave him a full paramilitary funeral when he died later in the year from a huge drugs overdose.[83]

Crude but effective defiance of Adair's Lower Shankill power base began to appear even on walls and hoardings quite close to it. As the first and inevitable killings began, one message read: 'How many more must die for Adair and his drug empire?' Another proclaimed:

Join the Lower Shankill UFF and see the world.
1, Exotic holidays.
2, Top of range cars.
3, Luxurious homes.
PS, Only apply if you are prepared to poison children with drugs.

These taunts were there for all to see but the UVF was careful to photograph them to use in its magazine, as well as one with the ominous message: 'The war has just begun.'[84]

It had indeed, and the first victims died at the hands of a single gunman as they sat talking in a car outside a betting shop on the Crumlin Road on 21 August. They were Jackie Coulter, whose main involvement with the UDA was in prisoners' welfare work, and his friend Bobby Mahood. He ran the

Sportsman's Bar, a popular venue on Snugville Avenue, close to his home. He came from a family with well-known UVF connections but was on good terms with many UDA members. No statement of responsibility for the double killing was made but PUP spokesmen admitted that they were the work of the UVF. The next day Peter Mandelson, the Secretary of State for Northern Ireland, revoked Adair's early release and he was arrested and flown by helicopter to Maghaberry prison.

Despite Adair's removal from the scene and heavy deployment of troops and police on the Shankill, the killing continued until the beginning of November, claiming five more victims. Two were UVF members and three had UDA links. All were easy targets in a squalid and unheroic cycle of reprisals in which, as so often before, gunmen simply arrived to do their work at the their victims' homes then disappeared into the night. The first was Samuel Rockett, who was killed at his girlfriend's home in Summer Street in the Oldpark area just two days after the Coulter and Mahood murders. His two-year-old daughter was sleeping close to him on a sofa and he was sitting drinking tea with his partner as his killers kicked in the front door and opened fire. Five days later there were ugly scenes, witnessed by the author, as UVF men arrived to strip the house of its furniture then set it alight. Only the arrival of the security forces prevented a violent confrontation with UDA members who also turned up at the Oldpark address. This was 'scorched earth' tactics in action to deny the house to the enemy.[85]

Rockett's friends said that he had been associated with a UVF 'team' nick-named the 'Liverpools' because they met and drank in a Liverpool support-ers' social club off the upper end of the Shankill Road. Naming 'teams' or units after pubs and clubs they were associated with was a Belfast Loyalist tradition which was kept up in some cases even after premises were bombed or demolished for redevelopment. Regardless of what he may or may not have done, Rockett was a target but had friends in the UDA and accepted assurances that he would not be attacked while visiting his girlfriend and child at the house in Summer Street. This fuelled the anger caused by his death and John White admitted that the UDA had carried it out.[86] Yet another large paramilitary funeral followed and the UVF has more recently dedicated a mural to Rockett's memory.[87]

Killing went on hold, as it often did, to allow for the funerals of victims. Few in Loyalist areas thought that Adair's return to prison would bring any immediate peace.

Sammy Duddy somewhat over-charitably took the view that Adair 'had been doing some good in the community. Hoods and muggers weren't getting it all their own way with him around but there was the wild side to him as well. He orchestrated attacks at interface areas, we all knew that. He said he still supported the peace process but what Johnny says and what he does are different things. Mind you, the mood has changed among Loyalist people over the Belfast Agreement and Johnny is tuned in to that change of mood.'[88]

Asked about White's role, Duddy confirmed the closeness of his relation-ship to Adair:

> Neither of them was coming much into the office I work from. Johnny did a lot of his interviews from John White's office but now that the UVF have blown it up he's going to move down the road to Boundary Way. They're fitting up a wee place right opposite Johnny Adair's house. You can read what you want into that.[89]

Questioned the following day about whether he was indeed Adair's mentor, White's evasive response was that he and the Adair family 'went a long way back' and he repeated his claim to have tried to 'involve him in community projects' after his release. As to the current cycle of violence, he denied any responsibility for it, describing it simply as 'the UVF doing what they've always been good at, killing other Prods'.[90] This was before a search by the security forces through the debris of his demolished office revealed weapons and ammunition which they concluded had been hidden in the building, pos-sibly under floorboards. No charges were pressed against White over this and he was able to continue his almost daily pronouncements and interviews, as ever relishing the attention of the media.

Even as White spoke, UDA brigadiers from outside West Belfast had made contact with the UVF to make clear their disinclination to be drawn into a fratricidal Loyalist war. This initiative came from Jackie McDonald in South Belfast but the East Belfast Brigade, while supporting it, let it be known that it would retaliate if any of its own members were attacked.[91] Proof that the violence could be localised came shortly afterwards when the UVF held one of its biggest annual commemorations at the upper end of the Shankill Road. This was in memory of one of its members, Brian Robinson, killed by under-cover army soldiers in 1989. Held close to the Woodvale and Highfield estates, where the West Belfast UDA's A and B Companies had a strong pres-ence, the event passed off peacefully.

Fears of violence resulting from it had been voiced in the media but a speaker in black beret, eye shades and combat kit, while denouncing the tyranny of UDA 'drug barons' on the Lower Shankill, also appealed to 'decent men and leaders' within its ranks to take action against C Company. He also paid a conciliatory tribute to the contribution 'sincere' UDA members had made to the Loyalist cause. Unusually, no volley by masked men was fired at the Robinson memorial but thirty-five bands were present and the parade was still on the Shankill two hours after it had assembled in a massive show of strength by the UVF.[92]

The lull in killing after the Coulter, Mahood and Rockett murders lasted for eight weeks, though violence and harassment continued despite appeals for an end to conflict from churches and community workers. There was also a march for peace down the Shankill Road in which families of victims of the Troubles took part.[93] Coulter's widow, however, still in shock and grieving for her husband, told the press that the UVF were trying to force her from her home by driving slowly past it to shout taunts at her and her family.[94]

Outside Belfast there was a near fatality in Coleraine when Charlene, the eleven-year-old daughter of former UDA prisoner Frank Daly, was caught in a burst of gunfire into the family home on the night of Monday, 28 August. The bullets smashed her ribs and caused a lung to collapse, putting her into intensive care for a period of weeks. It was clearly a UVF attack, and the fourth incident in Coleraine in as many days arising from the feud.[95] British troops were deployed in the town in support of the police and also in Carrickfergus, where twenty-five homes and several cars were damaged by Loyalist gangs on the Glenfield, Woodburn and Castlemara estates.[96]

The shooting of Charlene Daly proved to be a localised event. There were promises of retaliation but the UDA in both North Antrim and South Londonderry, as well as in South East Antrim, had little relish for being drawn into what they saw as a futile turf war started by C Company on the Lower Shankill. Jim Wright from Ballymoney, the UDP's North Antrim chairman, who had good contacts with the UDA, made this very clear to the author:

> What's been happening in Belfast makes me ashamed to be a Protestant at the moment. That parade past the Rex bar with the LVF standard should never have happened. It was provocation. There's people there with an agenda that has nothing to do with ours. There's poison that could spread out from Belfast if we let it, but we won't.[97]

Adair, it was widely assumed, would be held in prison for an extended period. His release on licence had been revoked by the Secretary of State only after he had seen a lengthy submission from the RUC's Chief Constable documenting his role in the current Loyalist feud as well as his part in co-ordinating attacks on nationalist areas. There were also press reports that the RUC Financial Investigation Unit was about to look into Adair's financial assets under the Proceeds of Crime Order, via which he could face further prosecution if he could not provide an adequate explanation of his income sources.[98] The police also let it be known that they were in receipt of an increasing flow of confidential information from the Lower Shankill which would assist their inquiries.[99]

From their point of view, Adair's continued detention could be justified because of this inquiry, as well as because of continued violence arising from the events of August. Even if this violence subsided, which it took time to do, they could argue that it was because Adair was safely locked up in Maghaberry prison. If it worsened, the case for holding him was even stronger. None of this deterred Gina Adair from pressing for her husband's release. On 9 September she picketed 10 Downing Street, accompanied, among others, by Thomas Potts, a convicted C Company gunman who figured prominently on video film footage of the violence outside the Rex bar.[100] She was also supported by London-based well-wishers to the UDA as well as members of Combat 18, the Neo-Nazi organisation notorious for its racist attacks in English cities.[101]

The end of October 2000 brought another death, that of 21-year-old David Greer, a UDA member, who on the night of the twenty-ninth was involved with others in a fight with the UVF in the Tigers Bay area. Soon afterwards he was found shot dead in Mountcollyer Street, a forbidding place where most homes were boarded up and abandoned, and those that were still occupied had wire mesh protecting their windows. Billy Hutchinson of the PUP claimed that in the aftermath of this killing people were being intimidated out of their homes by the UDA/UFF's use of what he called 'fascist' methods in response to the killing. The Housing Executive confirmed that some families had sought its help in finding new accommodation though not as many as Hutchinson had claimed.[102]

Greer's murder happened as secret talks to end UDA/UFF violence were held by representatives of the two organisations, though on the day before his death, the UDA's Inner Council had given out a statement dismissing reports of any early breakthrough being possible.[103] The killing was brutally avenged three days later. The chosen victim was 63-year-old Bertie Rice, who, before emigrating to South Africa in 1980, had been active in the UVF. He returned to Belfast only in 1999 and became involved with the PUP. At midday on 31 October, masked men broke into his home off North Queen Street and gave him a severe beating with baseball bats before one shot was fired into his upper body, in front of his wife. Rice died three hours later in the Royal Victoria Hospital following emergency surgery.

Nobody was in any doubt that this had been the UDA's work, though John White went through the motions of calling it 'deplorable'.[104] Retaliation came within a mere three hours, when Tommy English was shot dead in his home in Newtonabbey on the north side of Belfast. He too was attacked in front of his wife and children. For several years English had been a senior figure in the UDA's North Belfast brigade but had involved himself in political work and had been one of the UDA negotiating team in the talks prior to the 1998 Belfast Agreement as well as one of its delegation to Washington a few weeks earlier. He also had a violent reputation and at the time of his death was on bail and awaiting trial for his part in an attack on the Crow's Nest bar in the city's waterfront area.

The Crow's Nest had become a meeting place for gay men, and English and two friends had been charged the previous year with wrecking the premises and assaulting staff and customers with baseball bats a short time after being refused service. One victim of this incident, John Maskey, a quiet and inoffensive man, suffered severe injuries and traumatic shock. He later left Belfast and was reported five years later to have taken his own life.[105]

The UDA hit back with minimal delay, battering their way into the Rathcoole home of Mark Quail, aged twenty-six, and shooting him dead. His girlfriend, mother of his two children, was in the house but was unharmed.

Since his childhood, Quail had been a member of the UVF-linked Shore Road No Surrender Flute Band and had been involved three years previously in a Portadown bar fight with LVF members over which he still faced charges.[106] Another attack on a victim with UVF connections followed the next day but this time the killers only wounded Colin Gough in the butcher's shop where he worked on the Oldpark Road.[107]

The concentrated ferocity of this cycle of Loyalist killing simply added to North Belfast's existing problems. Traditionally a religiously mixed area, it had been ravaged by the Troubles, as a result of which the mix had changed with more Catholics moving in. New barriers and peace walls had to be erected and added to after the 1994 ceasefires as communal suspicions and prejudices seemed to harden. A survey by a University of Ulster social scientist published a little earlier documented in depressing detail the way crudely sectarian criteria dominated people's choices on where they lived, shopped and socialised.[108] A raw reminder of this, early in October 2000, was the decision of Translink, the city bus authority, to withdraw school services to the Shankill, Glencairn and Ballygomartin areas which had to pass up the Crumlin Road.

Stone-throwing attacks by Protestant pupils injured several girls from Our Lady of Mercy Secondary School as their bus passed up the Ballysillan Road on 3 October. Retaliation followed against pupils from the Boys Model School and a substantial force of police with armoured vehicles had to be used to escort pupils from school on foot up the Crumlin Road past the Ardoyne interface after their buses had been withdrawn. Even when the buses were restored to their school routes police escorts were still felt to be necessary.[109]

Teenagers, especially boys caught up in these clashes, were always open to the lure of the Loyalist organisations and one minister, the Reverend John Dickinson of Seaview Presbyterian Church, located midway between the UDA stronghold of Tiger's Bay and the UVF-dominated Mount Vernon estate, admitted in an interview to the existence of what he described as 'a much more perceptible paramilitary presence then there was when I came here thirteen years ago'.[110]

The current feud, Dickinson agreed, could spiral out of control, but he drew encouragement from new reports of UDA and UVF representatives being back in contact with each other. There was hope, too, in the fact that, as in August, the UDA as a whole was not involved in the ongoing violence. However, C Company, even with their leader in prison, felt free to operate and kill outside their West Belfast brigade area. Meanwhile, the dead still had to be buried, all of them in the same windswept cemetery, Carnmoney, with its panoramic view of Belfast Lough.

As always, the funerals were highly political events and shows of strength by both organisations. Once again, Frank McCoubrey, the Deputy Lord Mayor, came under attack for being present at a paramilitary occasion and for helping to carry Tommy English's coffin, flanked by a masked guard of honour in combat kit. His reply was the honest one that the dead man had been a friend.[111] Among the mourners were Paul Burton and Tim Carew, two Irish peace activists who had travelled up from Dublin. They later wrote of the welcome they were given at the wake for English, whom they had met and in fact liked, at conflict resolution courses as well as on a pilgrimage to the killing fields of the First World War, where they took part in the dedication of an all-Ireland memorial and peace park at Messines in Belgium.[112]

They did not claim any special sanctity for English, which would have been hard to do for someone with his record and the charges still pending against him at the time of his death. Yet they were ready to think of him as someone who could change and who, as they put it, 'had started on a long journey which was never straight or smooth'.[113] Their reception at his funeral 'told its own story of the decency and openness of our neighbours in the North – even in their worst moments of shock and grief. Maybe the real hidden Ulster, including the neglected and sometimes demonised streets of Tiger's Bay, has reserves of hope and courage that will yet see us all through to a better future.'[114]

The four funerals created a respite within which UDA–UVF talks continued. Gary McMichael and David Ervine used their influence, a diminishing commodity in the former's case, to encourage continued contact, and John 'Bunter' Graham, the UVF's commandant, was able to talk down hardliners who thought C Company of the UDA could simply be 'taken out'.[115] A truce was announced on 22 November and three weeks later a joint UDA–UVF statement spoke of an 'open-ended and all-encompassing cessation of hostilities.'[116]

This was followed by claims that a structure had been put in place to deal with future problems between the two parties. In a revival of a system used in the 1970s, each promised to appoint 'provost marshals' to act for individual companies in their own areas in response to any renewed violence. 'If that fails,' a Sunday newspaper was told soon after the ceasefire, 'it is moved further up the command structure and there is the possibility of it going to the very top, but at all times the discussions will be between representatives of both or all of the organisations involved.'[117] The word 'all' was a way of including the Red Hand Commando, which for all practical purposes had joined the UVF, while retaining its own identity, back in 1972.

The provost marshals, whose designation was borrowed from British army usage, were for the most part men able and willing to hand out severe beatings to anyone transgressing the ceasefire's terms or, in the case of the UDA's C Company, doing anything that might undermine the lucrative drug-dealing which went on under its jurisdiction. In fact, not long before the December ceasefire, Johnny Adair's own son Jonathan, or 'Jay' as he was often called, was badly beaten up not far from his home, after a robbery at an old age pensioner's dwelling nearby. RUC inquiries cast no light on what had happened. The UVF denied any involvement and one senior UDA man thought it might have been a case of mistaken identity by one of the organisation's punishment units. Jay Adair was left with a broken arm and leg in a brutal reminder of what vigilante justice from the UDA could mean.[118]

The premonition that any settlement, even a temporary one, of Loyalist enmities could lead to new attacks on the Catholic community was not far from the thoughts of its political spokesmen. 'Turning on the Taigs' had served before as a way of healing Loyalist rifts so only two days after the ceasefire, Pastor Jack McKee, a born-again Christian evangelist, felt he had to reassure Catholics. Well known on the Shankill for his commitment to the area and for his condemnation of paramilitary violence, he voiced his confidence that the ceasefire could hold while accepting that the LVF had not put their names to it. 'The Loyalist paramilitaries do not feel the need to make any statement to the nationalist community,' he argued. 'They are committed to the ceasefire and the peace process. The present feud had nothing to do with the peace process. Now they have resolved their differences, I don't think any statement to that effect needs to be given.'[119]

Others were not so sure. During the feud pipe and fire bomb attacks on Catholic homes in Belfast and elsewhere had continued. In Larne, police reported sectarian attacks, many of them on the mixed Seacourt estate. These, apart from bombings, included assaults, criminal damage, intimidation and incidents in which firearms had been produced. Not all the victims were Catholics, though most of the arrests and charges were of Loyalists and a superintendent in the RUC told the press that a total of 198 'anti-sectarian patrols and operations' had been carried out over the year.[120]

The Loyalist paramilitaries and especially the UDA were in fact still recruiting strongly from a new generation of working-class teenagers only too ready for violence and with increasingly easy access to drugs and alcohol. Only three months into the ceasefire, Jackie McDonald accepted that the UDA's youth wing, the UYM, had dropped its age of recruitment to fourteen because so many wanted to join. 'We're taking hundreds in South Belfast alone,' he told a journalist. 'They are growing up in a void and we've got to keep control and give them a sense of identity. We're not teaching them to shoot and bomb, we're trying to educate them about history, computers, job skills. Most of us were sceptical about this agreement [the 1998 Belfast Agreement] from the start and all six UDA brigades are against it now, but we do want peace.'[121] The atmosphere at the John McMichael Centre in Sandy Row, where McDonald could be located for interviews, bore out some of what he said, with its busy office and shop selling books and pamphlets on Loyalist history.

He also justified, though, the presence of the huge mural at the opposite end of the street. Inscribed on a bright yellow background and covering an entire gable wall, it helpfully advised visitors: 'You are now entering Loyalist Sandy Row, heartland of South Belfast Ulster Freedom Fighters.' The masked and armed figure on the mural still had as much allure for many young Loyalists as job skill courses and work placement schemes. The mural would never have gone up without McDonald's authorisation, given his seniority in the UDA, and in fact he was an effective brigadier who kept some real control over drug-dealing in his area and tried to hold young people back from sectarian confrontations. He could also talk seriously and intelligently about Loyalism's longer-term need to find a political role. However, his brigade area was only one of six and he needed little reminding of the need to keep a close eye on the others, not least West Belfast, where, on the Lower Shankill, Johnny Adair's writ still ran.

NOTES

1. K. Eide, 'Were the Northern Ireland media used as a tool to sell the Belfast Agreement?', unpublished B.A. Honours dissertation, Napier University 2001, pp. 14, 21.
2. Ibid., pp. 36–8.
3. S. Duddy, interview with author, 21 May 1998.
4. G. McMichael, interview with author, 9 February 2000.
5. *New Ulster Defender*, vol. 5, no. 5, 1998.
6. Ibid.
7. G. McMichael, *An Ulster Voice: In Search of Common Ground in Northern Ireland* (Boulder, CO/Dublin: Roberts Rinehart, 1999), p. 222.
8. Duddy, interview with author, 6 July 1998.
9. McMichael, interview with author.
10. Ibid.
11. *Fortnight*, December 1998–January 1999.
12. McMichael, interview with author.
13. *Guardian*, 7 November, 1998.
14. J. Cusack and H. McDonald, *UVF* (Dublin: Poolbeg, 1997), pp. 380–1.
15. *Irish News*, 4 November 1998.
16. *Irish News*, 28 November 1998.
17. *Independent*, 16 March 1999.
18. West Belfast UDA member, conversation with author, 9 April 1999. See also *Scotsman*, 12 April 1999.
19. *Observer*, 21 March 1999.
20. *Irish News*, 2 December 1999.
21. West Belfast UDA member, interview with author; *Scotsman*, 12 April 1999.
22. *Irish News*, 25 May 1999.
23. *Sunday Times*, 11 July 1999.
24. D. Ervine, interview with author, 6 May 2003.
25. R. Garland, *Gusty Spence* (Belfast: Blackstaff Press, 2001), pp. 243–6.
26. M. Dillon, *The Shankill Butchers: A Case Study of Mass Murder* (London: Hutchinson, 1989), pp. 158–61.
27. *Ulster*, December 1986.
28. *Combat*, vol. 7, no. 3, 1988.
29. Cusack and McDonald, *UVF*, pp. 244–5.
30. Ibid., pp. 284–5.

31. *Sunday Life*, 19 May 1996.
32. *Irish News*, 23 April 1997.
33. *Sunday Life*, 30 March 1997.
34. J. Gregg, interview with author, 16 October 2002.
35. *Irish News*, 30 October 1997.
36. *Warrior*, no. 12, 1998.
37. *Scotsman*, 12 April 1999.
38. J. White, *A Brief History of the UDA/UFF in Contemporary Conflict* (Belfast, 1999), p. 53.
39. Ibid.
40. *Irish News*, 15 September 1999.
41. Ibid.
42. Ervine, interview with author.
43. J. McDonald, interview with author, 7 October 2003.
44. *Irish News*, 25 May 1999.
45. J. Adair, letter to author, 10 November 2004.
46. *Irish News*, 29 January 2000.
47. Ibid.
48. Ibid.
49. J. White, interview with author, 10 February 2001.
50. D. Godson, *Himself Alone: David Trimble and the Ordeal of Unionism* (London: HarperCollins, 2004) p. 76.
51. J. Brown, former RUC detective sergeant, interview with author, 6 May 2003.
52. *An Phoblacht/Republican News*, 12 February 2004.
53. D. Lister and H. Jordan, *Mad Dog: The Rise and Fall of Johnny Adair and 'C' Company* (Edinburgh: Mainstream, 2003); H. McDonald and J. Cusack, *UDA: Inside the Heart of Loyalist Terror* (Dublin: Penguin Ireland, 2004).
54. *Observer*, 27 February 2000.
55. *Irish News*, 22 February 2000.
56. *Sunday World*, 23 April 2000.
57. *Irish News*, 26 July 2000.
58. *Sunday World*, 23 April 2000.
59. Ibid.
60. Ibid.
61. Ibid.
62. *Irish News*, 27 May 2000.
63. *Irish News*, 17 June 2000.
64. Ibid.
65. *Irish News*, 23 June 2000.
66. Adair, letter to author, 8 November 2004.
67. *Sunday World*, 9 July 2000.
68. Ibid.
69. White, interview with author, 11 July 2000.
70. Ibid.
71. Adair, interview with author, 11 July 2000.
72. *Irish News*, 18 July 2000.

73. *Guardian*, 25 July 2000.
74. *Sunday World*, 13 August 2000.
75. Ibid.
76. *Guardian*, 16 July 2000.
77. *Sunday World*, 20 July 2000.
78. Duddy, interview with author, 23 August 2000.
79. *Irish News*, 17 August 2000.
80. Adair, letter to author, 18 April 2004.
81. C. McGimpsey, interview with author, 28 August 2000.
82. *Independent*, 23 August 2000.
83. Lister and Jordan, *Mad Dog*, pp. 230–1.
84. *Combat*, Special Edition, 2000.
85. *Irish News*, 29 August 2000.
86. *Scotsman*, 25 August 2000.
87. *Combat*, no. 24, 2004.
88. Duddy, interview with author, 23 August 2000.
89. Ibid.
90. White, interview with author, 28 August 2000.
91. *Sunday World*, 27 August 2000.
92. Ibid., 3 September 2000.
93. *Irish News*, 15 September 2000.
94. *Irish News*, 30 August 2000.
95. Ibid.
96. *Irish News*, 31 August 2000.
97. J. Wright, conversation with author, 3 September 2000.
98. *Observer*, 10 September 2000.
99. *Sunday World*, 17 September 2000.
100. *Observer*, 10 September 2000.
101. *An Phoblacht/Republican News*, 14 September 2000.
102. *Irish News*, 31 October 2000.
103. *Irish News*, 30 October 2000.
104. *Irish News*, 1 November 2000.
105. *Sunday World*, 28 November 2004.
106. D. McKittrick, S. Kelters, B. Feeney and C. Thornton, *Lost Lives: The Stories of the Men, Women and Children Who Died as a Result of Northern Ireland's Troubles*, rev. edn (Edinburgh: Mainstream, 2004), pp. 1486–7.
107. *Irish News*, 3 November 2000.
108. P. Shirlow, 'Space, place and politics in Northern Ireland', *Political Geography*, vol. 17, 1998.
109. *Irish News*, 4, 5, 6, 7, 9 and 10 October 2000.
110. *Sunday World*, 5 November 2000.
111. *Irish News*, 6 November 2000.
112. *Sunday World*, 12 November 2000.
113. Ibid.
114. Ibid.
115. *Irish News*, 23 November 2000.

116. *Guardian*, 16 December 2000; also *Irish News*, 16 December 2000.
117. *Sunday World*, 17 December 2000.
118. *Sunday World*, 26 November 2000.
119. *Irish News*, 18 December 2000.
120. *Irish News*, 22 November2000.
121. *Guardian*, 3 April 2001.

11

Endgame for Johnny Adair

Mark Quail, who was buried with UFF honours on 7 November 2000, was the year's last victim of the hostilities unleashed by events in late August. His family issued a statement calling for an end to the Loyalist feud: 'Let Mark be the last one to leave a father and mother without a son and children without their father.'[1] Many such appeals had been made before by those bereaved by the Troubles and UDA/UVF attacks on each other did indeed stop. Only four weeks later, however, gunmen struck again, on Hesketh Road close to Ardoyne. Their victim was a Protestant taxi driver, Trevor Kell, who had begun work for a local firm only the previous night. Forensic tests showed that the bullet which killed the victim came from the same ammunition used by the IRA to shoot dead two RUC officers in Lurgan four and a half years earlier.

For Loyalists, the killing of a Protestant in such an area could only seem sectarian and it was avenged the very next day, 6 December. The victim was Gary Moore, a young Catholic building worker from Limavady who was employed on a contract on the Monkstown estate in North Belfast. Fifteen minutes later, another Catholic only just escaped death when gunmen opened fire on his taxi in Oldpark Road.

A murder twelve days later was again widely believed to be the UDA's work. James Rockett, the cousin of a victim of the Loyalist feud in August, staggered drunkenly out of a club in Rathcoole and was found the next day in the Ballysillan area, dead from a gunshot wound in the head, though he had also received a vicious beating before being shot. Rockett, found with £2,000 in notes in his pockets, had a lengthy criminal record which had caused him to fall foul of the UDA. He had taken refuge from them in Portadown but found few friends there.[2] His return to Belfast sealed his fate.

The last Troubles-related death of the year was at least a peaceful one. It was that of a man whose life and work had been a shining contrast to that of the increasingly nihilistic violence of the Loyalist paramilitaries. He was Ronnie Hill, the much loved former head of Enniskillen High School, who had been in a coma since soon after he was rescued, with terrible injuries, from the debris of the IRA's Remembrance Sunday bomb attack at the town's war memorial thirteen years earlier. He was one more of the IRA's 1,781 victims, twice as many as those of the UDA and UFF combined.

As a new year began, it was business as usual for many UDA units, something made clear in an excoriating newspaper article by Ed Moloney, who had been for many years a tireless observer of the paramilitary scene.[3] The police were, it is true, taking a tougher and more active stance on building site extortion and the running of drinking clubs which flouted licensing laws. By 2001, the UDA owned only one of these in the Shankill area. Its biggest and most lucrative venue, in Langley Street, had been closed as far back as 1996 after a large-scale RUC raid. Other income sources, such as the sale of stolen alcohol and money-lending at punitive interest rates and with often brutal consequences for those slow to pay back, continued and expanded, as did drug-dealing and, it was increasingly suspected, organised prostitution run by leading members of Johnny Adair's C Company.

Some UDA commanders could be strikingly casual about letting the organisation's cash reserves be seen. The author can recall arriving for an interview with Jackie McDonald a little later than this period, in the Sandy Row office he often worked from. He, as South Belfast brigadier, it should be repeated, took a much tougher line on drug-dealing than was the case elsewhere in the UDA, but on this occasion, with two young helpers, he was counting out on a table what could have been £2,000, which he described as the 'flag fund' though he did not elaborate on the source of the fund.[4]

The year's killing by the UDA began with a death that seemed to confirm what Moloney had written in his article. The victim, George or 'Geordie' Legge, was a man with a violent reputation who had for a time been in command of the East Belfast brigade of the organisation and had been implicated in several murders. Like others, he had been drawn into drug-dealing but a dispute over money raised from this source led to his expulsion from the UDA. This may have been the chance that enemies within it were waiting for as Legge was thought to have set up the 1992 killing of Ned McCreery, at one time a senior and much feared figure in East Belfast.

On the night of 5 January, Legge was lured to the Bunch of Grapes bar in East Belfast, where Jim Craig had been shot dead in 1998, though it was then called the Castle Inn. His body was later found beside a country road near Caryduff with multiple stab wounds and the head almost severed. Like Rockett three weeks before, Legge had a substantial sum of money on him but the Inner Council was still enraged that such a death could be inflicted on a former brigadier and ordered a full turn-out at his funeral. This was obeyed, except by the West Belfast Brigade.[5] Some thought Legge wanted revenge for his own demotion. One of those was McDonald, who later said:

> I knew Geordie Legge very well. We went a long way back and Geordie was a good
> Loyalist but he lost his way. He had plans to take out a senior figure in the organi-
> sation and that sealed his fate, but there was a time when he was well rated and had
> respect.[6]

Nineteen more killings followed in 2001 and the UDA were involved in several of them. On 3 April, Trevor Lowry, a 49-year-old father of two, died from a frenzied beating administered near the centre of Glengormley, a suburb on the north side of Belfast which had seen an insidious growth of sectarian tension. Lowry was a quiet man, known for his enjoyment of visits to the nearby Belfast zoo, who was making his way home from a bar when his assailants set upon him, mistaking him for a Catholic. Two and a half years later two men were convicted of his murder. One was a teenager who may have been a mere bystander but the other was Harry Speers, who had led the Ulster Young Militants in Glengormley. A Loyalist source described his role as being 'to groom teenagers into the mainstream UDA'.[7] Speers had been sentenced to seven years in prison in 1989 for armed robbery.

On 23 June a young Catholic, John Henry McCormack, was shot dead in his Coleraine home by two masked gunmen. He died in front of his two children as well as a niece and nephew.[8] His partner linked the killing to the UDA but the murdered man had been due to give Crown Court evidence in a forthcoming case arising from a UFF shooting in the feud of the previous summer. Less than ten days later, Ciaran Cummings, a nineteen-year-old Catholic awaiting an early morning lift to work in Newtonabbey, died at the roadside from shots fired by the pillion passenger on a motorcycle. What bore all the hallmarks of another sectarian killing was claimed by the Red Hand Defenders, which many took to be simply a cover name for the UDA. Police, however, had their suspicions that it might have been a case of the UFF using an identical flag of convenience.

Three weeks later Gavin Brett, an eighteen-year-old Protestant who had Catholic friends, was cut down by gunfire from a passing car as he stood talking to a member of St Enda's Gaelic Athletic Association club just outside the building. The club had been attacked before and had members murdered, but Brett died because his killers assumed he must be a Catholic. Again, they used the Red Hand Defenders name when they claimed the killing. Brett was yet another victim of the worsening sectarian atmosphere across North Belfast, although at his funeral and at joint church services in his memory, his friendship with Catholics was held up as a model for the area.[9] Police on the case worked on the assumption that the gunmen had UDA links though nobody was ever charged with the killing.

The protective cloak of the Red Hand Defenders name was used three more times before the end of the year. On 28 September, LVF gunmen murdered the *Sunday World* reporter Martin O'Hagan near his home in Lurgan and on 3 December, they shot dead a Catholic drug dealer, Frankie Mulholland. His killers believed he had double-crossed them over a transaction which required him to distribute and sell Loyalist-bought drugs in nationalist areas of Belfast.

The UDA, also using the Red Hand Defenders label, claimed their final victim of the year at 6.15 on the morning of 12 December. He was William Stobie, a short, bald and fat man aged fifty-one, an easy target for the lone gunman who lay in wait for him outside the bleak complex of flats he lived in on the Loyalist Forthriver estate. The five shots which killed him alerted his partner, who ran out from their ground-floor flat to hold him as he died. Stobie's days in were in fact numbered. He had been a member of the UDA with the rank of quartermaster, acquiring, hiding and making available weapons as and when they were needed without necessarily being told who the targets were. This had been his role in the murder of Pat Finucane in February 1989, but by then he had also become a police informer though by no means the only one in the UDA's Belfast brigades.

In November of 2001 he was brought to trial for his part in that murder but the case against him collapsed when a Belfast journalist who was a key witness was excused from giving evidence because of his fragile mental state.[10] Stobie then made some ill-advised statements to the media, culminating in an Ulster Television appearance in which he appeared to support an inquiry into the Finucane murder. By then it was anybody's guess as to which of his enemies would get to him first and he ignored police warnings about his safety. According to some reports he preferred, having for a time worked for C Company, to accept assurances about his safety from the imprisoned Johnny Adair.[11]

Stobie, on his own admission close to the time of his death, had become a pawn in a brutal game beyond his own control. During a secret meeting with one reporter, he joked grimly that he felt safer in nationalist areas of the city than in Loyalist ones.[12] His death was a clinical execution by an organisation which was no stranger to infiltration by security forces but which would not forgive anyone who appeared to give support to the case for an inquiry into the Finucane killing. As John White put it, in words which effectively justified Stobie's murder:

> By going on TV and making a broadcast about his involvement he created quite a lot of anger. On top of that he supported the inquiry into the killing of Pat Finucane. Most people within Loyalism see this as republicanism taking advantage of the death of Pat Finucane to undermine the credibility of the RUC and also undermine Northern Ireland as an entity.[13]

The total number of killings for 2001 was of course small in comparison with the worst years of the Troubles but it needs to be seen in the context of a relentless worsening in sectarian confrontations and attacks both at interface areas in Belfast and in smaller towns outside it. In January alone hardly a night went by without such incidents, thirty-five of which, with likely Loyalist involvement, were reported, and this pattern maintained itself for much of the year. Protestant homes and localities also came under attack but the police were in no doubt about the degree to which Loyalists and the UDA in particular were behind many of the incidents.

At many interface areas and in towns such as Larne and Carrickfergus, Catholic families took to sleeping in back rooms and attics for their overnight safety as well as keeping basins and buckets of water ready in case of petrol bomb attacks alternating with the even deadlier pipe bomb favoured by Loyalists. On 14 January 2002, the RUC's Chief Constable, Sir Ronnie Flanagan, stated that he had little doubt that in Larne the UDA was behind most of the ongoing attacks on Catholics there. He went on, however, to add that suggestions that the violence was centrally co-ordinated 'would misrepresent the situation' and he described the UDA 'as a loose collection of individuals'.[14] While it was true that nobody was exercising the kind of overall control of the UDA in the way Andy Tyrie had done in the 1970s and 1980s, few doubted that brigade areas such as West Belfast, especially its C Company, as well as South East Antrim, were quite literally calling the shots.

Attacks were very often the work of the teenage foot soldiers raised from the UYM and referred to in the previous chapter but their efforts were not unco-ordinated and could be turned on and off. Danny O'Connor, the young SDLP Assembly member for Larne and also a local councillor, suffered numerous attacks both on the local advice centre he worked from and on his home. He had little hesitation in blaming them on a new intake of youthful UDA recruits in the town.

Larne and Carrickfergus, like Ballymena, lay within the UDA's South East Antrim brigade area, where it claimed to have thirteen companies and 400 men. Its brigadier, John 'Grugg' Gregg, interviewed by the author three months before being shot dead by fellow Loyalists, had no problem about justifying necessary action to defend what he saw as a Protestant community increasingly under siege, with Belfast suburbs such as Glengormley having already 'gone nationalist' through rehousing and population movement. Any 'greening' of Antrim towns where Protestants still comprised the majority, let alone his own Rathcoole power base, was something which he was pledged to fight by any means necessary. 'Look at the White City estate just down the road from here,' he told the author. 'The people there, our people, get hassle every night, abuse, threats, stones and petrol bombs too from Catholic gangs on either side of them. But do the media report it? Those people are going nowhere. It's a Loyalist estate and that's the way it's going to stay, whatever it takes. We'll see to it. Retreats have to stop somewhere.'[15]

Gregg had a formidable reputation for violence towards anyone who crossed him and took pride in a tattoo of the Grim Reaper which covered most of his back. Unusually for Loyalists, he had studied Open University courses while in prison:

> We didn't all just pump iron in the gym. That's what the Provos put out about us but it's true that a lot of our boys did think that studying was for Fenians. I did my weights in the gym but I took courses as well. I had a run-in though with one tutor who marked me down on an essay on a community art project. I did a design of a shackled prisoner, to represent Loyalist Ulster but this fellow rubbished it. An OU counsellor though told me it was good.[16]

It would possibly have required very determined tutors to mark Gregg's work down too regularly.

Gregg's studies did little to dilute his hard-line views. While in prison he became strongly sympathetic to the Afrikaner cause in South Africa and also with that of Israel. This latter affinity distanced him, however, from the National Front. Like others in the UDA, though never more than a minority within it, he had made some contacts with them but was put off by the crudity of their anti-Semitism. In conversation he was much happier to describe his role as 'military' although he was prepared to discuss Ulster independence:

> I'd like to think we could achieve it, but there's the economics, isn't there? Mind you, it would be better than a united Ireland. It would be a Doomsday choice. For most of our boys here it would be too big a jump.[17]

The huge Rathcoole estate which was Gregg's fiefdom had originated as a mixed housing development in the 1960s but the onset of the Troubles soon changed this. Many Catholic families, like that of Bobby Sands, who had played with Protestants in a local football club,[18] were forced out and many Loyalist families from the Shankill with UDA allegiances moved in to replace them. As the Troubles worsened along with rising unemployment and social problems related to it, the UDA visibly tightened its control and the area acquired an intimidating reputation. Such private housing as there was spiralled downwards in value to the point where, by the mid-1990s, a family bungalow could be bought for under £8,000.

Local people had to learn to live with the reality of UDA power and Gregg had been an automatic choice for the position of South-East Antrim brigadier on his release from prison. He exercised much of his power from the Alpha social club, previously the Eastway cinema, where important UDA meetings were often held and it was always used as the rallying point for Remembrance Sunday band parades. The club was very clearly a place in which Gregg gave the orders to young and not-so-young Loyalists who congregated there. They included the Cloughfern Young Conquerors Flute Band, which used the club for practice sessions in which Gregg would join on the bass drum when his busy schedule permitted.

Gregg made little attempt to deny the UDA's readiness to kill. Asked by the author about the murder of Gavin Brett in late July 2001, his reply was straightforward and less than apologetic.

> That was a mistake we made. He was a Prod but he hung around with pals outside St. Enda's GAA club, nearly all of them Catholics. We knew that club was a pick-up point for republicans to be driven to interface areas like the White City and Glenbryn for attacks on our people. We'd checked it out, so the young fella Brett got it for being in the wrong place at the wrong time.[19]

On the issue of rampant drug-dealing on an estate where, with his power, he might have acted to stop it, Gregg was reluctant to be drawn. A leading UDA member in Ballymena was, however, prepared to give a view on this:

> I've a good relationship with Grugg but he's a tough bastard, as hard as nails. Nobody fucks him around. You'd only try it once. But with the drug business it's like this. Some of our brigades are actively involved, no question, but not all. They'll just look the other way. It's there but it's very hard to control, so we make sure a share of the takings comes our way. It's as simple as that.[20]

Not everyone in the area thought it was as simple as that. Mark Langhammer, grandson of a Socialist printer who had found refuge in Northern Ireland after defying the Nazis in the pre-war Sudetenland, was an independent Labour councillor in Newtonabbey, which incorporated the Rathcoole estate. His work brought him close to some of the havoc wreaked by drug-dealing and he campaigned tenaciously for a police presence on an estate which lacked a permanent station. His call for, at the very least, a 'police clinic' where local people might go with their problems was a challenge to the power of Gregg, who, on his own admission, hated police as much as he hated prison officers, 'for turning on their own and then expecting to live in Protestant areas'.[21] Langhammer's courage exposed him to a programme of intimidation, culminating in the destruction of his car outside his home in September 2002.

A year later, Langhammer had little doubt that the bomb used in this attack had been planted on Gregg's orders.

> My move to bring the police into the area, even half-day community clinics and workshops, was a threat. He saw it as a case of me posing a threat to his turf. Gregg wasn't in fact the worst of them, in the sense that he didn't live lavishly or push his money in your face, but he believed everything he said about the UDA's need to keep control. The bomb was a message, a warning shot from them to me.[22]

Tension in Rathcoole and other Loyalist areas rose steadily in the early summer of 2001. As so often, the parade by the Orange Order at Drumcree was a factor, though violence there in response to yet another ban on it going down the Garvaghy Road was much less than in previous years. Once again, C Company of the West Belfast UDA turned up in strength to support the protest but the prison authorities at Maghaberry kept Johnny Adair locked up in his cell and forbade him access to the media for comments which might have inflamed the situation.[23] Another massive operation by the security forces averted serious trouble at Drumcree, though on the night of 11 July in Portadown, police came under petrol and blast bomb attacks.

This violence was overshadowed by events on the Twelfth itself and in Belfast as Orange lodges from the north side of the city made their journey homeward in the evening up the Crumlin Road past Ardoyne but certainly not through it, as Republicans and their well-wishers in the overseas media were quick to claim. The early morning 'feeder' parade to join the main event starting from Carlisle Circus passed off without incident but at night the police had to hold back nationalist protests and what had every appearance of a well-orchestrated and prepared riot erupted. Two blast bombs and 263 petrol bombs were thrown, injuring 113 police officers and ten local people.

Leading Republicans, such as Sean Kelly, the 1993 Shankill bomber, were observed at the scene along with Brendan McFarlane, who had helped organise the dramatic 1983 break-out of IRA prisoners from the Maze. Both were seen using walkie-talkie radios at the height of the violence.[24] Kelly's presence was a particular provocation to Protestants, especially those living in the Upper Ardoyne enclave of Glenbryn, just across Alliance Avenue. Video camera footage of Kelly's role was later handed over to police by the press, leading to calls for the revocation of his release from prison, as had happened to Adair.[25]

No police action was taken against Kelly, though the Chief Constable, Sir Ronnie Flanagan, confirmed that IRA involvement in the events of the night of the Twelfth would be fully investigated.[26] To many, it was simply proof that in flashpoint areas like Ardoyne, communal violence was akin to a tap which could be turned on or off when the IRA wanted. That said, tension in Ardoyne had been high for several months since the murder of local taxi driver Trevor Kell, which Glenbryn Protestants and the police attributed to the IRA. Floral tributes to him were vandalised and, as the marching season got under way, Glenbryn Loyalists decked out their small area with more flags than ever.

This was, of course, a gesture of defiance against Republican Ardoyne from people who had suffered much in the Troubles and were still under regular attack from an enemy who were also their near neighbours. A security fence along the back of Alliance Avenue was insufficient to prevent these attacks, the proof of which was there in Glenbryn for journalists who wanted to see it in the form of damaged and boarded-up houses. What drove local tension to breaking point, however, was an incident in the afternoon of 19 June, when a car raced from Republican Ardoyne up the Ardoyne Road and rammed a ladder being used by a Loyalist to hang UDA flags on a lamp post beside the Holy Cross Catholic girls' primary school, which lay just a few hundred yards within Glenbryn.

Violent clashes immediately followed which brought people onto the streets in great numbers, and a large police presence was needed to separate the crowds. All this coincided with school closing time and the arrival of Catholic parents to collect Holy Cross pupils, only to find the school blockaded by angry Protestants. By Thursday, 21 June, after sustained rioting, police were advising the parents not to risk the short journey from their homes to the school and in fact only sixty out of the 230 pupils attended lessons that day.[27]

This violence came against a backdrop of high political tension. Once again, the peace process was on a knife edge. David Trimble talked of resigning as head of the power-sharing executive unless there was real movement by

1 July from the IRA over arms-decommissioning. Sinn Fein's response was to press its own demand for police reform and 'demilitarisation' of the province. The school holidays removed Holy Cross and its pupils temporarily from the spotlight as the usual tensions of July took over but the new school session in August saw an intensified Loyalist picket which lasted into the following year.

The sickening scenes which accompanied it were relayed on television footage around the world. Local camera crews and reporters hardened by the Troubles were shocked at the missiles and obscene taunts directed at small and terrified girls by some, and on occasion by many, of the protesters as pupils and parents made the daily journey to Holy Cross up the Ardoyne Road under massive protection from police and soldiers. They received no thanks for their work and the danger they faced in doing it from Sinn Fein spokesmen such as Gerry Kelly, who was regularly in attendance to talk to the media. Young Scottish soldiers to whom the author talked at the time admitted to being severely shaken by what they had seen and heard, especially the language used by women to two local priests, Father Aidan Troy and a younger colleague, who every day accompanied those parents, by no means all of them, who chose to brave the protest with their children.[28]

To call Holy Cross an own goal for Loyalism was an obvious understatement and some Glenbryn residents drawn into the protests could see this. One of them was Andy Cooper, a parent himself and a member of the Concerned Residents of Upper Ardoyne group. He described his community as living in its 200 homes under constant siege, unable to use the local shops or library without sectarian taunts. He also voiced his feelings about the school protests to a journalist after a massive police and army operation, carried out in the face of serious violence on Monday, 3 September, to keep the road to Holy Cross open and to hold back protesters behind solid walls of perspex shields.

> People say this is about children going up to school, but we've no problem with them – the problem's with the parents. The children are being used as human shields, allowing known Republicans to go up with them and taunt us. On Monday there was a group of seventy known Republicans who had no reason to be here, who weren't parents of the children, who were just here to goad us. One of them was a bomber out on licence and, as we were standing here, he threatened us: 'There'll be another Shankill bomb here.'
>
> This interface area is an open sore and Republicans are just rubbing salt into the wound. I grew up in Derry at the start of the Troubles, and the area where I was born is now nationalist. We feel 'greening' is now going on in North Belfast. They want our houses and they want us out.
>
> I'm totally sickened by what's happened – but the feeling before this was that we had to protest in some way. We feel what happened on Monday was propaganda. It was a media circus the moment Ronnie Flanagan said he'd get the children through. We know we've lost the PR battle, but people are so desperate they've gone beyond that.[29]

UDA members were without any doubt involved in the violence. Some of them were 'exiles' from the Shankill after the Loyalist bloodletting of the previous year. One of these was Jim Potts, whose brother had been caught on camera during the attack on the Rex bar at that time. Gary Smyth, a C Company gunman and old friend of Johnny Adair, was also seen on the Ardoyne Road during the protests and was later found guilty of making a hoax phone call to the media on behalf of the RHD, claiming that a car bomb had been left outside Holy Cross.[30]

Adair's elder brother James, who had served six years in prison for attempted murder, was arrested near the school and later convicted of throwing missiles at police.[31] The vulpine presence of John White was also noticeable, though he claimed he was only there to monitor the situation.[32]

One Glenbryn resident, Anne Bill, accepted that the UDA had a role in events. In a book she wrote which was published in 2002 but given little notice by the media, she tried to present the crisis from a working-class Protestant viewpoint but was clear in her own mind that 'Loyalist paramilitaries do not deny their involvement in these clashes and indeed some openly come out and put their hands up to it; but Republicans have relinquished any responsibility for the outbreak of violence'.[33]

In fact, many activists in the UDA knew a public relations catastrophe when they saw one. This was John Gregg's view[34] and also that of Jackie McDonald:

> We were up there at the height of it and some Glenbryn people wanted us to put 1,000 UDA men on Ardoyne Road. We had to ask them to think what might happen if just one of our boys was killed. We tried to talk the situation down, defuse it, but it wasn't easy. We told people not to walk into a trap set for them by Republicans. We began to get our message over. People could see guys who had been stoning Glenbryn homes the night before walking up to the school with the pupils and parents, with Gerry Kelly there to sweet-talk the media.[35]

Neither Gregg nor McDonald thought the picket should ever have been allowed to happen and it has been claimed that Adair too, on his release from prison in May 2002, threw his weight behind the decision to call it off.[36]

Doing this could not, of course, immediately heal the deep wounds left by months of violence and tension within such a small locality. Even so, relations between Holy Cross and the Protestant Wheatfield Primary School which almost faced it across the Upper Ardoyne Road remained amazingly good. These good relations had survived the worst of the Troubles but latterly they owed much to two quietly heroic school principals, Anne Tanney at Holy Cross and John Waugh at Wheatfield. Both were in post through the height of the crisis.

Waugh's example meant little to the young Loyalists who took part in what by late September 2001 became almost nightly riots barely a mile from his school. Police on the Crumlin Road and in streets opening off it regularly had to fire plastic bullet rounds, and the management of Brookfield

Mill industrial estate, whose thousand employees were mainly Protestant, announced that many jobs would be at risk if rioting continued. This was after one episode during which street violence had spilled into the complex itself.[37] The police were in no doubt that UDA members were involved and the organisation made little effort to deny it.[38] At least it was not directly implicated in the murder, in Lurgan on 28 September, of Martin O'Hagan of the *Sunday World*, the first journalist to be a victim of the conflicts, who had for long been an intended target of the LVF in the area where he lived.

Elsewhere in North Belfast hate continued to fester. A brutal reminder of this came in early September 2001 when Thomas McDonald, a sixteen-year-old Protestant, was killed by a Catholic motorist after he threw a half-brick at her car at the junction of Whitewell Road and Arthur Road. Alison McKeown, a young mother of five, was driving children to a nearby integrated school when the missile hit her windscreen. As McDonald left the scene on his bicycle she drove after him and up onto the pavement to strike him. At her trial the court was told that her vehicle pushed the bicycle for twenty-four feet before the teenager was thrown in the air, suffering a fractured skull from which he died shortly afterwards. The verdict, in February 2003, was that she had caused McDonald's death by dangerous driving. She was cleared of murder but found guilty of manslaughter and was sentenced to two years in prison followed by two years' probation.

Predictably, the court's decision enraged Loyalists and prior to it a local memorial at the spot where the teenager had died had been repeatedly defaced by nationalists[39] while mocking graffiti was sprayed on nearby walls. A website was also set up, using pictures of the scene of his death and of his mangled bicycle to taunt his family with offensive captions.[40] McDonald had played in the local Whitewell Defenders Flute Band, whose members formed a guard of honour at his funeral, and he had, without a doubt, been drawn into other sectarian confrontations near his home before his death.

Within just a few weeks another teenage 'ceasefire soldier' followed McDonald to an early grave. He was Glen Branagh, who through the UYM had a direct link to the UDA. Known to his friends as 'Spacer' for his often crazed attacks on Catholics along the North Queen Street and Duncairn Gardens interface between the nationalist New Lodge area and Tiger's Bay, where he belonged, Branagh had taken part in a UDA commemoration on Sunday, 11 November 2001, close to the Mount Inn on North Queen Street. After a period of drinking with friends and as darkness fell he joined a crowd of several hundred Loyalists for what had become a regular evening clash with nationalists who lived only a few hundred yards away.

As police and troops arrived on the scene missiles and petrol bombs were already being thrown. Branagh was killed when a blast bomb he was about to hurl exploded in his hand, ripping off one side of his head and much of his right arm. Eddie McLean, a Protestant community worker, claimed Branagh had picked up a device thrown from the nationalist end of the street, adding:

'He died a hero, trying to save others.'[41] The security forces on the spot denied this and Branagh's record suggested he would have been at the forefront of the action. As one UDA man, who did not wish to be named, put it: 'He was a good fellow. He just hated Fenians. We could do with hundreds more of his kind around here.'[42]

There is now a memorial plaque to Branagh almost directly across from the Mount Inn. Within a short time of his death, UDA emblems and floral tributes stretched for twenty feet on either side of the spot where he had received the dreadful injuries from which he had died. Ironically, the display included Rangers scarves, though in what seems to have been tolerated locally as an eccentric gesture of individuality, he had in fact claimed to support Celtic. He was buried with paramilitary honours on Thursday, 15 November. A beret and gloves were laid across his coffin along with wreaths that bore the description 'Tiger's Bay Young Gun'.[43] He was interred in Carnmoney cemetery the day before his seventeenth birthday. Branagh was not an innocent victim of the Troubles but a victim nevertheless, whose short life, unlike that of his relation, the actor Kenneth Branagh, had offered no escape from the bleak and violent streets of North Belfast.

Just before the funeral, Mrs Mandy Branagh received a hate letter telling her that the best Loyalist heroes were dead ones and wishing her son a happy birthday.[44] On the day of his burial Republicans on the New Lodge side of the cortège's route hung a large Irish tricolour from a high block of flats to taunt mourners. This prompted one journalist to observe that 'there is no respect for the dead in places where there is little for the living'.[45]

In this atmosphere of continuing violence the authorities came under growing pressure to review the whole question of whether the UDA should any longer be considered to be observing its ceasefire. On 29 September John Reid, who had succeeded Peter Mandelson as Secretary of State, announced that he would give the UDA 'one last chance',[46] claiming to have had assurances from its leaders that they would order members to withdraw from attacks and interface confrontations. He was criticised for accepting such assurances but stressed that his decision represented only a 'reprieve'.[47] Sammy Duddy was unimpressed:

> The Inner Council never made a formal response to Reid. The press dreamt that up. The UDA won't bottle out just because of a threat from him. Yes, we've been up the last few nights on the Crumlin and at Brookfield, shoulder to shoulder with the UVF, by the way, but that'll die down. Anyway, the UDA's illegal, so Reid can authorise arrests any time he likes but he won't be able to stop with us. Others are breaking the ceasefire.[48]

Just two weeks later, on 12 October, Reid changed his mind and announced that as far as he and the government were concerned the UDA ceasefire was over. This came in response to serious rioting the night before on the Shankill Road, when police searching houses for drugs and arms came under attack from a large crowd hurling petrol bombs and other missiles at them. Reid was promptly challenged by David Trimble over ongoing Republican violence and whether he planned to 'specify' the IRA's ceasefire in the same way, while a senior UDA member told the press that if the government followed up its announcement with arrests of UDA members, 'Tony Blair will not just have Osama Bin Laden to deal with – Northern Ireland will be out of control.'[49]

Arrests did not follow and UDA violence continued, in the immediate area of Holy Cross School where the local Loyalist blockade remained, at other interfaces in the city and in rural localities in North Antrim and South Londonderry. Inevitably the violence brought death in its wake. Less than one week into the new year of 2002, another teenage Loyalist, William Campbell, was killed when a bomb he had been handling close to his home in Coleraine exploded. The device was a pipe bomb, twenty-one of which had been used in attacks in the town over the previous twelve months. The dead teenager's father claimed he had done no more than play in a local flute band,[50] but John White told the press that he had been a member of the UDA.[51] Later in the year the organisation dedicated a mural to him in the Harpurs Hill estate, where he had lived.

On the same day that Campbell died, the North Belfast brigade issued a statement in response to worsening sectarian clashes on the Limestone Road, which links Tiger's Bay to the mainly Catholic Newington district. Constant trouble on this road had left many houses abandoned or with windows boarded up and the brigade communiqué singled out the area, calling for an end to the clashes from midnight on the fourth, after which, it said, 'any act of hooliganism or unprovoked attacks on the Limestone Road will be dealt with in a severe manner'.[52] The statement added:

> As an organisation we are still committed to our ceasefire but members of our community have acted on their own behalf in terms of defending their homes and families. The fuse is getting shorter and we are now faced with the reality of having to break our ceasefire in order that we can defend our community with the same means openly used by Sinn Fein/IRA to attack Loyalists over recent months.[53]

Within a week of the statement's issue, the organisation killed again, though using the cover name of the Red Hand Defenders. The victim was a baby-faced, bespectacled postman, Daniel McColgan, aged twenty and the father of a small daughter. He stayed on the nationalist Longlands estate very close to the fiercely Loyalist White City district. He might have lived had he gone ahead with his intention to ask for a transfer away from the sorting office in nearby Rathcoole, where he was an easy target for the gunmen who lay in wait for him at 4.45 on the morning of 12 January 2002. His murder was followed by threats to Catholic postal workers and teachers from the RHD but this did not deter thousands of people from attending peace rallies in Belfast and other towns to protest against sectarian killings.

Police arrested John Gregg to question him about the murder but his alibi
was a secure one, since he spent Saturday, 12 January in Glasgow to see
Rangers playing a home game. There were few who doubted the UDA's
involvement, however, and Jackie McDonald confirmed to the press that
members of the organisation, though not his own brigade, had carried it out
as a reprisal for Republican attacks on Protestant localities in Belfast. 'I'm not
saying it was the right thing to do but there had been so many attacks in North
Belfast on Protestants that people wanted a way to show the nationalist community they weren't going to put up with it.'[54] Two days later, the RHD
announced they were disbanding 'in response to an ultimatum'[55] from the
UDA, but many were sceptical of the UDA's condemnation of the threats
that had been issued to Catholics working in the public sector.

Police inquiries into the murder quickly hit a predictable wall of silence in
the Rathcoole area, where a number of local people, without feeling able to
identify themselves, expressed their horror at what had happened. One of
them was in fact the wife of a local UDA man:

> What are they thinking about? What's happening to us here? That fellow
> McColgan had a baby but he looked like a wee baby himself. But what can we do
> here in Rathcoole? We know where the power is and you can't say what I've just
> said in public.[56]

One local man who offered information about the McColgan killing to police
was Stephen McCullough, a former UDA member. He reportedly did this
while in police custody over a drink-driving charge. After being released from
Musgrave Street police station in the centre of Belfast, he was found dead
some hours later at the foot of Cavehill, the famous and precipitous rock formation which looms over the north side of the city. McColgan was not the
last Catholic victim of the UDA in 2002. Others targeted by them survived
but in late July, Gerard Lawlor, a nineteen year old with a job in Belfast docks
who was due to move into a house with his girlfriend and baby son, was shot
dead as he walked home from a bar. He was wearing a Celtic strip, though,
eight years into Northern Ireland's peace process, the direction in which he
was walking still identified him as a likely Catholic and thus a target for
murder.

The gunman who killed him at close range made his getaway on a motorbike. The Sunday on which Lawlor died, 21 July, had been a day of intensified violence across North Belfast, with a series of shootings, in one of which
a young Protestant in Glenbryn had suffered serious injuries. A UDA/UFF
statement claimed Lawlor's killing as 'a measured military response'[57] to
attacks on the Protestant community but he was simply another easy target.
He was the fifth member of his Gaelic Athletic Association club, St Enda's,
to be murdered by Loyalists. School pupils wearing the club jersey formed a
guard of honour at his funeral in Carnmoney cemetery. His grave, like
McColgan's, was very soon attacked and vandalised.

Questioned about these events by the author close to the end of his own violent life, Gregg seemed untroubled in justifying the murders of McColgan and Lawlor. Of the former he claimed:

> There was a lot of myth-making about him by the other side and by the media. He was no innocent. He took part in attacks on our people in the White City. We have a security forces source for that. After Thomas McDonald was murdered it had to be one for one. That's how it is here. There are no motiveless killings. McColgan had to go. There were sixteen other Catholics in that sorting office but we never touched them. There was no way we were going to let him carry on going into Rathcoole, it was as simple as that.'[58]

In fact, other Catholic postal workers in the Belfast area had received a generalised Loyalist threat and McColgan, the product of a mixed marriage, had enrolled his daughter, as soon as she was born, for Hazlewood Integrated College, which he himself had attended. Much of his time outside his post office shifts went on part-time evening work as a DJ in bars and clubs, including one owned by the British Legion.

Quite recently, McColgan has, however, been added to a Republican roll of honour on the nearby Bawnmore estate. The names on the memorial include both IRA volunteers and victims of Loyalist attacks. Local people deny that McColgan belongs to the former category but the central plaque is dedicated to 'all those from this area who played their part in the struggle for Irish freedom'.

Gregg took a similar view of Lawlor's murder: 'He was shot because IRA gunmen from Ardoyne hit and could easily have killed a young Protestant at Glenbryn that same evening. Young Lawlor wasn't so lucky. Again, it was one for one.' Asked if he thought the killers of McColgan and Lawlor would be found, Gregg replied by quoting the reward offered by the police for information on the McColgan killing:

> Did you see what's sprayed up on that wall across the road from here? £20,000, then a question mark, then Bloody Friday, La Mon, Teebane, Enniskillen. That says it all. They'll never pull in the boys who took out McColgan and Lawlor. I know they won't.[59]

Gregg's responses were chilling, though less so than those of another UDA man in Ballymena who was also willing to speak of the McColgan murder. When the point was put to him that, supposing it had been true that the murdered teenager had been involved in sectarian clashes with White City Loyalists, so had many others who had not been singled out for similar retribution, his reply was: 'He was easy to hit. Why make it hard when you don't have to?'[60] Asked about the vandalising of McColgan's grave in Carnmoney, his answer was: 'That wasn't us but if it had been we'd have dug the wee bastard up and hung what was left of him off a tree by his ankles.'[61]

For several weeks prior to Lawlor's murder and the July marching season undercurrents of unrest had been at work within the UDA. Press reports, though denied by Jackie McDonald, claimed that his South Belfast brigade was losing young members to West Belfast, who were anxious to 'join up' there in anticipation of Johnny Adair's release from prison.[62] Other reports told of higher levels than ever of UDA recruitment, especially in areas where there was serious sectarian tension such as North Belfast. A problem there was that 'Jimbo' Simpson, the 'Bacardi brigadier', had little real control and his behaviour had become a public liability to the organisation. At one point damage to the toilet doors of the Mount Inn was clearly visible after Simpson, in one of his many drunken rages, had hurled pool balls round the bar and had to be overpowered and ejected by customers.

Politically the UDA had lost any political direction it had ever had. The Ulster Democratic Party had, for all practical purposes, ceased to exist. It had held no area or constituency meetings for nearly two years and had failed to contest any seats as a party in the most recent council elections. Gary McMichael and David Adams in Lisburn, as well as Tommy Kirkham and Frank McCoubrey in Belfast, continued their work as councillors but sat as independent Loyalists.

One brigadier who did still talk about a political road for Loyalism was McDonald, who was acknowledged to have seniority on the UDA's Inner Council. Early in 2002 he gave a very full interview to Jim McDowell, a well-known Belfast newspaper editor and a shrewd observer of the paramilitary scene. McDonald admitted that the UDA had no political wing that could articulate its views but he did declare strong support for the new Loyalist Commission, which had been formed at the start of the year. David Trimble had pressed hard for its creation as a forum which could bring together the UDA and UVF and give them the chance for constructive dialogue with Protestant clergy and community workers from areas worst affected by recent sectarian violence.

> They are pooling their views and aims together. Look, everybody wants peace, nobody wants to go back to war. Everybody's got a family. We want a normal society for our children. And we want to play our part in that, through politics.[63]

He accepted that his own brigade area did not have the acute problems of North and West Belfast and reiterated claims he had made before that recruiting young Loyalists locally was a way of keeping some control over them and getting at least some of them to think politically: 'We're trying to educate young people that politics is the way forward, to keep them right, to keep them out of trouble.'[64]

However, what made the headlines for this interview was McDonald's readiness to talk about what remained unthinkable for most Loyalists, a united Ireland. Arguing that 'we're well on the way' to it, he went on to put the view that Republicans, having given up on an armed struggle, were prepared to sit back and wait. For Unionists, unity was the priority. 'I don't think we can stop a united Ireland. But, acting together, we can slow it down, at the same time promoting Ulster and making us secure within the United Kingdom as long as we can.'[65] Even if unification came, Ulster Protestants, he stressed, would remain a separate people: 'Just where would they fit us in? You can't define a people by boundaries. I don't care about the geography of it. It is, in the end about who we are.'[66]

There was an inevitably hostile reaction within much of the UDA, though not all McDonald's critics read the full interview carefully enough and, as events would soon show, he had the status and determination to survive much more serious challenges to his position. These were becoming imminent as Adair's release date drew near. His lawyers had failed in more than one attempt to bring this forward, using his hard work to set himself up at Maghaberry as a model prisoner. The day came on Wednesday, 15 May 2002, and at 7.30 in the morning 300 UDA members and supporters, all men with tattoos, medallions and many baseball caps, were in the prison car park to acclaim him, led by the organisation's serving brigadiers.

Adair stood silently beside the ubiquitous John White as he assured the press that Adair 'would make a positive contribution to the peace process'.[67] The hero of the hour was then taken to a car which led a noisy cavalcade of well-wishers back to a street party in Boundary Way on the Lower Shankill. Trestle tables were laid out with food and bottles of champagne labelled with UDA and C Company emblems as well as images of Adair. Flags hung off every house in the small cul-de-sac, not just paramilitary ones but others marking the Queen's Golden Jubilee year. The monarch herself was less than half a mile away as the party got under way, attending an inter-denominational service at St Anne's Cathedral.

Adair was not long in addressing the gathering.

> In the last couple of years we have started feeling as if we were wrong. We weren't wrong. Them people [the UVF] started the feud. We defended our people. We need to get it into our heads that we weren't wrong and we need to fucking get out of this wee square and get in to that Shankill Road where we belong.[68]

Huge cheers greeted these unscripted remarks. As always with Adair, the signals that went out were conflicting ones. Only two weeks later, he joined the Loyalist Commission for a special meeting in East Belfast with the Secretary of State. Tension was still dangerously high at flashpoint areas in the city and the talks went on for more than two and a half hours.

A smartly suited Adair arrived at the agreed venue with White and Mo Courtney, a West Belfast UDA member of forbidding appearance and with a ferocious reputation. The Secretary of State made no reference to Adair's contribution, if any, to talks intended to lower the level of sectarian violence, merely stating afterwards that he was ready to work with paramilitaries if, and only if, they shared his commitment to a resolution of Northern Ireland's problems.[69]

There had already been reports that Adair was stepping down from 'military' rank in the West Belfast UDA and that a successor had been sworn in as brigadier.[70] This was generally believed to be Courtney, not the most reassuring choice he could have made. In the first press interview after his release, Adair tried to find a conciliatory tone and gave assurances that he would not be present at the Drumcree parade scheduled for Sunday, 7 July.[71] This occasion was in fact accompanied by only a brief outburst of violence at the police barriers which once again closed off the Garvaghy Road, though serious trouble took place elsewhere, culminating in Gerard Lawlor's murder on the twentieth.

Just as after his previous release in 1999, Adair busied himself about the streets of the Lower Shankill, freshening up the paint on kerbstones and helping with the completion of yet more murals. There were also internal decisions to be made within the UDA, especially in North Belfast, where the deposed 'Jimbo' Simpson had to be replaced as brigadier. Adair was able to make the case to the Inner Council for the appointment of the UDA's youngest ever brigadier, Andre Shoukri, commonly referred to in the area as 'the Egyptian' because his father, who had died when he was a baby, was an Egyptian seaman who had settled in Belfast.

Shoukri, who with his brother Ihab was brought up in the fiercely Loyalist Ballysillan and Westland estates, was just seventeen at the time of the 1994 ceasefires. His mother was and still is a churchgoing woman who has won much respect for her community work, especially with young addicts, and she secured a place for Andre at Hazlewood Integrated College to complete his schooling. None of this stopped him and Ihab joining the UDA. 'It was a macho thing when I was hanging about with friends who were also getting involved,' he has said. 'The younger generation of UDA would be quicker to react if Protestants are attacked while older men caution them not to rush in. You need that mix of energy and experience.'[72] His involvement earned him two prison terms, one for malicious wounding and the other for extortion.

'I am not a bigot,' he insisted to a journalist. 'I don't believe in shooting people because of their views. But if they [Republicans] hit Protestants, it will be like for like. We have to defend our own people.'[73] He referred to recent attacks on the Protestant community in justification of his stance and argued that Loyalist paramilitaries were being unfairly judged by standards that were not being applied to the IRA:

> I don't see our ceasefire as having broken down because we are holding to the 'no first strike' policy agreed some weeks ago. But it is getting us nowhere. The government won't say the IRA has broken its ceasefire because they cannot put Sinn Fein out of Stormont. We don't have that card to play.[74]

Shoukri's swarthy good looks and urge to dress like a male model gave him almost a cult following among North Belfast Loyalists, especially women. He was also a martial arts specialist and a formidable kick boxer, capable of giving savage beatings to anyone who crossed him. One victim, the UDA's Woodvale company commander, Jim Spence, was described by witnesses as a 'bloodied wreck'[75] after clashing with him in a West Belfast club. Shoukri's credentials for a position of command commended themselves to Adair but he did not prove to be a reliable ally for long, as events would soon show.

Although attacks on Catholic homes across North Belfast and in other localities continued at a serious level into August and September 2002, the Holy Cross School blockade at least was lifted. Adair's role in halting it, alluded to earlier, was confirmed in press reports that he, in company with Andy Tyrie, who had earned much respect for his cross-community work in East Belfast, visited Glenbryn to impress upon residents the need not to cause any further damage to Loyalism's image.[76]

Violence close to the Adairs' own front door also became news when their eldest son, Jonathan, aged seventeen, was reported to have been the victim of a punishment shooting by the UDA. Conflicting stories about what had happened quickly circulated. One was that he had assaulted a young female shop assistant over her allegation of theft at a filling station forecourt on the Lower Shankill Road. Johnny Adair, it was claimed, arrived on the scene and exchanged blows with his son.[77] Shortly afterwards, a UDA punishment squad seized the teenager, accusing him of a record of anti-social behaviour dating back to a beating he had been given as a warning two years previously. This time he was shot in the soft tissue of his calves, not through any bones in his knees or ankles. A UDA source told a newspaper that

> Johnny Adair would not have been told and even if he had he would not have intervened. Of course he is upset at what has happened to his son but the UDA/UFF is not about one man. He has had to accept it.[78]

The truth that the UDA was 'not just about one man' was one that Adair would have been wise to keep uppermost in his mind but he was incapable of doing so. Had he been endowed with any of the heroic attributes of characters in the plays of Sophocles or Aeschylus, it might be possible to say that he was destroyed by the fatal flaw of hubris.

The final months of 2002 point simply to a disassociation from reality created by the coterie of sycophants who surrounded him, as well as by his ever-growing drug habit. The sinister role of his mentor, John White, an Iago-like figure constantly in attendance on his protégé, always listening and always ready to spread whispering campaigns against his critics and detractors, should not be ruled out either from any attempt to piece together the chronology of Adair's downfall.

Ironically, one source of growing tension within the UDA was Adair's attempt, much influenced by White, to reinvent himself as a peacemaker. Reports were even circulated, almost certainly by White, that he was considering putting his name forward as a candidate in the following year's Stormont assembly elections. Sending White as his emissary to meet Alex Maskey,

Belfast's first Sinn Fein Lord Mayor, without reference to the UDA's Inner Council, was one step too far. 'We made it very clear that it shouldn't happen but he defied us,' one Council member told the press.[79] The irony that Adair's C Company gunmen had done their best to kill Maskey on more than one occasion seems to have been lost on both White and Adair.

It was, however, Adair's continued links to the LVF which fatally undermined his position. This breakaway group of gunmen and drug dealers was still a target for a vengeful UFF which in March 2001 had shot dead Adrian Porter at his home in a village near Bangor in County Down. On 13 September 2002 they struck again. This time their quarry was Stephen Warnock, who had refused to clear a debt over a drugs deal to a North Down businessman, James 'Jonty' Johnston, who was also a local UVF commander. Warnock died in a hail of bullets fired by a masked pillion passenger on a motorbike which then sped away from the murder scene in the town of Newtownards. Warnock's three-year-old daughter, who had been in his car when the killers struck, had to be treated in hospital for severe shock though she was uninjured by the attack.

Some in the LVF were quick to place the blame for Warnock's murder on the East Belfast UDA, with whom they had been involved for some months in a turf war over drug money and territory. Adair acted promptly to encourage such talk when he visited the Warnock family home only twenty-four hours after the killing and Jim Gray, the UDA's East Belfast commander, was summoned to talks in the house as Warnock awaited burial. Shortly after he left, with Adair himself in the house, Gray was shot in the face at close range by a lone gunman.

Gray survived, though many hours of surgery were required to rebuild his shattered jaw and mouth. Adair added insult to injury by inserting death notices in the press paying tribute to Warnock and then by attending his funeral on Tuesday, 17 September. As far as the UDA's Inner Council was concerned, Adair had crossed a bridge too far, and three days later Jackie McDonald called upon him to explain his actions to a meeting of the Council in the John McMichael Centre in Sandy Row. Adair arrived with many C Company members who sealed off both ends of the street to foil the arrival of any assassins intending to eliminate their leader.

However, the Inner Council and McDonald in particular kept their nerve in a meeting which lasted more than two hours and even Adair's latest protégé, Shoukri, the newly appointed North Belfast commander, sided with the majority against him. They were incensed not only by events following upon the Warnock killing but by the appearance just two days previously of a defiant new mural in Adair's Lower Shankill fiefdom which proclaimed the UDA's C Company and the LVF to be 'brothers in arms'.[80]

An Inner Council member spoke to the press soon after the meeting finished:

> To say it was heated is an understatement. To the rest of us, an attack on a UDA brigadier is an attack on the whole organisation. But Johnny kept trying to justify it.

He claimed Gray wanted him dead and that Warnock was a good Loyalist and if anyone touched the LVF C Company would get involved. There's certainly no love lost between Adair and Gray but Johnny had no evidence against Jim except the word of some drugged-up head case. The UDA had nothing to do with his [Warnock's] death. Many of the LVF are just criminals, drug dealers, but if they don't bother us, we leave them alone.[81]

A few days later, after a further meeting at a social club on the Loyalist Taughmonagh housing estate on Wednesday, 25 September, the Inner Council announced the expulsion from the organisation of Adair, whom it accused of acting as an 'agent provocateur' who was using LVF/UDA tensions in pursuit of his own ends. White was also expelled and a predictably vicious war of words and graffiti ensued. Adair responded in a tone of injured innocence as posters began to appear in West and North Belfast declaring him 'guilty of loose talk, self-profit, drug-dealing, gangsterism and demeaning the proud cause of Ulster Loyalism'.[82]

Adair also insisted that he had widespread support within the UDA, though he was deeply resentful of Shoukri's desertion of him at the Inner Council meeting. 'Andre had the balls to stand up to him,' was how Sammy Duddy later put it. 'He had been his friend but he wasn't prepared to be his puppet. He had his own following too in North Belfast and Johnny was jealous of that.'[83] Soon after the Sandy Row meeting, Shoukri was arrested by police and charged with illegal possession of a firearm. This later earned him a term of imprisonment though some suspected that a C Company tip-off to police had helped to bring this about.[84]

Adair continued to hold court in his Boundary Way home or just fifty yards away from it in a local community centre which had become known as the 'Big Brother House'. The entrance to it was often guarded by the thuggish-looking Mo Courtney, while inside, incongruously, an after-school home-work club for children managed to function as tea and Wagon Wheel biscuits were dispensed to journalists and Adair and his minders came and went on C Company business. Gina Adair could often be found there and in mid-October 2002 she gave two press interviews, for which she neither received nor had requested any payment. She did her best for her husband during these interviews, calling him a 'good man, a real family man. He's a total softie with his children and me.'[85] She also spoke of her roots in the area. 'I hate leaving the Lower Shankill. I watch our flags as they get smaller and smaller and it makes me feel panicky . . . I wouldn't swop the Lower Shankill for anywhere else in the world. I love it here.'[86]

In fact, her days on Boundary Way were already numbered as Johnny Adair grew ever more paranoid about who he thought he could or could not trust. Even old comrades in the UDA's war were no longer safe. One of these was William 'Winkie' Dodds, his next-door-but-one neighbour. Back in the summer of 2002 Dodds's brother-in-law, William 'Muggsy' Mullan, had had to flee both the Lower Shankill and Northern Ireland itself after clashing with Adair over access to C Company funds. Dodds also had a cousin, Alan McLean, who had defected from C Company, taking some of its cash with him to the UDA's North Belfast brigade.

For Adair, Dodds's relationship to these offenders constituted guilt by association and Gina also had a personal grudge against Mullan's wife Maureen.[87] Dodds, who was partially paralysed from a stroke, was ordered to leave the area with his family. On Thursday, 21 November Sammy Duddy, who after many years of genuine community work on the Shankill Road had been evicted from his office at Adair's orders, arrived with Shoukri's brother Ihab and other North Belfast UDA members to help the Dodds family load up their possessions into a removal van. They were rehoused on the White City estate but their treatment caused much concern.[88]

Dodds had a long record in the UDA, sitting on its Inner Council and serving as West Belfast brigadier before his stroke. He had also served prison sentences arising directly from his activism in the organisation. Duddy put to the press his view that

> the fact that families were leaving the Lower Shankill showed how isolated Johnny Adair had become. Winkie Dodds is a living loyalist legend and I think that it is a disgrace that his family have been terrorised in this way.[89]

The services of another once-trusted C Company member were lost to Adair after a trial at Belfast Crown Court in early December 2002 found Andrew Robinson, who had been close to Adair, guilty of the sadistic murder of his girlfriend Julieanne Osborne two years previously. The court was told that he had inflicted nearly fifty knife wounds on her throat, neck and upper body in a frenzied attack after she broke off what had become an abusive and violent relationship. Amidst angry shouts from the victim's family, Robinson was given a life sentence. He was also a drug addict and had on more than once occasion been questioned by police about sectarian attacks in North Belfast.[90]

Outside the confines of Boundary Way and the Lower Shankill killing had continued after the Inner Council's decision to expel Adair and White. On Sunday, 6 October, Geoffrey Gray, aged forty-one and nicknamed 'the Greyhound', was killed by a lone gunman armed with a shotgun as he walked along Ravenhill Road, close to Dr Ian Paisley's Martyrs Memorial Church. Gray belonged to Portadown and had known Billy Wright and may have unwisely voiced LVF sympathies in the Bunch of Grapes pub, a scene of other UDA killings, where he had been drinking on the night of his death.[91] Police suspected UDA involvement in his murder but were unable to prove it, any more than they could in the case of Alexander McKinley, who was shot dead a week later in the Woodstock area of Belfast.

Duddy expressed his own certainty that the East Belfast UDA had killed both men because of their LVF links but added: 'We don't want any of that here in North Belfast, where I'm now based. We'll stay out of that for as long as we can.'[92] In fact the LVF as a whole had little relish for an alignment with Adair which would involve it in a major confrontation with the mainstream UDA, and by mid-October 2002 Duddy was predicting his downfall.

> He's committed treason against the UDA. He's told the LVF about Inner Council decisions. There's no way we can condone that. He went with White and Davy Mahood to talk to Alex Maskey [Belfast's Sinn Fein Lord Mayor] without Inner Council authorisation and there was the business of the Warnock funeral – all acts of defiance. He thinks he's bigger than the UDA. He's mad.[93]

John Gregg, talking to the author the following day, took an even more uncompromising line on Adair:

> He's finished, his time's up. There's only one way out for him now. He's on a huge ego trip. He's never done half of what he's claimed. OK, he shot Noel Cardwell, a lad with the mental age of a child. He could never keep his mouth shut. That's why he talked himself into his sentence and he's been living in fantasy land. When I got pulled into Castlereagh for questioning in 1997, the RUC quoted Johnny telling them I acted under his orders – total crap. I even once heard him say, with his hand literally on his heart, 'I am the Loyalist people', but he's lost the plot now. Even his own brigade are against him. We keep hearing about C Company but just wait until the A and B Company boys further up the Shankill make a move.[94]

Asked about Duddy's view that Adair had committed treason against the UDA, Gregg was in total agreement.

> That's exactly it and he knows the score. He'll be wiped out if he doesn't back down soon. We'll see where his real support is. It'll not be a straight UDA–LVF fight either, though that's what he's hoping for. We've got LVF boys up here in Rathcoole and in our brigade area but they don't want to get involved. We can sort out any problems with them but Johnny's a different issue. He's tried to use an element within the LVF against us because he thinks he's bigger than the UDA. He's not.[95]

Gregg's assessment of the growing weakness of Adair's position was correct in almost every detail but only three months after he gave it, C Company was still able to kill him.

Gregg's prediction that difficulties with the LVF could be resolved was also vindicated when a truce between the two bodies was announced early in November. In the statement that announced this, the LVF accepted that the East Belfast UDA had had no part in Stephen Warnock's murder. False information was blamed for recent tensions: 'Both organisations have therefore resolved any differences which may have existed between them and have initiated a policy whereby intermediaries have been set up to prevent any further recurrence of this sort of conflict arising again.'[96]

Even before this agreement the UDA's renewed confidence in disciplining known Adair supporters within its ranks became evident. On 1 November, on the Ballysillan estate in North Belfast, Mahood was shot in both legs. A statement was later read outside Laganside Magistrates' Court, where other UDA members were appearing on criminal charges. Duddy was the reader and the text admitted the UDA's responsibility for the punishment shooting of a man who had sat on the Ulster Political Research Group and had been an important negotiator with both the Dublin and the London governments earlier in the peace process.[97] His crime had been to gravitate dangerously close to the Adair camp and his shooting was clearly meant as a warning. The irony of the responsibility for it being announced outside a court was not lost on the media representatives who were there to hear it.

Two days later, however, C Company gunmen came calling for Duddy. Late in the evening of Saturday, 2 November, he and his wife Roberta escaped injury when shots were fired by two men through the front door of their bungalow in Carmeen Drive, Rathcoole. One of their dogs, Bambi, was killed in the attack and Duddy chased his assailants, one of whose weapons jammed as he tried to fire more shots.[98] Other attacks on UDA homes on the Westland estate also took place and on 8 November the UDA issued a warning to all Loyalists for their own safety to stay well away from Adair and his cohorts.[99]

Soon after this the organisation laid on a massive show of strength in West Belfast, ostensibly to mark Remembrance Sunday. Long columns of men in berets and combat kit marched up the Shankill Road behind bands and standards for a wreath-laying ceremony. With much media speculation as to what might happen, Adair let it be known that C Company, at full strength, would take part. They did so but in a tense stand-off the ceremony passed off without violence. The author and journalist Henry McDonald later recalled Adair speaking about the presence of A and B Companies of the West Belfast brigade: 'They've sat on the fence so long they've got splinters right up their arses.'[100]

Amidst this worsening tension within the UDA it was predictably Duddy who introduced a note of bizarre comedy to the situation by informing journalists that he was considering taking his once well-known drag act 'Samantha' back on the Loyalist club circuit. This was, he stressed, to help a special fund-raising Christmas concert for UDA prisoners and their families. Reminiscing about his heyday as Samantha, he told one newspaper: 'I wore a miniskirt many a time but it was usually a long dress, a straight black wig, a pair of falsies I bought in Blackpool and loads of make-up to cover my freckles.'[101] He also claimed on more than one occasion to have been propositioned by amorous soldiers and RUC men when, late for an engagement, he had put on all his finery only to be halted in his car at security checkpoints.[102]

After the Kincora Home scandal, in which well-known Loyalists had been convicted of the sexual abuse of boys in their care, Duddy recalled that Andy Tyrie had told him to give up his performances as Samantha and also to drop his voice and grow a moustache.

I started growing the moustache straight away and I've had it ever since. It was a pity, but I guess it had to end some time. I haven't decided whether the moustache will go off and the lipstick will go on. It's at times like this that your commitment to Loyalism is severely tested.[103]

Samantha's return did not in fact take place but the press had a field day with the story. 'Play it again Sam – one more time for drag queen and country.'[104] was how one Dublin newspaper headlined it and *The Times* ran it under the words 'UDA hard man lifts veil on life as drag queen'.[105] Its reporter in Belfast told of him admitting 'that he is only half the girl he used to be'.[106] A UDA member was quoted as saying: 'He wasn't so bad in the seventies but I dread to think what he'd be like now. His cheeks have gone a bit ruddy but we'll see what he looks like when he gets the wig on.'

While Adair carried on his losing battle for control of the UDA, sectarian attacks continued. Early in the morning of 22 December, one of them had a fatal outcome. David Cupples, a Protestant aged twenty-two from East Belfast, worked as a kitchen porter at the army's Girdwood Park base in North Belfast. His father dropped him off on the Lower Crumlin Road and he set off to walk in the darkness to his work on the predominantly Catholic Cliftonville Road. He was, however, under observation and eight years into the process, the direction in which he was going identified him as a likely Catholic and sealed his fate. He was set upon by assailants who left him with terrible head injuries. He survived until Christmas Day in the Royal Victoria hospital until his father agreed that his life support machine should be switched off.

A number of men were later charged with offences arising from his murder. One of the accused, in whose home police later found a bloodstained jacket and jeans, was accompanied by John White when he arrived at Tennent Street police station to make a statement.[107] A little over two years later, four men appeared in court on charges relating to the case and one made a plea of guilty to the murder. On the same day, John Cupples, a Presbyterian Church elder, gave a moving press interview about his son, revealing how he had hated sectarianism and had even thought of leaving Northern Ireland because of it. He also told of how, after David's death, he had agreed to some of his organs being used in two life-saving transplant operations.[108]

Just two days later, another equally innocent 22-year-old had his life brutally taken away only yards away from the scene of the attack which killed David Cupples. Jonathan Stewart was a victim of the feud between Adair and the mainstream UDA but his only crime was to be the nephew of Alan McLean, who had been forced out of the Lower Shankill after clashing with Adair over C Company finances. His girlfriend, Natalie Truesdale, whom he had been with for five years and planned to marry, was, however, the daughter of Ian Truesdale, a North Belfast businessman with interests in a taxi company and a hairdressing salon run by his wife. The premises of both these concerns had been shot up by the UDA because Truesdale had become a conspicuously loyal adherent of Adair.

On Boxing Day evening, Stewart went with Natalie Truesdale to a party in a house in Manor Street, just off the Crumlin Road. Not long after his arrival a lone gunman, with a zipper jacket pulled up to conceal his face, entered the house and shot him dead at close range in front of his girlfriend. It was a killing which incensed Protestant opinion in North Belfast. Duddy, speaking on behalf of the Ulster Political Research Group, was prompt in blaming elements linked to Adair and White: 'Jonathan Stewart had no paramilitary connections whatsoever but was killed because he is related to a senior Loyalist in North Belfast,' he told the press. 'C Company wanted to send a message to the McLean family and shooting this young lad was the way they went about it.'[109]

Truesdale's grief was deepened by the unavoidable thought that her lover had been taken from her by an assassin from the same dissident UDA unit with which her own father was associated. Like so many killings of the Troubles, Stewart's death had an almost incestuously local dimension to it, as one UDA member put it to a journalist:

> Part of the problem is that everyone knows who everyone else is and where they live. Like every feud you have families and neighbours on opposing sides and when they can't get the big players they'll go for an easy touch who takes a chance visiting a house in a dodgy area.[110]

Two years later, twenty five year old Wayne Dowie stood trial in Belfast Crown Court charged with Stewart's murder. The court was told that he lived in Manor Street, where the killing took place, and that he was a close associate of Adair, also that he had been present at the party but had left it in the early hours of the morning, returning masked and armed. Truesdale, the court heard, was present when the fatal shots were fired and later picked Dowie out at a police identity parade, despite the balaclava he wore during it, along with others similarly attired.[111] The trial was still in progress at the time of writing this book.

Duddy correctly predicted that any chance of mediation in the feud had been dealt a severe blow by Stewart's murder and the UDA hit back ruthlessly within a week of it. This was not simply revenge but a calculated response to Adair's boasts that he had support in other brigade areas outside West Belfast. One suspect in the South Belfast UDA was Roy Green, a drug dealer and former close associate of Adair, who was still thought to be feeding information to him. Jackie McDonald had Green's movements carefully monitored and on the evening of 2 January 2003 he was lured to the Kimberley Inn, off the Upper Ormeau Road, ostensibly to talk to senior UDA men from the area.

After a brief stay in the bar, Green left to return to his car but was shot dead by a gunman who emerged from a house which the UDA had taken over to set up the attack. Near it is a wall plaque in honour of Joe Bratty and

Raymond Elder, UDA men widely thought to have been implicated in the massacre of Catholics in Sean Graham's betting shop in 1992. Graphic press photos of Green's body appeared, showing him clothed in the Belfast drug dealers' 'uniform' of stylish tracksuit and expensive trainers, with his blood running on to the rain-soaked pavement. A UDA statement later claimed that Green had been 'executed for treason' but both he and his brother Charlie, who had lived in the Village area and had died of a drugs overdose, had also fallen foul of the hard line against drug-dealing taken by the South Belfast UDA and its brigadier Jackie McDonald.[112]

McDonald had confirmed this in a previous interview with the author:

> We do take as hard a line as we can in South Belfast. Three dealers have been shot here in the last six weeks, two in Sandy Row, one in Donegall Road. They knew the rules. Those boys weren't just punting cannabis, it was the hard stuff. In case you're about to ask, I didn't order it. It doesn't have to work that way. Taughmonagh don't have to call at my office in Sandy Row for permission. We accept it if they have the evidence and the intelligence and if it's a response to community demand. Let's be honest, though, paramilitary organisations can get drawn into the drug scene. You can't stay 100 per cent clean. It's impossible.[113]

McDonald's tight control over South Belfast and his proven readiness to stand up to Adair made him an obvious target for C Company's 'top guns'. By the start of 2003, however, they had someone else in their sights whose elimination rated as a higher priority. This was John 'Grugg' Gregg. Back in August 2002, unfounded stories of a successful coup against Gregg were run in a Belfast Sunday newspaper.[114] He subsequently claimed to the author that they were a result of Adair and White misleading journalists in order to undermine his position.[115]

'Black propaganda' was followed up by more direct methods. On 8 December, Gregg discovered a bomb under his car outside his home in Nendrum Gardens, Rathcoole. Army bomb disposal specialists defused it as part of a major security operation and the incident was widely seen as retaliation for the planting of a fire bomb at White's Carrickfergus home a day or two before.[116] Two pipe bombs were left in Gregg's garden over the next two weeks and shots were also fired at the Carnmoney home of Tommy Kirkham, a Belfast city councillor and spokesman for the Ulster Political Research Group.[117]

Menacing graffiti began to appear on walls in Loyalist areas, warning Adair that his days were numbered. One eye-catching prophetic work appeared in North Belfast:

> Mad Dog Adair is trying his best
> To stop his men leaving the nest
> But one by one they are flying away
> To re-unite with comrades in the UDA.

The day will come when he's no-one left
He better wear his bullet-proof vest
One thing for sure, that will come true!
Johnny Boy, the reaper's coming for you.[118]

This mural versifier was right about Adair's impending downfall, though Gregg, with his famous tattoo of the Grim Reaper on his back, would not live long enough to be the personal instrument of it.

Adair's inevitable rearrest came on the morning of Friday, 10 January 2003 after Paul Murphy, the new Secretary of State for Northern Ireland, was presented with an updated police assessment of his activities since his release in May of the previous year. A heavy police and army presence sealed off the Lower Shankill for the arrest operation but there was time for camera crews to capture Adair taking a fond farewell of his two German shepherd dogs outside his house. One C Company member confided his relief to the press the following day. 'Today was fucking great,' he said. 'It was the first morning for a while I have been able to roll over for a second sleep. Johnny has been hyper for a while. He would be round knocking on our doors every morning at eight o'clock, wakening everybody in the house, telling us to get out of our beds and round to his house. It was just a nightmare. We would be sent all over the city doing jobs for him. Then you would come back and tell him and he was happy. Hours later he would give you a bollocking for not carrying out his orders. But he had forgotten. He was starting to forget a lot of things over the last few weeks.'[119]

Others had noticed Adair's growing forgetfulness, a clear by-product of his renewed drug intake since his release, but this forgetfulness did not extend to Gregg. Adair remained, despite his return to prison, in telephone contact with White, who, in late January, met journalists outside his heavily fortified office in Boundary Way opposite Adair's house. Gregg, he told them, was no more than 'a bully boy and a moron' whose presence was an impediment to any resolution of the UDA feud, an outcome he claimed to support.[120]

White's language about Gregg was calculatedly inflammatory but it came as yet another of Adair's lieutenants was planning to desert him. Mo Courtney, who had often represented West Belfast on the UDA's Inner Council until Adair's expulsion from the organisation in September 2002, had been spotted in the company of a 'mainstream' UDA commander in the last week of January. He later fled with his family from his Glencairn home after learning of a death threat to him from C Company[121] and his rearranged loyalties would soon be much in evidence as events moved to their dénouement. His desertion was a huge blow to Adair. As one UDA man put it, 'Mo knows every brick in the Lower Shankill; he knows where the guns and the money are hidden; he even knows the minds of the men round Johnny.'[122]

In the final hours of his life Gregg, talking to a journalist writing for the Irish edition of a London-based Sunday newspaper, reiterated his support for the UDA's response to the behaviour of Adair and White: 'The sentences of treason on Adair and White will always stand – even two years down the line when Johnny is freed from jail.'[123] He admitted responsibility for the fire bomb attempt on White's home and said of Adair: 'No-one will ever know how close we were to getting him. We were so, so close when he was lifted.'[124] Gregg was talking on Friday, 31 January, before setting off with his son and Rathcoole friends for a Rangers game in Glasgow, a trip he made regularly.

They returned the following night on the Stranraer ferry to Belfast. Gregg, Rob Carson, his second-in-command in the South-East Antrim UDA, Gregg's eighteen-year-old son Stuart and another man took a taxi from the port terminal. Minutes later they were ambushed at traffic lights in Nelson Street close to the docks, two gunmen from another vehicle opening rapid fire with automatic weapons. Gregg and Carson were killed instantly and the taxi driver suffered serious injuries. Press photographs taken across police tape soon afterwards showed Gregg's bullet-riddled body slumped sideways across the car seat. Virtually overnight, graffiti in Republican areas of Belfast appeared with the message: 'Supporting Rangers seriously damages your health.'[125]

Adair was reported by prison officers to be jubilant when news reached him late that night of what he saw as a spectacular C Company hit, one which simply would not have been set up without his authorisation.[126] Police believed that the victims had been under surveillance during their ferry voyage home and that mobile phones were used to alert the two young C Company gunmen who carried out the attack.

Nemesis was now close at hand for Adair, White and their remaining supporters. There was now no road back for them and the Inner Council acted swiftly, leaking reports to the media that 10,000 men were ready to 'invade' and occupy the Lower Shankill to deal with Adair's family and his supporters. They were already a dwindling band after so many key figures had defected. The invasion story was a ruse to intimidate them and the Inner Council took over a social club in Heather Street, no distance from Adair's home and White's office. Those who wanted to formalise their break with the men were told to report there and hand over weapons and C Company cash to the leadership. The offer was quickly taken up, a steady flow of penitents making the short journey to Heather Street, to be greeted with much macabre humour by the waiting Inner Council members.

This in fact averted major bloodshed in response to the murders of Gregg and Carson, the latter of whom was buried on Wednesday, 5 February. Later that evening, towards midnight, scores of UDA men, possibly as many as a hundred, raced into the Lower Shankill in cars, then leapt out, heavily armed, to smash the doors and windows of known Adair supporters' homes and attacking any of them who could be identified. The violent chaos lasted for some fifteen minutes, without the intervention of police, who arrived on the scene to provide an armed escort for Gina Adair, her four children, White and fewer than a dozen C Company members. Before dawn they were all seen on to the Belfast ferry for Cairnryan in Galloway.

Boundary Way and the streets opening off it presented a sorry spectacle the following morning. The detritus of the previous night's violence lay all around outside wrecked and abandoned homes as Rebel and Shane, Adair's dogs, padded sadly up and down outside his house. New homes were later found for both of them but there was no immediate guarantee of this for Gina Adair, her children and the remnant of C Company, who left the ferry at Cairnryan at midday on Thursday, 6 February. No doors in Loyalist Scotland would open for them. The UDA there supported the Inner Council in Belfast and Sammy McCrory, Johnny Adair's oldest friend, who was living in Ayrshire, made no move to help them. On landing at Cairnryan, Gina Adair was relieved, by Dumfries and Galloway police, of a shoebox stuffed with £70,000 in banknotes.[127]

Within forty-eight hours of the seizure of the money, Stranraer Sheriff Court granted an interim order allowing police to retain it pending inquiries into its origins. Eight months later the court ordered its forfeiture on the grounds that it had been obtained through terrorism. This was the first case in Scottish legal history in which such an order was issued. It was done so under new proceeds of crime legislation enacted late in 2002 and the £70,000 was handed over to the Crown Office Civil Recovery Unit to be disbursed as it saw fit. Gina Adair did not contest the court's ruling. 'Johnny didn't want her to draw any more attention to herself, besides, seventy grand is nothing to them,'[128] a UDA source told a newspaper which covered the case.

On the morning of Gina Adair's arrival in Scotland, a few UDA men reappeared in Boundary Way to deface some of the murals which had gone up during her husband's reign in the Lower Shankill. One in particular, celebrating solidarity between C Company and the LVF, was singled out for the benefit of the cameras and Mo Courtney, to underline the recent reordering of his allegiance, was photographed hurling a pot of paint at it before driving off to Rathcoole for Gregg's funeral.[129]

It was a huge event, with close to 10,000 people estimated to have walked behind the coffin after a short service at the Gregg family home. Journalists were held well back by UDA stewards as the flag-draped coffin was carried into the street, where a salute of three revolver shots was fired into the air. Gregg's widow, who wept as she walked in the cortège with her children, had not wanted a paramilitary guard of honour but UDA brigadiers and other senior figures took it in turn to shoulder the coffin, as did members of the Cloughfern Young Conquerors Flute Band, in whose uniform Gregg was buried.

Gregg's grave at Carnmoney is well tended and the inscription on his stone describes him as a 'devoted son, husband and father, resting where no shadows fall'. The UDA motto, 'Quis Separabit', is carved on it, as is a Rangers badge. Also lovingly tended and not far from it, in a cemetery which is the final resting place of victims of the Troubles from both communities, are the graves of Daniel McColgan and Gerard Lawlor, the two teenage Catholics whose murders Gregg justified to the author and which he almost certainly ordered. The inscription 'True love never dies' from his partner Lyndsey is carved on McColgan's gravestone and around it are photographs of the infant child he left.

Lawlor also left a fiancée and a small child. On his stone are the words 'Those who we love and have lost are waiting for us in a place without parting where we'll never have to say goodbye again'. Unlike Gregg's grave, McColgan's and Lawlor's have been defaced and vandalised several times.

Asked how she felt about this, Siobhan, Gerard's sweetheart and mother of his child Josh, said:

> I don't think anything of these people who killed him because I don't know them or what made them do it. I suppose I feel sorry for them. God help them. What do they have? I get up every day and smile and say I'll do good today. They can't say that.[130]

NOTES

1. D. McKittrick, S. Kelters, B. Feeney and C. Thornton, *Lost Lives: The Stories of the Men, Women and Children Who Died as a Result of Northern Ireland's Troubles*, rev. edn (Edinburgh: Mainstream, 2004), p. 1487.
2. *Sunday World*, 24 December 2000.
3. *Sunday Tribune*, 7 January 2001.
4. *Sunday World*, 14 January 2001.
5. J. McDonald, interview with author, 3 May 2002.
6. Ibid.
7. *Irish News*, 25 September 2001.
8. *Irish News*, 2 August 2001.
9. *Guardian*, 27 November 2001.
10. *Irish News*, 13 December 2001.
11. Ibid.
12. *Scotsman*, 13 December 2001.
13. *Irish News*, 17 January 2002.
14. *Guardian*, 15 January 2002.
15. J. Gregg, interview with author, 16 October 2002.
16. Ibid.
17. Ibid.
18. Ibid.
19. Ibid.
20. Ballymena UDA member, interview with author, 6 July 2002.
21. S. McKay, *Northern Protestants: An Unsettled People* (Belfast: Blackstaff Press, 2000), p 100.
22. M. Langhammer, interview with author, 17 October 2003.

23. *Sunday World*, 8 July 2001.
24. *Sunday World*, 15 July 2001.
25. *Sunday World*, 22 July 2001.
26. *Irish News*, 24 July 2001.
27. *Guardian*, 22 June 2001. See also A. Cadwallader, *Holy Cross: the Untold Story* (Belfast: Brehon Press, 2004).
28. Members of 1 Battalion, Scots Guards, interviews with author, 2001.
29. *Guardian*, 6 September 2001.
30. *Irish News*, 23 March 2002.
31. *Irish News*, 13 June 2002.
32. J. White, interview with author, 5 October 2001.
33. A. Bill, *Beyond the Red Gauntlet: The Silent Voices of Upper Ardoyne amidst the Travesty of Holy Cross* (Belfast: Anne Bill, 2002), p. 107.
34. Gregg, interview with author.
35. McDonald, interview with author.
36. H. McDonald and J. Cusack, *UDA: Inside the Heart of Loyalist Terror* (Dublin: Penguin Ireland, 2004), pp. 361–2.
37. *Irish News*, 28 September 2001.
38. *Guardian*, 26 September 2001.
39. *Irish News*, 6 June 2003.
40. *Irish News*, 29 March 2003; *Sunday World*, 2 March 2003.
41. *Guardian*, 13 November 2001.
42. *Times*, 13 November 2001.
43. *Irish News*, 16 November 2001.
44. *Guardian*, 16 November 2001.
45. *Sunday Tribune*, 18 November 2001.
46. *Irish News*, 29 September 2001.
47. *Guardian*, 29 September 2001.
48. S. Duddy, interview with author, 3 October 2001.
49. *Observer*, 14 October 2001.
50. McKittrick *et al.*, *Lost Lives*, p. 1507.
51. *Irish News*, 5 January 2002.
52. Ibid.
53. Ibid.
54. *Guardian*, 14 January 2002.
55. *Belfast Telegraph*, 16 January 2002.
56. Rathcoole UDA member's wife, interview with author, 14 January 2002.
57. *Irish News*, 22 July 2002.
58. Gregg, interview with author.
59. Ibid.
60. Ballymena UDA member, interview with author.
61. Ibid.
62. *Sunday World*, 28 April 2002.
63. *Sunday World*, 27 January 2002.
64. Ibid.
65. Ibid.

66. Ibid.
67. *Irish News*, 16 May 2002.
68. *Magill Magazine*, June 2002.
69. *Irish News*, 3 July 2002.
70. *Sunday World*, 19 May 2002.
71. *Sunday World*, 7 July 2002.
72. *Guardian*, 14 August 2002.
73. Ibid.
74. Ibid.
75. *Sunday World*, 31 October 2004.
76. *Sunday World*, 1 September 2002.
77. *Sunday World*, 11 August 2002.
78. *Irish News*, 9 August 2002.
79. *Guardian*, 28 September 2002.
80. *Irish News*, 26 September 2002.
81. *Guardian*, 28 September 2002.
82. Ibid.; *Irish News*, 27 September 2002.
83. Duddy, interview with author, 15 October 2002.
84. *Sunday World*, 6 October 2002.
85. *Daily Mirror*, 14 October 2002.
86. *Daily Mirror*, 15 October 2002.
87. *Sunday World*, 24 November 2002.
88. *Irish News*, 22 November 2002.
89. Ibid.
90. *Irish News*, 10 December 2002.
91. *Sunday World*, 6 October 2002.
92. Duddy, interview with author, 15 October 2002.
93. Ibid.
94. Gregg, interview with author.
95. Ibid.
96. *Irish News*, 6 November 2002.
97. *Irish News*, 2 November 2002.
98. *Irish News*, 4 November 2002.
99. *Irish News*, 9 November 2002.
100. McDonald and Cusack, *UDA*, p. 376.
101. *Irish News*, 4 December 2002.
102. *Irish Independent*, 3 December 2002.
103. *Irish News*, 4 December 2002.
104. *Irish Independent*, 3 December 2002.
105. *The Times*, 3 December 2002.
106. Ibid.
107. McKittrick *et al.*, *Lost Lives*, p. 1513.
108. *Irish News*, 1 February 2005.
109. *Irish News*, 28 December 2002.
110. Ibid.
111. *Irish News*, 8 February 2005.

112. *Sunday World*, 5 January 2003; *Irish News*, 3 January 2003.
113. McDonald, interview with author.
114. *Sunday World*, 25August 2002.
115. Gregg, interview with author.
116. *Irish News*, 9 December 2002.
117. *Irish News*, 23 December 2002.
118. Ibid.
119. *Sunday World*, 12 January 2003.
120. *Sunday World*, 26 January 2003.
121. *Irish News*, 30 January 2003.
122. *Observer*, 9 February 2003.
123. *News of the World*, 9 February 2003.
124. Ibid.
125. Ibid.
126. *Observer*, 9 February 2003.
127. *Scotland on Sunday*, 9 February 2003.
128. *Sunday World*, 5 October 2003.
129. *Guardian*, 7 February 2003.
130. *Herald*, 25 October 2003.

12

A 'Post-War' UDA and the Issue of Collusion

∼

Soon after his return to prison in January 2003, Johnny Adair received a post-card from Dubai, where some UDA brigadiers and their families and supporters had flown for a package holiday, staying in the hotel where the Rangers team were preparing for a forthcoming European game. The card taunted Adair about his own pre-Christmas trip to Lapland with his wife. The 'greeting' on it read:

Woof Woof Daft Dog
Lapland Volunteer Force on tour (I don't think so)
Wish you were here (Aye right)
P.S. How is the food in the Maghaberry Beach Club
All the best, the Lads.[1]

The card reached Adair after John Gregg's murder. By then it was clear to almost everyone except him that he had gambled recklessly and lost. Yet even with plenty of time for reflection as he was held in the prison's isolation wing, Adair seemed to remain in a state of denial about the extent to which he had been the architect of his own downfall. This is apparent both in letters from him to the author and in an interview in Maghaberry which he gave on 9 June 2004, eighteen months into what was in effect the completion of his original sentence:

I fought for my country, for Ulster, but how have I been repaid? So-called Loyalists turned against me, so I'm cooped up here. I was ready to put my life on the line for Ulster, now I'm called a criminal and a drug dealer and it's other Loyalists doing it, people I thought were friends.[2]

Questions about his responsibility for unleashing the feud with the UVF in 2000 and that with the mainstream UDA two years later were brushed aside. So too were queries about the financial sources of his own and his family's lifestyle both before and following his sentencing in 1995: 'Listen, I've had just four holidays in my life. If you saw my passport, you would see just four stamps on it. I've got fuck all, I never even owned a house.'[3] Asked about police evidence of how his homes had been furnished far beyond his known financial means, his reply was: 'Everybody now has got TVs, stereos. I wanted nice things for my kids and Gina always kept a lovely house, something to be proud of.'[4] He declined to respond to questions about the source of the £70,000 she had been compelled to hand over to Scottish police at Cairnryan on her arrival there in February.

As before, he remained dismissive of questions about his own complicity in the deaths of innocent people:

> I've no apologies or regrets for what I did, none at all. Okay, I wish that 3,500 hadn't died in a fucking stupid wee war. The politicians fucked it up. They should have sorted it all out in 1967 and 1968. Was that my fault? I grew up in the middle of a war against my own people. What else was I going to do? I took the war right to them fuckers in the IRA and they knew it.[5]

Outside the walls of Maghaberry, killing as a direct result of the UDA power struggle stopped, at least for a time, but arson and pipe bomb attacks on Catholic homes continued. The UDA was accused of reigniting tension on North Belfast's Limestone Road and on Sunday, 9 February, army bomb disposal specialists had to seal off the nearby Newington Street to defuse explosive devices left there. 'Having sorted out their feud the UDA has returned to attacking nationalist homes which they have been consistently involved in for four years,'[6] claimed Alban Maginness, a North Belfast SDLP Assembly member.

Such attacks were almost inevitable as the UDA leadership struggled to make a reality of its authority after neutralising Adair's challenge to it. Just ten days later it was announced by the Inner Council that a supply of pipe bombs was being dumped in a park off the Crumlin Road, where the authorities would be free to collect them. This was the first time the organisation had taken such action, though it denied that it constituted decommissioning of its weapons. It did, however, urge people still holding such weapons 'to contact their local commanders who will initiate steps for them to be disposed of'.[7]

The dumped pipe bombs were in due course collected by the police and a bigger initiative quickly followed when a twelve-month UDA ceasefire was announced to the media at a hotel in East Belfast on Saturday, 22 February. Publicised, perhaps inappropriately, as the John Gregg initiative, this new departure was presented by political spokesmen of the UDA only, its brigadiers keeping well in the background. Jim Wright from Ballymoney, Sammy Duddy, Frank McCoubrey, Tommy Kirkham and Frankie Gallagher handled questions from journalists and expressed regret for the recent killings carried out by the organisation. Stressing that they spoke as the Ulster Political Research Group (UPRG), they ruled out any weapons-decommissioning until the IRA had demonstrably disposed of all its own firepower.

Internal restructuring was promised as well as mechanisms to monitor the ceasefire on a regular basis. 'It is the intention of the Inner Council not to have a public face any more and therefore the entire organisation will become faceless once again.'[8] Many thought that behind their balaclavas, the UDA's gunmen always had been faceless and there was no commitment to its paramilitary structure being disbanded. 'The Ulster Defence Association will as always be the last line of defence,'[9] the document concluded. It had, however, stressed a readiness to control and avert trouble at interface areas and offered an apology for the involvement of members in drug-dealing.

Responses to the John Gregg initiative were guarded and, within the nationalist community, sceptical. Duddy accepted this: 'We know our image had become a real problem,' he admitted when questioned about the 22 February statement. 'We've been working on this from well before Grugg got killed. Let's get it right, though, the six brigadiers are not going away. The UDA will keep its military structure. We have to until we know what the Provos are doing. The brigadiers may still talk to journalists they trust but the big stuff will go through the UPRG. We'll make sure we are active on brigade area committees, which will meet once a week. I'm still a UDA man but I'm prepared to play that down if it helps us find a new direction.'[10]

There was much premature speculation in the press about an immediate purge within the UDA command structure. In Duddy's view this did not happen because Jackie McDonald thought the new initiative would be obeyed.

> He's the main man now, he's got the seniority and the respect. We need a leading figure and Jackie fits the bill. He's widely seen as a father figure and the voice of reason. He's got my support, no question of it. I just want to do a bit of good if I can before I kick off this mortal coil. I'm fifty-seven years old and I've seen it all. We've got to go forward. There's no other way.[11]

'Going forward' had to mean taking a tougher line within the organisation against brigade areas which were known to be heavily involved in drug-dealing. East Belfast became a priority for McDonald because of the behaviour of Jim Gray, who had been brigadier since the murder in 1992 of Ned McCreery. Gray had become a farcical figure with dyed blond hair, a permatan and a predilection for pastel-shaded sportswear and gold jewellery as well as for frequent trips abroad and playing golf at expensive clubs, when he was not holding court in the Avenue One bar on the Lower Newtownards Road, which he owned. He made no significant contributions to debates about Loyalism's political future and allowed the area to be run by a vicious local gang known as the Young Newtons.

He was, however, jealous of any rivals to his own increasingly nominal position as brigadier and quarrelled bitterly with Michael Stone after his release from prison, seeing his return to the area as a possible threat. Many suspected him of having been implicated in the brutal murder in 2001 of George Legge [see Chapter 11], who had clashed with Gray's son over the control of local drug-dealing operations. The latter, often known by the nickname JJ, later died of a huge drugs overdose while holidaying in Thailand. In early March 2003, Gray was warned by the Inner Council to end his relationship with local drug dealers[12] and there were reports that he was planning to sell his bar in order to avoid an investigation of his lifestyle and income sources by the Assets Recovery Agency.

Questions about Gray's affairs were not encouraged by staff at Avenue One and his appearances there became less frequent. He was also conspicuous by his absence from the UDA delegation which met the Secretary of State at Stormont in November 2004, and five months later the Inner Council announced that Gray was being 'stood down' and that it was taking direct control of East Belfast. This was a dramatic intervention, given what had become the increasingly loose and devolved structure of the organisation, and there were reports of unease over it in East Belfast. Some wanted Stone brought in as a safe and clean pair of hands to run the brigade.[13]

Stone was quick to make it clear that he had no desire to be drawn back into a senior role. He told a newspaper: 'I'm a Loyalist. I'm not into gangsterism and I'm not into drugs and I'm afraid that is the legacy that is left there. If people are trying to clean it up, well and good but my war is over.'[14] Gray's days in power had been numbered since the Inner Council's warning to him in March 2003. There were reports that he had left for England but he was arrested by police near Loughbrickland in County Down, almost certainly heading in his car for the Irish border. He had substantial funds on his person and was held on remand on charges under the 2002 Proceeds of Crime Act.[15]

Just two weeks after the UDA's ultimatum to Gray, it acted to reduce the number of its flags and emblems on display across Northern Ireland and particularly in areas such as Tiger's Bay and the Westland estate in Belfast. There, members could be seen at work and even removing some ordinary Union flags as well as painting over red, white and blue kerbstones. Duddy, on behalf of the UPRG, described it as part of an effort to reduce sectarian tension and 'normalise' working-class Protestant communities.[16]

There was a guarded welcome for these moves from within the nationalist community but on the same day that it was announced, Albert McQuillan, a former RUC officer who had become director of the new Assets Recovery Agency, vowed to pursue UDA commanders who had acquired large fortunes from drug-dealing, extortion and racketeering.[17] The agency, modelled on the Irish Republic's Criminal Assets Bureau, had powers to seize assets and impose tax demands on those who could not prove that their income had legitimate sources. Although the new agency was arguably under-manned for its task, this was a clear warning to figures such as Gray as well as the Shoukri brothers.

The altered image the UDA was trying to create gained nothing from its active involvement in a boycott of the *Sunday World* newspaper's northern edition. Its editor, Jim McDowell, and reporters had, over an extended period, shown themselves to be fearless investigators of paramilitary crime, both Loyalist and Republican. Early in 1996, after the IRA's resumption of bomb attacks on English cities, the paper identified by name, and with photographs, the IRA's Army Council. Five years later, in September 2001, one of its reporters, Martin O'Hagan, who had been threatened on many occasions by the IRA, was shot dead by Loyalists. Tension had been created by articles in the paper alleging threats to Billy McFarland's position as brigadier in the North Antrim area because of his involvement in drug-dealing and illicit property deals.

Using the Loyalist Commission, the UDA set out its case against the *Sunday World* and even enlisted the support of its chairman, Reverend Mervyn Gibson, an East Belfast minister. Embarrassingly, he later had to admit to not even being a reader of the paper, but the Commission's support for a boycott of the *Sunday World* was then blatantly used as an excuse to threaten newsagents who sold it, as well as to seize and destroy bundles of the newspaper before it reached retail outlets. Posters echoing UDA claims about the paper's anti-Loyalist stance appeared in many areas and McDowell received death threats to himself and his family. Ironically, the editor came from a Loyalist background, having grown up in the Donegall Pass locality, and in boyhood had played for a time in a local flute band.

McDowell wrote a defiant editorial denouncing the boycott[18] though without naming the UDA, and received strong support from the respected Ulster Unionist Lord Laird of Artigarvan, who urged the Loyalist Commission to withdraw its support for the boycott. The issue was resolved after direct contacts between the newspaper and the UDA but the episode renewed widespread unease over the organisation's role which the John Gregg initiative in February had attempted to reduce. This unease was not allayed by the UDA's announcement, early in May, that it was dumping another quantity of pipe bombs for the security forces to collect from Alexandra Park in North Belfast.

Once again Duddy acted as spokesman, stressing the importance of lowering tensions at interface areas as another marching season loomed. He told the press that the decision to offload the weapons had come from recent talks between the UPRG and the UDA Inner Council. He was again careful to deny that it was an act of decommissioning but added the thought that 'these are deprived areas and the people need a break. Flashpoint areas shouldn't exist but if nationalists could do something similar, things could improve.'[19]

Instead of improving, however, things took a turn for the worse as a result of events in Bolton, in the north-west of England, where Gina Adair and her children, as well as around a dozen C Company activists, had taken refuge after their flight from Belfast in February. Settling there was a decision based in part on contacts Johnny Adair had made with the British National Party, which had a presence in Bolton and the Greater Manchester area. In fact, little real support materialised from this quarter for the Lower Shankill refugees. Adaptation to life in England required time for people who had only ever lived in one area of Belfast and it proved too difficult for one of them, 21-year-old Alan McCullough.

He was only three months old in October 1981 when his father, William 'Bucky' McCullough, a UDA commander, was shot dead outside his home in Denmark Street on the Lower Shankill. To this day, the gable end of the house, in which his widow Barbara still lives, is decorated with a UDA mural in his honour, naming him as one of its 'lieutenant-colonels'. Paramilitary Loyalism was part of the air the young Alan breathed as a boy and a teenager, and he grew up to idolise Johnny Adair, becoming one of his most loyal lieutenants. This loyalty quickly became strained by the reality of exile and separation from a girlfriend and two-year-old daughter.

Alan McCullough appears to have made contact with Mo Courtney, acting UDA brigadier in West Belfast, and offered him information about Gina Adair's Bolton location as well as where to find a cache of drugs C Company had brought into Belfast in late 2002. In return for this, he was led to believe he could return unharmed to Belfast, though some press reports suggested he might have been prepared for a punishment beating or even a shooting for his alleged involvement in John Gregg's murder.[20] To prove his good faith, he even opened fire on Gina Adair's rented house in Chorley New Road, Bolton, with a sub-machine gun provided by the Belfast UDA.

Soon after his return to Belfast, McCullough disappeared from his mother's home. A week later, after an intensive search, police found his body in a shallow grave near Mallusk on the northern edge of the city. He had been shot several times. Police inquiries revealed that he had left Denmark Street with three men who drove him to a hotel at Templepatrick, where he was bought a meal before being taken to the place of his execution.[21] Both the breach of faith and the calculated brutality of this first UDA killing since Gregg's murder three months earlier shocked Loyalist Belfast. 'Alan's fate was written almost from the womb,' a UDA source told one journalist. 'His father's murder was what drove him. He would have done anything for Johnny Adair and now it seems he may have paid the ultimate price. But someone will pay the price for that too.'[22]

Prior to McCullough's burial on 16 June, UDA graffiti justifying his killing began to appear in the Shankill area and his brother Kenny claimed to have received death threats because of statements he had given to the police during their hunt for the body. Several thousand people attended the funeral and the dead man's mother and four sisters were comforted by mourners as the coffin was carried out of the family home to the strains of the Liverpool football club anthem 'You'll Never Walk Alone' and also 'Simply the Best'.[23]

Kenny McCullough remained defiant, calling his brother's killers 'cowards and scumbags'. He urged people in the area to break with the UDA:

> The people of the Lower Shankill and North Belfast have been living under a dictatorship and we have had our basic rights denied. It's time for an end. It's time for all the decent people within the Loyalist community to stand together and unite as one. It is time to rid our community of the oppression and tyranny that has plagued us for so long.[24]

Ihab Shoukri and Courtney were later arrested and charged with Alan McCullough's murder. The charge against Shoukri was dropped but Courtney still awaits trial, though some think the killing was the work of a senior figure in the Rathcoole area who had been close to Gregg.[25]

Courtney's arrest and a six-year sentence for illegal possession of a firearm given to Andre Shoukri on 1 July removed two dangerous figures from the streets of West and North Belfast. This was an undoubted factor in reducing sectarian tension at interface areas during the 2003 marching season. So too was a very low-key protest by Portadown Orangemen at Drumcree. An *Irish News* columnist, Brian Feeney, seized upon the removal from the scene of Adair, Shoukri and Courtney by imprisonment and of Gregg by death as proof that more proactive policing involving the arrest and detention of UDA leaders could have reduced street violence much sooner.[26]

This was also the view of Mark Langhammer, the independent Labour councillor in Newtonabbey who had clashed with Gregg. He had long advocated a restoration of localised policing but he was aware of the problems of doing this and set them out in a discussion paper which he submitted to Paul Murphy, the new Secretary of State, in April 2003:

> There is a requirement for a warden level of policing. Since 1985, many RUC personnel have been intimidated from Protestant districts. The current PSNI has no significant organic connection with the people in the Protestant working class districts being policed. A natural information flow does not occur.[27]

Redressing this situation, he argued, and doing it through the new District Policing Partnerships set up under the Patten reforms, was one essential strategy for breaking UDA power.

Joining the District Policing Partnerships could make those who did so a target for reprisals from the UDA, especially if they had previously been active on its behalf if only in a political capacity. David Adams, whose public role had dwindled since he failed to win a seat in the 1998 Assembly elections, came under bitter attack in Lisburn. He had quarrelled with the local UDA over money they claimed he owed a local print company which some ex-prisoners were involved in running, but his decision to join the District Policing board without consulting them exposed him to threats, as well as an attack on his car[28] and then on his home.

Intensified police investigations into drug-dealing served only to underline the extent of the UDA's involvement in it. Early in August police drug squad officers seized a lorry at Carrickfergus which was carrying cannabis resin reckoned to have a street value of £2.5 million. The squad's senior officer told the press that there was strong evidence of it being intended for UDA and LVF men in the greater Belfast area.[29] There had also been reports of C Company members in Bolton seeking to move in on the existing drug scene there. In December Gina Adair, who had made more than one clandestine visit to her husband at Maghaberry prison, appeared before Bolton Magistrates' Court, charged with conspiracy to supply heroin and cocaine.

She appeared along with her nineteen-year-old son Jonathan and four others, including Benjamin 'Benji' Dowie, a well-known C Company gunman believed by some in the UDA to have been closely implicated in Gregg's murder.[30] Adair was subsequently acquitted of the charges brought against her, but not so her son, who was found guilty and later sentenced to a five-year term of imprisonment.

Johnny Adair himself continued to be available for interviews at Maghaberry's isolation wing. In mid-October, just a week ahead of his fortieth birthday, he boasted of the cards and letters from well-wishers which he claimed covered his cell walls. However, he also assured his interviewer that 'the people who betrayed me will have to face me some day. It's long runs the fox and they know that every day I'm here the clock is ticking away.'[31] He also used his contacts with a journalist on a Sunday newspaper to issue a series of threats to those he claimed had betrayed both him and the UDA by working as police informers, particularly Jim Spence, who was acting for a time as brigadier in West Belfast after Courtney's arrest, though his real 'rank' was as the commander of the West Belfast Woodvale Company.

There was no follow-up outside Maghaberry to these threats, and UDA violence remained at a relatively low level for the remainder of the year. Debates on the need for a political road to be found by the organisation were led by Jackie McDonald and continued intermittently on the Inner Council but were temporarily overshadowed by a short-lived crisis in the North Belfast brigade area. After his sentencing in 2003, Andre Shoukri was briefly replaced as brigadier by his brother Ihab until he too was arrested and charged with Alan McCullough's murder. A former Linfield footballer, John 'Bonzer' Borland, was then promoted to fill the position. He had a criminal record, having been jailed for three years with the Shoukri brothers over a bid to extort money from a North Belfast businessman.

'Jimbo' Simpson spread rumours about Borland's credentials and about whether he had ever really proved himself in the Troubles, though his own record made him ill placed to do this. He resented the way he had been 'stood down' at Adair's orders and saw an opportunity to retrieve his rank in the organisation. On 13 October around forty men who supported Simpson launched attacks on homes and business premises in the Ballysillan and Glenbryn districts and an unsuccessful attempt was made to abduct Borland. The 'putsch' failed, partly because of the rapid deployment of police and troops across North Belfast, though this did not prevent a series of punishment shootings in response to Simpson's move.

What also mattered was the prompt action of McDonald, who arrived on the scene to co-ordinate pre-emptive measures. He correctly saw the situation as much more than just a brigade problem and acted accordingly. Simpson's regime as brigadier had descended into one of drunken thuggery and intimidation in and around Tiger's Bay, where he lived. The protection rackets he was involved in had become an open secret and his wife 'Tootsie' was widely believed to be a buyer and seller of stolen goods. Early in October 2003 she was also found guilty of shoplifting at Marks and Spencer in Newtownards.[32] None of this deterred Simpson, after the Inner Council ordered him to leave Northern Ireland, from protesting at what he claimed was victimisation and expressing the hope that his return to Belfast might be peacefully negotiated.[33]

The episode at least caused no deaths but it did little for an organisation which had been attempting to alter its image since Gregg's murder. McDonald had shown more effective leadership than the Inner Council had been given credit for by many commentators but it was still possible for adverse comparisons to be made with the more centralised and predictable Shankill-based command structure of the UVF. In fact, the failure of Simpson's attempt to resume power in North Belfast simply cleared the way for Andre Shoukri, who reappeared in court on 13 November. Appeal Court judges rescinded his six-year sentence for illegal possession of a firearm and ammunition for it on the grounds that at the time of his arrest, in September 2002, he needed the weapon for his own protection against Adair.[34]

With the certainty of another sentence on a lesser charge being reduced, Shoukri's release was guaranteed and took place early in March 2004. This year had begun uneasily for the UDA with the imprisoned Adair using his contacts with a Sunday newspaper to launch repeated attacks on the role of Spence in West Belfast. He had reverted to being A Company commander in the Woodvale area after acting temporarily as brigadier following Courtney's arrest, but Adair accused him of being a Special Branch informer,[35] something he also claimed in letters to the author. This was in anticipation of the trial of Ken Barrett, a gunman who was due to stand trial for the 1989 murder of Pat Finucane. Adair clearly believed that in open court he would provide incriminating details on Spence's real role.

This did not happen because, ultimately, Barrett made a plea of guilty to the Finucane charge and thus made only a brief court appearance. Spence, of course, could not be sure of this in advance of the trial and enlisted Courtney's help in increasingly desperate attempts to ensure Barrett's silence.[36] His position in West Belfast was crumbling and Adair's continued accusations did little for the UDA's credibility. In yet another press interview in March 2004, Adair vowed vengeance on his enemies in the UDA, calling them 'criminals and ceasefire soldiers', adding:

> There are a lot of people on the outside who have a lot of questions to answer about what they did to my family and my friends. I have less time to do than I have already done. In ten months I will be out. The clock is ticking and the tables are turning.[37]

Most of his pronouncements and threats were simply bravado with not a lot left to back them up, as events would show. There were stories carried in the press later in the year of a breakaway 'Real UDA' loyal to Adair and of recruiting in the West Belfast brigade area in order to take on Spence and others who had risen to command positions over the previous year.[38] Little more was heard of it, however, and there were no clear signals of support from the Bolton 'exiles'. In Belfast though, there still remained some former C Company members who, despite having appeared to accept the authority of the mainstream UDA in February 2003, had not wholly abandoned their old allegiances.

At the end of January 2004 one of them is believed to have been responsible for a bomb which could easily have killed Sammy Duddy at the York Road office of the UDA's Prisoners' Resettlement Organisation. Duddy, with his well-developed instinct for survival, spotted the device taped to the door when he arrived in the morning to open up. An army bomb disposal unit needed four hours to clear the area and neutralise the bomb. Everything about it, the security forces later told the press, pointed to the work of Loyalists rather than Republicans.[39]

These tensions did not act as any impediment to the UDA's Inner Council deciding on an indefinite extension of the ceasefire they had committed themselves to at the end of February 2003. Once again, the announcement was left to the UPRG with brigadiers and 'military' men well in the background. The statement was read to the press by Tommy Kirkham and it was notable for its recognition of the increased vote achieved by Sinn Fein in the previous November's elections to the still suspended legislative assembly. It also offered a pledge to 'develop relationships with the broader nationalist community based on mutual respect and equity'.[40] There was also a promise to work with police and community workers to lower sectarian tensions as another marching season drew near. The announcement was clearly an attempt to influence the Independent Monitoring Commission (IMC), set up after the Belfast Agreement to monitor and report on continuing paramilitary crime. Even before it delivered its first report on 20 April 2004, Sinn Fein dismissed it as a creation of British 'securocrats' and their Stormont lackeys and it was indeed severe in its strictures on the IRA for the fire-power it retained, its continued recruitment and training and its involvement in serious crimes. However, its treatment of the UDA was equally severe. The report devoted one and a half pages to it, accusing it of being party to continued violence against the nationalist community and also blaming it for recent murders and arson attacks as well as extortion and drug-dealing. It cited the case of one building contractor who was believed to be paying the organisation over £2,000 a week in protection money.

'We are clear', it went on, 'that the UDA is involved in murders and other forms of criminal activity. Since 1 January 2003 the UDA committed some half of all paramilitary murders. We have no doubt that the UDA remains involved in paramilitary assaults and shootings, and in exiling people from Northern Ireland. We are satisfied that many of these activities are known to the UDA at "brigadier" level and so to the Inner Council.'[41] The report also blamed the UDA for the murder of 21-year-old James McMahon in Lisburn on

21 November 2003.[42] However, at the time of writing, nobody has been charged with it and police admit to being no longer certain of UDA involvement.

Privately some senior figures in the UDA claimed to be aggrieved at the tone and content of the IMC report, coming as it did within only a few weeks of the Inner Council's decision to extend their ceasefire. They were not, however, well placed to go public with any thoroughgoing denials of what the Commission had said. As July drew near, Duddy and, on occasion, Shoukri were to be seen out and about at interface areas and in contact with the police over how best to minimise street confrontations. The marching month again passed relatively quietly, though there was a five-day Loyalist blockade of the nationalist Ligoneil enclave in North Belfast prior to the Twelfth.

On the evening of 11 July, the UDA on the Westland estate in North Belfast staged what they described as a 'street party' for the community. This involved setting up a large platform decked out in the organisation's flags and emblems. Close to midnight this was taken over by masked men in combat kit who fired a volley with automatic weapons and revolvers.[43] Nearly all the following day's parades passed off quietly, partly because protests at Drumcree the previous weekend had been very low key. Only at Ardoyne was there any serious violence on the night of the Twelfth, when Orange lodge and flute band supporters were permitted by police to walk in a body several hundred strong back to North Belfast up the Crumlin Road and past the Ardoyne shops.

Some commentators even began to sound optimistic in their reactions to another relatively quiet marching season. 'The Shankill is not living in fear any more,'[44] wrote Pastor Jack McKee, who knew the area well. He claimed that the UDA's grip had begun to slacken, especially in the Lower Shankill. There, he stated,

> for the past eighteen months there have been no street lights put out; there have been no members of C Company sitting at street corners in the night time hours to protect certain homes; there have been no paramilitary vigilante groups walking the streets intimidating the residents by their very presence.[45]

The only two killings of the summer were isolated drug-related acts by the UVF and the INLA but tensions rose again in North Belfast in mid-September as the last remaining Protestant families abandoned the Torrens housing estate near Ardoyne. Claims and counter-claims were made about the sequence of events preceding this but the UDA and its political spokesmen saw it as self-evident proof of a relentless demographic stranglehold by nationalists being tightened around North Belfast's Protestant population. In a press interview, Duddy and John Bunting, who had begun working closely with him, cited events such as the 'loss' of Torrens as good reason for the UDA in the area recruiting better than ever.

Duddy referred to the speed with which Irish tricolour flags had been hoisted over abandoned homes in Torrens: 'Ten years after the IRA's ceasefire

Protestants admit to feeling no sense of relief in their entrenched areas. Indeed many have noticed very little change in their well-being.'[46] Bunting supported him, adding:

> Ask any Protestant what they think of Sinn Fein and prepare yourself for an eye-opener. They say: 'Sinn Fein is seen as the IRA in suits. They couldn't beat Protestants in a military fashion so they altered their agenda and are now trying to defeat us politically and geographically.'[47]

Both men agreed that the UDA was expanding for all the wrong reasons and that the way ahead for sorely tried Protestant communities lay in political education and activism. This was indeed the direction in which Jackie McDonald wanted to take the UDA and the possibilities of doing this had started to be considered in every brigade area for several weeks over the summer and autumn of 2004. Though McDonald was not keen to comment, newspapers got wind of this process and ran reports on it.[48]

A real problem in the path of this process remained that the organisation's firepower and military structure made the temptations of criminality hard to resist. In the second week of October 2004, a large force of police sealed off and raided the Insomnia nightclub, previously known as the Network, in Belfast's North Street. They seized ecstasy tablets with a street value of £20,000, and also large quantities of alcohol which were being sold illegally since the club had no late-night licence. Police told the press they were following a definite line of inquiry involving Loyalist paramilitaries[49] and Shoukri was popularly believed to have been closely involved in the recent takeover of the premises. Shortly afterwards the club had its licence withdrawn by Belfast City Council after a police inspector told councillors there was 'firm evidence that Loyalist paramilitaries were in control of it'. The council was also told that the previous legitimate licensee, Karen McGoldrick, had been subjected to a campaign of intimidation intended to force her into agreeing to hand over to 'new management'.[50] Shoukri's likely involvement in these events was widely known and many people were shocked at the audacity of such an operation within half a mile of the city hall.

An even more blatant episode followed the next month, when five men appeared in court charged with conspiracy to kidnap a bank official in North Belfast. Police believed that the kidnap attempt was in preparation for a major robbery but when the defendants were brought into court they were loudly cheered and applauded by around forty supporters, among whom were Shoukri and William 'Winkie' Dodds, former West Belfast UDA brigadier.[51]

Events like these came as no surprise to Mark Langhammer. In a conversation with the author, he enlarged on an analysis of Loyalist paramilitarism and the UDA in particular which he had already set out for the Secretary of State. In Rathcoole, which lay within the area he represented as a Newtonabbey councillor, the UDA's power, he argued, was a product of the collapse of old working-class structures as traditional industries had disappeared, congregations dwindled and churches closed and, as he put it, middle-class Unionism completed its 'retreat to the golf courses'. Areas such as Rathcoole, he stressed, had had minimal policing since the attacks on the RUC which followed on the 1985 Anglo-Irish Agreement, with hardly any police personnel living locally any longer.

This situation, he had already suggested, could be remedied by new policing strategies.

> Up in Rathcoole, the UDA could be policed in ever-decreasing circles until their hold on the area is broken. Over time, politics will make that possible but the new PSNI hasn't the will or the resources even though they have the UDA well infiltrated. The UDA is involved in more than enough crime to justify major police operations against them. The proof's there at elections. That's the only chance ordinary people have to show what they think of them. It can be hard on decent candidates like Gary McMichael but we know what happened to them.

The UDA, Langhammer continued, had given up on politics:

> What drives most of them still is getting stuck into Fenians and staying in control of areas where they have a presence. There's a generation with power now who are far removed from Andy Tyrie, Alan Snoddy and John McMichael. They had some sense of political possibilities for Loyalism though I don't really think they made many converts. Okay, Sammy Duddy can still talk the talk. He'll do his bit at the interfaces to lower tension, I accept that, but then they create interfaces themselves. Who puts up the flags and paints the kerbstones in the first places? Yes, Sammy worked hard for a 'yes' vote in 1998, I know that, but he'll walk round Tiger's Bay ordering graffiti to be painted over after he's let it go up in the first place.[52]

In fact Langhammer accepted that Duddy had done genuine community work in both West and North Belfast, and Duddy acknowledged that there were real issues about the UDA's future. Meetings about this became more frequent in the second half of 2004 with McDonald reportedly urging fellow brigadiers to face up to the need for a non-paramilitary future for the organisation. It was not an easy case to make. 'Jackie's taking flak from all directions,' Duddy thought. 'It's because he's being realistic. The problem is that there are so many on the take who don't want to let go of paramilitary structures that suit them fine.'[53]

He described a meeting he had attended in Ballysillan with Shoukri in the chair.

> I got up when he called for questions and he did pay a tribute to my long service, I'll give him that. But then I asked a direct question about exactly where all the money in North Belfast was going and I didn't get a real answer.[54]

Some of the audience would have had a fair idea, given reports that were carried in the press about Shoukri's huge gambling addiction. A few months later one newspaper told of him losing £10,000 in one day's betting.[55] 'It's all changed,' said Duddy, 'and it's because of money. I was put off the road for speeding, so I'd be at bus stops with the top men driving past me in their new cars. That would never have happened in the old days.'[56]

The rise of Shoukri, along with rumours of continued support for Johnny Adair on the Lower Shankill, reinforced the doubts that many had about the UDA's ability to stay on the course charted for it when its political spokesmen had announced the extension of its ceasefire in February 2003. At that time the Secretary of State, Paul Murphy, had not been ready to acknowledge that this decision might be genuine, but in early November he met Inner Council members at Stormont as well as spokesmen of the UPRG. Following upon this he took many in the media by surprise when he declared on 12 November 2004: 'I am persuaded that the UDA is now prepared to go down a different road, moving away from its paramilitary past.'[57]

He went on to stress that it remained an illegal body and that criminality by it would 'be pursued relentlessly by the police. I will continue to judge them not just by their words but by their deeds.'[58] It was clear that he was talking in expectation of a significant new statement from the UDA. This, he hoped, could help move the IRA to a bolder act of weapons-decommissioning which could be an essential prerequisite for reactivating the suspended institutions created by the Belfast Agreement.

Almost on cue the UDA responded with a statement heard by over 2,000 of its members at a Remembrance Sunday ceremony in Rathcoole, John Gregg's old power base. A colour party of men in masks and combat kit was present but the announcement was read out by Councillor Tommy Kirkham. While it offered a reiterated justification for the UDA/UFF's role in what it claimed had been the defeat of the IRA, it promised a 'wait and see' attitude on Republicanism's intentions. From there, however, the statement broke new ground by asserting:

> We have new enemies within the Loyalist community: they are poverty, social deprivation, injustice, drugs, crime, inequality and disparity. We intend to redouble our efforts into fighting these issues on a daily basis. From today we are prepared to move into a process, our commitment to that process will be to work towards the day that there will no longer be a need for the UDA and the UFF.[59]

Job creation, social inclusion and community politics were to be the new UDA watchwords, the statement stressed, though Unionist political unity would also be a priority. The document, it was emphasised, was meant to be supported by all the UDA's brigade areas and indeed in some of them it was read out on the same day, in Tiger's Bay, somewhat implausibly, by Shoukri.[60] Political reactions were predictably guarded and indeed sceptical, especially from Sinn Fein and the SDLP, but two *Irish News* columnists writing on successive days offered significantly different reactions.

Breidge Gadd called it

a hugely important statement, which if the leaders can deliver will move the vehicle of peace, currently cranking along in second, up to top gear again. Sunday was a good day for Northern Ireland, a day with the possibility of transforming our future.[61]

The next day, the always acerbic Brian Feeney mocked the statement and what he saw as the Secretary of State's naïve reaction. Giving the UDA a role in job creation and in the politics of social inclusion would, he argued, be akin to 'putting Dracula in charge of a blood bank'[62] because of the access ex-prisoners and other groups with paramilitary links would have to the generous EU funds available for urban regeneration.

The Lisburn-based UDA magazine the *Loyalist*, which printed the full text of the 15 November statement, commended it to members and indeed had gone some way to anticipate it earlier in the year with a call for the development of new relationships with the nationalist community based on 'mutual respect and equity'. The years of conflict were described as a 'painful legacy' which must not impede the emergence of 'a new Northern Ireland which is a warm house for both communities'.[63] Yet this same issue of a magazine edited by former UDA prisoners still echoed the dangerous crosscurrents within Loyalism. On its second-last page it paid tribute to a young Coleraine UDA member, William Campbell, killed three years before: 'It was on 3 January 2001 that William, on his way to rid his area of Catholic scum, was killed by a pipe bomb exploding prematurely, thus robbing us of a true Loyalist hero.'[64]

Five years on from their October 1994 joint ceasefire with the UVF, the UDA became caught up in a power struggle in two of its brigade areas which could have destroyed it. Intensive media coverage of this brutal drama was inevitable but it also served to refocus attention on the issue of the organisation's relationship to the security forces, especially the RUC's Special Branch and specific army intelligence units. For Irish Republicans, the word they now prefer to describe this relationship is the all-purpose 'collusion'.

Most dictionaries define 'collusion' as any secret agreement leading to action by two or more parties taken in concert. Much writing by Republicans and by well-wishers to their cause virtually defines paramilitary Loyalism in terms of its relationship to state forces, but 'collusion' of course is also a word which can be usefully applied to political Republicanism's relationship to an IRA murder machine which killed easily the biggest number of the Troubles' victims. Gerry Adams has managed to write two volumes of memoirs which make no reference to his membership of the IRA. Yet in his rise to a position of leadership within the Republican movement he can reasonably be accused of having built a successful political career out of a relationship of collusion with IRA killing, though a large and gullible element within the world's media is seldom inclined to put this accusation to him.

The modern IRA came into being to fight the British state and, after 1920, to end the partition of Ireland. Because of this it is readily categorised as an example of anti-state terror. Conversely, an organisation such as the UDA, which emerged to support Britain in its resolve to maintain a political settlement which a majority in Northern Ireland supported, has been described as a manifestation of pro-state terror. In one work on terrorist movements, published in 1994, which devoted part of a chapter to Northern Ireland, the UDA was not mentioned at all, though the author thought it important to stress the role of 'indigenous irregulars' who could be 'highly effective components of counter guerrilla operations'.[65] This was certainly a part in Northern Ireland's conflict aspired to by many who joined the UDA. Whether it really could have achieved such a role remains an issue largely neglected in a literature of global terrorism still much preoccupied with anti-state movements.[66]

This can serve to distort the key role played by pro-state terror groups, who in South and Central America have often been actively funded and armed by regimes holding on to power while under attack from Marxist guerrilla movements. Such groups can, if a state under attack is conscious of its own weakness, end up in competition with its authority. This was never a likely outcome in Northern Ireland, where the Stormont government and then, after its suspension, the British state directly always had the reliable manpower of the army and the locally raised RUC and UDR to call on for its security needs.

As the crisis worsened in 1971 and 1972, many in rural areas, who were uneasy over or repelled by the paramilitaries, could show their loyalty by enlisting in the state forces such as the RUC or the new UDR. They could do this on either a full-time or a part-time basis, depending on their family or work commitments. There were no such options for socially similar people in the nationalist community, who, if their political allegiance was strong enough, were much more tempted to take the paramilitary road.[67] It has of course not been unknown for senior figures in the UDA to have expressed a wish to join the 'legitimate' state forces. Two whose hopes of this were never going to be realised were Andy Tyrie and Johnny Adair. Their problem was always going to be that the RUC and the UDR could be rather more selective over their recruitment than any pro-state paramilitary body, though both had to draw from the same population.

Tyrie had at least served in the Territorial Army and, but for his rapid rise within the UDA, would have had a much better chance of being accepted by one or other of the state forces than a teenage Adair with a record of violent delinquency. For both of them and probably many others, an insight by the author of a major book on paramilitary Loyalism still has a precise application: 'The appeal of any terrorist organisation will depend in part on the existence of alternative expressions of the values which that organisation purports to embody.'[68]

A significant number of those who joined both the UVF and the UDA early on were former soldiers who, in Britain's slow withdrawal from empire, had learned something of the limitations of conventional warfare in confronting terrorism. Some of them were as a result schooled in covert counter-measures in places such as Cyprus and Kenya and brought their knowledge into the organisations they joined as the Troubles started. Disenchantment for many of them came with the realisation that 'their' army was in fact an actual impediment to them taking on the IRA in the way they wanted to. Over and above this was the experience of being arrested and imprisoned by the forces of the very state to which they had grown up to be loyal. This comes through powerfully in the testimony of Loyalist prisoners who ended up serving long sentences. Their disorientation and trauma was that of pro-state terrorists who realised that 'their' state was much readier to punish them than to reward them.[69]

Given this ambivalence in paramilitary Loyalism's relationship with the state, any support or co-operation from it was doubly welcome, whether it came with a wink or a nod or on a more structured basis. This book has not been lacking in evidence of this from quite early on in the UDA's emergence but when Brigadier Frank Kitson's manual of counter-insurgency was published in 1970, there were no specific references in it to Loyalist paramilitaries. He was commanding 3 Infantry Brigade in Belfast when his book came out and played a key role in operations against the IRA, including internment in August 1971. The UDA began to organise and to kill within this period but Kitson did not at any point in his book refer to political assassination as a policy, though two writers on what they called political murder in the early 1970s claimed that 'the spirit of Kitson's book would seem to countenance under certain circumstances a campaign of assassination'.[70]

The writers stressed that this would have had to be the work of specialist plain-clothes army units of the kind Kitson wanted to be trained.[71] The operations of such small units could easily enough in the killing times of 1972 and 1973 have been attributed by the nationalist community to the UDA but the matter remains one of conjecture. So too does the claim by the same authors that an element within the UDA close to Tommy Herron wanted the Official IRA, after its May 1972 ceasefire, to move against the Provisionals. Such an outcome, they argued, would have enabled UDA moderates to rein in the organisation's killers. In January 1973 the Republican Clubs, a front organisation for the Officials, did invite UDA participation in joint patrols to stamp out sectarian killings. Herron was not in a strong enough position to accept and murders went on relentlessly.[72]

Nobody active in the Official Republican movement in these years and to whom the author has spoken recalls according any credence to these feelers. Nor do they seriously entertain the thought of the Official IRA, despite its still formidable firepower, embarking on full-scale war with the Provisionals as an olive branch to the UDA.[73] Such a scenario, had the officials been prepared for it, might well have done terminal damage to the Provisionals but their propaganda machine would without question have claimed that the hidden hand of British intelligence was behind it.

Much writing on the Troubles continued to be driven by the belief that Loyalist counter-terror was facilitated by both army intelligence and the RUC's Special Branch. For Republicans of course such a belief was closely bound to their view of the very nature of a British state against which they had taken up arms. Loyalists' response was necessarily a more ambivalent one. Constant claims by the investigative media about their relationship to the state could seem a way of denigrating their paramilitary competence but it could also underpin what they saw as their own legitimacy and their ability to do the state's work for it.

Notable amongst this literature of collusion were books by the late Paul Foot, *Who Framed Colin Wallace?*, and Fred Holroyd, a former army intelligence officer, *War without Honour*.[74] Both titles came out in 1989 and made many allegations about black propaganda and disinformation tactics by British intelligence as well as an elaborate cover-up to protect the Loyalist perpetrators of the sex abuse scandal at the Kincora Boys' Home in Belfast. The Kincora story has yet to be told in full and subsequent events vindicated Foot's claims that Wallace, a staunch Unionist and former UDR officer, was set up on a murder charge to discredit him. Both authors, however, were on less firm ground with their talk of Loyalist terror being co-ordinated by British state agencies and neither had much to say about the UDA specifically.

This was also true of the even more spectacular allegations made in a Channel 4 television programme in 1992 entitled *The Committee*. Developed from some 1986 articles in the *Sunday World* by Martin O'Hagan, this hour-long purported documentary claimed the existence of an 'inner circle' of Mid-Ulster lawyers, businessmen and Unionist politicians acting in secret collusion with RUC and UDR officers as well as paramilitary killers, mainly from the UVF, to target and kill Catholics. A book with the same name as the programme and written by its maker, Sean McPhilemey, was later published in the United States and made further allegations. By then, McPhilemey had been drawn into extensive and costly litigation, losing a legal action brought against his production company by the RUC over his refusal to name sources used[75] but winning another over charges by the *Sunday Times* that the programme was no more than a hoax.[76]

Later in 2000, two Unionist businessmen named by McPhilemey in his book won a million dollars in a libel action they brought against him in an American court.[77] Both programme and book, which in fact drew little support from investigative writers such as David McKittrick and Martin Dillon or even from Sinn Fein itself, still seem symptomatic of an urge to prove that Loyalist killing was in some way dependent on an elaborate network of support from co-operative elements within the security forces. Yet the killings in the Lurgan and Craigavon area examined in the Channel 4 programme did not involve huge distances or arcane geographical knowledge which would have made Loyalists, in this case the UVF, beholden to the 'secret state' to reach their chosen targets.

What kept the collusion issue at centre stage was neither the programme nor the book but the revelations in open court and in the media about the double role of Brian Nelson as a UDA intelligence officer and British agent (see Chapter 7). His trial and conviction took place after the first Stevens inquiry into alleged collusion with Loyalists by personnel within the security forces and raised far wider issues than those identified by Stevens. His much-abbreviated report in fact never referred to the UDA by name, although prominent members of the organisation were among the ninety-four people arrested during the inquiry, fifty-nine of whom were later charged. Few who read it, however, had need to doubt that the UDA were the 'unauthorised persons' who had been given access to photomontages and other material on potential targets by well-wishers within the police and the UDR.

What had set in motion the first Stevens inquiry was the UDA killing of Loughlin Maginn in Rathfriland in August 1989. Despite Stevens and the arrests which the inquiry led to, Maginn's murder remained unsolved and there were nearly 2,000 others like it on RUC files at the time of the Belfast Agreement nine years later. The Agreement and the related peace process created new pressures for unsolved killings to be reinvestigated and the Republican movement and its supporters were highly skilful at ensuring that there was a strong focus on killings which they claimed arose from collusion between the security forces and Loyalists rather than, need it be said, the many more carried out by the IRA.

They drew encouragement from a BBC documentary made by Peter Taylor which was screened in early March, 1999. In it, Bobby Philpott, a convicted UDA killer who had held senior rank in the organisation and had met Mo Mowlam on her visit to the Maze prison in January the previous year, told Taylor that the UDA had been in receipt of regular information on potential victims' addresses, car registrations and even on the clothes they wore: 'I was getting documents daily. I was getting that many documents, I didn't know where to put them,'[78] he said at one point.

Philpott was by no means the first UDA member to have made such claims. Some RUC stations and UDR bases had always been sources of mostly low-level information which was passed on to Loyalists and as far back as 1982 a police raid on the UDA's East Belfast headquarters found an array of documents deemed likely to be of use to terrorists. Andy Tyrie later stood trial over this but was acquitted on the grounds that the Gawn Street office was used by dozens of people and so it could not be proved that he personally had conspired to have possession of the documents.[79] There are in fact few who have been active in the UDA who do not talk of information coming their way from police and army sources.

Just how good all this information was is another matter, as is the UDA's ability always to make maximum use of it. There is also the fact that the same police force and army had the awkward habit of tracking and arresting UDA members, hundreds of whom ended up as a result serving often lengthy prison sentences. Indeed if anything, the security forces had a rather higher success rate in taking Loyalist paramilitaries off the streets than they had against the IRA,[80] something not as a general rule mentioned by Sinn Fein.

Accepting unauthorised gifts of material from the security forces was one part of the UDA's relationship with them. The other of course was being pre-pared to act as agents for them within the organisation. Again, many who have been active in the UDA will talk of approaches being made to them to feed inside information to the police or army, who indeed needed such contacts just as they did within the IRA. Johnny Adair has, in his numerous interviews with the media both inside and outside prison, talked freely of the extent to which he claims the UDA was infiltrated, naming commanders such as Jim Spence in West Belfast as well as the late Tommy Lyttle.

These claims are well-founded in the cases of Spence and Lyttle but Adair also said that he himself was approached by the RUC's Special Branch with offers to work for them.[81] Whether Adair would have had the temperament to operate for them or a specialised army branch such as the Force Research Unit (FRU) has to be debatable given the way he ultimately incriminated himself. Since Adair's downfall, the UDA has not been averse to circulating rumours that he was working for the security forces. The trouble is, however, that this is what he thought he was already doing by using the cutting edge of C Company to hit targets they could not reach. This is clear from his constant boasting to both police and soldiers about his knowledge of the IRA, and when he was finally arrested and charged he was genuinely angry and uncom-prehending about his treatment.

It was of course the CID rather than Special Branch which finally drew the net around Adair in a masterpiece of surveillance and entrapment. Former Detective Sergeant Johnston Brown, the key player in this extremely danger-ous operation, was and remains highly critical of Special Branch. His own investigation of Adair was, he has claimed, at many points impeded by them, both from professional jealousy and because of an ethos which made them distrustful of his working methods and meticulous record-keeping. Brown went public with much of this after his retirement in a major newspaper article in which he made serious allegations about the way Special Branch used informers within Loyalist organisations.[82]

He wrote of a 'cancer within the structures of Special Branch'[83] and he repeated his claims in an Ulster Television *Insight* programme. One former Special Branch officer has, however, defended the way Loyalist agents and informers were handled:

> We never dreamed of aiding their twisted cause. There may have been some bad apples within the intelligence services who leaked files to the UDA and the UVF but the overwhelming majority of intelligence officers had nothing but contempt for the Loyalist terrorists. Not only were their actions morally reprehensible but

they also put an extra burden on an already-overstretched police force. Imagine if we had been able to divert all our resources to combating republican terrorism in the event of the inactivity of Loyalists. Surely more lives would have been spared as a result.[84]

There were high levels of suspicion between Special Branch and the rest of the RUC, as well as clear cases of police and army working at cross-purposes. A clear example was when the FRU's most vital agent, Brian Nelson, was arrested by the police in 1990. Events such as this call into question Republican belief in a monolithic and all-powerful British war machine co-ordinated from the top. The use and protection of Loyalist agents and informers was also part of a twin track strategy under which the IRA itself was infiltrated at the very highest level, as recently published work makes abundantly clear.[85] So too have newspaper revelations about the double role of 'Stakeknife', the nickname of Alfredo Scappatici, the former deputy head of the IRA's internal security unit.

The 1999 launch of the second Stevens inquiry gave new momentum to the Republican campaign directed at UDA and state collusion. In June of that year, a BBC *Panorama* documentary on the killing of Pat Finucane raised some leading questions and a succession of ensuing newspaper articles named names from the programme. One of them was Colonel, now Brigadier, Gordon Kerr, who had commanded the FRU at the time of the Finucane and numerous other killings carried out in the name of the UDA/UFF.

The Ministry of Defence fuelled suspicion with its ill-judged attempts to silence investigative journalists who in fact anticipated many of the new inquiry's eventual findings. *Daily Mirror* writer Nicholas Davies, after initially receiving confidential help from former army intelligence personnel for a book on the FRU, was then told that a High Court action would be brought against him to stop him from carrying on any further work on his project. After ten months of legal argument the action was halted and in 1999 he was able to bring out his book,[86] which, however, attracted relatively little attention from reviewers.

Davies used a different army code number for agent Nelson from that usually quoted and in his account of Finucane's murder, he said that the initial decision to set him up as a target was the UDA's and that Nelson's army handlers were very doubtful about it when first told.[87] This, Davies claimed, was several months before the actual hit. He stated that British intelligence operatives then made their own decision to put Finucane under close surveillance and then decided that 'he was working more closely than ever with IRA officers as well as Sinn Fein leaders'.[88]

This surveillance, Davies argued, cleared the way for the UDA attack on Finucane to be prepared. It was planned well ahead of the often quoted intervention in the House of Commons by the junior Home Office minister Douglas Hogg, who suggested that certain solicitors in Northern Ireland were unduly sympathetic to terrorists. According to Davies's sources, the operation was a straightforward one right down to the fact that the intended victim's home address was in the Belfast telephone directory.

Greatly at variance with Davies's account is that of the authors of the 2004 book *Stakeknife*. They maintained that the initiative came from Lyttle's Special Branch handler, who, they alleged, asked him: 'Why don't you whack Finucane?'[89] Lyttle, they said, then summoned Nelson to his home in the Shankill and told him to prepare an intelligence file on Finucane, not knowing that this was already being done. They described Spence picking the team and Billy Stobie providing the weapons for them. One of the team was Ken Barrett, who later, in 1991, confessed to Brown that he had fired the shots which were drilled into Finucane's face and upper body as he lay on his dining room floor in front of his family.

The authors wrote of a getaway driver and two other unnamed gunmen who made the short trip from the Shankill to the Finucane home, in the quiet and leafy Fortwilliam Drive between the Antrim and Cavehill Roads, on the early evening of Sunday, 12 February. In yet another and much fuller account of what happened, David Lister and Hugh Jordan, in their compelling account of the rise and fall of Johnny Adair, quoted at length from the testimony given them by one of the team that it was he who had killed the victim. This was 'Davy', the alias of a well-known West Belfast UDA man now held on remand on an unrelated murder charge. He was dismissive of Lyttle's involvement but confirmed the level of surveillance applied to Finucane's Republican contacts. In response to one question, he declared that killing him was 'the best hit' he had ever carried out.[90]

All these accounts, no matter how they differed on points of detail, implicated UDA members who were known to have been working for the security forces. Yet the fact remains that the UDA, emerging from the relative torpor of the mid-1980s and with a new generation of gunmen straining on the leash, could have reached and killed Finucane without the elaborate security forces' back-up which features in some versions of events. His house was within easy walking distance of a pub frequented by UDA men from the nearby and fiercely Loyalist Westland estate. Any claims that Special Branch and the FRU knew in advance that Finucane was a UDA target was, of course, a gift to the Republican propaganda machine. They could portray him as a politically uninvolved lawyer, the full investigation of whose death could be made into a test of the integrity of the peace process itself.

Republicans did not accord the same status to any of the IRA's victims. They were seen as agents of the British state who deserved to die because they wore its uniforms or simply tried to earn a living by cooking, cleaning or doing repairs at police and army bases. Either that or on Bloody Friday, July 1972 in Belfast, or in atrocities such as the La Mon House Hotel, Enniskillen or Frizzel's fish shop on the Shankill Road, they were simply in the wrong place when the IRA chose to slaughter them.

For the UDA, re-equipped and beginning to reorganise as it was doing by 1989, killing Finucane was both an act of war and a prestige operation directed at what they claimed was the brains of the Republican movement. It was also an act which cast a long shadow. Relentless media coverage kept the case at the centre of attention, as did the reconstituted Stevens inquiry. So too did the all-party talks at Weston Park in Staffordshire in the summer of 2001. At these, the Blair government gave undertakings to both the SDLP and Sinn Fein that the Finucane case, along with five others, including those of Billy Wright and Rosemary Nelson, would be the subject of special inquiries.

As the Stevens inquiry tackled its huge task, speculation intensified as to what its findings might be. In June 2002, two dramatic presentations which anticipated its outcome appeared on *Panorama*. In the programmes, powerful use was made of the testimony of police officers who had served on the original inquiry. They recalled the army's protracted denials that it even handled special agents in Northern Ireland as well as the numerous impediments placed in the path of their investigation. Johnston Brown spoke of threats from Special Branch over his co-operation with the new Stevens inquiry He also spoke of how he and a colleague had secured a taped confession, though one not made under caution, from Barrett of how he had shot Finucane dead. Brown talked of the later disappearance of this tape and reiterated his belief that prompt arrests and charges immediately after the murder would have been possible. In his view, they would have served to show that there was no structured complicity between the UDA and the security forces or at least not any which reached the latter's higher levels.[91]

There were a number of delays before the inquiry finally prepared its findings for publication. Prior to this, Brian Nelson, its most important source, died of cancer in the United States, where he had been living with his family under a new identity after his release from prison. Much of what he knew went to the grave with him, for Sir John Stevens later told a newspaper that in his opinion Nelson had held back a great deal of information.[92]

The report appeared in a drastically shortened form on 17 April 2003, inevitable perhaps, given the thousands of interviews the inquiry team had conducted. They had also sifted through more than 10,000 documents. Nelson, the inquiry concluded, through his work for the FRU and his dual role in the UDA, had been implicated in at least thirty murders. In many of these, it argued, the victims had not been directly involved in Republican terrorism. It singled out the Finucane killing as proof that the unit and elements of Special Branch had been operating without adequate accountability or control.

This was a conclusion sharply at variance with Republican claims that the FRU and units like it were run from the highest levels of the state. One ex-soldier who had served with the FRU said as much in a newspaper article the day before the report's publication. The writer was named as 'Martin Ingram', whose revelations about his undercover work had already involved him in legal proceedings and court injunctions:

In my six years in the FRU I never received advice or instructions from anyone outside the unit. It is true that ministers and prime ministers received regular intelligence briefings. But to conclude that a minister is involved in an illegal act because he or she reads a military intelligence source report – a sanitised version of the handler's contact form – shows a misunderstanding of the situation.[93]

Intelligence material, Ingram went on to stress, would be presented to ministers in much shortened form with salient points underlined and explained but without material about how the information had been acquired. 'There is a fire-break between government and the work on the ground. Do you honestly believe that politicians would have allowed themselves to be implicated in murder? They just don't have the balls.'[94] However, Ingram admitted that MI5 did share office space with the FRU and could thus feed selected information to ministers on their own account. His evidence demands respect, though it does not sit neatly with some of the more simplistic conspiracy theories about collusion. He has written elsewhere that he does not regret his role in the war against the IRA but is sorry that 'certain lines, certain moral boundaries were stepped over too many times and innocent people died'.[95] Whether some of the IRA agents and informers who were sacrificed were so innocent may well be another matter.

Amidst a spate of newspaper editorials demanding action to implement the report's conclusions, Stevens announced that he would be submitting twenty of the inquiry's files to Northern Ireland's Director of Public Prosecutions. The only legal proceedings to arise thus far have been against Barrett. He was settled in England under a witness protection programme after the Stevens inquiry began its work but was later arrested and taken back to Belfast for trial on the charge of having murdered Finucane. This was a huge embarrassment to the West Belfast UDA and to Jim Spence, its Woodvale company commander, who was widely believed to have been a Special Branch informer.

Intense pressure was put on Barrett by other UDA members in Maghaberry prison to say nothing in court about his contacts within the organisation. There were reports that Spence had offered a substantial sum of money to Mo Courtney to use his influence as a remand prisoner to ensure silence from Barrett when he finally appeared in court.[96] The trial was a non-event, as he changed his plea to one of guilty for the Finucane murder and eleven other charges brought against him. This outcome meant that most of the evidence against Barrett remained untested in open court. He was given life imprisonment with a recommendation by the judge that he serve not less than twenty-two years.

The sentence was only a notional one since, if he was willing to remain in prison in Northern Ireland and the authorities were prepared to keep him there, Barrett would be released under the terms of the Belfast Agreement because his crimes had been committed prior to the 1994 ceasefires. Outside the court, former police officers reminisced to journalists about Barrett, describing him as a cold and remorseless killer who had boasted to them of having killed ten people.[97] Whether Finucane was really one of them, despite Barrett's confession on tape to Brown, is something that many doubt. His change of plea was a little too convenient, both for the UDA and the security services. A few months after the trial, a Belfast Sunday newspaper claimed that in fact the fatal shots were fired by Courtney after Barrett's weapon had jammed.[98]

The April report was not intended to be the end of the Stevens inquiry. Apart from the exposure it had given to the security forces' infiltration into the UDA, it had also alluded to the handling of agents within the IRA and to one in particular. This was 'Stakeknife', whose true identity had become a matter of intense speculation well before the report in the Sunday People[99] and, a few days later, in the Irish Independent In the latter, the Dublin-based reporter Eoghan Harris argued that media coverage of Nelson's role was crowding out an even bigger story. He quoted respected colleagues such as Ed Moloney and Jim Cusack in support of his view that the press as a whole were avoiding naming Stakeknife because of the impact this would have on the Republican movement at a point when its support for the peace process was seen as vital by the British government.

Sinn Fein and the IRA faced acute embarrassment if the story became public of how an agent even more ruthless than Nelson had been operating for years at a high level within their own ranks. Even worse was the fact that this agent had set up and sanctioned the torture and execution of both real and alleged informers. Furthermore, he was also thought to have been behind the murder of key figures in the movement who were known opponents of the political strategy of the Adams–McGuinness leadership.[100] Harris also raised the question of why Nelson had not used his role to inflict more damage on the IRA. Where, he quoted Moloney as asking, was the pile of IRA bodies? Had Nelson and the FRU protected Stakeknife and, by extension, the Republican leadership from its own enemy within? If so, Harris argued, then they had materially contributed to the peace process.

The UDA's North Antrim and Londonderry brigade was quick to see the importance of Harris's article. Without ceremony or acknowledgement, they ran the whole of it in the autumn issue of their magazine Warrior.[101] This piece of plagiarism was their way of alerting a membership uneasy about the politics of the peace process to the deadly game into which the UDA had been drawn by the state and its agencies. Within a very few months of the recycling of Harris's article, Stakeknife's identity was revealed by newspapers, amidst predictable denials by the Republican movement which continued until Alfredo Scappatici, its former grand inquisitor and torturer in chief, made a permanent move from West Belfast to southern Italy.

At the time of writing, there is no reason to anticipate an end to revelations and allegations about Northern Ireland's secret war and the extent to which elements within the UDA became part of it. There is indeed a sense in which the whole issue takes us back to where this book began, with the formation of the UDA and its rapid evolution into a large paramilitary organisation. At that time and for several years, there were those on the British left who made a heavy intellectual investment in the view that since, by their definition, the IRA's war was an anti-imperialist one, then in such a context the UDA could only be an arm of the Unionist state and of the British state itself after the suspension of Stormont.[102]

Even if their explanation of the UDA's role had been correct, it would still have left unanswered the question of why so few members of the IRA and INLA, especially leading ones, were successfully targeted. One authority on Northern Ireland's paramilitaries has concluded that those least likely to die at Loyalist hands were precisely those who ought to have been their prime targets, i.e. active militarists within the Republican movement.[103] They were in fact at far higher risk from the SAS and other undercover units who, in the 1985–1992 period alone, killed twenty two IRA men in the Armagh and Tyrone area. This was not far off the combined UDA and UVF success rate against the IRA over the whole period of the Troubles. Only when Sinn Fein, which always had active IRA operators among its numbers, began to contest elections were the Loyalists able to start picking off some of its activists, because their public role made them easier to hit.

Yet it was never simply its relationship to the state which defined the UDA or brought it into being as a street-level working-class Loyalist organisation. To believe this is to accept a very simplistic view of the nature of Loyalism and to allow little for the variety of opinions, aspirations and above all fears within the UDA even at the point, early on, when real sectarian killers within it moved to centre stage. The dreadful crimes they committed can and must be explained, as this book has tried to do, but they must never be excused. There are now many UDA members out of prison who have a lifetime to spend with the memories of what they did. However, when the IRA unleashed its own brutal and sectarian war, ordinary men in Protestant areas confronted with an extraordinary threat to everything they believed simply did what they felt they had to do, like those who had gone before them. As Sammy Duddy put it in one of his poems,

Deeds deemed a crime
Vary with facts and time.
I can recall a time
When our acts suited the British stage –
Or have they torn out that page of history yet?[104]

NOTES

1. *Sunday World*, 2 February 2003.
2. J. Adair, interview with author, 9 June 2004.
3. Ibid.
4. Ibid.

5. Ibid.
6. *Irish News*, 10 February 2003.
7. *Irish News*, 21 February 2003.
8. Ulster Political Research Group, statement, 22 February 2003.
9. Ibid.
10. S. Duddy, interview with author, 24 February 2003.
11. Ibid.
12. *Sunday World*, 9 March 2003.
13. *Sunday World*, 3 April 2005.
14. Ibid.; *Irish News*, 31 March 2005.
15. *Irish News*, 11 April 2005.
16. *Irish News*, 25 February 2003.
17. Ibid.
18. *Sunday World*, 30 March 2003.
19. *Sunday World*, 4 May 2003; *Irish News*, 5 May 2003.
20. *Irish News*, 12 June 2003.
21. *Irish News*, 6 June 2003.
22. *Guardian*, 2 June 2003.
23. *Irish News*, 17 June 2003.
24. Ibid.
25. North Belfast UDA member, interview with author, 1 March 2005.
26. Irish News, 27 August 2003.
27. M. Langhammer, *Cutting with the Grain: Policy and the Protestant Community – What Is to Be Done?* (Belfast, 2003), p. 13.
28. *Loyalist*, vol. 5, no. 1, 2003; *Irish News*, 21 October 2003.
29. *Irish News*, 8 August 2003.
30. *Irish News*, 18 December 2003.
31. *Irish News*, 15 October 2003.
32. *Sunday World*, 2 November 2003.
33. *Sunday World*, 26 October 2003.
34. *Irish News*, 14 November 2003.
35. *Sunday World*, 11 January 2004.
36. *Sunday World*, 15 February 2004.
37. *Sunday World*, 21 March 2004.
38. *Sunday World*, 20 June 2004.
39. *Sunday World*, 1 February 2004.
40. *Irish News*, 25 February 2004.
41. *First Report of the Independent Monitoring Commission* (Belfast: Independent Monitoring Commission, 2004), p. 17.
42. Ibid., p. 37.
43. *Irish News*, 13 July 2004.
44. *Sunday World*, 1 August 2004.
45. Ibid.
46. *North Belfast News*, 18 September 2004.
47. Ibid.
48. *Sunday Life*, 3 October 2004.

49. *Sunday World*, 10 October 2004.

50. *Irish News*, 2 November 2004; *Sunday World*, 23 January 2005.

51. *Irish News*, 1 December 2004.

52. M. Langhammer, interview with author, 17 October 2004.

53. Duddy, interview with author, 5 October 2004.

54. Ibid.

55. *Sunday World*, 27 February 2005.

56. Duddy, interview with author, 5 October 2004.

57. *Guardian*, 13 November 2004.

58. Ibid.

59. *Loyalist*, Lisburn, vol. 5, no. 12, 2004.

60. *Irish News*, 15 November 2004.

61. *Irish News*, 16 November 2004.

62. *Irish News*, 17 November 2004.

63. *Loyalist*, vol. 5, no. 4, 2004.

64. Ibid.

65. L. Thompson, *Ragged War: The Story of Unconventional and Counter-Revolutionary Warfare* (London: Arms and Armour, 1994), p. 147.

66. J. Sluka (ed.), *Death Squad: The Anthropology of State Terror* (Philadelphia: University of Pennsylvania Press, 1999), p. 1.

67. K. Boyle, T. Hadden and P. Hillyard, *Ten Years On in Northern Ireland: The Legal Control of Political Violence* (London: Cobden Trust, 1980), p. 22.

68. S. Bruce, *The Red Hand: Protestant Paramilitaries in Northern Ireland* (Oxford: Oxford University Press, 1992), p. 273.

69. C. Crawford, *Defenders or Criminals?: Loyalist Prisoners and Criminalisation* (Belfast: Blackstaff Press, 1999), p. 116–61.

70. M. Dillon and D. Lehane, *Political Murder in Northern Ireland* (Harmondsworth: Penguin, 1973), p. 314.

71. F. Kitson, *Low Intensity Operations: Subversion, Insurgency, Peace-Keeping* (London: Faber and Faber, 1971).

72. Ibid., p. 174–6.

73. J. Lowry and D. O'Hagan, interview with author, 26 March 2004.

74. P. Foot, *Who Framed Colin Wallace?* (London: Macmillan, 1989); F. Holroyd and N. Burbridge, *War without Honour* (Hull: Medium, 1989).

75. *Guardian*, 1 August 1992.

76. *Guardian*, 31 March 2000.

77. *Irish News*, 13 May 2000.

78. *Irish News*, 6 March 1999.

79. H. McDonald and J. Cusack, *UDA: Inside the Heart of Loyalist Terror* (Dublin: Penguin Ireland, 2004), p. 124.

80. *Fortnight*, September 1992.

81. Adair, interview with author.

82. *Belfast Telegraph*, 19 June 2002; J. Brown, interview with author, 6 June 2003.

83. Ibid.

84. A. Barker, *Shadows: Inside Northern Ireland's Special Branch* (Edinburgh: Mainstream, 2004), p. 222.

85. E. Moloney, *A Secret History of the IRA* (London: Allen Lane, 2002).
86. N. Davies, *Ten-Thirty-Three: The Inside Story of Britain's Secret Killing Machine in Northern Ireland* (Edinburgh: Mainstream, 1999).
87. Ibid., p. 156–9.
88. Ibid., p. 160.
89. M. Ingram and G. Harkin, *Stakeknife: Britain's Secret Agents in Ireland* (Dublin: O'Brien, 2004), p.196.
90. D. Lister and H. Jordan, *Mad Dog: The Rise and Fall of Johnny Adair and 'C' Company* (Edinburgh: Mainstream, 2003), p.57–61.
91. *Panorama*, BBC, 19 and 23 June 2002; *Guardian*, 24 June 2002.
92. *Irish News*, 28 April 2003.
93. *Guardian*, 16 April 2003.
94. Ibid.
95. Ingram and Harkin, *Stakeknife*, p. 33.
96. *Sunday World*, 15 February 2004.
97. *Guardian*, 14 September 2004.
98. *Sunday World*, 27 March 2005.
99. *Sunday People*, 23 June 2002.
100. *Irish Independent*, 30 June 2002.
101. *Warrior*, no. 34, 2002.
102. G. Bell, *The Protestants of Ulster* (London: Pluto Press, 1976); D. Reed, *Ireland: The Key to the British Revolution* (London: Larkin, 1984).
103. J. Holland, *Hope against History: The Course of Conflict in Northern Ireland* (London: Hodder and Stoughton, 1999), p. 387.
104. S. Duddy, *Concrete Whirlpools of the Mind* (Belfast: Ulidia, 1983), p. 37.

13

Hands across the Sea: The UDA in Scotland

When Johnny Adair's family and remaining supporters arrived at the port of Cairnryan in early February 2003 there was a frenzy of speculation in the Scottish media about how Loyalist Scotland would respond and what support there would be for the exiles. Adair, like many leading figures in the UDA, was not a stranger to Scotland, certainly not to home games at Ibrox Park in Glasgow. There were also unconfirmed reports about the contacts he had made with criminal syndicates in the city as well as moves he had made to buy substantial property in Scotland.

One source told a Sunday newspaper how eighteen months previously Adair and other senior UDA members had been guests of honour in a pub in Glasgow's East End prior to a Rangers–Celtic game. According to him, several of the city's criminal godfathers with Loyalist sympathies arrived 'to pay their respects and do a little business. You walked into that pub and felt surrounded by power. The faces round that bar controlled thousands of foot soldiers, thousands of weapons. God knows what would happen if they ever joined forces.'[1] There was in fact little likelihood of this happening. Giving Adair celebrity treatment on a short visit was a different matter from letting him occupy any of the turf already controlled by local criminals.

A year and a half later there was no celebrity welcome for Adair's family and friends. On a later ferry than the one on which they had made their escape from Belfast, UDA Inner Council members crossed to a secret location in the west of Scotland for talks with the organisation's leadership there. At this gathering an order was passed on from Belfast that no doors should be opened to the exiles in Scotland. It was also made clear that any Loyalists with information on their whereabouts should immediately make contact with the UDA.[2] Adair in his cell at Maghaberry might rationally have expected little else after the murder of John Gregg, who had heroic stature in the eyes of Scottish UDA members, though he was then and still is in denial of any complicity in his death.

'Some of Adair's team are a bit tasty,' a Belfast UDA man was quoted as saying. 'The boys in Scotland don't really have the capability to take them on. So there's an all-stations alert out for them in Loyalist circles in Scotland. If anyone clocks them the information will be fed back to Belfast within hours. The UDA will take it from there.'[3] The Adair clan did not put matters to the test. After a brief stay in a hotel in Ayr close to the railway station, during which they threatened and then attacked a television crew,[4] they travelled south to Bolton, where many of them settled, after a fashion.

The UDA in Belfast, like the Scottish police, had been concerned at the continued presence in Scotland of Sammy 'Skelly' McCrory, one of Adair's oldest friends and an active C Company gunman. After his release from prison in October 1999 under the terms of the Belfast Agreement, McCrory had gone to live in Ayrshire but had maintained contact with Adair. He was seen on the Shankill Road in Belfast on Saturday, 19 August 2000, prior to the violence at the Rex bar which triggered the Loyalist feud in which Adair was the key figure. Death threats from the UVF followed McCrory back to Scotland and in May 2002 shots were fired at him in the town of Ayr.

He is known to have returned to Belfast in late January 2003 and to have visited Adair in prison just days before Gregg's murder. Interviewed by a Scottish newspaper, McCrory denied any involvement in the killing, insisting that 'I have nothing to do with what happens over there now. I haven't been in touch with anyone. I moved here to get away from all of that.'[5] Scottish police were not convinced and admitted that McCrory's movements were closely monitored. In Ayrshire, with its supportive network of Orange lodges, flute bands and Loyalist clubs, it would not be difficult for McCrory or others like him to keep his Belfast contacts.

Indeed, many years before his arrival, the county had been the focus of a report in the Scottish press that Loyalist paramilitary gunmen to whom elements in the security forces had 'obligations' had been spirited out of Northern Ireland and quietly resettled in Ayrshire under new identities. This story, with all it implications, was never followed up by the newspaper which initially ran it.[6]

Western and central Scotland's Protestant history, as well as the impact upon it of Irish migration and its historic links to Ulster both before and after partition, made it certain that any crisis 'across the water' would arouse strong emotions in areas where, since the late eighteenth and nineteenth centuries, there had been a rapid growth of an Ulster model of oath-bound Orange lodges. A Scottish Grand Lodge was formed in 1835 with thirty-five individual lodges affiliated to it. Since then the pattern has been of almost unbroken growth with Scottish Unionists reaping significant advantage from it as a working-class electorate emerged. Leading Scottish Unionists and Conservatives in the interwar years were active Orangemen[7] but the Orange vote which they could draw upon has broken up in recent years. However, during the Thatcher era, the melt-down of Conservative support in Scotland prompted some to argue a case for the party trying to recapture the Orange electorate.[8]

Economic fear of and prejudice against the Catholic Irish in Scotland well into the twentieth century were never hard to activate and they could be readily aligned to the cause of Protestant Ulster. This was apparent in the 1912–14

Home Rule crisis, when Glasgow saw big rallies in support of Sir Edward Carson and the formation of local UVF units posing as athletic clubs attached to Orange lodges.[9] All this was overtaken by the greater drama of a world war and the partial resolution of the Irish question by partition and the 1921 treaty. Nevertheless, sectarianism simmered on close to the surface of public and political life in Scotland, though receiving no serious academic analysis until the onset of Northern Ireland's Troubles in the 1960s.[10]

The Scottish Orange Order's first reaction to powerful media images of communal violence in Northern Ireland was a militant one. John Adam, its Grand Secretary, toured county and district lodge areas urging brethren with any military experience to be ready to give their services to Loyal Ulster. In July 1970, thousands of Scottish Orangemen and their supporters sailed for Belfast, and their Grand Master, Thomas Orr, before the Twelfth parade there, said of the worsening situation in the province: 'If it does erupt into civil war then I'm sure that many Scots will want to remain.'[11]

Support for embattled Protestant Ulster was always going to go beyond oratory, fund-raising and swelling the ranks at Belfast's Twelfth. What guaranteed this was the UVF's re-emergence and then the formation of the UDA. Their exploits encouraged a minority of Scottish Loyalists to organise on their own account, using their names, a development which the Orange Order felt it had to condemn.[12] Its devolved structure made it a problem, however, for the Grand Lodge of Scotland to control the practice of private lodges either accepting or keeping members with paramilitary links. It proved equally difficult to lay down the law about which of Scotland's many flute bands were hired by lodges for their parades. Some of these bands were quick to form paramilitary links and imposing discipline of any kind upon them became an intractable problem for the Orange Order.[13]

As in Northern Ireland, the UVF in Scotland was initially and for quite some time a better-disciplined body than the UDA. It built up a well-organised Loyalist Prisoners Welfare Association (LPWA), an active network in which one leading Scottish Orangeman took an active part for several years. The author was invited by him to be present on 3 August 1990 at an event held at a town hall in the east of Scotland which the organisation had booked under another name. Several hundred people were entertained by flute bands from Fife and Lothian who had been recently disciplined by the Orange Order. Lights were darkened as they made a thunderous entry to the centre of the hall, while spotlights picked out the bandsmen, to huge applause and cheers. One organiser reckoned that the evening would raise up to £2,000 for UVF prisoners. This goal was helped by a raffle in which the first prize was announced as a bottle of malt whisky. The second was a UVF plaque and the Orangeman already mentioned brought the house down when he announced that the third prize would be a week in Lourdes and the fourth prize two weeks there.[14]

The UVF and its back-up organisation in Scotland was much more successful than the UDA in producing and selling supportive literature. *Red Hand* was the most successful. Launched in 1989, it offered uncompromising and often rabidly stated support for the Ulster Loyalist cause. Those who produced it claimed they could sell up to 5,000 copies per issue. It came under threat of police investigation in 1991 after running articles printing the names, addresses and personal details of what it claimed were Irish Republican sympathisers in Scotland. Among those identified were the organisers, in Edinburgh, of what had become highly contentious annual marches to commemorate the birth there of the 1916 Easter week martyr James Connolly.[15]

Red Hand ceased publication in 2000. Some think this was in response to an order from the Belfast UVF, which, five years into the peace process, found its tone too warlike.[16]

The UVF was also ready to take the war to the Republican enemy in Scotland. On 17 February 1979 members bombed two pubs in Glasgow frequented by Catholics, the Old Barns in Calton and the Clelland bar in the Gorbals. These were claimed to be used for Republican fund-raising. Injuries but no fatalities resulted from the demolition of the two pubs, and in June of the same year nine UVF men from Glasgow's East End were convicted of these attacks and of other offences.[17] William Campbell, their leader, who received a sixteen-year sentence, became a hero in the eyes of the UVF in Belfast. He died there after his eventual release but in October 1995 his nephew, Jason, was sentenced to life imprisonment for slashing open the throat of a teenage Celtic supporter, Mark Scott, who bled to death from his wound.[18]

Happily, this was the only instance of a Loyalist pub bombing in Scotland, but there were a number of further trials of UVF members for illegal handling of firearms and explosives. West central Scotland, with its still sizeable coal industry, was a good source for the latter and significant quantities found their way to the UVF's Ulster-based units though they made less use of them than did the IRA. Unlike in Northern Ireland, there was little violent friction between the UVF and the UDA, though rivalry existed. There were also incidents in Glasgow's Barnlinnie prison in 1979 when both UVF and UDA men were on remand there awaiting trial.[19] Taunts and some insults were traded and prison officers had to keep the two groups apart.

At intervals during the years of the Troubles, UVF men appeared before Scottish courts to receive heavy sentences both for membership of the organisation and for illegal possession of arms and explosives. Further trials in Scotland took place after the October 1994 Loyalist ceasefire and reports started to appear in the Scottish press of the UVF seeking to move into an already lucrative local drugs market.[20] In June 2002 it was claimed that William Moore, who had served eighteen years in prison for his part in the serial murders carried out by the Shankill Butchers, had been seen in Edinburgh's Wester Hailes housing estate. Some thought he was lending his weight to a UVF bid to take over drug-dealing in the area[21] after the locality was terrorised by a ruthless six-man Belfast gang, who were sentenced by a Scottish court the following year. This gang had only tenuous links with the organisation[22] but

had made blatant use of its name, a capital offence in the eyes of the UVF leadership in Belfast, who made it known that death sentences on the men would
be carried out if they ever returned to the city.[23]

The UDA in Scotland recruited quickly and was soon boasting of a bigger
membership than the UVF. As in Northern Ireland, it was a legal organisation
and security sometimes seemed to be one of its minor priorities. The author
can recall an East Edinburgh acquaintance who openly wore a UDA lapel badge
and who would talk cheerfully in the street or on buses about dividing his weekends between Rangers games at Ibrox and military drilling and exercises on
Slamannan Moss near Falkirk. He was also active in the Edinburgh Loyalist
Coalition, which organised some violent disruption of events held in the city
in 1981 to give support to the IRA's H-block hunger strikers.[24]

June 1974 saw the first major trial in Scotland of UDA members, five of
whom appeared at Glasgow High Court charged with armed robbery and illegal
possession of firearms and explosives. One of those convicted was Andy
Tyrie's brother, Sammy. He received a shorter sentence than his co-defendants,
one of whom was given a ten-year term. This soon became a standard penalty
in Scotland for Loyalists found guilty of handling explosives.[25]

From early in the UDA's existence in Scotland, police and intelligence services were concerned to infiltrate it. This was facilitated by the use of known
criminals such as Arthur Thompson, who, at the time of his death from a
heart attack in 1993, was a dominant figure in organised crime in the west of
Scotland. He was also known for his Ulster Loyalist sympathies and as a man
who was ready to supply weapons to the UDA in Northern Ireland. Police
Special Branch and MI5 officers, journalists have claimed, were able to 'turn'
him by using their influence to secure a lenient sentence for him in a robbery
trial. The payback, they have also claimed, was that he would supply information on the UDA while still running weapons to them as a cover for his
relationship with Special Branch and MI5.[26] Thompson's son, known as 'Fat
Boy', worked closely with him, and one former Barlinnie prisoner who had
been involved with them declared: 'Over the years the Thompsons must have
shipped hundreds of guns and thousands of bullets to Ireland.'[27] It was a
high-risk operation for the UDA, without them knowing it, because of what
was being fed back to the security services in the form of useful intelligence
on their organisation. It also provided cover which helped Thompson expand
a formidable criminal operation based on extortion, money-lending, prostitution and drugs.

By the end of 1974 Roddy MacDonald, a former soldier, had emerged as
the self-styled UDA commandant in Scotland. The following year, on
September 21, he agreed to be interviewed on BBC Scotland's *Current
Account* television programme. He spoke openly about buying 'arms for
Ulster' in Scotland. When asked about the size of the UDA's membership, he
answered, somewhat implausibly: 'How many people do you get in Ibrox on
a Saturday afternoon? In a good game how many Rangers supporters do you

get? Well, half of them are members of the UDA.'[28] This ill-advised bravado landed him in serious trouble with the Orange Order, of which he was a member. His expulsion was called for by the Grand Lodge of Scotland but initially more than 300 members of this large and unwieldy body voted against it.[29] He was, in the end, forced out after senior office bearers had threatened to resign themselves.

MacDonald, after further injudicious media interviews and some well-publicised trips to Northern Ireland, was sentenced to eight years' imprisonment in 1979. This was the result of his being implicated in the robbery of a gun shop in the Gorgie district of Edinburgh in which a young employee was found guilty of murdering the shop's owner and then offering weapons stolen from it to MacDonald for the UDA's use.

There was some regrouping after MacDonald's removal from the scene but later in 1979 the UDA in Scotland received a devastating blow when twelve members of units based in Paisley and Dumfries were found guilty of charges ranging from conspiracy to illegal possession of firearms and assault. The trial was made possible through intensive surveillance work by Scottish Special Branch officers, which in the case of the Paisley unit had lasted for two years and had also involved its courageous infiltration by a Strathclyde Police detective sergeant. He gave evidence in court of witnessing vicious disciplinary beatings administered in a hall where the local UDA met. The favoured implement was a heavy pickaxe handle, painted red, white and blue and with the name 'Snoopy' inscribed on it.[30]

An element of levity crept into the audience when the court heard how one UDA commander in Paisley had 'pulled rank' in order to secure a free supply of electricity from a downstairs neighbour who was also a member of the local unit. This was done by taking out the cables for his television and other electrical appliances and leading them through the neighbour's windows to be plugged in to points in his flat. The trial and its outcome was an embarrassment to the Orange Order because several of the accused were also members of their local lodges. James Hamilton, MacDonald's successor as Scottish commandant, who was given a sixteen-year sentence, was not only an Orangeman but had served as an auditor for the County Grand Lodge of Ayrshire.[31]

What also emerged from this trial was that these particular UDA units had been of limited value to the Loyalist struggle in Northern Ireland. Incredibly, one particular package of explosive material was sent by them to Belfast by ordinary mail and with the sender's name and address on it. In addition, the weapons taken as a result of the Edinburgh gun shop robbery eighteen months earlier never reached the UDA in Northern Ireland and were in due course found by police in a Dumfries house, where they had lain for many months in a coal cellar.[32]

Despite the questions posed by this trial about the Scottish UDA's competence, surveillance by police of both it and the UVF continued, even though the level of UDA operations in Northern Ireland itself went into decline in the 1980s. There continued to be regular traffic of Rangers supporters heading to and from home games at Ibrox, as well as Scottish flute bands crossing by ferry in the summer months to join the Loyalist marching season in Belfast and elsewhere. All this movement had to be kept under observation but it was not always foolproof. As one Loyalist source told a journalist,

> when the flute bands and their followers go over on the ferries, many of them drunk on cider and wine and full of Orange fervour, the security people at the ports don't want to tangle with them. All kinds of things can be hidden in drums, flagpoles and the like.[33]

However, even incomplete surveillance could still impede the movement of suspect individuals and of items they might want to carry with them. It could also achieve arrests and convictions. In March 1987, five Glasgow men were found guilty of furthering the UDA's purposes by illegal means including the possession of arms and explosives. Weapons exhibited in court for the jury's guidance were said by Crown counsel to have been bought from Territorial Army soldiers, then buried in a field at Easterhouse on the east side of Glasgow. Police were guided to this cache by one of the accused and another, Andrew Robertson, a former Glasgow University student, was said in court to have co-operated with the police once arrested by them. This did not save him from a twelve-year sentence.[34]

Two years later, another six UDA men stood trial at Perth in the longest criminal case in the city's history. Once more, membership of the Orange Order emerged as a factor in the trial. For some Loyalists in Scotland, as in Ulster, joining a lodge or a flute band could mean trips to Northern Ireland and an urge developing to play alongside the 'big boys' there. All the defendants belonged to their local lodge, number 209, the St Andrew's True Blues, and were also members of their local Apprentice Boys of Derry club. The key figure was Erik Cownie from Wester Hailes, Edinburgh, who had recruited his co-accused to full UDA membership in Belfast the previous year. 'Until then,' a newspaper reported, all of them 'appeared to be normal family men, with a liking for a pint and an avid, almost obsessional, enthusiasm for Loyalist matters and paraphernalia.'[35]

What they had really contributed to the UDA's cause is open to doubt but they were all convicted of illegal possession of weapons and, in the case of Peter McQueen, a bullet-making machine, which he kept in his bedroom. This, according to evidence led by the Crown, turned out ammunition which was much more likely to endanger anyone trying to fire it than any intended victim. Their activities were described as 'the worst-kept secret in Perth'[36] but once again heavy sentences were passed on them, ranging from sixteen years for Cownie to twelve, ten, nine and seven years for his co-defendants. Two of them received ten-year terms.

One Scottish UDA organiser, who contributed to the UDA's *Ulster* magazine under the alias Colin Paterson, subsequently told the author that in his view the organisation in Scotland would need two or three years to recover from the effects of the Perth trial. He spoke with anger of defendants who had 'grassed' on each other to help the police and secure lesser sentences, though he exonerated Cownie from this charge. The LPA was, he declared, 'looking after' the families of Cownie and another prisoner whose wife was 'more than happy' with the financial support she was receiving.[37]

Paterson, who also answered to the name Charlie, came from Bonnybridge, near Falkirk, and had served in the Argyll and Sutherland Highlanders before settling in Belfast. His role, he said, was to co-ordinate funding in Scotland for UDA prisoners, subject to the orders of the Inner Council. The UVF, he conceded, were raising more money in Scotland than the UDA but he stressed that things were getting better. 'We can call up 1,000 collectors any time in Glasgow,' he claimed, 'but the vetting has to be good. Bogus collectors, guys on the take using our name can be a problem. They have to be given a wee talking to if we catch them.'[38] In some areas, he added, the Apprentice Boys of Derry would help out by holding dances or raffles from which the proceeds would be split evenly between the two Loyalists prisoners' organisations.

Ulster magazine, on its 'Tartan Talk' page, would regularly praise the fund-raising efforts of the Loyalist Prisoners' Aid organisation in Scotland and sometimes appeal directly to supporters there. In the summer of 1990, with many UDA men arrested under the Stevens inquiry, it urged Scottish well-wishers to raise their share of the £2,000 needed for a new minibus for prisoners' families.[39] *Ulster* also printed a letter from Orangemen in the Order's Falkirk district protesting at the opposition of some lodge office bearers to fund-raising for LPA. This was precisely the issue that created a crisis in relations between the Pride of Midlothian lodge (number 160) and the Grand Lodge of Scotland.

At the annual 1989 dance held by this lodge in Leith town hall in Edinburgh, two of its members, Shane Cameron and George Crawford, were seen to take a collection to augment the funds of the LPA. This became quite a *cause célèbre* within the Orange Order because of its reiterated condemnations of Loyalist paramilitary organisations. Lodge 160's initial disinclination to discipline the two members resulted in the Grand Lodge of Scotland invoking the full rigour of Orange jurisprudence to act against it. Its warrant, the basis for its authorised existence, was ultimately withdrawn by the Grand Lodge but this in turn was challenged by Lodge 160, which took the matter to the Scottish Court of Session. A judge ruled that the Grand Lodge had acted according to 'natural justice' in its handling of the matter[40] but in the end the lodge warrant was restored, only for the membership to transfer their allegiance to the Independent Orange Order.

Word of this case reached Northern Ireland through *Ulster*'s 'Tartan Talk' page, which included a letter from a former Scottish Orangeman who had left the Order in 1978 over what he had felt was its lack of real support for Loyal Ulster. 'Walking behind a band or going to a monthly meeting won't defeat the enemies of Ulster,' he wrote. 'In 1969 the Orange Order in Scotland were making plans to take women, kids, the old from Ulster if needed. It's about time some of this spirit was shown by the Orange hierarchy again. Support the men who are fighting for the Loyalist cause and you will find that your ranks will swell instead of shrink.'[41] *Ulster*'s next issue carried a letter supporting him and stressing that the UDA was still a legal body, though it would not be for very much longer.[42]

This case served to emphasise the role of UDA fund-raising in Scotland. It continued to be important, though the Pride of Midlothian case was a reminder that Orangemen who were well-wishers to the UDA needed to be circumspect over matters such as collections. Within the Apprentice Boys of Derry's approximately forty clubs across Scotland this mattered rather less, while some Rangers supporters' clubs and flute bands continued to be regular cash sources. This form of support did not, however, take over totally from questions relating to the UDA's 'military' role, despite the fiasco revealed by the 1989 Perth trial.

In July of that year, Tommy Lyttle, though soon to be arrested under the Stevens inquiry and openly revealed as the police informer that many in the UDA suspected him of being, talked to a journalist about the organisation's urgent need to reorganise in Scotland. He argued that there was too much 'wild enthusiasm', which could be counter-productive to the Loyalist cause. There had been too many major trials in which UDA members had been easily convicted, he stressed. To remedy this, Lyttle, using the seniority he could still cling to on the Inner Council, told his interviewer that the UDA's structure in Scotland was being reorganised. It would be split into different geographical areas, and soon into smaller units still. Each was to be assigned its own task, fund-raising, supporting prisoners or collecting what he laconically referred to as 'material'. He accepted that some Scots might not take to the changes.

> Then we have to say, this is how best you can serve us. In the end, the Scottish contribution to what we are doing will be more important and more effective. There is a role for them in this conflict. Scotland is our nearest and best friend in a world where we don't have many friends.[43]

Predictably, little was made public about this reorganisation though in May 1990 the UDA's magazine published a letter from a correspondent describing himself as the 'Commander Officer' of a new UDA battalion in central Scotland. He claimed that it recruited from Cumbernauld, Denny, Bonnybridge, Airdrie, Kilsyth and some other localities with a long history of allegiance to the Orange Order.[44] What this meant in manpower terms was not made clear. Paterson was prepared to be more specific when he told the author that a new unit on Benbecula in the Western Isles had been formed with, he said, 'two or three men'.[45]

Such paucity of information remained a problem for anyone trying to assess likely UDA manpower in Scotland. At the end of 1989, *Ulster* printed

Christmas and New Year greetings to its readers from what it called twenty-nine 'branches of the UDA and LPA'.[46] Apart from Inverness, Aberdeen, Dundee and Annan, all were in the west and central belt. There was no reference to any Benbecula unit and Perth, after the disaster of the High Court trial there in July 1989, was understandably absent from the list. There were no figures on unit and branch membership. Massive shows of strength could, however, draw on the support of those who did not choose active involvement. In May 1990, John McMichael's brother, along with his widow and her small son, Saul, were invited to Glasgow by the Dalmarnock No Surrender Club, an affiliate of the Apprentice Boys of Derry. A bannerette with a likeness of McMichael on it was dedicated and carried the next day, 19 May, in a parade during which more than forty bands with UDA links marched through the centre of Glasgow to the acclamation of large crowds lining the route. The guests of honour were later taken for lunch to the Rangers football club's hospitality suite.[47]

Rituals of commemoration like these continued to be important in the coverage of events in Scotland by UDA publications. The Scottish Orange Order's disciplinary response to flute bands suspected of UDA allegiance was also a matter for adverse comment by members and supporters on both sides of the water.[48] Unlike the UVF, the UDA had managed to remain a legal body and did so until August 1992. This was necessary for its fairly open fund-raising in Scotland but when the ban finally came it was applied only to Northern Ireland. Some anticipated that, because of this, more of the organisation's fund-raising effort would shift to Scotland but other commentators pointed out that the UVF had in fact been able to raise more cash there after it was proscribed.[49]

Of the UDA's cumulative effort in Scotland, a Belfast member was quoted as saying:

> It probably only accounts for ten per cent at the most [of total funds raised]. But with the ban in Northern Ireland it may well be that the UDA will have to rely on this part of the world for a higher percentage of their funding.[50]

He went on the speak of pubs in Glasgow's East End where collection tins or bottles for UDA prisoners were displayed as a matter of course and of other venues where money was raised 'by organisations other than the UDA. But everyone knows exactly where the money is going.'[51]

After the 1992 ban was announced, lawyers were quick to point out that UDA fund-raising in Scotland would not necessarily be affected.[52] Most of it was carried out in the name of LPA so it would be essential to prove that funds collected for it were in reality intended to further terrorist acts rather than simply to go towards the welfare of prisoners and their families. No immediate court proceedings in Scotland followed the ban, though the *New Ulster Defender*, the successor to *Ulster*, pointedly ceased to publish much information on localised LPA fund-raising in Scotland.

The Northern Ireland Office confirmed that Ian Lang, the Secretary of State for Scotland, and the Home Secretary, Kenneth Clarke, had been consulted about the proscription of the UDA at an early stage in the process. It also made it clear that any ban in Scotland or England would be a matter for them and would have to be justified under the Prevention of Terrorism Act. So too would any action to halt fund-raising by the organisation on the mainland.[53] No such legal action materialised between the time of the ban and the 1994 Loyalist ceasefire in Northern Ireland. A few weeks before, however, Henry Johnstone, who admitted in court to having worked for the LPA and to have been a member of the UDA, was sentenced to eight years' imprisonment for setting up a gun-running operation to Ulster. Originally from Glasgow, he had moved to Corby, Northamptonshire, where, within a significant steel industry workforce which was Scottish in origin, there had been for some time a degree of support for the UDA. He was arrested by police at a motorway service station in the Lake District, in the act of passing firearms to Glasgow accomplice Andrew Loan, a former flute band musician and Orange lodge member. A jury rejected their denials that the weapons were intended for Northern Ireland and the sentencing judge declared it likely 'that death and injury would have resulted if these weapons had been used in that unfortunate part of the United Kingdom'.[54]

Prior to this there had been rumours of reorganisation within the UDA in Scotland and when the Combined Loyalist Military Command finally issued its ceasefire statement on 13 October 1994, a declaration of Scottish support came from a newly designated body. This called itself the UDA's Scottish Central Office. It backed the CLMC's initiative while accepting the right of Ulster Loyalist people to remain sceptical about the IRA's intentions and it stressed to all 'Officers, NCO's and Volunteers' in Scotland that work would go on to support all Loyalist prisoners.[55]

Confirmation of a reorganisation came within a year of the CLMC ceasefire. The creation of a new and centralised Scottish brigade based in Glasgow was announced, though UDA sources assured the press that there was no link between the changes and the ceasefire. They claimed that the overhaul had begun in March 1994 because many fund-raising groups had become dormant or disorganised. 'We had to get rid of people who were living on the name and weren't doing the work. Certain units were disbanded.'[56] Much stress was laid on the support of the Inner Council in Belfast. 'It's now UDA policy, if you like, that everybody works through the central office in Scotland.'[57] The focus would now be entirely on prisoners' welfare work for around 160 jailed UDA men and their families.

One product of the reorganisation was the launch of a UDA magazine in Scotland. This was the *Scottish Freedom Fighter*, which displayed a Saltire and Red Hand emblem on its front page above the statement 'British and Proud'. Much of the first slim issue was taken up with messages to prisoners and reiterated support for the ceasefire as well as an interview with John White.

Readers were also alerted to increasing attacks on the Orange Order and its parades in the Scottish media and Glasgow's Labour-controlled council was described as a Catholic Mafia.

The second issue gave some information about the geographical distribution of LPA 'units' as it called them. Nearly all of those referred to were in the Glasgow area apart from Whitburn in West Lothian and Kirkcaldy in Fife. It also published a message to LPA members from the organisation's chairman, William McLeish.[58] Known by the nickname 'Bootsie', he had a long involvement in Loyalism in the East End of Glasgow and came to be regarded in Belfast as the senior figure in the Scottish UDA.

Five hundred copies of the first issue were published and 700 of the second, selling at one pound each. The third issue included special tributes to Joe Bratty and Raymond Elder, gunmen in the UDA's South Belfast brigade who were shot dead by the IRA a few weeks before its 1994 ceasefire. Bratty's widow, in a special contribution to the magazine, made much of his love of Scotland and his many trips to meet fellow Loyalists there until an exclusion order was served on him under the Prevention of Terrorism Act. She also commended the Paisley Imperial Blues flute band for its granting of honorary membership to her only son.[59] Three weeks prior to the publication of this issue, the Paisley band, well-known for its UDA links, had led a highly contentious Twelfth of July parade down Belfast's Lower Ormeau Road. The parade passed Sean Graham's bookmaker's shop, the scene of a 1992 massacre of Catholics widely believed to have involved Bratty and Elder, and a heavy police presence was required to hold back nationalist protest demonstrations.

Later issues catalogued IRA atrocities in Northern Ireland but also ran political interviews. One of these, published in two parts, was with Gary McMichael. He was asked by the magazine's editor whether, if the IRA went back to war, he would agree 'that the Protestant folk must instantly move for an independent Ulster' which could deal in its own way with renewed terrorism. In a limited reply he said that Ulster people 'must of course seek to determine their own future' if their democratic wishes were ignored and that they had full rights to their own self-defence.[60] The same issue also devoted two pages to a celebration of the doings of Johnny Adair, who had been given a long prison sentence the previous year:

> To the officers and men of the UDA in Scotland, Johnny Adair is and always will be a hero in our eyes. For taking the war to the Provos' doorsteps, ensuring an eye for an eye would mean exactly that, thanks, Mad Dog.[61]

Adair's bid to take over the UDA was still five years off and would command little support in Loyalist Scotland, but uncompromising sentiments such as these were a reminder of continuing doubts within the Scottish UDA about the peace process in Northern Ireland. 'A lot of people think this war is over and finished,' a UDA organiser told a Scottish journalist. 'Personally, I think this war has just got into a new phase. At the end of the day the government is going to sell us out anyway.'[62] Another activist agreed:

> We're just a wee bit suspicious of the whole thing. We still think they're aiming for one thing and that's a united Ireland, regardless of the Loyalists. If Britain sells us down the river then our only other option is an independent Ulster.[63]

The UDA's reorganisation in Scotland in the mid-1990s was not put to any immediate test as the Loyalist ceasefire in Northern Ireland continued to hold. Adair's bid to take control of the organisation could have provided such a test, had he not allowed himself to be implicated in the murder of someone as revered in the Scottish UDA as was John Gregg. That closed every door in Loyalist Scotland to Adair, his family and supporters after their flight from Belfast in early February 2003. The restructured Scottish UDA obeyed the Inner Council in Belfast, though there was criticism of McLeish, chairman and commandant in Scotland. He had been unwilling to deploy Scottish UDA men to exact revenge on Sammy McCrory, once one of Adair's 'top guns' who had moved to Ayrshire after his release from prison. There was even the suggestion that McLeish had alerted McCrory to the threat to him.[64]

The *Scottish Freedom Fighter* did not last long. Its editors, who could only be contacted through a Glasgow post box, grew increasingly wary of talking to the media as more evidence of Loyalist criminality emerged. In early March 1997, two brothers, Alistair and Stewart Woods, appeared with James Galloway at the High Court in Kilmarnock, charged with the abduction and shooting of Hugh Wyper from Kilwinning, Ayrshire, who had to have his right leg amputated after eight operations. All had been members of the Apprentice Boys of Derry in Kilwinning, a town described in court as 'a hotbed of Loyalist activity with links both to the UDA and UVF'.[65] Much of the evidence in the trial came from local Orangemen and bandsmen and pointed to brutal retribution on Wyper for allegedly indiscreet talk by him about his and the three defendants' affiliations.

Wyper had had links to both the Loyalist paramilitary organisations, not difficult to form in a small town like Kilwinning with its six Orange lodges, three flute bands and Scotland's premier and oldest Masonic lodge. After his release from hospital, Wyper left Kilwinning but told the court that he had received a series of phone calls 'from Scotland' warning him not to talk to the press about what had happened.[66]

Kilwinning was typical of many working-class localities across western and central Scotland, which saw themselves over the years of the Troubles as the engine room of support for Loyal Ulster outside Northern Ireland itself. How the real 'players', in both the UDA and the UVF, really rated the competence and effectiveness of Scottish support is another matter. More guns and ammunition than were intercepted by Scottish police and the RUC may well have reached Northern Ireland thanks to the networks of support linking it to Loyalist Scotland. Much of the Scottish support for the cause was and remained as 'parade Protestantism' – Scottish bands strutting their stuff on Ulster Twelfths and other anniversaries – and of course the high-octane fervour of the 'ninety-minute Loyalists' who supported Rangers.

Some of the biggest shipments of arms for the UDA came from South Africa and the Middle East, while in the early phase of the Troubles Canada too, with its history of Ulster Loyalist settlement in Ontario, was seen as a likely source of support, at least by theUVF.[67] Closer to home, English net-works of support for the UDA in Liverpool, Manchester and elsewhere were quickly and methodically taken apart by police action.[68] In more recent years, English support for the UDA has been political, with fascist movements such as the National Front, the British National Party and Combat 18 seeking to attach themselves to the UDA's cause and sometimes to that of the UVF as well.

With the UDA it has more often than not been a case of such support being offered rather than it, as an organisation, actively seeking it. Gregg's political views, at least for a time, made him more receptive to approaches from the far right than other UDA leaders, though its anti-Semitism alienated him because of his support for Israel. Going on a chaotic National Front march in Belfast in 1983 was one of Adair's first political acts while he was still a teenager[69] and the UDA's *Ulster* magazine gave intermittent coverage to National Front support in England for the Loyalist cause. Neither Andy Tyrie nor John McMichael accorded it much importance and the latter was extremely hostile to abortive attempts by them to seek support in Belfast. Charlie Sargent, a notoriously violent London racist and football hooligan who was convicted of murder in 1998,[70] professed to admire the UDA and made some contacts with it. In 1992 he split with the British National Party and joined the much more militant Combat 18. Its publications, such as *Blood and Honour*, sought to combine rabid and racist English nationalism with support for Ulster and the Union but the Hitler cult they espoused was repugnant to Loyalists brought up to revere their forebears' part in two wars against Germany.

The extreme racist right, while able to mobilise 800,000 votes in the 2004 elections to the European Parliament, has yet to achieve any real leverage in Scotland, even when it tries to play the Ulster Loyalist card there. Were polit-ical and sectarian tensions in Northern Ireland to resurface in the form of serious communal violence, Protestant and Loyalist Scotland would doubt-less reaffirm its support for Ulster and the Union in ways not dissimilar to those which defined its response to the recent Troubles.

NOTES

1. *News of the World*, 9 February 2003.
2. *Daily Record*, 10 February 2003.
3. Ibid.
4. *Scotland on Sunday*, 9 February 2003.

5. *Scotsman*, 10 February 2003.
6. *Sunday Post*, 22 March 1987.
7. T. Gallagher, *Glasgow: The Uneasy Peace – Religious Tension in Modern Scotland* (Manchester: Manchester University Press, 1987), pp. 143–50.
8. *Scotland on Sunday*, 27 September 1992.
9. S. Bruce, 'The Ulster connection', in G. Walker and T. Gallagher (eds), *Sermons and Battle Hymns: Protestant Popular Culture in Modern Scotland* (Edinburgh: Edinburgh University Press, 1990), p. 236.
10. Gallagher, *Glasgow, the Uneasy Peace*.
11. *Scottish Daily Express*, 11 July 1970.
12. W. Marshall, *The Billy Boys: A Concise History of Orangeism in Scotland* (Edinburgh: Mercat, 1996), p. 163.
13. *Scotland on Sunday*, 1 July 1990.
14. Author's recollections.
15. *Scotland on Sunday*, 13 October 1991.
16. Member of Grand Orange Lodge of Scotland, interview with author, 21 April 2005.
17. *Scotsman*, 17 June 1979.
18. *Herald*, 15 March 1996.
19. *Scotsman*, 27 June 1979.
20. *Daily Record*, 25 July 2002.
21. Ibid.
22. *Edinburgh Evening News*, 4 April 2003.
23. *Observer*, 6 April 2003.
24. *Glasgow Herald*, 29 April 1981.
25. S. Bruce, *No Pope of Rome: Anti-Catholicism in Modern Scotland* (Edinburgh: Mainstream, 1985), p. 173.
26. *News of the World*, 15 June 2003.
27. Ibid.
28. Bruce, *No Pope of Rome*, p. 175.
29. S. Bruce, *The Red Hand: Protestant Paramilitaries in Northern Ireland* (Oxford: Oxford University Press, 1992), pp. 158–9.
30. *Scotsman*, 27 June 1979.
31. Ibid.
32. Ibid.
33. *Scotland on Sunday*, 9 July 1989.
34. *Scotsman*, 6 March 1987.
35. *Scotsman*, 7 July 1989.
36. Ibid.
37. 'Colin Paterson', interview with author, 9 August 1990.
38. Ibid.
39. *Ulster*, July–August 1990.
40. Court of Session papers, 27 April 1990.
41. *Ulster*, June 1990.
42. *Ulster*, July 1990.
43. *Scotland on Sunday*, 9 July 1989.

44. *Ulster*, May 1990.
45. Paterson, interview with author.
46. *Ulster*, December 1989.
47. *Ulster*, June 1990.
48. *Ulster*, September–October 1990; *New Ulster Defender*, vol. 1, no. 2, 1992.
49. *Scotsman*, 11 August 2002.
50. Ibid.
51. Ibid.
52. *Scotsman*, 13 August 1992.
53. *Scotsman*, 12 August, 1992.
54. *Scotsman*, 17 August, 1994.
55. *New Ulster Defender*, vol. 1, no. 13, 1995.
56. *Scotsman*, 3 August 1995.
57. Ibid.
58. *Scottish Freedom Fighter*, vol. 1, no. 2, 1995.
59. *Scottish Freedom Fighter*, vol. 1, no. 3, 1995.
60. *Scottish Freedom Fighter*, vol. 1, no. 5, 1996.
61. Ibid.
62. *Scotsman*, 3 August 1995.
63. Ibid.
64. North Belfast UDA member, interview with author, 5 October 2004.
65. *Herald*, 20 March 1997.
66. Ibid.
67. Bruce, *Red Hand*, pp. 168–9.
68. Ibid., pp. 165–8.
69. *Observer*, 25 January 1998.
70. D. Lister and H. Jordan, *Mad Dog: The Rise and Fall of Johnny Adair and 'C' Company* (Edinburgh: Mainstream, 2003), p. 31; H. McDonald and J. Cusack, *UDA: Inside the Heart of Loyalist Terror* (Dublin: Penguin Ireland, 2004), p. 169.

Postscript

At present, Sammy Duddy is not writing as much poetry as he once did, though perhaps he should be. Over a decade on from the 1994 Loyalist ceasefire and almost eight years after a Belfast Agreement which he feels has given little to the working-class Protestant community, he is still working hard for the people of Loyalist North Belfast. This involves helping them on a day-to-day basis, whether their problems arise from the area's housing shortage, from teenage delinquency, from car crime or from sectarian tensions which have left Protestants and Catholics more segregated from each other than ever before.

Recently the UDA issued a statement which read:

> We have declared an Orange line around all Protestant areas. Whilst we realise that one community is growing faster than the other, we cannot allow another garden, another house or another street to be attacked. We can ensure to the utmost of our ability that Loyalists will not breach the Orange line. Will Republicans do the same?[1]

These words did not, it was stressed, apply simply to Belfast but to Londonderry's Waterside area, to the south of County Londonderry and to South-East Antrim. Duddy agrees that in a real sense there is now a border in his native Belfast not just physically in the form of new peace walls but also in people's minds.

This depresses him though he can see no alternative. However, he does believe that the latest UDA ceasefire can hold. If it does he is optimistic about European Union funds being brought to bear on North Belfast's problems and not just in Catholic areas. 'Catholic localities should get their fair share and we've got Dublin on our side over this. I've begun to think they understand us better than London ever has.'[2] He speaks here on the basis of personal meetings with the Irish President and her husband but he is not afraid to voice his thoughts on the UDA's future.

> We have to find a new role that's political and based on the needs of our communities. To do that we need changes. Right up to brigade level there are people who have to go and soon. We all know who.[3]

Duddy is someone who has seen it all since the Troubles started. In the Cavehill Inn, where he still likes to relax over a drink with journalists and researchers, he will recall how thirty years ago he arrived there late to meet a friend, just after IRA gunmen had raked the bar with automatic weapons, killing two men and wounding others. His memories are still vivid: one victim, whom he knew well, was propped up against a wall, visibly bleeding to death but struggling to get a wage packet from his top pocket so that it could be passed on to his wife. The man begged him to help, and he did so, removing £20 in notes already stained with blood, promising the dying man that he would 'see that his wife was OK'.[4]

Duddy can also be met on Wednesday evenings in the Mount Inn, where he often sings country and western songs and he keeps a bar newsletter going in which he makes bawdy fun of the regulars. Situated on North Queen Street and very close to the Republican New Lodge estate, the Mount is in fact a defiantly flag-bedecked outpost of Loyalist Tiger's Bay. Glen Branagh was ripped apart just across the street by his own pipe bomb in January 2001 (see Chapter 11) and eighteen months later a young Protestant, William Morgan, died from dreadful injuries when he was rammed against a wall only yards away by a stolen car which was later abandoned on the New Lodge. The Mount still has customers who were there in 1992 when a masked gunman from the Irish People's Liberation Organisation shot up the bar, killing a pensioner and seriously wounding two other people.

The narrow streets which lead away from it up to the Oldpark Road have bred a generation of boys into hardened killers ready to do the UDA's bidding. They were programmed to think they were fighting an unavoidable war created by all too immediate events, though it was also one deeply rooted in shared folk memories of an embattled past. The texture of these memories and fears are marvellously captured in some of the poetry of John Hewitt, who now has a pub named after him closer to the city centre but within walking distance of the Mount. He came of old Scottish planter stock, a breed still reviled by many Irish Republicans.

> Once alien here my fathers built their house
> claimed, drained and gave the land the shapes of use.

Hewitt wrote this of his forebears in 1942.[5] He was proud of what they had accomplished but knew too the hurt caused to the native Irish. This comes through powerfully in another poem, 'The Colony', written in 1950, in which he describes the settlers' primal guilt and premonitions:

> That terror dogs us; back of all our thought
> the threat behind the dream, those beacons flare,
> and we run screaming in our fear;
> fear quickened by the memory of quiet
> for we began the plunder – naked men
> still have their household gods and holy places,
> and what a people loves it will defend.[6]

Ambivalences such as these were savagely crowded aside by the awful momentum of events in 1971 and 1972 as the IRA extended its war against the Crown forces to working-class Protestant areas. That, for Duddy and thousands like him, was the time to 'join up' as old certainties fell apart while friends and neighbours were killed by car bombs and gunmen, events he has relived and captured movingly in his published poetry.

'Joining up' and rising within the UDA did not initially bring out the best in everyone. In some cases, as this book has shown, the opposite happened. Amidst the vast literature of the Troubles it sometimes needed women to say so. The UDA as an organisation gave them little real space or power, even though, just as in Republican areas, it was the women who held together families and communities exposed to the most destructive of pressures. In one of the finest books to have appeared about women's experience of Northern Ireland's conflict, 'Lily', which was not her real name, recalled her marriage to someone who joined the UDA in the 1970s: 'I've seen what a gun can do to a boy with no work. I've seen normal decent human beings turning into Hitlers overnight – and they act the part at home.'[7] She went on:

> The men are in control, there's no women's lib for us – you don't talk about women's lib, you'd get run out of the area. The men dominate completely. Women talk among themselves, but we might as well be back in the Middle Ages. You say things when you've drunk too much, but you cry for it afterwards.[8]

She recounted episodes of women who hid weapons and provided safe houses, as happened in Republican areas, but got little recognition from the men who held rank and power.

> I've seen them go into the bookies and think nothing of spending £100 on a horse. I couldn't put two pounds on a horse, if I get out twice a year I'm lucky. And then I'm watched. If I get up and dance with someone, that man's pulled – 'her husband's inside, leave her alone'. I can't even speak to a man. The women are completely dominated.[9]

Lily's reminiscences about the 1970s could as readily have applied to areas controlled by the IRA, some of whose members were notorious for domestic violence. Prolonged male absences from home through imprisonment could and did alter the nature of marital relationships and on occasion, Loyalist women could assert themselves, as they did during the 1974 Ulster Workers Council strike. Clubs and bars which stayed open were picketed and sometimes raided by the wives, demanding that if their men could drink during such a crisis for Ulster, they could also go home and mind their children.[10]

Attitudes began to change over time and women eventually took on important work in UDA advice centres and in its political organisations. However, they could also, it must be said, be brutalised by the Troubles, just as men were. In 1975, eleven women were jailed for their part in beating to death Ann Ogilby in a UDA club in Sandy Row (see Chapter 3) in July of the previous year. This may have been because the victim, a married woman with a small child, had been accused of taking parcels to and making friends with an unmarried UDA prisoner.[11] Her tormentors, all members or supporters of the UDA, battered her to death while her six-year-old daughter cried outside the door, within earshot of her mother's screams. They then continued their drinking session in a different club.

To this day, Ogilby's murder is an event hardly spoken of within the UDA. It was just one of many terrible crimes committed by both Loyalists and Republicans as part of a relentless downward spiral of cruelty that became inseparable from the political and ethnic conflict, Europe's worst between 1945 and the break-up of the Soviet Union and communist rule in the states allied with it. It was a conflict in which Republican paramilitaries killed more Catholics than the Loyalists and security forces combined, and its brutality alienated many nationalists, especially in the Irish Republic, from the idea of a united state. It also fed Protestant and Unionist fears of a united Ireland, as well as of Catholics in general and Republicans in particular.

Whether all this violence achieved anything at all in political terms is a question posed in one recent study. Its author argues that only the cessation of paramilitary violence in 1994 made possible movement towards even the tentative settlement embodied in the Belfast Agreement. He conceded, however, that the implied threat of renewed violence has, since then, been an effective means for the Republican movement to secure major political concessions. The UDA and Loyalists generally have, in his view, been much less successful at doing this, partly because they have always argued that their violence was reactive to the IRA's and would stop when it stopped.[12] Yet, for reasons explored in this book, between the second IRA ceasefire in July 1997 and the end of 2004, Loyalist violence has been greater than that of Republicans.

At the time of writing, however, there has been a marked decline in violence in Loyalist areas. Even a brief and melodramatic reappearance on his old stamping grounds by Johnny Adair, in late February 2005, following his release and removal to Manchester the previous month, caused no major reaction. Indeed it was an event overshadowed by the naked brutality of the murder of Robert McCartney by IRA members in South Belfast and the blatant intimidation used to stop witnesses from the Markets and Short Strand areas helping the police find and charge the culprits.

If Northern Ireland's conflict really is starting to slip into history there is more need than ever for its story to be fully and truthfully told. This book has tried to do so where the UDA's part in events has been concerned. 'Their only crime was loyalty' are words often inscribed on their murals beside the names and images of members killed in the Troubles. 'Loyalty' was something invoked by many who joined the UDA to excuse and indeed to justify truly terrible crimes. Some of them now wonder if their loyalty was to a Britain which had long since ceased to be loyal to them or to their vision of Ulster. Anyone who wants to make sense of what they did and what made them do it can do worse than be guided by Edwin Morgan's poem 'King Billy'.

He was moved to write it by the shared memory of sectarian violence in his native Glasgow in the inter-war years. Its final lines read as follows:

> Deplore what is to be deplored,
> And then find out the rest.[13]

NOTES

1. *Irish News*, 15 October 2004.
2. S. Duddy, interview with author, 5 October 2004.
3. Ibid.
4. C. Crawford, *Inside the UDA: Volunteers and Violence* (London: Pluto Press, 2003), p. 62.
5. J. Hewitt, *The Collected Poems of John Hewitt*, ed. F. Ormsby (Belfast: Blackstaff Press, 1991), p. 20.
6. Ibid., p, 77.
7. E. Fairweather, R. McDonough and M. McFadyean, *Only the Rivers Run Free: Northern Ireland – the Women's War* (London: Pluto Press, 1984), p. 303.
8. Ibid., p. 304.
9. Ibid.
10. Ibid., p. 302.
11. Ibid., p. 283.
12. B. Lennon, *Peace Comes Dropping Slow: Dialogue and Conflict Management in the Northern Ireland Conflict* (Belfast: Community Dialogue, 2004). The author contributed an article based on his work to the *Irish News* on 15 October 2004.
13. E. Morgan, *Collected Poems* (Manchester: Carcanet Press, 1990), p. 167.

Appendix A
Brief Biographies

ADAIR, GINA

Teenage girlfriend and later common-law wife of Johnny Adair, Gina Crossan married him in a prison ceremony in 1997. She fled to Scotland in February 2003 when the UDA decided to act against Adair's remaining supporters on the Lower Shankill estate. Scottish police confiscated from her a sum of almost £70,000. She lives in Bolton, Greater Manchester, with her family and was joined there by her husband in January 2005.

ADAIR, JOHNNY 'MAD DOG'

At the time of his arrest in May 1994, Johnny Adair had turned the UDA/UFF's West Belfast C Company into a ruthless killing machine. The following year a court found him guilty of 'directing terrorism' but he was released on licence under the 1998 Belfast Agreement. The blatant drug-dealing he permitted in his Lower Shankill power base led, along with his desire to take control of the UDA, to violent Loyalist feuds from late 2000 to mid-2003 and to his own rearrest and imprisonment.

ADAMS, DAVID

An active figure in what became the Ulster Democratic Party, and for a time one of its councillors in Lisburn. In 1994 he met US President Bill Clinton as part of a Loyalist deputation and represented his party in the talks which led to the April 1998 Belfast Agreement. He failed to win a seat in that year's elections to the new Assembly and after the break-up of the UDP lost his council seat in 2001.

ANDERSON, JIM

A glazier by trade, he was active in the original Woodvale Defence Association and then in the UDA itself. He was for a time co-chairman of the West Belfast UDA but stood down from that position in 1973. In September of that year he supported Andy Tyrie as a compromise leadership candidate and in November 1974 he survived an IRA attempt on his life.

BARR, GLEN

A trade unionist who chaired the co-ordinating committee of the Ulster Workers' Council during the victorious strike of May 1974. He acted as a political adviser to the UDA and was active for a time in the Vanguard Unionist Party but later settled for an independent political role. His work on youth employment initiatives in his home city of Londonderry helped to earn him an OBE in 2005.

CALDERWOOD, ALEX 'OSO'

A teenage recruit to the UDA's West Belfast C Company, he was given a life sentence in 1982 for the brutal murder of a young Catholic. In prison he achieved literacy and became a born-again Christian. On his release in April 1993 he urged all paramilitaries to lay down their arms.

COULTER, JACKIE

A UDA member from the Shankill who worked for a Loyalist prisoners' aid group and was for a time close to Johnny Adair. His murder by the UVF in August 2000 marked a dangerous escalation in tension between it and elements of the UDA controlled by Adair.

COURTNEY, WILLIAM 'MO'

Once a ruthless lieutenant of Johnny Adair, he transferred his allegiance in late 2002 to the UDA leadership. For a time he held a senior command in the West Belfast UDA but in the summer of 2003 was charged with the murder of Alan McCullough. A Belfast Sunday newspaper has claimed he was the killer of the lawyer Pat Finucane in1989.

CRAIG, JIM

He achieved a formidable reputation in the West Belfast UDA but increasingly used his position to operate lucrative protection rackets, for which he was named in a 1987 television programme. Rumours that he was feeding information on Loyalists to Republicans sealed his fate and in October 1988 he was shot dead in an East Belfast pub for 'treason' against the UDA.

DODDS, WILLIAM 'WINKIE'

An early recruit to the UDA, he was convicted of armed robbery in 1979. After his release he commanded C Company in West Belfast, one of his recruits being Johnny Adair. He was again imprisoned as a result of the Stevens inquiry in 1990 and later became West Belfast brigadier until he suffered a stroke. In late 2002 he took sides against Adair in the worsening feud within the UDA and was forced out of his home on the Lower Shankill.

DONAGHY, JIM

A shop steward in Short and Harland's shipyards, he joined the UDA on its formation, working on Loyalist prisoners' welfare. He also edited *Ulster* until near the time of his death in 1987. A master of his local Orange lodge, he was at one point trusted by spokesmen of the nationalist Short Strand area to negotiate the reinstatement of Catholics intimidated out of a local factory.

DUDDY, SAMMY

Apprenticed as a letterpress operator, he joined the UDA in 1971 and has survived a series of attempts on his life by the IRA and by Loyalists during the recent power struggle within the UDA. Never convicted of any terrorist offences, he is a wit and raconteur who has had a volume of poetry published. He also sings country and western songs and used to perform a drag act in Loyalist clubs. Since 1994 he has worked for the Ulster Democratic Party and on prisoners' resettlement schemes and also sits on the Loyalist Commission.

DUNN, HESTER

As a young mother and former dancer, she became active in local issues on the Loyalist Suffolk estate in West Belfast. Andy Tyrie gave her the chance to work for the UDA and she wrote regularly for *Ulster* on women's issues. Tyrie's fall from power in 1988 was a severe blow to her and she withdrew from further UDA involvement.

ELLIOTT, BILLY

An East Belfast activist who rose to the rank of brigadier and served on the UDA's Inner Council, he saw his role as military and had little enthusiasm for Andy Tyrie's concern to move Loyalism on to a political road. He was replaced as brigadier after his arrest under the Stevens inquiry and became suspected of being an informer. This led him to leave the organisation.

ELLIOTT, ERNIE 'DUKE'

A close friend and drinking companion of David Fogel in the UDA's early days, Elliott was implicated in some of its initial killings. Fogel promoted him but in December 1972 he was shot dead in a drunken fight between Shankill and Sandy Row UDA men over ownership of weapons secreted in a club. He was not killed because of his alleged espousal of socialist opinions. His death deprived Fogel of an important ally against Charles Harding Smith on the latter's return to Belfast at the end of 1972.

ENGLISH, JOE

He took over as South-East Antrim brigadier in early 1988 and remained on the UDA Inner Council after Andy Tyrie's resignation in March of that year. A new generation of young gunmen in West Belfast had little interest in his insistence on the UDA's need to find a political role. His position crumbled after the October 1994 Loyalist ceasefire and he was replaced as brigadier by John Gregg. He then fell severely out of favour over his criticisms of other UDA figures, especially over their condoning of drug-dealing.

ENGLISH, TOMMY

Although awaiting trial on criminal charges at the time of his murder by the UVF at the end of October 2001, he had achieved a role in the UDA's attempt to 'go political' and had been on the Ulster Democratic Party's delegation in the 1998 talks which led to the Belfast Agreement. In May 1998, at an Ulster Hall rally in support of a 'yes' vote in the referendum, he addressed the audience wearing an Ian Paisley face mask.

FOGEL, DAVID

A London-born ex-soldier who was active in the original Woodvale Defence Association and held senior rank in the West Belfast UDA until tension between him and Charles Harding Smith forced him to return to England with his family.

GRAY, JIM 'DORIS DAY'

He reached senior rank in the UDA's East Belfast brigade but in late March 2005 was 'stood down' by the Inner Council over rumours of his involvement in drug-dealing and corruption. Soon afterwards he was arrested and charged with serious money-laundering offences. He earned his nickname for his dyed blond hair and costly clothes and jewellery. After his release on strict bail conditions Gray was shot dead on 4 October 2005. Within the police and the media his murder was attributed to those in the UDA who had scores to settle with him and wanted to stop him giving damaging testimony at his trial.

GREGG, JOHN 'GRUGG'

A UDA hero for his part in a 1984 attempt on the life of Gerry Adams, he became South-East Antrim brigadier after his release from prison in 1993. He used his ferocious reputation to control the brigade area and was widely believed to have sanctioned attacks on and killings of Catholics. In February 2003 he was murdered as a result of the power struggle arising from Johnny Adair's ambitions. While in prison he started an Open University degree.

HARDING SMITH, CHARLES

A former shipyard worker and tyre salesman who was a founder member of the UDA. By early 1972 he was speaking as its chairman and was also West Belfast brigadier. Violent quarrels with other leading members terminated his leadership and Andy Tyrie replaced him in September 1973. After a failed bid to retrieve power in early 1975, he left for the north of England, where he remained until his death some years later.

HERRON, TOMMY

A prominent UDA spokesman in 1972 and 1973, his power base was in East Belfast and he often spoke as if he represented the whole organisation. He was shot dead in September 1973, possibly because his ambitions had antagonised Charles Harding Smith.

LYTTLE, TOMMY 'TUCKER'

He emerged in 1986 as the UDA's West Belfast brigadier and for a time, in 1988 and 1989, chaired its Inner Council and gave press briefings. In July 1991 he was given a seven-year sentence for withholding information likely to be useful to terrorists. By then his role as a Special Branch informer was widely known. He died of a heart attack in October 1995.

MCCREERY, EDWARD 'NED'

A notoriously brutal member of the East Belfast UDA, implicated in the early 1970s in the murder and torture of many victims, he was one of the first Loyalists to be interned in 1973. He became brigadier in the area and came to be seen by some as an opponent of racketeering and drug-dealing. This may have been a factor in his murder in April 1992.

MCCRORY, SAM 'SKELLY'

A childhood and teenage friend of Johnny Adair and a C Company gunman who, as a UDA prisoner, met Mo Mowlam in the January 1998 Maze prison talks. Released under the Belfast Agreement, he settled in Scotland but was seen in Belfast just prior to the start of the feud in 2000 between elements of the UDA and the UVF.

MCCULLOUGH, WILLIAM 'BUCKY'

An early UDA recruit, he helped make the West Belfast C Company a formidable killing machine in the 1970s. He was shot dead outside his home by INLA gunmen in October 1981, a murder widely thought to have been set up by Jim Craig. In late May 2003, his son Alan was killed by an element within the UDA who blamed him for his close association with Johnny Adair.

MCDONALD, JACKIE

Now regarded as a senior and experienced UDA Inner Council member, he was appointed brigadier of the East Belfast brigade by Andy Tyrie in 1988, and resumed the command after a prison sentence given in 1990 for extortion. He emerged over the period 2000–03 as a forceful opponent of Johnny Adair and is an outspoken supporter of Loyalism's need to find a political role.

MCFARLAND, BILLY 'THE MEXICAN'

He earned his nickname because of his moustache and swarthy appearance. He had overall command of the UDA's South Londonderry and North Antrim brigade at the time of the Belfast Agreement. He supported the leadership against Johnny Adair and has been associated with the magazine *Warrior*, which makes the case for Ulster independence.

MCKEAG, STEPHEN

One of the most feared gunmen of Adair's West Belfast C Company, who was entrusted with many of its killings. Near the end of his life he quarrelled with Johnny Adair and also developed a serious cocaine addiction. His death in September 2000 may have been the result of a huge drugs overdose.

MCLEAN, EDDIE

Active over many years in the North Belfast UDA, he admitted near the end of his life to active complicity in several of Johnny Adair's C Company murders. Latterly he worked on a Loyalist prisoners' resettlement project and other initiatives in his area. He served a term of imprisonment and was the last prisoner to be married in Crumlin Road gaol.

MCMICHAEL, GARY

Son of John McMichael, he became active in the Ulster Democratic Party and represented it on Lisburn council from 1993 until 2003. He strongly supported the 1994 Loyalist ceasefire and led the UDP delegation in the 1990 Stormont talks, but failed to secure a seat in the new Assembly. In 1999 he published a personal view of the Troubles and of the peace process, called *Ulster Voice*.

MCMICHAEL, JOHN

At the time of his murder by the IRA in 1987, he was second in command of the UDA and a ruthless co-ordinator of many of its attacks. He supported the formation, in 1981, of the Ulster Loyalist Democratic Party and stood unsuccessfully for it in a Westminster by-election the following year. He gave articulate support to the UDA's 1987 policy document, *Common Sense*. Claims are still made that his murder was set up by elements hostile to him in the UDA.

MURRAY, HARRY

A shipyard shop steward and chairman of the Ulster Workers' Council in the May 1974 strike, he worked closely at that time with the UDA although not a member. He split with the UWC and later came out in support of a form of power-sharing by constitutional parties.

NELSON, BRIAN

His trial in 1992 revealed his dual role as a UDA intelligence officer and secret agent for an army intelligence unit. He has been blamed for the 1989 murder of Pat Finucane and for many other killings, though at his trial an army colonel defended his record. He was released from prison in 1996 and went on to live under a new identity outside Northern Ireland. He is thought to have died from a brain haemorrhage in April 2003.

PAGELS, BOB

A trade unionist who sat as a member of the Ulster Workers' Council co-ordinating committee during the 1974 strike. For a time he held senior rank in the East Belfast UDA. After a period of imprisonment he left the UDA. In 2004 he claimed to an interviewer that the strike's real purpose was to secure Ulster independence.

PAYNE, DAVID

With John White, an early member of the UFF who acquired a chilling reputation as a sadist and torturer. He became a UDA brigadier in North Belfast
but proved difficult for others on the Inner Council to work with. He received
a lengthy sentence in 1988 for his part in a huge shipment of UDA weapons
into Northern Ireland from South Africa. He died following a period of
illness in March 2003.

ROBINSON, ANDY

A former Royal Marine who led the UDA's 1975 'amphibious' raid on the
Donegal port of Greencastle and was highly rated by Andy Tyrie for his military competence. He was given command of the Londonderry and North
Antrim UDA brigade but allegations about his involvement in two sectarian
murders led to him leaving Northern Ireland.

SHOUKRI, ANDRE 'THE EGYPTIAN'

Nicknamed after his father's nationality, he has acquired a major post-
ceasefire role in the North Belfast UDA and became its brigadier in May 2002.
With convictions for assault and extortion, in July 2003 he was jailed on a
firearms charge. Initially a supporter of Johnny Adair, he broke with him
in late 2002. Belfast newspapers claim he is heavily involved in drugs and
racketeering.

SIMPSON, JAMES 'JIMBO'

Also known as the 'Bacardi brigadier' in the Tiger's Bay area, he told a jour-
nalist in 2000 that attacks on Catholic homes that year were proof of the
UDA 'returning to its roots'. He was reluctant to join any feud with the UVF
at that time, but his erratic behaviour led to him being stood down as North
Belfast brigadier in May 2002. He was replaced by Andre Shoukri and in
October 2003 failed in a bid to resume his position.

SMALLWOODS, RAYMOND

At the time of his murder by the IRA in July 1994, he was chairman of the
UDP and an articulate exponent of policies based on the 1987 *Common Sense*
document. He served a prison sentence for his part in the attempted murder
of Bernadette McAliskey in 1981 and, while not a full convert to the case for
a Loyalist ceasefire, was ready to talk to Catholic clergy about the precondi-
tions for peace.

SNODDY, ALAN

Another early recruit to the UDA, he was by 1979 its South-East Antrim brigadier and a loyal supporter of Andy Tyrie. The cancer which would soon kill him necessitated his replacement on the Inner Council early in 1988, which, with John McMichael's death, seriously weakened Tyrie's position.

SPENCE, JIM

Commander of the UDA's West Belfast A Company in the Woodvale area and now widely believed to have been a police informer as well as having been implicated in the 1989 murder of Pat Finucane. In early 2003 he earned the bitter enmity of the imprisoned Johnny Adair through his part in driving his family and remaining supporters out of the Lower Shankill estate.

STOBIE, BILLY

A quartermaster who stored and supplied weapons for use by the West Belfast UDA, in late 2001 he was tried for his part in the 1989 Finucane murder. The trial collapsed because of the illness of a key witness but by then Stobie's role as a police informer was known and soon afterwards he was shot dead by the UDA.

STONE, MICHAEL

A legendary UDA member because of his single-handed attack on Republican mourners at Milltown cemetery in March 1988. This earned him several life sentences. He joined the UDA as a teenager in East Belfast but on his release in 1999 he stressed his 'war was over'. He has built up a reputation as an artist and in 2003 had a volume of memoirs published, called *None Shall Divide Us*.

TYRIE, ANDY

A former engineering factory worker and landscape gardener who, in September 1973, emerged as a compromise candidate for the UDA leadership. Over his fifteen years in command, he tried to improve military training and redirect more of its attacks to known IRA and INLA targets. He used his position to back major political initiatives including the 1981 formation of the Ulster Loyalist Democratic Party. His leadership style brought him enemies and in March 1988 he resigned as 'supreme commander' and Inner Council chairman.

WRIGHT, JIM

A Scottish-born trade unionist in Ballymena who emerged in the 1990s as a forceful figure in the political wing of the UDA's South Londonderry and North Antrim brigade. He stood at local elections for the Ulster Democratic Party and as an independent Loyalist but was close to the paramilitary leadership of the UDA, acting as a pall bearer at John Gregg's funeral in February 2003.

Appendix B
A Chronology of the Troubles

1966: 3 DEATHS

31 March   At Westminster general election, Gerry Fitt, Catholic standing for Republican Labour, wins West Belfast seat. Uses his victory to criticise discrimination in Northern Ireland and win support for views from some Labour MPs.

11 June   After weeks of tension over Republican commemorations of 1916 Easter Rising in Dublin, young Belfast Catholic, John Scullion, shot dead by re-formed UVF. Becomes Troubles' first victim.

26 June   Peter Ward, Catholic barman, shot dead by UVF in West Belfast. Within days, UVF declared illegal by Prime Minister Captain Terence O'Neill, already under attack from some Unionists for his reformist policies.

27 June   Matilda Gould, Catholic pensioner from West Belfast, dies from burns received seven weeks earlier in UVF fire bomb attack on her home.

10 November Sean Lemass replaced as Irish Taoiseach by Jack Lynch.

1967

29 January   Formation of Northern Ireland Civil Rights Association (NICRA).

7 March   Unionist government announces ban on Republican clubs.

1968

20 June   First direct action by NICRA. Stormont Nationalist MP stages sit-in protest in Caledon, County Tyrone over 'religious discrimination' by Unionist council's housing allocation.

24 August   First civil rights march from Coalisland to Dungannon, County Tyrone.

5 October   RUC uses force to break up civil rights march in Londonderry. Media coverage causes tension and prompts agitation, student groups calling for more militant action.

1969: 13 DEATHS

4 January   Loyalists attack march in support of civil rights from Belfast to Londonderry, organised by left-wing students.

17 April   Bernadette Devlin, one of marchers' leaders, elected as Westminster MP at Mid-Ulster by-election.

30 April   Terence O'Neill, who had begun reform programme of council house allocation policy and council voting rights, resigns as Prime Minister. Succeeded by Major James Chichester-Clark.

12–14 August Serious rioting in Londonderry's Bogside over controversial Apprentice Boys' parade. British troops called in as violence spreads to Belfast.

16 October   First RUC officer to die in Troubles shot dead by Loyalists in Belfast rioting in protest at plans to disarm police and disband B-Special reserve force.

28 December   IRA splits; birth of breakaway Provisional IRA. Those remaining become Official IRA.

1970: 25 DEATHS

1 April   Emergence of Ulster Defence Regiment in place of disbanded B-Specials.

18 June   Conservatives win British general election. Dr Ian Paisley elected for North Antrim.

26–7 June   Severe riots in West Belfast in response to Orange Order parades.

2 July   Lower Falls curfew by army in Belfast leads to serious violence and deaths.

31 July   Petrol bomber shot dead by army in North Belfast; five nights of rioting follow.

21 August   Formation of constitutional and nationalist Social Democratic and Labour Party.

23 October   Charles Haughey, dismissed from Irish government, acquitted along with three others after sensational trial involving charges of supplying guns to IRA in Northern Ireland.

1971: 174 DEATHS

6 February   First British soldier killed in Troubles in North Belfast.

11 March   Three off-duty soldiers lured from Belfast pub and shot dead by IRA.

20 March   Brian Faulkner succeeds James Chichester-Clark as Prime Minister.

13 May	Housing Executive set up to take away house-building, allocation and rents from council control.
28 July	As violence continues, Reginald Maudling, British Home Secretary, says 'a state of war' exists between army and IRA.
9 August	Internment introduced, prompting large-scale rioting, but most IRA leaders escape arrest.
5 October	Formation of Ian Paisley's Democratic Unionist Party.
4 December	In response to IRA bombs and attacks on bars, UVF bombs North Belfast bar, killing fifteen people.

1972: 467 DEATHS

30 January	'Bloody Sunday' shootings by army in Londonderry cause fourteen deaths at banned civil rights march.
22 February	Official IRA bombs Parachute Regiment HQ at Aldershot, killing six civilians and a Catholic chaplain.
24 March	Stormont Parliament suspended by Edward Heath. William Whitelaw appointed as Secretary of State for Northern Ireland.
29 May	Ceasefire by Official IRA.
26 June	Provisional IRA calls temporary ceasefire.
1 July	Ulster Defence Association appears in Loyalist areas of Belfast and sets up no-go areas.
7 July	Whitelaw and other ministers meet IRA leaders, including Gerry Adams, for secret London talks.
21 July	'Bloody Friday' in Belfast. Twenty-six IRA bombs explode, killing eleven people and injuring 130.
31 July	'Operation Motorman' by army to end IRA no-go areas in Belfast and Londonderry. Army strength in province reaches over 21,000.

1973: 250 DEATHS

1 January	The United Kingdom and the Republic of Ireland become part of the European Economic Community.
7 February	United Loyalist Council calls strikes over first internment of Protestants.
28 February	Fine Gael–Labour coalition formed in Dublin under Liam Cosgrave.
8 March	Referendum on continuation of border and partition boycotted by most of nationalist population but produces massive 'yes' vote. One killed, 243 injured by IRA bombs in London.
20 March	Fine Gael–Labour coalition government White Paper proposes power-sharing assembly and Council of Ireland.

16 June	Ulster Freedom Fighters emerge from UDA to intensify attacks on nationalist population.
30 June	Elections to new assembly give majority to parties ready to support power-sharing.
21 November	Power-sharing executive formed.
2 December	Francis Pym succeeds William Whitelaw as Secretary of State for Northern Ireland.
6–9 December	Sunningdale conference confirms powers of new executive, also creation of Council of Ireland.

1974: 216 DEATHS

4 February	IRA bomb attack on army bus on M62 motorway in Yorkshire kills eleven.
28 February	British general election returns Labour to office with Harold Wilson as Prime Minister. Eleven of Northern Ireland's twelve seats won by United Ulster Unionists Council candidates opposed to Sunningdale Agreement.
5 March	Merlyn Rees appointed Secretary of State for Northern Ireland.
4 April	Ban lifted on UVF to encourage it to 'go political'.
15 May	Ulster Workers' Council launches strike to bring down new power-sharing executive.
17 May	Massive UVF bomb attacks in Dublin and Monaghan kill twenty-seven. Death toll later rises to thirty-two, with 100 injured.
28 May	Executive resigns and new Assembly collapses.
29 May	Victorious UWC calls off strike.
10 October	Labour victory at general election but UUUC hold ten Northern Ireland seats.
21 November	IRA bombs in Birmingham pubs kill twenty-one, injure 180.
29 November	Prevention of Terrorism Act passed after seventeen-hour sitting.
8 December	Dissident members of Official Sinn Fein form new Irish Republican Socialist Party, from which grows new terror group, Irish National Liberation Army.

1975: 247 DEATHS

9 February	IRA announce 'indefinite' ceasefire but launches attacks on INLA.
25 February	Killings mark start of feud between INLA and Official IRA.
15 March	Temporary ceasefire between INLA and Official IRA.
24 May	INLA kills its first security forces victim.
5 June	Referendum shows UK majority for remaining in EEC.

24 July	Phasing out begins of internment without trial.
31 July	Three Miami Showband musicians, all Catholics, killed by UVF, one seriously injured.
2 October	Series of UVF attacks cause twelve deaths.
3 October	UVF again declared illegal.
9 October	Sixteen UVF men charged with murders of UDA members in feud.
29 October	Concerted Provisional IRA attacks on Official IRA.
13 November	Provisional and Official IRA agree to end feud after loss of thirteen lives.

1976: 297 DEATHS

5 January	Ten Protestant workers shot dead at Kingsmills, South Armagh. Republican Action Force claim responsibility.
7 January	SAS unit deployed by army in South Armagh.
13 January	IRA bomb in Belfast, followed by other attacks on security forces, signals end of ceasefire.
9 March	Constitutional Convention set up the previous year dissolved after a session ended in uproar and violence.
5 April	James Callaghan succeeds Harold Wilson as Prime Minister.
10 August	Three Maguire children killed by car after shooting in West Belfast. Horror of deaths leads to formation of Women's Peace Movement, which evolves into Peace People. Holds series of large peace rallies in Belfast and elsewhere.
10 September	Merlyn Rees replaced as Secretary of State by Roy Mason.
15 September	Special Category status for paramilitary prisoners phased out. Kieran Nugent first IRA prisoner to refuse to wear prison uniform.

1977: 112 DEATHS

3 May	United Unionist Action Council, strongly influenced by Ian Paisley, launches strike to secure return to Stormont majority rule and tougher security policies. It fails to get full support of UWC.
13 May	Strike called off.
27 July	New feud between Official and Provisional IRA – four killed, six injured.
30 August	US President Jimmy Carter declares support for any form of government in Northern Ireland commanding support across both communities. Urges Americans not to support paramilitary violence, clearly thinking of US-based Irish Northern Aid Committee (Noraid).

| 10 October | Betty Williams and Mairead Corrigan, founders of Peace People, receive Nobel Peace Prize. |

1978: 81 DEATHS

17 February	twelve die, twenty-three suffer severe burns in IRA fire bomb attack on La Mon Hotel.
26 March	Speakers at IRA commemorations of 1916 Easter Rising promise intensification of 'armed struggle'. Subsequent restructuring within IRA to create more effective cell structure.
1 August	Catholic Primate Archbishop Tomás Ó Fiach describes conditions of IRA prisoners in Maze H-blocks as 'inhumane'.
8 October	Serious rioting in Londonderry when Provisional Sinn Fein and other bodies hold march to commemorate civil rights demonstration of 5 October 1968.
28 November	Parliament agrees to increase Northern Ireland's representation from twelve to seventeen seats.

1979: 113 DEATHS

20 February	Eleven Loyalists with links to UVF and known as Shankill Butchers sentenced to life imprisonment for reign of terror which took nineteen lives in Belfast.
29 March	UDA publishes *Beyond the Religious Divide*, supporting power-sharing in an independent Ulster.
30 March	Airey Neave, Conservative opposition spokesman, killed by INLA bomb in London.
3 May	General election brings Margaret Thatcher to power.
5 May	Humphrey Atkins appointed Secretary of State for Northern Ireland.
7 June	Ian Paisley and the Social Democratic and Labour Party's John Hume win massive votes in European Parliament elections.
31 July	US State Department acts to stop private arms shipments to Northern Ireland.
27 August	Eighteen soldiers killed in IRA bomb ambush at Warrenpoint, County Down. Lord Mountbatten killed on boat by bomb off Sligo coast, which kills another three sailing with him, including two fourteen-year-old boys.
29 September	Pope at Drogheda, County Louth, appeals 'on bended knees' for peace in Northern Ireland.

1980: 76 DEATHS

| 7 January | Constitutional Conference opens at Stormont. |
| 24 March | Conference adjourns without agreement. |

15 April	Secretary of State Humphrey Atkins in talks with Haughey government in Dublin.
21 May	Margaret Thatcher and Charles Haughey meet at Downing Street. Communiqué pledges them to closer co-operation and stresses their countries' 'unique relationship'.
25 June	US Senator Edward Kennedy calls for 'end to divisions of Irish people' and all-party solution to conflict.
26 June	Dr Miriam Daly, prominent Republican member of National H-Block/Armagh Committee, shot dead by UDA/UFF.
27 October	Seven H-block IRA prisoners start hunger strike in support of demand, amongst other things, to wear own clothing.
8 December	Thatcher and three other ministers in Dublin talks with Irish government.
18 December	H-block hunger strike called off.

1981: 101 DEATHS

1 March	New H-Block hunger strike by prisoners, in support of five demands for full political status, led by Bobby Sands.
9 April	Sands wins Fermanagh and South Tyrone by-election.
28 April	US President Ronald Reagan says America will not intervene in Northern Ireland's worsening crisis but stresses his concern.
5 May	Sands dies after 66-day fast. Serious rioting and deaths follow in nationalist areas.
7 May	100,000 people attend Sands's funeral.
14 July	Irish government urges US to intervene and to seek to influence British policy on hunger strikes.
13 September	James Prior becomes Secretary of State for Northern Ireland.
3 October	Hunger strikes called off after deaths of nine more prisoners.
31 October	At Sinn Fein's Ard Fheis in Dublin, Danny Morrison tells audience that victory can be won with a ballot paper in one hand and an Armalite in the other.
6 November	Margaret Thatcher and the Irish Taoiseach, Dr Garret FitzGerald, agree to set up British–Irish inter-governmental Council of Ireland.
14 November	Reverend Robert Bradford, Unionist MP for South Belfast, murdered by IRA.
23 November	Loyalist 'Day of Action' in protest at so-called failed security policy. Ian Paisley announces formation of 'Third Force' of volunteers to back up security forces. Claimed it had between 15,000 and 20,000 members. Prior says private armies will not be tolerated.

1982: 97 DEATHS

18 February   Fianna Fáil victory in Irish Dáil elections.

17 March   Irish Taoiseach Charles Haughey, on St Patrick's Day visit to Washington, calls for US government to bring more pressure on Britain over issue of Irish unity. President Ronald Reagan says any solution must come from people of Northern Ireland.

22 April   Workers Party, which had grown out of the Official IRA, issues denial in Dublin of press claims that latter still active and involved in armed robbery.

20 July   Eight soldiers killed and fifty-one people injured by IRA bomb attacks on army in London.

20 October   Elections to new devolved Assembly set up by James Prior. Unionist candidates win biggest block of seats but Sinn Fein win five, though, like SDLP, they boycott Assembly.

4 November   Fall of Charles Haughey's Fianna Fáil government.

6 December   Seventeen people, including eleven soldiers, killed by INLA bomb at Droppin Well bar disco at Ballykelly, County Londonderry.

14 December   Fine Gael–Labour coalition formed in Dublin led by Garret FitzGerald.

1983: 77 DEATHS

11 March   Irish government announces it will set up all-Ireland forum on lines suggested by SDLP.

11 April   Fourteen UVF men sentenced to prison, two for life, on evidence of 'supergrass'. All freed on appeal the following year.

30 May   Inaugural meeting in Dublin of New Ireland Forum.

15 June   General election. Unionist parties win fifteen out of Northern Ireland's seventeen seats. John Hume wins Foyle for SDLP and Gerry Adams elected in West Belfast for Sinn Fein.

5 August   After lengthy trial of thirty-eight people charged with IRA terrorism on evidence of supergrass, twenty-two of accused given heavy sentences but four years later, eighteen of them freed on appeal.

25 September   Thirty-eight IRA prisoners escape from Maze, killing a prison officer. Nineteen recaptured within a few days but rest get away.

13 November   Major changes in Sinn Fein leadership carried at its Ard Fheis. Adams elected president of party.

21 November   Three shot dead, seven injured in gun attack on Pentecostal church at Darkley, County Armagh. INLA believed to be implicated but shootings claimed by 'Catholic Reaction Force'.

7 December   Dr Edgar Graham, Queen's University law lecturer and Unionist Assembly member, shot dead by IRA.

17 December   Five killed and eighty injured in IRA bomb attack on Harrods, London.

1984: 64 DEATHS

14 March   Sinn Fein President Gerry Adams survives UDA/UFF murder attempt in Belfast.

7 April   RUC Chief Constable denies cover-up over police killings of two INLA men, igniting controversy over whether police operate 'shoot to kill' policy.

4 June   President Ronald Reagan tells Irish Dáil and Senate that it is not US policy to intervene in Irish politics but praises New Ireland Forum and condemns paramilitary violence.

2 July   James Prior, speaking in House of Commons, rejects unitary state, federal Ireland and joint authority over Northern Ireland, all options set out by New Ireland Forum.

10 September   Douglas Hurd replaces Prior as Secretary of State for Northern Ireland.

29 September   Seven tons of IRA arms seized off Kerry coast on *Marita Ann*.

12 October   IRA bomb at Grand Hotel in Brighton kills four Conservative conference delegates; a fifth dies later. Thirty-four others injured.

19 November   Margaret Thatcher, after British–Irish summit meeting, reiterates government's rejection of all constitutional options set out by New Ireland Forum.

4 December   Hurd tells Unionist Assembly members significant moves needed to meet nationalist aspirations.

1985: 54 DEATHS

28 February   Nine RUC officers killed by IRA mortar attack on base in Newry, County Down.

3 July   Thousands of Loyalists demonstrate in Portadown over rerouting of Orange Order parade.

12–13 July   Violent clashes in Portadown over RUC's reversal of decision to ban Orange Order parade close to Catholic area.

30 July   BBC governors stop transmission of documentary featuring Sinn Fein's Martin McGuinness. Strikes in protest by BBC and ITV reporters.

2 September   Tom King succeeds Douglas Hurd as Secretary of State.

5 October   Fianna Fáil's Charles Haughey says his party will not accept any departure from principle of Irish unity set out in New Ireland Forum report and 1937 Irish constitution.

15 November Margaret Thatcher and Taoiseach Garret FitzGerald sign Anglo-Irish Agreement.

16 November All fifteen Unionist MPs announce they will resign seats in protest at Agreement.

23 November Huge Loyalist protest rally against Agreement in Belfast city centre.

21 December Progressive Democrats break away from Fine Gael and form new party group in Irish Dáil.

1986: 61 DEATHS

23 January Fifteen by-elections resulting from Unionists resigning Westminster seats. Total Unionist vote up from 1983 but the Newry and Armagh seat lost to SDLP.

3 March 'Day of action' against Anglo-Irish Agreement halts public services and much of local industry. Loyalist barricades go up in some areas and serious rioting breaks out later in day.

1 April Young Loyalist in Portadown killed when RUC fire on rioters with plastic bullets.

Main Protestant churches condemn Loyalist raids on homes of RUC officers. Official Unionist Party ends special relationship with Conservative party dating from late nineteenth century.

5 June Controversial decision taken to remove John Stalker, Deputy Chief Constable of Greater Manchester Police, from inquiry into alleged RUC 'shoot to kill' policy against IRA and INLA.

23 June Northern Ireland Assembly dissolved amidst angry scenes.

11–16 July Loyalist rioting in Belfast and Portadown accompanies Orange Order parades.

5 August IRA issues warning to contractors working for security forces and extends its list of legitimate targets.

2 November Sinn Fein Ard Fheis votes to allow successful candidates to take their seats in future Dáil elections. This significant move away from historic policy of 'abstentionism' results in former party leader Ruairi Ó Brádaigh and 100 supporters walking out.

10 November Ulster Resistance formed to 'take direct action as and when required' to defeat Anglo-Irish Agreement.

23 December Margaret Thatcher on visit to Northern Ireland reaffirms commitment to Agreement and states that change of government in Dublin will not alter it.

1987: 93 DEATHS

20 January Two INLA members shot dead in Drogheda hotel as a result of internal feud.

29 January	UDA publishes *Common Sense*, document calling for Ulster self-government based on power-sharing and bill of rights.
2 March	Ulster Clubs announce plan to set up alternative system of government by Unionist and paramilitary groups.
26 March	Two West Belfast priests announce end of INLA feud.
25 April	Lord Justice Gibson and wife killed in County Down by IRA car bomb. He is fifth Northern Ireland judge murdered by the IRA.
8 May	Eight IRA men shot dead by SAS in Loughgall, County Armagh.
12 June	Conservatives returned to power at general election. Only change in Northern Ireland is SDLP defeat of Enoch Powell in South Down.
1 November	150 tons of IRA arms and ammunition seized on French coaster *Eksund*, after tip-off to authorities.
8 November	Eleven killed and sixty-three injured by IRA bomb at Enniskillen war memorial on Remembrance Sunday.
22 December	UDA deputy leader John McMichael killed in Lisburn by IRA bomb, though tensions within UDA are also a factor.

1988: 93 DEATHS

8 January	RUC near Portadown seizes huge consignment of arms and ammunition intended for UDA and UVF.
11 January	John Hume and Gerry Adams hold talks in Belfast.
25 January	Government announces that eleven RUC officers investigated by Stalker inquiry will not be prosecuted for reasons of 'national security'.
6 March	Three IRA members shot dead in Gibraltar by SAS.
11 March	Andy Tyrie resigns after nearly fifteen years as leader of UDA.
16 March	Loyalist gunman kills three in gun and grenade attack on Belfast funeral of IRA members killed in Gibraltar.
19 March	At funeral of one of 16 March victims, mob in West Belfast attack and kill two soldiers.
1 April	Colonel Muammar Gadafy of Libya pledges support to IRA.
15 June	Six soldiers killed by IRA bomb in Lisburn.
28 July	All Northern Ireland parties oppose announcement in House of Commons of plans to privatise aerospace engineering company Short Brothers and shipbuilders Harland and Wolff.
20 August	Eight British soldiers killed by bomb attack on bus at Ballygawley, County Tyrone.
2 September	SDLP–Sinn Fein talks called off.
19 October	Government announces ban on all live statements on television and radio by spokesmen and supporters of paramilitary organisations.

1989: 62 DEATHS

12 February   Prominent Catholic lawyer Patrick Finucane murdered by UDA/UFF at his Belfast home.

14 February   Sinn Fein councillor shot dead by Loyalists in Magherafelt, County Londonderry. First of series of attacks on party officials and councillors.

22 March   Three Ulster Resistance members arrested in Paris and charged with trying to trade South African arms for missile parts stolen from Short's Belfast factory.

15 June   Elections to European Parliament return Ian Paisley, John Hume and Official Unionist Jim Nicolson for Northern Ireland's three seats.

7 July   Peter Brooke appointed Secretary of State for Northern Ireland.

25 August   Catholic Loughlin Maginn shot dead by UDA/UFF at home in Rathfriland, County Down. Death followed by UDA claims to have access to photomontage material on IRA suspects compiled by security forces. This leads on to Stevens inquiry into alleged 'collusion' between Loyalists and security forces.

22 September   IRA bomb attack kills eleven and injures twenty-one others at Royal Marines school of music at Deal, Kent.

19 October   Court of Appeal in London sets free four prisoners wrongly convicted of Guildford pub bombings by IRA in 1973.

3 November   Brooke tells media IRA cannot be defeated militarily and that he will not rule out talks with Sinn Fein if violence ends.

1990: 76 DEATHS

1 January   Fair Employment Act becomes law, setting up Fair Employment Commission and Tribunal and requiring all but small-scale employers to monitor religious composition of their workforces.

18 February   Martin McGuinness describes Peter Brooke as first Secretary of State 'with some understanding of Irish history' and urges him to spell out what steps he would take in response to a cessation of IRA violence.

17 May   Publication of summary of Stevens inquiry report into alleged collusion between Loyalists and security forces. It finds that collusion was 'neither widespread nor institutionalised' but calls for tighter controls over documents and more vetting of UDR.

20 July   IRA bomb at London Stock Exchange causes massive damage but no deaths or injuries.

30 July	Ian Gow, Conservative MP for Eastbourne, killed at home by IRA car bomb. He had resigned from the Government over 1985 Anglo-Irish Agreement.
24 October	Six soldiers and one civilian killed by IRA bombs on border near Newry and Londonderry. In each attack, abducted victim strapped into car loaded with bomb and forced to drive into army checkpoint for its detonation.
9 November	Mary Robinson elected Irish President. She had opposed Anglo-Irish Agreement and in her inaugural address says her supporters had 'stepped out from the faded flags of the civil war and voted for a new Ireland'.
22 November	Margaret Thatcher resigns as Prime Minister.
27 November	John Major declared Conservative leader and becomes Prime Minister.
23 December	For first time in fourteen years, IRA announces three-day Christmas ceasefire.

1991: 102 DEATHS

7 February	IRA mortar bombs fired at 10 Downing Street, narrowly missing Cabinet in session.
3 March	Three IRA men and one civilian killed in UVF attack on bar in Cappagh, County Tyrone.
14 March	Birmingham Six, Irishmen wrongly convicted of November 1974 pub bombings in city, freed by Appeal Court.
30 April	Combined Loyalist Military Command, representing UDA, UVF and Red Hand Commando, announces ceasefire for duration of all-party constitutional talks chaired by Secretary of State.
25 May	Sinn Fein councillor in Buncrana, County Donegal, killed by UDA/UFF raiding party operating from across border.
31 May	Three UDR soldiers killed by IRA bomb at Glenanne base, County Armagh.
3 June	Three-man IRA unit killed by SAS at Coagh, County Tyrone.
26 June	Members of Maguire family freed on appeal after convictions over 1973 London pub bombings by IRA.
3 July	Secretary of State announces end of all-party talks. Intensified UDA/UFF attacks resume; over year as whole, Loyalist killings surpass those of IRA.
15 November	Two IRA members killed at St Albans, Hertfordshire, by premature explosion of bomb intended for army band concert.

1992: 91 DEATHS

12 January	Secretary of State says IRA violence must end before talks with Sinn Fein possible.
17 January	Eight Protestant workers killed by IRA landmine at Teebane Cross, County Tyrone.
5 February	Five Catholics killed in UDA/UFF attack on betting shop on Belfast's Lower Ormeau Road.
6 February	Albert Reynolds becomes Fianna Fáil leader.
16 February	Four-man IRA unit killed by SAS at Coalisland, County Tyrone.
22 February	Split within Workers Party, formation of Democratic Left.
9 April	General election keeps Conservatives in power; Gerry Adams loses West Belfast to SDLP and Peter Brooke replaced by Sir Patrick Mayhew.
10 April	Three killed in huge IRA bomb explosion in central London.
10 August	As its attacks and killings increase, UDA declared illegal organisation.
4 September	North Belfast teenager killed by army patrol. Two soldiers convicted of murder but their subsequent early release and return to army causes bitter controversy.
3 November	Bill Clinton elected US President. Stresses his administration's strong commitment to working for peace in Northern Ireland.

1993: 90 DEATHS

2 January	After Dáil election, Fianna Fáil–Labour government formed in Dublin. Joint statement by John Hume and Gerry Adams on future of Northern Ireland.
31 January	Adams makes first visit to United States, talks to pro-Republican groups, also to advisers close to President.
8 March	IRA bomb kills two young boys in Warrington, Cheshire.
24 April	Massive IRA bomb explosion at Bishopsgate, central London, kills press photographer and causes many injuries and millions of pounds' worth of damage.
23 October	Ten killed and fifty-seven injured in IRA bomb attack on fish shop in Shankill Road in Belfast. IRA claims, wrongly, that UDA is using premises above it.
30 October	UDA/UFF attack on Rising Sun bar at Greysteel, County Londonderry, kills eight and injures eleven.
8 November	London newspaper reports secret talks between IRA and British government representatives, going back over previous three years.
27 November	Secretary of State admits to 'contacts' rather than negotiations having taken place.

15 December John Major and Albert Reynolds issue Downing Street Declaration, setting out case for joint British and Irish role in any settlement of the conflict in Northern Ireland and stress importance of wishes of a democratic majority in the North.

1994: 69 DEATHS

9 March Select Committee on Northern Ireland formed by House of Commons.

2 June RAF helicopter crash on Mull of Kintyre kills twenty-five, most of them British and RUC anti-terrorism experts.

18 June UVF attack bar at Loughinisland, County Down, killing six, including 87-year-old man.

11 July IRA kill Raymond Smallwoods, leading UDA political spokesman.

31 August IRA announces 'a complete cessation of hostilities'.

13 October CLMC announces ceasefire and apologises for innocent victims of Loyalists.

17 November Albert Reynolds resigns as Taoiseach after Labour ministers leave his government.

19 November Bertie Ahern elected leader of Fianna Fáil.

15 December John Bruton becomes Taoiseach at the head of Fine Gael, Labour and Democratic Left coalition.

1995: 9 DEATHS

22 February *Framework for the Future* document published by British and Irish governments.

15 June Ulster Unionists lose North Down to Robert McCartney, QC in by-election.

9 July RUC bans Portadown Orangemen from Drumcree Sunday parade along mainly nationalist Garvaghy Road. Protests and Loyalist violence follow.

11 July Orangemen allowed to parade into Portadown, led by Ian Paisley and David Trimble, Unionist MP for Upper Bann.

6 September Johnny Adair given sixteen-year sentence for 'directing' terrorism by UDA/UFF.

8 September Trimble elected leader of Ulster Unionist Party after resignation of James Molyneaux.

24 November Narrow majority for legalised divorce in Irish Republic referendum.

28 November Launch of twin-track British and Irish strategy to restart inter-party talks and set up 'international body' to examine issue of arms-decommissioning.

30 November President Bill Clinton visits Northern Ireland.

1996: 22 DEATHS

9 February	End of IRA ceasefire. Bomb at Canary Wharf, London, kills two, causes huge damage.
28 February	British and Irish governments try to restart talks process: all-party talks scheduled for 10 June.
30 May	Elections held for Northern Ireland Forum.
10 June	Stormont talks begin.
15 June	Massive destruction by IRA bomb in Manchester but no lives lost.
7 July	Loyalist violence escalates over new RUC ban on Garvaghy Road parade by Portadown Orangemen.
11 July	Widespread violence as RUC reverses its decision on Garvaghy Road parade.
13 July	SDLP withdraws from Forum.
10 October	IRA bomb attack on army HQ near Lisburn kills one soldier and causes many injuries.

1997: 21 DEATHS

30 January	Review body on parades and marches calls for creation of statutory Parades Commission.
12 February	Soldier killed by IRA at Bessbrook, County Armagh.
5 March	Adjournment of stalled all-party talks.
1 May	Decisive Labour general election victory. Tony Blair becomes Prime Minister. Mo Mowlam appointed Secretary of State for Northern Ireland.
16 May	Blair gives keynote pro-Union speech in Belfast.
2 June	Belfast City Council elects its first nationalist Lord Mayor, a member of the SDLP.
3 June	Multi-party talks resume at Stormont.
6 June	General elections to Irish Dáil lead to formation of Fianna Fáil–Progressive Democrat coalition led by Bertie Ahern.
6 July	RUC permits Orangemen once again to march along Garvaghy Road. Widespread violence and rioting in nationalist areas.
11 July	Orange Order reroutes contentious Belfast parades.
19 July	IRA reinstates ceasefire.
9 September	Sinn Fein joins all-party talks.
24 September	International panel on arms-decommissioning chaired by General John de Chastelain begins its work.
31 October	Mary McAleese elected Irish President.
10 December	Sinn Fein delegation meets Tony Blair at 10 Downing Street.
27 December	Billy Wright, leader of breakaway terror group the Loyalist Volunteer Force, shot dead in Maze prison by INLA. Death

launches a wave of reprisal killings by Loyalists and Republican counter-attacks which continue into the next year.

1998: 57 DEATHS

29 January	Demonstrations in Belfast and elsewhere in protest against renewed sectarian killings arising from the murder of Billy Wright.
20 February	Temporary exclusion of Sinn Fein from talks process because of recent IRA killings.
7 April	Tony Blair flies to Belfast to support the endangered talks at Stormont.
10 April	US Senator George Mitchell presides over completion of the Good Friday Agreement, setting out formula for power-sharing, parity of esteem for both communities, cross-border bodies and removal of Articles 2 and 3 from Irish constitution, which claim Northern Ireland as part of 'national territory'.
18 April	UUP endorses Agreement at meeting of its council.
10 May	Sinn Fein Ard Fheis also backs Agreement.
22 May	In Northern Ireland referendum, 71 per cent support the Agreement. In Irish Republic, figure is 94 per cent.
3 June	Announcement of independent commission on policing in Northern Ireland.
25 June	Elections to new assembly set up under Good Friday Agreement give majority of seats to parties prepared to support power-sharing.
29 June	New Parades Commission requires Portadown Orangemen to reroute their parade from Drumcree church away from Garvaghy Road. Loyalist protests again become violent and involve attacks on RUC and army.
12 July	Three Catholic Quinn children die after fire bomb attack on their home in Ballymoney, County Antrim.
8 August	LVF announces ceasefire.
15 August	Twenty-nine people killed in Omagh, County Tyrone, by Real IRA car bomb.
22 August	INLA announces ceasefire. Real IRA calls ceasefire.
16 October	John Hume and David Trimble awarded Nobel Peace Prize.

1999: 6 DEATHS

27 January	Eamon Collins, a former IRA intelligence officer who had written a book fiercely critical of Republican violence, murdered in home town of Newry, County Down.

16 March	Rosemary Nelson, prominent lawyer of nationalist sympathies, killed by car bomb in Lurgan, County Armagh. Responsibility claimed by Loyalist group, Red Hand Defenders.
17 March	Frankie Curry, once a leading member of UVF, shot dead in West Belfast.
5 June	Protestant woman married to Catholic killed at Portadown home by Loyalist pipe bomb, one of many such attacks during the year.
12 July	Orange Order parade in Belfast rerouted away from Lower Ormeau area.
21 July	IRA statement warns Britain of dangers of Unionists blocking progress on implementing Belfast Agreement.
9 September	Patten report published. Calls for new police service to represent both communities.
14 September	Johnny Adair released from prison, one of nearly 300 Loyalists whose phased release takes place under Agreement.
15 September	US Senator George Mitchell calls for devolved institutions proposed by Agreement to be set up ahead of paramilitary arms-decommissioning, though he stresses it should happen as soon as possible.
16 November	David Trimble accepts Mitchell's view but states need for arms-decommissioning. His response is significant move away from previous stance of 'no guns, no government'.
17 November	IRA promises to appoint representative to meet John de Chastelain and his arms-decommissioning body.
27 November	At special meeting of Ulster Unionist Council, Trimble wins 58 per cent of votes on issue of joining devolved executive but promises to resign from it if the IRA makes no real moves on decommissioning arms in New Year.
2 December	New all-party power-sharing executive meets at Stormont with Trimble as First Minister and SDLP's Seamus Mallon as Deputy. Two ministerial positions given to Sinn Fein and cross-border bodies called for by 1998 Agreement are rapidly set up.

2000: 17 DEATHS

11 February	Secretary of State announces suspension of new devolved institutions after report from John de Chastelain shows no IRA movement on arms-decommissioning.
12 February	IRA announces withdrawal from any further talks with de Chastelain but stresses ceasefire remains intact.
18 February	Two Protestant teenagers murdered near Tandragee, County Armagh. UVF widely believed responsible after murder of one of its commanders in Portadown by LVF.

21 February	Johnny Adair, with members of C Company, attends funeral of one of teenage victims. Seen as move to align himself with LVF and defy UDA leadership.
17 March	David Trimble in Washington gives impression he may lead UUP back into government, even if Belfast Agreement's May 2000 deadline for IRA arms-decommissioning not met. Hints he may instead settle for clear statement by IRA that its war is over.
25 March	Trimble defeats challenge to his leadership at annual meeting of Ulster Unionist Council, though Reverend Martin Smyth MP won 43 per cent of the vote. Result seen as blow to Trimble.
27 March	Saville inquiry into 1972 Bloody Sunday shootings in Londonderry holds its opening session.
6 May	IRA states that process will be initiated to 'completely and verifiably' put its arms beyond use and that it accepts inspection of some of its arms dumps by de Chastelain's commission. John Hume hails statement as proof that 'guns have been taken forever out of Irish politics'.
26 May	Shooting of North Belfast man with UVF links seen by police as indication of closer links being formed by elements in UDA with LVF.
27 May	Trimble wins crucial vote on Ulster Unionist Council on issue of rejoining Executive with Sinn Fein and others but majority is slender.
28 May	Ulster Freedom Fighters, UDA's 'military' arm, say they don't accept IRA's 6 May claims about arms dump inspection and query whether war is over. Well-known West Belfast drug dealer shot dead, one of several since 1994 ceasefire believed to have been killed by IRA.
31 May	Democratic Unionists say they will take ministerial seats on Executive but not sit around table with Sinn Fein or share collective responsibility for decisions with them.
1 June	London's Hammersmith Bridge damaged by Real IRA bomb.
26 June	Parades Commission announces further ban on Portadown Orangemen's Garvaghy Road parade.
1–12 July	Period of violent Loyalist protests at ban, over 300 attacks on security forces, injuring eighty-seven RUC officers and soldiers. Johnny Adair active in protests and appears at Drumcree with members of C Company.
12 August	Apprentice Boys of Derry parade passes off peacefully.
21 August	UDA's Loyalist 'culture festival' in Shankill leads to major violence and start of feud between Lower Shankill UDA and UVF.

22 August   Start of killings arising from feud; Adair arrested and returned to prison.
22 November Truce announced in feud after nine killings, though most of UDA's six brigades had kept out of it. Attacks on Catholic homes continue, carried out by young UDA members.
28 December Death of Ronnie Hill, former head of Enniskillen High School, in coma since 1987 Remembrance Sunday IRA bomb.

2001: 19 DEATHS

24 January   John Reid becomes Secretary of State for Northern Ireland.
3 March   Real IRA bomb attack on BBC Television Centre in London causes damage but no deaths or serious injuries.
4 March   IRA announces willingness to resume talks with John de Chastelain on putting its arms 'beyond use'.
31 May   Sinn Fein newspaper *An Phoblacht* carries IRA statement claiming it has accepted further inspection of arms dumps.
7 June   Westminster general election held amidst rising sectarian tension in many areas. Results weaken David Trimble's position with DUP gaining another three seats and Sinn Fein two more.
16–23 June   Serious street violence breaks out in Ardoyne and leads to Loyalist blockade of Holy Cross Catholic girls' primary school which carries on into next year.
1 July   Trimble resigns as leader of Northern Ireland Executive claiming no real movement from IRA on arms-decommissioning.
4 July   As sectarian violence increases, Catholic teenager murdered by Loyalists in town of Antrim.
12 July   After major Orange Order parades in Portadown, Belfast and elsewhere pass off peacefully, serious rioting breaks out in Ardoyne with police firing plastic bullets.
29 July   Protestant teenager in North Belfast mistaken for Catholic and shot dead by Loyalists.
2 August   Real IRA bomb explosion in Ealing, London, causes injuries and destruction but no deaths.
6 August   De Chastelain announces he is satisfied IRA willing to put arms 'completely and verifiably beyond use'. Dublin and London governments welcome the move but Unionist parties stress absence of a clear timetable for disarming.
10 August   Reid announces 24-hour suspension of Executive set up under Belfast Agreement.
12 August   Executive restored.
14 August   In Bogotá, Colombia, three men with known IRA and Sinn Fein connections arrested on suspicion of giving, in return for

cash, weapons and explosives training to anti-government guerrilla groups.

20 August Catholic bishops and SDLP announce their support for and readiness to join in administration of new police service to be set up by Patten report.

28 September Martin O'Hagan, *Sunday World* journalist, shot dead by Loyalists in Lurgan.

12 October Reid announces that, in his view, UDA ceasefire is over because of its role in sectarian violence and killings.

23 October De Chastelain and his Commission, after a new IRA statement on putting its arms 'beyond use', confirm they have witnessed a significant 'disposal' of arms.

5 November Formation of new Police Service of Northern Ireland, modelled on 1999 Patten report.

2002: 11 DEATHS

1 January IRA statement lays down conditions for further movement on arms-decommissioning. These include thorough reform of policing based on Patten report and 'demilitarisation' of Britain's presence in province.

12 January Catholic postman murdered by Loyalists in North Belfast.

17 March Break-in at East Belfast Castlereagh police building and theft of classified documents widely believed to be work of IRA.

1 May John Reid says IRA ceasefire not enough; must be a 'sense that the war is over'.

15 May Johnny Adair released from prison and makes defiant speech at Lower Shankill home.

1–8 June Serious rioting and gun battles in Short Strand area of East Belfast, Catholic enclave surrounded by Loyalist population.

1 July Belfast's first Sinn Fein Lord Mayor lays wreath at city war memorial in honour of those who fell at the Somme in 1916.

6 July IRA apologises for its role in the deaths of 'non-combatants' during the Troubles.

11 July Loyalists murder Catholic teenager in North Belfast amid rising sectarian tensions.

25 September Inner Council expels Adair from UDA in response to his open defiance of its leadership. Series of killings ensues.

4 October Police raid Stormont buildings, claiming confidential documents are being copied and removed by Sinn Fein for own use. Amidst claims of IRA spy ring at work within Executive, Unionists call for Sinn Fein's expulsion from it and Executive suspended once again.

24 October Paul Murphy appointed Secretary of State for Northern Ireland.

2003: 10 DEATHS

10 January   As UDA feud worsens, Johnny Adair rearrested and returned to prison.

1 February   John Gregg, UDA South-East Antrim brigadier, and another senior member shot dead in Belfast.

5 February   'Mainstream' UDA members arrive in force in Lower Shankill and expel family and remaining supporters of Adair, who flee to Scotland.

6 February   Huge show of support for UDA leadership at Gregg's funeral in North Belfast.

22 February Political spokesmen of UDA announce twelve-month cease-fire and restructuring within organisation as well as apology for drug-dealing by members and promise to work to reduce sectarian tension.

17 April   Stevens report, on alleged collusion between UDA, army intelligence and RUC Special Branch, published in abbreviated form. Some of report's files passed on to Northern Ireland Director of Public Prosecutions.

23 April   Tony Blair puts key questions to IRA about its intentions to end all paramilitary activity and whether, if all elements of the 1998 Belfast Agreement are implemented, there will be 'complete and final closure of the conflict'.

30 April   Gerry Adams, Sinn Fein President, repeats his view that IRA is determined to do nothing inconsistent with goal of finally ending conflict.

11 May   Alfredo Scappatici, former senior IRA security officer, named in press as British agent.

28 May   Another UDA killing of one of Adair's closest supporters who had returned to Belfast under 'safe conduct' promise from the organisation.

16 June   David Trimble survives 'no confidence' motion by critics on the UUP executive, but vote very close.

27 June   Three Ulster Unionist Westminster MPs suspended by party after their repudiation of Trimble's leadership.

1 August   Chief Constable of PSNI confirms his view that IRA likely to have murdered Armagh man last seen alive on 11 May.

21 October   John de Chastelain announces further major act of weapons-decommissioning by IRA but says he has agreed not to give details of its nature or extent. Unionist parties' response is that this devalues the move. Trimble declares it provides an insufficient basis for trust and he cannot recommend his party to resume power-sharing with Sinn Fein in the Executive after the Assembly elections scheduled for following month.

27 November Amidst continued deadlock on restoration of power-sharing executive, Assembly elections enable Sinn Fein to overtake SDLP as largest nationalist party. DUP also achieves significant increase in vote.

2004: 4 DEATHS

24 February UDA announces extension of ceasefire.

25 March UVF blamed for murder of man in Newtownards.

18 May UVF blamed for shooting dead LVF member in East Belfast.

20 April Independent Monitoring Commission, in first report, severely critical of IRA for continuing recruitment and involvement in serious crime. It makes similar criticism of UDA and UVF.

3 June Former INLA member shot dead outside school in South-West Belfast.

11 June In elections to European Parliament Sinn Fein wins two seats, defeating SDLP, which had held one of Northern Ireland's three seats since 1979. In local council elections in Irish Republic, Sinn Fein wins 126 seats.

12 July Rioting in North Belfast after police allow a Loyalist crowd to walk past Ardoyne in support of Orange lodges and bands.

19 September Joint statement by Irish and British governments after all-party talks at Leeds Castle, Kent. New negotiations promised in Belfast on IRA arms and on the restoration of devolved government.

29 September Young Protestant shot dead in Londonderry in UVF feud.

7 October Sinn Fein rejects claims by police, SDLP and Unionists that IRA has carried out major robbery at Belfast cigarette factory.

12 November Secretary of State Paul Murphy says he recognises UDA ceasefire and its readiness to move away from a paramilitary role.

14 November UDA statement that its priority must become the social problems of Loyalist areas and that it will work towards the day when there will be 'no need for the UDA and UFF'.

8 December Stormont talks come close to agreement with DUP and Sinn Fein expressing support for full power-sharing under terms of Belfast Agreement. DUP leader Ian Paisley demands photographic proof of any new and major act of IRA arms-decommissioning but Sinn Fein rejects it as means of humiliating Republican movement. This leads to break-up of talks.

20 December Over £26 million stolen from Belfast city centre branch of Northern Bank. IRA widely believed to have carried out robbery but denies responsibility.

Appendix C
Organisations and Initials

CLMC   Combined Loyalist Military Command: comprised UDA, UVF and RHC. First heard of in the summer of 1991 when it announced a temporary Loyalist ceasefire. In October 1994 it announced an extended Loyalist ceasefire but within three years was no longer in existence.

DUP   Democratic Unionist Party: formed by Dr Ian Paisley as hard-line breakaway Unionist group in 1971.

INLA   Irish National Liberation Army: formed in 1975 as ruthless Republican terror group.

IPLO   Irish People's Liberation Organisation: breakaway faction of INLA, disbanded in 1992.

IRA   Irish Republican Army: main Republican paramilitary group, closely allied to Sinn Fein. In 1970 it split from old 'Official' Republican movement. Often called Provisional IRA.

IRSP   Irish Republican Socialist Party: formed in 1975 as political wing of INLA.

LVF   Loyalist Volunteer Force: anti-peace process faction led by Billy Wright, who led split from UVF in 1996.

NUPRG   New Ulster Political Research Group: set up by the UDA in January 1978 to explore options for Northern Ireland such as full independence or devolved self-government.

OUP   Official Unionist Party: title first used in 1973 by Unionists opposed to Paisley's DUP and who wanted to stay clear of Unionist groups with paramilitary links.

PSNI   Police Service of Northern Ireland: instituted in 2001.

PUP   Progressive Unionist Party: grew out of and remained allied to UVF.

RHC   Red Hand Commando: formed in 1972 as affiliate of UVF.

RHD   Red Hand Defenders: 'flag of convenience' body for post-1994 ceasefire killings by UDA and UVF.

RIR   Royal Irish Regiment: formed in 1992 to replace UDR.

RSF   Republican Sinn Fein: 1986 breakaway group from Sinn Fein/ IRA.

RUC   Royal Ulster Constabulary: Northern Ireland's police force from June 1922 until November 2001.

SDLP Social Democratic and Labour Party: constitutional and mainly middle-class nationalist party formed in 1970.

UDA Ulster Defence Association: largest Loyalist paramilitary group, formed in 1971.

UDF Ulster Defence Force: formed by UDA in 1983 to give specialised 'military' training to a small and select group of members.

UDP Ulster Democratic Party: formed in 1989 as political arm of UDA.

UDR Ulster Defence Regiment: formed in 1970, absorbed into RIR in 1992.

UFF Ulster Freedom Fighters: illegal and ruthless 'military' wing of UDA, formed in 1973 and responsible for killings throughout the Troubles.

ULDP Ulster Loyalist Democratic Party: forerunner of UDP, formed by UDA in 1981.

UUP Ulster Unionist Party: for almost eighty years, Northern Ireland's biggest Unionist party.

UUUC United Ulster Unionist Council: set up in January 1974 to fight the Sunningdale Agreement. Its candidates won eleven of Northern Ireland's twelve Westminster seats the following month.

UVF Ulster Volunteer Force: re-emerged in 1966 and named after the original 1912 UVF.

UWC Ulster Workers' Council: formed in late 1973 to bring together Unionists, paramilitaries and trade unionists in opposition to the implementation of the Sunningdale Agreement.

UYM Ulster Young Militants: youth wing of UDA.

VUPP Vanguard Unionist Progressive Party: formed in 1973 by disaffected members of the Ulster Unionist Party who had joined William Craig's Vanguard movement.

WP Workers Party: formed in 1982 by former members of Official Republican movement to press for a socialist programme.

YCV Young Citizen Volunteers: youth wing of UVF.

Appendix D
Responsibility for Deaths, 1966–2003

Provisional IRA	1,781
INLA/IPLO	150
Official IRA	54
Real IRA	31
Other Republicans	142
UVF	558
UDA/UFF	430
LVF	18
RHD	6
Other Loyalists	87
Army	301
RUC and its reserve force	50
UDR/RIR	8
Others	87
Total deaths	3,703

I am indebted to Mainstream Publishing for their permission to adapt these figures from *Lost Lives*, which appears in this book's bibliography.

References and Sources

BIBLIOGRAPHY

G. Adams, *Before the Dawn* (London: Heinemann, 1996).

I. Adamson, *The Cruthin: The Ancient Kindred* (Newtownards: Nosmada, 1986).

I. Adamson, *The Identity of Ulster: The Land, the Language and the People* (Belfast Ian Adamson, 1982).

M. Arthur, *Northern Ireland: Soldiers Talking* (London: Sidgwick and Jackson, 1987)

A. Aughey, *Under Siege: Ulster Unionism and the Anglo-Irish Agreement* (Belfast: Blackstaff Press, 1989)

J. Bardon, *A History of Ulster* (Belfast: Blackstaff Press, 1992).

A. Barker, *Shadows: Inside Northern Ireland's Special Branch* (Edinburgh: Mainstream, 2004).

F. Barlet, 'Le visage changeant du Loyalisme 1974–1998', unpublished Ph.D dissertation, University of Paris, Vincennes/Saint Denis, 2001.

G. Beattie, *Protestant Boy* (London: Granta, 2004).

G. Beattie, *We are the People: Journeys through the Heart of Protestant Ulster* (London: Heinemann, 2002).

S. Belfrage, *The Crack: A Belfast Year* (London: Andre Deutsch, 1987).

G. Bell, *The Protestants of Ulster* (London: Pluto Press, 1976).

A. Bill, *Beyond the Red Gauntlet: The Silent Voices of Upper Ardoyne amidst the Travesty of Holy Cross* (Belfast: Anne Bill, 2002).

K. Bloomfield, *Stormont in Crisis: A Memoir* (Belfast: Blackstaff Press, 1994).

K. Boyle, T. Hadden and P. Hillyard, *Ten Years on in Northern Ireland: The Legal Control of Political Violence* (London: Cobden Trust, 1980).

C. Brett, *Long Shadows Cast Before: Nine Lives in Ulster 1625–1977* (Edinburgh: John Bartholomew, 1978).

S. Bruce, *No Pope of Rome: Anti-Catholicism in Modern Scotland* (Edinburgh: Mainstream, 1985).

S. Bruce, *The Red Hand: Protestant Paramilitaries in Northern Ireland* (Oxford: Oxford University Press, 1992).

S. Bruce, *The Edge of the Union: the Ulster Loyalist Political Vision* (Oxford: Oxford University Press, 1994).

A. Cadwallader, *Holy Cross: the Untold Story* (Belfast: Brehon Press, 2004).

A. Clark, *Contact* (London: Secker and Warburg, 1983).

B. Clifford, *Against Ulster Nationalism: A Review of the Development of the Catholic and Protestant Communities and Their Interaction with Each Other and with Britain: In Reply to Tom Nairn of New Left Review and Others* (Belfast: British and Irish Communist Organisation, 1975).

C. Crawford, *Defenders or Criminals?: Loyalist Prisoners and Criminalisation* (Belfast: Blackstaff Press, 1999).

P. Curno (ed.), *Political Issues and Community Work* (London: RKP, 1978).

J. Cusack and H. McDonald, *UVF* (Dublin: Poolbeg, 1997).

N. Davies, *Dead Men Talking: Collusion, Cover-Up and Murder in Northern Ireland's Dirty War* (Edinburgh: Mainstream, 2004).

N. Davies, *Ten-Thirty-Three: The Inside Story of Britain's Secret Killing Machine in Northern Ireland* (Edinburgh, Mainstream, 1999).

P. Devlin, *The Fall of the Northern Ireland Executive* (Belfast: Paddy Devlin, 1975).

M. Dewar, *The British Army in Northern Ireland* (London: Arms and Armour, 1985).

M. Dillon, *The Shankill Butchers: A Case Study of Mass Murder* (London: Hutchinson, 1989).

M. Dillon, *Stone Cold: The True Story of Michael Stone and the Milltown Massacre* (London: Hutchinson, 1992).

M. Dillon, *The Trigger Men* (Edinburgh: Mainstream, 2003).

M. Dillon and D. Lehane, *Political Murder in Northern Ireland* (Harmondsworth: Penguin, 1973).

J. Docherty, 'Imagining Ulster: Northern Ireland Protestants and Ulster Identity', Unpublished Ph.D. thesis, Queen's University, Belfast, 2001.

B. Donoughue, *Prime Minister: The Conduct of Policy under Harold Wilson and James Callaghan* (London: Jonathan Cape, 1987).

S. Duddy, *Concrete Whirlpools of the Mind* (Belfast: Ulidia, 1983).

K. Eide, 'Were the Northern Ireland media used as a tool to sell the Belfast Agreement?', unpublished B.A. dissertation, Napier University, Edinburgh, 2001.

R. English, *Armed Struggle: The History of the IRA* (London: Macmillan, 2003).

E. Fairweather, R. McDonough and M. McFadyean, *Only the Rivers Run Free: Northern Ireland – the Women's War* (London: Pluto Press, 1984).

R. Faligot, *Britain's Military Strategy in Ireland: The Kitson Experiment* (London: Zed, 1983).

B. Faulkner, *Memoirs of a Statesman* (London: Weidenfeld and Nicolson, 1978).

R. Fisk, *The Point of No Return: The Strike Which Broke the British in Ulster* (London: Times/Andre Deutsch, 1975).

W. Flackes and S. Elliott, *Northern Ireland: A Political Directory 1968–88* (Belfast: Blackstaff Press, 1989).

P. Foot, *Who Framed Colin Wallace?* (London: Macmillan, 1989).

T. Gallagher, *Glasgow: The Uneasy Peace – Religious Tension in Modern Scotland* (Manchester: Manchester University Press, 1987).

T. Gallagher, *Edinburgh Divided: John Cormack and No Popery in the 1930s* (Edinburgh: Polygon, 1987).

R. Garland, *Gusty Spence* (Belfast: Blackstaff Press, 2001).

D. Godson, *Himself Alone: David Trimble and the Ordeal of Unionism* (London: HarperCollins, 2004).

M. Goldring, *Belfast: From Loyalty to Rebellion* (London: Lawrence and Wishart, 1991).

D. Hamill, *Pig in the Middle: The Army in Northern Ireland 1969–1984* (London: Methuen, 1985).

S. Heffer, *Like the Roman: The Life of Enoch Powell* (London: Weidenfeld and Nicolson, 1998).

J. Hewitt, *The Collected Poems of John Hewitt*, ed. F. Ormsby (Belfast: Blackstaff Press, 1991).

J. Holland and H. McDonald, *INLA: Deadly Divisions* (Dublin: Torc, 1994).

J. Holland, *Hope against History: The Ulster Conflict* (London: Coronet, 1999).

F. Holroyd and N. Burbridge, *War without Honour* (Hull: Medium, 1989).

E. Hughes (ed.), *Culture and Politics in Northern Ireland 1960–1990* (Milton Keynes and Philadelphia: Open University Press, 1990).

M. Ingram and G. Harkin, *Stakeknife: Britain's Secret Agents in Ireland* (Dublin: O'Brien, 2004).

R. Jones, J. Kane, R. Wallace, D. Sloan and B. Courtney, *The Orange Citadel: A History of Orangeism in Portadown District* (Portadown: Portadown Orange Lodge District No. 1, 1996).

H. Jordan, *Milestones in Murder: Defining Moments in Ulster's Terror War* (Edinburgh: Mainstream, 2002).

D. Keogh and M. Haltzel (eds), *Northern Ireland and the Politics of Reconciliation* (Cambridge: Cambridge University Press, 1993).

F. Kitson, *Low Intensity Operations: Subversion, Insurgency, Peace-Keeping* (London: Faber and Faber, 1971).

B. Lennon, *Peace Comes Dropping Slow: Dialogue and Conflict Management in the Northern Ireland Conflict* (Belfast: Community Dialogue, 2004).

D. Lister and H. Jordan, *Mad Dog: The Rise and Fall of Johnny Adair and 'C' Company* (Edinburgh: Mainstream, 2003).

K. Livingstone, *Livingstone's Labour: A Programme for the Nineties* (London: Unwin Hyman, 1989).

J. Major, *The Autobiography* (London: HarperCollins, 1999).

E. Mallie and D. McKittrick, *The Fight for Peace: The Secret Story behind the Irish Peace Process* (London: Heinemann, 1996).

W. Marshall, *The Billy Boys: A Concise History of Orangeism in Scotland* (Edinburgh: Mercat, 1996).

R. Mason, *Paying the Price* (London: Robert Hale,1999).

E. McCann, *War and an Irish Town* (rev. edn) (London: Pluto Press, 1980).

H. McDonald, *Trimble* (London: Bloomsbury, 2000).

H. McDonald and J. Cusack, *UDA: Inside the Heart of Loyalist Terror* (Dublin: Penguin Ireland, 2004).

J. McDowell, *Godfathers: Inside Northern Ireland's Drug Racket* (Dublin: Gill and Macmillan, 2001).

J. McGarry and B. O'Leary (eds), *The Future of Northern Ireland* (Oxford: Clarendon Press, 1990).

M. McGartland, *Fifty Dead Men Walking: The Heroic True Story of a British Agent inside the IRA* (London: John Blake, 1998).

S. McKay, *Northern Protestants: An Unsettled People* (Belfast: Blackstaff Press, 2000).

D. McKittrick, S. Kelters, B. Feeney and C. Thornton, *Lost Lives: The Stories of the Men, Women and Children Who Died as a Result of Northern Ireland's Troubles* (Edinburgh: Mainstream, 1999).

G. McMichael, *An Ulster Voice: In Search of Common Ground in Northern Ireland* (Boulder, CO and Dublin: Roberts Rinehart, 1999).

S. McPhilemy, *The Committee: Political Assassination in Northern Ireland* (2nd edn) (Boulder, CO: Roberts Rinehart, 1999).

D. Miller, *Queen's Rebels: Ulster Loyalism in Historical Perspective* (Dublin: Gill and Macmillan, 1978).

G. Mitchell, *Making Peace: The Inside Story of the Making of the Good Friday Agreement* (London: Heinemann, 1999).

E. Moloney, *A Secret History of the IRA* (London: Allen Lane, 2002).

E. Moloney and A. Pollak, *Paisley* (Dublin: Poolbeg, 1986).

E. Morgan, *Collected Poems* (Manchester: Carcanet, 1980).

M. Mowlam, *Momentum: The Struggle for Peace, Politics and the People* (London: Hodder and Stoughton, 2002).

D. Murphy, *A Place Apart* (London: John Murray, 1978).

R. Murray, *The SAS in Ireland* (Cork: Mercier Press, 1990).

T. Nairn, *The Break-Up of Britain: Crisis and Neo-Nationalism* (2nd edn) (London: New Left, 1981).

R. Needham, *Battling for Peace: Northern Ireland's Longest Serving British Minister* (Belfast: Blackstaff Press, 1998).

S. Nelson, *Ulster's Uncertain Defenders: Protestant Political, Paramilitary and Community Groups and the Northern Ireland Conflict* (Belfast: Appletree Press, 1984).

M. O'Doherty, *The Trouble with Guns: Republican Strategy and the Provisional IRA* (Belfast: Blackstaff Press, 1998).

C. O'Leary, S. Elliott and R. Wilford, *The Northern Ireland Assembly 1982–1986: A Constitutional Experiment* (London: C. Hurst, 1988).

P. O'Malley, *Biting at the Grave: The Irish Hunger Strikes and the Politics of Despair* (Belfast: Blackstaff Press, 1990).

P. O'Malley, *Uncivil Wars: Ireland Today* (Belfast: Blackstaff Press, 1983).

T. Parker, *May the Lord in His Mercy Be Kind to Belfast* (London: Jonathan Cape, 1993).

S. Phoenix and J. Holland, *Phoenix: Policing the Shadows – the Secret War against Terrorism in Northern Ireland* (London: Hodder and Stoughton, 1996).

B. Purdie, *Politics in the Streets: the Origins of the Civil Rights Movement in Northern Ireland* (Belfast: Blackstaff Press, 1990).

A. Purdy, *Molyneaux: The Long View* (Antrim: Greystone, 1989).

D. Reed, *Ireland: The Key to the British Revolution* (London: Larkin, 1984).

M. Rees, *Northern Ireland: A Personal Perspective* (London: Methuen, 1985).

P. Routledge, *Public Servant, Secret Agent: The Elusive Life and Violent Death of Airey Neave* (London: Fourth Estate, 2002).

C. Ryder, *The RUC: A Force under Fire* (London: Methuen, 1989).

C. Ryder, *The Ulster Defence Regiment: An Instrument of Peace?* (London: Methuen, 1991).

C. Ryder and V. Kearney, *Drumcree: The Orange Order's Last Stand* (London: Methuen, 2001).

P. Shirlow, 'Space, place and politics in Northern Ireland', *Political Geography*, vol. 17, 1998.

H. Sinnerton, *David Ervine: Uncharted Waters* (Dingle: Brandon, 2002).

J. Sluka (ed.), *Death Squad: The Anthropology of State Terror* (Philadelphia: University of Pennsylvania Press, 1999).

A. Stewart, *The Narrow Ground: Aspects of Ulster 1609–1969* (London: Faber and Faber, 1977).

M. Stone, *None Shall Divide Us* (London: John Blake, 2003).

M. Sutton, *Bear in Mind These Dead: An Index of Deaths from the Conflict in Northern Ireland 1969–1993* (Belfast: Beyond the Pale, 1994).

P. Taylor, *Brits: The War against the IRA* (London: Bloomsbury, 2001).

P. Taylor, *Loyalists* (London: Bloomsbury, 1999).

M. Urban, *Big Boys' Rules: The Secret Struggle against the IRA* (London: Faber and Faber, 1992).

T. Utley, *The Lessons of Ulster* (London: Dent, 1975).

G. Walker and T. Gallagher (eds), *Sermons and Battle Hymns: Protestant Popular Culture in Modern Scotland* (Edinburgh: Edinburgh University Press, 1990).

J. White, *A Brief History of the UDA/UFF in Contemporary Conflict* (Belfast, 1999).

W. Whitelaw, *The Whitelaw Memoirs* (London: Aurum Press, 1989).

I. S. Wood (ed.), *Scotland and Ulster* (Edinburgh: Mercat, 1994).

NEWSPAPERS AND PERIODICALS

An Phoblacht/Republican News
Belfast Telegraph
Bulletin
Combat
Daily Record
Evening News (Edinburgh)
Fortnight
Glasgow Herald
Guardian
Herald
Independent
Ireland on Sunday
Irish Independent
Irish News
Irish Times
Labour Weekly
Loyalist
Magill Magazine
Monday World
New Ulster Defender
News Letter
News of the World
North Belfast News
Observer
Political Geography
Scotland on Sunday

Scotsman
Scottish Daily Express
Scottish Freedom Fighter
Sunday Business Post
Sunday Life
Sunday People
Sunday Post
Sunday Press
Sunday Times
Sunday Tribune
Sunday World
Tribune
UDA Bulletin
Ulster
Ulster Loyalist
Ulster Militant
Ulster News
United Irishman
Warrior
Woodvale Defence Association News
Workers Association Strike Bulletin
Workers Weekly

PAMPHLETS AND POLICY DOCUMENTS

Beyond the Religious Divide (Ulster Defence Association, 1979)
Building for the Future (Ulster Democratic Party, 1998)
Common Sense (Ulster Defence Association/New Ulster Political Research Group, 1987)
The Cook Report: An Internal UDA Inquiry (1988)
Loyalist Prisoners In Context (Prisoners Aid/Post Conflict Resettlement Group, 1997)
Supplementary Introduction to Documents for Discussion of Beyond the Religious Divide (New Ulster Political Research Group, 1980)
Ulster Defence Association/New Ulster Political Research Group Discussion Document (Undated, probably 1978)
What Happened on the Twelfth (Workers Association pamphlet, 1974)

OTHER SOURCES

Cabinet Confidential: Secrets of '74, BBC Northern Ireland television programme, 2 January 2005.
Cabinet Papers: PREM 15/10/13, letter from MOD to PM's office, 29 November 1972.
First Report of the Independent Monitoring Commission, 20 April 2004.
RUC Belfast Region: Terrorist Investigation – John James Adair, CID report compiled for Chief Constable, 1993 but undated.
M. Langhammer, *Cutting with the Grain: Policy and the Protestant Community – What is to Be Done?* (Belfast, 2003).

INTERVIEWS AND CORRESPONDENCE

Not all those with whom the author made contact for the preparation of this book wished to be identified. This wish has been respected and their names are not given here.

Johnny Adair
Joe Austen
Johnston Brown
Alex Calderwood
Professor Sir Bernard Crick
Sammy Duddy
Hester Dunn
Father Sean Emerson
Joe English
David Ervine
John Gregg
Mark Langhammer
John Lowry
Seamus Lynch
Tommy Lyttle
James G. MacLean
Rt Hon. Michael Mates, MP
Jackie McDonald
Chris McGimpsey
Eddie McLean
Gary McMichael
John McMichael
Dessie O'Hagan
Bob Pagels
Raymond Smallwoods
Andy Tyrie
John White
Jim Wright

Index